Shall We Play That One Together?

Paul de Barros

Shall We Play That One Together?

THE LIFE AND ART
OF JAZZ PIANO LEGEND
MARIAN MCPARTLAND

ST. MARTIN'S PRESS
NEW YORK

www.stmartins.com

Library of Congress Cataloging-in-Publication Data

De Barros, Paul.
  Shall we play that one together? : the life and art of jazz piano legend Marian McPartland /
Paul de Barros.—1st ed.
    p. cm.
  Includes bibliographical references.
  ISBN 978-0-312-55803-1 (hardcover)
  ISBN 978-1-250-01901-1 (e-book)
  1. McPartland, Marian. 2. Jazz musicians—United States—Biography. 3. Pianists—United States—
Biography. I. Title.
  ML417.M47D43 2012
  786.2'165092—dc23
  [B]

            2012028242

First Edition: October 2012

10 9 8 7 6 5 4 3 2 1

Contents

Acknowledgments   vii

1. "What Shall We Do with Her?" (1918–1935)   1

2. London (1935–1944)   27

3. "Oh, No! A Girl Piano Player!"(1944–1946)   51

4. Jimmy: "I Like You, Kid" (1907–1944)   75

5. Windy City Apprentice (1946–1950)   101

6. Getting to First Base with Three Strikes (1950–1953)   123

7. New York's Golden Age of Jazz, Part I (1953–1956)   149

8. New York's Golden Age of Jazz, Part II (1956–1958)   171

9. Loss (1958–1964)   191

10. Long Island Retreat (1964–1967)   215

11. Lost . . . and Found (1968–1973)   235

12. The Jazz Renaissance (1973–1978)   265

13. *Piano Jazz* (1978–1982)   295

14. Heyday (1982–1987)   317

15. Exit Jimmy (1987–1994)   345

16. Sweet Times (1995–2003)   375

Notes   403

Bibliography   449

Selected Recordings   457

Index   465

Acknowledgments

I am grateful first and foremost to Marian McPartland for having the courage to tell her story. Thank you, Marian, for graciously welcoming me into your memories and personal archive. I will always cherish the months I spent at your house on Long Island researching this book through innumerable interviews and your vast collection of papers.

Thanks, too, to Marian's great friend Tom Hampson, who made it possible for this project to move forward, to others he recruited—Nancy Christiansen, Merrilee Trost, Coby Hennecy, Dr. Jorge Cerruti, Ernest Wright Jr., Bernice MacDonald, Mary Kay Conwell, and Dr. Carl Oshrain—and to Elaine Freeman, executive director of The Friends of Marian McPartland, for providing the vehicle for that support. This book would not have been possible without them. Thanks also to my mother, Helen Smith, for her sustaining contribution and to Dan Morgenstern and all the folks at the Institute of Jazz Studies, who helped guide my research there, supported the project with a generous travel grant from the Morroe Berger–Benny Carter Jazz Research Fund, and gave permission for use of the material in Jimmy McPartland's 1972 interview.

I am indebted to earlier biographers James T. Maher and Irving Townsend, whose projects were not realized but whose research Marian wisely archived. Their interviews, notes, and sketches with Marian form the bedrock of the present volume. Thanks, too, to Marian's friend Joellyn Ausanka, for digging out the boxes of her transcriptions of the Maher and Townsend material and for her help in convincing Marian that her story needed to be told.

The pioneering research done by Clare Hansson in her Ph.D. thesis has also been a huge resource, particularly its comprehensive bibliography and perceptive musical analysis. Thanks also to Clare for her help with the date of Marian's arrival in Normandy.

It is the rare book that sees the light of day without the help of an agent, but labeling Anne Depue with this title obscures more than it reveals. Thank you, Anne, for not only championing this project and finding someone who loved it as much you did, but for your wise editorial suggestions and moral support. Thanks, too, to my editor, Michael Flamini, who shepherded the manuscript through St. Martin's Press and provided a judicious, close reading and editorial suggestions that improved and enriched it.

This book owes its genesis to Marian's former publicist, Don Lucoff, and Don's then-employee at DL Media, Brad Riesau, the two of whom brought me together with Marian in 2006. I am also extremely grateful to Marian's producer, Shari Hutchinson, for graciously offering me access to the studio for live sessions of *Piano Jazz*; for providing, through her assistant, Grant Jackson, compact discs of vintage shows and archival information; and for being a helpful friend throughout. Thanks, too, to jazz writer Ken Dryden for sharing his own archive of rare McPartland recordings and to Jim Carlton for sharing his father Ben's diary.

Many thanks to Seattle jazz pianist and transcriber extraordinaire Randy Halberstadt, for his musical analysis of Marian's tunes.

I take special note of Deborah Gillaspie at the Chicago Jazz Archive, whose help and guidance was instrumental in tracking down Jimmy McPartland's early life and work. I also thank, sadly and posthumously, the great Studs Terkel for pulling money out of his own pocket to pay for reproductions of his radio programs with Marian and Jimmy, held by the Chicago History Museum.

A special thanks to Max Batten of the Bromley Historical Society, for volunteering to research details of Marian's early life and to the Society's Tony Allnutt, as well. For help with archival material at St. George's Chapel, in Windsor, I extend my thanks to Kelda Roe and for research regarding the Dyson family, Chris Atkins, librarian at the Royal Borough of Windsor and Maidenhead. For other genealogy research and statistics, thanks to Lucien Rising. Thanks also to John Watson for sharing his Billy Mayerl research; to Alyn Shipton for his help with BBC jazz; to Loren Binford for his encyclopedic referrals to veteran Chicago musicians; to the man who goes by the Web moniker "Mr. Pilot" for clarifying certain World War II dates for me; and to the Smithsonian Institution Jazz Oral History Program for permission to quote librally from Marian's interview.

Researching this book required residence for extended periods in New York. Thanks to Kathy Nemser for providing a place to live and work on Long Island; and to Ray Neinstein, Andy Lilienthal, and Richard Cantor, in Brooklyn. Special thanks also to Marian's housekeeper, Gosia Gil, for her constant support and for providing emergency housing in the summer of 2011, and also to Bruce Kochis, Susan Davis, Mark Solomon, and Emily

Moore. Thanks also to Marian's archivist, Kathy Hart, for guiding me through the files and for her research into Marian's former addresses, and to Marian's assistant, Nancy Christiansen, for compiling and reproducing photographs, among many other helpful tasks.

Thanks to all the people (names listed in bibliography) who volunteered their time, insights, and information for interviews, but especially to Jimmy's grandchildren, Doug Kassel and Donna Gourdol, and to Marian's nephews, Mark and Chris Armitage, and Marian's niece, Sheila Prophet. Their extensive family archives—not to mention personal memories—have enriched this book.

Thanks to my superiors at *The Seattle Times*—Suki Dardarian, Carole Carmichael, and Lynn Jacobson—for granting me a leave of absence so I could write this book.

And for various and sundry other assistance along the way, thanks to Virginia A. Schaefer, Diana Schwartz, Ellen Rowe, Doug Ramsey, Chuck Sengstock, Bob Koester, John McDonough, Phil Brunner, Bert Vuijse, Nancy Christiansen, Merrilee Trost, Judith Stuyvesant, Willie Klewitz, John Litweiler, Neil Tesser, Anne Bolen, Dan Ouellette, Bill Crow, Daniel Griffin, Steve Perisho, Zane Knauss, Greer Rising, Lisa DeBenedittis, Rachel Dyson, Susan Pittman, Jill Atkinson, Howard Mandel, Charles Cross, Ira Gitler, Jill Johnson, Julie Porter, and Nick Phillips.

And, finally, thanks to my wife, Judy de Barros, for being there to hear every word as it was written, to offer suggestions and support and, especially, to have put up with the long absences that writing this book involved.

Shall We Play That One Together?

"What Shall We Do with Her?"
(1918~1935)

ON THE MORNING OF JULY 23, 1944, Marian McPartland stood on the south coast of her native England, looking across the English Channel. Part of a USO unit sent to entertain troops on the front lines in France, she was wearing combat boots and a helmet. She had spent the last month learning to pitch a pup tent and cook with a mess kit, rehearsing with a variety act called Band Wagon, fronted by an American comedian named Don Rice. On her way, she had stopped by her parents' home in Eastbourne to say good-bye and pick up the accordion her father had bought her years before, as she had been told there might not be pianos where she was headed. American troops had been flooding into England by the tens of thousands since early 1942, in preparation for the November assault on North Africa and then the continent itself. When the Americans arrived, a lot of British girls seemed to lose their minds. By the time the war was over, thousands had left home as war brides. Marian had met her first real beau in London, a handsome, dark-haired comedian and impressionist she'd worked with in a vaudeville outfit. They'd even lived together for a while in Camden Town, sharing a flat as well as the London stage. But David had shipped out to North Africa. Marian, like other young Brits, was smitten by American movie stars and swing musicians; she had even finagled a publicity photo of herself with Jimmy Cagney when he played for the USO.

The Normandy invasion originally had been planned for May but had been secretly postponed till June 6. On the evening of the assault, Marian had stayed up half the night, listening to thousands of planes passing overhead for hours and hours, a droning that seemed to go on forever. A month later, she found herself among the first entertainers assigned to bring good cheer and a few laughs to the men who survived those first few, bloody months. Twenty-six years old—an attractive brunette with a tall face, broad smile, and ready wit—she had been working as a professional pianist under the stage name Marian Page for six years, ever since dropping out of the prestigious Guildhall School of Music and Drama to play piano in a novelty act led by Billy Mayerl, a hugely popular English entertainer. After the war started, she had joined the Entertainments National Service Association (ENSA) but had switched to the American United Service Organizations (USO), where the pay—and the entertainers—were much better. Since 1940 she'd been barnstorming the provinces, entertaining soldiers in camps, mess halls, and vaudeville houses great and small.

But no experience in her background had prepared her for this moment. Born in 1918 near Windsor Castle and raised in a genteel, middle-class suburb in Kent, she had at first seemed destined for a career as a concert pianist. At seventeen, on the advice of an inspiring elocution teacher who had taken a special interest in her at Stratford House School for Girls, she had auditioned for the Guildhall in London. After three years, however, the lively beat of jazz and popular music had lured her away. Though Marian was by no means a jazz player yet, she had wide-ranging curiosity and a burning desire to learn.

As she looked across the Channel under the gray morning clouds, she wondered what lay ahead. The war was horrible, but surely there was something exciting there, too. She had never been out of England, so she had nothing to compare it with. But it somehow seemed so dull. Her parents were bound and determined to marry her off to a banker. Now that she'd seen life on the road, heard the applause, tasted the glamour—and, yes, felt the hard knocks and backstage boredom—she had found her path. She wasn't sure why. And she wasn't sure where it was leading her or what she might find. But as she stepped gingerly into the water and climbed aboard a small boat that would take her to France, somehow, she knew that making that crossing was something she needed to do. Little did she know that she was about to find her passion in life—and become a war bride herself.

Before that fateful morning, Marian's world had been almost entirely circumscribed by a thirty-mile stretch of the river Thames, from Windsor to Woolwich. As the river winds down from Oxfordshire, it picks up steam below the hill from which Windsor Castle commands the countryside. North lie the fields of Eton and the tenements of Slough. Widening into a great urban river at London's Victoria Embankment, it flows slowly past the Guildhall School of Music and Drama, becoming ever wider as its horseshoe turns meander beyond the Tower of London and are ornamented by the remains of the once vibrant industrial machinery of shipping, manufacturing, and the long shore, until, nine miles east, it reaches Woolwich, where Henry VIII established the Royal Arsenal in 1513. Just south of Woolwich is the leafy suburb of Bromley, once an important stagecoach stop on the road to Hastings. The river shortly thereafter flows into a great estuary before spilling its bounty of fresh water into the North Sea.

Marian's story began in Slough, where she was born Margaret Marian Turner at home, at 41 Sussex Place, March 20, 1918, eight months before the conclusion of the Great War and the year in which Englishwomen first got the vote. Marian's father, Frank Turner, a civil engineer, worked in management at the Royal Arsenal in Woolwich, but with the war on, the arsenal was a dangerous place, exposed to aerial bombings, zeppelin fly-overs, frequent accidents, and explosions. Because of that, it was probably decided that his wife, Janet, should bear her firstborn in Slough, across the river from Windsor.

Janet's people, the Dysons, had an illustrious history in Windsor, both musical and political. In 1855, Marian's great-grandfather Thomas Dyson had become a lay clerk—an adult singer—in the now world-renowned male choir at St. George's Chapel, on the castle grounds. Ten years later, Thomas founded Dyson and Sons, pianoforte dealers, and set up shop at No. 10 Thames Street, across from the castle wall. Thomas was elected mayor of Windsor in 1890. For his improvements to the city—in particular, refur-bishing a lovely promenade along the river—Dyson was honored with a pagoda-like memorial fountain of polished pink stone, which still stands at the corner of Goswell Road and Barry Avenue.

St. George's provided on-site housing for choir members and their families in the Horseshoe Cloisters, a stunningly preserved, two-story Tudor structure just across from the cathedral, with classic diagonal beams and wattle-and-daub walls of a redbrick hue. Thomas Dyson and his wife, Jane, lived at No. 14 with their seven children: Thomas George, Charles Frederick, Margarette Clara, Albert Harry, Arthur Edward, George Henry, and Sarah Annie. Marian's maternal grandmother was Sarah Annie (called Annie). Marian, who also went by her middle name, was probably named after her great-aunt Margarette. Thomas (the younger) and Charles Fred-erick (called Frederick) joined their father in the family piano business, as did young George. Frederick played cello in a local orchestra and for much of his life was connected with the nearby Eton College Musical Society. The rooms at No. 14 must have rung out with music daily, as Thomas and Frederick practiced their hymns, Frederick played cello, and Annie taught piano lessons.

Next door to the Dyson piano shop, on the posh commercial block that hugs the castle wall, at No. 9, stood Uncle (Albert) Harry's jewelry shop, operated by him and his son Cyril. Embedded in the sidewalk in front of the store was a working clock with a thick glass cover. A sign out front read, "By Appointment to Her Majesty." Among Cyril's duties were to repair the royal clocks and clean the family jewels. As a little girl, Marian remembered being shunted into a back room with her sister, Joyce, when King George came looking for an eggcup. As if in a fairy tale, the king thought the cup too small, so he requested that someone fetch an egg to test it. He was eventually satisfied, as Marian and Joyce peeked out warily from behind the shop's rear door.

Frederick, elected mayor in 1909, was knighted by King George two years later. As mayor, Frederick had just welcomed King George and Queen Mary back to Windsor after their coronation in London. As the royal procession marched down the High Street, the king descended from his carriage, put his sword on Frederick's shoulder, and publicly proclaimed him a knight. Harry's son, Cyril, also served as mayor and was knighted as well, in 1953. The Dyson line, then, boasted two knights and three mayors of Windsor.

"You can see how these associations might affect the family," Marian told a magazine reporter. "A good deal of attention was paid to my schooling and manners, and there was no nonsense about it. After all, when there's always the chance that your small child will go chasing her kitten and bump smack into the King of England. . . . I was quite a meek little nipper."

Marian's maternal grandmother Annie was born at the Cloisters in 1856 and in 1881 married John Payne, a banker from Wallingford, Oxfordshire, forty miles upriver. Seven years Annie's senior, Payne took her to Tunbridge Wells, Kent, where in 1885 their first daughter, Janet, Marian's mother, was born. John and Annie Payne eventually settled in Wantage, fifteen miles west of Wallingford, where Janet and her younger brother, Arthur, were raised. As a child, Janet contracted rheumatic fever, which left her with a weak heart. Not much else is known about her early life, but the Payne family seems to have been well-off, as Marian's memories of family visits to Wantage feature a rather grand house with lawn tennis courts.

Janet was a beautiful woman, about five feet seven inches tall, with small features, brown eyes, and black hair, which she tied in a bun. She always wore long earrings, which Marian loved to try on as a little girl. Janet studied piano with her mother but does not seem to have considered a career in music. Sometime during her twenties, Janet met the man with whom she would spend the rest of her life—Frank Turner. The youngest of four children, Frank was born in 1882 in Enfield, Middlesex. The Turners were solid professional folk. Frank's father, Henry J. Turner, was born in 1840 in Warminster, Wiltshire, and worked as a shorthand clerk;

Frank's mother came from Wellington, Shropshire, where she was born about 1842. Raised in Enfield, Frank studied engineering and went to work as an apprentice for the London North Eastern Railway in 1911. He then took a job at the Woolwich Arsenal, specializing in rifling, the spiral ridges inside gun barrels that spin a bullet (or larger projectile) to ensure that it fires straight and true. It was an auspicious career decision, for while Frank was by all reports a peace-loving, gentle man, sadly, the demands of two world wars would make the arsenal a secure employer for the rest of his life.

Frank was a handsome man, five feet ten and a half inches tall, with greenish brown eyes, black hair, and a stern, sometimes even solemn look. But he was quick to smile or even burst into song, and he had an easy sense of humor, which ran in the Turner family.

Frank and Janet married September 6, 1913, in Windsor Parish Church. It was a black-tie and top hat affair. Though Marian was born in Slough, by the time of her birth, Frank had found a house in Woolwich, at 63 Wrottesley Road. To an American, there is nothing particularly unfortunate about being born in a place called Slough, apart from the fact that it rhymes with "cow." But in England, the town is a national symbol of faceless mediocrity, famously skewered in a 1937 poem by John Betjeman ("Come, friendly bombs, and fall on Slough!") and more recently chosen as the setting for the British TV comedy *The Office,* adapted for American television. (The late comedian Steve Allen, original host of TV's *The Tonight Show,* used to tease Marian by pronouncing it "sluff.") This no doubt explains why Marian often told interviewers she was born in Windsor, then hastily moved the conversation to the Dyson lineage.

The object of Betjeman's derision was conformist suburban sprawl, but the destruction it suggested might suddenly fall from the sky was symptomatic of how central a factor war—and the specter of war—was to Marian's upbringing. The two world wars bookended her early life, and the nervous period between—which Britons call "the slump," a severe depression that started earlier and lasted far longer than its American counterpart—was the backdrop. During this entire span, the Turner household income was derived from the manufacture of weapons. This helps put in perspective the clichéd, tea-and-crumpets reminiscences Marian often provided the American press about her early childhood. In fact, the grim backdrop of her upbringing was much less a fairy tale. The Turners lived just a few hundred yards from the Royal Arsenal, a living embodiment of William Blake's dark vision of industrial hell, the "total war" engineered by the madness of the twentieth century. The arsenal was like a little city—1,285 acres along the river, with more than sixty-five thousand employees and forty-seven miles of private railway. One of Marian's earliest childhood memories is of those trains in the night—not romantic, mythic trains in the American South, hooting on a hot summer evening, but something rather more frightening.

"The heavy chuff chuff of the engine, the train whistle sounding as close as if it were in the room," she recalled. "These were slightly sinister to me. I sometimes dreamed about the train—that it was going right through the house—and then I woke to hear it in the distance."

Marian's first family home was modest, part of a long, institutional-looking row of attached, two-story brick houses, with white lintels and window frames, low brick walls, and chimneys with eight stacks each. In the spring of 1920, Frank moved the family up Shooter's Hill, a strategic high point from which the military had traditionally protected not only the Arsenal and London, but the nearby suburbs of Chislehurst and Bromley, where the family eventually moved. For a while, the Turners lived at 219 Eglinton Road; a few months later, Frank found a nicer house at 15 Eglinton Hill. McPartland's first vivid childhood memories are of that house, where she lived until she was six. The neighborhood afforded a panoramic view of London, the river Thames, the Arsenal, and the rather stately spire of the Woolwich Town Hall. After she moved to New York, Marian would accurately describe Woolwich as being "something like Astoria," Queens—a dense, urban mixed-use neighborhood.

The house at Eglinton Hill was a typical upper-middle-class dwelling with a fireplace and marble mantel with a brass candlestick at either end and an oval brown clock in the middle that ticked loudly and chimed the hour. At night, eight gas jets covered with green wire shades hissed and flared in the drawing room. Oil paintings of the Dysons hung on the wall. In the basement, maids boiled sheets, linens, towels, and diapers in a great cement container with a fire that glowed through a grate underneath. Marian spent much of her time upstairs in the nursery, which looked out onto a small garden. In early spring, her father encouraged her to plant seeds, which she sprinkled with water with a child's watering can, and later initiated Marian into the joys of weeding, cutting hedges, and tying up hollyhocks with raffia.

Marian spent many happy hours sitting on the back steps at Eglinton Hill, playing with woolly caterpillars, feeding them leaves from a lime tree in the front garden. In the early morning, when the flowers glistened, a dark ring would sometimes form in the grass. Her father told her it had been made by fairies dancing in the night. She remembered standing by the window in the winter when an occasional wet snow fell, nose pressed to the glass, watching the snow come down. She stood there for hours, daydreaming, and luxuriated in her fantasy world, which soon included the dream of music.

Marian's mother often played the family upright, not with any special fanfare, but casually sitting down to play Chopin's Waltz in A-flat or something by Grieg, while Marian's father read the newspaper in the sitting room. When Marian was three years old, after hearing her mother play Chopin, she climbed onto the piano bench and picked out the notes by ear. A few years later, while visiting her uncle Harry Dyson, Marian sat down at Harry's upright and had a transformational experience. This pale, thin girl with a serious, inward demeanor discovered that the melodies she heard in her head flowed easily from her mind down through her fingers to the black and white keys.

"It was like a vision," she later remembered. "I wasn't just toying with the keys. I could command them."

McPartland had been born with perfect pitch—the ability to pick out any note she heard and play it, the way other people might identify a color or shape. As she played, she became enveloped in the sound, forgetting everything around her. After that day, the world of sound she found that afternoon would be her refuge, her solace, her companion—and eventually, her profession and lifelong obsession. At six years old, she had discovered the world she wanted to live in.

If anyone had told Marian's mother her introverted little girl playing Chopin would one day become an American jazz icon, bristling with Manhattan bravado and the salty vernacular of the street, she probably would have scoffed—if not actually fainted. How Marian's private world of the imagination survived—flourished, even—in a stultifying landscape for the most part indifferent and, often, actively hostile to it is a challenging question.

Though Janet still played the piano for pleasure, she managed the household as her vocation. She had plenty of help. Alice came in the morning, another maid in the afternoon, and when Marian's sister, Joyce, was born in 1922, "Nurse Turner" was hired as well. Alice came to work in a blue coat and a blue straw hat with artificial cherries on it. After she arrived, she changed into a black dress, black shoes, and white frilly cap and apron. Marian took great pleasure in helping Alice with her chores, polishing silver, pressing handkerchiefs with a child-sized iron, and luxuriating in the fresh smell of wind-dried sheets. Marian also fondly recollected being held in her mother's arms before bed as they recited the Charles Wesley prayer:

Gentle Jesus, meek and mild,
Look upon a little child;
Pity my simplicity,
Suffer me to come to Thee.

But despite this seeming idyll, many of Marian's sharpest recollections of childhood were seasoned with a bittersweet sense of loss. A neighborhood boy trampled her caterpillar collection. When she was given a kitten, her mother took it away when Marian accidentally hugged it so hard it soiled her blouse. A beautiful doll sent by her uncle from China was stored away, with the explanation she was "too young" for it. Even her fondest childhood memories were notable for their solitariness. In her memoirs, there were few tales of games played happily with friends, but rather moments of sweet solitude—painting, writing stories, and playing the piano.

It seemed to Marian that just as she would become attached to one of the household help, her mother, impatient and hypercritical, would let the person go. Nurse Turner was sacked for taking Marian and her sister (still in a pram) to an "unsuitable" neighborhood. She was replaced by "Dunny"—Miss Dunston—whom Marian didn't care for. One Miss Clayton—"Claytie"—played games with Marian until she was summarily terminated as well, after some other "bust-up" with Marian's mother. Janet was critical of her children, too. Life was full of "Now, Margaret, sit up straight. You'll get round-shouldered." "Don't dash into things!" "If you do that, Mummy won't like you." Or worse, "You're pigheaded, just like your father!"

"Mummy did seem to find fault with everybody sooner or later," Marian said.

Class lines were very real in Britain in those days, and Marian's mother observed them strictly for her children. An erstwhile friend named Godfrey was nixed because he was "too rough." An encounter with a Cockney boy at Marian's first school, a Woolwich convent, led her mother to pull her out after a few weeks. Janet even referred to her brother Arthur as a "blue-collar type."

"I really have few memories of Mummy when she wasn't nagging me about something," declared Marian. "She was a chronic complainer. And yet her opinion, her judgment about things, was very important to me. Even now, after all these years, I think my decision making (or sometimes lack of it!) is affected by the strong hold she had on my feelings and my behavior. My parents, both of them, seem pretty opinionated to me now. At the time, of course, I believed everything I was told and pretty much *did* everything I was told."

Marian wrote an unusual story as a child, "It's Best to Be Good," which spoke with sterling clarity to this early internalization of parental authority. In language that would make a Freudian's day, "Little Doris" snuck out of the house on a rainy day when Mummy was out and was kidnapped by ominous "balloon men" with rubbery limbs who, *Alice in Wonderland*–style, shrank her so she could fit into their flying balloon. When the food they gave her burst in her mouth, and their ship suffered the same fate, Little Doris woke up to find her mother standing by. "You naughty girl! I said you were to stay in," she scolded. "So now," wrote Marian, "Doris thinks it best to do what she's told."

Marian said she learned early on that to be "liked" was important, and in order to achieve that, one must be "nice." When her mother brought back a dark green dress for her from one of her shopping trips to the John Barker department store in London, Marian didn't like it but dutifully put it on and didn't protest.

"She was overstrict and you had rows over things like you breaking her umbrella and [your] being 'critical,'" remembered Marian's sister, Joyce. "Being critical was not agreeing with Mother. . . . She admired your musical ability and at the same time seemed unable to come to terms with you as a person."

Marian's sister, Joyce Mabel Kathleen Turner, was born when Marian was four. Joyce was cheerful, had big eyes, straight hair, and a wide mouth, and from the outset Marian felt—in classic firstborn fashion—that Joyce was not only prettier, but the favored one. Her mother reinforced those feelings. Looking in the mirror, Marian saw not a little girl who was rather cute in a shy way, but a long, serious face, penetrating eyes, a prominent nose, and a big forehead. Joyce got sick a lot in the winter with bronchitis, and it seemed to Marian that her mother took an inordinate amount of time and pleasure in caring for her.

"They never heated the house," said Marian. "You could see your breath in the bedroom when you got up in the morning, it was so bloody cold. All you wanted to do was throw on your clothes and tear out of there. I was the big ox that never got sick."

Being ill carried a psychological premium in the Turner household. A diary Marian's mother kept in her last years revealed an obsessive interest in the health of family members, with every cough, sore throat, ache, and pain monitored with fretful detail. Janet's chronic complaining (later compounded by an actual, debilitating handicap) only amplified this obsession. If Marian got a cold, her father would bring her warm milk spiked with rum.

"I was Daddy's girl," said Marian. "If he had one."

McPartland's memories of her father—in contrast with those of her mother—were glowingly positive. In the morning, he would come into her room wearing a frayed green dressing gown and roust her out of bed, pounding on the bottom end of the mattress, saying, "Jump about! Jump about! Time to get up, old chap!"

"I've often wondered if it was a psychological slip with him, that he really wanted a son," said Marian. "He would always call me 'old chap.'"

Before he dashed off to work, Frank Turner would have two boiled eggs and toast. Marian by this time would already have finished her egg, and she would turn the empty shell upside down and put it in her daddy's eggcup. He would solemnly cut off the top, always pretending to be surprised to discover there was no egg inside.

Frank was not musical, but he liked to sing heartily in church and could often be heard humming "like a bumblebee" as he puttered away at woodworking projects around the house. He would drift about singing the nineteenth-century Irish ballad "I Dreamt I Dwelt in Marble Halls," then stop himself short, pretending to be startled, and say, "And then I woke up and found out I didn't!" The line always got a laugh. Sometimes when he was singing, according to Joyce, "Mummy would make some semicrushing remark that wiped the song from his lips." Frank loved to take long, brisk walks, and he often took Marian along, as well as the family's wire-haired terrier, Tim.

Good-natured and lighthearted as he was, Frank Turner held to a rigid Victorian work ethic. He brought work home with him and constantly seemed to be on the telephone or writing letters. His oft repeated motto was, "Fill the unforgiving minute," and it made a deep impression on Marian. He told her that while studying for his engineering exams, he read by candlelight till he fell asleep, waking up hours later to find the candle burned down to the end. An earthenware jug in the pantry sported another Protestant nostrum: "Success comes not by wishing but hard work bravely done." When Marian undertook the task of writing a letter—or an obligatory thank-you note for, say, the (unwanted) Dickens novel she received annually from her mother's relatives in Wantage (though she did make it all the way through *Oliver Twist*)—her father read every line. If she had crossed out a word or had forgotten to cross a "t" or dot an "i," he made her write the whole thing out all over again.

Beyond such fastidiousness, Marian's parents instilled in her many qualities typically associated with an old-fashioned English upbringing: a knack for keen, conversational wit and the cutting bon mot; a sentimental love of nature and animals; the proverbial British "stiff upper lip" in the face of adversity; an unflappable, understated skepticism about human nature; an appetite for hard work and good deeds; and a species of personal reserve that is particularly British—one that recoils from expressive intimacy but takes delight in gracious collegiality.

The Turner family was Church of England, but not deeply religious. If Marian asked to leave church before the sermon, her father usually said yes. They did not say grace before dinner, and religious icons had no place in the household. Church was simply something one did on Sunday but did not make a lot of fuss about. Marian despised Sunday school, where the teacher struck her as a dull "spinster."

In 1924, despite massive layoffs at the Arsenal, Frank Turner bought a stately, three-story detached house with front and back garden at 34 Cambridge Road, in the suburb of Bromley, about nine miles south of Woolwich, in Kent. Bromley then boasted a population of about thirty-five thousand and still had areas of open countryside. Most of the streets were unpaved, and milk and ice were delivered by horse and wagon. (The Turner family never owned a car.) Its two prominent historical features were the imposing brick buildings of Bromley and Sheppard Colleges in the old town center and a six-hundred-acre, eighteenth-century estate, Sundridge Park, whose handsome, pillared manor still serves as a hotel and rental for weddings and meetings. Marian's home on Cambridge Road lay a few blocks from the gates of Sundridge Park and just around the corner from Plaistow Grove, where another popular British entertainer, David Bowie, also spent part of his childhood.

The shops of the High Street—the British equivalent of Main Street—were close by. An East Indian family lived at the back of the large garden, which had a miniature castle and moat. Marian and Joyce were warned not to "mix," but they climbed a tree at the bottom of the garden anyway, and the neighbor kids climbed a tree on their side, and they all sat in the trees and talked across the fence. Out front stood a silver birch tree.

Shortly after the Turners moved to Cambridge Road, Marian's grandmother Annie moved in. She seems to have been in need of income. At one point she tried to sell some royal knickknacks from her Windsor days, including an umbrella that had belonged to King George IV. Marian remembered Annie as a "tyrannical" woman, imperious and critical, who wore long skirts and black shoes and kept a barrel of stout in the cellar. She would occasionally go downstairs to draw off a jugful to drink with lunch. The image of the demanding Dyson dowager living in the same household with her malcontented, critical daughter, Janet, and a soon-to-be-resistant granddaughter, Marian, suggested a painful level of domestic tension. The Turner household was not an expressive one, so that tension necessarily found its outlet in sarcasm, one-upmanship, passive resistance, and—at least for Marian—a determination to break free at the first possible opportunity. Annie lived with the Turners for just a couple of years, then moved to a nursing home. Marian remembered her grandmother waving to her in the morning as she walked past the home on the way to school. Annie died in 1929, an event that does not seem to have had much of an emotional impact on her granddaughter.

Outside the home, Marian found more nurturing influences, notably Miss Dorinda Hammond of Miss Hammond's School for Young Children, which Marian entered when she was six. Miss Hammond's was situated in a modest, one-story frame building on Minster Road and directed by two "spinsters," Miss Hammond, principal, and her stout assistant, Miss Agatha Cicely Grantham Nicholson, who shared a home at No. 5 Longfield. Miss Hammond and Miss Nicholson occasionally came to the house to play whist with Marian's mother. It was at Miss Hammond's that Marian first began picking out tunes on the piano for her schoolmates. The school was coed, and a 1926 class picture showed the boys in short ties and shirts and the girls in plain frocks. Marian, with a "fringe" of hair (bangs) her mother insisted she comb over her prominent forehead, gazed at the camera with a rather distant yet challenging look.

Opposite the school was a small footbridge over the railway and a path that led to Sundridge Park and Elmstead Woods, where Miss Hammond took her young charges on nature walks.

"I think that was quite an important part of my life," Marian concluded, looking back. "She made us listen to the birds and the wind and the water lapping in the brooks. I think it gave me the feeling I've always had about the environment. In retrospect, she was a wonderful person. She told us the names of the flowers and pointed out the birds and trees. I just loved knowing all this and bringing little things home and planting them."

Marian's father reinforced Miss Hammond's love of nature, teaching Marian to plant snowdrops and crocuses and daffodils around the base of the trees on the front lawn. He also wrote out pastoral poems for her in his own hand, such as this one, extolling the English countryside:

Where the flowers grow the sweetest
Where the brook goes singing by
Where the corn grows up the neatest
Grass and flowers lie.

Where the little lambs go skipping
Up and down the hills
Through the cooling woods they wander
Where the blackbird trills.

Marian especially looked forward to visiting her uncle Will and aunt Mabel in the rural village of Peaslake, Surrey, about twenty-five miles southeast of London, near the medieval town of Guildford. Will Turner had made his money in China (he had sent the doll), and he and his wife, who had no children, retired in Peaslake to a large, beautiful house with a field of sheep next door. Marian fondly remembered being allowed to hold a lamb there in her arms. But the highlight was walking with Aunt Mabel to a mysterious, beautiful spring called the Silent Pool. This serene Surrey Hills landmark has been venerated as a magical place since medieval times and is now a public park. Fed by an underground spring and enshrouded by poplars and gently drooping vegetation, the Silent Pool's uncannily glassy surface and pure, translucent water afford a view directly to the bottom, from which tiny bubbles rise. Red-wing red blackbirds chirrup in the trees, and when disturbed, partridges flutter up from the trail. The rolling countryside surrounding, especially by Albury, is idyllic, with a neo-Gothic Catholic church perched on a hill, fly fishermen plying the Tillingbourne River, red and white hawthorn spreading up the hills from the roadside, and great manor houses with a distinctive, baroque style of multiple chimneys that recall Toad Hall from *The Wind in the Willows*. "We would just stare at the pool," recalled Marian. "We didn't stay long, but long enough to take everything in." McPartland would later commemorate these pastoral childhood reveries by naming the title song of one of her albums "Silent Pool."

Marian's growing love of the natural world was accompanied by something else as old as Albion itself, a magical animism that invested nature with mystical power. Marian devoured illustrated books about fairies and also wrote some fairy stories of her own, printed in an immaculate hand

with astonishing sophistication and clarity—not to say botanical knowledge. Her story "Helpful Bluebell" told the tale of a fairy who lived inside
a hollow tree and read nursery rhymes to the young chicks of a bird called
a yellow hammer whose egg had been rescued after it fell from a tree. In
"The Lost Ball Dress," a fairy butterfly attended a dance in a gown made
from a yellow moon daisy.

In Marian's fantasy world, there were no scolding mothers—only happy
endings. Out in the real world, things were not so rosy. England's massive
public debt after World War I had led to a depression that would last
nearly twenty years. And while the Turners held on to their upper-middle-
class lifestyle during "the slump"—"I don't remember there being a depression for us," Marian said—thrift and moderation were bywords of her
childhood. Every piece of string that came into the house was unknotted
and saved, buttons were stored in a tin, everything was neatly folded and
reused. In 1926, in response to stagnant wages, the Labour Party called for
a general strike and public transportation ground to a halt. Marian's father nevertheless found his way to work and even volunteered to drive a
bus.

"It was a very long way from Bromley to Woolwich, which only shows
the great tenacity of the Conservative middle class of that time," wrote
Marian's sister, Joyce, in a memoir. "It never occurred to Father to stay at
home in bed with a book while the General Strike struck all 'round him.
Get to work if you can, said the Government, and that was enough to get
Father onto his bike, pedaling fast." On the last day of the strike—it went
for only nine days—Joyce added that someone stole Frank's bike.

Meanwhile, Marian had outgrown Miss Hammond's. In 1927, her
mother enrolled her in the Avonclyffe School, and the peripatetic Turners
moved again, to 50 Palace Grove, Marian's home for the remainder of her
childhood. Though not quite as grand as 34 Cambridge Road, Palace
Grove was another handsome, three-story detached house with front and
back garden on a pleasant street full of similar homes and a stone's throw
from the High Street.

Wrote Joyce: "When Mother wanted to move, we moved. The garden
was not so nice in Palace Grove but Father, patient and kind, set to, to make
it lovely. He built a summer house with stained glass windows. Those
windows were so beautiful. He also got two pennies, one with your year
of birth on it, and one with mine, and screwed them to the wall of the
summer house. He obviously thought we'd live there forever, because he
said that when young men were holding our hands in the summer house
we'd have to tell the truth about our ages, as there were the pennies for all

to see. In that garden Father used to write our names in flowers neatly planted, do you remember?"

Janet liked to have the maid bring tea out to the summer house—cakes, sandwiches, tarts, the whole lot—and Marian was astonished in retrospect how she and her friends could wolf down so much food at four o'clock and still eat supper. Six lime trees stood in front of the house, three on each side of the porch, the branches of which Marian's father violently pruned to stubby knobs every year, which annoyed Marian for the rest of her life. Frank grew wisteria on a wall that ran between his house and the one next door.

When Janet Turner had friends to tea, she sometimes asked Marian to play. She remembered one afternoon in particular when her mother's friend Nita Hookham came by. Mrs. Hookham and Marian's mother chatted throughout Marian's performance, then said, "Very nice, dear." ("They're still doing it," Marian noted sardonically of her audiences.) Nita and Felix Hookham and their daughter, Peggy, became family friends. Peggy was later known as the famous ballerina Dame Margot Fonteyn.

Palace Grove held a swirl of other memories familiar to many British children of the era: the smell of chloroform before a tonsillectomy in the upstairs nursery; mixing watercolors of blue and yellow to get just the right shade of green to paint a leaf; *Winnie-the-Pooh* and *Black Beauty* ("I felt so bad for that horse!—wound up drawing a cart"); cups of steaming hot cocoa; jigsaw puzzles; houses of cards that toppled to the floor; and windup toys that scurried across the great mahogany table.

"I was a dreamy sort of child, living in a half world of difficult schoolwork, reading a great deal, playing the piano a lot, and helping my father in the garden," she said.

And then there were family vacations. At the seashore at Herne Bay near Margate, Marian took her first—and last—puff on a cigarette. "I thought I must join the gang," she said. "I choked like mad and decided I was never going to do that." Janet's favorite getaway, though—and one of Marian's, too—was Limpsfield, a country village famous for its fields of bluebells. One year Marian was rushed home from Limpsfield, having caught the measles. When she later had a bout with pneumonia—serious business in those pre-penicillin days—Joyce recalled somewhat facetiously being "terribly cross" that her sister had arrogated her territory.

"Being ill, I felt, was my particular talent," wrote Joyce, "and why the hell couldn't you stick to playing the piano in a decent and forthright manner instead of taking up my role of the frail young girl . . . no one had time to ask what *my* temperature was. . . ."

Despite their good-natured competition, Marian got along well with her sister and one Christmas did her a good deed Joyce never forgot. Christmas in England was nothing like the extravagant material blowout it is in America. Nevertheless, the house was decorated with holly, carolers came to the door, and the family usually went to Uncle Ted's for a turkey dinner. However, Marian's fastidious mother drew the line at having a live tree. Every year an artificial Christmas tree was ceremoniously unfolded, its limp needles fluffed up and decorated. One Christmas when Joyce lay in bed, ill, she begged for a real Christmas tree with pine needles. When Joyce fell asleep, Marian surreptitiously opened up the artificial tree and to every limb tied a branch of real fir cut from the tree in the garden. When Joyce woke up, it was standing by the bed in a red pot with silver and gold ornaments and tinsel and a bird with a spun glass tail. Joyce never forgot this grand gesture of sibling affection.

Despite repeated requests from Marian, her mother refused to find her a piano teacher, arguing that she played so well by ear, she didn't need lessons, a curiously obtuse position for an accomplished pianist who had taken lessons as a young girl and come from a family of music teachers. When Marian was nine, her mother insisted she study violin, saying she had "violin fingers," whatever that meant—presumably that they were long and strong—and a teacher named Edith Jarvis was recruited. Edith unfortunately died and was succeeded by her assistant, Eleanor Izzard (who Marian sometimes cheerfully chanted under her breath might "die in a blizzard"). Under Miss Izzard's tutelage, Marian played her first public recital when she was ten. Though Marian despised the violin, she was a deferent, retiring, and obedient little girl who didn't dare complain. Such things simply were not done by "nice" children—especially little girls—in 1928. But she nevertheless longed to somehow muster the courage to assert herself against her mother's imperious dictates—instrumental and otherwise. Perhaps that is why her violin debut turned into such a disaster.

"It was in some parochial hall or church hall," Marian recalled, "and I had some woman play for me—I don't know why my teacher didn't play, because she was a marvelous pianist as well as a good violin player—but I remember this awful woman playing who couldn't play the piece at all. She got me lost. I think this was the first time I ever hollered at somebody. I said to her, 'You ruined my performance!' or something like that. I was in tears. I remember her just giving me a blank stare."

For anyone who grew up playing a musical instrument, the image of a ten-year-old girl bawling out her adult accompanist for making a mistake is rather startling. And to say so in front of other adults was even more bold and unusual. Marian's impulse to speak up for herself must have been driven by a powerful force, one at odds with everything her parents—and her environment—had instilled in her. For while she may truly have thought of herself as a shy, "nice," self-effacing little girl who always did as she was told, she also clearly had an unusually high self-regard—and extremely high standards—for a child. In that self-regard was the seed of a diva who—perhaps in self-defense—was developing a strong, stubborn will that could stand up to her mother. This push and pull between the need to be "nice" and please others—first her parents and then her friends, colleagues, and lovers—and an equally strong need to be appreciated, loved, and admired as an artist would establish the central dynamic of Marian's early life.

The scorching summer of 1928 sparked a fad in England for sunbathing, as well as Mexican straw hats, suntan lotion, and more daring bathing suits. Slimming became a cult. As a teen, Marian fell in enthusiastically with both trends, becoming an avid sunbather and fastidious dieter all her life. Frank's brother Harry, known in the family as the grumpy uncle (perhaps because his deafness was the worst of all the Turner men), most emphatically did not approve. When Marian and Joyce arrived at Eastbourne one summer for a weekend visit, Uncle Harry was scandalized by Marian's backless sundress.

Joyce's account was amusing:

"'What are you wearing?' he asked. 'A sundress,' you said, fairly enough, as it *was* a sundress. 'Go home at once,' he said, 'and put on some Proper Clothes.' You offered to hang a newspaper over your shoulders while visiting him, but we were ordered home, your flippancy disregarded."

Though Uncle Harry was exceptionally grouchy, Janet and Frank were overprotective and strict with their girls, too, forbidding them to wear makeup. Marian recalled once smearing something on her face—"I don't remember what, probably blackberry juice"—and presenting herself to her mother, who declared, "Margaret! Take that stuff off. You look like a clown!" Throughout her teen years, when Marian bought shoes, her father accompanied her to the shop.

"He would take a foot rule and measure the heel," she said. "I couldn't buy the shoe if he thought the heel was too high."

Even when Marian was seventeen, her mother insisted she insert a "modesty" at the front and back of a new dress she'd bought for a dance, because Janet didn't think the cleavage was "seemly."

Looking back, Marian chuckled, since the boy her mother had fixed her up with turned out to be gay.

"I didn't find that out till years later," said Marian. "Maybe Mummy knew and thought we were safe with them!"

But such issues concerning sexuality—and sensuality, for that matter—were simply not discussed. Adding to the sense of the forbidden, there were books on the shelf Marian was prohibited from reading. And while Frank had taken Marian aside at a certain point to explain "where babies come from," in classic schoolyard fashion, some of Marian's early knowledge of sex had come from a copy of *Lady Chatterley's Lover* surreptitiously slipped to her by Stratford House classmate Pamela Brown.

Marian's "flippancy," noted so keenly by her sister, was to become one of her most enduring character traits, particularly as she approached adolescence. It gradually blossomed into a steely determination to have her own way. It also wound up getting her into a pile of trouble at school. Though she had started out as a withdrawn and solitary child, by her teen years she was mouthy, stubborn, and flip. After two years at Avonclyffe—and just as the stock market crashed—Janet Turner decided Marian wasn't learning much, so she deposited her at the stricter Holy Trinity Convent, whose stern sisters led a prayer before every class. An imposing brick edifice along Plaistow Road with a great playing field in back, it stood adjacent to St. Joseph's Catholic Church, where Marian attended mass.

On the musical front, Marian had abandoned the violin by now but continued to enjoy being a "ham," as she put it, playing popular songs on the piano for the kids at Holy Trinity. One of the first tunes she learned—by ear, off the radio—was "You're Blasé," introduced by the singer Binnie Hale in the 1932 London stage show *Bow Bells*. A couple of classmates played, too, and Marian recollected "copping good chord changes" from one of them. Though she made friends at school—hanging out at the Sundridge sweet shop buying "gob stoppers" with her pals—Marian still felt something of a misfit. She relished being "accepted" for her music. "It was my claim to fame," she explained. At Holy Trinity, she also began to flourish as a vocalist, singing alto and soprano in the school choir under the tutelage of one Ada Bacon Haigh, who regularly displayed her students at recitals and music festivals around town, where Marian, with her perfect pitch, was often featured as a soloist or in duets and took prizes at local music festivals. In April 1933, the *Kentish Times* noted of her performance of the hymn "Dawn Gentle Flower" and Thomas Arne's setting of Shakespeare's "Where the Bee Sucks" that "Margaret Turner has a clear diction and produces her voice in a pleasantly effortless manner."

The course work at Holy Trinity was heavy, and while Marian excelled as a student, she routinely got low marks for "conduct" and "deportment."

One afternoon, her defiance prompted Sister Joseph to grab her by the scruff of the neck, take her out of the classroom, and lock her in the laundry room.

"She shouted at me in French," said Marian. "I don't know what I did. I really don't."

Pleas of innocence notwithstanding (certainly no one could have discovered she had a secret crush on the priest, who rode to school on a motorbike!), Marian's sister, Joyce, who also attended Holy Trinity, had a clear memory of the situation in general, if not of Marian's specific offense.

"I expect you can remember your life of crime at the Convent," wrote Joyce. "You were fighting well with Mother and so, I imagine, played up at school to compensate. Anyway, various reports came saying all the things they say when nuns are displeased, and there was a big family fight, and Mother said Boarding School was the answer. You must have been in a state of almost permanent hostility with Mother at that time."

And so it was, in 1933, that Marian was packed off to the Stratford House School for Girls, suitcase in tow. Founded in 1912, Stratford was a reputable day school in neighboring Bickley, with a boardinghouse next door to its primary, ivy-colored building. The school had about two hundred students, many of whom arrived each morning on the red, single-decker bus that ran through Bickley on its way from Bromley to Chislehurst, though Elspeth Campbell, daughter of local MP Sir Edward Campbell, was dropped off by car. Shortly after Marian entered Stratford House as a boarder, she began to develop violent migraine headaches, and her doctor advised her mother to switch Marian to day student status. Boarding school, that brutal English tradition, was not to become a lasting part of Marian's story. In a few weeks, her mother relented, though the headaches persisted for some time.

"There was lots of throwing up and feeling awful for days," Marian later wrote, realizing her childhood migraines were related to a syndrome of depression that persisted into adulthood. "After lying in bed for about three days, constantly vomiting and having Mummy ministering to me, I would finally come around, and I remember that first solid food (a boiled egg) as tasting just glorious."

The tone at Stratford House was set by Eva Georgiana Wilkinson, "every inch a headmistress," wrote Stratford House historian Susan Pittman, "a commanding presence with a gracious manner, who sailed along the corridors with her academic gown billowing behind, or with a ready smile and great charm, as she greeted parents on Sports Day wearing a flowered hat and flowing garments bedecked with innumerable strings of beads."

The school was well outfitted, with a chemistry lab, grass tennis courts, and a playing field where the girls—wearing pale blue cotton gym costumes called "jibbahs"—played field hockey and rounders and danced Eurythmics. The regular uniform was a navy blue dress with detachable beige tussore collar and tie. Miss Wilkinson took only "well-spoken and well-bred girls from good backgrounds," but girls from genteel families who had fallen on hard times during "the slump" were charged half the fee. Miss Wilkinson's noblesse oblige went only so far, however. When she discovered parents donating old uniforms to charity, she feared they would be worn "by children of the wrong type" and thereby bring discredit to Stratford House.

School began with a prayer and Miss Hollins, who taught art and geometry, persuading the girls to breathe deeply to expand their chests. After a hearty hymn, the girls marched out singing a Gilbert & Sullivan tune. "Solid" courses like algebra, German, English, and botany were offered, and there were outings to London to see theater, opera, and the symphony. At lunch, the girls might walk home and on the way back treat themselves at Mrs. Parfitt's Sweet Shop at Bickley Station.

Miss Wilkinson was also big on catering and domestic science.

"I feel sure," she reasoned, "that future husbands will profit thereby, for, if maidless, these girls will be able to do work efficiently, and, if fortunate to have domestics they will be able to train their maids correctly."

As Miss Wilkinson's remarks revealed so aptly, girls at Stratford House were being trained not for university—or careers—but for marriage. Nevertheless, Marian got a good education, one that would serve her well in later life. Under the watchful eye of Miss Hollins, Marian learned to paint meticulously crafted, botanically correct watercolors from nature—poppies, pansies, nasturtiums, roses, primroses, and violets—one of which was used for the cover of the school magazine. Marian later hung a framed set of these lovely watercolors in her house in Port Washington, New York, and used one as the cover art for her album *The Single Petal of a Rose*.

Marian also excelled in drama and debate ("elocution"). With her love of popular music, she hotly contested the resolution that "Composers of Jazz Have Rendered a Disservice to Music," "handily carrying the majority," reported classmate Doris Kidney. Ditto, the same year, for "The Cinema Is a Degenerating Amusement." Marian played the part of Bottom in Shakespeare's *A Midsummer Night's Dream* and, at the school's fall prize-giving ceremony in 1934, recited from the bard's *Henry VIII*, a program that concluded with "tea in the common room." Roles as Gratiano in

The Merchant of Venice and Aunt Imogen in W. Graham Robertson's *Pinkie and the Fairies* were hers as well.

When Marian entered Stratford House, the school was divided into two "houses," named for Queens Victoria and Elizabeth. The "Lizzies" and the "Vics" competed in sports. In 1934, with expanded enrollment, a third house, the Alexandrans, was formed and Marian took her place as house treasurer for the autumn term. Marian's suggestion that the Alexandrans adopt the sweet pea as its flower was accepted, and she painted the flower for the house crest. She also wrote the lyrics for the "house song," "Press On and Persevere," a maxim one could imagine her father heartily seconding.

While Marian embraced school activities with relish, her report cards reflected a desultory attitude toward core studies, summed up by the snippy Miss Wilkinson as follows: "Margaret has good ability and can do well when she likes. We wish she would make up her mind to work more seriously and also remember that she is a Senior member of the School."

"When she likes" would seem to have been the key phrase. For a budding young artist, it was, perhaps, not a bad trait, as making art requires focus. An inclination to pursue what she liked—music and art—and let the rest be damned probably hastened her development. It also reflected an increasingly entrenched willfulness and resistance to authority.

By this time, Marian had finally convinced her mother to give her piano lessons. She was sixteen years old. A local teacher, Gwen Massey, was recruited and Marian studied with her for better than a year. In May 1934, under the aegis of Holy Trinity vocal teacher Ada Bacon Haigh, Marian sang two songs written by Massey, "Elves" and "The Moon Maids," as well as "The Song of the Music Makers" by Martin Shaw, at Bromley's Robert Whyte Memorial Hall. The local paper praised her singing, noting, however, that she was "suffering from a cold."

Marian continued to entertain her mates at school, with increasing sophistication. Said Barbara Strudwick, a classmate who went on to a professional career as a violinist: "She used to sit down at the grand piano in the great hall at the school and just play and play and play. She was very good. I don't think she could read much. She didn't shine in music classes at all. That is, not from the classical point of view. She was 'jazzy.'"

Marian excelled at improvisation at quite an early age. At the 1934 Bromley Music Festival, she won the prize for "extemporization." That same year, she was praised in the *Kentish Times* for her "lyrical and sincere" vocal interpretation of Mendelssohn's "The First Violet" and took a junior prize at the piano for playing Frank Bridge's "Rosemary" "very well indeed."

"I was very keen to show them what I could do," she recalled, noting that the many prizes she won for piano, voice, and composition had by now made her something of a local teen celebrity.

Marian's teacher Gwen Massey was responsible for Marian's appearances at some of the festivals where she won prizes, but Marian's primary response to Massey was that under no circumstances did she ever want to become a piano teacher herself. Miss Massey lived with her mother and, like Marian's Sunday school teacher, had a "spinsterish" look about her. Though she wasn't quite sure what it was, Marian was beginning to have intimations of another, more glamorous order of existence beyond Bromley or Bickley, something she sensed in the jaunty popular songs and jazz she heard on recordings and on the radio and from a boyfriend named Ken Hughes. Ken had originally come around to see Joyce, but Joyce "lost interest" when Ken and Marian hit it off playing records. Joyce, after all, said Marian, could have her pick of boyfriends. She was "the pretty one," languid and comfortable in her own body, and to whom flirting came easily. Marian, more awkward around boys, had nevertheless blossomed into a young woman with an attractive figure, deep brown eyes, and a smile that flickered with wicked humor. Marian loved her parents' record of Bing Crosby singing "Please," but Ken's new jazz records made that seem tame. She and Ken pored over 78 rpm recordings by Duke Ellington, Sidney Bechet, Muggsy Spanier, the Benny Goodman Trio, and Bud Freeman's famous showpiece "The Eel."

"[Ken] made me really listen," recalled Marian. "He made me aware of the Ellington band's unique orchestral sounds, the quality and tone color of each soloist, Duke as a pianist, his way of voicing chords, the strong, exciting rhythms of the band. I absorbed it all, and from then on I was hooked! We'd discuss the records and say, 'What do you think of this and that? How did you like that chord?' Then I'd go to the piano and try to play it and take things off by Teddy [Wilson] and Duke."

Marian's Stratford House friend Margaret Cooper, also a pianist, introduced Marian to the music of the popular British piano ace Billy Mayerl, who had megahits in England with "Marigold" and "Ace of Hearts." Margaret and Marian played Mayerl's sheet music at Palace Grove after school, trading off playing for each other. Margaret began inviting Marian to play for parties at her house.

As at Holy Trinity, music provided an avenue to acceptance.

"I always felt like I was not with the in-crowd," she said. "I didn't have 'it,' unless I was playing, and then they all dug me. I would sit down at the piano and all the kids would crowd around. I needed approbation, and this was how I got it."

At a party, Marian met another young pianist with a yen for jazz, Ray Cobb, who had two pianos at his house. The two would play tunes for each other, comparing notes and having conversations about the music.

But by far the richest source for Marian of new popular tunes was the British Broadcasting Corporation (BBC). On the air since 1922, the BBC had from its inception made popular dance music a mainstay of its evening programming, forming an alliance in 1923 with the Savoy Hotel's Savoy Orpheans led by Carroll Gibbons and the Savoy Havana Band featuring Billy Mayerl on piano. Though it held no brief for jazz per se—in fact was passively hostile to it—the BBC saw the promotion of popular music as part of its mission to bring the social classes closer together. Popular music and jazz were broadcast under the rubric "dance music," considered respectable because of the upper-class tea dance and hotel venues where it was played. Marian most certainly heard these live broadcasts in the drawing room at Palace Grove, including the bands of Jack Payne, Jack Hylton, Henry Hall, Lew Stone, Bert Ambrose, and Roy Fox.

These groups played what jazz musicians call "sweet"—as opposed to "hot"—music. They didn't swing or improvise much. In fact, like America's Paul Whiteman (the paragon of a "sweet" stylist), they conceived of themselves as having improved on the "raw" jazz that had first appeared in England in 1919, when the Original Dixieland Jazz Band and Marion Cook's Southern Syncopated Orchestra (with Sidney Bechet) had first visited. These bands declined to even call their music "jazz," preferring "sophisticated syncopation." The BBC's monopoly of the airwaves and strict British union protection of local jobs guaranteed that sweet, "sophisticated syncopation" trumped "jazz" in the 1920s and 1930s. When the hot new big band music of Benny Goodman ushered in the swing era in America in 1935, Britain very nearly missed the movement altogether. British jazz itself wouldn't flower until the 1940s, when the policies at the BBC began to change.

Marian was introduced to jazz in this diluted form. Though she tried to copy what she heard on the radio, the idea of how to improvise in swing time was a mystery.

"I didn't know what was pop and what was jazz," she confessed. "I just learned the tunes. And I didn't have any kind of 'beat.'"

That Marian's early exposure to jazz was song-centered is extremely important in understanding her development. Many jazz artists could care less about tunes, so obsessed are they about the possibilities of harmony and improvisation. Marian always started with the song and never forgot it, lyrics included. This valorization of melody would become one of the hallmarks of her mature playing, even after her rhythmic abilities caught up. It accounts in part for her broad accessibility to the public, which has always responded more readily to the emotional punch of a good song than to complicated variations on it.

In the programs for the Ada Bacon Haigh vocal recitals as well as the school production of *Pinkie and the Fairies* was listed one Doris Mackie, L.G.S.M. Mackie became the most seminal influence on Marian McPartland's teen years and a lifelong friend who figured prominently in her life. A conservatory graduate—the L.G.S.M. after her name meant "licentiate of the Guildhall School of Music"—"Mac," as she was called, taught elocution at Stratford House.

Though married, with two sons, Mackie "had a masculine air about her," reported Marian's niece Sheila, and she had a close female friend, Nora, who ran a dance class in Bromley, for which she recruited Marian to play piano. It was de rigueur for English schoolgirls (and schoolboys, for that matter) in those days to have same-sex crushes on their public school teachers, and Marian developed a great crush on Doris Mackie. They became quite friendly, and Marian even remembered borrowing money from her to buy something she wanted at Harrods, in retrospect, something she saw as rather bold, but that Mackie was quite "carefree" about.

Mac became a familiar face in the Turner household and eventually took both Margaret and Joyce under her wing as a sort of surrogate aunt. She was just the kind of friendly champion Marian needed. Marian's parents had begun to worry about her future. According to Joyce, their mother wondered how such a willful girl would ever settle down to a nice life as a banker's or solicitor's wife and raise a family. With her interest in music, one supposed she could become a piano teacher, but Marian had already ruled that out. Marian remembered her mother looking at her directly in the eye at one point and saying rather sharply, "Well, you'd better decide what you want to do in life because we can't keep you."

"I guess I was about fifteen or sixteen, and it sort of hit me like a knock on the head," said Marian. "I remember the moment clearly. I had this awful feeling that something had changed—that childhood was over."

One night over dinner, when Mac was visiting, the subject of Marian's future came up and Frank Turner turned to the trusted teacher for advice. With an imploring tone, he asked, "What shall we *do* with her?" Mac was stunned. Had they never considered sending Margaret to London, to the Guildhall School of Music and Drama? And if not, why not? It was so obvious to her that Marian was a musical prodigy, it had never occurred to her that her parents hadn't noticed. Frank Turner was a reasonable man, but he knew little about such things. How was it done? Mrs. Mackie explained about auditioning and so forth and put Marian's father in touch with the right people. It was the spring of 1935.

Marian went down to London and auditioned for Sir Landon Ronald, director of the Guildhall School.

"I was shaking in my boots," said Marian, whose sight-reading skills had never been good. "I thought, 'They'll never take me. I'm not good enough.'"

"My girl," said Sir Landon, "you are sadly lacking in technique, devastatingly lacking. But you have rampant enthusiasm, God-given facility, and a dangerous surplus of imagination."

To Marian's utter surprise, she was accepted.

London
(1935~1944)

THE GUILDHALL SCHOOL OF MUSIC AND DRAMA is one of the top three conservatories in England today, but in Marian's era it had only recently achieved parity with its rivals, the Royal Academy of Music and the Royal College of Music. Upon its establishment in 1880, its initial goal had been to improve the quality of amateur music teachers of just the sort Marian had been exposed to in Bromley. Sir Landon Ronald, principal since 1910, had brought the Guildhall up to speed, raising the standards for new piano students, instituting a fixed curriculum, and hiring the composer Samuel Coleridge-Taylor, whose father was from Sierra Leone. When Marian attended, there were about twelve hundred students, though many were part-time. The school stood on the corner of John Carpenter and Talis Streets, near Victoria Embankment, by the river Thames. Its two neoclassical buildings had white stone façades, one with five porthole windows with the names of British musical lights engraved above them. Henry Purcell, the great baroque composer, took pride of place above the main doorway's scrolled lintel.

When Marian walked through that door in April 1935 after dropping out of Stratford House, she began a new routine, riding the train down to London three or four times a week—a forty-minute ride—then grabbing a cab from the station. The environment was formal. "When bass singer Norman Walker appeared in the School one day in grey flannel trousers and a tweed sports jacket, the Principal called him into his office and reminded him that as the holder of a major scholarship he was never to come again in 'week-end' attire," wrote Hugh Barty-King in a school history. "If he did not know where to go for a suit in London at a price within his means he recommended The Fifty Shilling Tailors in the Strand." A head porter in top hat greeted Sir Landon each morning, ceremoniously opening the door of his Rolls-Royce. A log fire crackled in the front hall in the winter, but students warming themselves were best advised to move along if they happened to be standing there when Sir Landon arrived.

Marian took piano instruction from Orlando Morgan, the first concentrated music lessons she had ever had. Morgan, a Guildhall professor since 1887, had an illustrious classical protégée in Myra Hess, the great British concert virtuoso. Fred Astaire and Noel Coward had also studied piano with him in the 1920s. Under Morgan's tutelage, Marian practiced eight hours a day on a Challen upright, using the Hanon method book to improve her fingering technique and to develop dexterity. She played Chopin, Debussy, Beethoven sonatas, Bach preludes and fugues, and the music of Edward MacDowell and Jacques Ibert. She was also exposed to the work of the British impressionist composer Delius, whose harmonies would later have an enormous impact on her. Marian's sight-reading skills—the ability to read music in real time from the page—probably reached their zenith at this point. But like many players with perfect pitch, she preferred to learn pieces by ear.

"There was no heat in the room where the piano was," she remembered. "You would light a fire. I sat in there with my coat on. It was always a great, painstaking thing for me to read music. I never was able to rattle something off. I learned everything very, very slowly at that time."

Morgan was a composer of note, having written song cycles and a light comic opera, *Two Merry Monarchs,* that enjoyed a 1910 run at the Savoy Theatre. He consequently stressed composition and improvisation as well as technique and sight-reading, the two former skills being especially important in Marian's development as a jazz musician.

"He showed me some things that were really quite valuable," she said. "How to put a piece together, how to refer back to the theme and build it up to a fine climax."

In 1936 and 1937, Marian received the school's Wainwright Memorial Scholarship for composition. Her piece "Valse Gracieuse" also earned her composition scholarships for two years from the Worshipful Company of Musicians, which would later award her one of its highest honors. Marian's father often came down to London to hear her recitals. Programs featured her own compositions; Rachmaninoff's "Polichinelle"; and "An Irish Dell" and "The Road Breaker," both by Harry Waldo Warner, the great viola player from the London String Quartet. The program for her final fall program noted she had been awarded the Chairman's School Composition Prize (divided) on October 29, 1937, by the Lady Mayoress of London in the School's Mansion House.

Guildhall classes ran from ten in the morning till seven at night. Marian studied vocal technique from retired opera singer Carrie Tubb, music theory, and sight-singing. The school required students to take up a second instrument, so she chose violin, presumably because she had already played it, though she continued to dislike the instrument. Worse, her teacher turned out to be something less than a gentleman. Though the doors of every classroom had windows—a Victorian precaution against "hanky-panky"—Marian's teacher apparently asked her to play standing on a chair.

"He was a dirty old man," she said. "I was uncomfortable about reporting one of the faculty, but I complained, I was so embarrassed. Anyway, that stopped. I didn't go there anymore."

As for more savory encounters with the opposite sex, Marian remembered being wooed by the Welsh tenor David Lloyd, who later became famous for his renderings of Welsh songs as well as his work with the Glyndebourne Opera Company and Sadler's Wells.

"That guy used to chase me all over the place," she said. "He was a fabulous singer."

While commuting to London, Marian continued to concertize in Bromley. On May 19, 1936, she played one of her compositions at a recital presented by Ada Bacon Haigh for Bromley's Conservative Club. She earned spending money playing piano one afternoon a week for her sister's dance class at Holy Trinity. Marian also continued to see her boyfriend, Ray Cobb, who played a little jazz piano, but it seemed to her father that all she did was practice until she was too sleepy to do anything else, then go to bed. Marian's apparent determination to make a career out of music worried him.

"Father said a girl could not have a secure life playing the piano," wrote Joyce. "How the hell can a girl have a secure life anyway, unless she refuses to go out, and then the ceiling may fall in, or the house catch fire? I can remember when Father said the Bank of England was a Nice Safe Job. Could you ever see yourself in the Bank of England, except as a cash customer?"

Looking back, Marian concluded she had no "teenage life at all, devoting every spare moment to practicing Hanon exercises and classical pieces, and competing for scholarships."

Marian's mother, for once, took Marian's side, at least on the practicing issue, which led to "rows" with Frank, as Joyce put it, and an increased level of tension in the Turner household over Marian's future. Strategically, Marian retreated into the world of music. But that world was changing. As she fastidiously practiced Bach and Beethoven, she began to realize that she responded much more urgently to the syncopated popular music she heard on the BBC, whether it was Billy Mayerl's glittering virtuosity,

Bob Crosby pianist Bob Zurke's raucous boogie-woogie, or Joe Sullivan's rambunctious stride piano. Though she couldn't articulate it, she sensed something driving this music that was more exciting, more glamorous, and more in tune with how she really felt about the world than the stuffy environment and limited musical outlook of the Guildhall. She also realized, day by day, that she had neither the will nor the skill to become a classical concert pianist. If that was not in her future, just what was it, she wondered, that went into the music of Teddy Wilson, Fats Waller, and Art Tatum? How did it work? With the same determination she had applied to the classics, she set out to decode this other music.

"I would sit down at the piano and try to duplicate Bob Zurke choruses," she recalled. "He had a kind of contrapuntal thing that he would play right down the length of the piano. I wanted to learn how to do that. Same with Teddy's runs. But it always used to puzzle me that it never sounded the way they did."

One day in London, she found a book of transcriptions of solos by Art Tatum and took it into the freezing practice room at the Guildhall. Tatum played with such speed and complexity that the pianist Jimmy Rowles later famously said that when he first heard Tatum's records he thought it was "four guys playing." As Marian pored over the tangled mass of black dots that supposedly represented Tatum's solo on "Humoresque," she heard a knock on the practice room door.

There was Orlando Morgan, with his great mass of white hair, glaring at her.

"Let's hear some of this discordant trash you call jazz," he said, his face reddening.

Marian played George Gershwin's "I'll Build a Stairway to Paradise."

Morgan listened. Without saying anything, he turned to leave.

"I'm sorry, sir," Marian said.

"Don't be," said Morgan. "If the Lord put that much rhythm inside you, he meant it to be heard."

For a moment, Marian was stunned but, ultimately, not surprised. Though ragtime sometimes accompanied Guildhall student gatherings (Sir Landon actually liked popular music), Morgan, like most classical musicians of his era, probably considered jazz to be a low, ephemeral gutter music played by Negroes. The problem for Marian was that there were no schools for learning how to play it. You had to pick it up on the bandstand, through personal contact with other players. Perhaps because she was a woman, and a timid, sheltered, suburban young lady at that (notwithstanding her "hollering" at her recital accompanist), the idea of venturing out to jam with London jazzers was unthinkable. True, one afternoon while skating at the Stratham Ice Rink with Mac ("by this time we were just friends; I had given up having a crush on her"), Marian had surprised even herself by asking to play a few numbers. But this had been a rare occasion. Marian didn't attend jazz concerts, much less ask to sit in. When Fats Waller played London in 1938, it never occurred to her to buy tickets, even though she'd seen a poster for the concert.

"I don't know why," she said. "I never did know how to gravitate towards any jazz musicians."

It's instructive to contrast Marian's experience as a proper young lady from Bromley with that of George Shearing, born male, working class—and blind—just outside London, in 1919. While Marian was practicing scales at the Guildhall, Shearing was jamming at the Nest in Soho, where he met and played with Coleman Hawkins and was introduced to Fats Waller. Apparently, Shearing's physical handicap was only slightly less daunting for him than the ones of gender and class were for Marian. But if she couldn't go out to clubs, how could a genteel young lady learn to improvise jazz? As she sat in the practice room pondering this question, Marian remembered an ad she had seen in *Melody Maker* magazine for a school operated by Billy Mayerl, the composer of "Marigold."

"Syncopated Piano Playing Can Be Taught," said the ad.

Though Mayerl's popularity had peaked in the 1920s, he was still a huge figure in British popular music, mostly as the ragtime-influenced composer of such novelties as "All of a Twist" and "Jazzaristrix." Billy's work wasn't exactly jazz, nor was it precisely classical; rather, it was somewhere in between, part of what the English call "light music," a mixture of classical and pops that takes in everything from Albert Ketelbey's "In a Persian Market" to ragtime brass quintets. In 1926, the entrepreneurial Mayerl and his partner Geoffrey Clayton had opened the School of Modern Syncopation, which offered lessons as well as correspondence packets. In less than a decade, Mayerl's school had more than three thousand students and branches in South Africa, New Zealand, India, and Germany. (The American crooner and heartthrob Rudy Vallée became a correspondence student.) The tone of the Mayerl courses was a curious blend of musical tips and unabashed commercialism. The Advanced Course in Modern Rhythm, for example, suggested pianists spice up their writing with "blue chords," such as a D-flat nine with a flatted five, a chord that wouldn't catch on in jazz till the 1940s. Yet in the Modern Popular Composition packet, Mayerl warned against writing music that was too complicated, because public taste was so simple-minded. With such obvious contempt for his audience, it's no surprise that while he composed more than three hundred piano pieces and scores for twenty West End musicals, Mayerl produced little, if any, music of lasting value.

When Marian knocked on the Mayerl school door at Hanover Square in early 1938, Billy had just begun to plan a new venture—a piano quartet to promote a gimmicky new instrument called the Multi-Tone, made by the Challen piano company, whose equipment Mayerl endorsed. A woman in the front office greeted Marian warmly and asked for a sample of her playing. After the audition, the woman excused herself and went into a back room. When she returned, Mayerl himself was with her. He asked her to play something else. Marian offered "Where Are You?" by Harold Adamson and Jimmy McHugh, a tune that had become popular in the 1936 show *Top of the Town*. Without fanfare, Mayerl immediately engaged her in an impromptu lesson.

Recalled Marian: "He showed me a certain way of playing the bass line, using split tenths. I think what he was trying to do was show me something that would make my playing more melodic. And he also said something which has stuck with me all these years, which was, 'When you're playing the melody to a tune, don't jump octaves. Play the whole phrase, or at least the first eight of the melody or the first part of it in the same part of the piano. Don't start it in one place and jump up or down to another.'"

After this brief exchange, Mayerl asked Marian a shocking question. Would she like to go on the road with his new quartet?

"I was just flabbergasted," she remembered. "I was very excited and confused, because I was going to the Guildhall and he wanted to start rehearsing for a tour that was coming up within the next few months."

On the train back to Bromley that night, Marian thought excitedly about the opportunity that had befallen her. An unknown, nineteen-year-old student at the Guildhall, aching to draw outside the lines of classical music but not quite knowing how to go about it, she had asked for a lesson from one of the most famous popular musicians in Britain and had been offered not a lesson—but a tour. It was difficult to even conceive of such good fortune. Though she had never traveled more than fifty miles from home, she decided she simply must go. It was her "big chance." When she broke the news to her parents, they were apoplectic. Sending her off to the Guildhall to become a professional musician had been a leap of faith. But a vaudeville performer?

"It is a stupid choice," her father declared, "racketing around the country with a lot of show people."

He peremptorily offered her £1,000 to change her mind. (This was a considerable sum, the equivalent of $40,000 in today's currency.)

"You'll come to no good. You'll marry a musician and live in an attic," her mother warned, furious that all her guidance and criticism had gone for naught.

In a tearful scene at the Guildhall, Orlando Morgan pleaded, "Don't throw your talent away," then, more placatingly, "Are you sure you're doing the right thing?"

But Marian was determined to go, even though leaving school meant she would earn only an associate degree, not the four-year licentiate she had been working toward. Eventually, after many "family councils," she promised to return to the Guildhall after the tour. Frank Turner met with Mayerl to see that his daughter was going to be treated like a proper lady on the road.

"He asked him all kinds of questions," said Marian. "'Where are you going to go? What kinds of dates are you going to play? What kind of money will my daughter be making?'"

Her pay, in fact, would be £5 a week, plus all travel and hotels, which was really not bad.

"In spite of my image of myself as a timid person," Marian later mused, "I've come to know that there must have been a stubborn or willful or driving side to my nature that I didn't really understand that led me to take off from the Guildhall, rashly promising that I would return . . . while knowing in my heart that I never really would."

In retrospect, Marian said her time at the Guildhall—in spite of rejecting a classical career—was one of the most influential experiences of her life. Her three-year immersion in the Western classics would have a profound influence on her musical sophistication, technique, and outlook. Under Morgan's guidance, she developed a classical touch both sensitive and firm, producing a bell-like tone and a feel for phrasing that pulled the listener naturally from the beginning to the middle to the end of a line. She learned to navigate the keyboard well in all keys, fingering scales, arpeggios, or successions of complex chords with apparent ease. Classical coherence and clarity became early hallmarks of her playing, as did a clear sense of developing an extemporized solo with compositional logic. Her immersion in the romantic music of Chopin—where she had started, after all—and the pastoral impressionism of Delius, especially in pieces such as "On Hearing the First Cuckoo in Spring," "Brigg Fair," and "Summer Night on the River," would color her solos for the rest of her life.

On April 23, 1938, just over a month after her twentieth birthday, Marian officially withdrew from the school. Later that year, she was awarded an associate degree (A.G.S.M.) with honors, with a bronze medal for the Chairman's Pianoforte Prize. Rehearsals for Billy's new act—Billy Mayerl and His Claviers—began that winter at a West End theater. The group featured four pianists—Billy, Marian, George Myddleton, and Kathleen Heppell—each playing specially made, gold-painted Challen pianos. Billy sat between two grands; the three other pianists played uprights. Each instrument was fitted with a Multi-Tone attachment, which enabled the player, with an extra pedal, to produce the sound of a harp, harpsichord, banjo, or mandolin. Always keen to try out new technology, Mayerl also played an early electronic piano called the Novachord. Before they set out, Mayerl's wife, Jill, outfitted the women with pinkish purple taffeta gowns, with frills on the bottom, cap sleeves with velvet trimmings, and shoes to match. Marian went to a posh London salon and had her hair styled.

Marian not only acquired new clothes and a new haircut, she chose a new name—Marian Payne. She had always preferred the flowing vowels of her middle name to the harsher Margaret—the family called her Maggie, Margie, or Mag—but the new last name was a curious choice, since one good reason for changing it was to avoid "blotting the family escutcheon," as she put it, with her new career. But Payne was her mother's maiden name. In a few months, no doubt realizing this contradiction, she changed her name again, to the more mundane Marian Page, thereby also avoiding, she said, vulnerability to clever pundits who might indeed find her a "Payne." But more important, in the time-honored tradition of show business folk—from Anthony Benedetto (Tony Bennett) to Robert Zimmerman (Bob Dylan)—Marian had made a symbolic break with her past. From this day forward, she would create a new persona. Margaret Turner, the shy English girl from Bromley who played Chopin on her uncle Harry's piano in Windsor, was no more. Marian Page, vaudeville pianist, had emerged. It was the kind of metamorphosis—and name change—her parents had hoped might happen when she married that elusive banker they had always had in mind. But Marian had married her music.

The transformation began immediately. The Claviers debuted March 26, 1938, at a venerable London artists' hangout, Pagani's Restaurant, and a rave review noted the show featured "two attractive young ladies," which must have done wonders for the self-esteem of a young Bromley girl who all her life had believed she was the ugly duckling. Four days later, the Claviers performed on the BBC's first prime-time comedy/variety show, Arthur Askey's hilarious *Band Waggon,* one of the most popular shows in British radio history. The next morning, the Claviers went into Abbey

Road studios (where the Beatles later recorded) to put down four sides—
released as two 78 rpm records—for Columbia.

The Mayerl sides—Marian's debut on record—were strictly novelty
fare, but notable for the uncluttered accuracy of the four piano parts and
how neatly they dovetailed, hocket style, as each pianist played notes from
a preassigned register of the melody. At times the quartet sounded like a
full orchestra, at others like chiming celestes, a plucked banjo, or an ice-
cream truck. When Mayerl reprised a medley of his hits "Sweet William,"
"Green Tulips," and "Marigold," the oddly speedy tempo made listening
a bit like watching an old silent film shot at sixteen frames per second projected at twenty-four. As corny and silly as this stuff was, it was also tricky
music, difficult to play.

After the session, the Claviers hit the road, giving their first performance outside London on April 4, at the Theatre Royal in Norwich. The
Claviers barnstormed the provinces, playing the Shakespeare Theatre in
Liverpool; the Embassy in Peterborough; the Palace in Hull; the Tivoli in
Aberdeen; the Argyle in Birkenhead; and pretty much every top variety
house in England from Birmingham to Bristol, winding things up with
an extended engagement at the Empire, as part of the Glasgow Exhibition,
in Scotland. Most of these old theatrical palaces have long since vanished,
but they were grand affairs, with velvet seats, great heavy curtains, high
ceilings, steeply raked balconies, and rococo Oriental motifs molded into
the stucco walls. The Claviers topped the bill, playing a week in each town
on a show that included caricatures ("both black and white," read one
review, suggesting minstrel comedy), top-spinning and balancing, vocal
impressions, dancing, acrobatics, and comedy. The critics loved the act.
"Easily the most interesting feature in this week's bill of variety is Billy
Mayerl's appearance in Norwich with his Claviers," crowed the *Eastern
Daily Press,* adding that all four "accomplished pianists provide a well
produced musical act of charm and entertainment upon their four golden
pianos."

A Pathé newsreel of the Claviers nicely conveyed the novelty of the act
and by its mere existence confirmed not only Mayerl's elevated status in
British show business, but his hunch that the Challen Multi-Tone would
make a good news hook. An elfish man with a gap-toothed smile and
pomaded hair, Mayerl, wearing a tux, sat between two grand pianos on
the lower level of a two-tiered, gleaming white stage set. The three side
players were stationed in a row above, on the second tier, playing uprights.
Marian, wearing a long skirt and a nearly backless top (what would Uncle
Harry think?), sat on the right; Myddleton, appropriately enough, was in

the middle; and the blond bombshell Dorothy Carless (who had replaced Heppell) sat at the left. Mayerl explained that the group would take listeners through three periods of history—the past, playing a Boccherini minuet, Multi-Tones pedaling in the sound of harpsichords; modern times, with Ruperto Chapí's lively, Latin-tinged "Bunch of Roses"; and the future—Billy's own jazzy "Bats in the Belfry." It was clever, if decidedly middlebrow stuff.

Marian took enthusiastically to the hurly-burly of life on the road. English variety acts in those days stayed in converted homes, which they called "digs."

"All these landladies would advertise in show business magazines," explained Marian. "There was one called the Stage. The ad would say 'all in,' which meant that you had the room and food. I remember having this fabulous landlady in Glasgow and she would ask me what I wanted for dinner or lunch, and she would go out and get it and cook it. It was all part of the deal. And very cheap. Thirty shillings—one pound ten. Usually these places were very comfortable, and they had a dining room table and usually a big roaring fire. She'd come in the morning and start the fire and bring the tea. You'd leave a call for what time you wanted to get up. There wasn't unlimited hot water. You had to have what was designated as 'bath night.' In a lot of places there'd be a washbasin in the room, and the landlady would come in with hot water in jugs. But we thought it was very comfortable."

At the beginning of the tour, the Claviers featured a dancer, Iris Kirkwhite, who shared stage secrets with Marian, helping her with the heavy, dark makeup the women had to wear. "We used some kind of junk on our eyelashes to make them stick out, with little beads of wax on the end," said Marian. "We'd use a pencil to extend our eyelids way out and put a little red dot in the corner." Marian usually roomed with Dorothy, a tall, buxom blonde who would later become a popular singer with bandleader Bert Ambrose. Marian and Dorothy became good friends, and Marian mimicked her behavior as well as her style of dress. Dorothy gave off a great aura of sexuality, and all the men "dashed around her," said Marian. "Whoever was left after everybody had made a pass at Dorothy, I would have to take." The night after the Norwich opener, everyone went to a pub. Still thrilled to have gotten through her first show without a mistake, Marian suddenly heard Mayerl shout across the room to Myddleton, "Hey, George, we've got a couple of virgins in here!" Everybody laughed at what was clearly a well-intentioned pun about her first time on the road, but Marian was chagrined.

"I didn't want to be thought of as a virgin," she said. "I wanted to be thought of as a person of sophistication. I was always trying to perfect my role, trying to pretend to be experienced, and probably coming off just as I was—a naive young chick."

Indeed, Marian's naïveté led her to tactlessly—if in all innocence—mention to Billy's wife, Jill, that she'd once seen Kathleen Heppell sitting on Billy's lap, which infuriated Jill and sadly soured Marian's relationship with Billy.

The Claviers concluded their run that summer. By tour's end, Marian would have played in dozens of England's major theaters, debuted on national radio with one of the most famous popular musicians in England, cut her first recordings, and appeared in a newsreel that played in theaters all over the country. She was launched. And she had started at the top, a pattern that would repeat itself in her career.

The experience with Mayerl exerted a lasting influence. He gave her a taste of the road, of show business and notoriety, all of which she found she liked very much. Going back to the practice room at the Guildhall was out of the question. In Mayerl she had also found a kindred musical spirit. Billy's two favorite composers—and his most serious influences—were Delius and Grieg. And while Marian eventually shed Mayerl's hokey style, his judicious balance of classical and jazz influences remained part of her aesthetic. One might also say, cautiously, that Marian's combination of contempt for popular taste and concomitant desire to write a hit song was a contradiction she shared with Mayerl as well.

By the time she got off the road with Billy, Marian's family had left Bromley, a move that had been in the works since Marian's third year at the Guildhall. Bromley and Chislehurst were on the aerial route from Germany to London, and fear of a surprise "knockout blow" by the German Luftwaffe was widespread. The Turners bought a house at 1 Victoria Place in Eastbourne, a seaside resort some twenty-five miles east of its more well-known cousin, Brighton. In October 1937, Janet also purchased a piece of property at 225 Willingdon Road in the adjacent village of Willingdon, tucked between the Sussex Downs and the sea. Frank designed the house and included a bomb shelter under the back garden stairs, made of enormous bricks the size of concrete blocks, creating a wall a foot thick. Joyce, now fifteen, enrolled at the Eastbourne Art School. She recalled the move with characteristic wryness: "Mother's arthritis was not getting any better and the War was coming nearer so Father thought it would be a good idea to get us out of London. So as Uncle Harry was in Willingdon, in a small sweet house, it occurred to Mother that she would like to live in Willingdon in a larger house, thereby putting Aunt Gertrude in her place, and making her vaguely discontented with her small sweet house. All this had no effect on Harry. He knew what he liked, and did it. I respect Uncle Harry despite the narrowness of his mind regarding sundresses."

Frank Turner may well have even had a firsthand look at Germany's airborne armada. Though no one in the Turner family seems to know what he was up to, Frank made frequent trips to Berlin, Munich, Czechoslovakia, and France starting in 1935, right around the time Hitler was playing chicken with Neville Chamberlain over the Sudetenland. Though there is no mention in the espionage literature of the Royal Arsenal playing an active role, Turner certainly was not on holiday on the continent, despite the cheerful picture postcards he sent to Marian. In 1939, a month after war was declared, he went to France with a special visa that read, "*affaires ayant trait à la défense nationale*" (business concerning national defense).

The white two-story house on Willingdon Road, called Kerrisdale, with leaded glass bay windows and a shingle roof, was doused in lovely sea air and had a more rural feel than the Bromley homes. Marian's father constructed a fish pond in the back garden and stayed busy with his flowers on the weekend. He used the bomb shelter, which he dubbed the "Spider Walk"—for its perennial inhabitants—as a shed for his garden tools. The house faced the road, and Marian's mother liked to look out from the small drawing room in front to see who was coming and going. This room, unfortunately, would become her "spot" for life. As the pain of her arthritis worsened, a doctor recommended a disastrous operation that promised to "cure" it by cutting a tendon in the back of her leg to relieve the pain.

"He must have been a hell of a doctor," said Marian. "He evidently felt she could walk on a straight leg. But she never did really walk again."

Confined to a chair with enormous wooden wheels, a laced-canvas back, and a black, felt-covered board that extended in front to support her stiff right leg, Janet would call for assistance by ringing a brass bell. She became a tyrannical presence, much as her mother had been before her, ringing her bell and demanding to be pushed from one place to the next in her great chair. Frank Turner, whose duties now included changing bedpans, was only too happy to be called out to the continent. (He once said to Marian, in a moment of particular exasperation, "I live the life of a toad under a harrow.") Frank rigged up each room with a system of buzzers and bells so Janet would never be stranded. But it was the little brass bell that jangled everyone's nerves.

Marian occasionally came down to Willingdon, though she never really lived at home with her parents again. "I was at loose ends," she confessed. "I didn't know what to do. I talked to agents, went around looking for jobs. They'd give you the once-over." She picked up some work on the BBC, accompanying singer Raquelle Dorne, who had enjoyed a hit with "Who Walks In" in 1934. At one point, she auditioned for the well-known group Ivy Benson and Her All Girls Band.

"I failed," she reported. "I'm damn glad I did. She probably found out I couldn't read. If I had gotten in, I'd probably still be there."

Eventually Marian got into a show in Stoke-Newington, playing orchestral, cocktail lounge–type arrangements with another female pianist, Roma Clarke, for a variety show. Variety, the post–World War I successor to the English music hall, had been given a new jolt of popularity by radio, with a fresh generation of stage and screen stars that included Gracie Fields ("In the Wood Shed She Said She Would") and George Formby ("When I'm Cleaning Windows"). Variety in turn spawned the slightly more lowbrow concert party, performed in Pierrot costumes—pom-poms and frills, plus a few minimal costumes such as a mustache or a hat—often presented in gingerbread Victorian theaters at seaside resorts like Brighton, Blackpool, and Margate. The serious British stage and screen bristled back to life during this period as well, with George Bernard Shaw's screenplay for *Pygmalion* (the play that inspired *My Fair Lady*), Noel Coward's *Blithe Spirit,* and Alfred Hitchcock's *The Lady Vanishes.* (The latter included a hilarious scene caricaturing the official British policy of appeasement in the person of two old coots who scoffed at the notion Hitler had anything in mind but peace.) British acting entered a golden age, with Vivien Leigh, Laurence Olivier, Ralph Richardson, and John Gielgud all in the spotlight.

Living in London during this fertile period, Marian drank in the riches of the stage and screen worlds and became part of London's theatrical milieu. She took in Vera Zorina in the musical *On Your Toes,* Noel Coward plays, and Irene Dunne singing "Lovely to Look At" (her father's favorite) in the film *Roberta,* and she slogged her way through one variety and concert party gig after another. She found the work challenging. Musicians had to cope with anything given to them, more or less on sight, and there was little time to learn the songs brought in by each new act.

"I really didn't know I was capable of doing that—rehearsing a pit band with the music of all these acts and telling them what went on with the different singers," Marian said. "I probably did more reading at that time than I've ever done since."

She later expressed embarrassment about the "square" and "commercial" music she played in those days—making a showpiece, for example, of a lugubrious tune like Lou Alter's "Manhattan Serenade."

"I'm sure if I heard it now, I'd blush with shame," she said, but added, "As I think back, I'm so glad I got to be part of that era. Those places were really fabulous in a way—great training, too."

Great training indeed. Few jazz musicians today can boast such a show business background. It would help her develop timing, presence, savvy, humor, fortitude, and—most of all—the ability to sell a show, whether she was onstage or on the radio. But stylistically, she was quite right about being "square and commercial." At this point, Marian was not a jazz pianist by a long stretch. She was a supremely versatile variety accompanist with a bouncy feel for popular tunes and a passion for boogie-woogie.

She also liked jazz-classical hybrids. One seminal influence in that department was the whimsical marriage of baroque counterpoint and jazz rhythms in the octets of American composer Alec Wilder, whose capricious song titles—"Jack, This Is My Husband," "Neurotic Goldfish," "The House Detective Registers"—were as intriguing as the music. Reginald Foresythe (an early Wilder influence) also caught Marian's ear with his avant-garde chamber jazz pieces "Dodging a Divorcee" and "Serenade to a Wealthy Widow," recorded in 1934 with Benny Goodman on bass clarinet. Marian saw Foresythe from backstage when she was on the road, as he accompanied the enormously popular African American singer Elizabeth Welch, the original voice of "The Charleston" and a veteran of black Broadway. The groundbreaking piano compositions of Bix Beiderbecke, notably "In a Mist," which also combined jazz and classical elements, became staples of Marian McPartland's repertoire as well.

During this period, Marian picked up songs from Afro-Caribbean café society pianist Leslie "Hutch" Hutchinson, a crisp, Fats Waller–type stride pianist and old-fashioned crooner with a big, hollow voice. But front and center was always Duke Ellington. A pianist, impressionist, harmonic genius, master of popular song, and scoffer at genre distinctions, Ellington remained the sine qua non of Marian's jazz pantheon. She even became friendly with ex-Ellington vocalist Adelaide Hall—or "Addy," as Marian and other friends called her—who moved to England in 1938. The two women performed at least once on the same variety bill.

By this time, serious British jazzers had begun to band together in "rhythm clubs"—hot jazz societies that met weekly to pore over the latest record releases from the United States—but they were typically dominated by men, who brought to them a peculiarly male obsession for collecting records and dissecting music. Marian did not join a rhythm club, nor does she seem to have been aware of Britain's first serious jazz movement, a Dixieland revival that began in 1943, centered around George Webb's Red Barn concerts in Kent. She did tune in to the BBC's *Radio Rhythm Club,* a weekly half-hour show that, finally, in 1940, began to highlight jazz, and she also ventured out to a few live shows. French violinist Stéphane Grappelli and Belgian Gypsy guitarist Django Reinhardt came to England during the war, and Grappelli decided to stay. Marian saw the hot jazz duo at a fancy London club called Hatchett's, on a date with a boy her mother set her up with. George Shearing played piano and Arthur Brown played the Novachord, the electric instrument Mayerl had used with the Claviers.

"I loved the music," said Marian, who spent the evening dancing foxtrots and waltzes. "But I hadn't the faintest idea who [Shearing] was. I was very green and callow and very unhip. I guess I was quite a good dancer, though."

Around the same time, Marian also got up the nerve to ask bandleader Carroll Gibbons if she could sit in at the Savoy Hotel.

"I remember he looked terribly surprised, but he didn't say, 'Get out of here,' or anything," Marian remembered. "He said, 'Yeah, well, why, yes. What would you like to play?' So I named some standard tune, and I played it to polite applause."

Other musicians who stood out in her memories of the era included Benny Goodman pianists Jess Stacy and Mel Powell; New Orleans soprano sax giant Sidney Bechet, Louis Armstrong, and Fats Waller. Female pianists Mary Lou Williams, Cleo Brown, Hazel Scott, and Britons Raie Da Costa and Winifred Atwell drew her attention as well. (Marian remembered getting furious with her father once when he asked her why she didn't "get a style like Winifred Atwell. I can understand the melody when *she* plays!")

Marian's early influences are striking for her lack of interest in the blues and black swing. Charlie Christian, Roosevelt Sykes, Count Basie, Jimmy Lunceford, Erskine Hawkins, and Andy Kirk do not figure in her recollections. And despite her enthusiasm for Ellington, Bechet, Armstrong, and Waller, at this point in her career, melody, elegance, and what she perceived as musical sophistication—including hybrids of jazz and classical music—trumped African American swing and blues feeling. Interestingly, much of her firsthand exposure to jazz had come from African American or Afro-British musicians such as Hutch, Foresythe, and Hall, but these were not hot, "in the pocket" swingers. White American jazz musicians at this time inevitably went through a period of envy and fascination regarding black players, looking to them for a deep well of specialized cultural knowledge.

"There was a mystique about black people [for young jazz players]," explained Marian's future drummer from Chicago, Rusty Jones. "She doesn't have that."

"As far as black and white I never gave it a thought," Marian said. "It didn't enter my head. Just that the people played—Hazel Scott, I didn't think anything about whether she was black or white. Same with Mary Lou. I didn't even sort of find out what was going on [along American racial lines] until I came to Chicago."

That Marian came to jazz as an outsider—as a Brit—without American social, racial, and class baggage is important. It allowed her to perceive jazz from the start as a high art, whether people were dancing to it, singing along, or listening intently to a concert. This quality of social distance would be essential to her development, not only as a jazz pianist, but in the tone and appeal of her radio program, *Piano Jazz*.

As Marian was absorbing all this music, events on the world stage were taking a dark turn. By the spring of 1939, it was clear Hitler's promises to Chamberlain had been a ruse to keep the British out of the war while the German dictator continued his expansionist program on the continent. In April, Britain and France abandoned their policy of appeasement and Britain began conscripting young men ages twenty to twenty-one. That summer, Germany and the Soviet Union signed the notorious Non-Aggression Pact, and on September 1, Hitler invaded Poland. Britain declared war two days later.

When war broke out, Marian was playing a concert party on the pier in the seaside resort of Felixstowe on the North Sea coast.

"One day men started putting up barricades and barbed wire on the beach," she said. "My sister was there with me and we both knew something horrible was going to happen. Everything became very ominous."

Recalled Joyce: "The weather was lovely and we went swimming and while in the sea I saw a crowd of people grouped round a radio on the beach, so being interested I came out of the water to listen. And the radio said to all those jolly British holiday makers that the Germans were bombing Poland, that War was coming, not in the distant future but now, on that sunny day. And I looked back for you in the sea and you had gone and

I thought, 'Oh, heavens, we've started to have a War and she's got drowned.' And I searched all over the beach, getting more distracted, when someone said you were in the Pub with friends. So that was how the war started for us, me with a fright and you with a few drinks. Do you think that is typical of us both?"

For the next year, Britain frantically prepared for war, rearming, building up the Royal Air Force, evacuating schoolchildren from London to the suburbs, rehearsing air raid drills, and handing out gas masks. But even as Germany rampaged across the continent, taking France the following May and pushing the British Expeditionary Force toward its famous evacuation at Dunkirk, there was at first no actual fighting. A curious lull ensued, which Brits call "the phony war." Schoolkids came back to London, and for a while, life went on as usual.

Marian, for her part, got work as a rehearsal pianist and performer with another concert party, this time with a sort of *American Idol* setup, called *Carroll Levis Discoveries*. Levis was a radio host from Toronto who had moved to England in 1935 and had reputedly hit upon the idea of using (free) local talent on the air when he recruited a boy from the audience to sing after one of his stars didn't show up. Levis took the concept on the road, "discovering" local talent all over England, including, he claimed, the hilarious comedian Terry-Thomas. Levis's eye for talent was apparently not always so keen. In the 1950s, he famously gave a thumbs-down to a group called the Quarrymen, later known as the Beatles.

Levis often traveled with an entourage of beautiful women. Marian remembered her father dropping by the dressing room when he happened to be in the same town as the troupe.

"He liked looking at the girls, I think," said Marian. "They all knew him. 'How are you, Mr. Turner?' I guess he liked that."

In his own way, Frank Turner had obviously come to terms with his daughter's choice of career.

During the Levis period, Marian moved to Frith Street in London, where she lived with another girl from the show. Though the Blitz had not yet begun, Marian could see it was only a matter of time before women would be called for national service. (Even the queen was doing her bit, after all, refusing to leave London, visiting hospitals, and rallying the troops.) Of the available choices, the most frightening to Marian was working on the barrage balloons, batteries of dirigibles lofted along the coast and tethered by cables meant to interfere with low-flying German aircraft.

"They had a bunch of very seemingly tough girls working those things," said Marian. "I thought, 'My God.'"

But for musicians there was an alternative—the Entertainments National Service Association. ENSA, as it was called, headquartered at the Theatre Royal on Drury Lane, had mounted its first show a week after war was declared. Not nearly as well-coordinated or professional as its American equivalent, the United Service Organizations (USO), ENSA was notorious for attracting second-rate, out-of-work amateurs from the provinces, though stars like Gracie Fields performed, too. ENSA almost immediately acquired an apparently well-deserved nickname: "Every Night Something Awful." Awful or not, Marian considered it far more desirable than the barrage balloons. In the fall of 1940, she signed up, touring military installations with a bassist, drummer, girl singer, two comedians, and a juggler.

It was a jolly good move. On September 7, 1940, at 4:55 P.M. on a perfect summer afternoon, just as Frank Turner had predicted, German planes flew down over Chislehurst and homed in on the Royal Arsenal. They attacked in three waves, dropping incendiary bombs, killing 53 people, injuring 247, destroying a new fuse factory and several storehouses, and leaving behind a fury of flames and smoke. That evening, the bombers came back and dropped more explosives into the fires. The Blitzkrieg had begun. From September to November, two hundred German planes flew over London every twenty-four hours, killing more than thirty thousand people, most of them civilians, half of them Londoners. Three and a half million houses were destroyed. (Though many theaters were bombed, interestingly, not one was ever hit with a crowd inside.) The Brits' unflappable determination to carry on as if life were normal in the face of this onslaught is legendary. Marian remembered most vividly walking down the blacked-out streets.

"We were all walking in pitch darkness, so it was kind of eerie, hearing all these voices," she said. "A few people had flashlights and they would occasionally put them on for a second. It was amazing nobody bumped into anybody. Air raid shelters were in the Tube. People would start coming down about five o'clock with blankets and stuff for the night. They'd all line up along the platform. Trains would come in and the passengers would step over them. And very few people got hurt. One big station got a direct hit and everybody was killed, but that hardly ever happened. It's amazing how cheerful everybody was. Everybody took it all as it just had to be. I don't remember even feeling that frightened about anything. We'd just go on with what we were doing. You just got used to it. Stepping off the train and stepping over those babies and their bottles."

Outside London, life could be just as dangerous.

"I remember being in Manchester and having lunch in some posh hotel and a siren went off and Beatrice Lillie was there in the room," said Marian. "She made some very funny remark and we just kept on eating and the waiters kept on serving food. It was pointless to go anywhere."

Even the house in Willingdon, with Frank's prescient bomb shelter, didn't escape the hostilities. According to Joyce's son, Chris, a "doodlebug"— a V-I cruise missile introduced late in the war that made an insidious buzzing noise as it flew over—crashed near Kerrisdale just as Marian's sister, Joyce, was leaving to walk the dog. The explosion threw her against the front door with such force it broke her front teeth. Marian also remembered a German plane getting shot down just as it passed Eastbourne. In another, lighter, family story, a bomb dropped by a German Messerschmitt lodged a piece of shrapnel in the garage door. Frank, ever curious, pulled it out and took it on the train with him to work. When he got there, he discovered it was still "live"!

But it was the food rationing that really got to people.

"We could only have a certain amount of meat, you could only buy x number of chops from the butcher, one egg a month," said Marian. "I don't remember being scared, but I do remember wishing I could have an egg and not being able to get one, except on the black market."

By 1943, unflappable or not, British morale began to flag.

"We were at the point when we thought they were going to come wading in from the Channel," said Marian. "We would talk about what we would do if we saw a German coming into the house. I was going to attack him with my pitchfork." But, she added, Winston Churchill's speeches "really pepped everybody up. Churchill was really loved during the war."

Throughout the hostilities, Marian's father—spared in the Arsenal bombings—spent weekdays in a rented room in Woolwich, coming home to Kerrisdale only on weekends. Marian later speculated that her father had fallen in love with his landlady, one Mrs. Franklin. Surprisingly, both Marian and her sister, Joyce, were quite forgiving—even sympathetic— about their father's peccadillo.

"I never knew till years later, long after Daddy had retired to Eastbourne to a life of drudgery, waiting hand and foot on Mummy, working night and day to keep the garden in trim, growing more irritable and nervous as the days went by, that he had a beautiful affair," Marian wrote in an unpublished memoir.

"I'm sure Mummy never knew anything about that," she added in a later interview. "Mrs. Franklin did everything for him that my mother didn't. She cooked for him and did his ironing and straightened out his papers.

All those wifely kinds of things. Jimmy and I went up to visit her once, and the way they were sitting on the couch, looking at each other, Jimmy thought there definitely was something going on. I don't know whether it was ever consummated."

Wrote Joyce of her mother and father: "It's a very great pity they married each other, as they did not laugh at the same things, and Father's way of life was not Mother's. He'd have liked to have an informal house where people just dropped in and were given whatever there was, but Mother liked the formal, come to tea next Sunday at four approach, and that's the way it had to be. It is such a sad thing that they stayed together, fighting, when had they tried living next to each other or even in the next road they might have found the whole thing easier to manage."

With such poor role models for intimacy, Marian's early relationships with men were awkward. Though full of desire, she held men at bay, almost by instinct. Her mother had warned her repeatedly that sex—and childbearing—was painful and, through her silence, shameful as well.

"I was so afraid of sex, and ignorant," Marian said. "No man could get near me!"

Perhaps because of her sexual reticence—or because she was such a resourceful and determined career musician—one of Marian's boyfriends early on dubbed her "Miss Independence," a moniker she attributed more to fear and ignorance than to any great self-confidence. It certainly didn't help that one of her first exposures to male desire had been with a child molester on one of her visits to Peaslake.

"One day," she said, "it was thought it might be nice if I went for a walk with a friend of Uncle Will's and Auntie Mabel's. But it turned out he wanted to take my clothes off. I ran home as fast as I could and told Auntie Mabel, 'That man tried to get my knickers off!' I was nine or ten. He was summarily banished from the house."

The English, with their famous reserve, have a notorious way of dealing with sexual repression—a long tradition of raucous, bawdy humor about bodily functions. One of Marian's most vivid memories of the war years was of a bold prank at a theatrical hangout she used to frequent, called Olivelli's. As she was sitting around with some actors and musicians, quaffing a glass of port or "shrub," a popular liqueur with a sort of sherry taste, suddenly a "sandwich" appeared on the table.

"A guy had put his member on the table between two slices of bread," she said. "He thought that was terribly funny. That's the kind of stuff that would go on in there. Nobody thought anything of it. There were various remarks on the size and shape of it."

Such an incident no doubt shocks some McPartland radio fans. But behind the genteel exterior of that voice on *Piano Jazz* lurked an irreverent, raunchy prankster who took particular delight in puncturing the balloon of propriety. Given the right audience, she could, and often did, swear like a sailor.

"She would always be saying, 'Motherfucker!'" remembered Marian's old friend in New York, Diana Schwartz. "She would say that after everything! And I would say, 'That just doesn't sound right coming out of that British mouth of yours!'"

Like so many Brits, for all her sophisticated repartee, Marian loved nothing better than bathroom humor. She was inordinately fond of asking people who inquired about her English background if they had ever tasted "spotted dick," an English dessert made of suet and currants.

But in spite of all this—the repressed humor, the molester at Peaslake, the lecherous Guildhall teacher, and her mother's dire warnings—Marian did not seem to have been deeply scarred by her upbringing. She fell into romantic liaisons as soon as she hit the road, even if they were somewhat strained. During the Mayerl quartet's extended stay in Glasgow, she met an attractive, happy-go-lucky young guy named Bill Eddy, who owned a fish market and came from a well-do-do family. Bill sent flowers and kippers (smoked herring fillets—still a McPartland favorite) to Marian's digs. It was the first time anyone had ever sent her flowers. She was "knocked out," but not quite ready for everything Bill had in mind.

"We would go to bed and do just about everything except the actual thing," she recalled. "I think he would have married me if I had either wanted to or been smart enough to know how to encourage him. My mother loved him. 'Why don't you marry this guy?' she said. He didn't want to marry me, he just wanted to get laid. He was sending flowers to other girls at the same time."

There were a couple of other "miniromances"—a doctor named Michael Buckloff, whom she met at an American army hospital in Tavistock, and another young fellow named "Reg"—but Marian met her first real beau in London. David Delmonte was a handsome, dark-haired comedian and impressionist who had managed the Carroll Levis outfit and who became her partner onstage as well as in real life. Delmonte had appeared in the 1939 Carroll Levis film *Discoveries* and shared the London stage with Marian in February 1942 in a show called *Sugar and Spice* at the Elephant and Castle. When Delmonte and Marian set up house together, sharing an apartment in Camden Town, a neighborhood north of Regent's Park, they even bought a little dog. Their relationship was quite formal; in the interest of modesty, they even put up a screen to divide the apartment in half.

"David was my first real affair," she said. "He was so patient and kind. He'd just say, 'When you're ready, darling.' He doted on me and I treated him badly. It was ages before I could let him touch me simply because I was scared stiff."

Delmonte was Jewish and thereby discounted by her parents as marriage material, but her father "tried awfully hard to like him," and her mother for once apparently put aside her prejudices as well.

"When I got the mumps and I was in bed in Kerrisdale, [Dave] came down and spent a couple of days," she recalled. "My mother really loved Dave. She thought he was great."

Delmonte eventually shipped out to North Africa. Before he left, Marian gave in to his amorous, if gentle, advances, a "first time" that does not seem to have left much of an impression, other than relief to have gotten it over with. She remained in touch with Delmonte throughout the war and for many years afterward.

In 1943, after David shipped out, Marian ran into another old mate from the Carroll Levis show, Zonie Dale.

"You ought to go with USO," Zonie told her. "You'll love it. They pay more [than ENSA]. It's better. And you'll meet some wonderful American guys."

To Marian, this sounded good—on all three counts. She called up the London office of the USO, open now that America had entered the war, and discovered that a lot of the USO shows coming to London needed a piano player. She eagerly put her name in for work and was soon back out on the road. Though there were still bad pianos, long bus rides, late (or canceled) trains, and trips that took ten hours when they should have taken two, the talent was better and so was the company. She performed with Cliff Hall, straight man to vaudevillian radio star Jack Pearl (aka "Baron Munchausen"), and Hollywood actor Sid Marion (*Lady of Burlesque, Colgate Comedy Hour*). When the USO sent out its star-studded Hollywood camp shows, Marian played the same stage as Edward G. Robinson, who was making a propaganda film for the RAF, and Jimmy Cagney.

"I was dying to meet Cagney," reported the starstruck pianist, who in an early example of what would become a striking facility for grabbing the spotlight finagled a publicity photo with him published in a USO rag.

England was awash in American soldiers—1.5 million of them. The "Yanks" brought their noisy self-confidence—and their noisy popular music. Described in the British press as "oversexed, overpaid and over here," American soldiers had access to all kinds of luxury goods, particularly liquor and stockings. "Yank hunting" at dances by young British girls became a popular recreation. By the end of this impromptu cultural exchange, there would be fifty thousand English war brides married to Americans.

Marian, with her love of jazz, got caught up in the fervor.

"We all thought then anything American—and meeting Americans—was always better than anything we had," she said. "I remember this as a kid, going through movie magazines and reading about the glamorous life of movie stars from Hollywood. When I finally went with USO I realized everything was done on a much higher level than ENSA was. I guess it's like I really found out about the American way. Everything is bigger and better."

Marian was assigned to a variety act called Band Wagon, possibly named after the famous British radio show (but with American spelling). Comedian Don Rice fronted the outfit, which featured Marian and a guitar player, the East Coast song-and-dance couple Ralph and Mary Carnevale, a female juggler, and—at one point—a magician and sword swallower with the improbable but highly appropriate name of Dolly Reckless.

The D-Day invasion had been originally planned for May 1944, but when it was postponed till June, ENSA and USO shows tried out their acts on the waiting troops.

"It was all very secret," Marian remembered, as no one was to know the actual date of the invasion. In addition to rehearsals and run-throughs, Marian and the rest of the troupe received basic training and were issued GI boots, helmets, and fatigues. On June 6, 1944, just after midnight, 24,000 troops were airlifted to France, followed by a landing force of 175,000 men at six thirty A.M. D-Day, the turning point of the war, had begun. Listening to the planes flying overhead, Marian remembered thinking, "They're all going over to smash the Germans."

"Smashing the Germans" in fact took considerably longer than expected, as the enemy put up ferocious resistance. It was not until July 9 that Montgomery triumphed at Caen and another nine days before General Omar Bradley took Saint-Lô. A week later, the members of Band Wagon embarked across the Channel, bringing up the rear behind Montgomery's assault on Caen. Marian's new life had begun.

3.

"Oh, No! A Girl Piano Player!"
(1944~1946)

October 19, 1944
Dearest Da,

   . . . thank heaven you have at last sent that barracks bag—please don't assume that we get anything over here; you have to be over here to know just what we can, and cannot get. I have to laugh at your indignation over us living in tents! Dear Pap, there's a war on! . . . Here's a typical day in our lives—Rise 7.30, muddle into damp Fatigues, feel around for matches and light stove (unless some good soul has already arisen and lit same). Put on coffee pot and attempt to make bed, throwing out all beetles, ants and pine needles meanwhile— Finally make bed, nearly upset coffee as I come into collision with Julie, returning from the fir trees, entirely roofless. Pour coffee, hastily butter slice of bread when light goes out. Fumble for matches, light candle when light comes on again! Eat bread, start to make up when yell comes from outside Tent (usually it's Willie) "Come on girls, time to go." We dash out, buttoning coats, through the driving rain, splashing through mud to where the weapons carrier is waiting— We all heave our cases into it, hang our carefully covered dresses in the center, and off we go! We drive through most impassable roads—thick creamy mud, huge ruts, bomb craters—anything! We sail through them all, and eventually arrive in a thickly wooded area, studded with tents of all shapes and sizes, rain dripping steadily through the trees, and we behold our stage—a hastily erected affair, covered with a tarpaulin, through which the rain plops at odd intervals— After a gloomy review of the situation, we trudge to the officers mess, if it can be called that, a long table set under the trees and shielded from the rain by a piece of canvas. There we gorge hungrily—roast beef, and everything that goes with it, gulp down our coffee, swallow our last piece of cherry pie, and away, to fix ourselves up as best we can— This particular day is an extra rough one, but the outfit we are playing to, do try. They have fixed a stove and a tiny dressing room, so everyone gets changed into evening gowns to give the boys a treat, and we get under way with the show. I am playing accordian [*sic*], so I'm able to hug the stove, while everyone on stage freezes! The poor boys sit out in the rain to watch, and despite it all, they are a wonderful audience. Combat troupes, just out of the Front lines—they surely deserve a show if anybody does, and we exert ourselves to see that they enjoy it. They do, and, finally packed up, back in Fatigues, with the satisfaction of knowing that our second show is cancelled, we head for home, and a hot meal— Arrived in the Tent, we light the stove, pull off our mud covered boots, comb our hair and prepare to mingle with officers and Red Cross girls already forming into a long line outside the mess tent—I decided to diet a little today, so I dash into the kitchen, past the watchful eye of the mess sergeant, grab a pork chop and put it between two slices of bread, return to our tent, and prepare to answer all my letters! And that dear Papa, is a brief account of today's doings— Rain still pours down, but I am warm, and in a mellow mood—so, I can be happy till about 7.30 tomorrow when the same old grind starts again!

Much love, Margaret

BY THE TIME MARIAN WROTE THIS letter from Belgium, she had been on the continent nearly three months and—though she didn't know it at the time—had just met the man she was going to marry. Before this, she had been spared any direct experience of the horrors of war, save those occasional hours in the London underground and, of course, the accumulating rubble left behind by the Blitz. As she advanced into the checkerboard fields and hedges in Normandy called the *bocage,* the grim reality began to sink in. Along dusty roads, she saw hedgerows with great holes ripped through them, where they had been breached by Allied tanks. The stench of corpses was everywhere. Whole towns had been razed, firefights leaving only piles of crumbled bricks and stone. Small-arms fire cracked in the distance as troops mopped up the northern battlefields on their way toward Paris. Marian later reflected on how odd she felt, even guilty, that she and her fellow entertainers were having a good time "when people were getting killed every five minutes. You knew that behind the hedge something or someone was dead there. It was really tragic, but somehow I didn't feel it as much then as I did afterwards."

Once, while she was sitting under a pear tree eating GI rations—a slab of meat with pineapple on top—a low-flying German plane suddenly appeared in the sky.

"It happened so fast that by the time you knew what was going on, it was over," she said. "He was flying so low, it's a wonder he didn't hit the trees. Nobody got hurt, and I finished the pineapple."

Band Wagon occasionally played from the back of a flatbed truck, sometimes for thousands of troops in a field. The show itself was straightforward, Marian's role not terribly different from what she was accustomed to, working out keys with the singers, playing dance numbers for the Carnevales and a few specialty numbers of her own—a medley of popular tunes, a classical interlude or a boogie-woogie. GIs with talent were sometimes invited to join in. Tunes included popular numbers like "Don't Sit Under the Apple Tree" or "Praise the Lord and Pass the Ammunition" in a symphonic or "jazzed-up" arrangement.

Marian was particularly impressed by the magician Dolly Reckless.

"She'd put a flock of razor blades and a paper of needles in her mouth, dance about, and suddenly pull them out of her mouth strung on a length of thread," said Marian.

The group was received with great enthusiasm.

"It's not that we were so good," she recalled with a self-deprecating modesty that became one of her trademarks. "It's just that the troops would be so ridiculously pleased to see anything or anybody. Especially to have some girls wearing skimpy outfits."

Female performers were told to dress with just enough allure to give the GIs a taste of home, but not so voluptuously as to frustrate them. Marian wore a backless satin gown with sequins.

After the Allies liberated Paris August 25, Band Wagon followed them into the City of Light. Chicago entertainer Willie Shore was now Band Wagon's comedian/emcee, and his wife, Julie, had joined the group, too. Shore was a dapper vaudeville hand, nicknamed "Five-by-Five" for his short and stout stature. He was famous for opening his show with:

Tea for two and two for tea,
And have you got some Scotch for me?

By this time, a slew of big-name entertainers—including Fred Astaire, Marlene Dietrich, and Bing Crosby—were flooding into Europe with the USO camp shows. (Marian recalled with some amusement meeting singer Dinah Shore as they sat side by side in an outdoor latrine.) Willie, Julie, and Marian were invited to tour with Astaire. Marian recalled one September night in Holland when the dancer's fabled agility served him very well: "He was a real good sport. He brought an accordion player with him and had three set routines. He would also chat with the boys during his performance. We played anywhere and everywhere—in an old castle or on a platform made of boxes—indoors and out, in any kind of weather. One afternoon when we had an outdoor stage made of planks, there was a downpour of rain. But Fred went right on and danced in the rain in his combat boots. Then we had a dinner one night and there was an air raid and we heard all this big noise overhead and he was the first guy under the table. I never saw anybody move so fast."

Back in Paris to celebrate the Allied victory on September 24, British, American, and French producers joined forces for a gala at the grand Olympia Theatre titled "Paris Presents Paris 1944." Emceed by British bandleader Jack Hylton, the lineup featured Astaire, Shore, Gertrude Lawrence, French cellist and actor Maurice Baquet, Django Reinhardt, and a grand finale of French can-can dancers. Band Wagon was subsequently invited to play with Astaire and Crosby at the Supreme Headquarters Allied Expeditionary Force (SHAEF) in Versailles, for Generals Dwight D. Eisenhower and Carl Andrew "Tooey" Spaatz.

Marian said she thought General Spaatz would "explode with wonder and admiration" over Dolly Reckless. At Ike's urging, Spaatz took out his guitar—which he played quite well, according to Astaire. Ike sang along and also, rather presciently, advised Marian to go to America, where he said her jaunty style would be widely appreciated.

In early October, as the Allies chased the Germans toward the Rhine, Band Wagon followed them into Belgium, where the group was billeted in tents in a bivouac area in St. Vith, a small town in the Ardennes forest, near the German border. St. Vith was still infested with German snipers. Allied companies regularly patrolled the countryside. One soldier assigned that onerous chore was a profoundly war-weary Chicago jazz cornetist named Jimmy McPartland. McPartland had plowed through Normandy just a few weeks ahead of Marian, fighting in the battles of Saint-Lô and the Falaise Gap. When he reached Paris, by a fortuitous coincidence, he had run into Willie Shore, an old friend from Chicago.

"What the hell are you doing with a helmet and a rifle?" Shore had asked Jimmy. "Where's your horn?"

McPartland was a jazz legend. At seventeen, he had replaced Bix Beiderbecke in the Wolverines, then played on the 1927 McKenzie-Condon sessions that put Chicago jazz on the map. Though his career had taken a dive in the Depression, he was riding high with the current Dixieland revival, had recently been written up in *Time* magazine, and was playing better than he had at any time in his life. Jimmy told Shore he had enlisted because he thought it was the right thing to do, but after what he'd just been through, he would now gladly trade his rifle for a microphone. Shore argued to his superiors that this famous jazz musician should be playing music, not shooting at Nazis in hedgerows. At the time McPartland was on patrol in the Ardennes, he was in the process of being transferred from combat duty to V Corps Special Services, so he could play in a band. When members of the army big band stationed in St. Vith got wind that McPartland was in the neighborhood, a buzz rolled through camp. The musicians organized a welcoming party for McPartland on October 14, in a large tent in the middle of a great field.

"Everyone in the band was saying, 'Jimmy McPartland's coming! Jimmy McPartland's coming!'" Marian recalled.

Though familiar with the records of some of Jimmy's childhood pals—notably tenor saxophonist Bud Freeman and clarinetist Benny Goodman—Marian had no idea who McPartland was. After the tent show, a jam session ignited and one of the musicians asked Jimmy to take out his horn. McPartland agreed on condition they bring him a bottle of Scotch. But when he looked at the bandstand, his enthusiasm took a nosedive.

"There was a girl sitting at the piano, and I thought, 'Oh, no, a girl?'" he remembered. "And she spoke with a British accent. I thought, 'This is not it,' you know. And sure enough, we played 'Honeysuckle Rose' and she was rushing like mad. After we had played a few jazz numbers, I said, 'Listen, let's play something pretty, like "I Never Knew Just How Much I Love You."' Because I could hear her harmony, her left hand, and she was playing some good stuff there. She played that and I heard those beautiful harmonies and I said, 'Oh, man, this gal is a killer.' I fell for her right then and there."

Marian, for her part, wasn't so sure. She found Jimmy dashing, but also a bit bombastic. He was a born emcee who loved to talk—"a sincere bullshitter," as Marian later put it—and always had a crowd around him, especially when the crowd was buying the drinks.

"I do remember very vividly looking across the tent at this very handsome man dressed like a paratrooper, trousers tucked into his combat boots, his helmet at a rakish angle," she said. "And he looked back at me. We played for hours. Other GI pianists sat in, then I played again. It was fabulous, such a heady feeling, and in fact my very first jam session. He was surrounded by musicians. I didn't get to talk to him much until later. We all went together to Eupen in this horrible vehicle called a weapons carrier and I looked at him and thought, 'Boy, you're so conceited.' I didn't realize until I found out later how he drank a lot that the little smirk he had was because he was half in the bag. I remember him remarking that I had great-looking eyes."

Warily fascinated by this larger-than-life musician who claimed to know all her childhood musical heroes on a first-name basis—Art Tatum, Fats Waller, Louis Armstrong—Marian agreed to go on a date with Jimmy to the resort town of Spa. After racking up a large bar bill, Jimmy, between assignments and therefore between paychecks, confessed he had no money. Marian was surprised, but not really angry.

"I think I had already begun to fall for him," she said.

Shortly after Marian met Jimmy, his transfer papers came through and he was asked to form a sextet combining USO and Special Services personnel in Eupen, about twenty miles north of St. Vith. Jimmy invited Marian to play piano in the band.

Eupen, a trading town of old stone buildings along the Vesdre River, was considered a quiet sector, so it was used as a training ground for new units and a rest area for ones that had seen hard combat. Troops would come in from the front and get a hot bath, a new uniform, and a home-cooked meal from Belgian families sympathetic to the Allies (not all were). Band Wagon was given "digs" in the Schmitzroth Hotel, a handsome, chalet-style affair with a dining room and wine cellar.

With Jimmy on cornet and vocals, Marian on piano, Chris Smith on bass, Joe Hardy on drums, Julie Shore on vocals, and the sword-swallowing Dolly Reckless also in the act, the sextet went to work. In the daytime, the group got up at the crack of dawn and rode out to the countryside, set up a stage, and played for the soldiers.

"We used to go right behind the front lines," Jimmy recalled. "You could hear small arms firing."

At night, in a pared-down quartet, they played for officers at the Schmitzroth. The group played cheek-to-cheek slow dances such as "Embraceable You," "Stardust," and "Body and Soul," with romantic vocals delivered by Shore, a pretty, diminutive brunette. Naturally, they also played the Glenn Miller wartime hit "In the Mood," as well as traditional New Orleans jazz numbers like "Royal Garden Blues," which showcased Jimmy's clarion cornet. Marian was knocked out by Jimmy's cornet playing, but she had had no prior experience backing up horn players.

"Just play organ," Jimmy told her.

"I never knew what he meant," Marian said. "Then I heard other trad players say it and I realized it meant 'Don't run up and down all over the piano.'"

Marian was learning from Jimmy how to "comp" (accompany) a solo, sparsely filling in the blanks as the horn "spoke," rhythmically driving it along. More important, she was learning how to internalize the beat and keep it steady—ultimately, how to swing.

Said Jimmy: "I just kept telling her, 'Look, you have the facility of the instrument and you're a fine musician, but you've got to learn how to swing, to hold that beat right steady where it is. It's called . . . it's time, you know, the Afro beat, it's the tom-toms. You have to feel it before you play jazz, just feel that time, feel that rhythm, that beat. Once you get the feel of it, you've got it.' So she just kept doing it and that's a girl that really did it."

From time to time, as a goodwill gesture, the Eupen USO presented shows for the general public, with former child actor Norman Tokar in charge. (Tokar later went on to direct episodes of *Leave It to Beaver* and more than a dozen Walt Disney films.) Tokar decided to put on a show at Eupen's Capitol Theatre. The only problem was, the piano was so terrible that Marian said she couldn't possibly play it. Jimmy got permission from Major Adams, the Special Services officer, to "requisition" a piano from a collaborator's home. Given eight men, a large truck, a tommy gun, and directions to a house known to have a brand-new grand piano, McPartland embarked on his mission.

"I went to the house and said, 'Here's the requisition.' The man says, 'Oh, you can't do that.' They were screaming bloody murder, you know. But who cares? Collaborators? Get out of here! So I just kept going. I said, 'Talk to the mayor. You'll get it back later. We're taking it to the Capitol Theatre.' So we moved the thing into the theater and Marian came in for rehearsal and here was the piano, like a bouquet of flowers. She told me later on, 'That's when I decided to really pay attention to you, you know.'"

Sixty years later, Marian still recalled how beautifully Jimmy played "Embraceable You" that night.

She was falling in love.

"Having lunch in the mess hall in Eupen," she recalled, "I started to get that feeling, when just being friendly suddenly changes to a sort of excitement and energy and the realization that I was unable to stop looking at him and drinking in every word he said, feeling so animated, wanting to be with him every minute. He was flirting and making jokes and probably wasn't as serious about me as I thought I was about him."

Yet something had awakened in Jimmy as well. Since a first, brief marriage in New York that had ended in disaster (and a daughter), he had had lots of girlfriends, but no one really serious. Marian was different. She was so elegant, so sophisticated, so witty and cultured, so, well . . . English!

Like his high school chums Bud Freeman and Dave Tough, Jimmy was enchanted by British refinement. He actually found it hard to believe Marian could even be attracted to a rough-hewn street kid from Chicago. But she was.

They started spending nights together at the hotel. Off days, the couple went out to the fields and forests, picnicking and talking about music and their lives. Marian recalled stopping once to peer into an abandoned house where the occupants had obviously fled in a hurry, leaving a meal still set on the table. Jimmy descended to the cellar and came back up with three bottles of liquor covered with cobwebs. Marian "requisitioned" a little cup and saucer, which she later displayed in her house.

By this time, Marian had begun to realize Jimmy—or Jamie, as she called him—had a drinking problem. Since USO performers were automatically conferred the rank of captain, Marian received a generous ration of alcohol—up to six bottles of Armagnac, gin, and whiskey a week. "Jimmy came up to my room in the afternoon," Marian remembered. "And I said, 'You're not interested in me. You're just looking for my liquor ration.' He laughed. Then I opened up the cupboard and got out whatever he wanted."

Having had no experience with alcoholics, she believed him when he made up various excuses for his drinking.

"He said things like 'I don't do that when I'm in the States. I drink like a gentleman. After all, there's a war on.' I was sure I was the one that would stop him drinking. Stupid broad."

In some ways, it wasn't so much the drinking itself she minded, but that whenever Jimmy drank, he was surrounded by a bunch of noisy guys.

"Any guy he would meet who would say, 'Do you want to have a drink,' they would sit down and get started and I would be left out," she said.

Sometime in November, not more than five or six weeks after they met, Jimmy proposed. Though Marian was the one with the reputation for being self-effacing, Jimmy's recollection of his tentative proposal later sounded almost apologetic.

"I said, 'Look, honey, let's get married. If it doesn't work out, you can always go back home. But let's get married anyway. Come to America with me.'"

"[The next day] I thought, I've got to get this straight," recalled Marian. "Was he sober? I really wanted to marry him. I stomped up the stairs to the place where all these guys were billeted and knocked on the door. He was there in bed, alone. 'Jimmy, I want to talk to you. Are you really serious?' He called out to the owner of the house, 'Peter! Peter! Bring me that bottle.' But then he reached under the bed and there was a bottle there. I said, 'No, leave the bloody bottle where it is,' and sat down on the bed. And he said, 'Yes,' he did want to marry me. We sat on the bed. And we hugged and we kissed and I climbed into bed with him."

The marriage of an Englishwoman in the USO to an American GI in Belgium in the middle of World War II turned out to be a more complicated proposition than simply saying "yes." Not only must a chaplain be secured, Jimmy's commanding officer had to give him permission. And here the run of unlikely names seems almost to have been invented by *Catch-22* author Joseph Heller, as the commander in this case was named Colonel Pecka. The colonel had some serious misgivings, not just about Jimmy's drinking, but about the fact that he and Marian had known each other so briefly. Marian's USO boss, Kitty Garlow, a stern-looking woman who had once threatened to let Jimmy go if he didn't stop drinking, was not keen on the union, either. Like so many English war brides who had hitched up with GIs in London, Marian would regret such a rash move, Kitty counseled. She should wait a while, cool off, and perhaps make her decision later.

Admittedly, they were an unlikely pair. (Trumpeter Roy Eldridge would later call them "the Odd Couple.") Marian was a well-bred, well-educated, upper-middle-class Englishwoman from the suburbs of London—slightly rebellious, but who grew up playing Chopin and painting watercolors, spoke the King's English, and wrote in an impeccable hand. She had absorbed a stoic work ethic from her father. Jimmy, by contrast, had grown up severely poor on the rough-and-tumble Near West Side of Chicago, spending his early years in an orphanage. A streetwise, fistfighting, fast-talking high school dropout, Jimmy loved to fish and box and swim. And drink. He was lazy to boot, a "natural" improviser who, Marian would discover, constantly required prodding to push his career forward. To makes matters worse, Jimmy had no legal proof he was even actually divorced. In the end, however, Colonel Pecka relented and love won out. On December 12, 1944, Marian signed an official document confirming she "acquiesced to his proposal."

The war, however, intervened. On December 16, the Germans secretly regrouped and set upon Belgium with the full fury of a wounded beast, attempting to pierce Allied lines in four places in a bloody encounter later known as the Battle of the Bulge. Ironically, the spot that proved most vulnerable was St. Vith. As the German panzer divisions advanced, civilians—Marian included—were sent packing from Eupen to Herve, twenty kilometers west. Jimmy, having had combat experience, was asked to stay behind at the Hotel Schmitzroth. The Germans bombed and strafed Eupen and even dropped in paratroopers. A few days later, an intrepid and worried Marian, accompanied by Willie Shore, hitched a ride to Eupen from Herve with an armed sentry on a weapons carrier over muddy, rutted roads, passing burning trucks along the way to reunite with her fiancé.

When she got there, she was told Jimmy was in a first-aid station. Certain he'd been wounded, she rushed to a hotel serving as a hospital. "Is he badly hurt?" she asked. "No, lady," was the reply. "Just fractured."

In room twelve, Marian found Jimmy with four companions, each with a bottle of wine in his fist, singing "I Had a Dream, Dear." When a bomb had hit the hotel, it had opened a locked closet door, revealing dozens of bottles of rare wine and champagne.

She told Jimmy the engagement was off.

Four days later, they were back in each other's arms and decided to get married before anything else could confuse them.

In the meantime, Willie Shore begged Major Adams to let him borrow Jimmy and a few other musicians for a Christmas show in Herve. Adams agreed. When Christmas arrived, however, it turned out to be anything but a "silent night." The German counteroffensive was still in full swing, and just as the band sat down to dinner, three Messerschmitt Bf 109 fighter planes started strafing the mess hall. Everybody hit the floor except Jimmy, who—at least according to him—ran outside, where he saw a truck with a .50-caliber machine gun on top of the cab.

"I was down on the ground, and these M109s were coming in and making passes at us," he said. "I asked the guy next to me, 'How a fifty?' and he said, 'Yes.' I said, 'Come on. I'll feed and you work it, or the other way around.' We got up in this thing and loaded it up and cocked it and started firing. Of course, other guys were firing, too, but he had it lined up just right, he was leading it just perfectly, and I could see those tracers going in there and we hit it. And he took a big zoom upwards, up through the sky and parachuted. Everybody was shooting at him. But I know we helped knock the thing down. Then we went back in and put on the show."

Fighting raged on through the winter, until the Allies finally beat back the German offensive on January 25, 1945. Marian went to Paris, where she dealt with the paperwork for the wedding. Jimmy, busted for the wine cellar incident, was promoted back to captain, perhaps because of his valor in Herve. Back in Eupen, Jimmy and Marian recalled gawking at Marlene Dietrich, saying "hello" as she passed in the lobby of the Schmitzroth Hotel. On February 3, escorted by a line of command cars full of helmeted soldiers, the couple rode to Aachen, Germany, to be married. Jimmy's commanding officer gave the bride away in a government military building. Colonel Pecka served as best man. That night, at the reception, Jimmy and Marian sat in with the band. Marian played accordion. It was a jolly affair, but as usual, Jimmy let himself be monopolized by "the gang," in particular a garrulous, hard-drinking guitar player known as "Happy" Norman.

"We went to the hotel room and he followed us and we couldn't get rid of him," she said. "I was dying to get in bed with Jimmy. 'Get him out of here!' [I said]. Finally, he did, but I can't remember what happened. I think we probably started off having a row."

The next day, General Leonard Townsend Gerow, head of V Corps, loaned Jimmy a command car and the newlyweds drove in style to Brussels, where they stayed at the Palace Hotel and spent the money Jimmy's outfit had taken up for the couple before the party. They honeymooned in Brussels for a week, where they sat in with some local bands. Marian wrote a dramatic letter to the English jazz magazine *Melody Maker,* announcing her marriage and their "narrow escape" from the advancing German army, demonstrating an early talent for self-promotion. The magazine duly repeated parts of her letter verbatim and accompanied it by a bare-shouldered head shot of Marian with the caption "Pianist Marian Page (Mrs. Jimmy McPartland) the first British bride in wartime Germany."

Remarkably, though she notified *Melody Maker,* Marian did not tell her parents anything about the wedding.

"I thought, well, if I tell them I'm going to do this, they'll somehow talk me out of it or my father will come over and kill Jimmy, or something will happen," she said. "They won't like it. So I'm going to do it and tell them afterwards."

In fact, she asked Colonel Pecka to break the news to her father, which he did, over lunch, in London. Frank Turner took it well, but Janet later told Marian she cried all day when she found out her daughter had become a war bride.

"I suppose unconsciously I wanted to be a rebel," she later admitted. "I couldn't help doing things that I knew would upset my parents, including going to France with USO."

The couple's honeymoon bliss was quickly interrupted by the exigencies of war. Days after their stay in Brussels, Jimmy was unceremoniously posted to a unit in the Alps, Marian sent to USO headquarters in Paris for reassignment to another show. For the next seven months, the lovesick newlyweds crisscrossed the continent, squeezing in visits between their respective tours, if only for a weekend rendezvous. Sometime in April, Marian was sent to Belgium and Germany with a jazz combo fronted by guitarist Jack LeMaire. A colorful New Yorker who had been a drinking buddy of Jimmy's in Chicago (and who would later serve as a stand-in for Colonel Sanders on TV commercials), LeMaire had been schooled on the guitar by the great Eddie Lang and had been a regular at the Hickory House on New York's Fifty-second Street, where Marian would later establish her reputation. LeMaire was hip to the new sounds in New York. Marian wasn't, but, as always, she was a quick study.

"She wanted to Americanize herself one hundred percent," said LeMaire. "She thought boogie-woogie was the thing. I said, 'Boogie-woogie is okay, why don't you try this?' I showed her modern chords and flatted fifths and stuff. That's a fact. Accent the second and fourth beat, blah blah blah. She played great rhythm. Her comps were fantastic. She'd pick out the right chords and that sort of thing. She'd say, 'What's that sound?' I'd tell her, 'It's a half-diminished.' If she heard something once, it was stamped. After months and months and months, she just tore the place up. She was that good a piano player. I forget the boogie-woogie number she played. She used to stop the show every night."

The LeMaire gang traveled in a truck with a canvas top and open back (affectionately known by the troops as a "douche and a half") with a two-jeep escort, one for protection and one for guidance. During the day, they were required to wear uniforms, in case they were captured. Like soldiers, they always wore dog tags. There was no bass player, just three rhythm—drums, guitar, and piano. The drummer was Joe Nardy, who would record shortly in London with Jimmy and Marian. Charlie Miller performed magic tricks, Beverly Allen (whom LeMaire later married) danced, and Chicago singer Dorothy Davis (later Nash) sang. Nash was impressed by Marian's pristine diction and vocabulary.

"I was describing some water in a pool at a house," she recalled, "and she said, 'Oh, you mean *pellucid*?' I'd never heard that word before. She was smart."

Dorothy's big feature was the 1944 Dinah Shore hit, "I'll Walk Alone," whose lyrics were just sentimental enough to remind the boys of home but bracing enough not to break their hearts.

"If you played 'My Buddy,' they'd all cry," said Jack. "It was a mistake to do that stuff. These guys were sad enough. . . . These beautiful German chicks would walk past and flip their skirts up. There would be a sign on their behinds that said, *'Das ist Verboten.'* The guys, they would flip. This was at the end of the war."

Indeed, the European theater was winding down as the Allies made their final drive into Berlin. On May 6, 1945, General Patton liberated Czechoslovakia, and Germany surrendered the following day. In a magnificent letter home dated May 13, Marian took stock of her situation—and the world's—conveying a dizzying mix of compassion, relief, curiosity, wonder, and even a sort of apology to her parents for having married in secret.

"Dearest Da, Mummy and Joyce," she wrote:

This afternoon I had a very interesting experience, flying all over Germany on a sort of reconnaissance flight. I thought of you because I'm sure you must have been well acquainted with many of the towns we passed, and to see them now—mere shells, is kind of an odd feeling. Our bombs have made of them mere heaps of rubble—Cologne cathedral stands starkly amid the shambles of the town; I'm glad it wasn't completely destroyed, I'm sure it must have been a lovely piece of architecture— We flew over Munchen Gladbach and thence into the Ruhr Valley, passing Krefeld, Essen—Dortmund—on to Dusseldorf, and so to Coblenz where we were scheduled to "meet" some other aircraft, which, however, did not show up, so we went on down to Frankfurt, on to Karlsruhe, then back up to Köln (sorry, Cologne, I was just looking at the map), thence to Aachen, through Eupen and back home.

This tour took us around 2½ to 3 hours—we were in a very fast plane, and it really is delightful I think to go zooming along at a low altitude—one can get a good view of everything. We passed a vast P.W. camp, and there were literally millions of Germans in it, and many of them were washing or swimming in the Rhine. The dust that blew up from this place was terrific—the guys must have been suffocating down there, and that plus their mental attitude must make their lives intolerable—

Don't the Germans love swimming pools! I saw dozens of them, and that Rhine looked wonderful for a quick dip!

Our tour over Aachen and Eupen was especially moving for me. I suppose it seems like turning the knife in the wound to you, but oddly enough, it made me feel very good to view the places where I spent so many happy months, from the air. I could see the church spire—the main street leading to our hotel, which was bedecked with flags—the theatre, the Special Service Office—these all passed beneath me in the space of a few all too brief moments, leaving me a score of wonderful memories which kept me busy until we landed. I'm not sure if I told you that Jamie and his outfit are now on the border of Czechoslovakia or did I? At any rate you can understand how I feel, being in this all too familiar territory—alone.

I am of course very worried as to the outcome of things, and I expect you are wondering what I am going to do. Well, that depends a great deal on what Jamie is going to do. I can't see him getting out for ages, and it looks as if we are going to have to grin and bear quite a number of things in the near future— However, a lot hangs in the balance these next ten weeks, both for him, and for me—I am of course (being me) trying to swing a deal to be with him, and I shall go all out until I do, or bust. Whether I do, or don't swing it, I shall be home for a while fairly soon, and don't imagine I shall make a dash for the States—even if I wanted to, it would take months of going through channels to get there, so that's out! Meantime, I hope Mummy got my letter asking for my birth certificate—this is most important— I must have it, or a reasonable facsimile.

Re you Joyce, coming over here. I can see no possibility of that until they make it possible for civilians to have passports once again. There is nothing I would like better than to have you with me, especially now when I feel the need so badly for a little moral support, and I would love you to visit one third of the places I have seen, and I hope one day you will.

This war has wrecked a million hopes, turned thousands of lives topsy turvy, but I regard myself, even in my present low state, as being one of the lucky ones—I have been able to do a small part in this great organisation, in fact, be a part of it—while doing work I love—I have a family—a home—friends—a husband whom I love and who loves me, and further opportunity to work, rehearse, and travel, while endeavouring to bring a little good cheer to a few people along the line. If that isn't lucky, I don't know what is—at any rate, writing it makes me feel a lot better, I can assure you!!

I often think of you, Mummy, saying "Don't do this" "don't do that" or "that's very dangerous" and then I laugh when I think what I've been doing over a period of ten months or so! I think I can safely say I've lived!

Did I tell you I flew up with a General from Cannes last week? I was stuck at the airport, couldn't get a ride, when along comes this guy, and takes me up in his private plane! I gave his aide your 'phone number, did he call you? Say, can't you get over to Brussels on business? If you could, I could get down there and meet you, and maybe Jamie could get time off, and come down, too. He is now recording and broadcasting regularly, and I have two records he made especially for me—haven't even been able to play them yet. I'm going to Brussels tomorrow, and shall doubtless meet all our friends, and will gossip in some café over a few beers, and end up visiting our favourite club. I have never been there yet without Jimmy, and don't know whether I'll feel like it when the time comes— Well—I must get this posted, else it'll take weeks—probably will anyway!

Much love to you and all, write soon.

Margie

After their wedding, Jimmy had been posted to Garmisch, Germany, a small Alpine town across the frontier from Innsbruck, Austria, then to Pilsen in the western district of Bohemia. There, Jimmy was given a choice assignment as personal orchestra leader for General Clarence Huebner, for whom the cornetist presented shows in a large theater, serving as emcee. He also entertained at private parties for visiting Russian and French delegations—once, for Czech president Edvard Beneš. Jimmy talked to Marian on army phones whenever he could—"like you see on $M*A*S*H$," she said—but they both soon discovered, with the constant air traffic, it was possible to thumb rides on planes carrying the mail or a load of GIs. Jimmy's commanding officer was sympathetic to his lovelorn situation.

"I used to say, 'General Huebner, my cornet needs repairing, and there's only one place to get it fixed, and that's in Paris, General.' He said, 'I understand, Mac, I understand.' He was marvelous to me."

Huebner took Jimmy along with him on a flight to Paris, but when Jimmy arrived, he discovered Marian was out on tour. Marian, meanwhile, hearing Jimmy was in Paris, convinced somebody to fly *her* there in a single-engine plane. Though she had no idea where Jimmy was, on a hunch, she went to a recreation hall where the Glenn Miller band was playing (minus the leader, of course, who had disappeared over the English Channel during the Battle of the Bulge). To her great delight, there was her Jamie, on the bandstand. The couple spent an idyllic week in Paris, listening to V-Discs at the USO canteen, drinking at outdoor cafés, and strolling under the plane trees and blossoming chestnuts. Pink blossoms fell over them as they walked along the Champs-Élysées. Marian rendezvoused with Jimmy again in Weimar and later got papers to visit him in Pilsen. In Pilsen, Jimmy's friends threw her a big welcome party, but the next day she had to fly back to Paris.

Sometime in late spring, Marian and Jimmy snuck in a few days in the South of France, riding bikes through the nearly deserted streets of Cannes. When Marian got back to Paris, she was hauled up to the head office of USO for "playing hooky." Fortunately, there was a shortage of piano players, so she was not fired. Jimmy went back to Pilsen. The couple finagled one more visit in June, on the solstice, spending a splendid weekend in Marienbad, at the Hohmhoel Egerländer Hotel. Marian sent a picture postcard home urgently requesting her birth certificate again. The war in the Far East, meanwhile, was finally tipping toward the Allies. On August 6, the atomic bomb fell on Hiroshima. A month later, on September 2, Japan surrendered. The war, which had started for the British almost six years earlier to the day, was finally over.

Jimmy, having spent the summer in Pilsen, began to work in earnest toward mustering out of the army. The good General Huebner suggested Jimmy apply for a discharge in Paris rather than waiting until he got back to the States. That way, he and Marian could be together until they found passage home. On September 27, 1945, Jimmy was honorably discharged, receiving, as he (and other GIs) called it, the prized "ruptured duck"—a cloth insignia of an eagle in a wreath, worn above the breast pocket by army personnel who were finally free to go home. A civilian once again, Jimmy got a job as the leader/emcee of a seven-piece USO band and—once again—hired Marian to play piano. Actress Celeste Holm came over from the States as the main attraction.

Holm had only recently become a star, having originated the role of Ado Annie, the girl "who cain't say no," in *Oklahoma!* on Broadway in 1943.

"I had to keep apologizing for being famous," she said, laughing. "'I got famous after you left,' I would explain. 'So you'll have to pretend that you know who I am.'"

The boys didn't care. She was gorgeous and funny, and she sang like an angel. And "I Cain't Say No" was just the message they wanted to hear. Holm also sang a hilarious novelty number she had worked up at a New York supper club, a sanitized version of the kind of bawdy song soldiers have sung for centuries. "Eunice from Tunis" began:

For a costume I wore a few beads here and there
And each night I came in a string and a prayer.

When Holm arrived, she had no idea whom she would be playing with, and there was little time for rehearsal. But she had nothing but praise for Marian.

"She could play anything," said Holm.

Holm also noted that Marian, though a year younger than Celeste, seemed "more grown up than I was. She was very professional. She knew exactly what she was doing."

The war had matured Marian quickly.

The Holm USO show traveled through France, Belgium, Holland, England, and Germany, including a stop at the Nuremberg Opera House. One freezing night in Rheims, when they were playing to six thousand soldiers on an open field, Holm slipped long underwear under her dress.

To the surprise of everyone, she flirtatiously flipped up her dress on-stage and told the soldiers, "I don't want you to worry about me. I'm not cold."

With the Holm outfit, Marian played again for General Eisenhower at SHAEF in Versailles. After their regular set, Jimmy asked Ike if he had any favorites he would like to hear. To Jimmy's great disappointment, the general requested "Red River Valley."

Jimmy's presence in Paris was exciting news to French jazz fanatics. *Le Jazz Hot,* the venerable jazz magazine, announced breathlessly that Jimmy had already visited the Hot Club and had promised to play with Marian at one of the organization's regular concerts at the L'École Normale. Marian vividly recalled visiting Hot Club honcho Charles Delaunay, the great French jazz critic and author of the first jazz discography, at his apartment on the rue Chaptal. Delaunay introduced her and Jimmy to Django Reinhardt, whom Delaunay was managing at the time. The famous critic also played them a new record from the States by John Birks "Dizzy" Gillespie and Charlie "Bird" Parker. This was Marian's first exposure to the new music called bebop, which was turning the jazz world upside down.

The new style had emerged in Harlem jam sessions but was now current on Manhattan's Fifty-second Street as well, where Jack LeMaire had been working. Harmonically, bebop was to swing what Ravel and Debussy's impressionism had been to classical music in the late nineteenth century—chromatic, slippery, complex, and full of new colors. Rhythmically, it was furious and fast, requiring new levels of technical agility. By contrast to the friendly, boisterous early jazz of Jimmy McPartland, bop expressed the anxiety of the age and the anger and frustration of African Americans, bitter about fighting a war abroad for freedoms not afforded them at home. Bebop also announced that jazz was no longer a dancer's diversion, but a high art. Because of the recording bans of 1942 and 1944, recordings of the new music had been delayed until February 1945, when

Guild Records issued Parker and Gillespie's "Hot House," followed in November by the dazzling "Koko." Listeners were stunned. The new music seemed to have come out of nowhere. Delaunay had ordered a copy of "Hot House." Marian couldn't believe that Parker and Gillespie and pianist Al Haig could actually invent such complicated phrases so fast.

"I was flabbergasted," she said. "That was the first time I heard that kind of comping, and I said to Charles, 'How do they do that? Is it all written out?'"

Marian would come to terms with the challenging new music soon enough. But dealing with Jimmy's drinking was proving much more challenging. At one point in Paris, she recalled complaining to another woman in a USO band that Jimmy was always drunk, running with his buddies. The woman advised her to get drunk, too, so Jimmy could "see how awful it looks."

"It was silly advice," said Marian. "I started to flirt with some officer— we were in this club where all the USO people were staying—and I did get quite drunk. I passed out in the ladies' room on the floor, because I remember some old French lady coming in to sweep up, who couldn't speak English, and looking at me like 'What are you doing here?' I struggled to my feet, and oh, God, it all came back to me. I ran up to the hotel and Jimmy bopped me in the face. He thought I was flirting with this guy. So then I had a cut lip. He apologized, and he quit drinking for three days."

A few days later, unable to drag Jimmy away from a party, Marian hit him on the head with the heel of her shoe.

"What'd you wanna do that for?" Jimmy asked, sounding like an injured little boy.

Jimmy's tone was a tip-off. He was indeed like a little boy who needed someone to take care of him. Marian had volunteered.

"I was just so in love with him," she said.

Why Marian married Jimmy has always been something of a puzzle— sometimes even to her. There was certainly no doubt, reading her letters, that she was absolutely smitten by her handsome new love.

"How do you like the pictures of my Jamie?" she wrote home. "Every time I look at them, I think of my wonderful week in Eupen . . . I miss my 'honey.'"

The carpe diem atmosphere of wartime no doubt had been a factor as well.

"Everybody was getting married," remembered Marian's friend Zena Collier, who had also grown up in a London suburb and later come to America as a war bride herself. "It was that feeling in the air. You never knew what tomorrow would bring. I got married because everybody was getting married. It seemed so exciting. And people in uniform seemed so exciting. Though the Blitz was terrible, and people were dying, men were getting killed, but at the same time I have to say to you that, in London especially, the ambience was so exciting and glamorous."

On the other hand, Marian and Jimmy were such complete opposites, and Jimmy had such obvious problems—not just the drinking, but his feckless boyishness—one wonders why Marian—overprotected, raised to be cautious and moderate, eminently sensible—would make such a move. Later on, she would cynically chalk up the marriage to "propinquity."

"There we were," she said. "It just sort of seemed like the thing to do."

At other times, she claimed to have had no agency, direction, or motivation at all.

"I was like something blown about by the wind," she said.

This most certainly was self-deception. For while she truly seems to have lacked focus before the war, by the time she met Jimmy, she had clearly become ambitious. In a 1951 interview, she even said as much, telling reporter Beverly Smith, "I didn't become ambitious until 1944." But outward displays of ambition were tricky for women in those days, opening them to charges of being "unwomanly," "shrill," or "strident." Better to sound uncertain, hesitant, "blown about by the wind." Ambition was touchy for the British, too, male or female, for whom self-deprecation and false modesty are a way of life. Americans wear their hopes on their sleeves, Brits feign indifference. For Marian, all of this was made even more complicated by the fact that British war brides were sometimes accused of opportunism. In one famous incident, wives being ferried to a fleet of ships to transport Britain's war brides to America were jeered by British men. Even Eleanor Roosevelt had come out publicly against American soldiers bringing home European wives, declaring it an impulsive act, borne of loneliness, that they would regret the rest of their lives. (The First Lady notwithstanding, the United States Congress passed a law in 1945 that waived all visa restrictions for war brides, gave them the opportunity to apply for U.S. citizenship after two years, and automatically conferred citizenship on their children.) Marian was understandably sensitive about being perceived as an opportunist.

"I certainly never thought about going to America," she said. "A lot of girls had married GIs to get to America. I'm still British. I never became an American."

But in fact, it's clear that by May 1945, when she wrote home asking for her birth certificate, Marian and Jimmy were making plans for a career in the States, plans that were even reported in the *Chicago Tribune* later that year, in a story about how Willie Shore had been the unwitting "cupid" in their marriage.

But Marian was particularly sensitive to the accusation that her marriage was cynically motivated. She often even preempted the question. In her interview with the Smithsonian Jazz Oral History Program, without prompting, she said, "Some people think that I was guilty of some kind of skullduggery, because I married Jimmy. They all thought . . . it was a ploy to come to the States, because a lot of women did do that. But . . . I didn't do it for that reason. . . . I didn't think further than that we would work together."

It's certainly understandable why McPartland would want to distance herself from the war bride stereotype. But she protests too much. In fact, she was enchanted with America and Americans, and the opportunity to go to the United States must have seemed like a gift from the gods. Britain, after all, hadn't exactly been a wonderland to grow up in between the wars, and now that World War II was over, it was even bleaker. Rationing continued, work was scarce, and the city of London was in ruins. America lay untouched. And rich. It was the land of promise. And the land of jazz.

And Jimmy was the open sesame into that land. He had opened the door to the world of jazz and improvisation Marian had been trying to find since 1938, when she knocked on the door of the Billy Mayerl school in London. Jimmy was the guy who could show her how to make those licks of Bob Zurke's and Teddy Wilson's sound the way they did on the records. He had that magic "beat," the feel of the thing, and the blues, and he was delighted to share it all. Just the fact that Marian wrote a letter to *Melody Maker* about their wedding would seem to confirm she knew exactly what the market value of her new name really was. So while it would be cynical, unfair, and incorrect to say Marian married Jimmy McPartland to get to America—or, worse, that she didn't fall in love with him, since she clearly did—it would be naive to say it never occurred to her that going to America was part of the excitement and attraction of the package.

Besides, in England she had never quite fit in anyway. As Jenel Virden points out in her book about British war brides, *Good-bye, Piccadilly,* "Those who chose the path of immigration were oftentimes the people who were 'out of step' with their societies."

The notion of Marian McPartland as an emigrant is sometimes underplayed, but it's important. George Wein, the American promoter who started the Newport Jazz Festival and would become a great champion of the McPartlands, noted the "tremendous incentive and drive" Marian must have had to emigrate from England to America to make her way in the jazz world. It was a courageous leap of faith.

But before Marian could make that leap, she needed to take Jimmy home to meet her parents. Guessing they would assume a jazz musician would be irresponsible (and probably out of work), she had tried to create a good advance impression by stressing in her letters that Jimmy was "recording and broadcasting with his band." Jimmy, for his part, composed one of the few letters he ever wrote in his life, an inelegantly scrawled but disarmingly courtly missive addressed to Marian's father:

> I am afraid I'm not a very good writer and I have been in some doubt as to how to start, but I want you to know that I love your daughter and will try to make her happy for the rest of our lives. She is such a fine musician and a lovely person withal, I know you are going to enjoy hearing us play together and we will even play "Drink to me only with thine eyes," as Marian tells me it is your favorite tune. I'm looking forward to meeting you and the family, but will probably tremble in my boots on the way over! However it looks like I won't have much of a chance of getting to England for a while, but when I do, I hope I can bring our girl with me if the South of France can spare her! Please give my love to Mamma, and Joyce and thank you for giving me your daughter, she is the most wonderful thing in my life.
>
> Hoping to see you all soon.
>
> Love, Jimmy

In November 1945, Marian and Jimmy finally made their way to Eastbourne. On the way, the couple stopped in London to see Max Jones, the jazz writer at *Melody Maker* who had published Marian's letter earlier that year. He now wrote a longer piece, noting the couple's "fetching uniforms." The magazine ran a photograph of them sitting in their "browns," looking fresh and young and happy. Jimmy had a thin mustache and Marian was wearing an army cap.

At Kerrisdale, for all Marian's trepidation, Jimmy's first meeting with Marian's parents turned out to be quite ordinary.

"He had the drinking thing under control when he was there," said Marian. "My mother was in bed. She couldn't get up. Jimmy came over and gave her a big kiss and said, 'It's great to meet you.'"

Janet later remarked to Marian, "He's not at all like an American. He's polite."

Frank took Jimmy fishing in Eastbourne, and they came back with a fine catch. Marian's father cooked. He and Jimmy went to the movies. Joyce and her boyfriend, Tony, came for dinner.

"Visiting Marian's parents was like being in an English movie to me," Jimmy later told *The New Yorker*. "They were mid-Victorian in style. Her mother was in a wheelchair and very well dressed and very particular. Everything at a certain time, everything regulated. Tea at four, dinner at eight. If I was late coming back from fishing or golf, Marian's mother would say, 'James, you're late. We've started our tea.'"

Mrs. Turner was more than charmed. Soon, Jimmy was teasing her like an old pal from Chicago. Sensing her stuffiness, he would occasionally peer around the door to her room and ask, "You want a little poke?"

"Oh, Jimmy," she'd say in a faux scandalized tone. "How can you say those things?"

While the couple was in England, Jimmy contacted British guitarist Vic Lewis, whom he had known in New York. Lewis played in the house band on the *Radio Rhythm Club* show on the BBC and had even made some records in New York with Jimmy's buddies Eddie Condon, Bobby Hackett, and Pee Wee Russell. Vic invited Jimmy and Marian to record. On January 6, 1946, Lewis featured them on their first recording together. It was Marian's studio jazz debut, though it would not be issued until 1986, when it came out as *Vic Lewis Jam Sessions, Volume 3: 1945–1946,* on Harlequin Records. Drummer Joe Nardy, whom Marian had worked with in the Jack LeMaire outfit, was also on the session.

Marian acquitted herself well enough. With a pumping sense of time appropriate to classic Chicago jazz, she delivered a perky, clean solo on "The World Is Waiting for the Sunrise," managed a few Fats Waller–ish licks on a ridiculously up-tempo version of "I Got Rhythm," and decorated "Rose Room" with some bluesy thirds and tremolos. On a title called simply "Blues," however, she was unconvincing. Listening to these sides in the summer of 2008, she insisted the solo on "Rose Room" was by Jerry Schwartz, an American who had been playing in the Army Air Force Band in London and who shared piano duties on the session. When she got to "Blues," she joked, "Does it have to be me?"

Interestingly, Marian said she was neither nervous nor intimidated by the session, as it felt like what she'd been doing with Jimmy for the past year.

"I knew the tunes, I didn't have to read anything," she said. "So I'm sure I didn't feel anything but happy to be playing."

In February, *Down Beat* noted that Jimmy and Marian had gotten married and wrote, perhaps with some exaggeration, that Jimmy had been "barn-storming the British Isles and the continent, carrying the spirit of Bix in his heart." As they awaited passage back to the States, Marian and Jimmy returned to the continent, taking a skiing holiday at the Zugspitze, Germany's highest peak, and on March 14 attended the Nuremberg trials, which had begun the previous November. Marian remembered the sinister Hermann Goering, commander of the Luftwaffe, which had rained down all that destruction on London, sitting across from them, eerily laughing, as if nothing really serious were at hand. On the drive to Nuremberg, Marian's jeep got into an accident and she broke her wrist, which effectively ended her involvement in the USO. In April, the couple finally secured passage on a Victory ship sailing from Le Havre. The voyage took fourteen days. Marian spent most of the trip "deathly sick," she said, "and all Jimmy could talk about was what he'd had for lunch."

On April 23, Marian, her forearm wrapped in a cast, and Jimmy, trim in his army uniform, sailed into New York Harbor.

"When we saw the Statue of Liberty, everyone crowded around the rail," Jimmy remembered. "I'll never forget it."

"Nothing could take away the excitement I felt at seeing New York for the first time," said Marian. "Moving from war to peace that first night in New York was the most exciting beginning in my life."

4.

Jimmy:
"I Like You, Kid"
(1907–1944)

FOR MARIAN, NEW YORK was virgin territory. For Jimmy, it was ripe with memories—some ecstatic, some excruciatingly painful—recalled through a haze of Prohibition booze, cascades of cash, and dizzy musical invention. Twenty years earlier, Jimmy had been a teenager in Manhattan. None other than Bix Beiderbecke had passed him the baton of classic jazz. Then Jimmy had shared the bandstand with the future stars of the swing era—Glenn Miller, Benny Goodman, and Tommy and Jimmy Dorsey. In jazz—and on Broadway—Jimmy knew everyone and everyone knew Jimmy. His days had been filled with glamorous showgirls, Broadway pit work, and almost weekly recording sessions. But like so many who had lived to the hilt in the Roaring Twenties, he—along with the stock market—had crashed and burned. By the time he met Marian, Jimmy had lived what for other people might have felt like several lifetimes.

James Dugald McPartland was born March 15, 1907, in Chicago. His father, James Clement McPartland, was an Irishman born and raised in Burlington, Iowa. A big, athletic man, Jimmy's father grew up on a farm, worked as an oarsman on the Mississippi River, boxed as an amateur, and once tried out for Cap Anson's Colts, the precursors of the Chicago Cubs. He also learned to play a variety of instruments, including cornet, clarinet, saxophone, and violin. During the Spanish-American War, he served as an army bandmaster, then opened a music store on Chicago's Near West Side, where he sold instruments, taught lessons, and headed up a local band in the parks. An erratic, sometimes violent alcoholic who could not maintain a steady income, he often took out his frustrations on his wife and children.

Jimmy's mother, Jeannie Munn, had come to Chicago with her parents from Paisley, Scotland, near Glasgow, in the 1880s. She worked variously in a grocery store, as a schoolteacher, and as an interpreter in civil courts for immigrants. She also played piano. Jimmy's middle name, with a slight spelling variation, was derived from Jeannie's father's name, Duigald

Munn. Jimmy was known all his life to family members as Dugald. Jimmy was the baby of the family, preceded by Ruth, Ethel, and Richard. They grew up poor in a mostly Italian, inner-city neighborhood near Lake and Paulina Streets, a district famous for Jane Addams's Hull House and, later, Prohibition bootleggers. The area also produced clarinetist Benny Goodman, pianist Art Hodes, and reedman and jazz chronicler Milton Mesirow, known as Mezz Mezzrow.

Every Sunday, Grandfather Duigald read the Bible to Jimmy in a burr so thick, he couldn't understand it.

"But he paid me fifteen cents," said Jimmy, "and afterward I'd shoot craps under the el."

James McPartland taught Richard and Jimmy to box and taught all of his children to play musical instruments. For his fifth birthday, Jimmy was given a violin his father fashioned from an orange crate. Two years later, he and Richard got real violins. Ruth and Ethel played piano. Jeannie, who had sung alto in a choir in Scotland, taught the boys to play "Blue Bells of Scotland" ("Oh where, tell me where, is yo-ur Highland laddie gone?"). It would become one of Jimmy's enduring themes. Jeannie also taught her children that racism was wrong, that "colored people" no more liked being called names than Jimmy liked being called a "shanty Irishman."

In 1914, when Jimmy was seven years old, Jeannie left her husband to protect herself and her brood from his drunken violence. Unable to support her children, she sent Ethel, Richard, and Jimmy to the Central Baptist Children's Home in Maywood, a suburb west of Oak Park; Ruth lived with an aunt. When the other two children found homes in a few months, Jimmy was left in the orphanage.

"I really felt left alone," he remembered. "And I do think that this has affected me throughout my life somehow. . . . I was very mad at everybody. . . . I remember one of the matrons—I'd done something, I'm not sure what it was—she put me in this attic and closed the door and she told me the tigers were going to get me, and the animals really scared the heck out of me. I remember pounding on the door and crying, and that's the last thing I remember because I evidently went to sleep."

Not long after this incident, McPartland got into a fight with the superintendent's son and knocked him through a glass door. It was snowing that day. The superintendent wrapped Jimmy's clothes in a brown paper bag, gave him three cents carfare, and sent him packing to his father's house in Oak Park. Jimmy later told Marian this experience made him vow to never let anybody or anything "get to him" again. He developed a happy-go-lucky exterior and rarely let on when anything bothered him.

Jimmy's parents eventually reunited on the Near West Side, where Jimmy and Richard fell into the street life, modeling themselves on local gangsters like Dago Lawrence Mangano and Mike de Pike Heitler. Jimmy stole a .45 automatic out of a Cadillac parked in front of a saloon where the hoods hung out, and he and a buddy started stealing chickens in the suburbs, selling them door-to-door in Chicago. One night in Cicero, someone fired a shotgun at them. Jimmy fired back. A neighbor later ID'ed Jimmy, and he and his brother were hauled off to jail. When the boys' case came up, Jeannie's familiarity with the courts turned out to be a godsend. The judge told her that if she moved her children out of the gang-infested neighborhood, he wouldn't send them to reform school. Jeannie moved to Austin. Before Jimmy left, he sold the .45 for $25.

A quiet, middle-class suburb annexed to Chicago in 1899, Austin was just the change of venue Jimmy and his brother needed. Mezz Mezzrow, the colorful Chicago clarinetist, would later write that Austin was "a sleepy-time neighborhood big as a yawn and just about as lively." Jimmy enrolled at John Hay Elementary School, and a well-to-do uncle, Fred Harris, took Richard and Jimmy on fishing trips and taught them how to swim. Swimming, fishing, and boxing—and later golf—would become lifelong passions. In the fall of 1921, Jimmy entered Austin High School. There, he and Richard fell in with some other boys—Frank Teschemacher, Jim Lanigan, Bud Freeman, and Dave North—who liked the frenetic new music called jazz that was sweeping the country. Jazz had first flourished in New Orleans, but in the 1920s, in part because of the Great Migration north of a million and a half African Americans, the epicenter of the music had moved to Chicago. To accommodate the new nightlife, a "sporting district" of bars, clubs, restaurants, theaters, houses of prostitution, and gambling dens emerged on the South Side in a district along State Street called the Stroll. Among the musicians who came to Chicago were the New Orleans Rhythm Kings, a band of white players who took up residence at the Friar's Inn in downtown Chicago in 1922, where they were known originally as the Friar's Society Orchestra. Jimmy and his friends first heard them on a windup Victrola with a green-and-gold-fringed lampshade over the turntable at an ice-cream parlor across the street from Austin High called the Spoon and Straw.

"I think the first one we heard was 'Farewell Blues,'" said Jimmy. "Boy, when we heard that—I'll tell you we went out of our minds. Everybody flipped."

The boys were so inspired, they decided to start a band of their own. Jimmy's father provided musical instruments—and lessons—for everyone.

The McPartlands, Teschemacher, and Lanigan already played violin; North and Lanigan played piano. But for the band, Jimmy chose cornet, in part because he was entranced by the work of the Rhythm Kings' Paul Mares, but also because it was the loudest instrument and was played by the leader. With his gift for gab and easy confidence, Jimmy was a natural-born front man. His brother Dick, more introverted, chose the banjo (a rhythm instrument in early jazz). Tesch, as Teschemacher was known, the most accomplished musician of the bunch, already played alto saxophone (and banjo, too), so he was assigned the clarinet part. Lanigan took the bass (tuba, then bass fiddle), and Dave North came in on piano. Freeman had had no musical training whatsoever and later confessed it was the stylish clothes and spastic moves of the era's "Frisco dancers" that piqued his interest. But when Bud saw a fellow playing a diamond-studded saxophone in Paul Biese's band at the Senate Theatre, he decided that was for him.

The boys learned to play the music of the New Orleans Rhythm Kings in the most awkward, painstaking way, listening to the records over and over, copying one phrase at a time until they could string together a tune. McPartland said it took them four to six weeks to learn their first song. Calling themselves the Austin Blue Friars, the group started out playing school functions, "tea dances," and college fraternity parties. Soon McPartland and his colleagues came to be known as the Austin High Gang.

"We were ruffians," said McPartland. "If some of [the fraternity boys] didn't like us, or said, 'That stinks,' we'd say, 'You don't like us? Come on outside. I'll explain it to ya.' . . . That's how we got the reputation: 'Don't fool around with that Austin High Gang. They're rough!'"

During this period, dozens of other white Chicago youngsters were smitten by jazz, too, in particular a precocious young drummer from nearby Oak Park named Dave Tough, who was dating a girl from Austin. He was invited to join the "gang." Tough was taking literature courses downtown at the Lewis Institute and also frequented the Green Mask cabaret, where he had participated in jazz and poetry sessions by Langston Hughes and Kenneth Rexroth. A sophisticated drummer who had absorbed the style of King Oliver's man Warren "Baby" Dodds, Tough had been reading the sarcastic essays of H. L. Mencken in the *American Mercury* and was a buff of French culture. Tough introduced the boys to the idea that jazz was a calling, an act of artistic rebellion against middle-class norms. The notion that jazz was an antibourgeois art played for art's sake, and that popular dance music was "commercial," was a powerful message that became a permanent feature of McPartland's worldview.

However, McPartland quickly moved from amateur to professional. In the spring of 1923, he joined the musicians union so he could play with a band led by Al Haid at a Chinese restaurant, earning $35 a week. That summer, the band played the Fox Lake Casino fifty miles northwest of Chicago. It would be the first of many resort gigs, which combined three of Jimmy's great loves—jazz, swimming, and fishing. And if there was a bottle of gin around—and a girl in a swimsuit to share it with—better yet. Jimmy had no trouble getting girlfriends. He was a handsome guy with rugged features—wavy black hair, blue eyes, a big nose, a dimpled chin, and a boyish grin that showed all his teeth. Barrel-chested and just under six feet tall, he spoke with casual confidence in a gravelly Chicago street cadence that conveyed both enthusiasm and authority. He had prizefighter's manners, opening doors for ladies and respectfully addressing older women as "ma'am." His open, expectant face could turn from friendly to hostile in a trice. He was a player.

After Fox Lake, Jimmy went with Paul "Frisco" Hasse at the Hawthorn roadhouse in Cicero. A couple of the guys in the band took music lessons at Hull House, where they told Jimmy there was an unbelievable young clarinet player, still in knee pants, named Benny Goodman. Benny sat in and knocked Jimmy out on clarinet, then proceeded to borrow Jimmy's cornet and play "Rose of the Rio Grande." McPartland was floored. The Hawthorn was a tough dive owned by ex-prizefighter Eddie Tancil, who foolishly refused to buy beer from an up-and-coming gangster named Al Capone. Jimmy, now playing till three A.M. on weeknights and falling asleep at school, decided to quit the band. It was a fortuitous decision. Tancil was killed in a gunfight with Capone's hoods.

Goodman, meanwhile, brought Jimmy in on higher-paying jobs for fraternity parties at the University of Chicago and Northwestern University. Jimmy bought Benny his first pair of long pants for one of those jobs, holding his hand as they crossed the street to Marshall Field's department store. Jimmy and Benny both took up golf around this time, and it remained one of Jimmy's lifelong pleasures. He once shot a 73 in high school. Playing frat parties, Jimmy met a hip university pianist named Bill Grimm who told Jimmy about an astounding cornet player from Davenport, Iowa, named Leon "Bix" Beiderbecke, who was attending Lake Forest Academy in Evanston. Grimm also took the Austin High kids down to the South Side to hear African American players King Oliver and Louis Armstrong at the Lincoln Gardens. It is hard to overestimate the influence this experience had on McPartland.

In a memoir, Chicago banjo and guitar man Eddie Condon remembered it like this: "It was hypnosis at first hearing. Everyone was playing what he wanted to play and it was all mixed together as if someone had planned it with a set of micrometer calipers . . . there was a tone from the trumpets like warm rain on a cold day. Freeman, McPartland, and I were immobilized; the music poured into us like daylight running down a dark hole."

"We knew that we were hearing the real thing for the first time," observed Freeman.

McPartland became a regular, befriending Armstrong and absorbing his rhythmic inventions, swing feel, and deep gift for original, coherent soloing. But it was Beiderbecke—like Jimmy, a disciple of both Armstrong and Paul Mares—who would ultimately have the biggest influence on McPartland. Though Jimmy never heard Bix play in Chicago, the records Beiderbecke made in 1924 with a band formed by Chicago-based musicians from Michigan, the Wolverines, cut straight to his heart. Bix's warm, full sound, sweet attack, lyrical phrasing, and sophisticated harmonies would be Jimmy's musical model for life. (Eddie Condon later famously wrote that hearing Beiderbecke was "like the sound of a girl saying 'yes.'")

Around the time Jimmy heard the Beiderbecke recordings, he hooked up with a University of Chicago outfit called the Maroon Five, with whom he spent another idyllic summer in the woods, playing Lost Lake Resort in northern Wisconsin. At night, he played music; days, he fished for muskie and walleye and worked as a fishing guide. Though he was the only high school kid in the band, Jimmy was the front man.

"I was always a cocky guy, you know?" he said. "I wasn't bashful."

With all the money he was pulling in, Jimmy bought a Model T Ford. He also began drinking heavily, a habit Bud Freeman said McPartland had acquired in high school.

"One day he passed out in front of my house," wrote Freeman in his autobiography. "I called my father and he and two others carried Jimmy inside and put him into my father's bed. My father loved Jimmy. I'll never forget him lecturing Jimmy the next day. 'This is terrible what you're doing to yourself.' Jimmy looked up at him and said, 'Mr. Freeman, do you have a beer?'"

When McPartland got home from Lost Lake, he grandly displayed his new car, two quarts of gin, and his "loot" from the summer. No doubt because of the extreme poverty he had experienced growing up, and despite his uncompromising attitudes about playing jazz, making money was always a matter of pride for him. Jimmy was known for picking up pennies on the street, even after he became an adult. He often sounded astonished that people would pay him to play music, which he thought of as simply having fun. There was something of the con artist about him, as though music were just another hustle.

If it was, it was certainly panning out. On October 12, 1924, just as Jimmy returned to Austin High for his senior year, he received a telegram:

CAN YOU JOIN WOLVERINES IN NEW YORK REPLACING BIX
BEIDERBECKE AT SALARY OF EIGHTY-SEVEN DOLLARS FIFTY PER
WEEK QUERYMARK ANSWER IMMEDIATELY STOP.

At first, McPartland thought it must be a gag. But then he remembered that on the previous New Year's Eve, he had played a gig out in Lincoln Park West with Vic Moore, the drummer in the Wolverines. Moore had told Jimmy he sounded like Bix and, indeed, had recommended the seventeen-year-old cornetist for the job. The Wolverines had opened in September at New York's Cinderella Ballroom, at Forty-eighth Street and Seventh Avenue. But a month into the job, Beiderbecke had been hired away by bandleader Jean Goldkette. Bix agreed to stay until a replacement could be found.

For McPartland, this was the opportunity of a lifetime. His brother Dick sent a wire back that said YES, adding, just to be sure it was all for real: SEND TRANSPORTATION. A money order for $35 arrived, with directions to the Somerset Hotel in Manhattan. Three days later—after a milk run that included a missed connection in Buffalo—the bedraggled McPartland arrived and was told he would be rooming with Beiderbecke. After running through a few tunes at an informal audition, McPartland spent the next few days hanging out with Bix. Noticing Jimmy's beat-up horn, Bix took him to a music shop and bought him a new Conn Victor cornet. Jimmy vowed he would pay Bix back. Bix waved him off, saying, "I like you, kid. You play like me, but you don't copy me." McPartland would repeat this line like a mantra the rest of his life. For the next few days, Bix played in the band alongside Jimmy, showing him the lead parts. Up in their hotel room, Bix showed Jimmy some of his tricks—lip slurs and different ways to finger the same notes to get through difficult passages in the music.

The Wolverines played at the Cinderella till the end of the year, then headed for Florida. But before they left town, the band recorded two sides, "When My Sugar Walks Down the Street" and "Prince of Wails." On the first tune, clarinetist Jimmy Hartwell was supposed to take the solo after Dave Harmon's jaunty vocal but unexpectedly handed it off to Jimmy. Because of a midsong key change that put Jimmy in the awkward key of E, he accomplished little beyond outlining the melody, though to his credit he sounded confident and sturdy, with a natural, buoyant sense of swinging time. The ensemble, unfortunately, played with a sodden feel. "Prince of Wails" was even less inspiring.

After the sessions, the band was booked into a Miami speakeasy in February 1925, but the feds shuttered the joint before the Wolverines could open. Broke, Jimmy wired home for train fare, and he and the band's pianist and leader, Dick Voynow, reinvented the Wolverines as the Austin High Gang redux. Dave Tough replaced Moore, and Bud Freeman and Teschemacher came aboard. At Cleveland's Palace Theatre, the boys shared the bill with the great tap dancer Bill "Bojangles" Robinson, who taught McPartland a step to do while he sang the Charleston number "Oh! What a Girl!" Voynow left the band, and under Jimmy's leadership, with the help of a sharp agent, the group moved into a lucrative six-week engagement in Des Moines, Iowa, at Riverview Park, which had a man-made island in a massive swimming pool with sandy beaches. The band played a return engagement in May 1926. Midsummer, the Wolverines moved to White City, a South Side Chicago amusement park that had opened during the World's Fair the previous year. The band had so much fun, the manager had to ask the guys to stop playing through intermissions and give the dancers a rest!

What a time it must have been—a Jazz Age fantasy. On his night off, Bix, playing with saxophonist Frankie Trumbauer and clarinetist Pee Wee Russell down at Hudson Lake in Indiana, drove eighty miles north to Chicago to see Jimmy's band. After the gig, the boys prowled the South Side clubs. King Oliver was at the Plantation; next door was the Nest, where clarinetist Jimmy Noone held forth with the great New Orleans trombonist Kid Ory and drummer Zutty Singleton. Louis Armstrong, playing at the Dreamland Café, occasionally fell by White City to hear McPartland and the boys. Mezz Mezzrow joined them onstage on weekends. On Thursday and Saturday nights, Sig Meyer's band, which included Chicagoans Muggsy Spanier, Rosy McHargue, and Jess Stacy, shared the stand with Jimmy's group. From time to time, McPartland and the gang would drive down to Hudson Lake. Bix and Pee Wee were rooming together in a little yellow cottage in back of the hotel. On an old piano, Bix played a brilliant new piano composition, "In a Mist," the very piece that would excite Marian in London a decade later.

Bix's piano pieces were heavily influenced by the French impressionist composer Maurice Ravel, and the Frenchman had in turn been influenced by jazz. Ravel himself turned up in Chicago in January 1928, and after conducting a debut with the Chicago Symphony of his deliciously jazz-influenced Sonata for Violin and Piano, he visited the South Side clubs. At the Nest, Jimmy met Ravel, listening to clarinetist Jimmy Noone. No wonder, looking back at this era, Condon said there was so much jazz being played in Chicago, "you could hold an instrument in the middle of the street and the air would play it."

Or so it may have seemed if one had been taken to a club by Mezzrow, who was as much a missionary for marijuana as he was for jazz. One night after the White City gig, Mezzrow turned Jimmy on to "muggles," then took him to the Dreamland to hear Louis.

"It really got me floating," Jimmy remembered. "Everything was like a slow-motion picture. I half closed my eyes and listened to Louis weave in and out on 'Dippermouth' with Little Mitch [George Mitchell, cornet]. Each note Louis blew came out of his horn like a colored bubble. The bubbles changed their shape and drifted around the dance hall. On short fast passages Louis's cornet would squirt out a whole bunch of small bright red, green, and yellow ones. They were bigger and darker—blue, purple, and maroon—during slower passages. It was a beautiful sensation, but I was afraid to try it again."

Jimmy apparently got over his fears. When he stopped drinking, like Louis, he became a lifelong pot smoker.

While the Wolverines were at White City, bandleader Art Kassel invited them to join some of his men at the fabled Greystone Ballroom in Detroit, but the boys found Kassel's music corny. Jimmy and Dave Tough mutinied. When Kassel called a sweet dance number like "When My Baby Smiles at Me," Tough whispered, *"Le Rat Mort,"* which meant "Shim-Me-Sha-Wabble," and away they went. After a week or two, Kassel fired the cheeky Chicagoans.

McPartland and Lanigan—who by now had married Jimmy's sister Ethel—had spent many a night as underage youngsters standing on the sidewalk in front of the Friar's Inn, listening to the New Orleans Rhythm Kings. Now, Jimmy and his brother-in-law found themselves playing there in a band led by Bill Paley. The Friar's was owned by Mike Fritzel, who wittingly hosted gangsters in the club, including Al Capone. One night, his hoods shot up the place, including Lanigan's bass. Jimmy complained.

"I happened to know [Jim] had laid down $225 for [the bass], but I said $850," said Jimmy. "Believe it or not, in five minutes Mike came over with $850 in cash. The torpedo just peeled it off a roll. You know these Prohibition guys were loaded with loot."

In the fall of 1927, McPartland and Lanigan got on at the Blackhawk Tavern with drummer Ben Pollack, formerly with the New Orleans Rhythm Kings. Pollack had one of the first hot swing bands, with Goodman on clarinet and Glenn Miller on trombone and writing arrangements. In the meantime, Dick Voynow, now at Brunswick, recorded a new version of the Wolverines. This time, on "Royal Garden Blues," McPartland sounded zippier and the rhythm section had left behind the sludgy sound of its first recordings. The sides also featured what the boys called "the explosion"—a full-on attack by the whole band between solos—which would become a signature of their style. Bix, now playing with Paul Whiteman, came to Chicago for three weeks in November. Beiderbecke called Jimmy at eight o'clock in the morning the day the band arrived, asking if he could borrow a tuxedo, explaining he'd left his at the cleaners in the previous town. Jimmy never saw the tux again, but while Bix was in Chicago, he gave Jimmy $100 toward the price of a new Bach cornet. He also made a point of taking Jimmy to hear the great singer Ethel Waters, famous for her versions of "Dinah" and "Sweet Georgia Brown."

While Whiteman was at the Chicago Theater, Bix started hanging out at a shabby saloon at 222 North State Street called Sam Beers My Cellar, with a sawdust floor and a beat-up piano. Bix's reputation was such that Goodman, drummer Gene Krupa, Bing Crosby (also with Whiteman), and other musicians flocked to the joint. The place was eventually dubbed, in jest, the Three Deuces, a reference to the Four Deuces, a popular gangland whorehouse. One night at the Three Deuces, when Condon was extolling the superiority of Chicago jazzmen over New York "hacks" like popular trumpeter Red Nichols, a kazoo-playing hustler named Red McKenzie challenged Condon to prove his point—on record. McKenzie had access to the Okeh studios and had already recorded a novelty hit for them with the Mound City Blue Blowers (which later featured Jimmy's brother Richard). Condon picked up the gauntlet. He rounded up four Austin High boys—McPartland, Freeman, Teschemacher, and Lanigan—plus pianist Joe Sullivan and eighteen-year-old Krupa. The McKenzie and Condon's Chicagoans sessions of December 8 and 16, 1927, put Chicago jazz—and the Austin High Gang—on the map. There were only four sides—"Liza," "Sugar," China Boy," and "Nobody's Sweetheart"—but their obsessive, nervous drive, their use of the saxophone (instead of trombone) as a solo instrument, their emphasis on individual solos, and their "explosions" between choruses and sudden "flares" in front of a drum kick created a sensation.

One of the things that made the records stand out was that Krupa's whole drum set—including the bass drum—was recorded. Prior to that, most jazz recordings had left the bass drum at home, because it caused the recording needle to jump out of the groove. By covering the bass drum with blankets, Krupa and the session engineer managed to get a fuller drum sound. Today, the records sound raw and perhaps overexcited, but with a kind of lift, a floating quality—particularly from McPartland himself—that reflected the influence of Beiderbecke on the whole crew. On "Sugar," Jimmy seemed to caress the notes as Condon's chunk-a-chunk banjo buoyed him along. Jimmy's solo on "China Boy" had an organic flow, a natural-sounding contour to its phrases. "Liza" showcased something else important about McPartland. Even at this early date in the history of jazz soloing, he was crafting his own, original melodic phrases, not just decorating the melody.

After these records came out, the French jazz critic Hugues Panassié credited the white Chicagoans with forging a new style, devoting an entire chapter of his *Guide to Swing Music* to "Chicago jazz." For a variety of reasons, historians later distanced themselves from this idea. How, they asked, could a "Chicago style" be exclusively the province of white musicians, when black players such as Oliver and Armstrong, not to mention Noone, the Dodds Brothers, and Earl Hines, were playing in Chicago at the same time? And since these mostly New Orleanian African American musicians hadn't started recording until they left the Crescent City anyway, what was "New Orleans jazz" and what was "Chicago jazz"?

Whether it was a new style or not, Richard Sudhalter, who played this music as well as wrote about it, probably captured the spirit of the young white players best when he wrote, "These players are young men in a hurry, crowding the front of the beat like rush-hour commuters muscling their way into a subway car. The New Orleans men, it must be remembered, were playing for their audiences in a city whose long and varied tradition of showmanship continues to this day. For the young Chicagoans the audience was at best an inconvenience: if they understand and like us, fine—if they don't, to hell with them. The difference is real and discernible in every phrase."

When Maurice Ravel had come through Chicago in 1928, McPartland and Freeman were still with Ben Pollack at the Blackhawk Tavern. That year, the Chicago city fathers started to shutter the South Side clubs as a moral nuisance, and a great exodus of jazz musicians to New York began. For the next six months, Jimmy scuffled with Pollack in the Big Apple, playing first at the Little Club, managed by John Popkin, who later owned the Hickory House. When the job at the Little Club went dark for the summer, Pollack found an engagement at the Metropolitan Theater in Brooklyn, set up by a Chicago shake dancer named Bea Palmer, known as "the Shimmy Queen." Jimmy had a torrid affair with Palmer while she was estranged from her husband. Palmer got the hungry musicians invited to a Park Avenue do where they hoped to dine on hors d'oeuvres. Unfortunately, only cocktails were served. At the party, Bix, in town with Whiteman, came to the rescue, peeling a hundred-dollar bill off a roll and handing it to Jimmy. At one point, the boys were so down on their luck that Bud, Jimmy, Benny, Glenn, and several other Pollack sidemen all shared the same suite in the Whitby Apartments on West Forty-fifth Street, sleeping on chairs, couches, or the floor. Freeman took an offer to sail to Europe. Pollack cobbled together a few more dates, notably at a theater gig in Oakmont, Pennsylvania, just up the Allegheny River from Pittsburgh. It was here, in the summer of 1928, that Jimmy fell in love with a teenage singer named Dorothy Williams.

Dorothy and Hannah Williams had been doing a sister act since childhood, famously working in the early 1920s with the Scranton Sirens, the launching pad for Tommy and Jimmy Dorsey. In December 1926, singing with Pollack in Chicago, they had scored a minor hit with a catchy, jazzmatazz vocal, "He's the Last Word." Vacationing in their hometown of Scranton, the sisters and their mother decided to go up to Oakmont to say hello to their old boss, Ben Pollack. Backstage, something clicked. At just five feet tall (and wearing a size four shoe), Dorothy was petite, had a cute, high voice, and was drop-dead gorgeous, with dark hair and black eyes. Jimmy and Benny Goodman invited Dorothy and Hannah on a double date. They went swimming at the Willows, an artificial pool near the Oakmont Country Club, and later boated on the river. When the sisters had to go Washington, D.C., for a theater engagement, Jimmy and Benny talked a rich pal from Princeton into flying them to D.C. in his private plane. Back in New York that fall, Jimmy and Dorothy became an item.

Meanwhile, Condon and McKenzie showed up from Chicago, moving into the Whitby Apartments. Jimmy's other Windy City pal Pee Wee Russell turned them all on to a trombone player he had played with in Texas back in 1924—Jack Teagarden, who replaced Miller in the Pollack band that summer. That fall, Pollack scored a plush gig at the Florentine Grill of the Park Central Hotel at Seventh Avenue and Fifty-fifth Street. Pollack played at the Park Central nearly a year, drawing huge crowds and filling his sidemen's pockets with more cash than they had ever dreamed of. Jimmy, Benny and his brother Harry, and alto saxophonist Gil Rodin moved into the Bender Apartments on Fifty-fifth Street, and Rodin hired his own cook. In November, when the mobbed-up gambler Arnold Rothstein, reputed to be the architect behind the infamous Black Sox scandal, was shot at the entrance to the Park Central, people started calling the hotel the Shooting Gallery. It didn't seem to hurt business. The following month, the day after Christmas, Pollack's band was hired to double in the pit of a new Broadway musical, *Hello, Daddy,* written by up-and-coming songwriter Dorothy Fields as a vehicle to showcase her father, Lew Fields. It was a hit, running through midsummer. Jimmy and the boys collected two checks every week.

"It meant starting at the hotel at six thirty, doing a broadcast and playing until eight, then going to the show from eight thirty to eleven," said Jimmy. "After that, back to the hotel, where we finished around one thirty. That was our routine. . . . I was making between five and seven hundred dollars a week."

In addition to collecting checks for the Park Central and *Hello, Daddy,* in the daytime Jimmy earned money playing for short films in Astoria, Queens, and on a dizzying sequence of recording dates under Pollack's name or capricious rubrics made up on the spot, such as "Benny Goodman and His Hotsy Totsy Gang." Between late 1927 and mid-1929, the cornetist went into the studio with Pollack and/or his sidemen forty-two times and recorded nearly one hundred sides, mostly forgettable popular tunes of the day. Done off the cuff, and sometimes with severe hangovers, McPartland's recordings on these small-group sessions did not represent his best work, but they highlighted his ability as a solid section leader with a robust, singing tone and an irresistible feel for swinging a melody. There were a few jewels. On Teagarden's minor blues, "Makin' Friends," the cornetist played in a middle register sometimes lower than Teagarden's famously high trombone, creating an irresistibly slinky mood. The growling influence of Duke Ellington trumpeter Bubber Miley was obvious on "Jungle Blues," which featured Benny and Jimmy in a vigorous musical discussion. Jimmy also offered some nice muted work on "Futuristic Rhythm," a song from *Hello, Daddy,* and his softer, Bixian side showed up on "Since You Went Away," with Jimmy kissing and pushing the notes with a lilting swing. As the British jazz writer Humphrey Lyttelton noted, for all the talk of Chicago players being hard-boiled, McPartland's sound was surprisingly "soft-centered." But McPartland could also sound direct and rough, and, as Richard Sudhalter has pointed out, "more savage, more aggressive," than Beiderbecke.

While Jimmy was playing at the Park Central with Pollack, Louis Armstrong appeared in a Harlem song-and-dance revue *Hot Feet* that in

June 1929 was moved to Broadway and renamed *Hot Chocolates*. Jimmy and Louis occasionally hung out. One night after they had both finished work, they hopped into a taxi and headed up to Harlem to sit in with pianist Willie "the Lion" Smith at Pod's and Jerry's. In the cab, Louis taught Jimmy one of the tunes Fats had written for *Hot Chocolates* and they sang it together. If that cabbie was a jazz fan, he was no doubt delighted to have been one of the first to hear Waller's classic "Black and Blue."

Hello, Daddy went dark in July, and the Park Central closed down for the summer, so Jimmy took a fishing trip in the Rockies with his uncle Fred. When McPartland came back to New York, he and Pollack fell out over what he and other band members considered to be the leader's tilt toward commercialism. Things came to a head at the Fox Theatre in Brooklyn when Jimmy and Benny, after playing handball on the roof of the theater, came onstage with their shoes scuffed. Pollack gave Jimmy two weeks' notice. Goodman said if Jimmy was fired, so was he. They both left the band, which broke up shortly thereafter.

But the party of the Roaring Twenties was just about over, anyway. In October, the stock market crashed, and for the next few years, jazz languished in a sort of suspended animation. McPartland stayed alive by doing theater work, including a stint with a successful romantic comedy called *Sons O' Guns*. The show starred the five-foot-two-inch French firecracker Lili Damita, with whom Jimmy fell into a hot romance while Dorothy was out of town. (Five years later, Damita married an unknown actor named Errol Flynn.) Come February, McPartland suffered an attack of appendicitis and Dorothy rushed back to New York. As it turned out, she had medical news much more drastic than his. At his hospital bedside, she informed him she was pregnant.

McPartland was twenty-two years old. A carousing alcoholic far from ready to settle down, he nevertheless decided to marry Dorothy, who was younger than him and no more ready for family life than he was. The couple wed in New York in February 1930 and moved into the Cardinal Hotel on West End Avenue. On July 13, 1930, their daughter, Dorothy Hannah McPartland, was born. On nice afternoons, McPartland and Jimmy Dorsey pushed their babies in perambulators across Central Park, then left them in front of Plunkett's, the speakeasy on West Fifty-third Street where Jimmy had first heard Jack Teagarden, while they had a drink. Or two. Or three. Back at the hotel, during jam sessions, Jimmy and his pals tossed the baby back and forth to the rhythm of the music. Little Dorothy would spend the rest of a very rocky early childhood in bars, hotels, dressing rooms, and theaters, surrounded by self-involved, hard-drinking thespians and jazz musicians.

Sons O' Guns closed in August, and Jimmy found work that fall in the pit for *Sweet and Low,* a Billy Rose revue starring his wife, Fanny Brice, and George Jessel. Dorothy's sister, Hannah, also got into the act, popularizing Rose's song "Cheerful Little Earful." In January 1931, Hannah married millionaire bandleader Roger Wolfe Kahn, son of Otto Kahn, the financier, at his estate in Cold Spring Harbor, Long Island. They flew to Florida for their honeymoon in one of Kahn's six planes. Otto Kahn did not want his daughter-in-law working on the stage, so Dorothy replaced her in the show. *Sweet and Low* lost money, so Rose rewrote it and renamed it *Crazy Quilt,* which ran through July. The following month, Jimmy ran into Bix at Plunkett's. He was living in Queens. Alcohol had taken its toll.

"He was all run down and miserable," recalled Jimmy. "[He] had been drinking excessively and not eating much . . ." Jimmy suggested Bix drink some silver fizzes (gin and egg whites) to get something nutritious inside him. After they drank six of these, with some sugar, Jimmy discovered Bix was broke. He gave Bix some money. "I felt good to be able to repay him in some measure for his kindness to me."

A few days later, on August 6, 1931, Bix Beiderbecke was dead. He was twenty-eight years old. Not well-known to the general public during his lifetime, his original harmonic and lyrical style would eventually become legendary. Bix's death was the first of several blows that led Jimmy to a complete breakdown. In March of the following year, his old pal from Austin High, Frank Teschemacher, was killed in an automobile crash. The next year, Jimmy came home after a road trip with crooner/bandleader Russ Columbo to discover Dorothy, unhappy with their income and being a housewife, had filed for divorce so she could marry the son of a building contractor. (She said she was inspired by her sister, Hannah, who had divorced Kahn in Reno to marry the heavyweight prizefighter Jack Dempsey.) Jimmy fell apart. Bingeing, he worked briefly with bandleader Horace Heidt, then spent half of 1933 in New Orleans at the Club Forrest, playing in a band organized by Glenn Miller and fronted by ex-Pollack vocalist Smith Ballew. When he got back to New York, he tried to rekindle the flame with Dorothy but discovered she had already remarried. Jimmy cashed in an insurance policy and headed for the Caribbean.

"I had a nervous breakdown," he said. "The only time I could eat—I had a nervous stomach—was when I was really drunk."

He also lost heart for music.

"I didn't know how to cope with the situation," he said.

At some point during this dark interlude, McPartland worked on a cruise to Havana with the Clicquot Club Eskimos, led by crackerjack banjo man Harry Reser, who had been in the Pollack outfit at the Blackhawk. But mostly, Jimmy spent this "lost weekend" of several months drinking in various Caribbean ports such as Havana, Caracas, and Colón. After an early 1935 engagement on Long Island, Jimmy tried to renew his relationship with Dorothy yet again, as she had separated from her new husband. Jimmy and Dorothy spent time with Hannah and Jack Dempsey at Jack's restaurant, across the street from Madison Square Garden, where Jimmy delighted in talking to Dempsey about boxing. But when Dorothy stood Jimmy up for a Broadway high roller, he finally accepted that his life with her was over. A wire came from his brother Richard, inviting him to replace the trumpet player in his lounge quartet in Chicago. Just as he had done a decade earlier, when the Wolverines fell apart in Florida, Jimmy headed home to Chicago.

With the repeal of Prohibition and the 1934 World's Fair, work for musicians had picked up in the Windy City. Dick had put together an act called the Embassy Four at the Celtic Bar of the Sherman Hotel, doing novelty numbers, vocals, and comedy. When McPartland came into the band, it moved into the Victorian-appointed Empire Room of the Palmer Hotel. Jimmy stayed with the group fourteen months, alternating sets with "sweet" music bandleader Ted Weems, who had a new kid singer named Perry Como. The band did run-outs to Kansas City, Joliet, Illinois, Cincinnati, and even New Orleans, but Dick was a family man and didn't like to stay away long. He had seen firsthand what the jazz life could do to families. He even refused to give his four children music lessons.

Jimmy, for his part, tried to recover his equilibrium. Apart from family members, the one person who offered him moral support was a jazz-loving, piano-playing LaSalle Street attorney named Edwin M. "Squirrel" Ashcraft III, who had co-founded the Rhythm Club of Chicago in 1935. Jimmy had known Squirrel since the 1920s. Ashcraft had played accordion in an amateur group at Princeton called the Triangle Jazz Band. He lived in Evanston in a great white mansion, where he threw house parties to which he invited locals as well as visiting jazz stars to jam in the library. His Monday sessions became a regular affair and were often recorded.

F. Scott Fitzgerald famously declared there were no "second acts" in American life, but Squirrel didn't agree. He advised Jimmy that if he wanted to escape his brother's lounge band and play real jazz again, he should get together his own group, do a concert, and make a recording. Squirrel said he would stake him to the project. After hearing Benny Goodman's wildly successful new big band at the Congress Hotel that December, Jimmy recruited Benny's trombone player, Joe Harris, and his tenor saxophonist, Dick Clark. With some other Chicagoans, Jimmy presented a show with Muggsy Spanier at the Pershing Hotel. In April 1936, McPartland made his first recordings in five years.

These records didn't come out until 1939, on Ashcraft's Hot Record Society label, and were not particularly noteworthy musically. But their release coincided with an avalanche of nostalgic "hot jazz" reissues that spurred what came to be called the "Dixieland revival." In late 1939 and early 1940, the idea of Chicago jazz as a historically precious heritage—with Jimmy McPartland as one of its heroes from a bygone heroic age—was cemented in place by producer George Avakian's *The Chicago Jazz Album,* which featured two records each by three white groups—Eddie Condon and His Chicagoans, Jimmy McPartland and His Orchestra, and George Wettling's Chicago Rhythm Kings. The night before Jimmy's session, he came down with an infected wisdom tooth, to which he applied his usual remedy for everything—in this case, brandy. Despite this "medicine"—or perhaps because of it—McPartland put down the most relaxed, vigorous musical recordings of his career to date, a preview of what was to come in his mature years. On "China Boy," he was all over the horn, creating a logical, melodic solo that sang. On "Jazz Me Blues," the band conveyed a delightful sense of fun, as Jimmy blithely carried the melody like a tray of drinks through the polyphonic crowd, then wooed the listener with sudden soft, low notes on his solo, adding a bluesy smear for good measure. His lead on "Sugar," the classic from the McKenzie-Condon sessions, was tender, his solo packed with drama, and the rhythm section drove with the Chicago fire Jimmy adored. After dropping to a series of slow, pushed notes as if he were cutting the time in half, he burst back dramatically on "The World Is Waiting for the Sunrise," making the most of dynamics.

The reaction to *The Chicago Jazz Album* was immediate and intense. *Down Beat* selected "The World Is Waiting for the Sunrise" as jazz record of the year. The album set the stage for McPartland's comeback, a process already under way in Chicago clubs. In January 1939, Jimmy was back in the basement of 222 N. State Street, where he had jammed with Bix in the twenties. The room was now called the Off-Beat, a project of *Down Beat* editor Carl Cons, who had invited an unknown singer named Anita

O'Day to open the room, backed by vibes player Max Miller. When Miller left, Jimmy's band, with seventeen-year-old guitarist George Barnes, came in. Anita and Jimmy didn't get along rhythmically—she found him old-fashioned—but they agreed to disagree and drew good crowds. Upstairs at the Three Deuces, Art Tatum held forth. Later that fall at the Off-Beat, Jimmy shared the bill with Billie Holiday. She packed the place, and she and Jimmy struck up a friendly relationship. In December, McPartland went into the Panther Room of the Sherman Hotel, where he alternated sets with Fats Waller. On the gig, Fats taught Jimmy his song "I'm Gonna Sit Right Down and Write Myself a Letter," which became one of the more delightful staples of McPartland's vocal repertoire. He and Fats developed a routine in which Jimmy would bring Fats a bottle of Gordon's gin, Jimmy holding a white napkin over his forearm and carrying the bottle on a tray. The audience thought it was water, but in fact, it actually was gin. Waller was notorious for downing a bottle—or more—every night, on- or offstage.

Alcohol continued to play a big role in Jimmy's life, too. He gained weight, his face filled out, and he got paunchy around the middle. The drinking and carousing were sore spots with Dick McPartland's wife, Lenore. Their daughter, Lenore Gibbs, recalled Jimmy "crashing" at the house one night when he came in drunk. As a seven-year-old girl, she was shocked and not a little fascinated to discover this huge man flopped on a bed, snoring, his underwear not quite covering him up. Jimmy often came back to the house with glamorous showgirls. Gibbs remembered one named Angel who had a pet monkey on her shoulder.

But there were happy times, too.

"On Sunday afternoons," remembered Jimmy's niece Diane Lanigan, "they'd invite musician friends and we'd bring a covered dish. Ethel would make a roast. They'd play in the kitchen because there wasn't room in the living room [where the piano was]. Everybody'd bring their kids. They'd play until about five thirty or six, then Mom would serve the food. They always played 'Blue Bells of Scotland.'"

In the fall of 1940, Eddie Condon invited Jimmy, whom Condon nicknamed "Scotchie" for his poison of choice—to join him at Nick's in New York's Greenwich Village, as cornetist Bobby Hackett was leaving the band to join Glenn Miller. Squirrel Ashcraft encouraged Jimmy to go, counseling him that it would be a good opportunity to visit his daughter, whom he had not seen since she was four years old. Condon and other Chicagoans had been playing at Nick's since 1938 and had been instrumental in establishing the traditional jazz revival. The club was patronized by artists and writers, many of whom, such as John Steinbeck, John O'Hara, and Stuart Davis, publicly celebrated the emotional directness and honesty of the music. Condon, a savvy publicist, had even engineered the publication of a lavish, eleven-page story in *Life* magazine on August 8, 1938, which gave the revivalists a huge boost, featuring photos of Armstrong, Condon, Beiderbecke, Pee Wee Russell, and Bud Freeman. That same year, Dorothy Baker's wildly romanticized (and very popular) fictionalized biography of Bix, *Young Man with a Horn,* added an extra glow to Jimmy, whom *Down Beat* had begun to refer to as a "Bix disciple" as early as November 1937.

While in New York, Jimmy took Squirrel's advice and visited his daughter. According to an unpublished biography of McPartland by Chicago newspaperman Bentley Stegner, to prepare for the reunion, Dorothy's mother described Jimmy as the trim and sturdy athlete she remembered. When Jimmy arrived, Little Dorothy turned to her mother and whispered, "Mama, who's that fatty?" Little Dorothy had had very little contact with her father. Her mother had occasionally written Jimmy, but a January 28, 1937, letter she sent to New Orleans, while Jimmy was playing there with the Embassy Four, suggested he had rarely reciprocated. Its tone also implied that Big Dorothy—as the family now called her—was still ambivalent about their breakup:

"Jimmie Darling," she wrote.

I wrote you from the train but as usual didn't receive an answer.

Please angel write to me as I am so anxious to hear from you. We are with Hannah and Jack in Miami—it is so lonely here and I do wish you were with us. Write me in care of Dempsey's Vanderbilt Hotel Miami Beach, Florida. Little Dorothy is fine.

My love to you, angel,

Dorothy

That summer, Jimmy sent a gift to Little Dorothy for her seventh birthday, and Big Dorothy wrote a fulsome thank-you, enclosing a society page article from Scranton that covered the birthday party as well as the news that Hannah was getting back into show business. Three years later, in a letter dated July 18, 1940, Dorothy reminded Jimmy to send a birthday present to his daughter. She came across as less needy this time but implied she had moved in with her sister and had no return address of her own. In fact, Dorothy Williams's life was falling apart. Depressed and lonely, she was a promiscuous alcoholic whose show business career was over. Little Dorothy would later tell her own daughter, Donna, that she often came home to discover her mother drunk on the sofa, the light bill unpaid. Jimmy's grandson, Doug, said his mother told him she spent her childhood in hotel rooms with her mother and that they would go to the movies all day long.

Diane Lanigan, Jim Lanigan's daughter, put it more bluntly.

"Dorothy had a mother who was cuckoo. . . . She was sleeping with men. Little Dorothy could hardly wait to get out of there and get to Aunt Ethel's because Ethel had a family."

In fact, going to Aunt Ethel's was exactly what Jimmy had in mind for his daughter. When Condon got the band booked in Chicago at the Brass Rail in July 1941, Jimmy and Pee Wee Russell hopped into Jimmy's 1936 Plymouth sedan and put Dorothy in the backseat, sandwiched between the luggage, a cornet, and clarinet. They drove at night and slept during the day, stopping along the way at movie theaters and saloons. The trip took four days. When they got to Chicago, Dorothy moved in with Jim and Ethel in Lombard, west of Chicago, and that fall enrolled in school with the Lanigan kids.

"It was the only family Dorothy ever had," said Gibbs.

Dorothy stayed with the Lanigans through Christmas, then returned to New York. Sometime around the end of the war, she came back and stayed with the Lanigans until she got married.

Meanwhile, *Time* magazine took notice of the gig at the Brass Rail, where trombonist George Brunies occasionally dared customers to stand on his belly while he played "Tiger Rag" lying on the floor.

"The Chicago jazz style, rough nervous, backed by a driving pulse, got its start when the Austin High Boys played in their gym on Friday afternoons in 1923 and 1924," the article began. "The Brass Rail boys have always played hot, intricate, free-ranging music, without ever making much money for it. Benny Goodman dressed Chicago jazz up, quieted it down and turned it to profit."

And thus were the terms of the Dixieland revival laid out: Early jazz was an earnest, authentic, and communal music played for the fun of it; swing was a commercial, overorganized dilution of the real thing, done for profit. Jimmy McPartland rode the wave of the revival for the rest of his life.

It's fair to ask why McPartland chose the revivalist route, particularly when some of his contemporaries—Bud Freeman, Jess Stacy, Gene Krupa, and Dave Tough—changed with the times, playing in the new, looserlimbed big band style of the thirties popularized by Goodman. Why didn't McPartland get a piece of the new action? Dick Wang, a scholar of Chicago jazz and a longtime friend of both Jimmy and Marian, speculated McPartland's sight-reading skills may have been too limited for the big bands. But McPartland's long stint with Pollack and deep résumé of recording sessions suggest he could read down an arrangement as well as anybody. More convincingly, Wang argued that "Benny was a perfectionist. . . . Jimmy's freewheeling spirit would not have fit in. He enjoyed the free spirit of the Chicago style. That was his home base, rather than being glued to the charts." Perhaps more important, McPartland was not an ambitious man. He did what came most easily, and that was playing the music he knew. And he enjoyed being a leader, not a sideman. Whatever his motivations, Jimmy—and Eddie Condon—spent the rest of their careers idealizing (and mythologizing) the past or, as Sudhalter put it kindly, "looking over their shoulders."

After the engagement at the Brass Rail, Jimmy worked with Jack Teagarden, his old pal from the Pollack days, who took the band to Los Angeles. Back home on a break in June 1942, Jimmy and his brother Dick and Jim Lanigan played for the Austin High School prom at the Stevens Hotel in a band they called the Austin High Gang Summa Cum Laude. After the dance, the three alums were awarded the Austin "A," the equivalent of an honorary degree. Ironically, not one of the Austin High Gang musicians had ever graduated, and according to a *Chicago Tribune* article, some had been expelled several times!

By this time, America was deep into World War II. Jazz musicians were madly auditioning for armed forces bands so they could avoid combat while also making a contribution. But McPartland, a street fighter by nature, seemed to take the attack on Pearl Harbor personally. When Squirrel put out the alert that the draft board was looking for him, Jimmy enlisted as a regular combat GI. McPartland often told interviewers—perhaps to cover for what he later concluded was a foolish decision—that he had been a "drunken patriot." In fact, he had made his decision quite soberly.

"How are you going to win the war if nobody joins the army?" he asked when *Melody Maker* brought up his military service. Everybody else, he said contemptuously, "was trying to duck the services."

At Camp Hahn, near Death Valley in California, an incident between McPartland and new recruit Dave Brubeck—who would later become one of the most famous jazz musicians in history—made Jimmy's motivation crystal clear.

"Man, you're one of the greatest trumpet players I've ever heard," Brubeck told Jimmy after he sat in with his group. "Wouldn't you want to stay in our band?"

"I'll never forget what he said," Brubeck recalled. "And I don't think I'll say it now. But he said, 'I'm here to go out and kill . . .' And I'll leave it blank."

McPartland was inducted in Chicago on October 27, 1942. He went out in style: One of Ashcraft's friends chauffeured Jimmy to the draft board in a Rolls-Royce. In California, Jimmy trained to fire a machine gun with the 462nd Antiaircraft Artillery. In February 1943, he trained with the U.S. Army Rangers at Camp Gordon Johnston in Carrabelle, Florida, crawling under machine-gun fire three feet over his head, doing high dives with a full pack into burning water, and practicing amphibious landings. Perennially late and insubordinate, McPartland was demoted on what seemed like a regular basis for such indiscretions as playing "Reveille" in swing time and coming back late from a weekend in Los Angeles to see Goodman, Krupa, and Crosby.

On the condition that he bring back a signed photo of Jack Dempsey, his captain on the East Coast gave him a three-day pass to see his ex-wife and daughter in New York. During this visit, according to Marian, Jimmy told Dorothy that if he survived the war, he wanted to get back together with her. In November, McPartland shipped out of Boston for Europe. On the way, the ship's chaplain asked Jimmy to organize a show. After he played, the third mate said, "Say, soldier, you sound just like Jimmy McPartland." "That's funny," Jimmy replied. "I am." The third mate had a healthy supply of booze, and Jimmy got permission to move in with him. When the ship pulled into Greenock Harbor, Scotland, Jimmy was three sheets to the wind. Thinking to honor his mother's homeland, he went on deck and serenaded the Scotsmen lined up on the dock with "Blue Bells of Scotland."

"It was so quiet in this bay that, man, as soon as I blew this 'Blue Bells of Scotland,' well, all the bagpipes started going on shore," he said. "And the people all started hollering. You could hear them all that distance."

After they pulled into port, Jimmy's colonel approached him. Jimmy thought he was in dutch again. But the colonel said, "Great stuff, McPartland. You know, cementing relations with our allies."

Jimmy was a sergeant again.

After more exercises in Pembroke, Wales, Jimmy's unit waited in Southampton for the call. On D-Day plus four, they hit Normandy beach. McPartland said soldiers around him were "picked off like pesky insects."

Jimmy's unit pushed south to the town of Saint-Lô under the leadership of Lieutenant General Omar Bradley. Firing a .50-caliber machine gun mounted above the covered cab of a "half-track" armored personnel carrier—half-jeep, half-tank—McPartland shot his way through the *bocage,* the same territory Marian would traverse several weeks later. German machine gunners and antitank units had set up hidden nests in the hedgerows. Ferreting them out was one of the great challenges of that long and bloody battle. "We'd go into a hedgerow and just fire," Jimmy remembered. "I never got hit. A lot of guys got it."

In fifteen days of fighting, Bradley's Thirtieth Division sustained nearly four thousand casualties. After Saint-Lô was won, the 462nd remained to fight in the decisive battle of the Falaise Gap, during which Canadian, American, and British forces encircled the German divisions and cleared the way for the liberation of Paris. At Falaise, the tables were turned, and it was the Germans, Jimmy said, whom he and his buddies "killed like flies." Jimmy's unit was sent to Paris, then to Charleroi, Belgium, where he watched with horror the execution of two girls who had collaborated with the Germans.

Through all this, McPartland survived without a wound. But the impulsive patriotism that had led him to enlist for combat duty did not. He had had enough. Jimmy decided that henceforth, if he possibly could, he would carry on the fight against fascism with his horn. Fate was on his side. That's when he had run into Willie Shore, who had set the stage for his first encounter with Marian in Belgium. It felt like half a lifetime since their jam session at St. Vith, but it had really been only eighteen months. From the Battle of the Bulge to the atomic bomb and the Nuremberg trials, the world had changed drastically and rapidly. And so had Jimmy's and Marian's lives. No longer a couple in a wartime romance, they were married now—she for the first time, he for the second—and they were embarking on a new life together in America. Though they were headed for Chicago, they decided to spend a couple of weeks in New York first, then visit Washington, D.C., where Squirrel was now working for the Central Intelligence Agency. In Manhattan, they checked into the Victoria Hotel on Seventh Avenue and Fifty-first Street. After a quick Chinese dinner, they headed down to Greenwich Village, where Condon now ran his own nightclub. Marian's left wrist was still in a cast from the jeep accident, but she was determined to sit in, to hold her own with "the boys."

"My fingers were sticking out of the end of this thing," she said. "It didn't matter so much, because being my left hand, I could sort of take care of the bass and play enough things in my right hand."

Apparently she did all right.

Clarinetist Tony Parenti, on the bandstand that night, recalled:

I'll never forget the first time I heard Marian Page. It was a couple of nights after Easter in 1946 . . . Jimmy McPartland and Marian were just back from the war. They walked in wearing officers' uniforms with USO patches on their sleeves. None of us even knew they were married. Eddie Condon called them to the stand. Then they sat in with us, and we were amazed. Marian picked the numbers, "Muskrat Ramble" and a whole set of Dixieland. Her chords were big and fat and honest. She played like a man. We had begun by thinking we'd do Marian and Jimmy a favor, but they wound up by doing the favor for us. They tore the house down.

At a club called the Aquarium, they ran into Louis Armstrong, who hailed Jimmy with a hearty "Mac-*Part*-land!" in his trademark Satchmo voice. Marian shook her head in disbelief. Jimmy hadn't been making it up.

"I was thrilled beyond belief meeting these people I'd dreamed about or read about or heard on records," she said. "They were so friendly with Jimmy, and he knew everybody. God, I remember being in a place where Jimmy was playing, and meeting Fletcher Henderson. I was like a kid in a candy store. I couldn't believe all this was happening to me."

During most of their visit to New York, the McPartlands stayed with Gene Krupa and his wife, Ethel, in Yonkers. Jimmy took Marian to see Gene's band at the 400 Restaurant, and Goodman vocalist Peggy Lee and trumpeter Charlie Spivak came along. Gene threw a party for Marian and Jimmy and invited pioneering bop vocalist Buddy Stewart.

Their life during those first weeks in America was a party every night— a hangover every morning. At Condon's, Marian saw firsthand that far from being a wartime aberration, heavy drinking was as much a part of Jimmy's scene as the music. Between tunes, the waiters brought great trays full of drinks to the band. As the night wore on, everyone sank—or rose, depending on their chemistry—into a haze. Marian, anxious to work, to learn, to meet everyone, found Jimmy just wanted to party every night. One evening while they were at the Victoria, Jimmy disappeared. When he came back, he was loaded. He told her he had gone to see Dorothy and his daughter, now fifteen. Marian was shocked, first that he would visit Dorothy at all, but second that he would come back and drunkenly justify it. Apparently he wanted to tell Dorothy he was married and that any prior talk of a reunion was off, and, understandably, he felt awkward doing so with Marian around. But had it not occurred to him that Marian desperately wanted to meet his daughter?

"He wasn't very bright in some ways," said Marian. "He probably didn't think about how I would feel."

Marian was angry, hurt, and disappointed. The man she had married clearly carried a lot of baggage.

Before Jimmy and Marian left New York, Condon offered Jimmy a regular spot at his club. He turned it down. He wanted to go back to Chicago.

"I just got out of the army," he said. "I want to see my family. I want to relax. I don't want to work."

When the couple got to Chicago, Marian discovered Jimmy wasn't kidding. She spent the next four months trying to get him back onstage so they could begin the musical life she had been planning so excitedly in Europe. Their marriage very nearly ended before it got started.

5.

Windy City Apprentice
(1946~1950)

MARIAN AND JIMMY LIVED IN CHICAGO more than four years. It was a critical growth period—a musical apprenticeship for Marian and an emotional one for her and Jimmy as a couple. Through wit, keen observation, and sheer force of will, Marian emerged from Chicago a modern jazz player. She also began to get a glimmer of recognition beyond the shadow of her famous husband. Her marriage, already fragile because of Jimmy's alcoholism, survived its roughest period, including one dismal juncture when she gave up on it altogether. Years later, she would complain that she and Jimmy should have stayed in New York in 1946 when Condon had offered Jimmy a job there, but in many ways, Chicago had been a better choice. The Chicago scene flowered in the late 1940s, giving her an opportunity to grow at her own pace—in the limelight, but not directly under the glare of the Big Apple's unforgiving spotlight. Chicago was good for Jimmy, too. It was home, for starters, and showing off his new bride to family and friends was just the right medicine after the war.

Before the couple left Europe, Jimmy had netted a sizable homecoming stake selling money orders to soldiers at a 300 percent profit. He got the idea from a young lieutenant who tried the scam on him.

"It was not a nice thing to do," he confessed. "But this officer burned me up."

With this substantial cushion, Marian and Jimmy did not need to work right away. They didn't have to pay rent, either, as they moved in with his sister Ethel and her husband, Jim Lanigan, in Lombard. Lanigan had gone legit and was now playing bass with the Chicago Symphony. Jimmy settled in for what he envisioned as a long and well-deserved vacation, hanging out at the house, jamming on weekends, seeing old friends, and drinking beer. The McPartland clan welcomed Marian with enthusiasm and curiosity. The kids were especially fascinated by her accent, which, according to Jimmy's niece Lenore, was "so thick nobody in the family could understand her."

"She was very excited and interested and outgoing," recalled Jim Lanigan's son, John. "We had a grand piano and we would make her play, over and over, *Rhapsody in Blue*. We were such Anglophiles. She'd never heard of an English muffin. We couldn't get over that. And she had never heard of a teabag! We'd always like it when she would fix something for dinner—haddock, broiled with Cheddar cheese and dill."

"The family talked for years about how she could eat chicken with a knife and fork, like she was operating," recalled Jimmy's granddaughter, Donna. "That's one of the reasons my grandfather was so proud of her. That she had lots of talent, but she was so elegant. Had so much class. My grandfather, coming from where he came from, I think, really wanted to be upper-class or something. He would always say to me, 'Look at her, she's such a great dame.' And he meant 'dame' in French—a great lady."

In June 1946, Marian made what was probably her Chicago debut on a concert billed as "Swing vs. Jazz," sponsored by the newly formed Hot Club of Chicago. Staged at the Moose Lodge on North State Street, the show pitted a trad band featuring members of the Austin High Gang—Jimmy, Richard, and Lanigan—against the renowned swing band of Charlie Barnet, who had had the 1939 hit "Cherokee." People packed the place and welcomed Jimmy home from the war.

Marian, who had grown up with such a compulsive work ethic—"Fill the unforgiving minute!" she heard her father's voice in her head—was finding her enforced "vacation" extremely trying. Years later, she said with undisguised contempt, "Jimmy always talked about 'relaxing.' I suddenly sort of woke up and said, 'My God, when are we going to start working and stop all this carrying on?' The money just evaporated. Jimmy kept handing it out. Gave money to his brother. We would sit in the backyard and drink till the beer ran out, then someone would go for more."

As it happened, Jimmy's brother Richard was now running a small booking agency. Itching to work, Marian talked Richard into finding her a solo gig that summer at the St. Charles Hotel in a pretty suburb along the Fox River, about fifteen miles west of Lombard. She also managed to drag Jimmy out to the Glenbard Firehouse in Lombard for a jam session organized by Jim and Ethel that featured none other than Warren "Baby" Dodds, the drummer who had turned the jazz world upside down with Joe "King" Oliver back in the 1920s. Dodds, always a great showman, was having a heyday with the Dixieland revival.

"I was thrilled," Marian said. "It was just a small affair. But my God, Baby Dodds. He sounded pretty good."

After four months lying idle, that fall Marian finally talked Jimmy into going back to work. The couple moved to the Croydon Hotel, favored by musicians, then to their own apartment on Dearborn Street. Their first regular gig was decidedly low profile—in a South Side bar attached to a bowling alley called the Rose Bowl, down near 119th Street on Michigan Avenue.

"Jimmy would very proudly introduce me for my number, which might be 'Claire de Lune,'" said Marian. "There weren't that many people in the bar, but I would be playing, and somebody in the bowling alley would get a strike, and everybody would *roarrrr*."

Dick Wang, a high school trumpet player at the time (and later a distinguished jazz professor), recalled seeing Marian and Jimmy there while Wang was playing a gig nearby with pianist Audrey Morris.

"I was just knocked out," said Wang. "First of all, Marian had really good piano chops. . . . She played the stride style left hand. . . . She had listened to Jess Stacy and to Teddy Wilson. She was throwing in these harmonies, and this was what fascinated Audrey. It was always explorative, the chord voicings especially."

Jimmy's bass player at the Rose Bowl was Ben Carlton, who became a lifelong family friend of the McPartlands. In January 1947, when Ben's second child was born, he and his wife, Eileen, bought a house, and to pool expenses, Jimmy and Marian lived with them.

On November 10, 1946, Duke Ellington came through town showcasing the Belgian Gypsy jazz guitarist Django Reinhardt, on his first and only tour of the United States. Marian and Jimmy, who had met Django in Paris the year before, paid their respects backstage at the Civic Opera House and *Down Beat* snapped a photo. Reinhardt was notoriously absent without leave on this tour, and Chicago was no exception. He came on late and played only four tunes, but the crowd nevertheless awarded him a thunderstorm of applause before he slipped out with Ben Carlton to hear Chicago saxophonist Eddie Wiggins. Later that evening, Django dropped by the Capitol Lounge to see Jimmy and Marian.

Toward the close of 1946, the McPartlands moved to the Taboo on the North Side, then in February 1947 back to the Capitol Lounge, across the alley from the Chicago Theater, on the Loop. The Capitol Lounge had a white picket fence and, like many Chicago clubs, a raised stage behind the bar. Dizzy Gillespie and other jazz stars had played there; the audience came to listen as well as to drink. There were no bowling balls. *Down Beat* editor Eddie Ronan dropped by and opined in print that Jimmy was fronting a great band and "playing the greatest trumpet he has in the last ten years" and that Marian played with imaginative harmonic colors.

Ronan also noted that Jimmy was no longer playing "Dixieland" exclusively, but had begun to include music geared to a general audience, such as vocals, popular songs, and even some solo classical features by Marian, such as excerpts from *Rhapsody in Blue* or Ted Mossman's "adaptation" (that is, theft) of Rachmaninoff's Second Piano Concerto, "Full Moon and Empty Arms." Jimmy presented Marian with a grand flourish in a faux British accent as a sort of show business novelty act along the lines of Hazel Scott, a virtuoso "piano professor(ess)" who could play everything from Beethoven to boogie-woogie. With her music hall background (and real accent), this was an easy role for her to adopt. The band's other repertoire included a hip, modern arrangement Marian made on "How High the Moon," interpolating Dizzy Gillespie's bebop line "Ornithology."

"People started to notice me because I was with Jimmy," Marian said modestly. "He was very proud of me—he did show me off . . . and in his better moments introduce me in such a way as to make me sound like the greatest thing since the wheel."

In his *Down Beat* review, Ronan compared Marian to Mary Lou Williams, rare praise. Women instrumentalists were largely dismissed by critics in that era. ("If you had a dress on, it meant you couldn't play," observed Audrey Morris.) But Williams, who had written, arranged, and played for Andy Kirk's Clouds of Joy, the great black swing band from Kansas City, commanded great respect. When Jimmy's band moved to the Brass Rail, also on the Loop, writers continued to notice Marian. In May, *Down Beat* ran a feature noting that she "displayed unusual versatility" and published a sample of her chord voicings. In her comments for the *Down Beat* piece, Marian made it clear she now preferred modern sounds to traditional jazz. Her playing was undoubtedly a work in progress, as she leapfrogged from Jimmy's four-on-the-floor trad to the more abstract and complex style of bop, effectively skipping the swing era altogether. The result in the long run would be an eclectic, personal style described perceptively by one musician who hung around the Brass Rail in those days, accordion player Charlie Rex, as "homemade."

Though Marian was rolling along musically, life on the home front was rocky. Having learned of the seedy life Jimmy's daughter was living with her mother in New York, Marian had suggested the previous summer they send Dorothy to a Virginia boarding school, St. Agnes, for the 1946–1947 school year. Little Dorothy was now writing home repeatedly to say she was lonely and unhappy. Marian, apparently having forgotten that boarding school had given *her* migraine headaches, urged Dorothy to "buck up," among other platitudes that had little resonance for a seventeen-year-old girl. By the end of the term, it was decided Dorothy should come back to Chicago to live with Aunt Ethel and Uncle Jim again. Jimmy and Marian, scuffling from gig to gig and apartment to apartment, were in no position to provide a home for her.

Marian would later regret the boarding school episode.

By this time, Dorothy—or "Dot," as she called herself—had blossomed into a stunning beauty, with the high cheekbones, facial structure, and glowing complexion of a young Ingrid Bergman, with jet black eyes and a slightly dark complexion that made her even more alluring.

"Both men and women loved to be around her," recalled Richard Lanigan, who along with his two brothers became very close to their cousin. "She was like a sister."

According to John Lanigan, their other brother, Jim, fell tragically in love with his first cousin, putting up pictures of Dorothy on his bedroom wall and refusing to go out with other girls.

"They had a Romeo and Juliet love affair," said John. "He was a kind of mentor to her. He exposed her to a lot of cultural things. They were madly in love. He had a sample of her perfume in a cotton ball."

Marian was aware of the relationship, but it's not clear how seriously she and Jimmy took it. In any event, something happened in the interim that made it all moot. Back when the band had been at the Rose Bowl, a young student named Don Kassel, who was going to Chicago's Ray Art School on the GI Bill, had pleasantly surprised Jimmy by requesting the classic from the McKenzie-Condon sessions, "China Boy." Kassel had grown up in Moline, Illinois (across the river from Bix's hometown of Davenport, Iowa), where he had started a "hot club," and he was now active in the Hot Club of Chicago. When Dorothy tagged along to clubs to hear the band, Jimmy designated Don as a sort of chaperon. One thing led to another—including secret "make-out" sessions at Jimmy and Marian's apartment—and Dorothy and Don became an item. According to John Lanigan, his brother Jim was crushed.

"He never got over it till the day he died," said John. "He never dated or married."

In the meantime, Jimmy's drinking was becoming more and more of a problem, despite Marian's continual protests and his empty promises to quit. It finally got to be a sort of sick game of cat and mouse, with Jimmy sneaking booze any way he could. Frank O'Connell, a labor relations lawyer who befriended the McPartlands in Chicago, recalled asking Jimmy if he could buy him a drink one night. Jimmy told O'Connell to tell the bartender, who in turn deposited a huge glass of gin in the men's room, where Jimmy could retrieve it in secret during a break. At the Lanigans', Jimmy hid bottles in the backyard and in the toilet tank. During a family jam session, Marian became so frustrated she decided—as she had in France one night—to "protest" by getting roaring drunk herself.

"I drank down a pint of white rum," she recalled. "Then I lay down on the davenport. I woke up in bed, vomiting, about ten hours later. Dorothy was holding my head. She was like a little mother to me.

"'Marian, are you all right?' she asked. I'm puking into a basin. I said, 'Where's your dad?' 'Oh, he went to play a gig. He and Richard just went out.'

"We were supposed to play somewhere that night and they just got another piano player and went off. It didn't make any difference to him."

On another boozy night at the Lanigans', Marian ran stark naked out of the bedroom into the backyard.

"It was five A.M. and I remember in the midst of my misery and anger what a beautiful morning it was—still and barely light yet. A bird chirruped. One part of my brain took in the beauty, the rest of it was bent on getting Jimmy to follow me."

Looking at a home movie of the couple shot in the deep winter of January 1947, one would never guess anything was amiss. Posing and mugging for the camera, Jimmy, in fedora and overcoat, affectionately places earmuffs on Marian, looking radiant in a fox fur jacket. She receives a buss from Jimmy as they ride in a car toward Salem, Illinois, to visit Abraham Lincoln's hand-hewn log homestead. (Ever the patriot, Jimmy no doubt wanted to show Marian this political landmark.) Marian was inspired to write her first love song, "He's the One," with the opening lyric "I never dreamed that someday I'd meet somebody so completely right for me."

But the images and romantic hyperbole belied the truth. Things came to a head in the spring of 1947 when the couple was invited to play an afternoon concert with the recently rediscovered New Orleans trumpet player Bunk Johnson. After the show, Bunk and Jimmy disappeared. Several hours later, Jimmy showed up quite drunk at the Brass Rail, late for the gig. Marian was furious. She and the band (and Don Kassel) were waiting on the corner of Dearborn. Marian and Jimmy got into a "knockdown, drag-out" fight on the sidewalk, said Kassel. She wound up socking him in the nose and going back into the club to play without him. For a few days, the band carried on, but without Jimmy the group had little marquee value and the band was fired.

Marian decided she had had enough.

"I wanted to keep the marriage together, but at the same time I kept making these devious, small attempts to show Jimmy I wasn't going to stand for it. But I was very weak about it. I finally said, 'If you don't quit, I'm going to leave.'"

She took a room at the Sherman Hotel. Jimmy's response was to go to a ball game with his brother, get loaded, then burst into the room, accusing her of seeing someone else. He gave her a black eye and left. They later made up on the phone and he came back to the hotel, but the house detective threw him out. After much protest from Marian, Jimmy was allowed to register at the hotel and they were together again.

But not for long.

In August, Marian's sister, Joyce, concerned about the letters she had been receiving from Marian, came to Chicago to offer moral support. Or so Marian thought, until she saw Joyce at the station. Joyce was five months pregnant. Two weeks before she arrived, she had married her boyfriend, Tony Armitage, the father of her child-to-be, with whom she had been living at the house in Eastbourne. To conceal her advanced pregnancy from her father (she suspected her mother already knew), Joyce had decided to visit Marian in America. So there they were, two proper, upper-middle-class girls from Bromley, Kent, descendants of Dyson choirboys, whose parents had sent them off to the Stratford House School for Girls to be groomed for nice husbands. One was pregnant out of wedlock; the other was nearly penniless, married to an alcoholic jazz musician.

"My mother's dire prediction," wrote Marian in an autobiographical essay, "that I would marry a musician and live in an attic [well, not quite an attic, but the Dearborn St. apartment was close], had come true."

Commiserating with her sister, Marian determined that the situation with Jimmy was unsalvageable. She decided to go home with Joyce and booked passage on the *Queen Elizabeth*. As things turned out, however, Joyce helped Marian find her backbone instead. One night when the three of them went out with a gang of musicians to the Rag Doll to hear Jack Teagarden and Louis Armstrong, Jimmy did his disappearing act again. This time, when he came home, at Joyce's insistence, Marian refused to let him in the house.

"He was beating on the door," she recalled. "We called the police and had him arrested. I said, 'Let his sister come to the jail and get him out.'"

When Jimmy got out of jail, he phoned Squirrel Ashcraft, who called a meeting at his office with Jimmy and Marian. Squirrel suggested Jimmy join Alcoholics Anonymous. Jimmy contritely agreed, vowing to get sober, even though "it was obvious," Marian recalled with disappointment, "he had had a drink, even then."

Drunk, Jimmy could be belligerent, crude, loud, sloppy, and sometimes violent. He didn't seem to care about anything but carrying on with his men friends, drinking himself into a stupor. Sometimes he had even passed out on the street. Sober, he was like a different person. "He was just really loving," Marian recalled at eighty-nine, in a tone that sounded as vulnerable and sweet as a little girl's.

Both Jimmy and Marian began to attend AA meetings in 1947. Marian liked the philosophy of the organization, with its emphasis on humility and self-reliance and its relentless insistence on facing the truth about oneself. For a while, the couple enjoyed happier days. They even found time to go fishing up in Wisconsin and "sit there by some lake and cook fish and eat them and watch the sun rise."

Marian canceled her ticket to England and Joyce sailed home alone. Jimmy's sobriety didn't last long. Though the band was hired back at the Brass Rail, a few months later Jimmy "went off on one of his great toots," Marian said. "He went to Wisconsin this time. Squirrel had a place up at Pike Lake. I have never forgiven Squirrel for this, because I tried to get them on the phone and I couldn't. I sent a wire to Squirrel asking him to please just let me know that Jimmy was up there. And he never answered. There was just a bunch of hard-drinking guys up there, having a ball and going fishing. Eventually he came back. And then he would have these terrible hangovers where he'd be in bed. It would be like an illness. It would take him days to taper off. He would have to be drinking the first day, and the second day a little less. Then I remember a guy named Tom Culhane from AA coming over and sitting with him and saying, 'Serves you right, you SOB.'"

Over the course of their marriage, Jimmy McPartland never did beat his alcoholism, though he often stayed on the wagon for three months at a time and went to AA meetings religiously. Why Marian stayed with him is a subject that obsessed her for years. In a series of remarkably self-perceptive interviews she did for an unpublished autobiography, she reflected that the qualities that attracted her to Jimmy—his childlike good nature, his sunny view of the world, his sense of adventure—also appealed to her need to protect, nurture, and mother him. Putting Jimmy's needs above her own played into her desire to please others, instilled in her since childhood. But in direct conflict with that need was Marian the performer, the pianist who wanted to be honored for her own talents, praised, and even adored, the Marian who had asserted herself so boldly when her accompanist had failed her in Bromley.

"I've always been what some people would call just plain bossy," she confessed. "Being with somebody you think you can have control over—in Jimmy's case, he always seemed to be messing up a good thing by getting drunk—so I saw how I could be 'superior' to him, since I wasn't messing up the job. I remember saying to him—'Gee, what a shame, you've got the whole thing—you're out of combat, which you wanted to be, and you've got a real good thing now. It seems such a shame to spoil the whole thing by drinking so much. It's really a drag.' But I guess I was taking on the 'mother' role."

Marian's urge to nurture others would play out in her relationship with Jimmy—and with others—for the rest of her life. So would the conflict between her desire for notoriety and Jimmy's perpetual need to be bailed out.

Jimmy and Marian worked at the Brass Rail till the end of 1947. By this time, the Chicago jazz scene had exploded. Clubs sprouted up everywhere, in the Loop and on the North and South Sides. Every brand of jazz was played: Dixieland, big band, swing, piano trios, and—of particular interest to Marian—the new bebop she had first heard in Paris.

"Randolph Street was just like Fifty-second Street in New York," remembered Joe Segal, longtime owner of Chicago's venerable club the Jazz Showcase. "The first time I came here, I was stationed in the army down in Champaign. I'd get the weekend off and grab the IC [Illinois Central] right up to Randolph Street. Joe Sherman's Down Beat Room, which was in the Oriental Theatre, had Henry 'Red' Allen and J. C. Higginbotham. I was in hog heaven. And then Red Saunders was there, who was at the Club DeLisa a long time. Then across the street was the Brass Rail. And the Band Box, that was the one that was underneath."

Musicians flocked to the city because of all the work, not just jazz but advertising jingles and radio and TV jobs as well. Jazz at the Philharmonic came through with Roy Eldridge and Ella Fitzgerald. Jazz Ltd. featured Dixie revivalists, and the Blue Note had the modern cats. Eddie Heywood ("Canadian Sunset") played at the Detour, and bassist John Kirby, pioneer of the "little big band" sound, played the College Inn at the Sherman Hotel, following boogie-woogie piano man Freddie Slack. Los Angeles bebop trumpeter Howard McGhee tore up the Argyle, and Sarah Vaughan hit the Pershing Ballroom.

For Marian, Chicago was like an open university. She went out to hear everyone, setting her sights on learning how to play modern. And Chicago was going modern fast, the seeds having been sown by local boys such as pianist Lennie Tristano and bandleaders Bill Russo and Jay Burkhardt. The singer in Burkhardt's band was a straw-voiced lass from Milwaukee named Jackie Cain, who, after she hooked up with vocalist/pianist Roy Kral, went to work with the Charlie Ventura Octet. Jackie and Roy forged a personal style of bop singing that incorporated scat, witty lyrics, agile melodies, and a light, airy sound. Their slinky, exotic "East of Suez" with Ventura knocked everybody out. Jimmy's bass player, Ben Carlton, hipped the McPartlands to Jackie and Roy. They all jumped into Chick Evans's car and raced down to the Bee Hive on the South Side to hear the new duo. Jackie and Roy returned the favor, dropping in on Marian and Jimmy at the Brass Rail. They all became fast friends. Kral's advanced but accessible approach to bop, which honored the song while venturing into new harmonic territory, was right up Marian's alley. She literally hovered over his shoulder, studying the way he comped, learning to add ninths and altered intervals to her chords. As Marian pointed out later, this was the way jazz was "taught" in those days.

"Jazz education," she said, "consisted of someone saying, 'That's not the right chord.' 'Play more like Count Basie because you're getting in my way.' 'Don't play down in there where the bass player is playing because you're covering up his notes.' Listen, learn, and adapt."

Around this time (early 1948), Jimmy signed with the notoriously Mob-connected booking agent Joe Glaser, who handled Louis Armstrong. One of Glaser's Associated Booking agents, Freddie Williamson, sent Jimmy's quartet off to the hinterlands to play in cocktail lounges with names like the Flame, the Club Flamingo, and the Zebra Lounge, occasionally with a girl singer named Adrienne, and also got them high-profile gigs in Chicago working opposite singers Billie Holiday, Sarah Vaughan, and Anita O'Day. Marty Dennenberg, who owned a new club on North Clark Street called the Hi-Note, thought it would be a good idea to reunite Jimmy with O'Day and vibist Max Miller, to commemorate O'Day's debut back in 1939. Jimmy and Marian opened for a week at the Hi-Note with O'Day on March 4, 1948. It was a nice idea, but everyone seemed to have forgotten that the temperamental O'Day hadn't really been happy with Jimmy's "old-fashioned style." Now she that was a stone bopper, O'Day was even more difficult to deal with.

"She would start a tune, and then she would stop and look around at us, like 'What the hell are you doing?'" said Marian. "We weren't doing *any-thing*. Then we would start all over again. She always managed to do something outrageous to make us look bad."

The intermission entertainer on the O'Day gig was singer/pianist Jeri Southern, who also caught Marian's ear. Like Kral, Southern incorporated the new, modern language of bop with a softly contoured edge and an ear to the melody. She later had success in the 1950s with her sultry, whispered version of "You Better Go Now."

Marian continued to pick up tricks of the trade from Jimmy, too, especially how to "flirt" with the crowd and, most important of all, to "be yourself."

"His main thing was to be individual, not to copy anyone, sound like yourself," said trumpeter Scott Black, one of Jimmy's protégés.

Hearing and playing music live was the best way to learn, but radio played a big role in Marian's Chicago apprenticeship, too. Dave Garroway, who went on to pioneer television's *Today* show in New York, was a Chicago deejay at the time. On his WMAQ show *The 11:60 Club,* he championed the hip new sounds, spinning Dizzy Gillespie's "Groovin' High," Nellie Lutcher's "Fine Brown Frame," and, in 1949, George Shearing's hit "September in the Rain" and Lennie Tristano's famous free-improvised version of "I Can't Get Started." Marian often spent intermissions listening to Garroway's show in Chick Evans's car. What she didn't hear on the radio, she heard on Ben Carlton's portable record player, which he brought with him wherever they traveled. Carlton turned her on to Woody Herman's bebop band and bassist Chubby Jackson's septet with Dave Tough, playing barn burners like "Northwest Passage" and "Four Brothers." Marian learned from these recordings what she could not get from Jimmy: bop harmonies that included dissonant upper extensions of the chords (altered ninths, elevenths, thirteenths); the new, laconic style of "comping" pioneered by Bud Powell; the light, even-handed touch of Lester Young's disciples; and how to think about forging a middle ground between the transgressions of bop and a commercial sound. Over the years, all of this information would, in one form or another, come out in her own playing.

Carlton also introduced Marian to one of the recreational distractions of the bop life. Unlike many musicians of this era, though she drank her fair share, Marian wasn't much for drugs. Marijuana made her sleepy, and the one time she tried cocaine, she said it did nothing for her. (Dizzy Gillespie told her she'd probably gotten some "bad shit.") But Marian did like the buzz of Benzedrine. Carlton showed her how to remove the paper from over-the-counter Benzedrine inhalers and soak them in a glass of Coca-Cola.

"The first time I tried this," she said, "I was awake for two days, and so nervous and jumpy I had to have a few beers to 'come down.' Finally I learned the proper amount to take, and then was able to get a pleasantly alert feeling, an 'edge,' just enough to titillate my brain a little."

Benzedrine inhalers were eventually taken off the market.

It had been more than two years since Marian had seen her family. In the spring of 1948, she decided to "make an appearance" and sailed solo for England on the *Queen Elizabeth*. Eleanor Roosevelt happened to be aboard, and Marian played an impromptu concert attended by the former First Lady. In Eastbourne, Marian was delighted to see Joyce's daughter, Sheila, for the first time. Marian proudly showed off her reviews. Though her parents were still puzzled by her decision to play jazz in America, by now they had accepted it. During the course of a two-week stay, Marian was invited to play a jazz concert in Windsor—well received, though Marian said the audience was "shocked to have it come from a native." On the voyage home, by a strange coincidence, Mrs. Roosevelt was again on board. While Marian was resting in her stateroom, a messenger knocked and told her the former First Lady had requested "some more of that English-American jazz." Marian complied, met Mrs. Roosevelt, and got her autograph.

When Marian got home, to her great disappointment (but probably not surprise), she found Jimmy drunk. She also discovered that Dorothy and Don Kassel were engaged to be married. Dorothy was only eighteen and while sophisticated for her years was still an emotionally immature young girl. That's why they had asked Kassel to look after her in the first place, to "protect" her from guys who might get the wrong idea when they saw her hanging out in a jazz club. Now Don had become the very person they had meant to protect her from! Dorothy, for her part, having had such a paltry family life, was dying to get married if only to have a family of her own. Marian and Jimmy liked Don, but he was a feckless individual and did not seem like a promising son-in-law.

But Dorothy had made up her mind. In November, the couple married and moved into a house on Hudson Street. Don got a job as a commercial designer for the Southworth and Bentley agency. The McPartlands lived a few doors down, in a coach house behind the Lanigans, who had left Lombard for a brownstone in the city. When Dorothy had been a needy teenager, Marian had felt the unwanted weight of parenthood shifting to her, thanks to Jimmy's gross incompetence as a father. (Dorothy would later complain to her cousin John Lanigan about how useless Jimmy was as a parent. "I got the father with the pink center," she said, referring to the candy in the box no one wants.) Alas, boarding school—how English a solution!—hadn't worked out. But now that Dorothy was "grown up" and a neighbor to boot, Marian found the relationship much easier. Marian and Dorothy became great pals and would remain so for years.

Jimmy was always sentimental about family, and he and Marian spent a good deal of time with the extended McPartland crew. In 1947, when Jimmy's brother Richard moved out to Elmhurst, a relatively undeveloped suburb, Jimmy gave Richard $5,000 to build a new house. Marian and Jimmy helped dig the foundation. Richard and his family spent one horrible winter there, before the walls were up, struggling to stay warm. Come summer, family jam sessions resumed, sometimes including some of the old Chicago gang, like trombonist Floyd O'Brien.

"Marian and others would come out," remembered Richard's son, Haydon McPartland, a teenager at the time. "I remember we'd put the piano on the deck and they'd sit on boxes and crates and bushel baskets. The food and drink were served off the back of a station wagon—drop the back, set up the tray, hot dogs or spaghetti. Those were fun times."

On the business front, Joe Glaser's office kept the McPartlands' dance card full. Starting with an engagement at the Stage Door in Milwaukee, they began a year-and-a-half whirlwind with a quintet. On clarinet they had Jack Golly, a talented player who later worked with musical comedian Spike Jones; Golly was succeeded by Don Kruswick, then Lou Ranier. On drums, Elmer "Mousie" Alexander came into the band after Chick Evans left. Originally from Indiana, Alexander had been studying music at Chicago's Ray Knapp School and would become a lifelong McPartland sideman. Bassist Ben Carlton remained over most of 1948 and part of 1949, during which time he kept a journal that nicely captured the bipolar swings of life on the road—flushes of exhilaration on stage alternating with the tedium, uncertainty, and loneliness of days in hotels. He was particularly disconsolate about spending Christmas and New Year's in St. Paul, "away from home and not knowing anyone."

Between small-town lounge dates, Jimmy's band played more high-profile gigs in Chicago, opening for the featured attraction. One of the most important venues they played was Frank Holzfeind's Blue Note, which had opened in the fall of 1947. The name had been inspired by a fictional club featured on Dave Garroway's radio show. The Blue Note was the first Chicago club devoted specifically to jazz and—like, say, Café Society or Birdland in New York—catering to a hip, racially integrated audience. (Before this, as in other cities, Chicago music venues were not jazz clubs in the way we understand that term today; they were cocktail lounges and/or restaurants that happened to feature jazz.) In June, Bud Freeman, who had been playing the Blue Note with Eddie Condon, was invited to stay on with Jimmy and Marian. The reunion of Bud and Jimmy drew great notices and was also the occasion for Marian's first feature in a daily newspaper focusing on her and not her husband. Interestingly, Marian was apparently still using her stage name, Marian Page.

In the June 10, 1948, *Chicago Sun-Times,* Betty Walker described Marian as "one of Chicago's most versatile and vibrant new citizens," praising her as "one of England's foremost jazz pianists" and "the heroine of a love story as full of red-white-and-blue romance as any yet screened by Hollywood."

Not exactly an in-depth critique, and definitely smacking of some planted publicity (such as Marian's bogus status in England as a famous swing pianist), but a career milestone nonetheless.

Marian and Jimmy stayed on at the Blue Note. Later that month, Billie Holiday came into the club as the star attraction. Holiday had been off the scene, serving time at Alderson Federal Prison in West Virginia for drug possession. Released in March, she had given a much-hailed homecoming concert at Carnegie Hall. Demand for her was high, and Chicago's jazz community was abuzz. She opened at the Blue Note June 14 and played through the Fourth of July, packing the place every night. Jimmy and Billie got on famously, as reflected in a photograph of them together, with Billie smiling affectionately at the Chicago cornetist.

"She had a soft spot for him," said Marian. "She didn't talk to him the way she did to some people—curtly and with a sort of contempt."

Billie's accompanist, Bobby Tucker, was frustrated because Billie refused to rehearse new tunes, but Marian would go down to the club in the daytime and listen to Tucker going over songs by himself, "stealing his changes," she said.

In a rare buoyant mood, Holiday delighted Ben Carlton one night by signing the sheet music of "Some Other Spring" for him, a song she had made her own. After Holiday left the Blue Note, Jimmy's band stayed on through the summer. Guitarist Mary Osborne, one of the few top-notch women jazz instrumentalists of the era, came in as the featured artist. Business fell off, but Marian—always alert to other women players—befriended Mary and would later hire her to work in an all-female combo. Around this time, Jimmy's old friend Dave Tough swung through town with Jazz at the Philharmonic. Tough had made quite a name for himself, working with Woody Herman, Tommy Dorsey, and Benny Goodman, but he had a severe drinking problem. Jimmy suggested Dave join AA—and Jimmy's band, too. Tough was a confirmed modernist who disparaged the revivalist cult and had skewered Jimmy in a *Down Beat* "Blindfold Test," a feature in which musicians are asked to identify and give star ratings to other musicians' records. He probably would not have been happy in the band. It hardly mattered. He was found dead on the street in Newark, New Jersey, December 9, 1948, the victim of a drunken fall in the snow.

Jimmy's band continued its regular association with the Blue Note. In July, when Sarah Vaughan opened there, Marian snagged another sparkling review.

"There are only three women jazz musicians worth tooting," wrote Ted Hallock of the *Chicago News*. "Mary Osborne, Marian (McPartland) Page and Billie Rogers." (Rogers was a California trumpet player.)

In late October 1948, Jimmy's band was co-billed again with Holiday at the Silhouette, a club in the North End where Marian heard George Shearing's groundbreaking quintet for the first time. The Silhouette was owned by a shady character Marian suspected had Mob connections, an opinion she later naively aired in a live radio interview with Studs Terkel. ("Easy now, Marian," Studs cautioned.) But she may have been right. Though the Capone era was long gone, some Chicago clubs were still tied to organized crime, an assertion all but confirmed later when an airtight union contract Marian had with another club was suddenly canceled. When she called Joe Glaser to complain, he said, "Marian, there's nothing I can do about it. Take my advice and forget it. The guy's a bad man. You don't want any part of that." When she persisted, asking how the club could get away with such a thing, Glaser became impatient. "Forget it," he yelled, and banged down the receiver.

Whatever connections the Silhouette had, they didn't help to draw a crowd for Billie Holiday, possibly because she had just been in town. (The distraction of the presidential election, in which favored challenger Thomas Dewey was wrongly announced as the winner over Harry S. Truman, may also have been a factor.) Holiday was in a foul mood. She walked out early on one set, leaving Jimmy's band to play for almost two hours while she and her husband took in a baseball game. Eventually fired, she was reinstated, according to Carlton's diary, because she had a "no cut" clause in her contract.

Around this time, Marian got the notion she and Jimmy should start their own record label. They called it Unison. The 1940s was the heyday of independent labels, such as Dial, Savoy, and Chess, which brought the new bebop and R&B to the public. But it was unusual for musicians to bring out their own records. The quartet recorded two sides in 1948 that were not released until much later. But on March 24, 1949, they recorded four more sides, issued as two 78 rpm records: "Royal Garden Blues" backed with "Singin' the Blues," and "In a Mist" backed with "Daughter of Sister Kate." Marian, Ben, and Mousie made up the rhythm section; Jack "Duff" McConnell played reeds, and Harry "Slip" Lepp played trombone.

In terms of Marian's musical development, the only track of any importance was her arrangement for horns of the Bix Beiderbecke masterpiece "In a Mist." With its impressionist piano intro, change-ups of tempo, and lovely, Ellingtonian trombone solo, it was the prototype of the kind of "classical jazz" set piece she would later incorporate into her live performances. The sides got mostly good reviews and, thanks to Marian's irrepressible knack for publicity, lots of them. Studs Terkel, in a column called "Hot Plate" for the *Chicago Sun-Times,* noted with pleasure that Jimmy played with "joy and good humor" and that "Marian Page (Mrs. Mac) . . . is a good musician in her own right."

Down Beat and *Metronome* were pickier, the former fretting that Lepp's trombone solo was "[Paul] Whitemanesque" (a comment Lepp never got over), the latter grading the sides from "B" to "C+." In England, where the records were licensed by the Harmony label, *Musical Express* critic Steve Race rated Marian's "In a Mist" arrangement "brilliant," her playing "excellent," and the records altogether more "modern" and "up to date" than one might have expected from the band of a revivalist hero. One reviewer did complain that one "needed a Geiger [counter]" to find the Unison sides, which of course spoke to the problem of distribution. Any musician can cut a record. Marketing and distributing it are entirely different matters. Though the Unison sides were later reissued by Marian herself, these two 78s were effectively the beginning and end of the label, which makes one wonder why the McPartlands made them in the first place. One guess is that it was to advertise an upcoming trip to Europe.

Jimmy had been invited to play the Paris Jazz Festival in May. Parisian bohemians and intellectuals had embraced jazz from the beginning, making a star out of the dancer Josephine Baker in *La Revue Nègre* and idealizing the blackness of jazz musicians such as Duke Ellington, as evidence of an authentic and spontaneous primitivism they called "Africanisme." Jazz record collectors were legion in the City of Light. For the new generation of postwar existentialists, the music was a badge of hipness, and French fans of bebop were called *zazous.* Jean-Paul Sartre's novel *La Nausée* included a leitmotif of the central characters listening to Bessie Smith and Louis Armstrong. The French not only loved jazz, but as with all the arts, they loved a good fight over its fine points. French critics had at first rejected bebop as an aberration (note Sartre's characters are listening to Bessie and Satchmo, not Bird and Diz), and as fans took sides in this latest debate, the Paris Jazz Festival was staged as an arena for settling the argument. The festival had started the year before along more traditional lines, but this time, modernists Miles Davis and Charlie Parker, who had never played Europe, were much-anticipated headliners. The bill also included Sidney Bechet, Django Reinhardt, Oran "Hot Lips" Page, the Swedish All-Stars, Toots Thielemans, Don Byas, and Vic Lewis, the McPartlands' old recording mate from London. Jimmy was booked to play a "Chicago jazz" set with a band led by English drummer Carlo Krahmer. Marian decided to come along for the ride.

After spending the day in the studio, Marian and Jimmy closed their gig at the Hi-Note (where they had been playing with Anita O'Day again) and the club threw them a champagne farewell. The McPartlands went to New York, where Jimmy reportedly did a TV show with Eddie Condon, then set sail for England. In Eastbourne, they visited Marian's parents, where Jimmy took in a few rounds of golf, then the couple went up to London and sat in April 30 at the London Jazz Club on Oxford Street with trumpeter Humphrey Lyttelton's band. Because the musicians union had effectively kept American jazzers out of England, British fans and critics flocked to the Paris festival to see the new American stars Davis and Parker. The festival ran May 8–15. The trad vs. bop drama began immediately. On opening night, Vic Lewis, now playing "modern," was booed offstage after two numbers. And while Charlie Parker was received more respectfully, the fans made it clear they preferred Sidney Bechet. Davis, according to Steve Race of *Musical Express,* looked "young and a little scared" and, clutching a canvas trumpet case, delivered one of the high spots of the festival with his solo on "Don't Blame Me." Jimmy played not with Krahmer as planned, but with a pickup group whose sidemen were not mentioned in reviews.

Back in London, Jimmy did some broadcasts from the Palladium with British bandleader Ted Heath. Marian and Jimmy also did a tribute to Dave Tough with an English band for the BBC, then on May 30 recorded six tunes for Krahmer's Esquire label. Krahmer was a big name on the London club circuit. Nearly blind, he had played with Shearing in Claude Bampton's Blind Orchestra back in the 1930s and now led the Nuthouse Band (so named for the club where it played). He was known for his enormous record collection and impromptu recording sessions, which eventually led to the formation of his own label. Esquire brought out some of the first bop records in England. Krahmer must have had some magic as a producer. For the first time on record, Marian sounded truly confident and relaxed. She absolutely sparkled on Earl Hines's "Blues in Thirds," playing spirited runs and muscular tremolos, zippering back up the keyboard with élan, then closing the cut with a tender touch.

Back in Eastbourne, the couple was the star attraction at the Terminus Hotel in a concert presented by the newly formed Eastbourne Rhythm Club. In a sweet, local-gal-makes-good review, Marian was referred to as a "Willingdon girl." Before sailing from Southampton on June 15, Jimmy sent a letter to Ben Carlton, urging him to join them when they got back for a gig at the Zebra Lounge in Green Bay.

"I am having a ball playing golf every day and am getting a little more consistent," he wrote. (He was being uncharacteristically modest. A scorecard from the Willingdon Golf Club showed him shooting a 78.) "Will be looking forward to having a game with you when we get back. We arrive in New York the 20th of June. I do hope you will be with us because I know we shall all miss you terribly if you don't. I have made quite a few speeches with my AA and I've thoroughly enjoyed it. At least I'm still sober and am enjoying life."

Despite Jimmy's warm invitation, Ben declined in favor of steady, full-time work at television station WGN. It wasn't jazz, but it was a job and it was close to home. Besides, Ben Carlton's wife, Eileen, was now working across the street from the station at the Carson Pirie Scott department store. (*Down Beat* disparaged Carlton for leaving jazz to play "cowboy music" for the Curley Bradley show.) Before Marian and Jimmy trekked up to Wisconsin without him, she pitched a story to *Down Beat* editor Ned Williams about the Paris Jazz Festival and with little fanfare began what would become an important secondary career—as an astute, winning, and very readable jazz writer. The article ran July 1, 1949.

Very few jazz musicians over the years have been able—or willing—to write coherently about the music. Musicians, after all, choose the medium of sound, not words, to express themselves. In this particular era, especially, as the style of "cool" emerged, there was also a premium on artists to sound even more incoherent than they actually were. A jazz musician who could articulate clearly what he was up to was probably a square. Better to just say, "You know, like, I just dig it." Possibly because of her schooling, or because she was such a voracious student of the music— almost an ethnographer of style—McPartland never bought into such cool evasions. She valued precision and clarity. Though writing didn't come as easily to her as music, she displayed great confidence and skill with a pen and had a distinct knack for journalism, delivering tart, succinct, compelling, and accurate articles. The manuscript she submitted to *Down Beat* required minimal editing. It had a great lead, which painted a vivid picture but also established her intriguing status as an insider: "Backstage at the Salle Pleyel, an excited crowd shuffled back and forth. Musicians were warming up, stage technicians barked last minute directions, critics and kibitzers conversed excitedly and craned their necks, as, fifteen minutes late, a French emcee sidled in front of the curtain and announced, 'Le Festival Internationale de Jazz est ouvert.'"

Marian conveyed the contentious mood of the event and, as she had in her wonderful letters from the front, offered keenly observed details of the Miles Davis appreciators in the crowd: "Bespectacled, goateed Parisians nodded bereted heads sagely at each exciting harmonic change, screaming and whistling their approval of every soloist. . . ."

What she wrote next—an out-and-out plug for her own husband—would not be permitted in today's journalism. But jazz critics such as Leonard Feather and John Hammond often worked as promoters, publicists, and record producers in those days and seemed to have little concern over conflicts of interest. "Jimmy McPartland," wrote Marian, "with a French group ambiguously called the New Sound Chicagoans, brought down the house with his driving choruses on 'China Boy' and 'Singing the Blues,' which he dedicated to Bix Beiderbecke. In the battle of trumpeters with Miles Davis, Bill Coleman, Roland Greenberg and Aimé Barelli, McPartland and Lips Page stood out for sheer showmanship and facility of phrasing."

Down Beat dropped one comment from Marian's original manuscript, a criticism that most of the French and English bands, "though technically proficient and desperately in earnest, couldn't seem to find that easy groove." As she heard these European players, how could Marian have helped but think, There but for fortune . . . No longer a European, Marian was now a veteran of American swing. How far young Marian Page had come since meeting Jimmy McPartland in Belgium and taking first-hand lessons in "groove"! What's more, in journalism Marian had also discovered a potential resolution to one of her deepest conflicts—between her desire to please and her need to be praised herself. What better solution than to put oneself in the limelight by promoting others? Along with her dual status as a participant/observer—standing backstage, both performing and reporting—it was a paradigm that worked. Collaboration would become a key strategy in her success.

When Marian and Jimmy got back to the States, she wrote another piece for *Down Beat,* taking up the cause for British musicians, railing against union restrictions that prevented them from hearing the latest in American jazz. (These restrictions would not be lifted until 1956.) In October,

Glaser's office sent Marian and Jimmy out to Columbus, Ohio, where they opened Mike Fleisch's new cocktail lounge, the Forest Room, at the Grandview Inn. It would be the first of many return visits for the group to this jazz-loving watering hole. Four days later, Dorothy gave birth to her first child, Douglas. Keeping it all in the jazz family, the birth was announced in *Down Beat*.

Marian got off a caring, helpful letter to Dorothy from Columbus, noting in passing that she would probably put off visiting until after Big Dorothy had come and gone. Interestingly, she also referred to drinking recreationally, though presumably she was referring only to herself and not to Jimmy.

Dearest Dorie,

I was just amazed when Don called us. I couldn't believe everything would be over so quickly—so soon. Well, how does it feel to be a mama? Lucky girl, & not too much trouble either. You bloody McPartlands do everything so easily! We shall be through here Oct. 22nd so will be home the 23rd. I don't think I shall try to make it to Chicago before that, because your Ma will be there & I would rather be around when I can be useful instead of just standing around ineffectually, making clucking noises. Grandpa took the news very proudly. I can hear him already. "My grandson Douglas" etc. etc.

Are you going to stay long in the hospital? I imagine they will let you go within a week, won't they? How about sending out cards? (I fully intend to ask you about it when I call you but will probably forget.) Do you need a list of addresses? Maybe someone will send you something you need—I feel sure Squirrel and the aunts will kick in with something. . . .

The weather is terribly hot; & all my summer clothes are put away, so I'm sweating, & hoping for cooler weather. I feel terrible about not having left a number where we could be contacted. Wouldn't you know the one night we were out things would happen! Pa played golf all day & we were at a country club for dinner. I phoned the hotel & said we were there, but then we got in a big spin & went to about five different houses for drinks, & to listen to records, so I got in rather an intoxicated condition, it being our night off. . . .

All our love to you both, & the boys send their congratulations. Will buy a bottle tonight & celebrate.

Mag & Dad xxxxx

When the band got back to Chicago, they recorded three tracks with vibist Red Norvo, but unfortunately they had no money to pay for the studio time and the owner refused to release the tapes. Spring found the group in Toronto for the first of what would become regular visits to the Colonial Tavern, and Jimmy did a promotional spot with Bing Crosby at the National Tobacco Dealers Convention in Chicago. A gag promotional photo pictured Bing playing Jimmy's cornet and Jimmy singing. But the McPartlands' sights had begun to turn east. The Dixieland revival that had supported Jimmy's career so handsomely in Chicago had begun to wane in the Windy City. Marian, inspired by Shearing and Tristano, was thinking about striking off on her own in a more musically advanced direction. Ever generous toward his wife's career, Jimmy encouraged Marian to move ahead, though he would later acknowledge that he worried, even then, that parting ways musically might drive a stake into their relationship. Marian was conflicted as well. It was comfortable working with Jimmy as leader, and she feared—with good reason—he could not stay sober on the road without her. She also worried that Jimmy wouldn't find a supportive AA group in New York (and she turned out to be right). Nevertheless, after seeing all the bop musicians at the Paris Jazz Festival, she decided New York was the place to be.

"I think I was the one that got ambitious," she said later. "And he wanted to go, too."

That fall, they made the move. On October 25, on the road out east, they played in Philadelphia at the Rendezvous with clarinetist Omer Simeon. New York's Local 802 required musicians to wait several months before working, so Jimmy suggested the couple lie low in Long Beach, on the south shore of Long Island, where Jimmy had worked with Condon back in 1935. A gorgeous stretch of sand with a wooden boardwalk as wide as a street and a view south to the horizon across the great Atlantic Ocean, where freighters and tankers and fishing boats plied, Long Beach is just east of what was then known as Idlewild Airport, and a scant hour from Manhattan on the Long Island Rail Road. During the swing era, it had been a prominent dance resort, where Bob Crosby, Bunny Berigan, and Tommy Dorsey had played. Dorsey was now at the Statler Hotel in Manhattan, and the McPartlands dropped by to say hello. Marian and Jimmy took an apartment in a residence hotel called the Commodore at 55 West Broadway, one of dozens of old hotels just a hop from the boardwalk that looked as if they were dropped into New York from Southern California.

"It was like a vacation," Marian said. "It was right on the beach."

On Fridays, the couple popped into the city to play at the Stuyvesant Casino, a cavernous Manhattan Dixieland haunt pioneered by Bunk Johnson, and another Dixieland venue, the Central Plaza. Marian had spent four years paying dues in the Midwest, working in clubs from Peru, Illinois, and Columbus, Ohio, to Toronto, Ontario. She was a bona fide road warrior. She had played alongside Anita O'Day, Billie Holiday, and Sarah Vaughan, recorded in Chicago and London, and written her first articles for *Down Beat*. Her marriage wasn't perfect, but she had found a way to keep it alive. On Christmas Day 1950, as she and Jimmy strolled along the boardwalk, she wondered what the future would bring.

6.

Getting to First Base with Three Strikes
(1950~1953)

WHEN MARIAN AND JIMMY MCPARTLAND MOVED TO New York in 1950, the city was entering one of its great heroic periods. It is difficult to imagine a more thrilling place to have been. Untouched by enemy bombs, on an economic growth spurt that would last two decades, the city had become the undisputed capital of the Western world, brimming with hope, optimism, and energy. As a symbol of that optimism stood Le Corbusier's sleek, slim United Nations building overlooking the East River. Beneath it, a system of expressways designed by Robert Moses surrounded the island of Manhattan, connecting it to Long Island, Westchester County, New Jersey, and Connecticut for the great postwar expansion to the suburbs. In midtown, international-style office towers shot up like steel-and-glass weeds, creating the hard-edged landscape of the Manhattan we know today. New York's abstract expressionists had displaced Paris as the capital of the art world. The Broadway musical had reached its zenith, with some of its greatest works on deck, including *West Side Story*. Americans such as Leonard Bernstein were finally conducting American symphony orchestras, and Tin Pan Alley, though breathing its last gasp, was grinding out tunes from the Brill building, offering, along with Broadway, daily grist for the jazz mill. The New York Yankees were on a six-out-of-seven winning streak at the World Series. And despite the tensions of the cold war—and the hot war with Korea that had begun in June—despite the palling chill of McCarthyism, the fear of atomic war, and a decidedly revisionist atmosphere for women's rights, the 1950s marked the beginning of the peak of the American century, an era that looked to the future with robust—if often unexamined—confidence.

Jazz, too, would soon enter a golden age, though in 1950 there was a decided lull. The swing boom had ended, but the general public had rejected bop, turning to sophisticated singers (Frank Sinatra, Peggy Lee) or, for dancing, the tough backbeat of rhythm and blues—renamed rock 'n' roll in 1956. "Cool," which found expression in the Method acting of Marlon Brando and James Dean, was in keeping with the emotionally restrained mood of the heroin drug culture that emerged. But in 1950, middle-class folk who had survived the war—now raising families in the suburbs—were not interested in bebop or cool jazz. They sought intimate settings where they could drink a cocktail, converse, and listen to a piano trio on a night out in a low-lit room. It was that milieu—and the consolidation of the piano trio as a standard ensemble in jazz—that would offer Marian McPartland a platform for success. Less than three years after her arrival, Marian established herself as an independent voice in modern jazz on the sophisticated Manhattan cocktail circuit.

One of the first things Marian did when she got to New York was seek out Lennie Tristano, the blind pianist who had pioneered an icy, even-handed style associated with "cool." Marian brought two acetate recordings of her playing to Tristano's apartment.

"I'd heard that Bud Freeman went to him and took some lessons," Marian said. "I found him very forbidding. It was like going to a church and seeing some kind of mysterious being. He had it all dark, and smelling of incense. I was very spooked by the whole experience. He asked me to play. . . . [He said] I had very erratic time. He said, 'If you want to be a romantic kind of player who plays rubato and roams all over the piano, that's one thing. But if you want to be a jazz player and have good time, you better go home and play with the metronome.' I was crushed, but I felt that it was a valid criticism. I wanted to play like Mary Lou [Williams], but I probably didn't keep good time."

Marian did not go back to Tristano for any more lessons, but she took his advice to heart. She dutifully bought a metronome and began to do what every good jazz player must—internalize the beat so that it's there, inside you, whether or not anyone else in the band, drummer included, is playing good time. Eventually, though she always enjoyed playing in the loose, elastic manner known as rubato, especially on ballads, her jazz time became rock solid.

Even as she explored modern sounds, Marian continued to play with Jimmy. Throughout the fall of 1950, on weekends, the couple drove into the city from Long Beach to play one of two social halls on the Lower East Side, the Stuyvesant Casino and the Central Plaza, booked by Jack Crystal, co-owner of the Commodore Record Shop, which specialized in jazz. The Stuyvesant was a boomy room, the din from the crowd deafening and the upright piano out of tune, with broken, scratched, and yellowed keys. One night Joe Sullivan became so disgusted he spat on the keyboard right before Marian played. As at Condon's, alcohol was endemic to the scene. (According to one wag, George Wettling was notorious for being "the best drummer you ever worked with—for the first half hour.")

Outside Jimmy's circle, Marian began to meet a new set of friends in high society. The most important was the polymath and multimillionaire Sherman Fairchild, a pioneer in the semiconductor industry, an early investor in IBM, and inventor of the aerial camera, who also had a hand in new recording techniques. Fairchild loved jazz, particularly jazz piano, which he played himself. At his luxurious Manhattan apartment at 17 East Sixty-fifth Street, Fairchild had two modified, white Steinway pianos bolted together like a love seat, as if they were one instrument. The pianos were miked to a private recording booth. Fairchild would often invite piano royalty—including Hoagy Carmichael and Joe Bushkin. At one of Fairchild's soirees, Marian hit it off with the highly regarded hotel pianist Cy Walter. Playing a duet, they challenged each other with complicated licks; Walter invited her to appear on the WJR radio show *Piano Playhouse*. Marian played on the show December 3, 1950, her first radio appearance in Manhattan.

Unable to work regularly in New York until Jimmy had completed his six-month "waiting period" for Local 802, Jimmy and Marian plotted three months of work outside of town, playing Boston; Columbus, Ohio; and Toronto, through February 1951. In Chicago, they had found a replacement for Ben Carlton in ex–Stan Kenton bassist Max Wayne, who migrated to New York with them. Max was an easygoing guy with a southern drawl who was fond of telling people he was from West "By God" Virginia. In the Big Apple they met another Kenton alum, drummer Bob Varney, a storied protégé of Buddy Rich. With Wayne and Varney they headed for Boston, where they played at a new club called Jazz at 76 Warrenton with trombonist Vic Dickenson and clarinetist Buster Bailey.

"That's where I learned to drink whiskey out of the bottle, backstage with Vic and Buster," Marian said.

While they were in town, the band recorded for Prestige, which was inaugurating a traditional jazz line to supplement its bebop catalog. Prestige also agreed to reissue the two Unison 78s from Chicago. With Gene Sedric on clarinet, the band recorded material for two 78s: "Come Back, Sweet Papa" backed with "Manhattan," and "Use Your Imagination" backed with "Davenport Blues." Jimmy sounded robust and Marian played a beautifully phrased solo on the lighthearted Rodgers and Hart classic "Manhattan" ("It's very fancy / On old Delancey / Street, you know . . ."), though the recording quality was so poor that the critic at the *Chicago Daily Tribune* declined to review it.

The new year found the McPartlands back at the Grandview Inn in Columbus, Ohio. New Yorkers sometimes thought they were too hip to play such midwest gigs, but Marian said she had some of the best jam sessions of her life in Columbus.

"There's a fellow there, Hank Harding, and after our shows we'd go back to his house and stay up all night playing," she said.

Unfortunately, this time their engagement ended rather abruptly, as the club burned down. (Luckily, the fire happened in the wee hours and no one was injured.) The band moved to the nearby Regal, where Marian received a remarkably perceptive review.

"Someone with a Chopin complex must have been her first teacher," said the critic, "for she rhapsodizes the Kern number ["Yesterdays"] with the touch of a concert stage artist and breaks down into all the key strumming of a 'Basie boogie' with the same number. She is truly remarkable."

Marian's mother and Bob Zurke were clearly still strong colors in Marian's musical palette. The band then headed for the Colonial Tavern in Toronto. Jimmy and Marian had earned a strong following there on run-outs from Chicago. Marian had also developed a good relationship with local jazz critic Stan Helleur at the *Telegram,* making a point of writing him thank-you notes, one of which was so full of news that he published it. Marian's chipper, civilized, and literate cordiality would become a signature and must have come as a quite refreshing surprise to journalists. This time around, the band was booked opposite pianist Oscar Peterson and bassist Ray Brown. A flashy, swinging Canadian disciple of Art Tatum, Peterson was the most-talked-about young musician in jazz, thanks to a "spontaneous" invitation to sit in at Carnegie Hall in 1949, a stunt staged by his manager, the impresario Norman Granz. Marian feared Jimmy's traditional approach might get in the way of making a good impression on Peterson, but somehow her modernity must have peeked through. According to Helleur, Peterson liked Marian's playing better than Shearing's. Such praise from peers was golden. It also translated into opportunity. When the Peterson duo left the Colonial in February, Jimmy's band became the headliner.

It seems fitting that at this turning point between her Dixieland past and her modern future, Marian changed her stage name again—for the last time. Abandoning the name Page, which she had adopted in 1938 to play with Billy Mayerl, she would henceforth be known, she told the Toronto press, as Marian McPartland. *Down Beat* printed the announcement that April. It's ironic she took Jimmy's last name publicly just as she was separating herself from him musically, but her motive was quite pragmatic. In New York, she had discovered there was another Marian Page who played piano and sang.

When the couple returned to Long Beach, it was only a matter of days before Marian, never comfortable sitting around "relaxing," began to get restless. In March, a new club called the Embers had opened on East Fifty-fourth Street and become the talk of the town. Art Tatum and Joe Bushkin christened the place and the papers said Tallulah Bankhead was "swooning" over Bushkin. Though Marian was appalled that the noisy crowd completely ignored Tatum (he didn't seem to mind), she got it in her head that she wanted to form a trio and play there herself. Jimmy got the ball rolling. He approached Irv Braybeck, an agent he knew at MCA, who said he could get Marian into the club but that she should first make a recording. Braybeck contacted King Records, an important R&B label with a subsidiary called Federal, which hit the jackpot in 1956 with the James Brown smash "Please, Please, Please." It was hardly the right fit for Marian, but it would be her first record under her own name. She leapt at the chance.

On March 15, 1951, Marian went into a New York studio and recorded material for two 78s: the Cole Porter classic "It's De-Lovely" backed with "Flamingo," the 1941 ballad made famous by vocalist Herb Jeffries; and "Four Brothers," the hurtling theme song for four tenor saxophones from the Woody Herman band, backed with a pop version of Franz Liszt's love song Liebesträume No. 3. Drummer Don Lamond, recently of the Herman herd, played drums. Bob Carter, whom Marian had known in Chicago when he worked with Charlie Ventura, played bass. Marian wanted to play bop but was also still smitten by the idea of "classical jazz." She asked if she could record with cello and harp. Braybeck hired the gifted young arranger Tom Talbert to write charts. Though Talbert used the cello smartly on "It's De-Lovely," the overall result was sugary. Marian, as always, played with forthrightness and clarity, at least when the tinkling of the harp and the groan of the cello were not in her way, but on "Four Brothers" her time was poor, the feeling wooden. Tristano had been right.

"I was dashing about like an idiot," she said, listening to the records many years later, adding, "I'd never play that record again as long as I live."

Far more interesting than the music were the marketing considerations that went into it. The harp and cello—as well as the choice of Liszt—"feminized" the record, playing on the image Jimmy had created in Chicago of an elegant lady who didn't mind dipping her feet in the mud now and then with a little boogie-woogie. Though this approach had putatively gone out of style with Paul Whiteman, mixing classical forms with jazz had become all the rage again, this time in progressive circles. Shearing was doing it, and so was a young pianist in California named Dave Brubeck. Marian herself would soon be playing a Bached-up fugue arrangement of "All the Things You Are," "borrowed" from pianist Johnny Guarnieri, which would become a lifelong staple of her repertoire.

The cello and harp also may have been chosen for commercial reasons. Having an identifiable instrumental "sound" sold records, such as those by Shearing's brilliant, carefully arranged quintet. Though Shearing used vibes and electric guitar, his sound was gauzy and romantic; perhaps cello and harp could achieve a similarly soft contour. Though they did not, in fact, sell well, Marian's first two records were a huge critical success, which speaks to the mode for "classical jazz" at the time. *Metronome*'s Barry Ulanov fell all over himself, declaring hyperbolically that Jimmy's "brilliant spouse" had taken "a firm hold of her place in jazz history with these sides," in "the most refreshing of all the many attempts to give Shearing competition."

Whatever the merits of these assessments, as Braybeck had hoped, the records worked hand in glove to promote Marian at the Embers. For the gig, she bought some great-looking new clothes ("quite expensive," she remembered) and kicked off the engagement on May 8. The Embers was a long room with soft lighting and a fireplace at the back, with glowing coals that gave the club its name, a far cry from the saloons and steak houses the McPartlands had been playing on the road.

"It was the epitome of the chic jazz room, like a very posh supper club," recalled pianist Barbara Carroll, who later played there opposite Tatum and others. "For one thing, it was on the East Side. All the places on Fifty-second Street were on the West Side. There was a panache, if you will. They had great food. . . . Celebrities and movie stars came to the Embers all the time. Society people, musicians, and singers."

The club was owned by Ralph Watkins, an ex-musician and veteran club operator who had worked at the Royal Roost in the glory days of Fifty-second Street. Watkins had hired Eddie Heywood to replace Joe Bushkin, but when business fell off, Watkins offered Heywood three marquee sidemen, tenor saxophonist Coleman Hawkins, trumpeter Roy Eldridge, and vibraphonist Terry Gibbs. For whatever reason, Heywood preferred to play alone, so Marian inherited the sidemen. When one considers that she had never worked as a leader in New York, this was a remarkable stroke of good fortune. Thanks to Jimmy's connections, Marian had once again started at the top.

"I never went through any of the real apprenticeship that people like Barbara Carroll had to go through," she said.

Nor had she worked as a leader, since Jimmy had always taken care of that. Now she had to learn how to front a band, play with new sidemen, pay them, deal with hecklers and fan requests, and present herself to an audience.

"I used to be a nervous wreck," she recalled. "I had a hard time just saying, 'Thank you, ladies and gentlemen. Now we'd like to present Eddie Heywood.' I had it written on a piece of paper."

She also had to learn how to speak on the radio. To advertise the gig, Marian played a half-hour show on WNEW hosted by the famous deejay Al "Jazzbo" Collins.

"I was quite nervous, and when Al would speak to me I would be so shy about answering I must have sounded ridiculous," she said. "Jimmy always told me, 'Be yourself,' but it was hard. I wanted to be liked and admired, yet I was seldom really relaxed in those first months."

Beyond dealing with the microphone, Marian was intimidated by Hawkins and Eldridge. To her great surprise, she found them both to be pussycats.

"They were so nice," she said. "They were wonderful. Roy always talked about [the Embers gig], every time I saw him, as if I had done *him* a favor!"

It was probably during this engagement that Marian starting using her left foot to pedal so she could do a half turn on the bench and make eye contact with the crowd. She had noticed Bushkin doing something similar at the Embers, sticking his right leg out and "more or less flirting with the audience," she said. Mary Lou Williams pedaled with her left foot for the same reason. Whether it came from Bushkin or Williams, Marian picked up this device and was first noted for using it in New York.

In 1951, the trio format of piano, bass, and drums wasn't standardized the way it is today. Many trios, such as the ones led by Art Tatum and Nat Cole, used guitar instead of drums. Oscar Peterson and Ray Brown played as a duo, then later added guitar. Billy Taylor used both guitar and drums. For her trio, Marian chose bass and drums. She had excellent players: Don Lamond and the much-admired bassist Eddie Safranski, who had left Stan Kenton to do studio work. Marian may have chosen drums rather than guitar because she preferred the clarity and freedom of the format. She later told the critic Nat Hentoff that she liked this setup because it was less harmonically restrictive. "The only person I, as a trio pianist, have to worry about is the bassist," she said. A drummer also probably made Marian feel more secure. Tristano had told her to be sure to always play with other musicians who had very good time. Lamond and Safranski were good choices, both having anchored big bands for years.

As for hiring and firing sidemen, that was a whole new responsibility. She didn't like her first bass player at the Embers, but it took her a long time to get up the courage to tell him. (Jimmy told her, "Well, that's easy. Just fire him," which she eventually did.)

"I know I was a pretty inept leader," she said. "I've never liked being one, and in those days I relied heavily on the sidemen to make suggestions to me about how to play tunes."

Marian's gig at the Embers was only moderately successful, but the press took notice, if not always in the most complimentary way. The entertainment sheet *Variety,* in its famous shotgun shorthand, said, "Gal handles the 88 with imagination and assuredness despite fact that she is still searching for proper styling." The *Sunday Mirror* ran Marian's photo along with other "nightclub stars" appearing around town, including her old USO chum Celeste Holm; the powerful gossip columnist for the *Post,* Earl Wilson, noted Marian at the Embers as well. Marian had "arrived."

She had also been noticed by a pair of promoters in Boston named George Wein, who played piano, and Charlie Bourgeois, who adored piano players. They invited Marian to play at their club, Storyville. Marian and the guys flew up for the gig, getting back to New York just in time to play the Embers. The trio was then invited back for a Saturday afternoon date, June 2, and the performance was recorded live. Bourgeois liked the tapes so much that (without McPartland's knowledge) he took them to Herman Lubinsky at Savoy Records, an important independent label bringing out the new bop sounds, including Miles Davis and Charlie Parker.

Marian signed with Savoy in 1951. Over the next two and a half years, she recorded thirty-seven sides for the label on six sessions. At the time, recording formats were in transition, so Marian's efforts were released on no fewer than twenty-one different records in a dizzying array of formats, including 78s, 7-inch EPs, 10-inch LPs, and 12-inch LPs. (By 1952, 12-inchers would evolve as the standard album format.) Marian's first Savoy recordings were the 7-inch EPs *Jazz at Storyville Vol. 1* and *Jazz at Storyville Vol. 2,* featuring material recorded live at the club: "Gypsy in My Soul" backed with "Strike Up the Band," and "These Foolish Things (Remind Me of You)" backed with "Get Happy." Nat Hentoff, a deejay in Boston on radio station WNEX at the time, emceed the concert and at one point indulged in some borscht belt humor, jokingly announcing

"These Foolish Things" as "These Meshugganah Things." Marian didn't like her playing on the tracks and said the piano was out of tune.

But like most musicians starting out, she was happy to have something in the stores. And while the recording quality was tinny and, indeed, the piano slightly out of tune, the recordings were not bad. Stylistically, Marian burst with ideas, and her playing was clean and crisp, if episodic, as if she were trying to play everything she knew in five minutes. But there were graceful, Teddy Wilson–style lines, cushiony, Shearingesque block chords, an interlude suggesting classical music, and, on "Gypsy in My Soul," one of those big, splashy, two-handed dissonant chords that would become a signature. Lamond and Safranski offered excellent support.

Savoy's packaging revealed a lot about what the company thought it was selling. Graphic designer Burt Goldblatt, who would later design record covers for Miles Davis and Charles Mingus, executed a vivid, swirling line drawing of Marian seated at the piano, head thrown back, eyes closed, wearing a white backless dress, arms arching over her head, palms extended over a wavy keyboard. The image was variously printed over full-bleed backgrounds of hot green or pink. The feeling evoked nightlife and ecstasy at same time that it was cool and hip and sexy. Hentoff contributed exuberant liner notes.

In July, British jazz critic Leonard Feather, who had moved to the United States in the late 1930s, published a breakthrough article about Marian in *Down Beat*. Feather praised Marian highly but embedded his compliments in a conceit that, like the early Savoy recordings, would haunt her for the rest of her life. Marian, he began, had "three hopeless strikes against her"—she was white, she was female, and she was British. The Feather article has become something of a legend in the McPartland story, invoked time and again by interviewers as evidence of the chauvinist critical prejudice she had to overcome. And indeed, the context of the article itself said a lot about the status of women in jazz at the time. Published July 13, 1951, under the now amusingly sexist—but then intentionally minimizing—title "Girls in Jazz," the story ran with pictures of three singers—Helen Forrest, in a bathing suit; Connie Russell, at a makeup mirror; and Janet Blair, having her hair done. In this era, jazz was decidedly a man's world, portrayed by the male gaze. If a woman instrumentalist was noticed, her looks, figure, outfit, and hair would be highlighted as a matter of course. Marian's notices during this period rarely failed to mention that she was female, British, or white, sometimes all three. (*Variety* even referred to her as a "British import" and "an ofay," a black slang expression for whites taken up by white hipsters.) And if she played with strength, as Marian did, it would be said that she either "played well for a girl" or that she "played like a man."

The notion that women could not play as well as men was part of the orthodoxy of the period's music criticism. Rudolph Elie, a classical critic who had praised Marian in print in Boston, would later fume that the Boston Symphony had hired a woman as first chair flutist. In 1958, Barry Ulanov, a champion of Marian, nevertheless wrote an article for *Down Beat* with the straight-faced title "Is There a Place in Jazz for Women as Instrumentalists?" In 1962, Harold C. Schonberg of *The New York Times* declared women could not "dominate" their instruments the way men could. In 1964, Whitney Balliett, jazz critic for *The New Yorker,* though he made an exception for Mary Lou Williams, asserted that women had "decorated" stringed instruments in jazz over the years but lacked "the physical equipment and poise" needed to "blow, beat and slap instruments like the trumpet, bass, and drums." The idea that jazz was a masculine music was deeply ingrained and posed a distinct barrier for women instrumentalists. (Singers were okay, especially if they were cute—and they usually were.) Jazz musicians were sexualized males, wielding their "axes" to seduce women with the blues or woo them with a ballad. If a woman played in that same, erotically charged, blues-drenched way, her virtue was suspect. Novelist Robert Ruark once approached McPartland after hearing her play and observed, "My God, the way you play jazz, you can't be a respectable woman." McPartland took it as a compliment.

Though there were a few female pianists on the scene in the early 1950s—notably Williams, Carroll, Jutta Hipp, Dardanelle, and Adelaide Robbins—it was difficult for women to get a hearing.

"When I first came to New York, I had a friend who was a pianist," reported Carroll. "I didn't have any work. He had an engagement for a Saturday night, but if somebody called and asked him for another gig, he would try to get it for me. But he couldn't tell them I was a girl, because they wouldn't hire me. So instead of saying, 'I'd like to send Barbara Carroll,' he'd say, 'Listen, Bobby Carroll could do this gig.'"

Sometimes, even if you did get heard, male musicians snubbed you. Marian encountered this at least once, at Birdland, playing with an all-black, all-male band.

"Nobody spoke to me," she said. "They'd just count off a tune. It so happened I knew all the tunes. But they obviously were not pleased to have this particular piano player there. And their backs were turned to me the whole time."

Carroll acknowledged that once other players heard her, being female could actually be a plus.

"It almost became a commercial asset, in a sense; you were regarded as unique. . . . Cocktail dress, a little cleavage, if you were fortunate enough to have it, bare shoulders. Sultry and glamorous. Photographers took these marvelous photographs with lighting and shadows."

Carroll, in fact, went so far as to have her nose bobbed—a gambit crassly embraced by a *Down Beat* writer as a great career move. "Six months ago she was just a musicians' musician—and let's face it, looked like one," he wrote. "Today . . . her handsome portrait has gazed down at a million passengers from posters in every Fifth Avenue bus. . . ." Clearly, the message was that girls were there to be seen as well as heard.

And Marian, though in no way a tease, was a strikingly beautiful woman who didn't hesitate to show what she had.

"She was thirty-five, and we were in our twenties," recalled Norton Wright, who as a college kid at Yale would go see McPartland in Manhattan. "But here was this sexy, buxom babe who played dynamite jazz piano. It was like our exultation in life."

The prejudice against women in jazz was part of a much larger social context that developed during the post–World War II era, which Betty Friedan spelled out in her 1963 book, *The Feminine Mystique.* This was the period, Friedan explained, in which the first wave of feminism, which had secured women the vote, took a body blow from advertisers, industry, pop psychologists, and even scholars, who idealized the new suburban housewife, whose sole fulfillment in life was meant to be purchasing goods, taking care of her husband, and raising children. Magazines such as *Ladies' Home Journal* and *Life* were stuffed with ads picturing happy housewives with their new refrigerators and self-help articles advising women to relieve their "anxiety" by throwing themselves into motherhood and housekeeping, when in fact their "anxiety" stemmed from having been excluded from meaningful lives. Even serious female scholars such as Margaret Mead, in books such as *Male and Female* and *Coming of Age in Samoa,* idealized motherhood and warned women that careers would "masculinize" them. This kind of language was very much in the air when Marian came up, so it was no surprise that the discourse about what was "masculine" and what was "feminine" seeped into jazz criticism. It was the cultural background noise behind an article like Feather's.

But if it was difficult for women instrumentalists to be heard, and even more difficult to be taken seriously, it was also true that Feather, in his article, meant to buck the trend rather than endorse it. For in fact, he actually didn't say he believed McPartland had "three strikes against her." What he did say was that French jazz fans—notoriously dismissive of white jazz musicians, particularly Brits—might feel that way, but he didn't. Feather was setting up a straw man (straw woman?) in his article, all the better to blow it down. In reality, he argued, "if you ask Coleman Hawkins, Roy Eldridge, Ed Safranski, or any of the other cats who worked with her at the Embers recently, you'll know from their enthusiasm that Marian has nothing to worry about. She's a fine, swinging pianist and one of the most talented girls in jazz."

Notwithstanding the unintended sexism of that last phrase, Feather clearly meant that anyone who held prejudices based on race, gender, or nationality was wrongheaded. He had, after all, designed the *Down Beat* "Blindfold Test" in part to expose just such hypocrisies and had long championed women players, with the specific agenda of pointing out biases that existed against them. Blindfolded, he argued, one could not tell whether a jazz musician was white or black, male or female, American or "foreign." Nevertheless, his article has been held up for years to prove that he—like all the other chauvinist critics—did not support McPartland, when obviously he was one of her earliest champions.

What's ironic in all this is that McPartland herself probably did more to keep the article alive than anyone else.

"It was a good piece of publicity," she said.

It certainly was, since in addition to outlining the real obstacles she faced as a woman, it painted an appealing portrait of an intrepid artist for whom any obstacle would make her that much more determined. What might have been a crushing blow for somebody else, McPartland shrewdly turned on its head and used to her own advantage.

"I was pleased to be written about," she said, "and I just sort of took it as an accolade. I was somebody who kind of went barging ahead, no matter what."

McPartland was not always so sanguine about sexist critics. In a 1952 interview with Ben Gross at the New York *Daily News,* she lashed out at the ghettoizing of women players.

"I know any number of women musicians who can play as well, if not better, than the men," she said. "Talent is talent, regardless of sex, and it should be recognized as such. . . . If a girl can withstand all the rigors of war and marriage, why can't she exhibit a simple little quality like talent? Sex has nothing to do with artistry. . . . I defy anyone listening to any of my recordings, on the basis of hearing alone, to detect whether the pianist is a man or a woman. The fact is that all human beings are equally endowed by our Creator."

Asked if she didn't agree, nevertheless, that men were stronger, she replied hotly, "I certainly don't. We females are capable of enduring more pain than you men. We have babies, don't we?"

Later that year, McPartland's views were reinforced by Nat Hentoff, who wrote an article for *Down Beat* in which he chalked up such attitudes to "male chauvinism," a vanguard use of a phrase that would become commonplace in 1968 but certainly had not been used previously in jazz criticism. McPartland, he said, was proof positive that a woman—even a woman from Britain—could play "authentic jazz."

Sometimes, however, for all her "barging ahead" and bravado, Marian wasn't as sure of herself as she pretended to be. Privately, she often compared herself unfavorably to other female players. She was particularly intimidated by Carroll, who had been established in New York since 1947, when she had worked at the Down Beat on Fifty-second Street opposite the Dizzy Gillespie Big Band. Carroll was the only other woman—apart from Mary Lou—who had wide respect as a solid modern jazz pianist. The jazz press had even nicknamed her "Barbara bebop," and in 1951, Atlantic Records put her on a par with Williams by releasing an album, *Ladies of Jazz,* shared equally by the two. When Marian played the Embers, she said she felt she was "playing second fiddle to Barbara Carroll, who got raves in *The New Yorker* every week from Popsie Whittaker." (Whittaker wrote for the unsigned front section of *The New Yorker* called "Talk of the Town.")

"I always felt somewhat inferior to her," McPartland wrote in a letter to record producer Irving Townsend in 1975. "There was a sort of rivalry there (at least in my mind—probably she was unconscious of it—she has always seemed very together). Every time she was booked on TV (Kate Smith Show, 'Tonight Show' with Steve Allen, etc.) I would call Larry [Bennett, Marian's agent] and ask him when my next date was going to be. I always felt Barbara was way ahead of me, & I had to catch up."

Carroll would later drop out of jazz to raise a family, then reemerge in the 1970s as a supper club singer/pianist. But in this period, she was indeed the more swinging pianist of the two. She had mastered the sinuous lines, percussive touch, and blues-based feeling Bud Powell had set as the gold standard for modern jazz piano.

"Barbara could swing you right out of the room," recalled Billy Taylor. "She was the kind of player that, male or female, you admired."

Marian, by contrast, was awash in rubato pastels, block chords, and classical mannerisms. And when she did try to swing, it sometimes sounded more like bouncing.

Besides Carroll, Mary Lou Williams was the only other pianist McPartland inevitably compared herself to. Williams was a giant. She had not only played with Andy Kirk, she had taught herself to arrange and compose, then, serving as a mentor to Thelonious Monk and Bud Powell in the 1940s, had absorbed bop. Williams was like a walking, living history of jazz. Marian desperately wanted her respect. It was not easily won. In September 1952, Marian sought Williams out at Le Down Beat on Fifty-fourth Street near Eighth Avenue, where Williams was playing with Oscar Pettiford (bass) and Kenny Clarke (drums). Though McPartland always portrayed their relationship as "friendly," in fact, Williams was condescending and dismissive.

"She had no use for Marian," said Daniel Griffin, later a very close friend of Marian's who squired Williams around campus at Bates College in the late 1970s, when the school awarded Williams an honorary degree. "She didn't take her seriously. She didn't think she was a jazz artist."

"[Mary Lou] liked Barbara Carroll," said Peter O'Brien, a priest who would later manage Williams and look after her legacy. "But, see, Barbara Carroll is a true bop pianist and would have been working on Fifty-second Street the same time Mary Lou was. There was also this compelling forward motion. It's a different animal from Marian."

In what would become a standard modus operandi, McPartland simply refused to take no for an answer.

"I think Marian was always a little concerned whether Mary Lou really accepted her," said Dan Morgenstern, on the scene at the time and later director of the Institute of Jazz Studies. "Mary could be very tough. . . . Mary really liked Marian and she respected her, but there was also a little jealousy there, the competitiveness, because there weren't that many women in jazz and it's the same instrument. And although Mary was an arranger and had been a bandleader and all that, she still felt a little standoffish. So I think there was a kind of warmth that one might have expected that didn't show. But she always said nice things about Marian."

Maybe not always. Drummer Joe Morello, who later worked with Marian at the Hickory House, recalled sitting with her in the control booth at a radio station where Williams was being interviewed. When asked, "What do you think of Marian McPartland?" Williams said, "She just can't play jazz. No jazz."

"Whoa," said Morello. "[I'm thinking] there's going to be a big scene here. But no, in comes Marian and she says, 'Mary Lou!' and they're hugging each other and all this bullshit. And I'm saying, 'What kind of crap is this?' So I told Marian later, 'Do you know you're hugging this woman and she's saying you can't play?'"

Clearly, this was a complex relationship. Over the years, it would have many ups and downs. However, there was little time for it to develop in 1952, as Williams went to Paris that November and didn't return to New York until 1954. The two women's paths would cross again; often, sparks would fly.

After establishing her trio at the Embers, Marian left MCA and went back to Joe Glaser's Associated Booking Corp. She and Jimmy began to take separate engagements outside of town, with Larry Bennett handling Marian's account. To beef up her press packet, Marian requested endorsements from supporters. Dave Garroway happily complied.

"Marian honey," he wrote, spacing his words on the page as if they were a lyric poem:

> *Take your choice—*
> *Plays like a strong pearl necklace.*
>   *Or*
> *You can count the great women jazz artists on the fingers of*
> *Marian's fine right hand—and in my book, she gets two fingers.*
>   *Peace,*
>   *Dave*

Unlike some artist couples who purposely forgo parenthood in favor of nurturing their art, the McPartlands had been trying without success to have a baby. In Philadelphia, on their way from Chicago to New York, Marian had even consulted a doctor to ask why she was having trouble getting pregnant. The doctor told her there was nothing physically wrong. Marian wondered—perhaps facetiously—if she weren't her "own best prophylactic," because her mother had made her so afraid of childbirth. In Boston, however, she discovered another problem. She had cysts on one of her ovaries. Its removal in a Boston hospital pretty much put an end to whatever hopes she had of having children. Though deeply disappointed at the time, in later years McPartland said she had no regrets.

"I think I would have been a terrible mother," she said. "Like my mother. Perfectionist. Want to have everything just so. I'm just glad I didn't."

Marian wasn't all that fond of children anyway. Though generous and thoughtful at holidays (Jimmy's granddaughter remembered getting dresses from Saks Fifth Avenue at Christmas), she was not reflexively maternal—except toward Jimmy—and preferred the company of adults. If they had had kids, the burden of parenthood inevitably would have fallen on her, and they needed two incomes to get along. Besides, as Dizzy Gillespie's wife, Lorraine, had said when she was asked why she didn't have kids: "I've already got one at home."

In Boston, Marian got some welcome news from Larry Bennett. In February, she was to open at the Hickory House in New York. The Hickory House, at West Fifty-second Street and Seventh Avenue, was one of the oldest clubs on "Swing Street" and, along with Jimmy Ryan's, the only other survivor of the street's heyday. John Popkin and a partner, Jack Goldman, had opened the place in 1933. Popkin was a Lithuanian immigrant who had managed speakeasies during Prohibition, among them the Little Club, where Jimmy had played with Ben Pollack in 1928. Popkin started booking music at the Hickory House in 1934, doing a robust business with traditional jazz throughout the Depression. Marian's former USO cohort Jack LeMaire had played there with Joe Marsala; Gene Krupa and Buddy Rich played the club as well. After the war, in keeping with the subdued mood of the country, Popkin stopped hiring horn players, toned down the music, and put more emphasis on his dinner business. It became a haven for sophisticated supper club pianists, including Joe Bushkin, Billy Taylor, and the French genius Martial Solal. Popkin also featured many ensembles led by women: Mary Osborne, Hazel Scott, Jutta Hipp, Toshiko Akiyoshi, Mary Lou Williams, Marjorie Hyams, and, of course, Marian herself.

The Hickory House, which in a previous incarnation had been a used-car showroom, was a barn of a room with a forty-foot ceiling, leaded glass windows, and a maroon awning on the sidewalk. Popkin installed an imposing fireplace at the back made of white brick, with stained glass doors to showcase the hickory logs he had delivered from upstate New York, over which steaks were cooked.

"The food was terrific," said Marian. "Chicken in the pot, boiled beef with dumplings, steaks broiled over hickory logs."

Duke Ellington, a great lover of steak whose publicist, Joe Morgen, also worked for Popkin, ate there often. A spotlight illuminated a glassed-in refrigerator full of fresh meat. The bandstand stood aloft an enormous, oval-shaped bar of varnished black walnut, with a canopy and pillars at either end. Liquor bottles festooned circular shelves around the pillars. The bar seated seventy-five, and they were the best seats in the house. The feeling was bustling, noisy—"more like a Broadway pinball parlor at times than a nightclub," said Marian—and with a decidedly masculine sporting theme. Amateurish paintings of baseball stars, boxers, and even a foxhunt adorned the walls. Autographed celebrity glossies lined the walls. A dozen or so booths were arranged along the sides of the room.

On February 2, 1952, the night before her seventh wedding anniversary, Marian opened at the club. She wore a strapless gown of orange brocade with Asian-looking floral patterns. (Fifty-six years later, it was still hanging in her closet.) Max Wayne played bass. Mel Zelnick, an alumnus of the Chubby Jackson and Lennie Tristano bands, played drums the first few weeks until Mousie Alexander could break free from Chicago. Marian was nervous. Guitarist Mary Osborne had preceded her at the Hickory House and hadn't done particularly good business, so Marian felt she had the burden of picking up the trade. But Bennett assured her everything would be fine: He had her booked for a month solid. McPartland did all right. She wound up playing at the Hickory House for nearly a decade, putting a virtual "lock" on the room and becoming a midtown institution.

Marian's longtime friend Bernice MacDonald remembered the pianist, perched on the elevated stage.

"Seeing her up there in the center of that bar, I always remember you could see her foot on the pedal," said MacDonald. "You were looking up at it. Her playing was scintillating. I remember her playing 'A Nightingale Sang in Berkeley Square.'"

"At times I felt like Miss Seagram of 1952, sitting there among the bottles, trying to make my piano playing cut through the various sounds," said Marian.

The trio played from nine P.M. till three A.M., including Christmas and New Year's, spelled by "intermission pianist" Ellie Eden. On breaks, there was no escape from the bar, as there was no dressing room, so the band chose an inconspicuous booth to hang out in.

Popkin was a colorful boss. An inveterate gambler who played the horses daily, he was known for his mercurial moods. The publicist for the club, Joe Morgen, a short and melancholy-looking fellow, once said, "John would bet you a thousand dollars any hour on whether the next passing car had an even- or odd-numbered license plate." If Popkin had had a bad day at the track, it was best to keep out of his way.

"When he was feeling good, he'd come by and give me an enormous slap on the back," said Marian. "But when things weren't going so well at the track, he'd complain that I was taking too long an intermission."

On slow nights, Popkin would complain, "Look at them! Beer drinkers!" Then he'd glare at Marian as if it were her fault. Sometimes Popkin's niece Roberta sang a tune or two.

"The whole family sat at the bar, gazing proudly at her," said Marian. "When she had finished, they would return to the back of the room and resume talking at the tops of their voices."

The headwaiter, Julius Artman, was short and unctuously polite, and he carried himself "like a storm trooper," Marian recalled. When Joe Morello later joined Marian's trio, to get Julius's goat, Morello would turn a ratchet on one of his drums—crunch! crunch! crunch!—in time to Julius's goose step. According to bassist Bill Crow, who also later joined the trio, the Greek chef was temperamental and prone to tantrums. After overhearing Popkin complain one night that he had "nothing but t'ieves" working for him, the chef dramatically demanded an apology in front of the customers, throwing his white chef's hat and apron to the floor, then filled a coffeepot with Scotch and stomped back into the kitchen.

The Hickory House was slightly out of the price range of scuffling young jazz fans, but it did draw some regular joes, as well as celebrities, show people, students from Yale or Princeton on dates, and, later, when the Americana Hotel (now the Sheraton Hotel) opened across the street, conventioneers. It was publicist Joe Morgen's job to keep the place full.

Balding, with bulging, hyperthyroid eyes, Morgen was a rude, old-school pro from the Walter Winchell school of celebrity whom one writer described as seeming to have wandered in from the set of *Guys and Dolls*. Morgen had little regard for the truth, and countless items he planted in the New York papers were often out-and-out lies. But it wasn't long before Morgen's magic began to work.

"Tallulah Bankhead is such a jazz enthusiast," wrote Nick Kenny in the *Daily Mirror* in March, "that she shuttled between the Hickory House and the Embers half a dozen times a night just to hear Marian McPartland and her trio at the Hickory House and Marian's hubby, Jimmy, with his hot combo at the Embers."

Morgen eventually snagged articles for McPartland in *Time, The New York Times,* and Dorothy Kilgallen's column in the *New York Journal-American.* He also enticed Garry Moore to come by, and Moore subsequently booked Marian on his TV variety show on CBS.

By this time, Marian and Jimmy had left Long Beach for an apartment at 341 West Eighty-eighth Street on the Upper West Side, between West End Avenue and Riverside Drive, though she and Jimmy still weren't sure if they had come to New York to stay. Mousie arrived—none too soon, as Zelnick, Marian said, didn't seem that interested in the job. Mousie found an apartment nearby, and Marian began to settle in to her new job.

It wasn't long before she started to notice Duke Ellington coming into the club, usually around midnight, with an entourage that included his sister, Ruth; other musicians or colleagues; or, later, his girlfriend, Beatrice "Evie" Ellis. Duke always sat at a booth for eight in the corner of the room and ordered steak, grapefruit, and a cup of hot water with lemon peel. An elegant flirt, Ellington would sometimes invite Marian over to his table, cut a little piece of steak, and offer it to her on the end of a fork.

"He had so much sex appeal it was almost frightening," said Marian. "I was so naive and shy that I couldn't ever figure out how to act with him, although I enjoyed being with him."

One night, Marian boldly asked Duke what he thought of her playing.

"You play so many notes," he said.

"I thought about it and after a while I thought, 'He probably is telling me I'm playing too many [notes],'" she said. "It was one of the best criticisms I ever had."

Marian repeatedly invited Ellington to sit in, and after a year, he finally consented. In return, Marian would often play a medley of Ellington's own compositions when he came in. With the prodding of Joe Morgen, she even learned Duke's abstract, unusual composition "Clothed Woman," an odd tune that sounds as though it is full of wrong notes. Ellington was thoroughly delighted.

Marian's gig at the Hickory House put her at the epicenter of the Manhattan jazz world. In April, Leonard Feather again acknowledged her success, conducting a "Blindfold Test" with her and Jimmy for *Down Beat,* the first of several over the years. The interview was notable for Marian's 360-degree awareness of what was going on in the jazz world, from Bud Powell, Miles Davis, and Barbara Carroll on the East Coast to Shorty Rogers and Dave Brubeck out west. Her role as both participant and keen observer of jazz was coalescing.

In April, dissatisfied with the live recordings from Storyville, Marian went back into the studio with Wayne and Zelnick. Savoy issued a redo of "Strike Up the Band" on EP, backed with the Gershwin song "Our Love Is Here to Stay," just popularized by the Gene Kelly film *An American in Paris.* Marian's fleet technique drew strong reviews, including her first notice in *Time* magazine, which praised, in the beret-and-goatee slang of the day, her "wig-flipping rhythm." But McPartland's playing on these records still sounded impatient, and as Duke had observed, she played too many notes.

That fall, Marian and Jimmy returned to Boston to play for George Wein. There, for the first time, Marian heard the much-talked-about progressive Dave Brubeck. The horn-rimmed-spectacled pianist was scheduled to play a matinee on Sunday, October 12, but his bass player had tied one on the night before ("he had to sober up in the bathtub," said Dave), so while Dave and alto saxophonist Paul Desmond were waiting, they started to improvise. Tape was running and the result was a glorious duo version of "Over the Rainbow" that became a Brubeck classic. Marian would later write extensively about Brubeck, defending him against the virulent criticism he often encountered. The respect was mutual. The two even wrote tunes for each other.

Jimmy, meanwhile, had been working in and out of New York in a variety of Dixieland venues, including Child's Paramount in Times Square and Lou Terrassi's, a West Forty-seventh Street club where Henry "Red" Allen held forth. When Jimmy took his own group on the road, Marian worried he wouldn't be able to stay sober without her around. Her worries were entirely justified. George Wein recalled playing a gig with Jimmy in Montreal. McPartland insisted that they room together.

"He couldn't be alone," recounted Wein. "We wake up in the morning and order breakfast and he says, 'Would you like a brandy Alexander for breakfast?' Fine, I'll have a brandy Alexander, too. I go in and brush my teeth and he had drunk his brandy Alexander and my brandy Alexander. I never did taste it. I like a brandy Alexander. I'd pay for one every morning, but I never did get one."

In December, Jimmy recorded a session arranged by Leonard Feather called *Hot vs. Cool,* pitting Jimmy's "hot" traditional jazz against Dizzy Gillespie's "cool" (actually "hot," but never mind) modernism. Recorded live at Birdland, the album was a gimmick, but it generated a lot of publicity for Jimmy with its bop and trad versions of familiar standards such as "Indiana," "How High the Moon," and "Muskrat Ramble." An image of Jimmy and Diz jokingly "crossing swords" with their instruments conveyed the warmth and respect that existed between these two musicians all their lives.

Despite Jimmy's inevitable tumbles off the wagon, Marian decided to go to England by herself for the Christmas of 1952. Joyce was pregnant again, due in January, and Marian hadn't been home in nearly three years. Before leaving, she and Jimmy sent out a humorous Christmas card designed by Don Kassel that pictured Jimmy, Marian, and Santa. Jimmy's dialogue balloon said, "OK, so his tone is nowhere and he plays out of tune—but think of the terrific name he has!" "Name indeed," replied Marian. "Already the old boy wants December 25th off." Inside, the festive message: "Have a real gone holiday."

Before this, Marian had crossed the Atlantic only by ship. But she was making good money now—$200 a week, eventually $800—so she decided to fly, boarding a plane for London December 8. Before she left, George Shearing and his wife, Trixie, presented her with a bouquet of roses. Marian was nervous about the flight, but it turned out near perfect—that is, until it reached England, where the fog-bound London airport caused the plane to be diverted some one hundred miles to the southwest. When a bedraggled Marian, clutching her bouquet of roses, finally crawled into Victoria Station, an emissary from *Melody Maker* greeted her, then sent her on her way to Eastbourne.

The visit was primarily social, though she did appear on a BBC program called *World of Jazz* and was feted at a BBC Christmas party, publicity shots of which depicted Johnny Dankworth, under the mistletoe, planting a buss on the pianist. *New Musical Express* ran a gag picture of her playing a toy piano along with Lord and Lady Donegall playing harmonicas. (The Donegalls had come to hear her and Jimmy play at the Hi-Note in 1949 in Chicago.) In January, *Melody Maker* saluted Marian's success at the Hickory House with a front-page story.

When she returned to New York, Marian decided to pay a visit to the great Bud Powell, who had been in and out of mental hospitals since 1945, after being allegedly beaten over the head by police in Philadelphia. Powell was incarcerated at Creedmoor State Hospital on Long Island. Marian persuaded Bud to play the hospital's decrepit piano after she performed "A Nightingale Sang in Berkeley Square" at his request.

"In spite of the defective keys," Marian said, "he seemed to get wonderful tonality out of the piano and seemed to be able to play around the defective keys. As I left Bud turned to me and plaintively inquired, 'Marian, has everybody forgotten me? Do they still remember me?'"

Francis Paudras, the French graphic designer whose friendship with the troubled pianist was fictionalized in the film *'Round Midnight* (the saxophonist in the film is meant to be a composite of Powell and Lester Young), later described Marian as among the few musicians to reach out to Powell during this difficult period. She would later reach out to Mary Lou Williams, too, when Williams was in need. McPartland clearly regarded herself as a self-appointed ambassador for the health and welfare of the music and its practitioners. Her self-image reflected both humility and pride, for while she always took the high road, keeping her eye on the genius of other musicians, putting aside insults or injuries, she also set herself above the fray, projecting an almost regal sense of her status before she had actually earned it. It was a quality most people responded to well but to which a few took exception, finding it phony or self-serving.

When Powell was released from Creedmoor, McPartland invited him to sit in at the Hickory House so her friend Sherman Fairchild could hear him. Fairchild was a regular at the Hickory House and usually came in flanked by two beautiful girls. Marian would play one of his favorite tunes, "Lover," by Richard Rodgers. Years later, in 1955, Fairchild invited Bud to record at his home studio and Marian came along. It was a fascinating session, featuring two duets, on "Lullaby of Birdland" and the George Gershwin standard "Embraceable You." After a skittering, double-timing solo by Powell on "Lullaby," Marian edged the duo toward a classical pulse, which Powell fell in with easily. Though the result was a bit scattershot, the ending a bit of a jumble, it was a remarkable sound capture. Powell's dissonant, hymnlike solo version of "It Never Entered My Mind" was extraordinary, showing a kinship between Powell and Monk that was not always obvious at other times.

Over the years at the Hickory House, personnel in Marian's trio inevitably shifted. In 1953, bassist Bob Carter, who had played on Marian's record for Federal, replaced Max Wayne. In the spring, Marian discovered a new drummer who would have a profound effect on the trio and on her future—Joe Morello. Born of French and French Canadian parents in Springfield, Massachusetts, in 1928, Morello had taken up drums in high school, playing with local chums Phil Woods (alto saxophone) and Sal Salvador (guitar). After studying in Springfield with Joe Sefcik, Morello had gone to Boston for more lessons from George Lawrence Stone. Born with a severe visual handicap—he eventually became legally blind—Morello wore thick glasses and was a compulsive practicer who developed outsized technical skills as a young man. In the understated tradition of Dave Tough and Jo Jones, Morello played intricate, precise, subtle, and melodic figures, teasing out specific sounds from each drum and cymbal as if it were a special friend. He also introduced complex figures that played with the time while never losing where it was. His visual impairment led him early on to be a somewhat introverted yet also wickedly witty man. In 1952, Salvador encouraged Morello to join him in New York. When he arrived, Sal took him to hear Marian.

At first blush, Marian was singularly unimpressed by this young man with the crew cut and Coke-bottle glasses.

"He looked more like a chemist than a jazz musician to me," she said.

Feeling she must be polite, however, she invited him to sit in.

"I knew when I first sat in with her that time I felt like I should have been there," said Morello. "I felt very comfortable with her. I knew how she played and I knew how to deal with it, you know?"

McPartland felt the same way. After playing a couple of Monday nights at Birdland with Carter and Morello, she decided she simply must have the drummer for her trio.

"With a good drummer," she later wrote of Morello in a memoir, "you feel a lift that is both physical and psychological, as he anticipates every nuance of the music almost before it reaches your fingers. You find yourself trying things you were afraid to try, playing beyond your own capabilities, smiling at the end of the tune before the audience quite realizes what it has heard. Joe was that kind of drummer." Later, she wrote in *Down Beat,* "Within a matter of seconds everyone in the room realized that the guy with the diffident air was a phenomenal drummer. Everyone listened. His precise blending of touch, taste, and an almost unbelievable technique were a joy to listen to. He played with a loose, easy feeling interspersed with subtle flashes of humor reminiscent of the late Sid Catlett. Everyone knew that here was a discovery."

Morello hooked up nicely with Carter, too.

"They would play against the beat, setting up two or three different rhythms simultaneously, while I would just float in and around their rhythmic figures. It felt great!" said Marian.

Mousie was so intimidated by Morello, he asked Joe for lessons.

Joe said, "Aw, come on."

Wary of being accused of trying to steal Mousie's gig, Joe stopped coming around. But Mousie saw the writing on the wall. He made a plan to go with the Sauter-Finegan Orchestra. Meanwhile, Morello was hired for two weeks at Birdland by the great guitarist Johnny Smith, who then took the group into the Embers. There, Morello got a call from Salvador, telling him Stan Kenton's drummer needed to have an operation. Did he want to play with Stan?

"I said, 'Sure, I don't care,'" said Morello. "So ten minutes later the phone rings. 'This is Stan Kenton,' and I said, 'Yeah, I'm Benny Goodman.' I thought he was kidding. He said, 'This really is Stan Kenton.' He was working at Birdland and he said how about— I said, 'You've never heard me play. I'll come down to Birdland to sit in.' And he said, 'No, you don't have to, I've heard all about you. Shelly Manne told me about you.' I had never met Shelley. So I said, 'I think I'd like that.' Then the phone rings again. Now it's Marian McPartland. She said, 'I hear you're going with

Stan Kenton.' I said, 'Only for a month.' She said, 'Do you want to go with my group?' I said, 'Sure, I don't know, whatever.' So she starts saying, 'How about this? How about that?' Trying to talk about money. Then Jimmy gets on the phone with me. I said, 'I'll be through on Tuesday, with this month of work.' She said, 'That's great because I'll be through here and I'm going to Chicago.'"

Morello played his first job with Marian at the Blue Note in May, with Charlie Traeger on bass. Morello stayed with the trio for nearly three years, lighting a fire under her that markedly improved her playing. His musicianship also helped put her in the limelight, which soon shone brightly in the form of a write-up in *Time* magazine, September 21, 1953.

Describing Marian as "long, lean, and suntanned," the keenly observed review praised the pianist for her "larruping climaxes" and "distilled dissonances" in a set that came in three flavors: pensive and slow; breakneck and "quivering"; and concertized production numbers, including one on "Slaughter on Tenth Avenue." Her work, said *Time,* was "some of the cleanest, most inventive 'progressive jazz' to be heard anywhere."

Accompanied by a glamorous head shot, the article was followed by a rave record review in *The New York Times* by jazz critic John S. Wilson of the 10-inch LP *The Magnificent Marian McPartland at the Piano* (Savoy MG 15021). Her strongest work on record to date, the album was composed of six tracks from a 1952 session with Mousie and Max. The arrangements were outstanding, the trio swung—politely, to be sure, but swung nevertheless—and though there were still a few cocktail flourishes in it— broken chords, grace notes, turns, and the ubiquitous block chords Shearing had seemingly made de rigueur—Marian was starting to sound like a modern jazz pianist. Her arrangement of "Moonlight in Vermont" was especially hip, with a vamping bass figure that reached up for a dissonant D-natural against the key of D-flat, anticipating Marian's beautiful substitute chord change. She grabbed the old warhorse "Limehouse Blues" by the scruff of the neck and galloped with it, perfectly executing crisp, long lines with her right hand à la Bud Powell.

Even the cover art announced a new, hipper, Marian. Gone was the cocktail lounge sketch that had adorned the singles and EPs. Goldblatt's image now was more hard-edged, abstract—with white title letters printed on black bands, surrounded by nine beseeching blue hands—women's hands, with long fingernails—reaching toward the center, as if to say here was someone with a serious intent, reaching for something artistically fresh and important.

Time jumped on the album in May, praising "Limehouse Blues" as "fast and fantastic," "Hallelujah" "wild and gay," and "Moonlight in Vermont" "cool and wistful." In October, Wilson wrote in *The New York Times* that the now popular LP format had spawned a plethora of mediocre piano LPs, but that Marian's was worth singling out. Marian also began to be noticed in the annual poll conducted by *Down Beat* magazine, which in 1953 had added a critics poll to the one cast by readers. In a category called "Piano—New Star," the critics placed Marian second, behind Billy Taylor. Readers voted her thirteenth in the piano category, not exactly a coup, but a confirmation of her legitimacy in a massively competitive field. (The top six pianists were Oscar Peterson, Dave Brubeck, Bud Powell, George Shearing, Erroll Garner, and Art Tatum, in that order.) Perhaps even more significant, Marian's trio placed in the combo category (won by Peterson), a slot that the year before had acknowledged Barbara Carroll but had ignored McPartland. McPartland was gaining traction.

She was even mentioned in a new jazz history by critic Barry Ulanov published in 1952, in which she was singled out—along with Paul Smith, Johnny Guarnieri, Stan Freeman (of *Piano Playhouse*), and others—as part of a jazz/classical "school" spawned by Shearing. In October, Marian began a live broadcast from the Hickory House three times a week on radio station WOR.

This exposure, along with her well-reviewed albums on Federal and Savoy, allowed the trio to begin touring in places like Detroit, Cleveland, Boston, and, of course, her old standbys, Chicago and Columbus.

"That's where I really got started," she explained. "When I went out on the road, I already had a built-in audience."

The trio made the road trips in Marian's gray Hudson.

"It had a rack on top so we could all pack into it and get everybody in," she said. "We couldn't afford to fly in those days."

Taken all together—the touring, the polls, reviews in *Time* and *The New York Times,* the radio broadcasts, her record contract with Savoy, and a gig at the Hickory House that appeared secure for as long as she wanted it—Marian had accomplished precisely what she set out to do in New York: She had become recognized as a modern jazz pianist. A review of her album in the *Chicago Tribune* by Fred Reynolds summed it up nicely: "I won't go so far as to say that Mrs. MacPartland [*sic*] is magnificent," wrote Reynolds, "but she is a good modern jazz pianist." A fair assessment. The former Long Beach visitor who had been commuting with Jimmy to play Dixieland at the Stuyvesant Casino was now a glamorous fixture at one of Manhattan's central jazz spots. She was talked about by gossip columnists, at the vortex of the jazz scene, where she was meeting all the major players from Duke to Bud, and playing with one of the greatest new drummers in jazz. On the personal side, the musical break with Jimmy was working out. They were getting along, and his career was going well. The future looked bright, as it did for the great city of New York, as if it could only get better. And, for a while, it did.

All photos courtesy of Marian McPartland except where noted.

Janet and Frank Turner. Marian's mother, Janet Payne, and her father, Frank Turner, on their wedding day, September 6, 1913, in Windsor.

Marian and Joyce. Marian and her sister, Joyce, in 1924, two years after Joyce was born. Marian always felt her sister was "the pretty one."

Miss Hammond's School. Marian, fourth from right in the second row, in her 1926 class picture. Miss Hammond's School for Young Children was on Minster Road, near Sundridge Park. Marian fondly recalled being taken on nature walks by Miss Dorinda Hammond to Sundridge Park and Elmstead Woods.

Promotional head shot, London, 1939. After she got off the road with Billy Mayerl, Marian continued her show business career in England's vaudeville theaters, working concert parties and variety shows.

USO with Fred Astaire, Maastricht, Holland. 1944. Shortly after her arrival in Normandy, Marian's USO troupe was asked to perform with Fred Astaire, in Maastricht. Marian (fourth from left) is standing next to Colonel Black. Astaire is third from right.

Marian and Jimmy, Belgium, 1945. Marian met Jimmy McPartland in St. Vith, Belgium, in the fall of 1944, after he had fought in the battle of St. Lô. Jimmy transferred to special services so he could stop fighting and play music. He and Marian played in a band at the Hotel Schmitzroth in Eupen, Belgium, and were married in February 1945.

Marian and Jimmy riding bicycles in Cannes, 1945. Days after their honeymoon in Brussels, Marian and Jimmy were posted far away from each other, Jimmy to Czechoslovakia, Marian to Germany. They rendezvoused whenever and wherever they could, hitching rides on military planes. One weekend, they met Cannes.

Marian accompanying Celeste Holm, 1945. After mustering out of the army in the fall of 1945, Jimmy went to work for the USO and hired Marian to play in a seven-piece band that accompanied Broadway actress Celeste Holm. Holm had just had her first big hit as Ado Annie, in *Oklahoma!* On the USO tour, she sang "I Cain't Say No" and "Eunice from Tunis." *(Photo courtesy of Celeste Holm)*

Jimmy McPartland, 1946. When Jimmy came back from World War Two, he found himself still a celebrity in Chicago, where he was revered as one of the founding members of the school of "Chicago jazz."

Jam session at the Lanigans, Chicago, circa 1948. Weekend jam sessions were a regular feature of McPartland family life. "On Sunday afternoons they'd invite musician friends and we'd bring a covered dish," remembered Jim Lanigan's daughter, Diane. "Ethel would make a roast. They'd play until about 5:30 or 6, then Mom would serve the food." Left to right: Jim Lanigan (bass), Dick Lanigan (holding microphone), Jim Lanigan Jr. (bass clarinet), Floyd Town (tenor saxophone), Jimmy McPartland (cornet), Dick McPartland (guitar), Marian McPartland (piano). Audience: Ethel Lanigan (standing in doorway), John Lanigan (hands on face).

Marian and Jimmy with Oscar Peterson in Toronto, February 1951. During the 1940s and early 1950s, Marian and Jimmy often played the Colonial Tavern, in Toronto, where they had a strong following. At one point they shared the bill—and apparently the piano itself—with new Canadian star Oscar Peterson, pictured here with bassist Ray Brown.

Jimmy and Marian at 341 West Eighty-eighth Street, Manhattan. The sleek minimalist furniture in their Upper West Side apartment places it unmistakably in the early 1950s and the Christmas tree and cards on the table indicate this was the holiday season. This was their first apartment in Manhattan. *(Photo courtesy of Robert Parent)*

Marian and Joe Morello at the Hickory House, circa 1956. Marian and Joe first fell in love with each other's music; the rest seemed to follow naturally. Not everyone knew what was going on, but as singer Helen Merrill put it, "You could see the rays coming out of her eyes." *(Photo by William "PoPsie" Randolph)*

Marian and Art Tatum, Cleveland, 1956. While Marian and Jimmy were playing the Theatrical Lounge, in Cleveland, they were invited to an after-hours speakeasy, where Art Tatum was playing. Marian was struck by how attentive the audience was, as opposed to the noisy crowds at the Embers, in New York.

Marian and Duke Ellington, Hickory House, 1950s. Duke Ellington was a huge influence on Marian's approach to the piano. He came by the Hickory House to eat often, as the club's publicist, Joe Morgen, worked for Duke, as well. Duke liked to flirt. "He had so much sex appeal it was almost frightening," said Marian.

Marian with Benny Goodman on *The Tonight Show with Johnny Carson*, 1963. Goodman had a reputation for being difficult to work for, but Marian, intrepid as always, said yes when he invited her to go on the road. They kicked off their tour in New York, then went south, just in time for the Dallas assassination of President Kennedy. It was an awful experience. Benny and Marian clashed so badly Marian often joked that Goodman drove her into therapy.

Marian playing with Jimmy (cornet) and Joe (drums), 1956. Marian often found herself playing—even recording, as she is here—with both her husband and her lover at the same time. "I enjoyed the playing and turned off my feelings as much as possible," she said.

Marian's trio at Strollers Theatre Club, 1964. When British political satire became all the rage in America, The Establishment crossed the Atlantic to play in New York. Marian's trio, with Eddie Gomez (bass) and Dottie Dodgion (drums), played incidental music for the revue, then retired to the lounge for sets of jazz.

Marian and Alec Wilder, Rochester, circa 1977. Marian's friend and mentor Alec Wilder was a child at heart. Their mutual friend Lou Ouzer captured this quality nicely in his photograph of Alec and Marian in front of Ouzer's shop in Rochester, New York. *(Photo courtesy of Lou Ouzer)*

Marian and Mary Lou Williams, *Piano Jazz,* **1978.** "I should have this show," Mary Lou Williams tartly told Marian's producer, Dick Phipps, when she taped the very first episode of *Piano Jazz*. Despite Mary Lou's decidedly unfriendly mood, Marian managed to pull off a fascinating interview with her hero. *(Courtesy of South Carolina Educational Television [SCETV])*

7.

New York's Golden Age of Jazz, Part I
(1953~1956)

TALK OF "GOLDEN AGES" often has the unintended consequence of
diminishing the present in favor of the past, implying that paradise, alas,
has been lost. But with the caveat that no such implication is intended, it
must be said that when Marian McPartland played at the Hickory House
in New York, jazz was enjoying a golden age. Between 1953 and 1966,
artists such as Miles Davis, John Coltrane, Sonny Rollins, Thelonious
Monk, Dave Brubeck, Charles Mingus, and Ornette Coleman, among
others, produced some of the best work in the history of the music—
nearly all of it in one city, New York, in one loosely configured community. Clubs proliferated. In midtown, there were Birdland, Basin Street,
Jimmy Ryan's, the Embers, the Hickory House, the Composer, the Royal
Roost, Child's Paramount, and the Metropole. In Greenwich Village, you
had Condon's, Café Bohemia, Café Society, the Five Spot, the Half Note,
and the Central Plaza. Beyond New York, the music rumbled into living
rooms on TV sound tracks—notably for *Peter Gunn*, the 1958 detective
show with Henry Mancini's wailing saxophone theme—and in mainstream motion pictures a few years later with Quincy Jones's sound track
to *The Pawnbroker*. Resident jazz bands played on late night talk shows—
indeed, *Tonight Show* host Steve Allen was himself a jazz pianist—and jazz
musicians, including Monk, Dizzy Gillespie, and Marian herself, were
regular guests. Louis Armstrong appeared on *The Ed Sullivan show* and was
interviewed by Edward R. Murrow on *Person to Person*. Monk, Dave Brubeck, and Duke Ellington appeared on the cover of *Time* magazine. Broadway sparkled with jazz influences, particularly in Leonard Bernstein's score
for *West Side Story,* and Bernstein himself went on TV to explain how jazz
was an American treasure. Unlike today, at that time musicians playing
jazz could make a decent living. Though never as lucrative as rock 'n' roll,
jazz was still as commercial, in the best sense of the word, as it had been in
the swing era. Jazz festivals, first in Newport and then in Monterey, California, offered a wholesome, outdoor atmosphere where families could
hear the music. Histories and encyclopedias of jazz were published—and

read. Leonard Feather and Ralph Gleason syndicated jazz columns in daily newspapers across the country. The Institute of Jazz Studies was founded. University music departments—slowly, to be sure—began to allow jazz into their hallowed halls.

"Respectability has indeed come to the unique art form called jazz," wrote Robert Fulford in Canada's *Mayfair* magazine in 1956, with a picture of Marian illustrating the phenomenon. "In the last five years jazz has been lifted out of its guttersnipe existence as a poor relation of concert music to a dazzling new position as the gleaming Cinderella of the arts."

Who can say why an art form flowers? But the social context, in addition to the great confluence of talent in this period, clearly helped. The civil rights movement, for one, created a lens through which the public, both black and white, could understand jazz as an expression of the black struggle for freedom. As the doors to political and economic power slowly opened for African Americans, jazz offered an appropriate new image of black men, magnified on jazz album covers, as thoughtful fellows brooding over their art, wearing long wool overcoats and fedoras, a far cry from the servile stereotypes of black minstrels of the past. The cold war helped, too. In the ideological battle against communism, America's Achilles' heel was its slaveholding past and Jim Crow present. To counter this image, the State Department sent jazz musicians abroad, black and white, including Armstrong, Gillespie, Jones, and Brubeck. This period also witnessed a youthful revolt against American conformity and materialism by a generation who—like Jimmy's in the 1920s—saw, rightly or wrong, something rebellious, free, and idealistic in African American music. If you had a few jazz albums on your shelf in 1955 and were going to college—where Brubeck had introduced the music—likely you were liberal, aspired to be slightly bohemian, and welcomed not only racial integration, but the liberation of African colonies from their European masters. This mainstreaming of liberal politics and cultural "cool," once the private domain of a tiny minority, allowed jazz to symbolize a new zeitgeist that would eventually flower in the 1960s—though jazz, sadly, would be eclipsed by the populist fervor for rock later in that decade. While Marian did not play a generative artistic role in the golden era of jazz, she was at center stage, playing, recording, touring, and, as ever, alert to the music around her, its constant public champion. When, in 1958, *Esquire* magazine serendipitously commissioned photographer Art Kane to take a group photo of everyone he could find working on the New York scene, McPartland was there, standing next to Mary Lou Williams, one of only three women in the picture. (The third was Maxine Sullivan.) It became an icon of the era.

One of the highlights of the period for Marian was playing and record-ing with Joe Morello. The drummer brought a lift to her trio and jetted some much-needed air between the instruments. He treated the drums not as a mere rhythm machine—though he certainly swung—but as a delicate and intricate musical system. He was exact, but never clinical. Obsessed with technique, he worked at it constantly.

"I remember once I was driving to the Hickory House," Marian said. "Suddenly, a cab went by at a furious rate. Joe was in it—practicing like mad on a practice pad in the cab. I broke up. It just looked so funny."

With Morello, less was more. He often used brushes instead of sticks. (Dave Garroway said the sound of Morello's brushes against a cymbal was like the touch of a "butterfly's wing.") If Marian had had a tendency to overplay before—hammering away at chunky block chords and decora-tive lines—Morello (and, later, bassist Bill Crow) weaned her from this fulsome style. Slowly, she abandoned the "hot" eagerness of Chicago for something more laid-back and "cool."

McPartland still found hiring and firing musicians uncomfortable. When she had wanted Morello, rather than cutting Mousie loose, she had waited for him to leave on his own accord. Sometime in the summer of 1953, she began to feel the need to rid herself of Bob Carter. Though his playing was "fabulous," she said, he was "really wild, drunk, and disor-derly." Marian eventually plucked herself up and replaced Carter with Vinnie Burke, a Newark-bred musician who had switched to bass (from violin and guitar) after losing a finger in a wartime factory accident. Though he had a good résumé (Joe Mooney, Sauter-Finegan Orchestra), Burke turned out to be even more unpleasant than Carter.

When Burke came in for his first rehearsal, Marian kicked off a medley she'd worked out from the popular Richard Rodgers/George Balanchine ballet, *Slaughter on Tenth Avenue*.

"I thought this was a jazz gig," Burke said sullenly.

"He was a jerk," said McPartland. "[At the club], Vinnie would stop playing, glare at somebody in the audience who wasn't paying attention, and shout, 'What's the matter? Don't you like the music?' Back would come the reply: 'Why don'tcha smile?'"

While Carter and then Burke were with the trio, Marian made her last recordings for Savoy, two 10-inch LPs, *Moods* (Savoy 15022) and *Jazz at the Hickory House* (Savoy 15032). The former featured Marian's first recording of what would become a standard ballad in her repertoire, "Willow Weep for Me." Ann Ronell, the composer, was a regular at the Hickory House. Though McPartland gave it a slinky, mysterious treatment, she would later play it as a blues. For the latter album, McPartland asked Herman Lubinsky if she could record live at the Hickory House. The studio environment, she said, made her tense and inhibited. Savoy agreed. In 1953, on-location recording was not as common as it is today, but McPartland pulled a lucky card when the company hired one of the great jazz engineers of all time, Rudy Van Gelder. The resulting album featured six tracks recorded at the club. Its black-and-white cover, designed by Bob Parent, conjured an urban, after-hours mood, with a photo of Marian playing the keyboard superimposed over a silhouette wash of the Hickory House awning and marquee. For the first time, Marian wrote her own liner notes, striking a genteel, personal tone that would become another trademark, as if she were inviting fans into her living room for a private concert.

Morello's brushes buoyed the clean, lyrical lines of Marian's fine solo on the opening track, "A Foggy Day," and the two traded crisp exchanges— Joe with sticks—on an up-tempo "The Lady Is a Tramp," with Morello's witty cross-rhythms a highlight. On "Manhattan," an audience request, she essayed a new, Basie-like simplicity, milking the tune for its sweet nostalgia. But on the rest of the tracks, the old, busy Marian snuck in. "Four Brothers," the classic Jimmy Giuffre line, taken at a brisk tempo, felt stiff and jumpy. That jumpiness—almost a hopping quality—also crept into her otherwise fine solo on "The Lady Is a Tramp." Though she played with enviable "enthusiasm, optimism and mischief," as one observer would later write, Marian was still not yet as cool and laid-back as she wanted to be.

Critics liked the album, though, particularly for the novelty of the live setting.

"It's so realistic," wrote Hy Gardner of the *Herald Tribune,* "by the time you finish listening to the recording you expect to have a waiter hand you a check."

In December 1953, much to Marian's relief, Vinnie Burke gave notice and Marian at last found the perfect third corner for her musical triangle— Bill Crow. Originally from a suburb of Seattle, Crow had come up playing valve trombone in the late 1940s on the local after-hours scene along Jackson Street, where Ray Charles and Quincy Jones had cut their teeth, as well. Crow moved to New York in January 1950 with the great northwest drummer Buzzy Bridgeford, who convinced Crow to switch to bass on a gig in upstate New York. After migrating to Manhattan later that year, Crow was hired by Stan Getz, with whom he recorded in 1952.

Crow was a careful observer of the scene, made manifest later in two books, a beloved collection of musicians' stories called *Jazz Anecdotes* and a more conventional autobiography. Crow was by his own admission still learning his craft back in the 1950s, having just taught himself the proper left-hand positions on the bass by trial and error, while working with Claude Thornhill. This did not stop Crow from being opinionated.

"I was full of youthful hubris," said the bassist. "The Basie rhythm section had the feeling that I approved of."

Crow and Morello both found Marian's sense of swing slippery. Crow took particular exception to the way she articulated the Lester Young tune "Tickle Toe."

"I had trouble getting her to phrase that whole line in the way I was used to hearing Lester Young play it in the Basie band," said Crow. "And it took her a while. She wanted to play it in little four-note groups instead of one long thing."

"It wasn't really swinging jazz," recalled Morello of Marian's style at the time. "She was over from England and she had her own way of playing. She still does."

Marian sometimes found Crow somewhat intimidating, he was so sure of himself.

(Crow later told a Canadian magazine he didn't think Marian's swing feel was so hot, which stuck in her craw. Forty years later, in a radio profile, she tartly asked interviewer Nancy Wilson to ask Crow if her time hadn't improved!)

Fortunately, McPartland, in spite of her hurt feelings, was a perennial student, always receptive to suggestions, even from sidemen. She was— and remained—a highly collaborative leader.

"She was always looking for more knowledge," said Crow.

Much of the repertoire from Tin Pan Alley and Broadway is written in the flat keys—F, B-flat, E-flat, A-flat, and so forth. Marian, by contrast, loved to play songs in bright, sharp keys like E, B, and F-sharp, which are often difficult. As Crow was learning the cross-fingerings on the bass, these keys posed a challenge, but, like Marian, he learned on the bandstand. Crow said Marian was as easy with the business side of the trio as she was with the music. She paid generously and at one point fronted Crow $150 toward a new French bass, which he still plays to this day. She was an easygoing leader.

"[Joe] would always have these terrible excuses," remembered Marian. "I remember this one time he showed up late and said, 'The train blew up.' The humor was the excuse. Anytime Joe was late after that, we would always say, 'The train must have blown up.'"

Practical jokes—a fad in the 1950s—were a regular part of the McPartland band's vocabulary. Crow found a fake faucet with a rubber suction cup in a joke shop and attached it to the piano. It remained there for months. He also bought a stuffed animal called a "Pluto dog" and planted it on the post supporting the lid of the grand piano. After intermission, Crow found it on the scroll of his bass. The dog made the rounds, turning up in all sorts of places.

During their half-hour breaks, the musicians enjoyed slipping over to Birdland to hear whoever was playing. If they came back late, they would inevitably discover that the intermission pianist, Ellie Eden, had played her half hour to the minute, refusing to cover for them, leaving the club silent. Owner John Popkin would give them "the fish-eye" as they slunk back in. With John Mehegan, who succeeded Eden, they had the opposite problem. Mehegan would get so wrapped up in what he was playing that he would lose track of time, leaving the trio little room for its last set. Mehegan headed the jazz department at the Metropolitan Music School and was something of a stuffed shirt. Fed up, Crow at one point bought an alarm clock at the corner drugstore, the old-fashioned kind with two large bells on top. He hid the clock under the music of the piano and set it to ring in half an hour. When it did, Mehegan's face filled with "absolute panic," said Crow. Like many jazz pianists, Mehegan kept time by stomping his right foot. Crow had a little airline pillow in his bass case. One night he slid the pillow under Mehegan's foot while it was in the air.

"When his foot came down silently, John was so disoriented he stopped playing altogether," Crow said.

Morello was something of a card himself. When Marian sat down at the piano, she could see him behind her in a long mirror placed on a pillar. He would sometimes comically accompany her movements by cranking the ratchet he also used to torture the headwaiter, Julius. At the end of a tune, when Marian and Crow would trade four-bar solos back and forth with the drummer, Morello's "solo" would occasionally consist of simply dropping his brushes on the floor and picking them up again. Other times, he would play a figure that appeared to transpose the first beat of the measure to the second, which totally confused Marian, who would start accenting the first and third beats instead of the second and fourth, a gaffe jazz musicians refer to as "turning the time around." Eventually this gambit became a standing joke, which the trio referred to as "the chicken."

Because of Morello, the Hickory House became a mecca for young drummers. When Marian noticed Joe's fans in the house, she would give him extra room to blow. Popkin would leap up, rush to the bar, and shout, "Stop that banging!" Morello didn't take well to hero worship. He got so tired of people comparing him to great drummers like Buddy Rich and

Max Roach that he invented an imaginary drummer, Marvin Bonessa, whom he said with deadpan seriousness was "better than all of them." Joe added that, like the legendary Texas pianist Peck Kelly, Bonessa rarely played out, so it was impossible to ever really hear him. Marian and Joe went along with the ruse, nodding solemnly whenever Bonessa's name came up. Crow claimed Bonessa eventually got a few votes in a *Down Beat* poll, so far did his reputation spread.

The bandstand at the Hickory House was surrounded by liquor, so when Marian came down from the piano, she sometimes helped herself to a shot of Scotch, "not because I wanted it, but just because I could." Popkin usually let it slide, but if he'd had a bad day with the horses, he was less sanguine.

"We would go in the kitchen and get coffee and he would tell us, 'Get out of here! I can't keep you in coffee!' " said Marian.

McPartland did her share of drinking in those days, especially when customers insisted on buying her cocktails. From time to time, after she'd had a few too many, she'd ask Crow, "Did I do anything bad last night?" "No," he replied one night, "but you played all ballads, and when you played 'Polkadots' you couldn't end it. In fact, you never *did* end it. We just stopped."

One night Marian's uncle Cyril (Sir Cyril, now, since his 1953 knighthood) made an appearance with his wife, Sylvia. They had been attending a conference of mayors in Windsor's namesake city in Ontario, Canada. As he looked up at his niece on the elevated stage, surrounded by whiskey bottles, his eyes popped out.

"Does your father know what you're doing?" he asked.

The Hickory House did great business, but sometimes only a handful of people would be left in the club at two A.M. To amuse themselves in the wee hours, the trio once played an entire tune lying down. On other dull, late nights, they distracted themselves by pretending they were playing for an imaginary circus, complete with balancing acts and clowns.

"The waiters thought we were crazy and would look at us in bewilderment, wondering why we seemed to be killing ourselves laughing," Marian said.

Norton Wright, the Yale undergrad so smitten with Marian's good looks, fondly remembered late nights at the club.

"At about one A.M. Julius would lock up the revolving door and look at us severely to get us to leave," he said. "Then Tony Scott would knock. Then there'd be another knock. Jackie Paris. Then Sal Salvador, Kenton's guitarist. Pretty soon, there'd be an impromptu jam session taking place, and Julius wasn't licensed for that. Then maybe one thirty or one forty-five Jimmy would have finished up at the Metropole and he'd tap on the door and he'd bring his tenor sax man up, Bud Freeman, and they'd come in and we'd have some Dixieland licks. This would go on till six o'clock in the morning. We were about twenty years old, and to be surrounded by these jazz greats, it was just dynamite."

Popkin viewed most musicians with suspicion. His main aim was to sell steaks, a preference revealed by the fact that the meat refrigerator had better lighting than the stage. ("Why don't you shine some light on the other meat?" Marian quipped.) Crow eventually took matters into his own hands: He went to a theatrical shop and bought some miniature spotlights, which he mounted above the bandstand. Using a switch box he found on Canal Street, he rigged the lights so he could control them with his foot, moving the beam from player to player when they traded fours. (As he became more adept at this, he sometimes purposely trained the spots on the wrong player.) He could bathe all three in soft light and also make a blackout on the last note of the tune, then bring the lights back up for applause. On ballads, he used a fourth pin spot to highlight Marian.

The crowds kept coming in, month after month. Marian, ever charming, built a loyal following, including show business celebrities. Steve Allen, who was courting Jayne Meadows, would sit in a booth at the back, sipping martinis. Sometimes Allen would sit in. Rosemary Clooney, who thanks to her smash hit "Come On-a My House" had graced the cover of *Time* in February 1953, dropped by in December of that year with her fiancé, actor José Ferrer. The great dance team Marge and Gower Champion, who had recently choreographed *Make a Wish,* were so impressed they sent a telegram to Marian and Jimmy saying how much they loved the show.

Earlier that year, Henry Fonda opened on Broadway in *The Caine Mutiny.* Fonda became a fan, and Marian returned the favor, going to see the play. British ambassador Sir David Ormsby-Gore brought Jacqueline Kennedy by one night; Commander Edward Whitehead dropped in, too, and asked to use her arrangement of "Greensleeves" for his Schweppes television program because it "sounded so cool and refreshing." Jazz royalty, past and future, fell by the Hickory House. Ben Webster, former tenor saxophonist with Duke, asked to sit in and stayed on the bandstand for half an hour; a week or two later, he came back for more. When avant-garde pianist Paul Bley sat in, Marian was mystified that he strayed from key to key—on the same B-flat blues—yet never lost his sense of the form. Other guests included Oscar Peterson, Benny Goodman, Artie Shaw, Bucky Pizzarelli, Oscar Pettiford (who sat in often in 1955, sometimes on cello),

Barbara Carroll (popping over from the Embers), Cy Coleman (playing up the street at the Mermaid Room), Kenny Clarke, Wilbur Ware, and the harmonically brilliant pianist Steve Kuhn, who came when he was only fifteen years old. Steve had just played on *The Tonight Show* for Steve Allen, and his father, Carl, asked Marian if his son could sit in.

"I just played a couple of tunes," said Steve. "But every time I came to New York after that she let me sit in, sometimes for a whole set."

The New York jazz press continued to embrace McPartland. In April, 1954, writing in *Down Beat,* Nat Hentoff perceptively praised her for refusing to "abandon the left hand in laconic chords," à la Bud Powell, instead creating "flowing counterlines" with her left hand. He singled out "strength" as the keynote of her style, describing her as a "girl . . . with the heart of a stomper."

This assessment accurately placed Marian in the two-handed piano tradition of Duke Ellington, Art Tatum, Earl Hines, and their stride predecessors and set her apart from the more widely imitated Powell, who improvised long, sinuous Charlie Parker–like lines with his right hand, while his left blipped and blopped out chords. Like Tatum, McPartland wanted to ring out sound from the whole keyboard. In this she was something of a stubborn holdout.

While Marian was busy getting famous at the Hickory House, Jimmy often played a few blocks away at the Metropole, on Seventh Avenue above Forty-eighth Street. The Metropole "stage" was a long, shallow ledge above the bar where the musicians—at one point the entire Woody Herman band—stood side by side, as if they were in a police lineup. The place was so popular—there was no cover and no minimum—that the beer-happy crowd often spilled out to the sidewalk, where patrons would congregate, listening to "When the Saints Go Marching In" and "St. James Infirmary" blaring out the doors and windows. One spring, on Marian's birthday, Jimmy surprised her by filing through the revolving door of the Hickory House with the whole band from the Metropole behind him.

"They marched around the bar, serenading me with a wild version of 'Happy Birthday' and then marched out again, playing their way down Seventh Avenue. That was the kind of thing I loved about Jimmy. He was full of surprises, and often they were wonderful."

Though not making as much money as Marian—he was paying Pee Wee Russell and George Wettling $80 each, so as leader he must have been making around $100 to $150 a night—Jimmy was working steadily. He had recently released the best album of his career and appeared in a documentary film that would come to be regarded as a classic. The album, conceived and produced by Bob Thiele and called *Shades of Bix* (Brunswick BL 58049), was an homage to Jimmy's lifelong inspiration and featured eight tunes associated with the great Davenport cornetist. Jimmy played with warmth and confidence, emitting pearly lines in a rich, burnished tone, managing to sound rough-and-tumble and tender all at once. His legato delivery on "I'm Coming, Virginia," with a languid, three-against-two "puh-puh-puh" at the finish of his solo, was pure Bix—and pure Jimmy, too. Jimmy's solo on "Singin' the Blues" was, intentionally, pretty nearly Bix's note for note, one of the few times Jimmy "copied" Beiderbecke for effect. *Down Beat* awarded the album four stars, and it made *Metronome*'s Records of the Year, along with discs by modernists Chet Baker, Lee Konitz, Ben Webster, and Dave Brubeck.

Hard on the heels of these notices, Roger Tilton, a thirty-year-old film history teacher at Columbia University, took a crew and sound equipment down to the Central Plaza, where Jimmy was leading an all-star band with Russell and the cigar-chewing Willie "the Lion" Smith. In three hours, on a budget of $10,000, Tilton shot a vivid documentary at this exuberant Dixieland palace. With its shadowy ambience, emotional immediacy, and rhythmic editing, this black-and-white short became a legendary early example of cinema verité. Rubber-legged Lindy Hop champion Leon James appeared in the film with another Savoy Ballroom legend, Will Minns. The camera moved from candid shot to candid shot: a girl in sweater and wool skirt, taking a drag on a cigarette; shoes with ballet laces; a close-up of drummer George Wettling smiling; the Lion wiping off the piano bench. Though this was hot music, there was something cool and bohemian about the scene, as patrons solemnly quaffed beers, danced, or stared into the existential middle distance. The film climaxed with the Lion shouting, "Oh, when the saints," and the crowd answering back, "Go marching in!" as dancers mounted the chairs and the Lindy Hoppers led the band in a snaking parade through the crowd. *Jazz Dance* was received with wild approval, playing at the Paris, the wonderful little movie house by the Plaza Hotel. Bosley Crowther of *The New York Times* called the film a "beautifully photographed report on the atmosphere and personalities in a genuine shrine of jazz."

With Jimmy playing so well and Marian securely ensconced at the Hickory House, the couple's experiment to part ways musically but keep the home fires burning seemed to be working out.

"We were both working, making money, and Jimmy was proud of me," Marian told Irving Townsend. "Perhaps this was the proper mixture of dependence and independence at last. We could hold hands without clinging. We could enjoy our separate successes in mutual ways. The Hickory House could be just the therapy our marriage needed."

Marian was particularly gratified they could go home together every night, since this was her insurance Jimmy would stay sober. Once they got home, they divided domestic duties in a quite progressive way. Marian did all the bookkeeping, business, and "secretarial work"; Jimmy cooked. They were a thoroughly modern couple, defining a dual-career marriage in their own way. Yet traditional values tugged. Marian felt guilty for leaving Jimmy's band and feared—with some justification—it would lead to her reputation eclipsing his and to their growing apart. She wanted fame and acclaim, but not at Jimmy's expense. It felt unseemly, particularly in light of all the doors he had opened for her. It was a delicate dance.

The press delighted in celebrating the royal couple. In its twentieth anniversary issue, *Down Beat* ran biographies of both Marian and Jimmy, and *Metronome* offered a two-part series about their lives. But in the midst of all this acclaim, the inevitable happened. Eddie Condon invited Jimmy over to Fort Monmouth, New Jersey, where he often hosted trad jazz sessions, and for several days, Jimmy simply disappeared.

"That was sort of a shocker," Marian said. "It did more damage to our fragile new relationship than either of us realized then."

Jimmy eventually came home and there were the usual remonstrances, apologies, and AA meetings. Marian talked to Jimmy's sponsor, who told her she needed to get on with her own life and not worry about Jimmy. But Marian's impulse to take care of Jimmy was as strong as—perhaps stronger than—her will to take care of herself. When she made bookings out of town, she tried to arrange for jobs where Jimmy could play, to make sure he'd stay off the booze. He went along with it, but their marriage suffered. "This was," she later reflected, "when the rot set in a little bit."

Having done so well in the United States, Marian and Jimmy decided to see if they could gain some traction in the United Kingdom. In the summer of 1954, the couple went to England for ten weeks. Jimmy was invited to play on the BBC programs *World of Jazz* and *British Jazz* but developed a fever blister on his lip. Unable to play, he gave an impromptu lecture about Bix, with Marian playing a tune or two. Invited to perform with Ronnie Scott and Georgia Gibbs at the Royal Albert Hall, Jimmy was told by the Department of Labour that, as a visiting American, he would be allowed to appear only as an emcee. Marian, forced to renew her membership in the British musicians union, could generate little interest for bookings.

Despite being strongly championed by the British jazz press, Marian never developed a substantial audience in England. Jimmy, by contrast, was fussed over obsessively by the small but loyal trad crowd. This disparity in popularity may simply have been a matter of audiences' preference for the exotic. In Britain, Jimmy was an appealing American type, a brash Chicago innovator who had palled around with Louis Armstrong and Bix Beiderbecke. By contrast, Marian, with her English accent and Mayfair manners, may have been exotic to Americans, but certainly not to her fellow countrymen. If anything, her style was perhaps a little too familiar. Ironically, the kind of prejudice Leonard Feather had accused the French of having back in 1951—that only American males (preferably black) could play jazz with "authenticity"—may have been at work among English fans, too. Europeans typically overvalued Americans and undervalued their own players. How could an Englishwoman really play jazz?

When the McPartlands returned to New York in the fall of 1954 to resume their respective posts at the Metropole and the Hickory House, *Billboard* reported a "boom" in jazz record sales and jazz-only deejays began to make inroads at mainstream stations. The city was abuzz with news of a wildly popular new star, Dave Brubeck. The California pianist's album *Brubeck Plays Brubeck* was a big hit on college campuses and had made his cool, progressive jazz all the rage. The eager, experimentally minded pianist was playing at Basin Street, around the corner from the Hickory House. Marian and Joe wandered over to check him out and were duly impressed.

Brubeck and Miles Davis recorded for Columbia, but Capitol Records had started reaching out to more jazz artists as well. Started by songwriter Johnny Mercer in 1942 and specializing in sophisticated vocalists (Nat Cole, Frank Sinatra, Peggy Lee) and cast recordings of Broadway musicals (*The King and I, Carousel, Oklahoma!*), Capitol had approached Marian before the trip to England, signing her to a five-record deal. Moving from Savoy to Capitol was a huge step. A young, aggressive company with a fresh approach to album design and production, the label had considerable revenue from number one chart hits—and its absorption of the English label EMI—that eventually would allow it to establish a foothold in Los Angeles, where in 1956 it constructed its famous disc-shaped Hollywood tower.

Marian's first two albums for Capitol, though tasteful and remarkably well received, both featured harp and cello, carrying forth her image as the genteel, "classical jazz lady." That said, she and Morello and Crow played some solid, swinging trio jazz on the first one, a 12-inch LP titled *Marian McPartland at the Hickory House* (Capitol T574). Crow clearly had made his point about articulating "Tickle Toe." Critics, possibly dazzled that McPartland had signed with a major label, hailed her as a new star. *Metronome* was so enamored of the recording that it named her trio Small Group of the Year. George T. Simon, who had made his reputation as a chronicler of the big bands, wrote a glowing feature, noting that the year 1954, with the rise of Brubeck and Marian, had been "a pianist's year." He ended his review with an astonishing hyperbole, calling Marian's trio "one of the most attractive organizations in the history of jazz." *Down Beat,* which hailed Morello as the year's new star on drums (presenting him with the award on Steve Allen's TV show), gave the album four stars but noted tartly of the four tracks with cello and harp: "Too much sugar."

It's tempting to speculate that strings were thrust on McPartland by a producer, but, to the contrary, she seems to have embraced the concept enthusiastically. She even discovered the harpist Ruth Negri herself. Negri, principal harpist for the New York City Ballet, was Marian's landlady on the Upper West Side.

"I heard her practicing," said Marian, "so I asked her to be on the album."

Always savvy with business, McPartland later told Hentoff she wanted to use the cello and harp "as a wedge to get into places that aren't usually receptive to jazz," possibly an allusion to the college market so lucrative for Brubeck. It's telling, however, that reissues of the album (by other labels) later uniformly drew negative comments about the strings and that Capitol never issued the material on CD.

Capitol spent money that year advertising its jazz list in *Billboard,* which included Stan Kenton and Lennie Tristano among others, but the sales charts showed little return for their money. Django Reinhardt and Jonah Jones were selling records, and so were Erroll Garner and Dizzy Gillespie. But not Marian McPartland. For the second album, released in 1956 as the 12-inch LP *After Dark: The Marian McPartland Trio with Strings* (Capitol T699), the company nevertheless held to the same strategy, with the strings appearing on eight out of twelve tracks this time. The overall effect was upscale cocktail music—or "mood music," as it was called then (Capitol was doing a land-office business with the dreamy albums of Jackie Gleason)— though not many pianists were playing Billy Strayhorn's complex ballad "Chelsea Bridge." One of the best tracks was "Easy Come, Easy Go," which showcased her knack for drawing pathos from a ballad, as did her moving version of Alec Wilder's "I'll Be Around," which would become a standard in her repertoire. Marian's sympathy for ballads seemed to arise magically from some quiet, interior place one can't help but associate with her solitary childhood, listening to the radio, practicing, and staring into the Silent Pool in Surrey. *Billboard* liked the album a lot, praising it as "classy" and "elegant."

While she was recording her first Capitol album, in November 1954, Doug Watt, a writer for *The New Yorker,* reviewed the Hickory House trio, praising her for her "cheerful composure," "sunny personality," and "rare good taste." Watt was so enchanted he stayed through the third set, noting Marian slipped the melody of *Rhapsody in Blue* into her version of "How High the Moon" and ended it with "a suggestion" of "Clair de Lune." She also played a chorus in the manner of Scarlatti. "All in all," he said, "a wonderful recital." Recital indeed. Clearly the jazz lady with classical leanings—or was it the classical lady with jazz leanings?—was still part and parcel of Marian's image.

With McPartland hailed as a new star by *Metronome* and Morello touted by *Down Beat* as the best new drummer in jazz, Marian's trio was too hot not to tour. Through the spring, summer, and fall of 1955, McPartland played extended engagements in the Midwest and along the eastern seaboard and appeared on Steve Allen's *Tonight Show* on October 15 (and again the following year, on January 20). In July 1955, Marian and Jimmy played the Newport Jazz Festival, the outdoor extravaganza Boston promoter George Wein had spearheaded the year before, with the help of Newport, Rhode Island, resident Elaine Lorillard. (Marian and Jimmy hadn't played the inaugural spree; they were visiting England at the time.) Newport's second edition offered a stellar lineup, including Brubeck, who was highly impressed when Morello sat in with him. Marian and Jimmy were billed as "a marriage of modern and traditional, both literally and musically."

It was during this period that Marian's relationship with Morello began to change dramatically. Before Joe had met Marian, he had been living in New Jersey, playing at a dance hall in Seaside Heights, and dating Ellie Schneider, whom he had met on the beach. Joe and Ellie married in 1954, shortly after he joined Marian's trio. When he started playing at the Hickory House, if Joe missed his bus back to Jersey, Marian occasionally would ride in a cab with him to Penn Station and hang out with him until train time. Sometimes she even drove him home. They soon found themselves spending quite a bit of time together, taking walks in Central Park or having drinks at the nearby musicians hangout Charlie's Tavern. She had always found him attractive, particularly his deadpan wit and quirky irreverence.

She enjoyed his unusual compliments.

"He said I was like Carole Lombard. I was not in the least like Carole Lombard."

At some point things boiled over—Marian thought it may have been during a gig in Rochester in February 1956—and Marian found herself hopelessly in love with her drummer. What had been a mere flirtation turned into a full-blown affair.

"At first it was a kind of 'hero worship,'" she told her friend Jim Maher in the 1970s. "Joe is probably the only person I can talk to, in a certain way—no holds barred. It came out of left field . . . [but] we both started to enjoy it, and we both felt terribly guilty. . . . I had no idea what to do about it, no idea where it would lead. I knew only that he was funny and tender and a great musician, that I couldn't bear to lose him any more than I could bear to end my marriage."

When she fell in love with Joe, Marian came to singer Helen Merrill for solace and counsel. Helen had gone through a divorce, so Marian looked up to her as a woman of experience. Marian and Jimmy had befriended Helen in New York after hearing her version of "What's New," from her famous debut album with trumpeter Clifford Brown, on a car radio. The McPartlands had been so impressed, they had pulled to the side of the road to listen. Helen and her son, Alan, would occasionally celebrate holidays with Marian and Jimmy.

"He was a good cook," said Helen. "He'd make these big hams and turkeys and then he'd invite us over. And we'd have a wonderful, simple, lovely holiday. I was a single mom, and she and Jimmy sensed that I didn't have much of a family to support me."

Helen confided in Marian as well.

"I used to call her Ma Perkins," said Helen, referring to a radio personality who dispensed advice. "I could talk to her about anything. She had this wonderful British humor. In the middle of a sentence would come the most foul word. And it would sound like 'Good morning!' And she'd say something terrible! It used to break me up, never missing a beat."

Joe and Jimmy were very different, but Helen could see how they fit into Marian's scheme of things.

"Jimmy was the storybook love of her life," she said in an interview at her Manhattan apartment. "Joe was the fantasy love . . . Jimmy was her husband—home, cooking, husband and wife. Joe was the romance."

Jimmy was a leading man—big and brash and bold, like his cornet. Joe was quiet, sly, and gentle—like his drumming. More intellectual. He liked messing with the time, messing with people's heads, as he did with those deadpan tales of Marvin Bonessa. Being around Joe was like being in a secret society. And in some respects, because of his poor eyesight, he was in a secret society. As Marian grew to love him, she wanted to experience the world from his point of view. After the engagement at the Grandview Inn, in May 1955, the trio did a pro bono concert at the Ohio State School for the Blind. Back in New York, Marian volunteered to read books aloud to the blind.

Marian and Joe developed a set of private jokes about his handicap.

"Sometimes I might knock something over," said Joe, "and two or three days later she knocked something over and she said, 'See, it can happen to anyone.' That was nice."

"One of his characteristics was to make fun of his bad eyes," said Marian. "Once we were making one of our clandestine visits. . . . I had checked into the Park Plaza. Joe came over, we had breakfast, we stayed around for a while, then I took him back to his hotel. The street was heavy with traffic. I pulled up to the curb, let Joe out to go into the hotel (it was the Lord Simco), but instead he went in the wrong door and into the bank next door! He walked around for a while, obviously looking for the elevator, still thinking he was in the hotel. I was sitting in the car, dying laughing. Finally he realized, spoke to an attendant in the bank who showed him where the hotel entrance was, and he went in, not perturbed, but grinning like I was. It took me about five minutes to get back to my hotel and into my room. As I walked in the phone started ringing. It was Joe. He wasn't talking, just roaring with laughter into the phone. Finally, he gasped, 'You saw that, didn't you?' I was laughing just as much. Really it was funny, the expression on his face of blank amazement. . . . We must have just laughed and giggled for five minutes."

In New York, when Marian went to see Joe, she sometimes told Jimmy she was visiting Merrill. In Chicago, Dorothy and Don's house became a favorite rendezvous. Dorothy and Don were now the proud parents of a daughter, Donna, born in April 1953, but even with two children they lived a somewhat bohemian lifestyle. Joe was welcomed into the clan like a new member of the family, though the "cover story" was that Joe came by because he enjoyed Dorothy's company. An album of snapshots taken in the modest Kassel living room in the spring of 1955 suggests that Marian and Joe—and little Doug, who would have been six years old—had some wild times. In one of them, with a cornet that had belonged to Bix on the mantelpiece in the background, Don Kassel stood on his head on the living room rug, with a paintbrush in his mouth. Joe pretended to drive a drumstick into Don's foot with a hammer, and little Dougie played a drumstick as if it were an end-blown flute. In another, Joe sat on the rug wearing a fake turban, looking beatific as Don, Marian, and Doug bowed down to him as if he were a holy man.

Perhaps the family favorite in the photo album was one of Marian, wearing a skirt, sitting on the couch, throwing her legs up—spread-eagled.

"This proper British woman was like one of the boys, you know," said Don. "Cussin' and dirty talk. But with this accent. It was wild."

One of Joe's contributions to these gatherings was a famous British comedy album called *The Great Crepitation Contest of 1946,* in which the contestants grip a "farting post," bend their knees, and let fly. Commentators narrated the action with the whispered reverence of golf announcers.

When he was older, Doug sometimes brought out his *MAD* magazine belching record, "It's a Gas."

"It was just such a fun, crazy household," remembered Donna. "It was just kooky and the ladies were up drinking at night, partying, laughing, listening to either Frank Sinatra or jazz records. They had the greatest sense of humor, and I would hide on the stairways and listen to them. They used to dress Doug up as a French bartender when he was like eight years old. My father would put this big mustache and white apron on him and have him serving drinks at these wild parties where they played conga drums in the living room. Marian was Mom's best friend. And I loved Joe. We all really loved him. I always thought he was my uncle from somewhere."

In a more serious vein, Morello offered drum lessons to Doug.

"Joe would show me stuff, how to hold the brushes," said Doug. "He was very sweet to me. He gave me the first practice pad I ever had, which I still have, and my first snare drum and brushes."

The lessons took. Doug became a jazz drummer and later worked at the Jazzschool in Berkeley, California.

Marian naturally worried whether Jimmy suspected anything. If he did, he didn't let on. But Jimmy was always chary of showing his feelings, especially if he had been hurt. Marian and Joe seem to have been somewhat discreet. Bill Crow, who worked with the trio till the end of 1955, said he was never aware of the affair. On the other hand, Merrill and George Wein said many people on the inner circle of the New York jazz scene knew what was going on. "It was such an obvious thing," said Merrill. "The rays coming from her eyes, especially. No coochy-cooing. They tried to have it not obvious. But just the exchange of conversation and the sophistication of the exchange."

Things got awkward from time to time, especially when Marian invited Jimmy to play with the trio—or when she found herself recording with her husband and her lover at the same time.

"I enjoyed the playing and turned off my feelings as much as possible," she said. "Joe was married and he obviously wanted to keep the marriage going, and I was married and Jimmy was there on the road. But Jimmy always had all kinds of activities that I wanted no part of. He always wanted to meet people in the club I thought were boring and go out and play golf. And this sort of threw Joe and myself together, which was exactly what we wanted."

"Oh, we were in love," Joe said with absolute candor years later. "We did have a nice affair."

Morello made it sound like a brief entanglement. In fact, he and Marian carried on—in fits and starts—for nearly a decade. For Marian, it was probably the first time in her life she had ever really let go. The sometimes tormented journals she wrote about it revealed that she found it terrifying, thrilling, guilt-producing, and unbelievably fulfilling. The affair brought out a vulnerability in her she had never been able or willing to show, even to her most intimate friends, from whom she habitually hid behind a façade of temperance, discipline, and wit. Along with Jimmy and *Piano Jazz,* Joe Morello was probably one of the best things that ever happened to Marian McPartland. Looking back, in language that recalled the sensuous, celebratory intensity of one of her favorite writers, Colette, McPartland wrote that the affair led her into a "fanatical, unreasoning desire . . . an insane, besotted love.

"Ecstasy—that's the most that can be said about any love affair! I had always thought I must be frigid—now I knew I wasn't. It just took the key to unlock the door. We promised each other we'd never talk about it or discuss it in a disparaging way. Even when it was over, we'd know we'd had something special and lovely. It was childlike, gauche, utterly improbable, with moments of ecstasy, yet no doubt no different from any two people who fall in love while married to other people and feel guilty about it. But we thought we were the only people in the world. Sufficient to say it colored my days and nights, changed my playing, got me out of my brainless rut, made me think, put me through some terrible changes, but it was all worth it."

At the close of 1955, Bill Crow gave Marian notice, after getting an offer from baritone saxophonist Gerry Mulligan. Marian hired Bill Britto (pronounced Breeto), a marvelous bassist from Toronto who had a sound as big as Crow's and a solid sense of swing. Britto, whose wife, Carol, was a respected jazz pianist in Canada, stayed with Marian nearly three years. When winter hit New York, Marian, ever the sun worshipper, customarily did her best to find a gig in Florida, and 1956 was no exception. In February, she and Britto and Morello played Miami Beach's Saxony Hotel. In April, they were back in Detroit, and the following month they opened at Chicago's London House, a club on Michigan Avenue that had been competing for years with the Blue Note for A-list acts. (Indeed, the week Marian opened, Shearing played the Blue Note.) The London House, a plush steak house with good sight lines, attentive patrons, friendly management, and a pleasant staff, became one of Marian's favorite places to play.

After the gig, Marian received a gushing fan letter praising the "dignity, warmth, sincerity, intelligence and originality" of her playing. Marian's performances often prompted such reactions, particularly from women, who were charmed by her welcoming intimacy. Marian always responded, tirelessly building her following fan by fan, until, twenty years later, she had fifty to one hundred "friends" like this in almost every major American city.

In the first half of 1956, Marian took time out from touring to record a couple of albums with Jimmy—*After Hours* (Grand Award 33-334) and *The Middle Road* (Jazztone J1227). The latter was most significant, because it marked the first time Marian recorded one of her own tunes. Marian was at first a reluctant composer but eventually was goaded into composing by the veteran song publisher Jack Robbins ("Blue Moon," "Sing, Sing, Sing," "Moonlight Serenade," and others). Performers don't receive royalties when their records are played on the air, but composers do, so getting one's compositions recorded and/or played is advantageous. That's why so many jazz artists insisted—and still do—on recording at least one of their own tunes on their albums (and why aggressive producers like Leonard Feather insisted that *their* songs be recorded). It's also why "song pluggers" habitually came by the Hickory House trying to convince Marian to play their material on the radio.

When she first started composing—she would eventually write nearly fifty songs—McPartland lacked confidence, so much so that when she played the ballad that appeared on *The Middle Road,* "Stranger in a Dream," she told the trio it had been written by someone else! Robbins prevailed upon Marian to show him the tune and he sent it to Irving Caesar, who had written the words to "Tea for Two." Marian didn't like the lyric. (Apparently, neither did anyone else; no singer has ever recorded it.) In any case, it was an inauspicious debut. Mistitled "Stranger in the Night" on the album jacket, it was a moody thirty-two-bar ballad in E minor with a haunting opening theme that took a fetching dive in the first four bars down to the pleasantly unexpected sixth note of the scale, but the melody meandered and never seemed to reach a climax.

Marian often scolded Jimmy for not being ambitious enough, but now he was flying high. In February 1956, he appeared with Bud Freeman on *The Tonight Show,* and in June *The Alcoa Hour,* a TV show featuring original scripts every week, cast Jimmy in a teleplay called *The Magic Horn.* Though the plot was flabby, McPartland was superb, a natural, and *The New York Times* agreed. After the show, RCA Victor issued an album under Ruby Braff's name, on which Jimmy was featured to good advantage. A 12-inch LP version of *Shades of Bix* also came out in 1956 with four additional tunes, including a gorgeous new Dick Cary arrangement of "In a Mist," featuring strings, some tasty writing for bassoon and oboe, and a lovely solo by Marian. Jimmy explained in the liner notes that the idea for the arrangement had been inspired by an evening he spent at the symphony with Bix, listening to Debussy and Ravel.

That summer, Jimmy and Marian played Newport again, where they witnessed Ellington's "comeback" concert, when Paul Gonsalves played his famous twenty-seven-chorus tenor sax solo on "Diminuendo and Crescendo in Blue." After the festival, Marian's trio recorded its third album for Capitol—this time with no strings attached. *The Marian McPartland Trio* (T785) was by far the best album she made for the label, a truly swinging affair that has held up so well, it's a shame Capitol has never reissued it. McPartland, Britto, and Morello interacted with immediacy and élan, seeming to have swept aside all considerations of the "classical lady" of the past. The trio burned through jazz tunes, such as Oscar Pettiford's springy "Bohemia After Dark," which Pettiford had played for her at the Hickory House, and Marian applied a bluesy English to her attack that suggested the influence of the "funky" hard bop of Horace Silver, cleverly interpolating phrases from the melody into her solo and into the lively trades she took with Morello. The disc also featured the can-kicking samba "Carioca," on which Morello clanged the nipple of the ride cymbal. The only throwback to ingratiating cocktail music was a gimmicky version of the ballad "Symphony," a tune that had sentimental value for Marian, as it had been wildly popular in France right after the war. The album also showcased another McPartland original, "There'll Be Other Times," her first on a record released under her own name. This new composition, one of her best, had come to life after an incident with Joe.

"Joe and I were going to meet somewhere," she recalled. "We couldn't for some reason get together and he said, 'There'll be other times.' I thought that was such a nice title I made a tune out of it."

As with so many of Marian's originals, the motif mimicked the rhythm of the syllables that inspired it. In the first languid, slightly nostalgic five-note phrase—two notes up, three down—one could hear the words *there'll be other times*. Marian played around with some ideas for a lyric but didn't really get anywhere. Then serendipity intervened. She played the song at the Hickory House, casually commenting it would be really nice if it had words, and a girl came up from the audience and said she had written a lyric. The woman's name was Margaret Jones. Her lyric was nothing to write home about ("This love of ours will never die / It's not good-bye, it's not good-bye"), but Mayfair Music published sheet music to the song as a "Hit Parade" extra in 1957. Jones later came to Marian's house, where they swapped tunes and tried to write some more, but nothing further came of their collaboration.

Significantly, the liner notes to *The Marian McPartland Trio* were written by Father Norman O'Connor, the famous "jazz priest" from Boston who wrote a jazz column for *The Boston Globe* and served as emcee for the Newport Jazz Festival. In her guilt over her affair with Joe, Marian had confided in O'Connor. In his notes, O'Connor wrote sympathetically about Marian as a woman who had excelled in a field dominated by men and who had overcome, additionally, a background ill-suited to producing a jazz musician. As a humorous aside, he joshed that while a convent education might not have been conducive to jazz, it might well have led to her "good taste."

The day after the trio finished the album for Capitol, Marian flew to England. She had decided it was time for a break—emotionally and musically. From Eastbourne, she wrote long, passionate, confused love letters to Joe, who picked them up secretly at general delivery. Marian confided in Joyce and also did some business in London, appearing on the BBC shows *Jazz Band Ball, World of Jazz,* and *In Town Tonight.* Though McPartland was usually careful in interviews to project an image of domestic bliss between her and Jimmy, in a chat with the *Record Mirror* she allowed one of her pet peeves to slip out. Jimmy, she said, always wanted to watch sports on TV, while she preferred to listen to music "full blast" on the hi-fi. Marian also gave an uncharacteristically candid interview to her old friend Max Jones at *Melody Maker.* In New York, she said, you needed "staying power" and a "strong stomach" to resist the competition and deal with the "do-you-downers" on the scene. That went double and triple if you were a woman, which was considered "infra-dig" (1950s British slang for uncool). Customers sometimes came into the Hickory House, she said, and asked where Jimmy was. Upon discovering it was her trio, they walked out.

On a more positive note, she gave a quite accurate assessment of her own progress as a player. America, she suggested, had helped her to "drop the old school reserve." She didn't feel she had "broken it down completely" but said, "I'm getting a little closer to it." Most Brits played stiff, she said, and in an uncharacteristic lapse of diplomacy, she added that even less well-known musicians in the United States were better than top-of-the-line Brits. All in all, it was a refreshingly honest interview.

Marian stayed in England for a month. When she got home, she was greeted by three nasty surprises. Joe's wife, Ellie, had discovered her letters. Joe had been hired by Dave Brubeck. And Elvis Presley's "Hound Dog" was the number one record in the country.

8.

New York's Golden Age of Jazz, Part II
(1956~1958)

BEFORE MARIAN LEFT FOR ENGLAND in the fall of 1956, Dave Brubeck and his svelte-toned alto saxophonist, Paul Desmond, had begun to drop by the Hickory House on a regular basis. Marian was flattered.

"I never dreamed they were going to cop my drummer," she said.

Joe had been with the trio more than three years, felt he was no longer growing, and had eyes to play with a name big band, a glaring hole in his résumé. Unbeknownst to Marian, he had already received offers from Benny Goodman and Tommy Dorsey. But when Brubeck promised to showcase Joe as a soloist, he accepted.

Marian was crushed. She was losing not only her drummer, but her lover, though some sensible part of her also welcomed this stroke of fate as perhaps a way out of her romantic dilemma. Awkwardly, the trio still had an outstanding commitment in Toronto. She and Joe were scheduled on the same flight. When they met at the airport, he said, "Gee, I have some things to tell you that are really going to shake you." Joe told her about Brubeck, then also explained that someone—they later determined it was their bassist, Bill Britto—had told Joe's wife he was picking up mail at the post office. Ellie found a stack of Marian's letters from England. On opening night in Toronto, Ellie called Marian.

"This chick had a lot more moxie than I thought she had," said Marian. "She had a lawyer and she was going to sue me for alienation of affection and she was going to blast this thing all over the newspapers. I didn't know what to say. I was shocked. She was just awful on the phone. I sort of froze, to the extent that I answered her very quietly and said I was sorry she had found out about it. . . . I was feeling like the bottom had dropped out of the whole world."

In a small spiral notebook—one of Marian's sporadic attempts to keep a daybook that would usually last a month or two—she wrote: "September 10. Toronto. $1,000. My last week with Joe."

As soon as she hung up the phone, Marian called Father O'Connor in Boston. She was scheduled to play there next, with Jimmy, at Storyville.

O'Connor offered consolation and support and suggested he and Marian get together when she came to town. It then occurred to her that Ellie might well call Jimmy next, so she decided to get to him first. Jimmy's response to Marian's confession stunned her.

"Oh, you don't have to tell me," he said. "I know about it already."

"He had a nice, fatherly attitude about it," Marian said, "which didn't make me feel much better. I said, 'If you've known about it all along, how could you stand it? Why didn't you do something about it? Maybe things would have changed if you had made waves.' He said he thought nothing would do any good, but then it's not in his nature to make waves."

In Toronto, Joe and Marian reluctantly agreed they should end their relationship. In Boston, she told Jimmy, and somehow they got through the gig at Storyville, hiring the house drummer, the swinging Jake Hanna, as a replacement for Joe. In October, Morello opened with Brubeck in Chicago, ironically at the Blue Note, where he had first worked with Marian. When she got home, Marian began seeing an analyst.

"I was really hurting inside," she said. "I felt total rejection, and I had some unreal idea that this woman [the analyst] would solve all my problems right away. I said I seemed to be making a mess of my life and I just didn't feel I was getting anywhere, and I'd been involved in this ridiculous affair, which went on and on and I couldn't seem to get over it."

The analyst turned out to be something of a free thinker. She told Marian she was a charming and attractive and funny person and asked her why she thought she shouldn't have this wonderful guy.

"She condoned the whole thing," said Marian. "She even met with Joe and his wife. She was kind of dangerous. I thought she'd help me get over Joe. I wanted to. I felt so hurt and rejected and foolish. I felt [Joe] no longer cared for me. I let her con me into the idea of continuing the affair."

In fairness to the shrink, it must be said that Marian did not need a whole lot of encouragement. She was still madly in love with Joe. It was only a matter of weeks before the pair took up where they had left off.

"We both spent a fortune on the phone, and we would make dates whenever he would come to town," said Marian. "It got to be just as bad as before, or worse. I would plan and plot to be somewhere Brubeck was."

Morello would mischievously book himself into hotels as "Mr. Miller," so Marian didn't have to ask for him by name. Brubeck seemed only vaguely aware of what was going on, but then it wasn't in his sunny nature to dwell on such things.

"Paul and I suspected something," the pianist said later. "One night we were coming home from a job outside of New York, and coming across one of those bridges from New Jersey, and when we got on the New York side, Joe said, 'Oh, pull over here.' I said, 'Why, Joe? Aren't you staying in town?' He said, 'This is my favorite place to get a milkshake. Leave me here.'"

Brubeck chuckled, recalling another incident.

"I remember we were going on a tour, maybe to Europe, and Marian came to the airport to say good-bye and I noticed that she was in one phone booth—you know how they'd be lined up?—and Joe was in another. But they weren't together. They were on the phone for a long time. You're giving me a clue to maybe what they were talking about!"

Among Marian's intimate friends and family, Marian's affair with Joe Morello simply became a fact of life—in Chicago, New York, Florida, California, even England, where Joe became a frequent visitor to Joyce's household. Periodically, she and Joe would swear each other off, but then they would once again find the attraction irresistible.

"They were star-crossed lovers," said Helen Merrill. "They couldn't stop what was happening. Marian was willing to give up everything for Joe. But Joe was encumbered. . . . I guess she felt lonely, even though Jimmy was her best friend."

In February 1957, Marian wrote in her daybook: "Part of me clings fiercely to every thought and memory, part of me wants the whole thing to be over, wants to show affection for J. as I once did. Not perhaps the fanatical, unreasoning desire I have felt for T. [she used "T." for Joe, presumably because "J." stood for Jimmy], but a solid, sound feeling of affection. Guess I don't want the romantic storybook type of love to slip away from me, leaving only solid, sensible down to earth feeling. . . . I wonder if I would love T. so fanatically after living with him for a year or two? Yes, I think so. I have never had such a deep affection for another man. I sometimes wonder if it will take some terrible jolt to change my feelings. I must start accepting the fact that T. is going to stay with Ellie in fact I should wish for this & wish for his happiness and hers and then try to turn to J. and make him happy instead of yearning after something I cannot and should not have."

"She felt very guilty," said George Wein. "Marian was not a 'swinger' per se, you know what I mean? She was a deeply thoughtful person. A spiritual person. She was never a promiscuous person."

Guilty or not, Marian continued to see Joe every chance she got. Oddly, Joe and Ellie, who had now moved to San Francisco, struck up a friendship in their own right with Dorothy and Don Kassel in Chicago. Joe carried on a warm and lively correspondence with the couple and their son, Doug, whom he encouraged to keep practicing drums. Morello's idiosyncratic sense of humor came through in line drawings, jokes, and a predilection for using the word *pip!* which he would throw in after a clever remark, the way a drummer might toss in a "ba-da-boom!" after a vaudeville joke. Mysteriously, he signed his letters "M.I.T."—which meant "Morello in Town."

At one point, Morello sent Don a postcard of Alcatraz.

"Thought you'd like to see my apt.," he joked, signing off, "M.I.T. Pip!"

In another, he included a "droodle," a form of cartoon riddle that had recently been popularized by the comedian Fred Allen. Joe's droodle pictured a large triangle moving across a horizontal line toward a smaller triangle. The answer (printed upside down at the bottom of the page) said: "Ship arriving too late to save drowning witch."

Joe even brought Ellie out to Chicago to meet the Kassels. That Ellie would befriend the stepdaughter of her husband's lover seems odd, even if Joe had led her to believe it was all over between him and Marian. But perhaps it only goes to show just how unconventional and bohemian Marian and her milieu really were in those days. As the years wore on, she and Jimmy developed what she even referred to occasionally as an "open marriage," though that probably made it sound more blasé than she really felt.

"I think in a way the relationship they had was ideal," said Merrill. "It didn't force him to divorce or force her to divorce . . . and I think Jimmy always knew he could not fulfill everything that she needed. It was an understood thing. Since Joe was married, I think Jimmy didn't feel that threatened. But I think he loved Marian very, very dearly, so it was a very hurtful situation for him."

Indeed, Jimmy vacillated between passive acceptance and occasional bursts of outrage. But it's possible he was so afraid of losing Marian, he felt he had no choice but to go along with her disloyalty.

"There were periods when he would act as if he was very resentful," said Marian, "But he was very passive about it. And then he'd drink again, and that relieved my guilty feelings and I could excuse the fact that I was seeing Joe."

Jimmy, of course, was no babe in the woods. A consummate ladies' man, he had done his share of fooling around.

"He was a good-looking guy and a con man," said Dr. Carl Oshrain, a Rochester doctor who later became a close family friend. "I would sit down with him after we'd played some golf and he'd have six waitresses telling him how adorable he was."

While Marian had been in England in the fall of 1956, writing mad love letters to Joe, Jimmy had had a casual affair with a young African American woman. In 1957, she had given birth to a baby girl. Though Jimmy apparently provided support for his love child, he never publicly acknowledged her, nor did she ever come forward. She was apparently raised by her mother on Long Island. Marian's reaction to Jimmy's infidelity was curiously muted, possibly because she felt so guilty about Joe. But it was complicated. She told Jim Maher that she was so in love with Joe that at one point she had hoped to have a child with *him*, no matter the consequences.

"Jimmy always said, 'Well, it was a very casual thing with me and I didn't mean it to turn out the way it did,'" she told Maher. "'Whereas the thing I can't stand with you and Joe was that you really loved him, it was really a big affair.' And I would say, 'Well, I can't help it, it just turned out that way. I needed something and he gave it to me, and vice versa.'"

Marian later noted in the margin of the transcript of this interview: "But he didn't seem to worry if the woman got pregnant. In fact, he told me she said she wanted to have his child. In that way, she accomplished what I wanted to accomplish with Joe."

Somehow, the McPartland marriage withstood this new challenge. "For some reason," said Marian of Jimmy's peccadillo, "I kind of let it go." She wasn't sure why. Was she so committed to Jimmy that she just couldn't bring herself to let him go, no matter what? Or was it that she cared so little she couldn't be bothered? She didn't know. For Jimmy, the hurt never really went away. Even as late as the 1970s, when it was all over, he would sometimes ask, "Well, how's your boyfriend Joe Morello?" But the marriage endured, even if it was no longer the vital and central union it once had been. Ultimately, it could not last.

By the time Morello went with Brubeck, Marian and Jimmy had moved to Yorkville on the Upper East Side, to a pleasant, one-bedroom, fourth-floor apartment on Seventy-ninth Street between First and York Avenues. But Marian and Jimmy continued to tour together. In October 1956, while she and Jimmy were playing at the Theatrical Lounge in Cleveland, they had the distinct privilege of hearing the great Art Tatum at a late night gig with a guitar player at the Sky Bar. Afterward, Tatum invited them to an after-hours speakeasy. Marian, who had previously seen Tatum only at the Embers, where no one listened, was struck by how differently he played in this freer environment.

"Gone was the slightly bored, perfunctory attitude he would sometimes adopt in a club where people weren't into giving him their full attention or where the clattering of dishes disturbed him," she said. "He played for himself and for all of us listening to him—for me it was an unforgettable experience."

They stayed until nine o'clock in the morning.

Marian had met Tatum the year before in Washington, D.C., while playing a matinee at Olivia's Patio Lounge, where the great singer/pianist Shirley Horn famously held forth. When she saw Tatum walk into the room with his manager, Joe Marsolais, she got very nervous. Tatum was like a deity for pianists; whenever he came into a club, musicians even said, "God is in the room." After the set, Marsolais introduced Marian to Tatum, who was quite complimentary about her playing. Later, however, Marian heard from a third party that "God" had been "disappointed." She was crestfallen. Nevertheless, she remained devoted to him. When he died a month after the Cleveland after-hours experience, Marian sent an unsolicited obituary in the form of a letter to the editor of the *Detroit Free Press*. In the piece, she hailed the passing of a great artist but also made a point of saying Tatum had offered her encouragement and advice, thereby placing herself squarely in the Tatum lineage.

With her obvious talent for writing, Marian increasingly used her by-line to enhance her own public profile. In 1957, Charlie Bourgeois introduced her to an editor at *The Boston Globe,* where she published articles about Dave Brubeck, the Modern Jazz Quartet, Helen Merrill, George Shearing, Erroll Garner, and Duke Ellington. She reestablished ties with *Down Beat,* for whom she profiled Morello, Paul Desmond, Mary Lou Williams, and others. Putting one's opinions of colleagues into print can be a treacherous business, but McPartland was careful to be diplomatic—often to a fault—championing and celebrating her subjects rather than evaluating them. A bigger problem—and one of which she seemed unaware—was conflict of interest. She wrote extensively about Morello and Brubeck, even though she had an obvious interest in touting their careers because of her own associations with them. As with the Tatum obituary, her knack for quietly promoting herself even as she promoted others became a hallmark of her public style.

Though McPartland's approach may appear cynical and calculating, it was also a survival strategy well suited to the mores of her time. Had Marian brazenly touted herself as men were expected to do, she most certainly would have been branded "mannish"—one of those "masculinized" career women excoriated by Margaret Mead. But by writing about others—and by advocating and celebrating jazz as an important art form—she appeared to be putting herself on the back burner even as she kept her name in lights. It was a shrewd solution to a problem not of her own making. And besides, who else was going to promote Marian McPartland if she didn't do it herself? Billy Taylor, who would similarly position himself as a public advocate for jazz, spoke eloquently to this question.

"She watched all the other women that sang and played go down swinging because they didn't speak up for themselves," said Taylor. "They didn't have the opportunity to say, 'Hey, fellas, I can do this.' And she did!"

The best part, of course, was that McPartland was genuine. A perennial student at heart, she really was interested in other players in a way that many musicians, absorbed in their own art, are not. And she adored serving as a public advocate. That's one reason her articles were so good. "I'd rather feel that I'm doing something for the general good, rather than just doing something for myself, playing in a hall and getting money," she would later say, a remark that reflected not only the noblesse oblige of her upbringing, but the idea that jazz itself was a *cause,* a notion also dear to Jimmy's Chicago gang. So what if she had mixed motives? So what if she got a little publicity out of the deal? It was a "win-win" for everybody.

McPartland found another avenue as a jazz advocate in the fall of 1956. It all started somewhat by accident. While playing a trio gig in Rochester, New York, at the Band Box, she was approached by a local deejay from radio station WVET named Willie Moyle. He invited her to do a workshop at his son's high school. Marian was skeptical at first. The kids were thirteen, fourteen years old. They wouldn't be interested. But Moyle insisted. After getting a warm response for "Lullaby of Birdland" and "Stompin' at the Savoy," Marian asked the kids what else they would like to hear. In a story she often reveled in recounting, she said: "With one voice, they all yelled, 'You Ain't Nothin' but a Hound Dog.' It was like a bolt from the blue. They didn't know anything or want to know anything about jazz. It just felt like an entire atomic cloud or something. It just took over from the jazz scene."

What the kids were responding to, of course, was the July 13 release of Elvis Presley's sizzling remake of the Big Mama Thornton jump blues "Hound Dog." The record had catapulted to number one. By fall, Presley had appeared on *The Ed Sullivan Show,* during which his sensual, shaking hips had given notice that, once again, African American blues was knocking on the door of the white American middle class, just as it had in Chicago, Illinois, in the 1920s. Marian saw the writing on the wall. If the only popular music kids heard on the radio was rock, jazz was doomed. Schools might save the day. Though her experience in Rochester was a catalyst,

Marian's work in schools did not begin in earnest until much, much later, when it was a matter of survival, not only for her, but for countless other jazz musicians. But the experience in Rochester made her aware of the problem, and she began to do school workshops from time to time after that.

Marian's label, Capitol, was slow to jump on the rock 'n' roll band-wagon (though it would later find a gold mine in the Beatles), but it was retreating from jazz. In January 1957, arranger Bill Miller suggested to Marian's label liaison Andy Wiswell that they record McPartland with a string quartet and harp. Wiswell had served as vice president at Muzak and would later go on to produce some classics, including Nancy Wilson's timeless debut album with Cannonball Adderley and the Grammy-winning cast album of *Hair.* But when Marian visited Wiswell at his home in Bronxville to discuss the project, his commercial outlook made her uneasy. She felt rushed into the project. She told Wiswell she wanted to name the album after a song she'd just written for Joe, "With You in Mind," but when her label-mate Nat Cole suddenly came out with a song titled "With You on My Mind," she was told she would have to use a different name. The label brought out albums by Shearing and Joe Bushkin with a full string section but offered Marian only the quartet. She was jealous.

"I wasn't a hot property," she said. "I must have gotten a label along in there somewhere that stuck in everybody's head—'nice cocktail piano, semi-jazz, nice player, great for the Hickory House.' I just sort of stayed in a middle category."

Marian McPartland with Strings (T895), recorded in January 1957, was a bland album that pandered to the lowest common denominator of Marian's base. The cover featured a gauzy picture of a pensive blonde in a peasant blouse leaning against a tree, apparently in a reverie about her man. String quartet and harp were slathered over everything, sometimes taking the lead on the melody. McPartland noodled on top. Marian even included that cloying warhorse of the light classical repertoire, Beethoven's "Für Elise," as well as nods to the commercial folk music revival then getting under way, with dreamy versions of "Black Is the Color (of My True Love's Hair)" and "Greensleeves," both of which Marian had been performing in her regular set. This was background music, romantic movie music. There was very little jazz feeling. After the swinging *The Marian McPartland Trio,* the disc was a profound step backward. *Billboard* agreed, noting the record "takes Miss McPartland further than ever from the jazz scene."

"I think I was trying to—or they were—get something that would sell," she said.

The album's one saving grace was the song originally cast as the title track, "With You in Mind," a lingering, nostalgic ballad written for Morello. It was a beautiful tune and played with a level of feeling and commitment noticeably absent from the rest of the tracks. Marian had been contracted to do five albums for Capitol, but the strings record, her fourth, would be her last. Poor sales and a paucity of reviews for the third and fourth albums suggest she was probably dropped from the label. McPartland recalled receiving no royalties from Capitol, which also supports this conclusion.

In February, Helen Merrill invited Marian to accompany her on four tracks of an album with the Hal Mooney Orchestra, another dreamy production in a quiet key. Merrill picked the Jule Styne–Sammy Cahn ballad "The Things We Did Last Summer" particularly for Marian, knowing what she was going through, but Marian could barely be heard over the harps and strings. In May, she championed Merrill in an article for *The Boston Daily Globe.*

Marian also became a staunch defender in print of Dave Brubeck, often attacked in his early career as a player who couldn't swing or play the blues. There was a volatile racial subtext to this criticism that stemmed from the commercial success of "cool" or "West Coast" jazz—played mostly by whites—which irked many black musicians as well as hipper-than-thou whites, such as John Mehegan, Marian's intermission pianist, who piled on with a vicious article about Brubeck in *Down Beat*. The piece sparked a bonfire of angry letters, the most incisive of which was a hilarious riposte from Marian herself, who facetiously suggested Brubeck challenge Mehegan to a "piano duel." The categories, she said, would be "Count Basie: good time, relaxed feeling; Duke Ellington: interesting tone colors, harmony and voicing; Billy Taylor: touch, choice of chords, and harmonic interest; Oscar Peterson; technique, facility and development of ideas; Horace Silver; funkiness. The loser would play a guest shot on the Lawrence Welk television show (without pay). Winner gets a Fats Waller piano roll. Okay, fellas—start swinging!"

"That is exactly Marian," said Billy Taylor. "She has a sense of humor that really is unlike anybody I know. Just to take that and to write that at the time we're talking about, that's very perceptive. That's not one piano player talking about another one, that's somebody who has looked at the field and who really was telling those of us in the field to respect one another."

In an amusing article Marian wrote in August 1957 about Brubeck for *Melody Maker,* he was quoted as saying that Mehegan's critique had "done more good than harm in the long run," as it had rallied his fans and sparked a firestorm of publicity. Like Marian, Brubeck was clearly from the "the only bad publicity is no publicity" school. When Marian wrote the article, she was working opposite George Wallington at a supper club on Fifty-eighth Street called the Composer, down the block from the Paris Theatre, where *Jazz Dance* had played. The Brubeck piece was essentially a chronicle of cab rides up and down Manhattan between her gig and Dave's at Lower Basin Street in Greenwich Village. At the Composer, Marian wound up "interviewing" Joe. If all this seemed a bit incestuous to those in the know, it nevertheless caught the spirit of the times nicely, with jazz rooms buzzing all over Manhattan—there were now six clubs in the Village alone—and a fan base that cared deeply about its heroes.

A month after her piece on Brubeck, Marian was herself the subject of a two-part cover story in *Down Beat,* written by Dom Cerulli. McPartland was pictured, hands at the grand piano, her head turned slightly left toward the camera, smiling warmly. Her hair was short and coiffed, lashes long, a costume jewelry earring on her left ear. The impression was elegant and dignified. Without sounding strident—or, heaven forefend, "shrill"—Marian was strikingly outspoken, offering uncharacteristically open comments about issues of identity and self-confidence, her parents and upbringing, which suggested that analysis was having an effect.

"I never would have been able to find myself if I had stayed in England," she told Cerulli. "Several weeks ago I went for a ride on Bill Crow's motor scooter. That was something I'd never have done in England, and I'm a bit surprised I did it here." Her father, she said, would have called such a thing "undignified," and her mother would have fretted: "Don't fall off and break an arm!" In America, she had learned, slowly, to become more assertive and less concerned about what other people thought. George Shearing had even told her that her "natural reserve" held her back, for fear of hurting people's feelings.

"He was right," she said. "But I'm changing, I think. If I have something to say now, I pretty often say it, if I think it's right. On radio, it used to be that Jimmy did all the talking. Now he has to really work to get his 10 cents in."

Zena Collier, the English novelist and American "war bride" who later befriended Marian, observed: "I think America gave her permission to be who she wanted to be. If you came from England in that time, life was planned out. I don't think she would have been such a great success in England."

No doubt Collier was right. Yet Marian still carried a lot of England with her, notably a deep nostalgia for the lush and peaceful garden community she had grown up in. Though she and Jimmy had spent their entire married life in Chicago and New York, neither was, at heart, an urban person. Even Jimmy, though he had started out on Chicago's Near West Side, had grown up in suburban Austin and loved the outdoors—fishing, swimming, golf, and fresh air. In the fall of 1957, when an opportunity serendipitously presented itself to move to Long Island, the McPartlands jumped at the chance. The connection was an old variety show companion of Marian's from her ENSA days, Zonie Dale, who lived with her mother in a modest duplex on Webster Street in Merrick, a small community not far from the McPartlands' old stomping grounds in Long Beach, on the south shore. Zonie and her parents were moving to Florida. In October, Marian and Jimmy bought the place for $13,500. It was a pleasant enough house, with a big backyard and a roomy kitchen, where Jimmy enjoyed whipping up pastas, roasts, and chowders for company, and a duplex unit upstairs they could rent out. The neighborhood was an ordinary grid of bungalows, with a commercial district right around the corner on the town's main drag, Merrick Avenue, which sported an A&P, a luncheonette with a counter where you could buy an egg cream, a butcher shop, and a dry cleaners. In the summer, kids played stickball in the street till dusk, and there was little traffic. This was North Merrick. South of Sunrise Highway was the more upscale beaching-and-boating district, with its waterfront inlets.

Having a place to come home to where she could feed the birds, listen to the wind, dig in the garden, and sunbathe in the backyard was a welcome change. She had been on the go since 1938, when her parents moved to Eastbourne, living in hotels, on the battlefront, in apartments, and at other people's houses. She loved having a garden. Jimmy would later report that it was not unusual to find Marian working out in the garden in Merrick at four or five in the morning, after coming home from a gig. Long Island, with its golf courses, beaches, gardens, swimming pools, and fresh air, made perfect sense for both of them. It was only a thirty-to-forty-minute ride into the city, but the McPartlands kept the apartment on Seventy-ninth Street for those occasions when it would be easier to stay overnight in town.

When Marian wrote home about the move, her mother's response was,

"What a low-class address. It sounds very *common*." (No doubt if they had given the house a name—like Kerrisdale—her mother might have approved.) For Jimmy, however, who had known poverty, humble as the Merrick house was, it was a big deal.

"I've never had a home of my own before," he told a reporter for a Long Island paper shortly after they moved in.

"There were good times," said Marian, "when we would pack a lunch basket and take it to the swimming pool. I remember the days when I was a sun worshipper and would lie in the chaise lounge in the garden. Jimmy would bring me cups of tea, and sometimes he would join me outside."

"She was very brown, for years," remembered Doug Kassel. "She'd put on the bandanna and the black goggles and sit under the sun. For years she looked like she was East Indian or something. She had the blond bouffant hair and the very dark skin."

The idyll on Webster Street did not last long. Weeks after Jimmy and Marian moved in, they got the jolting news that Dorothy and Don were splitting up. Having married at eighteen, Dorothy had no skills and no means of support. Impulsively, Marian and Jimmy invited Dorothy and her children to live in the top floor of the duplex. They stayed for nearly a year. Dorothy took the train into Manhattan, where she took a course in speed-writing with the idea of getting office work. For a while, Jimmy rented a car for her. Doug enrolled at Camp Avenue Elementary School, and Donna, four years old, was looked after at home. When they were not on the road, Marian and Jimmy minded the kids or they were ferried to the home of Jimmy's ex-wife, Big Dorothy, now married to her third husband and living in Levittown, the famously monotonous-looking suburban "planned community" on Long Island. Sometimes Dorothy dropped the kids off in Levittown for the weekend. Doug remembered a traumatic experience there.

"The Good Humor truck used to come winding down the streets every day and I ran out of the house with my quarter and chased the truck down the street," he recalled. "Then I turned around and I had no idea what house I came from. They all looked the same. Eventually I kind of looked in some windows and I figured which one was us."

Doug had gotten to know Grandma Dorothy and her sister, Hannah, during their occasional visits to Chicago.

"Hannah had been more successful in show business," he said. "My grandmother would be like Cher's Laverne, wearing the rhinestone glasses and the shorts and the horrible purple shoes. She always had a can of beer.

Then Hannah would show up and she'd be like in a mink stole, coming to say hello to her dear sister. And every once in a while, Hannah and Dorothy would break into song. Aww, Grandma!"

According to Doug, family members kept their distance from Grandma Dorothy, even at holidays.

"She wanted to be more a part of [Jimmy's] life than he wanted, but I think she was always after money, too," said Doug. "Marian didn't want to have anything to do with her. Grandma Dorothy was always kind of needy and whiny."

Doug's child's-eye view of his days on Long Island offered an interesting window into the McPartland household. He remembered being told by his mother that he and his sister always had to be very quiet in the morning, as Jimmy and Marian worked at night and got up late. Once everyone was up, it was quite a different story.

"People were always playing music and always inviting us over to spend the weekend, swim in the pool, or go fishing," he said. "We used to get invited to all these multimillionaire jazz fans' places."

That included Sherman Fairchild's palatial home on the north shore in Lloyd Neck, an estate that resembled a medieval castle with its long hedgerows, where he hosted piano parties with another set of bolted-together Steinways. At one point Marian took Doug to the Hickory House, where he sat in on drums.

"He could play, too," Marian said.

Doug remembered the war as being one of Jimmy's favorite topics: "Sometimes after he'd had a few, we'd be sitting in the backyard—he had like a croquet thing set up there—and he'd talk about how he stormed Normandy Beach with his horn and everybody would start rolling their eyes—especially Marian. . . . He had a lot of friends, and he would always make a big deal out of the fact that they were secret superspies—OSS and CIA stuff. He'd take us fishing. I remember always being around water with him. Lake fishing. I think we may have gone up to Wisconsin at some point, too. Everything was fish and water and seafood and a lot of clams. He liked to cook. I remember we were terribly grossed out when he took the Bowie knife and popped the eye out of a fish and popped it in his mouth."

Doug also recalled discovering Jimmy's stash of *Playboys*.

"I can't imagine what I was thinking at eight years old," he said. "They had a spread of Jayne Mansfield. I put this pinup on my wall in my room. And my mom comes in and . . . they thought it was cute. He used to have a Jayne Mansfield hot-water bottle."

Donna, who was much younger, remembered feeling "reassured" being around her grandparents.

"We were always so happy and so family with them," she said. "It's still the only the family I have. Oh yes, and we would always be diving for quarters, wherever we were. It was just so great to have a grandfather to play in the pool with you."

But there were darker memories, too, said Doug.

"I remember my mom got a splinter in her foot and [Jimmy] went out and got his Bowie knife and he was going to take the splinter out with this twelve-foot knife and she was like running away from him and he was chasing her with this knife, saying, 'Gr-r-r-gh!' He thought he was doing the right thing, but he was in no shape to do it. I remember him in similar states and it was always very unsettling, because this dark, brooding personality would come over my very sweet grandfather. On the bandstand he was a ton of fun, but all of a sudden there was this [growling sound], and it was definitely unsettling. I don't remember a lot of that, but I do remember some."

A sensitive eight-year-old, Doug Kassel picked up on the tension between his grandfather and Marian, particularly over work habits. Marian continually prodded—or, to use her favorite word, "nagged"—Jimmy to practice.

"She's very business-oriented and Grandpa was, 'Hey! Let's swing,'" said Doug. "He'd rather sit in his bathrobe and watch TV. He would only practice when he had a gig coming up. On the other hand, he had been playing professionally since he was seventeen. And his attitude was much different about life. 'Do it with class. Just keep swinging.' Everything was like this [finger-popping]."

One of the gigs Jimmy did practice diligently for that year was an excellent—and very successful—album called *The Music Man Goes Dixieland*. With the Meredith Willson show a smash on Broadway and the Dukes of Dixieland shoveling records out the door, a producer at Epic Records, having noticed Jimmy's natural ability as a stage actor, approached the cornetist to do this concept project. Jimmy had to memorize a good deal of patter for the session and was nervous he wouldn't be able to remember it. Doug recalled helping him rehearse.

"Marian would write the lyrics on shirt cardboards, little cue cards," said Doug. "He was running lines all the time . . . 'Well, you got trouble, right here in River City . . . and that rhymes with P, and that stands for *pool. . . .* ' After the five hundredth time, you just wanted to scream! The energy he had always reminded me of Jackie Gleason."

When Jimmy got to the Epic studios in December 1957—a converted church where, in 1959, Miles Davis would record *Kind of Blue*—Jimmy discovered he had a much more serious problem than remembering his lines. He put his instrument to his lips and the only sound that came out was a kind of, well, crepitation. Befuddled, he took the horn apart and discovered it was full of half-chewed peanuts! Little Doug had decided to experiment with Grandpa's cornet. Once Jimmy figured out what was going on, the problem was easily solved.

The Music Man Goes Dixieland was a fine record—a little cutesy, but entertaining and upbeat—with an all-star cast that included Eddie Condon, Pee Wee Russell, George Wettling, and Bud Freeman. Pianist Dick Cary crafted lively, smart arrangements with clever transition figures and key changes. Jimmy blew with a beautiful, buttery tone, and his talk-singing vocals—in that inimitable, alcoholic-adenoidal Chicago rasp—exhibited the timing of the old vaudevillian he was. Marian played on five of the album's twelve tracks, delivering a lyrical solo on "Till There Was You."

The reviews were strong. But a telegram from Meredith Willson himself, sent to Jimmy March 17, 1958, was worth a thousand write-ups: "IT's A 24 CARAT GAS. . . . THE COVER PICTURE IS TOO GOOD TO BE TRUE."

Willson was referring to a picture of Jimmy in top hat, vest, yellow bow tie, and plaid pants, shooting pool, cornet cocked on his belt, as a guy behind him with bushy mustache, vest, and bowler chalked up his cue.

The record prompted a *Down Beat* Q and A in which Jimmy offered shotgun answers to trivia questions that evoked a nice snapshot of the era, including references to TV comic Ernie Kovacs ("thumbs up"), filter cigarettes ("like smoking cornsilk"), Secretary of State John Foster Dulles ("a rough job, trying to outcute the Russians"), cocktail parties ("horrible, everyone is talking at the same time about nothing"), and Stan Getz ("he's a blowin' boy").

Newsweek caught up with Marian at the Hickory House in December. The article, titled "Clean and Cool," was accompanied by a crisp photograph supporting a description of her as a "tall, cool-looking brunette in a close-fitting blue sequin dress." (McPartland, always stylish, seems to have stepped up the glamour factor at this point. A photo from Chicago in November showed her as a rather regal blonde, wearing a sleeveless gown and large bracelet. "I went blond from the sun," she later said, "and then I decided to stay blond for a while.") She was particularly pleased when the writer quoted Duke Ellington, who happened to be in the club that night.

"It doesn't matter if it's a symphony or bebop or a man or a woman playing," said Duke. "If it's good, it's good, and Miss McPartland is wonderful."

With Jimmy and Marian both in the limelight, *Down Beat* ran another "Blindfold Test" with the jazz couple. This time, Feather played them the cuts separately, perhaps suspecting that when they were together they influenced each other's opinions. He may have been right. Marian liked modern bopper Hampton Hawes, but Jimmy found him "confusing," and when it came to Dixieland, Marian's views had hardened. Jimmy gave Muggsy Spanier four stars; Marian didn't recognize the trumpet player and gave him two.

When Marian went back into the Hickory House for the winter of 1958, Manhattan was a beehive of jazz activity. Thelonious Monk had opened a long engagement at the Five Spot, marking the start of his triumphant ascendance. Marian made the mandatory pilgrimage. Later, when she ran into Monk on the street, with her usual chutzpah she told him she had been playing his tune "'Round Midnight" and invited him to the Hickory House. He showed up with a friend on a rainy night.

"[They] wore raincoats down to their ankles, and carried umbrellas," remembered Marian. "They looked very sinister, wearing berets and dark glasses. They sat in a back booth. They talked through the entire set and drank brandy. I kept looking to see if there was any reaction. Then they got up and walked out, left me with the check. I don't know if he heard ''Round Midnight' or not." McPartland later reflected that "it was a dumb thing, to invite Monk to hear me play his music." Dumb or not, she repeated the story often, apparently feeling that to be dissed by Monk was better than to have been ignored by him altogether. Once again, publicity was publicity, especially if it involved a celebrity.

A more receptive Hickory House visitor was Duke Ellington's right-hand man, Billy Strayhorn, who came into the club once or twice a week, always sitting in the same spot, the last stool on the right side of the bar. Whenever she played his brilliant ballad "Lush Life," Strayhorn would turn to face her, raise his cocktail and his eyebrows high in a toast, and say, "Aaaah!" Like Strayhorn's "Chelsea Bridge," "Lush Life" would become a jazz standard. McPartland, as always, was ahead of the curve in picking out enduring songs. Doris Duke, who would later become a major jazz philanthropist, was also a regular. Duke lived across the street from the Lorillards (who bankrolled the Newport Jazz Festival) and was a closet pianist who sometimes played anonymously in uptown clubs. Being in the theater district, the Hickory House often attracted Broadway types. One night, after Marian had played a set that included the ballad "Ill

Wind," a man walked up to her and slipped her a note. It said, "I'm Harold Arlen, and I love your playing." Arlen, of course, had written the song, along with dozens of other evergreens, including "Over the Rainbow" and "Stormy Weather." Marian never threw away Arlen's note.

Early in the summer of 1958, Marian booked a series of gigs at a chain of Indiana hotels, but the tour fell through. Marian took some time off in Chicago, and Bill Crow left the trio for good. The last night they played together at the Hickory House, the bassist decided to leave a memento for John Popkin. After borrowing Marian's lipstick, he climbed up on a chair and drew a discreet penis on one of the horses on the wall paintings. Ten years later, when the Hickory House closed, the painting was still there, exactly as he had left it.

The 1958 edition of Newport has been forever memorialized in the Bert Stern film *Jazz on a Summer's Day,* which features Anita O'Day's spectacular improvisation on "Tea for Two," as well as performances by Louis Armstrong, Mahalia Jackson, Thelonious Monk, Chuck Berry, and the Jimmy Giuffre 3. Doug Kassel remembered everyone driving up from Merrick to Newport, Rhode Island, in one of Jimmy's "aircraft carrier"–sized cars—probably a Chrysler wagon. Doug was particularly thrilled to meet Kansas City blues shouter Jimmy Rushing backstage. Marian did a trio set with bassist Milt Hinton and drummer Ed Shaughnessy (of the *Tonight Show* band). ('This "lesser known group . . . almost stole the show," wrote the *Christian Science Monitor*.) Jimmy played with Pee Wee Russell. At some point, Marian also sat in with baritone saxophonist Gerry Mulligan, playing Ellington's "Don't Get Around Much Anymore" and "C Jam Blues." A recording was later issued, and Marian sounded confident and clear. In its coverage of the fest, the *Providence Journal* rang a cold war note, quoting Voice of America jazz broadcaster (and Newport emcee) Willis Conover saying, "Jazz is a potent weapon against communism."

That summer, Jimmy and Bud Freeman also played the Randall's Island Jazz Festival, which had been revived in 1956 after its 1938 splash as the first big outdoor jazz festival in America. The lineup of stars at Randall's Island was breathtaking—from Count Basie and Lester Young to the Modern Jazz Quartet and Billie Holiday. But New Yorkers were probably blasé: This was simply what jazz was in 1958. And as with all periods of abundance, who ever thought it would go away? One enterprising magazine editor, Harold Hayes at *Esquire,* saw presciently that the jazz scene in New York had reached critical mass and ought to be documented for posterity. Hayes decided to devote a whole issue of *Esquire* to the music. The graphics editor, Robert Benton, enlisted Art Kane, art director for *Seventeen* magazine, to take the photographs. Kane suggested they round up every jazz musician they could find in New York and take a class picture. The result was the historic photograph *A Great Day in Harlem*.

Before this auspicious August 12 shoot, the magazine sent out letters, made phone calls, and put out the word to club owners and Local 802. Nat Hentoff also alerted as many musicians as he could, including Marian. The call was for ten A.M. Gerry Mulligan later said he doubted anyone would come that early, given the hours musicians usually kept. (Bud Freeman famously quipped in a documentary about the photo, "I didn't know there *were* two ten o'clocks in each day.") At the appointed hour, fifty-seven musicians—arriving on foot and by taxi, subway, and private car—congregated in front of a brownstone on the north side of 126th Street, in the block between Fifth and Madison. Among them were Count Basie, Lester Young, Dizzy Gillespie, Thelonious Monk, Oscar Pettiford, Bud Freeman, Johnny Griffin, Coleman Hawkins, Hank Jones, Maxine Sullivan, Jimmy Rushing, Chubby Jackson, Roy Eldridge, Art Blakey, Rex Stewart, Gerry Mulligan, Gene Krupa, Vic Dickenson, Red Allen, Mary Lou Williams . . . and Marian McPartland. Wearing a fetching yellow sundress and holding a briefcase-sized handbag in her right hand, arm distended, her left hand stretched across her waist to her right forearm, Marian stood in the front row next to Mary Lou, who was flanked on the other side by Monk.

The musicians spread out in a T formation, the top of the T forming on the sidewalk and the stem climbing the stoop of the brownstone. Seated on the curb was a gaggle of neighborhood kids who insisted on being in the photograph. Basie joined them there.

"I hadn't seen Mary Lou in such a long time that we spent practically the whole morning catching up," said Marian. "Once we got over the novelty of seeing each other again, it was like old-home week, a comfortable family get-together."

It took a while for Kane to get all his subjects to stop "catching up," but after much delay he snapped one of sixty exposures printed as the final photo. When the shutter clicked, Marian and Mary Lou appeared to be continuing their conversation, Marian's head cocked ever so slightly upward, listening. Gillespie, at the far right, one leg crossed casually over the other, stuck his tongue out at Roy Eldridge, who, standing in front of Diz, had just turned around to speak. The whole impression was one of a gathering of friends.

And so it was.

Conspicuously absent was Jimmy, who, when Marian had urged him to come that morning, had said, "That's too fuckin' early," turned over, and gone back to sleep. *A Great Day in Harlem* was published in the January 1959 issue of *Esquire*. Few musicians even bothered to keep a copy. Later they kicked themselves, for there would be precious few opportunities again to gather such a stellar assembly in New York. The golden era would soon be over.

9.

LOSS
(1958–1964)

WHEN MARIAN TOOK HER PLACE next to Mary Lou Williams in the historic *Esquire* photograph *A Great Day in Harlem,* she had no reason to believe her career would not continue to flourish. Since she had moved to the city with Jimmy in 1950, everything, apart from getting dropped by Capitol Records, had gone her way. She was performing in the heart of a thriving, creative scene; had become a swinging, respected modern jazz pianist; had embarked on a successful journalism career; had met most of her childhood heroes; and was touring regularly. She was getting great print media exposure and regular appearances on TV and radio. And while her marriage was less than ideal, it was stable. Over the next decade, Marian's life and career slowly and inexorably fell apart, until, by 1968, she hit bottom. Her engagements at the Hickory House wound down. She made a motley series of albums for a variety of shotgun labels. And while she grew exponentially as a pianist, her best work went undocumented; her popularity in the jazz polls plummeted. Her relationship with Joe Morello finally ground to a halt after years of agonizing self-questioning. For Marian, the 1950s had been a period of vision, growth, and expansion. The 1960s were etched by loss.

On the personal front, things began to go downhill just a few weeks after the *Esquire* photo shoot, when Marian got word that her father had collapsed from a stroke. He died a week later at St. Mary's Hospital in Eastbourne, on August 30, 1958. He was seventy-six, had lived through two wars and one of England's worst economic declines. Marian was profoundly affected by her father's death. He had instilled in her an unstinting work ethic, intolerance of poor craftsmanship, love of nature, a sense of humor, and—perhaps most important of all, for all his sternness and formality—a sense of playfulness. Life, Frank Turner had suggested, was a source of pleasure, whether it be from a phrase well-turned, a children's poem, a beautiful song, the magic of a flower springing up in the garden, a music hall number, or a silly joke. And if indeed he had wanted a son instead of a daughter, his chauvinism had ultimately worked in Marian's favor, for he had passed along "masculine" skills that served her well—hoeing in the garden, pouring cement, taking brisk walks, and taking pride in a job well done. She may have been Daddy's girl, but he didn't ask her to *act* like a girl. Marian was unable to attend the funeral and felt guilty that her sister was now burdened with their mother's care.

On the home front, losses loomed as well. After a year in Merrick, Jimmy's daughter, Dorothy, decided it was time to go back to Chicago. In September 1958, booked for a run at the London House in Chicago, Marian packed everyone up in the car and drove the thousand miles to the Windy City. Though Marian was fed up with having a second family in the house, Dorothy was also her best friend. They often discussed books together. Karl Menninger's *Man Against Himself* and *Love Against Hate,* Erich Fromm's *The Art of Loving,* and Khalil Gibran's *The Prophet* were favorites, as well as other books about psychology and human development, inspiring biographies, and novels about relationships and the lot of women generally.

Dorothy and Marian treated each other like girlfriends and shared their fears and anxieties and their desires to improve their knowledge of themselves. They also laughed a lot, sharing an offbeat, irreverent sense of humor.

Since Dorothy knew Joe so well, she was a prime confidante for Marian about her long-standing love affair. In 1961, when Morello finally divorced Ellie, Marian called Dorothy. She was utterly confused as to what she should do. Needless to say, Morello was none too happy about her indecision.

"He wanted to marry me," Marian said. "But I couldn't make up my mind. I was going to this analyst, and she said, 'Well, now you've got Joe all to yourself. You can marry him.' And suddenly it was like, 'Jesus, I can't do it.' My thinking was so confused. I guess I had a lot of guilt on that score, but also in a way I didn't feel that sure of Joe. I thought, 'Oh, my God, I'm ten years older than he is, he'll go for a younger woman and I'll be devastated.' And Joe could be so ridiculous—undependable—late—drank a lot, very childish. I saw Jimmy in him, too. And I also felt responsible for Jimmy, and fond of him. Jimmy and I were still on and off, and then he started seeing an airline stewardess—I really can't blame him for seeing somebody else. We were both on the road all the time.

"But then [Joe] started being very bitter, accusing me of—which was right—'Why don't you do something with your life?' and 'You're messing me up' and 'You're still married to Jimmy.' I had to start facing it.

"But still and all, we'd get together and then we'd start to fight and argue. It was never really finished. It was always that whoever would cut it off—it would usually be me—I'd storm off in a tantrum and then wait for him to call."

In the early 1960s, Dorothy began to have marriage problems of her own again. She fell in love with a developer named Bill Komlos, who, unlike Don Kassel, was outgoing and social, lavishing her with jewelry and a trip to Europe. Unfortunately, he also beat her up. He had three sons from a previous marriage who were, like him, robust and macho and could not relate to the more sensitive Doug.

Marian remembered him as "just insufferable—conceited, self-important, and really unkind to Doug."

Marian stopped coming around. So did Joe.

"[Dorothy's husband] came to see me when I was playing in Chicago," recalled the drummer. "He said, 'I got a deal. Sign this, right here.' 'Sign what?' They were building houses in Mexico. 'You're gonna be a million-aire.' He had a big mouth. He was rude to the kids, too. Really a domi-nating guy. Somebody should have slugged him right in the puss."

As it happened, no one—in Chicago, at least—would get that chance. In the summer of 1963, Dorothy and her new husband moved the family to Cuernavaca, Mexico, then Mexico City. The family was away for two and a half years. When Dorothy came back, she and Marian would have a major falling-out.

Before Marian had deposited Dorothy and the kids back in Chicago, she had cut a deal with Argo, a subsidiary of Chicago's fabled Chess Rec-ords, to record live at the London House. Her trio—which still com-manded a respectable fee of $1,100 a week—now featured, in addition to Bill Britto on bass, a masterful, mustachioed young New York drummer named Joe Cusatis, later a noted percussion teacher and owner of the Modern Drum Shop in Manhattan. Argo had a good stable of jazz artists, including Ahmad Jamal and Ramsey Lewis. *At the London House* (Argo LP S640) turned out to be a swinging, unpretentious affair, one of Marian's better straight-ahead jazz records. Particularly attractive was her version of "Sweet and Lovely," on which she altered the chords of the first four bars in a very hip way, creating an upward chromatic movement within the progression. Her voicings were open, rather than the crowded block chords she had overused before, giving her playing a much more modern sound. A new thirty-two-bar tune inspired by Morello, "So Many Things," had a strong melodic arc and very cool harmonic movement in the bridge. The Argo album was the last really good record McPartland made for a decade.

Marian spent the Christmas of 1958 in England, where she visited her old elocution teacher, Mac, and paid her respects at Lullington, where her father's ashes had been scattered. Janet's diary from the period suggested she was slightly peeved by the celebrity life Marian was now leading—dashing to the post office, making long-distance phone calls to London (each call dutifully noted), getting her hair done, and staying in fancy Mayfair hotels. It's possible Janet was right. In a *Melody Maker* article she wrote after jetting home on a Pan American 707, Marian referred to Barbara Carroll rather condescendingly as a "warm, witty girl with a delicate Dresden China approach to jazz," which suggested that any intimidation she had once felt about "Barbara bebop" had evaporated. After boasting of having breakfast in London and dinner in New York, she offered a blithely cosmopolitan roundup of the jazz scene from Palm Beach to New York, Chicago, and Toronto. Her astonishingly comprehensive, briskly annotated survey covered pianists Billy Taylor, Dave Brubeck, Ramsey Lewis, Dave McKenna, Don Shirley, Terry Pollard, and Pat Moran; vocalists Lurlean Hunter and Ella Fitzgerald and Lambert, Hendricks, & Ross; saxophonists Bud Freeman at the first Playboy Jazz Festival and Sonny Stitt and Georgie Auld in Florida; the wildly successful revivalist group ($3,000 a week, she noted) the Dukes of Dixieland; trumpeters Jonah Jones and Bobby Hackett; drummers Gene Krupa (with visiting British jazz pianist Ronnie Ball) and Buddy Rich; and Red Norvo with Frank Sinatra. Few, if any, other jazz musicians have been so alert to the scene.

Marian's writing talent attracted the attention of another British jazz journalist, Sinclair Traill, who invited her to write an essay for the third installment of the annual compilation *Just Jazz*. McPartland's contribution, "Playing Like a Man," reflected a substantial shift in her thinking. The lingo of gender wove relentlessly through the fabric of reviews of the day, whether positive or negative. The quite complimentary article about Marian in *Newsweek,* for example, had referred to her playing as "masculine and aggressive." A subsequent rave in Chicago declared, "Jazz demands a strong, aggressive hand . . . not the one that traditionally rocks the cradle. Man is cast in the role of the aggressor, the creator in this male–female world. Woman is the tender, watchful partner. Most jazz fans are glad this didn't work in the case of Marian McPartland . . . a friendly, gentle lady who can match most men note for note when it comes to improvisation on a piano." (*The New Yorker* listings, more subtly sexist, described Marian as "half modern décor and half Queen Anne lace.") In her piece for Traill, Marian complained that these compliments were backhanded. She asked, "Can't we women make our own contribution to jazz by playing like women but still capturing the essential elements of jazz—good beat—good ideas—honesty and true feeling?"

Later that year, McPartland expanded on this idea in an interview with syndicated jazz columnist Ralph J. Gleason.

"I don't want a woman pianist who plays like a man at all," she said. "I want a woman pianist who plays like a woman, with the warmth, sensitivity, feeling, perception and all the womanly virtues, plus a little masculine saltiness in humor, surprise and accent.

"Play like a woman," McPartland advised her female counterparts. "There's nothing wrong with that at all. And as for being a woman in a man's world—I love it."

McPartland's ideas about gender were remarkably advanced for their time. Four years before the publication of *The Feminine Mystique* and nearly a decade before the second wave of feminism, the idea that a woman could be *equal* to a man but not *like* a man was quite progressive.

Sometimes critics stumbled on gender when they actually had something critically substantial to say. On a 1959 jaunt through the States, the perceptive British writer Steve Race, who a decade earlier had covered the Paris Jazz Festival, reviewed Marian at an intimate club called Top o' the Pole, an adjunct to the Metropole, the boisterous Dixieland hub where Jimmy played. While acknowledging Marian was "delightful and charming," Race complained there was "still something or other that comes between her and complete keyboard mastery. Marian is not quite assured as she sits down at the keyboard; not quite monarch of all she surveys, as she flexes her fingers and decides what to play first. The piano is a proud independent beast, and will soon have you fretting and frustrated if you don't show it a firm hand."

Wasn't this just another variation on Balliett's assertion that women lacked the "physical force" to play good jazz? Indeed, such words as "mastery, "assured," "monarch," and "firm" suggested obvious male stereotypes, while "charming," "delightful," and "fretting" conjured female indecisiveness and insecurity. But in spite of the gender connotations, there was an essence of truth to what Race was saying. For rarely at this point in her career—unlike Mary Lou Williams—did Marian McPartland play a solo that radiated that quality of inevitability one associates with, if not "mastery," creative originality. On the contrary, she often gave the impression that what she played was simply one of many choices that amused her. In that sense, her great talent as a mimic—her ability to absorb almost instantly what she heard around her—had become as much a liability as an asset. For Marian, it was not so much an issue of "mastery" at this point as a matter of making up her mind about who, precisely, she wanted to be.

And who, indeed, was Marian McPartland? There were a few clues to her tangy personality in her answers to a list of questions in *Down Beat*'s amusing "Cross Section" feature, in 1959, the same section of the magazine that had focused on Jimmy two years earlier.

Kippers: "You can't get a decent kipper here. American kippers are bigger and saltier—like some Americans I know."

Wanda Landowska: "I hope I can have half her musicianship and spirit when I'm her age."

Electric pianos: "Indispensable on the road . . . more important than the bedside table. The earphones are great, too. No neighbors are banging on the walls. And at home, Jimmy won't have to be banished for wanting to watch TV."

John Clellon Holmes: "Of all the people who have tried to write about jazz, he's done the most convincing job. The other books border on absurdity. [Apparently no fan of Jack Kerouac, she!]"

TV westerns: "Never watch them. I don't care for TV at all. I only watch to see a jazz group."

Football: "No interest. Not even in cricket."

The New York Times: "I'm not a good newspaper reader. I only read John S. Wilson [the jazz critic] and the theater-music section."

U.S. foreign policy: "I'm a visitor."

What an interesting surprise that Marian—literate, educated, an avid reader and conversationalist—took no interest in the front page or American foreign policy! Later in life, Rachel Carson's *Silent Spring* would exercise an enormous influence on the pianist and inspire her to become an environmental activist. But apart from environmentalism, McPartland had little interest in politics, the world of ideas, or even other art forms. She was a talented painter yet rarely visited art museums or took time out while traveling to visit cultural sites. As a reader, she liked pop psychology and certainly read novels of the day, but she had no interest in "literature" per se. (Many years later, when she moved to Port Washington, close to the setting of F. Scott Fitzgerald's *The Great Gatsby,* a friend lent her the book; she told him she found it dull and didn't finish it.) Music and the music business consumed her life.

"Somebody told me I was very narrow-minded, because I really don't have hobbies as such," Marian told pianist James Williams in her Smithsonian Jazz Oral History program interview. "It seems like everything I do is connected with music, because if I go out, I like to go to a club where there's music, so that I can hear either somebody new coming up, or somebody that I know. . . . I guess I'm a workaholic."

During the late 1950s, Marian engaged Jack Teagarden's wife, Addie, as a manager, the first (and only) time she ever entered into such a relationship (Joe Glaser's office had served as a booking agency, not management). In June 1959, Addie booked Marian into an East Fiftieth Street venue called the Roundtable, where Marian shared the bill with Jack. (The Hickory House, which Marian did not play the entire year, meanwhile opened up to pianists Pat Moran and Billy Taylor.) Addie also sent Marian and Jimmy on a midwest tour, the highlights of which were a gala concert in Chicago, headlined by the smash hit comedy team Mike Nichols and Elaine May, and, in August, a Newport-sized jazz festival in French Lick, Indiana, presented by George Wein. French Lick was dangerously close to the Kentucky border—what Roy Eldridge called the "Cotton Curtain"— and Art Farmer and Dave Bailey were hesitant about using the hotel swimming pool. Dizzy Gillespie and Jimmy changed their minds.

Wrote Bill Crow: "Dizzy, wearing bathing trunks from the French Riviera, an embroidered skull-cap from Greece and embroidered slippers with curled-up toes that he'd picked up in Turkey, a Sheraton bath towel draped over his shoulders like a cape fastened at the neck and a jade scarab pin from Egypt, Chinese ivory cigarette holder in his left hand and powerful German multiband radio in his right, said, 'I've come to integrate the pool!'" Dizzy and Jimmy, arm in arm, then proceeded to walk to the end of the diving board and jump in. Everyone else, black or white, soon followed.

Addie also got Marian a gig at the Taboo in Palm Beach, Florida, a popular resort for the rich. The Duke and Duchess of Windsor (whom Marian despised, not because of the duke's famous 1937 abdication, but because of his fascist politics) dropped by, and so did Pierre Salinger, secretary of state to recently elected president John F. Kennedy. Salinger, an amateur jazz pianist, occasionally sat in. He also took Marian out on the presidential yacht, though, to her regret, not with the president. Marian was excited about Kennedy's promise to present jazz at the White House and his plan for a national support organization for the arts. She sent him her two most recent albums, for which she received a formal thank-you on White House stationery. Kennedy kept his word. On November 19, 1962, jazz was played at the White House for the first time, by the Paul Winter Sextet, further proof that jazz was finally being honored in its country of origin.

Teagarden also found Marian her first gig on the West Coast. In December 1959, she played the very club where Brubeck had become so popular in San Francisco, the Blackhawk. A supremely hip spot in San Francisco's Tenderloin district, the Blackhawk was a destination for serious, finger-popping hipsters, not a supper club. Marian's trio featured Jake Hanna and the left-handed bass player Earl May, a New Yorker who had worked with Billy Taylor. Though she didn't make a huge splash in the West, she would eventually be invited back.

In New York, Marian began her penultimate engagement at the Hickory House and played there the rest of the year. The trio featured Hanna and a swinging new bassist from the Nashville area, Ben Tucker. Marian had fallen in love with Hanna's swinging, Kansas City style when he'd served as house drummer at Storyville in Boston.

"There is an easy flow, a logical, methodical purpose to everything Jake does," Marian wrote in yet another *Down Beat* profile of one of her own sidemen. "He is a pleasure to watch; there is no wasted motion, yet he is a flamboyant performer and does everything with a flourish, plus a jaunty good-natured air."

Hanna had a wicked sense of humor. He nicknamed Jimmy "Major Hoople," after the paunchy, fatuous cartoon character from the *Our Boarding House* strip.

Marian's new bassist, Ben Tucker, was an ebullient character upon whom the fickle gods of the music business would shower great gifts. Tucker had played on the West Coast with "cool jazz" figures Shorty Rogers and Art Pepper, eventually landing with Lennie Tristano disciple Warne Marsh. After a three-week European tour with Ella Fitzgerald, he found himself in a walk-up on the Lower East Side, down to his last few dollars. When he saw Marian was working at the Hickory House, he boldly asked to sit in, hoping he could audition his way into a job. It worked. When he got home, she called him at three thirty A.M. and invited him to join her trio. He worked with her eight months.

"I looked forward to going to work every night," said Tucker. "We had a ball. I learned so much playing with her. Dexterity, timing, crossing from three-four to four-four. Marian could just groove, line after line. . . . Lay it down and groove the meter, like a rubber ball, floating on water. . . . A lot of guys say she has no balls, no guts—female player, all that—but we got down with her! We would drive her crazy! The time and the groove was so strong, Marian would be out of her mind."

As a leader, McPartland had clearly become comfortable with asserting her authority.

"She was very dominant," remembered Tucker. "She was very adamant about where these changes are going to go. There it is. You go to change keys, she'd go into a modulation . . . [it was] like Tiger Woods playing golf."

The money was good, too. In town, Tucker made $600 to $700 a week; on the road, up to $1,000.

"She was all business," recalled Tucker. "She never played around with the bread. You do your job, boom, here it is."

Marian's new trio got a loose and bluesy sound, which was not lost on veteran record producer Bob Shad. Shad had come up with Savoy, done well with "exotica" and "mood music" in the 1950s, and in 1960 founded an independent jazz label, Time, with a roster that included Max Roach and Carmen McRae. McPartland's trio made two albums for Time, one in 1960 devoted to the compositions of Leonard Bernstein—whose *West Side Story* was then enjoying a Broadway revival—and a 1963 album more cynically directed at the marketplace. On the Bernstein album, Marian played fashionably behind the beat and was attractively limber on single-note lines, tender on ballads. But while pleasant, the album was ultimately undistinguished. *Down Beat*'s Frank Kofsky found it "bland."

Though rock 'n' roll was moving relentlessly toward market domination, it was still possible for jazz artists to score an instrumental pop hit. Brubeck had "Take Five"; Stan Getz had turned the world upside down with the bossa nova "Desafinado"; Ahmad Jamal had "Poinciana"; Erroll Garner had his evergreen album, *Concert by the Sea;* newcomer Ray Bryant had "Little Susie"; Ramsey Lewis would hit big with "The In Crowd"; Vince Guaraldi with "Cast Your Fate to the Wind"; and Steve Allen with "The Gravy Waltz." The real money in the music business, as Ben Tucker discovered, was in getting one's songs published, played on the radio, and/or recorded by others. Tucker had one night tossed off a gospelish groove tune called "Comin' Home, Baby," recorded live at the Village Gate with flutist Herbie Mann, and with that one song (later recorded by Mel Tormé) he created a lifetime sinecure.

With such possibilities in mind, in 1963 Marian, Tucker, and drummer Dave Bailey (who would later direct the jazz education organization Jazzmobile) went back to the studio with Bob Shad. The result was *Bossa Nova + Soul*, a fairly obvious bid at cashing in on the "soul jazz" trend scorching jukeboxes at the time. Combining two marketplace buzzwords in a not particularly clever knockoff of Ray Charles's *Genius + Soul = Jazz* album, it featured Marian on Wurlitzer electric piano, which Charles had also popularized. Marian had signed an endorsement deal with Wurlitzer as early as November 1959, with full-page ads appearing in *Down Beat* and *International Musician,* featuring her in a tiered Spanish dress, with the caption "The only thing square about my Wurlitzer Electronic Piano is the carrying case." Ironically, McPartland didn't even like the sound of the instrument—she would ultimately far prefer the Fender Rhodes—but as a novelty kept the Wurlitzer (donated by the company) on hand at the Hickory House.

Bossa Nova + Soul started off with a stereo gimmick—Marian trading licks with herself between electric and acoustic piano—then proceeded through an uninspiring cover of Tucker's hit song, another tune by the bassist and a six-eight blues collaboration that ended with a fade. Marian also included two of her own tunes, the aimless ballad she had recorded with Jimmy, "Stranger in a Dream," and another version of her much stronger song for Joe, "With You in Mind," which unfortunately came off like background music in a Latin lounge. The only track worthy of her was a clever, up-tempo version of Thelonious Monk's "Straight, No Chaser," which she laced with a Ray Charles–like riff using sharp nines the way James Brown or Charles himself might. Had she truly embraced this soul/jazz style throughout, the album might well have been a success, but clearly her heart wasn't in it. As it happened, the album not only bombed, Marian herself never saw a penny from it.

"Bob Shad had a private jet," said Helen Merrill, who had worked with him on the Hal Mooney album. "But he never paid royalties."

It's worth asking why McPartland was unable to make even a modest hit record during this period—or, for that matter, at any time in her career. Bassist Eddie Gomez, who would later work with Marian, speculated that McPartland's penchant for constantly changing sidemen—not to mention her own style, which was always evolving—prevented her from developing a recognizable "sound." It was precisely that element that had made Shearing's quintet such a great success.

Or perhaps it was simply a matter of temperament. In a revealing interview given much later about jazz education, McPartland said, "Some people have an insatiable drive to make a commercial success. I don't know if I'm lazy or not motivated . . . but somehow I really don't have that kind of drive to spend hours trying to find a tune or walking around to publishers' offices or making a record and playing it for everybody. And I guess people do do this, they knock their brains out if they have a tune they think is going to make it. I just do things I like to do."

There was, perhaps, in this an element of resistance to popular taste itself. Marian often said she purposely played obscure tunes and resisted the familiar. She disliked Ellington's "Satin Doll," for example, because it was always requested, and she dismissed Tucker's hit "Comin' Home, Baby" as "a nothing song." In all of this there was an odor of elitism that recalled her old boss, Billy Mayerl, a composer who desperately wanted a popular hit but could never lower himself to write one.

After her second disc for Time, Marian would not record another album under her own name for five years. However, a month after the Bernstein album, she and Jimmy made another gesture toward commerce with an LP for a budget imprint of the Pickwick label, Design, titled *Jimmy and Marian McPartland Play TV Themes* (Design DLP-144). Potentially the most shallow of all Marian's grasping 1960s output, this album actually was the best of the lot—even today a solid, thoroughly enjoyable Dixieland record. In 1963, Marian also managed to place one of her songs with a top artist, when Sarah Vaughan recorded "There'll Be Other Times" on her album *Star Eyes* (Roulette), but the Divine One took the tune at a sludgy tempo and it was slathered with syrupy strings.

If one listened only to her sporadic recordings of the 1960s, it would be easy to conclude that Marian was a lively, robust player with a feeling of good cheer and a bluesy twist. Live, however, her playing was undergoing a profound shift. As early as June 1961, she had publicly championed Bill Evans during an interview with Studs Terkel on his radio show, on which the Chicago pundit played and discussed records with his guests. By then, Marian had seen Evans with bassist Scott LaFaro at the Village Vanguard, where his set ended an hour later than hers at the Hickory House. With the help of LaFaro and drummer Paul Motian, Evans had developed a new approach to the jazz piano trio, marked by countermelodies from the bass, intense interactivity among all three instruments, and a freer sense of rhythm that, while swinging, breathed with oceanic ebbs and swells. His careful approach to harmony and voicing, like Marian's, was highly influenced by the piano music of Chopin and Debussy. Because of his extreme lyricism, Evans had sometimes been unjustly criticized for lacking blues and swing feeling, but McPartland disagreed.

"What Bill was doing was definitely jazz," Marian said after Terkel played Miles Davis and Evans performing "Someday My Prince Will Come." "The feeling, the harmony. It has a poignant air to it."

Evans was not so much an "influence" on McPartland as a sort of liberator of a quality she already possessed, since she had been influenced by the same composers. There was an undercurrent of the gender issue here, too, in that Evans clearly allowed a "feminine" side of himself to show, the same side Bix Beiderbecke had allowed to come out in his music two generations back. McPartland would later famously say that if a woman played with strength, people said she "sounded like a man," but no critic ever dared to say that Evans "played like a woman," when he clearly did. Ironically, it would be a man who gave Marian "permission" to luxuriate in her own harmonically sophisticated, lyrical, and sometimes melancholy feminine side.

McPartland's absorption of the Evans style was abetted by two exceptionally gifted young bass players highly influenced by LaFaro—Steve Swallow and Eddie Gomez. Ironically, Marian met Swallow, who had played in a Dixieland band at Yale, through Jimmy. They all played together in 1961 with Pee Wee Russell in Pittsburgh. A few months after Marian opened her last engagement at the Hickory House (May–November 1962), she hired Swallow and, on his recommendation, an extraordinary drummer named Pete La Roca—a polyrhythmic player who had worked with LaFaro and Sonny Rollins, among others, and who later left the jazz life to become an entertainment lawyer. Just as President Kennedy was facing off with the Soviets over their installation of nuclear missiles in Cuba, the trio played opposite Buck Clayton at the Living Room in Cincinnati, a bona fide piano bar with built-in seating around the contours of the grand piano. The reviewer at the *Cincinnati Post & Times-Star,* Dale Stevens, apparently familiar with Marian's work, immediately noticed a change.

"La Roca and Swallow add a dimension to Marian's trio because they are not merely timekeepers," he wrote. "Swallow . . . plays lengthy, probing figures behind Miss McPartland and prefers the bottom note that is harmonically surprising."

Surprising indeed. At one point, Swallow played a D-flat under Marian's C chord.

"I was flirting a lot with dissonance," recalled Swallow. "I found Marian especially receptive to that kind of thing. For one thing, her ears were magnificent. She knew it was a D-flat, not just a dissonance. And she was making a computation in a nanosecond, what that signified and what the possibilities in that would be. There was a kind of impish quality to her that loved the wrong note at the right moment and relished it and threw it back at me. She was fearless."

As in verbal communication, Marian welcomed the opportunity to pointedly answer such a musical punch. She had already become used to this idea, rhythmically, with Morello, whose playing was conversational, melodic, and cuttingly witty. But such wildly anticipatory voice leading by the bass player was new. In the manner of Evans, it offered Marian a more advanced sense of the jazz piano trio as a musical conversation, rather than a group led by an orchestral pianist supported by two rhythm players.

After working so hard to advance from swing to bop, Marian now had to confront yet another trend—the "new thing" of Ornette Coleman. Coleman was an alto saxophonist from Fort Worth, Texas, who had developed a new style of improvising, sometimes called "free jazz," that summarily tossed aside chord changes. Lennie Tristano had actually done it first, in 1949. But free jazz really took off after Coleman's extended gig at the Five Spot in 1959, the same place Thelonious Monk had made his comeback. Every jazz musician in New York went to hear Coleman (which the *New Yorker* listings snottily dubbed "a lecture in Sanskrit"), including the ever-curious McPartland.

Marian confessed she didn't understand what Coleman was doing. But she was intrigued. Other players scoffed, calling Ornette a charlatan. Yet others embraced the style as the "next big thing." (Paul Desmond said listening to Ornette was like "living in a room where everything's painted red.") Coleman's record company marketed him with provocative titles like *The Shape of Jazz to Come,* to suggest that disliking him would be tantamount to turning one's back on the future. And this was an era when the future—optimism, idealism, progress—was the prevailing zeitgeist. Though Marian's trio still played on chord changes, it sometimes ranged so freely through substitute harmonies, anticipations, vamps, suspensions, and ostinatos, it felt kin to free jazz.

"I'm interested in absorbing parts of the new bag," Marian told Dale Stevens. "There has to be a change in music. You have to move forward. You can't just sit there and say, 'Things aren't the way they used to be.'"

Unfortunately, Marian's trio with Swallow and La Roca never recorded. It would be fascinating to hear what they were up to. Because of her own recording hiatus, the "new Marian"—customarily but inaccurately declared a Bill Evans disciple—would not emerge on record until the end of the decade.

In the fall of 1963, amid all this stylistic turmoil, Marian got a call from Benny Goodman, who told her he was putting together a band for a month of one-nighters in which he would play both classical music and jazz. Was she interested? Benny was notoriously difficult to work for—a perfectionist so wrapped up in music and so lacking in social skills that he had acquired a well-deserved reputation among musicians as rude, petty, pathologically self-involved, cheap, and even mean. Nevertheless Marian was thrilled to get the call and told Jimmy she was sure she could deal with Benny's eccentricities. She soon got a taste of the notorious Goodman persona. During informal sessions at his house, Benny disappeared. After an hour of noodling at the piano by herself and poking through his record collection (she was surprised to find albums by rock groups and John Coltrane), she went looking for him.

"I found him in another room, a sort of office where his secretary worked, and as I stuck my head in the door, he looked up.

"'Oh,' he said. 'Are you still here?'"

Before Marian accepted the gig, she called her friend John Bunch, a wonderful musician from Indiana who had played intermission piano at the Hickory House for Marian and had traveled with Goodman the year before on his groundbreaking tour to the Soviet Union. Marian asked John how much money she should ask for. Bunch told her $500 a week. When she told Benny, he said, "Oh, Marian, you people go out and work for hospitals and places like that for free." But she got the money.

Working for Goodman was a good move careerwise—he was still a very big name—though musically it made no sense. He was an old-fashioned player, even as Marian was striving toward modernism. And while healthy eclecticism would always be a McPartland hallmark, her decision suggested a confusion about her aspirations as an artist. Was she interested in developing her own voice, in making a mark in the music, or only in notoriety? Either was an honorable choice. But she needed to make up her mind. Was she an entertainer? Or an artist? As the decade wore on, this aesthetic conflict—along with her personal ones—would lead to a dramatic crisis.

Marian's new gig was considered newsworthy enough that Dorothy Kilgallen announced it in her column. On October 24, the new Goodman septet played *The Tonight Show* to publicize the tour, and Marian had her photograph snapped with host Johnny Carson. (A women's page article reported—facetiously, one presumes—that Marian planned to "knit a sweater" on the band bus because she wouldn't be playing poker with the guys.) Soon after the group's New York debut at Lincoln Center, on November 5, 1963, Marian began to feel uncomfortable. During rehearsals, she noticed Benny giving her a funny look—a stare jazz musicians famously called "the ray." When Marian played an inversion or slightly altered chord, Benny would hunch up his shoulders "like he had been stabbed in the back," she said.

"It was unnerving, to put it mildly. Once, after we had played 'Rose Room' or a tune equally familiar to me, he asked, 'Marian, do you know that tune?' And I said, 'Well, we just played it, didn't we?'"

Dissatisfied, Goodman designated trumpeter Bobby Hackett to tell Marian to back off the modern stuff, particularly on "Body and Soul."

Marian told Hackett she thought she was playing the right chords and added, "Anyway, if Benny doesn't like what I play, why doesn't he tell me himself?"

"Oh, he doesn't want to hurt your feelings," Hackett said.

As the tour moved through the eastern seaboard toward the South, she screwed up her courage, and with the help of a few drinks, sitting next to Benny on a couch at an after-the-gig party, she turned to the clarinetist and said, "Benny, I know you don't like my playing. Why did you ever hire me?"

"I'm damned if I know," he answered.

"Well, why don't you get somebody else, and I'll just play my trio numbers with the rhythm section?"

"Oh, you don't mind? That would be great."

Goodman hired John Bunch. But with Benny, nothing was ever straightforward. The first night Bunch showed up, Benny turned to him and said, "Oh, let Marian play the show. You can play tomorrow." Goodman then made the mistake of calling Bunch out for a four-handed duet with Marian.

"We broke it up," recalled John. "I played a sort of boogie-woogie with both hands, the low part. We both really pounded on the piano. Of course, that's an audience pleaser."

Jealous that Bunch and McPartland had gotten so much applause, Goodman never featured the duo again.

For the remainder of the tour, Marian played a few numbers with a trio, and Bunch played with the larger ensemble. When the band reached Texas, however, something far more dramatic brought the tour to a halt. On November 22, President John F. Kennedy was assassinated in Dallas.

The band was stranded in a small Texas town for several days, not sure what the fallout of the tragedy would be.

"The bus driver was black," said Bunch, "and he immediately quit because he thought [the assassination] had been racial. The agent didn't know what to do. We had to cancel some one-nighters. We were there three or four or five days. It was extremely upsetting. It was just a terrible time. The bus went right through that area where he was shot. There were police all around."

Marian remembered being glued to the motel TV. But she took time out to write a letter to *Down Beat* to express her sympathy and praise the Kennedys' support of the arts. The Goodman tour eventually resumed, playing Houston and Shreveport, Louisiana, but the combination of the assassination, the conflict with Goodman, and the general confusion in her life pushed Marian desperately close to a nervous breakdown. It was getting near the Christmas season, a time she always found depressing anyway, as she was usually touring, alone in a hotel room somewhere. "I could no longer cope," she wrote. Knowing the tour would end in Topeka, Kansas, Marian wrote a letter to the Menninger Clinic there, asking for help. When the tour ended, she checked into the Jayhawk Hotel, asked Jimmy if he would come out to offer moral support (he declined), and went up to the pastoral grounds of the clinic to try to recover her shaken equilibrium.

Starting with his 1930 book, *The Human Mind,* Karl Menninger's writings had gone a long way toward normalizing and popularizing psychoanalysis. Menninger and his two brothers had founded their clinic with the idea that an asylum—or sanitarium, as it used to be called—was not merely a place to warehouse crazy people but should offer active analysis, testing, and treatment. Marian found it a rejuvenating, inspirational experience.

"I was so unhappy," she wrote. "I felt I was a failure in life. I thought, 'Christ, here the guy that you think you love gets a divorce, and there has to be something wrong with you, because you stand on the brink and you don't marry him, and you don't let the other guy go.' I was beaten down by Benny Goodman. I felt inadequate as a musician and as a person. I was becoming more and more upset with myself, feeling I wasn't getting anywhere. I remember telling the doctor there, 'I'm stepping all over myself. I'm not doing myself any good. I really don't know what I'm doing. I was miserable, lonely, angry, rejected, guilty, unsure . . . I was hurting inside. I needed help!"

Marian spent two weeks as an outpatient at the Menninger Clinic. She found the shade trees, garden paths, and tennis courts of its grounds "fantastic" and after a few days felt she never wanted to leave. Indoors there was a great piano, and she played a concert for the patients. There were music magazines (even *Down Beat*), and Menninger himself—or "Dr. Karl," as he was called—taught a Bible class, which Marian attended. After a battery of tests, however, she began to get the sorts of violent headaches she had had as a girl. Marian was soon presented with some startling news. She was told she had a "cloud of depression" over her.

"This was amazing to me," she said. "I'd never thought such a thing about myself. I realized I felt depressed a lot, though I always acted cheerful."

The doctor also told her, "You're somebody who could be very important to a lot of people."

At the end of two weeks, a doctor recommended a psychoanalyst on the north shore of Long Island. Dr. William Benjamin had a beautiful home in Glen Cove, near Oyster Bay, with an office on the side of his house. On December 19, 1963, after returning to Merrick, Marian began an intense, fruitful, six-year relationship with Dr. Benjamin. The doctor in Topeka who recommended Benjamin had told Marian she needed someone very strong: "You have a way of kind of turning people around your little finger." It appeared Dr. Benjamin was tough indeed. He also seems to have been a pretty straight-ahead Freudian who took Marian through her childhood, her feelings about her mother and father, early friendships, betrayals, traumas, and so on.

"I'd avoid talking about things he wanted to get into," she recalled, "but Dr. B. made me do it. He was strict, tough, mean. He made me think. I'd thought I was a very honest and forthright person, and I didn't realize how I was deceiving myself and conning myself and bullshitting myself about so many things, and copping out."

While she had been running all over the country hooking up with Joe, she had even committed the unforgivable show business sin of missing a gig.

"I went to see Joe and he was playing at some god-awful place in Michigan, with Brubeck, and it was in winter. I had to drive back to Detroit and catch a plane to Omaha," she said. "I missed the gig because there was a snowstorm and the plane I was waiting for never left." She later wrote in the margin of this transcript, "There's no excuse for missing a gig except death!"

One of the things Dr. Benjamin made her think about was the contradictory nature of her self-perception. On the one hand, over the last ten years, the little girl from Bromley who had tried to please everyone and be liked had also developed a façade of self-confidence and bravado, often expressed through cutting wit or stiff-upper-lip good cheer. The episode with Goodman was a prime example. Looking back, she saw herself as having been timid with Goodman, but in fact she had actively resisted him in a way that was entirely inappropriate for a side player, refusing to do as he asked, insisting that she was "right," then confronting him with the same smart mouth that had gotten her kicked out of Holy Trinity and upstaging him in a competitive display. Marian may have felt herself to be a shrinking violet, but in the spotlight she had become a preening rose. The ten-year-old girl from Bromley who had opened fire on her grown-up accompanist during her violin recital was still very much alive.

Yet beneath that veneer of confidence lurked a voice of perfectionism and self-criticism—in short, her mother—who never stopped telling her she really wasn't good enough. Goodman, after all, was notorious for hiring and firing musicians as casually as he changed reeds. Had Marian possessed genuine self-confidence, she would have shrugged off his ugliness the same way John Bunch and Teddy Wilson had. But it devastated her. Her task with Dr. Benjamin was to reconcile the wobbly, self-questioning, worried, and anxious little girl inside with the steely and determined woman on the outside who had such a canny ability to—at least most of the time—get exactly what she wanted.

Psychoanalysis required that Marian change her lifestyle dramatically. In the past, she had gone weeks, even months, without walking through the front door of the little duplex on Webster Street. She needed to stay home for a while.

"I was doing anything I could to stay in town and not go on the road and scrape up enough money to pay the analyst," she said.

Luckily, an opportunity conveniently presented itself when a British political satire revue called the Establishment opened in New York at an Anglophile venue called Strollers Theatre club, across the street from the Embers. The Establishment called for a jazz trio to play incidental music. The original pianist was Teddy Wilson, but in January 1964, Wilson passed the gig to Marian. Strollers was a supper club with a flat floor, a low stage, and, according to Marian, a somewhat sketchy kitchen. (She remembered watching chefs pour a red sauce over the meat to make it look "rare.") Playing the Establishment's quick-change theater score came easily to her, as it reminded her of her concert party days back in England. After the stage shows, the trio would move to the pub in back and play for revelers.

For the Strollers gig Marian hired eighteen-year-old Eddie Gomez, a second-year student at Juilliard, and Dottie Dodgion, a hard-swinging drummer married to Marian's friend alto saxophonist Jerry Dodgion. Marian auditioned Gomez at his apartment but after ten minutes knew he was perfect. She later wrote that with his glasses, long blue overcoat, homburg, and lace-up shoes, he "looked like a rabbi." Gomez had recently married. After working till three A.M. with Marian, he would get up early to go to school. Gomez had a speaking part in one of the skits, in which Eleanor Bron (who later played the high priestess Ahme in the Beatles film *Help!*) played Queen Elizabeth. As the queen arrived in a gilded carriage with Prince Philip, a woman's voice offstage said in a thick Cockney accent, "She's every inch a queen," to which Eddie added, "And so is he."

The pub at the back of Strollers was a sophisticated midtown room where one might spot Rex Harrison, John Gielgud, or Pierre Salinger dropping in for a grog.

"It was absolutely lovely," recalled Bron. "We'd all go there after the show. It had cushiony velvet banquettes and this sort of curved mural of Victorian-type singers. Gerry Mulligan would come in, Paul Desmond, and Dizzy."

Bron, twenty-five at the time, recalled being slightly awed by Marian, an admiration that only expanded in later years as they became good friends.

"She never let her giant appetite for work get in the way of being a delightful companion," recalled Bron. "She seemed to take great joy in everything she did."

It also made a "terrific impression," said Bron, that Marian had a female drummer. Dodgion was the first woman Marian had ever hired. Dottie was well up to the task. Mentored by Dave Brubeck bassist Eugene Wright, she had moved from California to New York in 1961, and one of her first gigs there had been with Benny Goodman. With a brash sense of humor and a hearty smoker's laugh, Dottie was happy to find that her sense of where to "divide" the beat fit Marian's exactly. She was all about swing.

"Stick with me, baby!" she would shout, beating the bass drum, whenever she thought Gomez was dragging the tempo.

Gomez toed the line, though his virtuosity in the high register and advanced harmonic choices, like Swallow's, suggested where he would ultimately make his mark—with Bill Evans. With her black dress and pearls, Dodgion apparently became something of a conversation piece, though she staved off unwanted admirers by staring straight ahead. Marian, on the other hand, as leader, needed to charm the crowd and had developed a different set of tactics. At the Hickory House, she had discovered that her English accent was sometimes a good shield. When Steve Swallow had played with her, he noticed that her accent thickened whenever she had been faced with "a potentially difficult patron. It enforced the tone, that forbade overstepping."

Swallow also noted that Marian's bawdy sense of humor and uninhibited language not only made her "one of the guys" with band members, but served as a warning to male fans that she could defend her turf. Indeed. Dodgion recalled one evening at Strollers when a particularly obnoxious drunk began to hover around the piano and make requests.

"She was so ladylike," recalled Dottie, "but this one night she's sitting there playing and this drunk comes up and starts babbling incoherently, and she turns to him and very calmly says, 'Fuck off, ducks,' and just kept on playing. She didn't whisper it, either."

Marian continued to see Dr. Benjamin. After she had debriefed the Goodman disaster, her first order of business was dealing with her hopelessly confused love life. What was she going to do? Leave Jimmy? Break it off with Joe? Or go on the way she had been? Not only was it confusing, but her indecisiveness made her irritated with herself, particularly after Morello had become available. It was also becoming more and more difficult to sustain their secret. While playing in Palm Beach, Marian had engineered a rendezvous with Joe as the Brubeck Quartet made its way to the Caribbean. Much to her embarrassment, a mutual friend spotted them together.

Marian continued to be one of Morello's most ardent public champions, publishing two affectionate profiles of him in *Down Beat*. Anyone reading between the lines could sense she knew the drummer in a way that was far from merely professional. Yet she was unable to make up her mind. Dr. Benjamin apparently made short work of Marian's indecision, forcing her, so to speak, to face the music—and dance. He made her see that her relationship with Joe was a convenient way to avoid dealing with her problems with Jimmy: As long as she was with them both, neither relationship could ever be resolved. After nearly a decade of trysts in hotel rooms on two continents, clandestine phone calls and letters, secret passwords, tantrums, arguments—the lot—in the spring of 1964, McPartland finally decided to end her relationship with Joe Morello.

"Joe had been calling for days," she remembered. "I told him what I had decided and he said, 'Thank you for telling me.' It was really awful, and I felt terrible doing it to him. Then I felt guilty, after all I'd put him through. I felt so sad; I couldn't stop caring. I felt brokenhearted, but I stuck with it."

Why Marian never married Joe Morello is a question she was never quite able to answer for herself.

"In a way, I wanted someone to take over and take care of me, but I always picked people that couldn't," she said.

Or maybe she didn't want someone to take care of her but just thought she did. In a flash of unguarded candor, in 2009, McPartland said, "It's a good job I didn't marry Joe. I wouldn't have had a career. He would have been the big-shot drummer and I would have played in his band."

Morello, for reasons of his own, agreed later, somewhat bitterly, that marrying Marian would have been a mistake. "Everything was her," he said. "With Marian, it was all me, me, me, me."

But as the Chinese poet Li Po once wisely wrote, "There is no end to things in the heart." Marian McPartland and Joe Morello remained close friends all their lives (Morello died in 2011), often talking for hours on the telephone, confiding in each other in ways they had found impossible to do with anyone else. Though they never resumed their affair, Marian never stopped loving him, either. In fact, when asked in her nineties what the most important question was in her story, she answered, "How a woman could be in love with two men all her life."

Nineteen sixty-four continued to be a year of losses. Marian's mother, whose condition had been deteriorating for years from severe arthritis, developed breast cancer early in the year. Marian had been a dutiful correspondent, writing letters on almost a weekly basis. In May, she took a quick trip to England, knowing it might be the last time she would ever see her mother. Janet complained about the food in the home where she was staying; when Marian got back to New York, she sent a "care package." Janet went home to Kerrisdale on June 25 and spent the summer receiving friends and family. On September 16, Janet Turner died at Downside Hospital in Eastbourne. She was seventy-nine years old. A few days later, Joyce wrote Marian a longish letter, a line of which made it clear Joe Morello was still very much a part of the family, despite the split with Marian.

"Maggie dear," wrote Joyce. "I am so sorry that I had to ask you to phone it must have been horrible for you . . . by Tuesday she was very far gone and unable to speak. However I sat with her as long as I could telling her how fine everything was and how well everyone was and that you were happy and Jimmy was happy and that we would all wrap ourselves up in cold weather and do all the things to prevent colds that she advised and so on. . . . I phoned Joe and told him and he was sweet, very kind and sensible. I gave him your message and he seemed happy with it. I didn't talk with him for long because I was so tired. I still am I suppose but what the hell there's so much to do. . . . We are having a service at Willingdon Church and then on to the crematorium. . . ."

As always, Joyce—capable, warm, supportive, sweet—had come through, in just the right emotional key. Her letter must have been a comfort to Marian, who now had to absorb the inevitable but still always shocking and life-changing reality that, after losing one's parents, one is alone in the world. A few months later, Marian received another letter of consolation from her cousin Ted Turner Jr. It was notable for painting a strikingly different picture of Marian's mother than the one usually painted by Marian, or even by Joyce, for that matter.

"She was the wittiest, the sharpest, the most clear thinking of her generation that I knew well," wrote Ted. "No humbug, no pretence, no Jonesmanship marred her. Directness & honesty & fearlessness were her qualities & they were lovely."

He went on to praise Janet for having been so "up to date" about young people and so vigorous and vital, despite being confined to a wheelchair.

"I suppose it all boils down to courage & to that elusive word—character," he wrote. Then, sounding so British you could hear the accent on the page, he asked, "I wonder if we are still breeding enough of her sort?"

Ted closed his condolences by praising Marian for having, like her mother, a sense of "meaning and purpose" in her life and an "appreciation of the tiny, the everyday & simple things. You have got the secret, Meg, perfectly."

Marian had been at odds with her mother all her life. Obviously two very strong, willful people, they had apparently also been very much alike, often a recipe for disaster. Psychoanalysis would gradually reveal to Marian that the hypercritical negativity and even intolerance she had found so unpleasant in her mother lived on in her. But it would also help her see that her mother had passed on some of her strength of character. Janet, for her part, had eventually come to embrace her daughter's career, affectionately referring to her as "Granny's blue-eyed girl" to her grandchildren and pointing with pride to friends at the photograph of Marian sitting at the piano with a young student in Washington, D.C. It would be many years before Marian could step back from her animosity and recognize that it had been her mother, after all, who had inspired her to play the piano in the first place, who had rocked her to sleep, singing lullabies and reciting prayers, and who had also passed on the perspicacity, clarity, and eye for detail that would serve her so well.

While she had been in England bidding farewell to her mother, she had done a few of the usual career rounds, including an interview with Max Jones, in which she talked about Brubeck. ("They say he writes a tune a day," said Marian—she waited a beat—"and some of them sound like it.") But the most striking feature of the May 30, 1964, *Melody Maker* in which her interview appeared had nothing to do with jazz at all. On nearly every page, there was a huge photo or article about John Lennon, Paul McCartney, George Harrison, and Ringo Starr. The Beatles, already huge in England, had cracked the U.S. market, with twelve songs on the *Billboard* singles charts, including the top five slots. They were soon followed by the Rolling Stones, Dave Clark Five, the Kinks, Yardbirds, and others. The "British invasion" was on.

When rock 'n' roll had first hit in the 1950s, jazz musicians had pretty much shrugged it off as simple-minded music for teenagers. But with the Beatles, everything changed. As college students turned to the new, sophisticated rock, jazz clubs began to close all over the country. Avant-garde jazz, difficult listening at best, and linked (in some cases unfairly) to black militancy, had further driven away the white, mainstream audience. Jazz was hanging by a thread. It didn't help that John Lennon, a brilliant songwriter but an angry, working-class chap, pointedly disliked jazz and said so publicly, associating it with "a lot of old blokes drinking beer at the bar, smoking pipes and not listening to the music." Jazz, once the bastion of "cool," was now as uncool as a bad cardigan sweater. Marian would spend the next several years figuring out how to survive this seismic cultural shift.

10.

Long Island Retreat
(1964–1967)

MARIAN'S RESPONSE TO THE 1960S DOWNTURN in the jazz market was enterprising and agile and, as usual, showed a remarkable ability to see around the corner. Refocusing her life on the home front as much as possible, she found a job in a Manhattan piano bar; did "club dates" (weddings, bar mitzvahs); took pretty much any gig that came her way on Long Island (often with Jimmy); became a full-time record reviewer for *Down Beat*; started a jazz radio show; and—perhaps most important, in the long run—began to serve in earnest as a jazz educator, getting in on the ground floor of a movement that would ultimately succeed the jazz club culture that had nurtured her career. Though her new persona as an educator would temporarily eclipse her profile as an artist, ultimately it would help revive her performing career as well.

During this period of career transformation, Marian also made a decision about her marriage. Anyone reading a 1964 profile of the couple in the Long Island daily *Newsday* would not have been overly surprised. Written by veteran reporter Al Cohn (not to be confused with the jazz tenor saxophonist of the same name), the article portrayed Marian and Jimmy as leading quite divergent—if not openly conflicted—lives, though with a patina of domestic tranquillity. Though they spent time together at home—cooking (Jimmy), sunbathing (Marian), golfing (Jimmy), gardening (Marian), watching TV (Jimmy), swimming at Lookout Point, and gabbing pleasantly—they often went out for days or even weeks at a time on separate gigs, to separate places.

Cohn described Marian as tall, blond, and British, "buzzing back and forth from the living room phone to the bedroom phone," brimming with an "implacable ambition" confirmed by her friends Dottie Dodgion and Father Norman O'Connor. Jimmy, by contrast, lolled on the couch, complaining he was tired after a nine-hour drive from Buffalo. Though he acknowledged the new competition from rock'n'roll and folk music, he came off as complacent, dismissing the "new bag"—avant-garde jazz—as bitter and angry, declaring he would "just sit around and wait" for his style of music to make a comeback. Perhaps remembering how baffled she had been by bebop the first time she heard it in Paris, Marian countered that she didn't "get" Dizzy the first time she heard him, either, but that it was "only a matter of time" before the new bag caught on. Wondering out loud how long she could survive the ups and downs of the jazz life, Marian then got off one of her classic bon mots:

"'It really would be something if I were playing in a nightclub at 70.'"

She waited a beat.

"'Old bag plays the new bag.'"

A photograph portrayed Marian and Jimmy on the back steps of the Merrick house, with a cat on Marian's lap and Jimmy feeding a rather brazen squirrel. Tippy the cat, whom Jimmy called his "baby," had recently become a permanent member of the household, lending a feeling of domesticity to the scene. The cat had come into the McPartland household earlier that year, when Marian was playing Minneapolis with Dottie at a disagreeably noisy club with a seafaring theme, complete with porthole windows, called Davey Jones Locker Room. The owner of the club had given her one of his cat's kittens.

Tippy, who had long fluffy hair, was an unusual cat. He not only had a propensity for falling over, but he didn't mind car travel. Jimmy got a harness for him and took him along on gigs. (Apparently Marian did, too. Trombonist Phil Wilson reported that if there were roses in the room she would put them in the closet when they were playing, because the cat liked to eat them when nobody was around.) Tippy was the first of many felines to prowl the Merrick house and yard. Jimmy became obsessed with the cats, spoiling them with fresh liver and treats, feeding them the eyes of fish he caught, and brushing their coats. After Tippy came a ginger male named Red and a stray tossed over the back fence, named Scooter.

So she wouldn't have to go far from home (and miss appointments with Dr. Benjamin), Marian took a variety of modest local jobs, for a while working weekends with Jimmy at the Office in Freeport, a south shore boating mecca with a huge fish market and a long commercial pier. Former Woody Herman bassist and bandleader Chubby Jackson, who hailed from Freeport, was offering Saturday jazz clinics for young players there. He invited the McPartlands to teach. In March 1964, at one of the sessions, Marian met a music educator named Clem De Rosa, who would have a huge impact on her career. A drummer with Stan Kenton–ish good looks and a commanding, old-school presence, De Rosa had grown up in Huntington, a north shore community not far from Lloyd Neck, where Sherman Fairchild had his estate. De Rosa had freelanced in Manhattan with

Thad Jones, Teddy Wilson, and even Jimmy from time to time, and he had recorded with Charles Mingus. After earning a master's degree in percussion at the Manhattan School of Music, De Rosa turned his attention from performance to education: In 1955, he started the first elementary school jazz band in the United States, while serving as director of instrumental music in Huntington. De Rosa expanded the program to all the grades, acquiring a huge portfolio of arrangements by inviting musicians to test-drive their sheet music with his student bands in exchange for free copies. De Rosa's bands became legendary, appearing on *The Tonight Show Starring Johnny Carson*. In 1961, De Rosa was recognized as Teacher of the Year by the state of New York.

Clem invited Marian to do a guest shot in Huntington with his Alumni Jazz Band. De Rosa was so impressed, he invited her back repeatedly. Despite a childhood aversion to "old maids" who taught piano lessons, Marian discovered she really enjoyed working with kids. In her workshops, rather than concentrate on technical or formal issues, she asked students to respond to tunes emotionally, in their own language, sometimes even asking them to make a painting, or poem, or story about how the music made them feel. De Rosa did not have to teach her how to work in the classroom.

"She had that ability to communicate," he recalled. "Always smiling and happy and always positive. Just a natural. . . . I've seen a lot jazz musicians work in the classroom, but there weren't a lot who did it as well as Marian."

McPartland and De Rosa were among a handful of musicians and activists who saw the future of jazz in the schools. In 1964, Billy Taylor, who had succeeded Marian at the Hickory House, founded Jazzmobile, a school on wheels that brought jazz to kids in Harlem. That same year, Long Island jazz fan Ann Sneed founded the International Art of Jazz, which brought professional musicians to the schools. In 1968, De Rosa and a group of other visionary music educators founded the National Association of Jazz Educators, which eventually tied everything together, from grade school to university and the music industry itself.

Marian had been speaking out about the need for jazz education for a long time, publicly endorsing the Berklee School of Music in Boston, where jazz was taught, and describing her own work with schoolkids in a 1961 piece for *Down Beat* titled "Jazz Goes to Grade School." As early as 1960, in a TV broadcast with young musicians from Ohio State University, she had declared prophetically, "Tomorrow's top musicians will come from college campuses."

"She knew instinctively sooner than a lot of pros that education was the place where it was going to be," said De Rosa.

Teaching jazz in the schools appealed to Marian for obvious reasons, which she later spelled out in notes for an article. She had no children of her own and found that kids kept her "on my toes." She was also indignant that rock music dominated the radio; she wanted to expose them to jazz, thereby perpetuating the audience for the music.

In 1966, De Rosa moved from Huntington to nearby Cold Spring Harbor High School, where he served as supervisor of music and secured a federal planning grant of $51,000 to develop a performing arts curriculum enrichment (PACE) program for eight school districts in Huntington Township. The grant led to Marian's first full-time, paid jazz education gig.

As Marian developed skills as a jazz educator, she also sharpened her pencil in the media, contributing stories to *Down Beat* on a regular basis. Her subjects included more of her own sidemen and also a second profile of Mary Lou Williams, Brubeck's alto saxophonist Paul Desmond, and Benny Goodman. In the spirit of her new role as educator, she also wrote how-to columns (variously called "Woodshed" or "Music Workshop") about the music of arranger/composer Quincy Jones, Bill Evans, John Coltrane, and, in some instances, her own compositions.

As a writer, McPartland came across as urbane, clear, fair, informed, curious, and absolutely delighted by her subjects. She also seemed to intuitively understand the skills of music journalism—gathering disparate (or even contrary) opinions, drawing people out in interviews, doing her homework about their background, and presenting a well-organized, balanced story with just enough attitude to keep it interesting. She had a rich vocabulary and a gift for metaphor. Her editors in the 1960s were the late drummer Don DeMichael and, after 1967, Dan Morgenstern, who would go on to serve as executive director of the Institute of Jazz Studies at the Rutgers University campus in Newark, New Jersey.

"There wasn't much editing to do at all," recalled Morgenstern. "It was very clean copy. Writing was something that Marian enjoyed and did very well. But it wasn't something like us guys who are professional journalists could just knock off. She worked very seriously on it. She was a very good interviewer."

When she set about writing her 1960 piece about Paul Desmond, she discovered he was a reticent subject, so she resorted to a classic journalistic strategy. She showed him what she was going to write if he wouldn't talk. Desmond opened up. McPartland's articles could have come across as "gotcha" exposés, as she was privy to much insider information, such as the fact that Desmond had initially threatened to quit Brubeck's band when Morello joined because he was jealous. Somehow, however, McPartland managed to reveal a lot without sounding invasive. But writing honestly about one's colleagues could be challenging, as Marian discovered when she did a piece about Goodman. Attempting to balance her high regard for him as a musician with the anger and hurt she felt after playing in his band, she wound up writing a hypocritical piece in which she quoted the modern classical composer and pianist Morton Gould saying Goodman was "a very warm and compassionate human being" and that her time working for Benny had been "a great experience." As always, she wanted to smooth things over. She also needed to protect herself.

"Benny was far more powerful than she," said Helen Merrill. "She's very careful of her career. She knew we never speak out against musicians. We do it privately, but we will not do it publicly."

McPartland later acknowledged that she had been "far too nice" to Goodman.

"I really didn't want to come right out and say what an asshole he was," she said.

Writing about one's colleagues could have unintended consequences, too. Such was the case when McPartland profiled a pianist who often played the Hickory House when Marian was on the road—Toshiko Akiyoshi. Championed by impresarios Norman Granz and George Wein, Akiyoshi had come to America from Japan in 1956, marrying American alto saxophonist Charlie Mariano three years later. In her article, McPartland described Mariano effusively ("fresh jets of sound . . . with a dry-ice quality spurt from his horn"), but her writing about Akiyoshi was oddly tepid and even slightly condescending. In an earlier piece, a program note, McPartland had said Akiyoshi worked "in her native costume, a colorful kimono with a wide obi sash, her black hair drawn back slightly from her face," and that she loved to shop, host parties, and cook "exotic Japanese dishes." A good deal of the *Down Beat* article focused on appearances, too, including the remark that it was curious so "small and slim" a pianist played with such "fire and intensity" and that Akiyoshi had elected to stop wearing traditional Japanese clothes onstage. The whole thing had an air of ethnic stereotyping.

Nearly fifty years later, Akiyoshi still remembered with displeasure that McPartland had talked more about her hairdo and clothes than her music. This was not surprising. If Marian had a triple handicap—being white, female, and British—Akiyoshi faced even higher hurdles, being Asian. Many people didn't know what to make of her, and she was sensitive

about it. McPartland was enjoying relative success; Akiyoshi was struggling. In Japan, she told Marian, no one had ever commented about her
gender. Unfortunately, jazz is a small world and rumors travel fast. One
night, McPartland made a random comment at the Hickory House that
apparently made the rounds.

"I made a remark—not to her, but to somebody else—that I wished
when Toshiko played she would wear that wonderful [Japanese] outfit,"
said Marian. "She got very annoyed. She said, 'I suppose when Marian
McPartland plays she should wear a tweed jacket and have a pheasant slung
over her shoulder.'"

It made for a cute party story, but according to Akiyoshi, it was entirely
fabricated. Marian nevertheless was always sure that Akiyoshi later refused
to appear on *Piano Jazz*—one of the few musicians who ever declined to
be on the show—because this comment had gotten back to her.

"I am amazed at her story," said Akiyoshi in a 2010 letter. "In those
days, I didn't speak English that well. . . . I didn't know about 'tweed
jacket' or 'pheasant slung.'"

In fact, the reason Akiyoshi never appeared on *Piano Jazz,* she said, was
that when Marian called her in the 1980s, she was busy on the West Coast,
composing for her big band.

"I asked her to give me a little time and I would tell her when I came
to New York. People don't believe me, but I was also insecure about my
piano playing."

The straw that broke the camel's back was a phone call from George
Wein's right-hand man and Marian's old Boston pal, Charlie Bourgeois.

According to Akiyoshi, Bourgeois said, "George said you should play
Marian's program."

Toshiko felt she was being strong-armed and resolved never to play the
show.

"I am not used to being ordered like a soldier," she wrote.

Akiyoshi nevertheless closed her letter by saying, "For what it's worth,
I have great respect for [McPartland] for being in the forefront of the scene
for so many years."

It was an unfortunate misunderstanding, particularly since McPartland
and Akiyoshi were both such important role models for young women in
jazz. McPartland, grieved that she had made Akiyoshi angry, later approached her to be on the show, but without result. Today, in these politically correct times, McPartland no doubt would have gotten it right the
first time.

If the Akiyoshi profile highlighted the dangers of musicians writing about their colleagues, McPartland's 1964 reprise about Mary Lou Williams served as a reminder of just how useful such writing could be. Titled "Into the Sun," the piece remains one of the finest articles ever written about the great Pittsburgh pianist, composer, and arranger, despite the fact that McPartland had many reasons to feel uncharitable toward her long-time inspiration. By this time, Marian had come to know Mary Lou rather well and was all too familiar with her dark moods, cattiness, martyr complex, paranoia, and envy of musicians she thought less deserving of success than she. In France, Mary Lou had experienced a Catholic religious conversion and for a while had renounced music altogether for charitable activity, including running a thrift shop.

"This was the start of the hostile feeling that came along," Marian said later. "She had this Bel Canto Foundation, and through lack of organization she just couldn't make money out of the thrift shop. She met me in a nightclub and said, 'Why don't you send me some stuff? You pay a lot of money for your clothes.' She always laid this one on me. I went down there with a big suitcase full of stuff."

Marian felt Mary Lou had gotten in her own way at least as often as racial prejudice and shortsighted club owners and record executives had. In her article, Marian pulled no punches, describing Williams as withdrawn, sulky, chary of suffering fools, and poor at handling her career. Yet with a novelist's sense of character, Marian also presented Williams as an irresistibly fascinating, sympathetic person—brilliant, idealistic, fragile, and unconditionally committed to the art of jazz. The writing had a pulsing cadence, with a quote from Mary Lou running through it like a leitmotif—"Anything you are, shows up in your music"—that captured her mysterious aura and conviction.

"She is like a child who dreams of a good and perfect world and cannot quite tolerate the fact that it isn't that way," wrote Marian. "Here is a woman who is conscientious, introspective, sensitive, a woman who, with her quiet manner, and at times almost brusque, non-committal way of speaking, has been misunderstood. . . . A woman vulnerable. A woman hurt so many times she tends to withdraw from, and be suspicious of others . . . she is still confused, still searching, still figuring things out for herself."

Perhaps at this point in her own life, McPartland identified with Williams's confusion and vulnerability, feeling "misunderstood" herself. Or perhaps she was still seeking Mary Lou's approval. For whatever reason, she painted a compassionate, empathetic, enduring, and penetrating portrait of a difficult colleague. Marian never heard whether Mary liked the article or not.

Up to this point, McPartland's work for *Down Beat* had been more testimonial than critical. But in 1966 she was enticed to become a record reviewer, thrusting herself into the role of bona fide critic. Marian was well aware of the dangers of such an enterprise. But *Down Beat* liked the idea of using musicians as record reviewers and had already brought on vocalist Carol Sloane and trumpeter Kenny Dorham. (It was a great staff all around, which included Michael Zwerin, later widely recognized as the jazz columnist for the *International Herald Tribune* in Paris; veteran critic and jazz encyclopedia editor Ira Gitler; and Harvey Pekar, the innovative comic book author of *American Splendor*.) Figuring this was one more thing she could do while still staying at home, Marian signed on the dotted line.

During her two-and-a-half-year career as a reviewer, Marian rated thirty-four albums, from pianist Denny Zeitlin's dazzling *Live at the Trident* (five stars) to *New Thing at Newport* by John Coltrane and Archie Shepp (three and a half stars). Her output was heaviest in 1966, when she sometimes wrote as many as three reviews per issue. McPartland's reviews showed that a working musician approached an album with a different ear from that of the average critic. She praised drummer Ed Thigpen's record *Out of the Storm* as "well planned and organized," a comment that could only have come from someone who had planned an album of her own. In a three-star review of Oscar Peterson's *Something Warm,* she wrote perceptively of bassist Ray Brown's note choices. (By contrast, bassist Dave Kniss often "bypassed logical changes" with Don Friedman.) McPartland's attention to repertoire also highlighted her musicianly outlook. She praised the Dwike Mitchell–Willie Ruff duo for rejuvenating the shopworn "I Got Rhythm" by playing it as a ballad and disguising it with altered chords. But she took Nat Adderley to task for tarting up Ellington's "Satin Doll" with a "go-go" beat ("Preposterous!" she raved) and for playing nearly every song in F minor, which would bore lay listeners, even if they didn't know why. McPartland brought her reviews to life with expressive vocabulary and vivid metaphor. Of the Bill Evans/Jim Hall collaboration, *Intermodulation,* she wrote, "Without a banal note, and soft as thistledown, the delicate probing figures are like tendrils of sound that curl around the melodies with a wispy, ethereal quality." Vibist Cal Tjader's music was as "perfect as a hand screened print." Bobby Hutcherson's vibes sounded "like tinkling glass."

But the most revealing aspect of McPartland's record reviews was not her taste per se, but what they said about her aesthetic. Though she came from a classical background, she didn't think of music as an absolute, self-contained system that created its own reality and perspective, the way the music of Bach (or, for that matter, Bud Powell) did. Nor, on the other hand, did she hear music as simply a descriptive program meant to evoke a picture or panorama, though she often used pastoral imagery (particularly water images—streams, pools, waves, hurricanes, storms) to describe music she liked. A disciple of neither absolute music nor program music, McPartland seems to have heard music as an expression of character. Over and over, she described solos as if they were actual people, involved in quite tangible human dramas. Roy Eldridge played "in his mettlesome manner, his effervescence seeming to affect the other players like champagne." The "zesty" and "jovial" Les McCann gave "Arabella" a "gentle touch" before she was "taken for a ride in the McCann Hot Rock, careening along at a furious rate. Finally they set her down with a light caress and a tip of their sombreros." Frank Foster's "Skankaroony" was not just a "raunchy girl," but "must have a degree of hipness, a good sense of humor, and a brash, cheerful air." A piece called "Joy" played by Stan Kenton came "skipping in with a glad feeling, like children running free, with hops and skips . . . but mischief rather than joy . . . *Games People Play* set to music!"

Over the years, when people asked McPartland what attracted her to jazz, she often said it was the freedom to improvise, which classical music didn't allow. That sense of jazz as a music in which the individual could defy the "authority" of the composer appealed to her rebellious side, and it was no doubt a trait that attracted her to Jimmy as well. But beyond this cliché, clearly what Marian also heard in jazz was an opportunity to actually express who she was in a way she found difficult to do in daily life. Music was a way of talking, feeling, thinking, and interacting with other people, like characters on a stage, and indeed, in her own best work, she created precisely such emotional pageants.

During the years Marian wrote record reviews for *Down Beat,* 1966–1969, jazz, like America itself, was experiencing a violent struggle for change, a conflict between old and new values, some of which were utopian and idealistic. It was a visionary time, laced with the language of nonviolence and peace but a reality of deadly confrontation. After the 1963 assassination of John F. Kennedy came the murders of Malcolm X, Bobby Kennedy, and Martin Luther King Jr. Whole areas of Los Angeles, Detroit, and Newark were incinerated by race riots. The streets of Chicago exploded into anarchic violence at the 1968 Democratic convention. Black militancy fragmented the civil rights movement. Whites fled to the suburbs. Hundreds of thousands of people took to the streets, protesting the U.S. war against North Vietnam. Underground terrorist groups emerged at home, executing anarchist actions of a sort the country had not seen since the early 1900s. Tens of thousands of young Americans fled to Canada to protest the war and evade the draft. Others "dropped out" to the countryside, imagining a pastoral, psychedelic-fueled utopia that could exist "off the grid." And as the decade closed, the second wave of feminism—militant, angry, impatient—began to emerge, as did the struggle for gay rights and for the preservation and protection of the environment.

Throughout "the sixties" (an era that actually extended into the early seventies), one could feel this turbulence whirling through the pages of *Down Beat*—in coded, polemical language. Critics and readers argued heatedly about whether the new, black avant-garde was great music or just the "angry squalling" of inept amateurs; whether the new rock, spurred by the Beatles, had value or was "merely dance music" (also played by amateurs); and whether jazz was an American or African (and therefore "world") music. As a jazzer, one's positions on the avant-garde ("the new thing"), rock, and world music were defining touchstones. Marian, unsurprisingly, showed a profound condescension toward rock typical of her generation. Music whose primary element was rhythm simply did not interest her. She made an exception for the Beatles, since Paul McCartney was obviously such a gifted melodist, and, later, for Stevie Wonder. But by and large, she dismissed rock as pop cultural trash.

As for "the new thing," McPartland tried to keep a more open mind but often had to hold her nose. In her earnest review of the Coltrane-Shepp album, *New Thing at Newport,* she bent over backward trying to be fair to music she obviously found unsettling. The album had been recorded during separate sets at the 1965 Newport Jazz Festival, an edition Marian and Jimmy had missed. (She did hear Shepp and Coltrane that August at the *Down Beat* Jazz Festival in Chicago, where Doug Kassel recalled the whole family walking out before the set ended.) Coltrane had begun to move into a realm of pure sound—not pastoral sound, but abrasive, assaultive, sometimes high and piercing sound that was often mistakenly interpreted as militant black "anger."

"Like method acting," she wrote, "it is raw, real, spontaneous, yet it also seems to have elements of a sort of calculated crudity about it," a "graphic portrayal in sound of emotions and feelings not usually brought so strongly into the light of day."

There was a suggestion here of a (British?) reserve that implied some things were simply better left unsaid. Ditto for the more straightforwardly political protests of Shepp, whose sensibility she found laden with a "Kafka-like preoccupation with the grotesque." (Fair enough: One piece was about lynching; another, heroin.) "At times," she wrote, "one wants to cry out, 'Yes, yes, I hear you; now, please stop!'" McPartland respected Coltrane too much to pan his work. With Shepp, however, she went in for the kill with an elaborate literary pun: His music was just "'Who's Afraid of Virginia Woolf' in Shepp's clothing."

Coltrane died in July 1967 but would come back to haunt Marian. As posthumous albums such as *Meditations, Om, Expression,* and *Live at the Village Vanguard Again!* were released, Marian was asked to review one—she does not remember which—but after listening, she declined.

"I couldn't stand it," she said. "And I thought, 'Gee, if I'm going to say I don't like John Coltrane, that will be terrible. I can't do that.'"

The Coltrane offer marked the end of Marian's formal career as a critic. She would later look back on her stint as a record reviewer as having been a "very bad" decision, brought on mostly by a shallow desire to see her name in print. But she had for the most part walked this tightrope with balance and dignity. Though her name continued to appear on the masthead for months, after a September 5, 1968, four-star review of pianist Joe Zawinul's *The Rise and Fall of the Third Stream,* McPartland published no more record reviews.

She did, however, continue to write for *Down Beat,* changing hats to become an instructional columnist—an extension of her role as jazz educator. To fulfill what she may have felt was an obligation to Coltrane, she wrote a workshop piece about his groundbreaking tune "Giant Steps," which came from a period of his work she loved and understood. In 1971, she contributed a "Woodshed" column about her new composition, "Ambiance." McPartland's transcription of the tune, a gorgeous modal ballad inspired by Herbie Hancock, so delighted Dottie Dodgion's husband, Jerry, the alto saxophonist wrote an arrangement of it for the Thad Jones/ Mel Lewis Jazz Orchestra.

"He didn't say a word to me," she said. "He went ahead and made the arrangement, then he called me up and said, 'We just recorded your tune.' I was *floored.*"

It was a gorgeous arrangement. Such was the upside of writing for *Down Beat.*

During her Long Island retreat, Marian was recruited as another sort of critical gatekeeper when she served on the Grammy screening committee with Dan Morgenstern, Father Norman O'Connor, and others. For a while, she was quite active in the National Academy of Recording Arts and Sciences, the industry association that produces the Grammy Awards. In 1965, she and Jimmy attended the East Coast Grammy Awards ceremony at the Astor Hotel on Times Square, and in 1967, her trio performed at the ceremony in the Grand Ballroom of the Hilton Hotel.

She also started promoting other musicians' music on the radio. New York City's WBAI 99.5 FM, one of three Pacifica stations (the other two are in Berkeley and Los Angeles), is a politically radical radio outlet that in 1966, thanks to then general manager Chris Albertson, was broadcasting a good deal of jazz, as well as experimental music, folk music, and anything else "on the edge." Albertson, raised in Denmark, had come to the United States in 1957 and worked for Riverside and Prestige Records before becoming an announcer at WBAI. (He would later become jazz editor for *Stereo Review* and write an authoritative biography of Bessie Smith.)

"I had this slot open every Saturday at two o'clock, so I decided to do two hours of jazz," recalled Albertson. "I gave the two hours over to somebody every week. They could do whatever they wanted. They could play live, play records, bring people in for interviews. Toshiko [Akiyoshi] was on for one week. Jimmy Rushing. Eddie Condon."

And Jimmy McPartland.

After hearing Marian with Jimmy, he invited her to do a show.

"I remember her saying she didn't think she could do it. [She said,] 'Who wants to hear me on the radio?'"

Starting in May 1966, Marian did a Saturday show for two years, when the station was located in a brownstone in Murray Hill, at 30 East Thirty-ninth Street. She called her program *A Delicate Balance.*

"I would bring an armful of records and just play what I felt like playing, whether it be Maynard Ferguson or a record of Jimmy," Marian recalled. "I mixed it up. Then one day Bill Evans walked in and obviously wanted to be interviewed. I was scared stiff. But somehow I struggled through it because he's such a voluble talker. It was easy, really. I thought, 'Well, why not have a few guests?' I had Benny Goodman. And Alec Wilder. Herbie Hancock."

She was a natural.

"She just had a certain charm," said Albertson. "That English voice. Everybody loved that. And she knew some very interesting people, and she knew what she was talking about."

"That did sort of get me into the radio thing," Marian later reflected. "So when I started *Piano Jazz* I pretty much knew what I was doing."

After Bill Evans appeared on her show, Marian interviewed the pianist in London, then wrote a workshop piece for *Down Beat* about his beautiful ballad "Very Early," reproducing a manuscript copy of the tune as he wrote out it for her. The article is a fascinating read, because it was so obviously a dress rehearsal for what would become the classic interview she did more than a decade later with Evans for *Piano Jazz*. Marian treasured the manuscript of "Very Early" and later asked Evans to sign it a second time.

Though McPartland spent a good deal of time teaching, writing, and broadcasting during this period, she did take a night out to see the famously filmed Richard Burton version of *Hamlet* on Broadway. She also worked locally and did a little touring. But times were tough. Even name players such as Roy Eldridge and Buck Clayton, pals from her Embers days, were doing weekend "club dates" on Long Island, sometimes for as little as fifty bucks a pop. Marian often joined them.

"We'd have to play for cocktails before, in another room, and I'd be playing on this terrible piano," she remembered. "It didn't even have eighty-eight keys. It was really rather degrading. We didn't get to hang with the posh folks. We stayed in the kitchen area. Roy always took a belt of Scotch at twelve noon or whatever time it was. I said, 'How can you do that?' And he said, 'I can't go on unless I do that.' [Bassist] Roger Page and the drummer, in the middle of a tune, would be talking about the stock market. And I said, 'For God's sake, play, I want to enjoy the tune!' Roy, by that time, was half in the bag."

Around this time, Marian's agent out of Joe Glaser's office wanted her to go back into the Hickory House, but Marian said she was "burned out" on the place and wanted something more intimate and quiet. In 1966, she started working through an agent Jimmy used, Max Cavalli, who had started out with Dixieland but eventually picked up Teddy Wilson, Bobby Hackett, and Red Norvo and became the booker for the posh East Side venue Michael's Pub.

"We called him Max the Mayor," said Marian. "He had a Brooklyn accent that was so thick you could cut it with a knife."

Cavalli was so brusque on the phone that he usually hung up without saying good-bye. (This idiosyncrasy led to a private joke between Marian and one of her bass players, Frank Tate: Whenever they felt the conversation was over, one or the other would say, "Max Cavalli," and hang up.) Max landed her a month in January 1966 at Les Champs on East Fortieth Street, where she worked with Jake Hanna and Eddie Gomez. Later that year, she went into a Sutton Place supper club on Second Avenue at Fifty-sixth Street called the Apartment. No doubt named for the touching 1960

Jack Lemmon comedy about an executive love nest (the "Theme from *The Apartment*" became a huge "easy listening" hit), the Apartment was a low-lit room with a plush midtown mood, if not the best piano—an upright—or the most attentive patrons. There were only a couple of tables between the bandstand and the bar, so most of the crowd congregated far from the music. Working opposite Marian was Charles DeForest, a Bobby Short–type singer/pianist who, like Marian, took a jazz approach to the Great American Songbook.

Marian put together a new trio featuring bassist Linc Milliman and drummer Jim Kappes. Milliman, originally from upstate New York, was another Scott LaFaro disciple who, after being on the road and recording with Maynard Ferguson, was dying to play intimate trio music. Kappes had just recorded with pioneering bebop pianist Al Haig. On opening night in October, Jimmy and Squirrel Ashcraft came along, and so did Broadway columnist Jack O'Brian of the *New York World Journal Tribune*.

"Marian's not just a fine 'woman pianist,'" wrote O'Brian, "but one of the great jazz-mood stars of any sex. . . ." When the holidays arrived, O'Brian saluted the McPartlands in his annual Christmas poem:

> All hail to McPartlands Jim and Marian
> Her piano so cool, his horn so clarion

After her annual winter flier to Florida, in February 1967, the trio reopened at the Apartment, where for the next several years Marian played two- and three-month stints. The Apartment attracted a first-class clientele. Pierre Salinger, whom Marian had met in Florida, dropped by, and so did the restless inventor Sherman Fairchild, who tried out a new kind of "fast" film at the club, which resulted in some excellent photographs of Marian taken in near darkness. Tony Bennett fell by one night, too, and "sang and sang," reported the *New York Post*. Another frequent visitor was the composer Alec Wilder. Marian had recorded Wilder's tune "I'll Be Around" on her 1956 Capitol album, *After Dark,* and Wilder had come by the Hickory House to check her out. But at the Apartment, they connected.

"Alec Wilder came prowling around one night and told me how much he liked that album," said Marian. "He would come and sit at the bar. One night, he had a record under his arm of the Swingle Singers [a sparkling French vocalese group that had just recorded with the Modern Jazz Quartet]. . . . I said, 'Oh, Jesus, I really wanted to get that record. That's a good record.' And he gave it to me. He insisted."

Wilder was sometimes described by critics as a "musicians' musician," and Marian seemed destined to join him. Or so it seemed to Marian's perceptive editor at *Down Beat*, Don DeMichael, who in another manifestation of the era's journalistic incestuousness dropped by the Apartment and wrote a glowing write-up in which he wondered aloud why, if Marian was so good, so few people seemed to know who she was. She had never made it commercially, nor, he noted sadly, had her trios made much of an impression among jazzers. Perhaps it was because she, like the Apartment, was "warm and friendly," but not a "hard seller." DeMichael went on to catalog a wide-ranging set that included a "sensitive" "Stella by Starlight," an "abstract, off-the-wall" "Dearly Beloved," a "jolly, Oscar Petersonish" "On Green Dolphin Street," a "stark and touching" edition of Bill Evans's "Blue in Green," and a lively "I'm Old Fashioned." After praising her blues feeling on "Willow, Weep for Me" he noted that she "turned all-feminine" on her own tune, the pretty bossa nova "Twilight World," and ended with a Duke Ellington medley that featured Milliman doubling the melody on a speedy edition of "Cottontail."

Marian's Cleveland write-ups had hinted at the influence of Bill Evans. DeMichael came right out and said it, noting that Milliman often led the way and that Marian's playing had "evolved from its 1946 schizoid state of half bop and half swing into a predominantly Bill Evansish mode." Even more fascinating was his use of the description "abstract, off-the-wall." Surprisingly, it was during her engagement at the Apartment that McPartland began to experiment with "free" or "outside" jazz. Musically, this covered a lot of territory, including playing "outside" the chord changes of a tune; playing in two keys at once (like Charles Ives or, for that matter, Delius); stacking disparate chords, which she had described Coltrane and Shepp doing at Newport; playing with no chord changes at all, like Ornette Coleman; or improvising completely atonally, like Cecil Taylor. By this time, McPartland, ever curious, had ventured out to hear Taylor, who asserted that the pitch of the piano keys was no less important than their percussive value in creating clusters and aural shapes. Marian's Virgil in this journey had been Patti Bown, a vigorous, classically trained pianist from Seattle who had worked in the 1960 Quincy Jones big band before moving to New York.

"Both of us wanted to be educated," Marian said. "This was at Town Hall. [Cecil] was doing pretty much things that he does now, except I remember he had on some kind of a sports outfit and sneakers. He had a little knit cap which he has had ever since. He would get up . . . and run around to the other end of the piano and strum the strings. Then he would run back to the keyboard. We were fascinated. I didn't quite know what I was listening to, but I was interested in it. I liked it."

Marian's drummer, Jim Kappes, urged her to play more "outside," and so did Jimmy.

"I would say, 'What do you mean, outside? What's outside?'" Marian remembered. "I must have been very conventional in those days. 'Just forget about a key signature,' [Jimmy said]. 'Just . . .' I don't know. He kept nagging me. All of a sudden I found I was doing it. I suppose it's like riding a bicycle. All of a sudden you know how it's done. I started finding that I could just go away from whatever tune I was playing. Even something like 'I Got Rhythm.' All right, so we're in B-flat and then again you start playing in B or A or just anywhere away from that key and maybe not even playing any bass notes associated with that tune. But in your head, you know where you are in the tune. You can get crazily away from the entire tune and the harmony altogether, but at will, you can come back and fall right back into the tune again."

While these changes were taking place in Marian's music, her work with Dr. Benjamin was proving equally transformational. It was the 1960s, after all. There was a feeling in the air—a mandate, even—that things simply had to change. Though she had finally broken it off with Joe, Marian was still unhappy in her marriage. Talking to Dr. Benjamin forced her to think deeply about why she had married Jimmy in the first place and why she was still with him. Even though they shared many of the same values—rebelliousness against authority, nonconformity, bohemianism, and, of course, the music itself—they were also very different people.

"He was a very good-natured guy, like a W. C. Fields, making little jokes, and funny, and kind of like you'd think he's not taking any of this all that seriously," said Eddie Gomez. "Whereas Marian was very much the English lady. . . . She had to take the position of keeping him on a short leash, keep him tethered to reality. I remember doing a concert with them once, it might have been with Dottie, and being in the car, coming back, I remember Jimmy said, 'Pull over to the side, I gotta go to the bathroom.' Even as a young kid [I was startled that] he wanted to stop off and take a leak on the street, and she was kind of looking the other way. [I thought], like, 'Who is this person?'"

No doubt Jimmy had been drinking, though Marian was always loath to admit how often he fell off the wagon.

"His drinking was a terrible problem," said Jimmy's niece Lee Gibbs. "I was in New York on one of these vacation trips and Jimmy was playing at a bar . . . down some stairs. And after he got off the set and was done for the night, Marian and Dugald and I went to a little restaurant and she told him, 'You've got to stop drinking.' And we got to him. And he did stop after that. He'd drink tea."

For a while.

And then he'd fall off the wagon again.

Jimmy's sponsors at AA helped Marian see how her role as Jimmy's caretaker was doing neither of them any good. She couldn't solve his problem. He had to.

"I was so positive I was going to be the one who would change him," she said.

The relationship was further complicated by the fact that Marian was also secretly looking for someone to rescue *her.*

Dr. Benjamin asked, "When will you wake up and finally realize you expect Jimmy to come to your aid and he's never going to? You just can't get this through your head that he's just not capable of doing this thing that you want, that you're looking for. You're looking for a knight on a white charger, and you're looking in the wrong place."

In fact, the doctor made her see that it was Marian who was doing all the rescuing. She had set herself up for failure. The hard truth was that in Marian's eyes, fairly or unfairly (and given her compulsive appetite for work, it's possible she might have felt the same way about any man she had married), Jimmy lacked ambition, while she had her eye on the main chance. It was as if Jimmy had climbed up to a plateau, found the view to his liking, and simply sat down to enjoy it. Being tethered to him had begun to feel like a burden.

"I wanted to move to a better house and couldn't get him to move," she said. "He had quit drinking . . . [but] I'd go to the doctor and say I hated Jimmy. Jimmy didn't like to work, he was always 'relaxing.' I always worked hard, every minute, and cleaned the house and did the garden, too. To get him to do something was very hard. I even asked him if he'd come to the doctor with me one day and he did and that was the time he went into a big diatribe about how there was no sex in our relationship."

Indeed, the marriage had been fractured, not just by Marian's long affair with Joe, but by Jimmy's dalliances as well.

"We were always fighting and not really enjoying anything," she said. "Just sort of being quarrelsome and not really caring. Putting the marriage back together was like putting the toothpaste back in the tube."

One afternoon, after sitting in a chair talking to Dr. Benjamin about all this, Marian got a phone call from the city.

"Oh, I just got back to New York the other day," said her friend. "I just went out for Joe Morello's wedding."

"It was like somebody hit me in the chest," said Marian. "I sat there and listened while he told me who Joe had married, and I froze."

This was 1966. Joe and Marian had not seen each other—at least romantically—for almost two years, yet she realized how much he still meant to her. Somewhere, somehow, she must have held out the hope—the fantasy?—that she and Joe might still get together. And yet once she got over the shock, she realized that Joe getting married was somehow liberating, too. Because if she wasn't waiting around to marry Joe, what was she doing with Jimmy?

"It wasn't long after that," Marian said, "I remember saying to the doctor, 'Gee, this thing with Jimmy is just ridiculous. I don't know what I'm doing there. It's not satisfying either one of us.'"

The doctor suggested one of the reasons she hung on to Jimmy was that she didn't have anyone else. Even Jimmy had told her that. It was complicated, though. Jimmy and Marian were comfortable. They bickered, but they also loved each other and enjoyed each other's company. He was charming, chivalrous, good-natured, and funny. (Sometimes when he greeted a couple he would say to the wife, "I see you brought your father with you.") Though they worked together on the road only five or six times a year now, they were still a salable act. They always got a great reception, from the public and the press. In Cleveland, one reviewer dubbed them "the Lunts of the saloon circuit," another "hand-holding Honeymooners." ("Your jokes would kill me if you ever set them to newer arrangements," Marian quipped onstage.) There was a lot about their life and career together that worked. Tossing it after all these years just seemed too difficult. And scary.

And then, of course, there was the sense of debt. Though she had worked hard, Marian still felt she somehow owed Jimmy. He had taught her, firsthand, everything he knew about jazz. The first night she was in America, he had introduced her to Louis Armstrong. He had arranged her first trio gig, her first record date, her first agent. How could she possibly leave Jimmy without feeling horribly guilty? And what an opportunist she would appear to be—not that appearances mattered, but still—to have married this guy, milked him for everything he had, then left him? It not only didn't look good. It didn't feel good.

"It was a torture in her life because she didn't want to have to, but she knew it was the only way to save herself and maybe save him," observed Jimmy's granddaughter, Donna. "It was not easy to deal with Grandpa.

I think she probably just said, 'I've got to get my life in control of my career."

As always, Marian confided in Helen Merrill.

"I always felt a little guilty about it," said Helen, who had already been married and divorced. "I think [Marian] was inspired by my strength. I think maybe that she thought, 'Well, if Helen can do it, maybe I can do it, too.'"

Of course, lifetime monogamy was up for a rather vigorous review during this era anyway. Marian's friend Jim Maher proposed that marriage really was an invention of the Catholic Church and should be a three-year "renewable contract." Indeed, Marian told Maher she felt the negative example of her parents—"living together till the end of their years and hating each other"—was an incentive to choose a different route.

In the spring of 1967, Marian broached the subject of splitting up.

Dr. Benjamin asked, "Are you sure you can stand the possibility of him going downhill when you leave, or drinking again? Can you stand that?"

Marian said she thought she could.

True to form, Jimmy took the news impassively.

"Well, I guess I wouldn't blame you," he said. "Maybe you should."

"That sort of cut the ground out from under my feet," said Marian.

She should not have been surprised. She knew it was impossible for Jimmy to let on when he was hurt. It was part of his nature and had been ever since the orphanage days. This was just another rejection. And ultimately, she confessed to herself later in a marginal note on one of the old interview transcripts, "I expected things of him he never has been capable of & I'm still surprised when he doesn't react the way I wish he would!"

That summer, while Marian worked nights at Shepheard's in the Drake Hotel, just a few blocks from the Apartment, she and Jimmy began to seriously discuss during the day how, after twenty-three years of marriage, they would untangle their lives. The couple went to a lawyer and drew up separation papers. Marian found an apartment, and Jimmy refinanced the house on Webster Street and bought her out. Later that year, the attorney sent Marian off to Juárez, Mexico, with a batch of other clients for a quickie Mexican divorce. The night before she left, "in the friendliest way," she recalled, "Jimmy took off to Wisconsin to fish."

"It was as friendly a divorce as ever took place," recalled Marian's old friend Frank O'Connell, the attorney who had befriended her in Chicago. "No acrimony whatsoever. It was simply a professional disagreement. I think they simply seemed to founder on the issue on how hard they wanted to work. . . . But I think that they were genuinely in love and each respected the other enormously."

When Marian moved into her new one-bedroom apartment on the seventeenth floor of 305 East Eighty-sixth Street, she was exhilarated.

"I never realized until I moved out how much I valued having space," she said. "I never realized that I never really had space. I value it more and more—I like to have room to get away from everybody and have silence. No TV."

Looking back, Marian could see that her sessions with Dr. Benjamin— and the seriousness with which she took them—had been the decisive factor.

"Analysis changed my life," she said. "It gave me strength, a better sense of my own worth. Courage. Strength. And knowledge of myself. I learned to want better things for myself."

Without this assertion—and acceptance—of herself and her career as the center of her life—instead of Jimmy—Marian quite likely would never have developed into the successful and mature artist, radio celebrity, and integrated person she became.

In November, Marian took the trio from the Apartment to Chicago, where they played three weeks at the *Showboat Sari-S,* a riverboat at the foot of Ontario Street that usually featured Dixieland. Two years earlier, she and Jimmy—in what was perhaps an augury—had played there, too, in separate groups, in separate rooms.

When she got home, news of her split with Jimmy had hit the papers. On December 15, 1967, in lieu of mentioning them in his annual Christmas poem, Jack O'Brian ran this simple item: "McPartlands Are Parting."

Marian now had a room of her own.

II.

Lost . . . and Found
(1968~1973)

ONE OF THE FIRST PROJECTS Marian threw herself into after the divorce was figuring out a way to get her music heard on record. With all but a few companies having abandoned jazz, many players had resorted to starting their own labels, among them George Shearing, Stan Kenton, Tony Bennett, Blossom Dearie, and Anita O'Day. As a rule, jazz artists aren't adept at this sort of thing, but Marian had a knack for business and an enthusiasm for getting things done. She was also extremely savvy about promotion. In 1966, she had met a traditional jazz fan named Hank O'Neal. An imposing, gently charming man with a confident, carefully modulated manner, O'Neal loved opera and ballet as well as jazz. He worked for Jimmy's old friend Squirrel Ashcraft in the CIA and often threw jazz parties at home, in Washington, D.C. When he was transferred to New York in June 1967, he was dazzled by Marian's connections, which included John D. Rockefeller's private secretary, Mary Packard, who invited Hank to sit in the Rockefeller box in the grand tier at the Metropolitan Opera. O'Neal was also nonplussed when Marian took him backstage at the ballet and introduced him to her childhood chum Peggy Hookham—aka Margot Fonteyn. As their friendship blossomed, Marian and Hank discovered they had a mutual friend in Sherman Fairchild, whom O'Neal knew through the CIA. Fairchild had an abiding interest in the technical side of sound reproduction. Agreeing that there was something decidedly wrong with a music business that turned up its nose at Earl Hines and Teddy Wilson, Fairchild, O'Neal, and McPartland began to discuss forming an independent label devoted to jazz pianists.

Financially, Fairchild was the only one with the wherewithal to bankroll a label, but to keep things democratic, he proposed each partner pony up $500 and take responsibility for separate parts of the venture. He would provide, gratis, administrative support out of his corporate Manhattan office as well as the use of his home recording studio on East Sixty-fifth Street. Hank—who had been making recordings of his house parties—would engineer the albums, Marian would select material for her own records, and the three partners would decide mutually what else they wanted to release. The label's business would be primarily mail order, but Marian would also sell records at gigs. In February 1968, Fairchild's office filed incorporation papers for the company, and Marian came up with the name Halcyon, in Greek mythology the daughter of Aeolus, god of the winds. There was a story: When Halcyon's husband died in a storm at sea, the gods turned them both into kingfishers and Aeolus saw to it that every winter, the sea remained calm for seven days so kingfishers could mate and lay their eggs. These days were later called by the Romans "halcyon days." Marian liked the image of calm seas and regeneration suggested by the myth; the phrase *halcyon days* with its combination of nostalgia and optimism also suggested her feelings about her own music. During a trip to Chicago, Marian asked Dorothy's ex-husband, Don Kassel, to design a logo. Don came up with a simple, understated design, a line-drawn circle with a dot in the middle that resembled a vinyl record, with a small kingfisher perched on a branch at about four o'clock on the dial. Kassel designed several jacket covers for Halcyon.

As Marian, Hank, and Sherman plotted Halcyon's future, Marian got an offer from a small label called Dot to do an album based on the songs of Sam Coslow, composer of the hits "Flamingo" and "Cocktails for Two." *My Old Flame: Marian McPartland Performs the Classic Hits of Sam Coslow* dramatically highlighted the desirability of McPartland taking the reins of her own recording career. Over its bland cocktail flourishes, the label dubbed a female vocal chorus that offered Ray Conniff–style "dits," "doo-wahs," and occasional great curtains of "ooohs" that rendered irrelevant whatever good the trio (Ron Carter, bass; Grady Tate, drums) may have accomplished. The cover art featured a gauzy color photo of a mascara-brushed, full-lipped model who very much recalled the girl (and mood) on Bud Shank's album of Beatles covers, *Michelle,* plus a blurry close-up of a kerosene lamp (get it?—"My Old Flame"). Of the more than sixty albums McPartland made in her career, this was the one record she regretted. It was the last commercial album she would record for six years.

By contrast, Marian's debut disc for Halcyon, *Interplay* (Halcyon 100)— and the label's debut as well—seemed to have been made by an entirely different musician. It was a spare duo effort with Linc Milliman, mostly recorded live, in July 1968, at a club in Rochester, New York, then finished up in August at Fairchild's studio. In instrumentation, spirit, harmonic approach, rhythmic feel, and downright seriousness, *Interplay* departed so dramatically from anything McPartland had done on record before that critics who had not been following her development, live, could not believe their ears. The album kicked off with a nicely crafted, bittersweet tune Marian had composed while working at the Apartment, "Twilight World"—probably the best song she ever wrote—then ranged through a variety of material that would form the bedrock of her future repertoire: a mix of originals, Ellington, early jazz (Hoagy Carmichael), a modal tune (by Miles Davis), a healthy selection of standards from the Great American Songbook, and a contemporary jukebox hit. She and Milliman interacted flexibly, with the bassist making conversational, LaFaro kinds of moves. The music breathed as they played with the time, moving lithely from rubato to swing and back. Marian's attack was percussive and sure and swinging, yet reflective and moody. Though Milliman's bass was too high in the mix, they hit their stride on the standard, "Close Your Eyes," which featured a long, two-handed break by Marian that didn't return to regular time for quite a while and recalled Bill Evans without mimicking him. She and Milliman even put their own stamp on Glen Campbell's then popular country hit by Jimmy Webb, "By the Time I Get to Phoenix."

But the most important aspect of this album wasn't so much in the details as in the spirit of the thing. It was as if, suddenly—at the age of fifty—Marian McPartland had decided to play music the way she wanted to hear it, instead of how she thought everyone else wanted to hear it. Gone was that busy, eager-to-please cocktail lady who bounced all over the piano with block chords or got gooped up with syrupy singers or strings. McPartland was clearly playing to express her real self—reflective, bittersweet, moody, but also cheerful and robust—and let the market be damned. The result, of course, was that she was far easier to love, having found out, finally, who she really was.

None of this went unnoticed by reviewers, among whom were the observant Dan Morgenstern at *Down Beat* as well as writers for *Stereo Review, High Fidelity, Jazz Journal,* and *Saturday Review,* all of whom recognized the album as a breakthrough.

"Some months ago I reviewed an album on Dot featuring pianist Marian McPartland," reported *High Fidelity.* "The Dot album turned Miss McPartland into Miss Peppermint Stick. She played the part so well that I ignored the blandness of the album. This one is another story. This is Miss McP saying, 'Get out of my way and let me play.'"

As for Halcyon itself, the Canadian jazz magazine *CODA* remarked that any new label "should wish for such an auspiciously and musically valuable first release; or second, or third, or fourth."

Marian was having a ball running this new cottage industry—finding studios, looking for artists, choosing tunes, designing and packaging the albums, getting them reviewed, and mailing them out to stores. Marian hatched the idea for the design of the first album, multiple exposures of a piano with blue and white hands on the keyboard, strung out like a hand of cards, a visual apposite of the music's series of overlays. A designer from Rochester, Joe Hendrick, executed the idea. The company pressed one thousand copies of the LP, which would become Halcyon's standard run.

Even Fairchild, the multimillionaire tycoon, seemed to be having the time of his life. In 1970, he personally designed a Christmas brochure for the first three records.

"I feel like a kid again, selling penny lemonade in front of my house," Fairchild told Marian.

"He taught me the fun of getting things done cheaply with Halcyon," Marian said. "He had such a positive attitude. I learned from him to be 'all business' on the phone, to just say what you have to say and hang up. He had tireless energy and was a perfectionist."

Marian wrote the liner notes for *Interplay* in her usual warm, welcoming style, as she did for her next Halcyon album, *Ambiance* (Halcyon 103), even more of a departure than the first. Recorded in July 1970 at Fairchild's studio and released late that year, it featured Cincinnati bassist Michael Moore and his pal, drummer Jimmy Madison—both of whom Marian had hired for the Apartment gig when they moved to New York. They played mostly original material by Marian and Moore. *Ambiance* was a gorgeous, oblique, in some cases nearly free-improv album with a thread of mystery running through it, much like the style developed by Miles Davis and Herbie Hancock. It remains a classic in McPartland's discography, one of the best albums she ever made. The title track, a sixteen-bar tune with a four-bar reprise of the first theme, was a mysterious, hauntingly modal piece that made a surprise substitute resolution to a C-major ninth under the gorgeously dissonant melody note of F-sharp, then did the same thing again, except the chord resolved to B-flat minor under an A-flat melody note. By the end of the second eight, the key migrated a step and a half away, to E-flat, which gave the whole thing the floating, atmospheric quality suggested by the title. She was quite open about the influence of Hancock's "Maiden Voyage" on the tune. But the era was rampant with such atmospheric pieces, in which unpredictable modal motion, atmosphere, and color trumped singable melodies. The difference here was that Marian had also written a *memorable* line. The trio gave it a light bossa feel.

But "Ambiance" was just the beginning. "Glimpse" (featuring the creative Billy Hart on percussion) had no chords at all (though it was credited to Moore as composer) and had been worked out onstage as a free-improv piece. Marian's "Aspen" evoked the rattle of leaves with icy percussion and atonal, trinkle-tinkle piano. The opener, "What Is This Thing Called Love?," languidly ambled toward a swing feel, suggesting Paul Bley in its propulsive cut-and-paste deconstruction as Marian snatched patches of the tune's melody and harmony, stringing them together in whatever order she felt like. Madison's drumming had that inner, probing feel of Paul Motian, another Bill Evans alum. Marian debuted another dreamy original on the album, "Afterglow."

Hendrick's softly psychedelic cover art, a collage of sunflower tones with a bright orange border, alluded to Marian's background, with Little Bo Beep in a storybook English landscape, as well as her love of nature, with butterflies and wildflowers. When Marian played *Ambiance* for Bill Evans, he was shocked. "My God, Marian, how come you're playing like that?" Then he unintentionally tossed her a sexist left-hand compliment: "Who did that for you? The boys?"

Moore was quick to credit McPartland.

"She really wanted to experiment," he said. "It was very much a conscious effort on her part to have an album like that."

Said *CODA:* "It looks as if Marian McPartland has finally arrived and it has turned out to be a welcome arrival."

During this period of exponential growth, Marian also threw herself into jazz education, partly out of missionary zeal, but also to keep the wolf from the door. In January 1968, the proposal Clem De Rosa had submitted two years earlier for the Huntington schools materialized into a $288,600 grant for the PACE program. In January and February, Marian did twenty-eight demo/workshops in fifteen junior high and high schools with Milliman, drummer Jim Kappes, and flugelhornist Ray Copeland. The work gave her a new appreciation for teachers.

"To play a piano in a night club is infinitely easier than teaching school," she wrote in a journal she kept for the project. "One has to improvise constantly, change, delete, add, adapt, be flexible. Every situation is different. Schools are different. Teachers are different. Time of day makes a difference in the attention span. Sometimes by 2:20 everyone has had it—just waiting to go home. Then you really have to work hard, arouse them, draw them out, but it's rewarding. Being a teacher is the hardest job in life."

Marian quickly realized that the fastest way to turn kids off was to tell them the pop music they liked was "trash," even if that's how she felt. Driving to schools, she listened to rock stations on the car radio, learning songs like "Eleanor Rigby" by the Beatles, "You Are the Sunshine of My Life" by Stevie Wonder, "Sunny" by Bobby Hebb, and the feel-good classic Burt Bacharach had written for the film *Butch Cassidy and the Sundance Kid,* "Raindrops Keep Fallin' on My Head." Later, she even learned Led Zeppelin's "Stairway to Heaven," though she drew the line when Mrs. Miller's class at Oldfield requested Iron Butterfly's "In-A-Gadda-Da-Vida"!

One of the big payoffs in the schools was discovering young talent. At Cold Spring Harbor High, Milliman and Marian taught a precocious thirteen-year-old named Jon Burr, who would later play with Tony Bennett, Houston Person, and Stéphane Grappelli and write arrangements for Marian.

"Here was an established professional telling me I should continue pursuing music," Burr said. "She was one of the early missionaries of jazz education. . . . She broke down the wall of exclusivity that jazz seems to have, that jazz [was] elitist and forbidding and male and black, or whatever preconceptions people might have had about inadmissibility to the club. Marian put all that stuff to rest through her work. She was a real game changer."

From Long Island, Marian's teaching fanned out to the rest of the country. In 1968, De Rosa recruited her as a judge at a St. Louis intercollegiate jazz festival, and his associate Ken Morris, who had started the first National Stage Band Camp in 1959 at Indiana University, invited her to participate in a summer jazz education program the following year. For the next few years, Marian would teach on a circuit that included some combination of Seattle, Portland, Sacramento, Long Beach, the University of Utah, Illinois, Oklahoma, Indiana, and Storrs, Connecticut. These camps were among the only places a young musician could get hands-on professional help in those days, and numerous players who attended them, such as Gary Burton, would become stars. The faculty included players such as Herb Pomeroy (trumpet), John LaPorta (reeds), Alan Dawson (drums), Buddy Johnson (piano), and Phil Wilson (trombone), the last of whom shared Marian's love of tennis and the outdoors and became a close friend.

Dave Peck, an Oregon-born, Seattle-based pianist who has enjoyed some success (and has appeared on *Piano Jazz*), recalled studying as a teenager with McPartland at camps in both Washington and Oregon.

"Of all the people on that thing, she could really kick butt," recalled Peck. "She was all over the piano. She did things there you never heard on those [Hickory House] records. That's where it all started for me. Left-hand voicings for the blues, arranging, improvisation. It wasn't like anything else you could get in those days."

Noreen Lienhard, a pianist from Racine, Wisconsin, who became a jazz educator and also appeared on *Piano Jazz,* vividly remembered Marian's 1970 workshop.

"It was so thrilling to be in the room with this wonderful woman," she said. "She had an arrangement of 'Giant Steps' with all the voicings written out. You got to hear the faculty play every night. When you come away from something like that, you have stuff to last for years and years. It was very inspiring."

For someone accustomed to going to bed at four or five in the morning for more than twenty years, doing school workshops at nine A.M. was a grueling change of pace. *Newsday* painted a crisp portrait of teacher Marian on Long Island:

"Marian's driving a yellow Pinto on the Northern State Parkway, trying to learn the words to a new Top 40 song," wrote Howard Schneider.

> She's on her way to Northport. . . . She's dressed in knit slacks, lavender blouse and matching scarf, her long English face impeccably made up and her blonde hair stylishly coiffured. When she uses words like "gig" and "swinging" she sounds like a butler trying to be hip. . . .
>
> From February to May, the routine had been the same. Up at six o'clock in the morning for the drive out to Northport, where she was an artist in residence. Concert, then individual classes. Duet on "Heart and Soul."
>
> Back to New York, The Cookery, falling asleep at 3 a.m.

Schneider closed with a quote from "Raindrops," suggesting Marian's inspirational—and intrepid—attitude toward her crazy workload: "The blues they send to meet me, won't defeat me. . . ." Sometimes, though, the blues won out. For while the separation from Jimmy allowed her the space to grow, it also brought on periods of deep depression, during which Marian realized she was not only unhappy on her own, but often missed Jimmy terribly. In the first years after the divorce, she spent many a night mooning about him in Manhattan—and Joe Morello, too, for that matter—and for a brief period even started drinking heavily herself.

In a laconic daybook detailing her expenses and activities during the summer and fall of 1968—alongside quotidian notes of the cost of cabs, hair coloring (she was still dyeing her hair blond), and fees—appeared stark, brief notations of loneliness, confusion, and even an anomalous run of hangovers. After an unpleasant gig in Beverly Hills, she registered "absolute despair." When she got back to New York, she drove out to Merrick to go to the beach with Jimmy but on September 28 woke up "hung over and ashamed." According to sidemen who worked for her in the 1960s and 1970s, she was very much "one of the guys," no less reluctant to hop into the sack from time to time than most male jazz players. (Bassist Ron McClure reported that Marian seduced him on a couch at Bunch's apartment when he was twenty-three; she was forty-six.) And why not? One of the things that gets lost in discussions about women in jazz is that part of what was meant by jazz being a "man's world" in those days was that when men went out on the road together, they talked dirty, they talked about women, and they often scouted for women to sleep with. How was a woman to deal with that? Marian's solution was to join the crowd. If she was truly the equal of men, why deny herself the sexual freedom universally accepted as part of the jazzman's life? As Marian put it sarcastically in regard to one ex-road boyfriend with whom she had an extended, rather sweet affair, "We played music, we drank, we played tennis—that was just one more thing we could do."

But as laissez-faire as she tried to sound—and behave—whenever she went out with other men, Marian discovered to her great dismay that, far from feeling liberated, she felt even lonelier. Or just confused. Notes she made to herself suggest that at one time she had been attracted briefly to bass player Billy Taylor Sr., who had worked with Duke Ellington in the 1930s and whom she met through Jimmy on the trad scene. "Should I have gone ahead?" she wondered. On the phone with Jimmy, she would find herself saying, "Gee, I feel so lonesome," and, "Gee, now that I'm here [in Manhattan], I realize that a lot of things I blamed you for are my fault."

"I always blamed him because I could never get any work done," she said. "But it wasn't true."

Dr. Benjamin had warned her this would happen.

"You can't seem to cut him loose," he said, "so you're just going to have to learn how to live with him."

In a longer, surprisingly contemporary-sounding journal entry from this period, Marian morosely registered the conflict she felt between career and romance, as well as a growing anxiety about her income.

"Music takes up your whole life," she wrote. "I understand why musicians are so weird—there's no time for anything else. To lead a reasonable life you have to cut down on music and that means less money. To form a relationship takes time. A close relationship—not an occasional lay. . . . How do you organize your life? Practice. . . . Feel as if I'm getting intolerant of the city, dues you have to pay. . . . I guess I do want companionship. . . . Nothing lined up to do after the Apartment. Apathy. . . . Everything seems too much."

From time to time, Marian would call Joe Morello, at one point noting she had spoken with him for two hours. One night, her musings migrated into a nascent song lyric about him, even as she wagged her finger at herself with Ben Franklin–ish nostrums:

I'm lonely.
But I'm also learning how to be alone
Be with young people, listen to them listen to their music
    don't put them down or ridicule them.
While others come and go like shadows in a play
The memory of our love is bright as day [crossed out]
He's still the one I think about
And turn to in my dreams
No day goes by
That I don't see him in my mind's eye
Feel him in my heart and mind.
He's still the one no matter who I see
Only him for me. [crossed out]
Dr. B said Listen to yourself
Eric Fromm: "Don't be with zombies."
So starved for real love and good sex.
Compliments that seemed real, sex life that made me know I was a woman.
diet and exercise
no junk food
use today's fashions your way

In the past, when Marian felt down, she had called Dorothy. But the two had fallen out. Dorothy had finally left her second husband in the summer of 1966—sneaking out of their house in Mexico City in the middle of the night with both kids—and had filed for divorce in Chicago. Ever hapless in love, Dorothy had promptly fallen for her Spanish instructor, a seminarian-turned-teacher named Eliseo Cuevas Nava, known to Dorothy and others as "Cheo." Dorothy invited him to Chicago and announced her intention to marry him.

Cheo was ten years younger than Dorothy and was described by family members with patronizing diffidence as a "pleasant," "sweet," "well-mannered" man with gold teeth. Marian, whose dislike of Dorothy's second husband had already strained their friendship, was more straight-forward. She told Dorothy that marrying Cheo would be a terrible mistake. Dorothy did not take kindly to her stepmother's advice.

"She said something very snippy, like 'Don't tell me how to run my life,'" said Marian. "She loved Mexico."

Sadly, the disagreement ended their friendship.

Dorothy and Cheo married in 1968. Marian and Jimmy did not attend. Dorothy bought a new Volkswagen station wagon with a small settlement from her divorce and drove back to Mexico to a remote mountain village south of Cuernevaca called Jiquilpan, where Cheo had gotten a teaching job. In June, after Donna finished her freshman year of high school, she joined them. Doug, who by this time had started college, remained in Chicago.

Dorothy was clearly in a confused state of mind.

"I remember her saying she had $10,000 and we should take this $10,000 and go to Acapulco and live on the beach, and when the money's all gone, take a bottle of Seconal [a popular sleeping pill]," said John Lanigan.

On July 19, 1968, Marian took a BOAC red-eye to England. A few days later, she was having drinks with Eleanor Bron at Ronnie Scott's, London's premier jazz club, then merrily chatting over lunch with Joyce in the city. She and Joyce had a lot to talk about. Marian had been on her own for almost a year now. While she was sure she had made the right decision, she was hurt that Jimmy had not put up more of a fight for her. If he had, she told Joyce, maybe they never would have split up. On the other hand, it was starting to feel as if she had never left. Jimmy was constantly doing her favors, lending her his station wagon when she needed to get out to various schools on Long Island, picking up stamps for her, driving her to the airport, coming over to visit at East Eighty-sixth Street. She even found herself occasionally staying overnight in Merrick.

Joyce had her own tales to tell. She, too, had married a man who drank too much, repeating with fatal precision the family dynamic—a dominant woman in control of a passive man. And Joyce, too, had become involved in a long-term affair with a younger man. It had gone on for fifteen years. Ultimately, Joyce had lovingly cast him out, telling him he was wasting his life with a married woman and should find a wife and children of his own. The story reminded them both of Colette's novel *Chéri,* in which the courtesan Léa agrees that her lover, Chéri, should leave her to marry a

younger woman. (Thankfully, Joyce's story didn't end tragically, like Colette's novel; Joyce even attended her ex-lover's wedding.) But that was the
past. Though her husband definitely spent too much time at the Wheat-
sheaf, the pub below Wish Hill, Joyce had a lovely family. Sheila, twenty-
one, was studying nursing in London; Chris, fifteen, was doing okay in
school; and twelve-year-old Mark was a confirmed Beatles fan.

On July 29, Marian had lunch in London with young British jazz critic
Valerie Wilmer, and that night they went to see Don Ellis, the experimental composer/bandleader who had electrified his trumpet and was
experimenting with wild new time signatures that made Brubeck's "Take
Five" sound like an old-fashioned waltz. When Marian got back to Eastbourne, she received a long-distance phone call in the middle of the
night. It was Don Kassel, in Chicago.

"Dorothy is dead," he said.

Fun-loving, beautiful Dorothy, Jimmy's sweet daughter, who had been
dragged from green room to hotel room to relatives' homes to private
school and back, who at thirty-seven had been married three times, had
killed herself. Donna had been in her bedroom when her mother came in
and said she had taken "forty or fifty" sleeping pills. She died in the village hospital the next day. Don Kassel and Doug flew down a few days
later for the funeral. In standard McPartland fashion the family had a party.

"We drank—and they drank—and they laughed and we told stories and
everybody danced and we talked about all the good things about my
mother, and it was really lovely," said Donna.

In the fall, Donna went back to live with her father in Chicago and
started her sophomore year at Senn High School.

"It was as if I had just been on vacation," she said.

The "as if" part of Donna's description wasn't just a conceit. For years,
no one in the McPartland family acknowledged Dorothy had taken her
life. Jimmy even lied in jazz oral history interviews, declaring his daughter had died in a car accident. The stigma of suicide—and his own apparent guilt—was too great to bear. The suicide, in fact, cut a deep swath
between the McPartlands and Jimmy's grandchildren, a wound that would
take years to heal.

"For a long time after this, we didn't see Marian," said Donna. "I couldn't
figure out why Grandpa disappeared. He was such a big, strong character,
why didn't he show up? I thought he was going to come and save us. But
they [Jimmy and Marian] disappeared into their own problems."

When Marian received the news of Dorothy's death, she felt a combination of deep sorrow at losing her best friend and fear that the suicide

would knock Jimmy off the wagon. Her fears were justified. When she got back to New York, Jimmy had gone on a serious bender that lasted several weeks. He had a gun in a drawer and was muttering, "If I had the guts, I'd shoot myself."

Marian called an AA hotline to try to get some help and eventually reached a woman named Patti Sarka. A jazz fan, Sarka knew Marian by reputation.

"Are you *the* Marian McPartland?" Sarka asked.

"I guess I am," Marian replied sarcastically. "I'm calling because my husband has a drinking problem. He's drinking because his daughter—in Mexico—has committed suicide."

Sarka recommended a hospital in Freeport with a rehab program. Jimmy had tried to dry out there before, but this time, though he stayed there for only a week, the cure seemed to take. Jimmy had been an alcoholic for more than forty years. Though he would have a severe relapse a year later, Dorothy's death sobered up the Chicago cornetist.

He was sixty-one years old.

After Dorothy's death, Jimmy had a spectacular year of sobriety. In 1969, he began to gear up for his first gig off the sauce, at the Down Beat, a club on Lexington and Forty-second Street, near Grand Central Station. One morning, however, he picked up the horn to practice and found his hands were shaking so badly he couldn't play. As an alcoholic, he was only too familiar with this condition and he resorted to the only cure he knew. When he called Marian to tell her what was going on, it sounded as if he were drunk. Marian called Hank O'Neal.

"You've got to help me with something," she said. "Something is really wrong with Jimmy. You've got to go to Merrick."

Hank and Marian drove out to the house. Marian went to the front door, Hank to the back.

"I looked in the kitchen door window and I see Jimmy," remembered Hank, "who is walking around in his boxer shorts—and in those years, Jimmy had a stomach that was pretty substantial—anyway, he had a big, big glass of brownish liquid of some kind, probably Scotch, in one hand, a big one, I mean, just cut the top off the bottle—and a pistol in the other one."

Hank knocked, gently let himself in, and the two of them talked Jimmy down. He put the gun away and Jimmy went back to rehab.

"What we figured out later was that Jimmy was really trying to get into shape," said Hank. "He was exercising, going to the beach, swimming, doing his calisthenics, push-ups, and sit-ups. And what he did was, he exercised a little too hard with the push-ups or something. And when he had tried to play the trumpet, he was shaking. It was muscle fatigue, but he was thinking that something was happening to him and 'if I have a drink I can get rid of this.' "

There was a happy ending. O'Neal called Pee Wee Irwin to have a second trumpet player on hand, just in case, but Jimmy made the date. And as far as anyone knows—except at the very end of his life—that really was the last time Jimmy McPartland took a drink.

Never one to be left out, Marian followed Jimmy into the Down Beat, where, in the political spirit of the times, she staged a "jazz-in" November 8, 1969, inviting two hundred junior high and high school students to play, including kids from Cold Spring Harbor, directed by Clem De Rosa.

After Jimmy quit drinking—possibly because his sobriety made it easier, possibly out of habit, but most probably because she never had really wanted entirely to leave him—Marian gradually drifted closer to Jimmy, recalibrating their separation into a rather unusual relationship that was not quite marriage but not quite divorce: best friends, sometime lovers, socializing and working together as a couple, yet living in separate homes.

For Jimmy, the split had never been quite real, anyway.

"He was always married to Marian in his head, even when they got divorced," Donna said.

"In a way," Marian said, "I don't know why I got the divorce, because we would still be always hanging out together. There was something childlike about him. He would always call me if anything happened. Once or twice he got sick and I went out and took care of him. And he never found somebody else. I don't know. Maybe if he had, I would not have been so blasé about the whole thing."

On March 15, 1969, without telling him why, Marian invited him over to her apartment. When he got there, Eddie Condon and a gang of friends—including Eddie's wife, Phyllis, Hank O'Neal, choreographer and American Dance Guild president Marilyn Danitz, and another doctor friend, Herb Ogden—leapt out to sing "Happy Birthday." That summer, Marian terminated her analysis with Dr. Benjamin. She had come nearly full circle. And so had Jimmy.

Marian's emergence in the late 1960s as a pianist with a distinctive voice was unfortunately not supported by robust opportunities for live performance. On the contrary, the era began with the closure of the very club where she had gotten her first great opportunity—the Hickory House—which went dark just as 1967 merged into 1968. Billy Taylor, who had become a fixture at the venerable steak house, was on the stand for the last hurrah. He invited Marian to sit in.

"I felt so sad that I just couldn't play," reflected Marian. "I knew that with this room went almost forty years of jazz history. . . . I never went back. . . . There has never been another place like it, and there never will be."

Though work in New York was drying up, Marian occasionally found jobs out of town, through Max Cavalli. In September 1968, she flew out to Beverly Hills to play a new club called the Jazz Suite on Rodeo Drive, a cooperative venture started by a group of Angeleno jazz lovers. Marian brought bassist Ron McClure, with whom she had worked in the Midwest and Florida and who had contributed "Nimbus" to her book. (She had also written a very complimentary piece about McClure and Eddie Gomez for *Down Beat* in 1966.) One of the new crop of harmonically nimble LaFaro-ites of the sort Marian adored, McClure had come to New York from Connecticut in 1963. The idea at the Jazz Suite was to take jazz out of the noisy, smoky club environment and put it into a respectful listening situation, a notion also taking hold on New York's budding "loft" scene. Unfortunately, the atmosphere turned out to be far from respectful. One night, two drunks approached Marian on the bandstand and, pointing to the front cover of the menu, which had some musical notation printed on it, said, "Play this!" Marian took the challenge, cheerfully hoping they would settle down and laugh it off. But McClure was outraged. He gathered his things and walked offstage. On the way, he complained to the management, asking why they hadn't intervened.

"It was just too much cocktail lounge bullshit," said McClure. "I said, 'Fuck this, I'm going home.'"

The next day, Marian hired Los Angeles ace Andy Simpkins. She had to stay over an extra night just to get paid by the club, and she left rather upset. When she got back to Manhattan, she thrust herself back into Long Island school workshops with Milliman and Kappes. Milliman had begun to grumble about money. After an engagement in Canada, he said Marian paid him only $25, declaring she had spent the rest on legal fees to get him into the country. (Milliman had indeed been busted there for marijuana, playing with Maynard Ferguson, and Marian had hired a lawyer to get Milliman across the border.) Things came to a head the following February 1969, when Milliman's girlfriend, a student at Hood College in Maryland, arranged for the trio to play there for a fee of $1,500. When Marian sent Milliman a check for a hundred bucks—and gave his girlfriend a watch—he was livid.

"Send $300 and we'll send back the watch," he wrote, enumerating his complaints with what he called Marian's "excessive parsimony."

Though she said later she felt bad about the incident, McPartland never worked with Milliman again, which was a shame, since she sounded so great with him. Was he right? Did she habitually lowball her sidemen? It's possible she did, at least in this period, as she was scrimping to pay rent because of the split-up with Jimmy. And it's certainly true that she specialized in hiring great young musicians who naturally would work for less than seasoned pros. But Milliman was the only sideman (of dozens interviewed) who ever complained that she paid worse (or, for that matter, better) than the going rate. Most reported she was quite fair—and prompt. Milliman appeared to have been the disgruntled exception.

More important, these two incidents illustrated that McPartland finally was comfortable being in charge. She had become less obsessed with being "nice," seeking approval from others when she needn't. So she fell out with a couple of bass players? So what. In the early days, she had negotiated, waffled, danced, or procrastinated when it came to firing musicians. Now she was confronting the business head-on, with no apologies. This assertive, practical mind-set would become an even more prominent part of her character in the 1970s.

Not long after the McClure and Milliman episodes, Marian received an invitation to celebrate Duke Ellington's seventieth birthday at the Nixon White House—on April 29, 1969. Marian got a booking at the Washington, D.C., club Blues Alley and spent the evening shuttling between the gig there and the gala East Room affair in a White House limo. The rather grand guest list of two hundred took in Duke's family, including his sister, Ruth, with whom Marian often chatted on the phone when Duke was on tour; Ellington's personal physician, Arthur Logan; Willie "the Lion" Smith, who never took his cigar out of his mouth the whole night; and a gallery of illustrious musicians that included everyone from Benny Goodman and Cab Calloway to Harold Arlen and Paul Desmond. Marian wore a white satin gown with a rhinestone collar and beads around the bottom, made especially for the occasion. After the receiving line, cocktail party, and formal dinner—during which the unctuous Ellington turned to Pat Nixon and said, "It's illegal for a woman to be so pretty"—a ten-piece band performed, then a jam session ensued. When Marian noticed someone had left a drink on the eagle-legged White House piano, she removed it and wiped off the surface, a fussy gesture duly reported the next day by *The Washington Post,* much to her embarrassment. She also recalled Duke goading her into hopping onto the piano bench—not that she ever needed much prodding to sit in—because Willie "the Lion" Smith was monopolizing the keyboard.

"I suppose you want to play," said Smith.

"Yeah, I'd like to," she said, moving in a little.

"Okay," Willie said, then walked off in a sulk.

Ellington stood in a corner, chuckling to himself.

Nixon thanked Marian for playing several of his favorite ballads, two of which came from the Sam Coslow book—"My Old Flame" and "In the Middle of a Kiss"—but then nudged *her* off the bandstand so he could play "Happy Birthday" for Duke. Nixon retired before midnight and the session went on till the wee hours, with the musicians becoming progressively inebriated on free White House booze. (Marian knew it was getting late when even Urbie Green had to play leaning against the wall.) Someone joked that the president was going to have to come down in his pajamas and throw the crowd out. But, in fact, recalled Marian, "it was really a very pleasant and happy party," and she finished off the evening with a fourth set at Blues Alley. "Sorry I'm late," she apologized cheerfully. "I'm also doubling at the White House!"

A few months after the White House gig, in September 1969, Marian found herself playing in Rochester, New York—the home of Kodak, about seventy-five miles east of Buffalo, on Lake Ontario—with bassist Michael Moore and ex–Thelonious Monk drummer Ben Riley, at a new club called the Monticello Room. A large restaurant and bar in the Rowntowner Motel, the Monticello was surrounded by shopping malls and automobile dealerships in the blue-collar suburb of Henrietta. When Marian heard Alec Wilder was in town, she left him a note at his hotel, inviting him to dinner. It was the beginning of a deep and lifelong companionship.

A curmudgeonly, urbane malcontent with a wicked sense of humor, severe alcohol problem, nasty temper, and purist's contempt for commercialism, Wilder had grown up in Rochester and on Park Avenue, the scion of three generations of bankers. Thanks to a trust fund, he kept a room at the Algonquin Hotel (albeit a modest one) but also spent time in his hometown, where he had studied at the Eastman School of Music. Wilder composed classical music, popular songs, and a vast amount of uncategorizable material in the vein of the octets that had struck Marian so deeply growing up. For a while, he had toiled in the very maw of the popular music machine, working as staff arranger for CBS's *Ford Theatre Hour*. But he disliked the business and ultimately became known as a "composer's composer," though millions heard his bittersweet classic, "While We're Young," on the B side of Tony Bennett's hit on Hank Williams's "Cold, Cold Heart." Wilder's songs "I'll Be Around" and "It's So Peaceful in the Country" were often recorded. In 1946, Frank Sinatra had released *Frank Sinatra Conducts the Music of Alec Wilder.*

When Wilder came to hear Marian's trio at the Monticello, he was dazzled.

"In three unplanned minutes," he later wrote, "she can, and consistently does, invent rhythms, harmonic sequences and melodic flights which would take me three weeks to achieve as a composer. And even then, not half as well."

Wilder kept coming back to the Monticello, night after night. As he was leaving one evening, he said, "I'm going to write a piece for you—I'll bring it next week."

"I was pleased, but I didn't really believe him," said Marian. "I forgot all about it until the next time he showed up at the Rowntowner. He airily tossed me a sheet of music, on which was written, 'Jazz Waltz for a Friend—a small present from Alec Wilder.' I was delighted, and I couldn't wait to play the piece. It had a haunting melody that had a way of turning back on itself that I found fascinating. It was deceptively simple to play, yet hard to memorize and improvise on. Many of Alec's pieces are that way, but they are rewarding, for as you delve into them and explore their intricacies, you find fresh ways to go."

Though Sinatra and Bennett were two of Wilder's staunchest admirers, he could be a difficult person to champion. For Wilder, music was a personal affair, the music business a nasty inconvenience. He often made gifts of his compositions. It was an idealistic, if regal, attitude that had immense appeal for McPartland, who despite her business acuity felt much the same way about the personal nature of music. They also shared an antipathy for rock music. Rock, they felt, had rendered them obsolete outsiders, a situation that led Alec to a rather noble self-pity (composer Warren Benson called Wilder "the Errol Flynn of losers")—which magnified as he became progressively inebriated—despairing that "good music" would ever again get a hearing. Marian, as an educator, was more upbeat but nevertheless pummeled rock whenever she got the chance. "These poor American children," she lamented in a Washington, D.C., interview in her best Jazz Nanny tone. "They grow up hearing this awful rock and roll. They've never heard any of America's real music." (As if Robert Johnson, Muddy Waters, B. B. King, and Elvis Presley weren't America's "real music.")

Over the years, Alec wrote many lovely tunes for Marian, including "Jazz Waltz for a Friend," "Homework," "Lullaby for a Lady," "Inner Circle," and "Why," as well as the modern classical piece *Fantasy for Piano and Wind Ensemble.* (He also wrote a song originally titled "The Marian

Kind," but when she laughed at the title, he petulantly rededicated it to Mabel Mercer, changing the title to—ironically—"Be a Child.")

No one in America had thought more about songwriting than Wilder, as the world would see when the book he and Jim Maher were writing, *American Popular Song,* was published in 1972. This groundbreaking, idio-syncratic, phrase-by-phrase analysis of the composers who wrote what would later be called the Great American Songbook—Irving Berlin, George Gershwin, Harold Arlen, Cole Porter, and all the rest—was an original that treated this body of work with the high seriousness one might bring to Schubert or Chopin, without ever losing sight of the fact that the purpose of it all was to entertain. Rather than "elevate" popular music to the level of the "classics," Wilder reminded readers that classics were also meant to be *popular.*

But for all his philosophical adherence to accessibility, Wilder's own songs were often rejected by the public. As Wilder's biographer Desmond Stone put it, they "were not cut from common cloth." They were, rather, "leaping and lovely, sinuous and sequestered, elusive and wistful. All the top vocalists would record and praise them, but not many people would sing along."

Impressed by Marian's mercurial imagination, Wilder was convinced that if she applied herself, she could write good songs herself. He encour-aged and criticized her, lavishing generous attention on her work, nag-ging her by telephone to finish things she'd started. He even gave her a set of notebooks in which to jot down her ideas. His hectoring bore fruit. Between 1966 and 1974, McPartland penned "Ambiance," "Willow Creek," "Illusion," "Twilight World," "Afterglow," "Lost One," "Time and Time Again" "A Delicate Balance," and "Solace." Some of these songs found a degree of success. "Afterglow," which she first recorded on *Ambiance,* found its way into Peggy Lee's book, when the singer wrote some fine lyrics to it and changed the name to "In the Days of Our Love," recording it on her 1979 album, *Close Enough for Love.* Lee's lyrics uncan-nily evoked Marian's lingering feelings for Joe Morello—which she had had in mind when she wrote the song—as the narrator stared into the ashes of a past love. "Twilight World," which reviewers began to note with pleasure in Marian's live sets around 1967, received the gift of a lyric by the great Johnny Mercer. In 1971, Tony Bennett picked up the song for a marvelous album, *With Love,* with arrangements by Robert Farnon, a record that was, unfortunately, poorly distributed.

As a composer, Marian shared Wilder's affection for bittersweet ballads, which in her work often evoked the emotion Brazilians call *saudades,* a feeling somewhat more complex than mere nostalgia or sadness and in some ways similar to the blues, in that it evokes the sadness of missing something that has passed at the same time that it celebrates how wonderful it was when it was at hand. Marian performed such songs, appropriately, with a quietly understated bossa nova beat. Unfortunately, she was also prone to meandering and cloud gazing, so in some ways Wilder's oblique sense of melody was probably not the best influence on her. She often started tunes with a three-to-five-note idea based on a spoken phrase, then, rather than attaching the theme to the spine of a traditional thirty-two-bar AABA song, she developed the melody in a free-associative way, returning obsessively to the same short phrase. The results were sometimes stringy, lacking a memorable aesthetic arc. "Afterglow," though far better than the earlier "Stranger in a Dream," had that problem: No matter how many times you listened to it, even with lyrics, it was hard to figure out where it started and where it ended. An odd length—twenty bars, with a first melody of ten bars, a second of six, and a four-bar reprise of the beginning of the first ten. McPartland sometimes seemed to almost purposely avoid catchy hooks, but she definitely knew how to create a mood, and in "Ambiance" and "Twilight World" she had written two songs of lasting value.

Wilder and McPartland shared a love not only of music, but of language, nature, books, and a spirit of mischievous rebellion. Wilder was an avid crossword puzzler (he even composed them), and they both prized—and used—large vocabularies and self-consciously correct grammar and diction. When Marian interviewed Alec for her show on WBAI, he joked about how Jo Stafford's record company was upset by the poor grammar of Alec's song title "Who Can I Turn To?"

"The BBC probably would have made it 'To Whom Shall I Turn?'" Marian quipped, then added—ever one for self-improvement—that she was reading Edwin Newman's new book, *Strictly Speaking,* and trying to stop saying "you know" unnecessarily.

Marian and Alec enjoyed an active social life in Rochester, mixing with a rare circle of friends that included Wilder's pal the photographer Lou Ouzer; newspaper editor (and subsequent Wilder biographer) Desmond Stone; lawyer, aspiring drummer, and radio host Tom Hampson and his wife, the English novelist Zena Collier; Father Henry Atwell, a radical priest and former editor of the *Catholic Courier;* Dr. Carl Oshrain, who played excellent saxophone in the style of Paul Desmond, and his wife, Margaret, a sometime singer; the late trumpeter Sal Sperazza; and Ray Wright, director of jazz studies at Eastman. In 1971, Wright invited

Marian to work with piano students at an annual summer arranging workshop. It was the beginning of a long relationship with Eastman, which would develop into a series of special concerts and Marian's classical debut. Marian would eventually elect to have most of her archive posthumously donated to the school.

Three-quarters of the mail Wilder got at the Algonquin came from the Audubon Society or other environmentalist organizations, and though Marian by then had read Rachel Carson's groundbreaking 1962 book, *Silent Spring,* her environmentalism seems to have flourished under Wilder's influence. Alec and Marian enjoyed taking walks through a Rochester park full of rhododendrons. Outside of town, along a stream, Wilder introduced her to the sound of small frogs in the area he called "peepers." At one point, Hampson took Wilder bird-watching, to expose him to the call of the olive-backed thrush, the echo of which Hampson said he heard in one of Wilder's melodies. ("By God, you're right!" Alec exclaimed when he heard the thrush.) When Phil Wilson moved into a new house, in 1972, Marian sent him four live trees, including a white birch and an apple tree. Like Alec, she joined a bevy of environmentalist groups, giving many of them large sums of money, especially the Sierra Club.

Despite his outward crustiness, Wilder had a childlike quality—not like Jimmy's boyishness, but more Peter Pan, a careful preservation of a child's sense of wonder. In keeping with that side, one of Wilder's favorite pastimes was blowing soap bubbles through a five-and-dime plastic hoop. Lou Ouzer's camera caught Wilder and Marian blowing bubbles on a Rochester street, smiling with glee.

"A guy was looking at us, disgusted," recalled Marian. "'You'll never grow up, Alec Wilder,' he said. And Alec said, 'No, I never will.'"

Being difficult was part of Alec's style. As much as he admired improvisers, he was adamant that the melody of a song be sung or played at least once precisely as composed. No cheating. When Peggy Lee recorded one of his tunes and changed the melody slightly, he wrote her a letter, saying, "The next time you want to record one of my songs, when you get to the bridge, jump off." At the top of "Jazz Waltz for a Friend," he wrote, "Kindly McPartlandize!" (his code to Marian for ad-libbing), but he was careful to note where she was "allowed" to do so, scribbling on the manuscript, "Okay, school's out!" One night in Raleigh, North Carolina, Alec made a rather snarky remark about the tonsorial disarray of Marian's drummer, Joe Corsello, whom he described as "a raccoon peeking out of a bush." When the trio arrived in Rochester for a monthlong engagement at the Monticello, Marian summarily sent Corsello and bassist Rick Petrone to Dr. Oshrain's house for haircuts, administered by his wife.

Marian was crazy about Alec. Had his sexual preference—ambivalent at best, apparently indifferent most of the time—been less repressed, he and Marian might well have become lovers.

"He used to come up to my room in the hotel and lie on the bed," said Marian. "I always had two beds, one for me and one for the suitcase and other stuff. Even though he was gay, I always thought, 'Well, you never know.' I said, 'You don't know how dangerous it is for you to lie on that bed like that.' And he said, 'Oh!Ho!Ho!' [scoffing laugh] I guess if I had leapt on him, he would have screamed!"

Mitch Miller's wife, Fran, was wild about Alec, too. After she divorced Mitch, she invited Alec and Marian to her place in the Cayman Islands. Marian recalled how she and Fran ogled Alec—who, despite his drinking and smoking, kept fit—in his bathing suit.

"Fran and I sat on the beach knowing there was no hope for either of us," Marian told Zena Collier. "And Alec went off to swim."

Though Wilder never expressed his love for Marian physically, he did write her an extraordinary letter revealing his affection.

"Dear Marian," he wrote. "In the event that you respect my judgment, my awareness and my occasional maturity, then believe me when I tell you that you fulfill all those requirements which one sensibly demands of anyone whom one loves and respects. You are very talented, you are witty, warm, good, ethical, tender, tolerant, angry, responsible, elegant, stylish, strong, steadfast, womanly, understanding, romantic, demanding, and sensitive, civilized, a trustworthy, generous, indeed a sensible example of the potential splendor of human kind at its best."

"It's the closest thing he would ever come to writing a love letter," Marian said. "I kept it in my purse for years, until it finally fell apart. I wonder if he knew how much that letter would mean to me, how I'd look it over when I got depressed and insecure, and decide maybe I wasn't so bad after all!"

Though Marian and Wilder were close, their relationship was subject to extreme ups and downs. When Marian played for the inauguration of President Nixon's second term, in January 1973, Wilder was livid. McPartland opposed the Vietnam War, certainly, but she had been invited to the White House by Len Garment, the man who had organized the Duke Ellington celebration in 1969 and to whom she had also recently suggested that money be found for her to present jazz workshops in the Washington,

D.C., schools. It would be not only bad manners to refuse the invitation, but impolitic. Wilder considered Marian's acceptance of the gig—perhaps not without justification—as cynical careerism. But for Wilder, as always, it was also personal. In the early 1970s, he had composed an elaborate antiwar piece for Tony Bennett and a children's choir, "The Children's Pleas for Peace," which Bennett's label, Columbia, had refused to record. For Nixon's inauguration, Marian played the ball at the Smithsonian Museum of History and Technology, where she sat in with "sweet band" leader Lester Lanin. Ironically, a traffic jam prevented her piano from arriving, so she had to have Wurlitzer send an electric keyboard.

"It was a very dull gig," she said. "I didn't feel very good about doing it. Alec didn't speak to me for months."

Jimmy seems to have shared Marian's indifference to politics. In February 1972, he agreed to play with local Dixielanders at the Queen's Tavern in Durban, South Africa, at a time when most jazz musicians were boycotting the country (notable exceptions being Ray Charles and Chet Baker). Jimmy played in Durban on his birthday, March 15, and telephoned Marian that day while she was doing a workshop at Dickinson School on Long Island. Jimmy was so delighted by his reception in Durban that he agreed to a return engagement in July.

"Jimmy didn't think about a lot of things," said Dr. Carl Oshrain, who had become a golf buddy of Jimmy's in Rochester. "Jimmy was a happy-go-lucky guy. He was out in space most of the time."

Nobody could have known that better than Oshrain, who received a mysterious package from South Africa with no return address.

"I didn't know who it was from," said Oshrain. "I opened it up and inside was a substance that smelled like pot, but it wasn't. I took it to the lab to have it analyzed and they told me it was hashish. Jimmy had sent me a package of hashish from South Africa."

Marian said he had brought back another brick in his cornet case.

"He could have got arrested for life for that," she said, shaking her head with a combination of admiration and disbelief at Jimmy's boyish daring.

Though work was scarce, Marian was booked in 1971 for a two-month run at a marvelous new spot in Greenwich Village called the Cookery, opened by Barney Josephson, owner of the late and lamented Café Society, where Billie Holiday had first sung "Strange Fruit." On University Place near Eighth Street, the Cookery was a smart restaurant with good food and sophisticated clientele. Mary Lou Williams had opened the club the previous November, and Marian had written a favorable review of her—and the club—in *Down Beat*, saying she was "better than ever."

Marian followed Mary Lou in June, with yet another great young bassist, Jay Leonhart. Bernice MacDonald, who had been a McPartland fan since the Hickory House days, painted a vivid picture of Marian at the club.

"She would come in, and it was like she was coming right off the sand," recalled MacDonald. "She'd have her hair tied back, and she'd be very tan and she'd have a sundress on and it looked as if she had almost come from the beach. She was in a gay kind of mood."

John S. Wilson of *The New York Times* described Marian's sets as "free-flowing" and "full of fresh ideas."

Though Marian and the Cookery were a smashing success, her tenure there led to more friction with Williams, who brusquely snubbed Marian when she brought her a bouquet of roses.

"She was very terse, curt, didn't have much to say to me at all," said Marian, who couldn't understand what the problem was.

Mary Lou's bass player, Brian Torff, whom Marian had taught at a Bloomington workshop that year and who would join her trio in 1976, confirmed Marian's observation.

"Marian would come in and be sweet and Mary Lou would be very cold to her," said Torff. "Mary Lou was jealous, and envious. She was that way about a lot of people."

In retrospect, Williams's manager, Peter O'Brien, had a hunch what was bothering Mary Lou specifically.

"Mary had established the place with Barney, and then Marian came in with her agent, Max Cavalli," said O'Brien. "People began hovering around to get the job. They were all sniffing around. But to come in with an agent! That's pretty bad! That's not a visit. That's scoping out the scene."

Williams took such things personally and with a decided racial slant. In her view, white jazz "copycats" who made more money than black innovators—like herself—were an outrage. She was by no means alone in her thinking, particularly during this era of cultural nationalism and black separatism, but for Marian, this line of thought—and Williams's deep and unshakable personal resentment—was incomprehensible. Perhaps because she had not grown up on the American racial scene, she simply refused to look at jazz this way. To her, it was only about the music—black or white, male or female, British or American. As always, though hurt, she refused to let Williams's rebuff embitter her toward the woman she admired most in jazz. Williams responded by telling interviewers McPartland had even "copied" her device of pedaling with her left foot.

While Marian was at the Cookery, Louis Armstrong died. Marian and Jimmy attended the memorial at the New York National Guard Armory, an event that drew twenty-five thousand people. The pallbearers included Bing Crosby, Ella Fitzgerald, Duke Ellington, Dizzy Gillespie, and Frank Sinatra. Jimmy fondly remembered in an interview about Armstrong's passing that whenever Louis had seen him, he would shout, "Mac-*PART*-land!" just as he had that first night he and Marian had run into him in New York in 1946.

Nineteen seventy-one brought more disappointments, this time at Halcyon, as Marian discovered that collaborating with two partners as strong-willed as she was proved to be more difficult than she had envisioned. The first recording sessions for Halcyon had reflected the original mission of the label, to record players being passed over by the industry. That included an obscure Harlem stride pianist who lived in upstate New York named Bobby Henderson, who had accompanied Billie Holiday in the 1930s; a solo effort by Earl Hines, reprising the classics he had waxed in 1928 for the QRS label; an album of duets by Marian and Teddy Wilson; and a live recording of Willie "the Lion" Smith from Blues Alley in Washington, D.C. Sherman Fairchild complained that Teddy Wilson's performance on what would eventually be released as *Elegant Piano* (Halcyon 106) was tired and stale, and he told Marian so in a letter. Though she knew he was right, she was hurt, and in a hot reply she insultingly inquired if Fairchild had actually listened to the record. Fairchild also observed that the recording levels on the Earl Hines album (Halcyon 101) were too low and noted they had forgotten to print the word *Stereo* on the cover. But Fairchild's most urgent complaint was that Marian and Hank had not come through with three thousand names for a mailing list they had promised. Fairchild was also concerned that records were going out willy-nilly, with no coordination between Marian and Hank and an employee Fairchild had designated on Long Island to take care of distribution.

"This is a real emergency situation," Fairchild said in a long letter to Marian.

Marian, for her part, had begun to distrust Hank O'Neal, who she felt had begun to take on projects without consulting her, the Bobby Henderson record being a case in point. "Hank slipped that one in," she said. Now, she complained, O'Neal was telling people all over town that Halcyon was about to record another O'Neal obscurity, Don Ewell, the pianist who had worked in Chicago with Bunk Johnson back in the 1940s.

"I got the feeling he was taking over," she said. "He's a cunning kind of a fox. He kind of insinuated his way into a friendship with me. And I thought he was a nice guy. He *is* a nice guy—very persuasive and very pleasant. I found myself introducing him to Eddie Condon and Sherman

Fairchild, and pretty soon he was joining up with Halcyon Records and I found myself recording people I didn't even want. . . . He just wanted to get in."

In fairness to O'Neal, Marian did not introduce O'Neal to Fairchild; the label did not start out as her project, it was a cooperative from the beginning; and Marian and O'Neal were close friends for many years before falling out. O'Neal readily confessed, however, that his zeal probably did get the best of him.

"It's extremely unfortunate," he said. "I was probably too enthusiastic about wanting to record everybody in town. Because all these people were not being recorded. And Marian, justifiably, was primarily interested in recording Marian, as well she should have been. . . . Marian has always felt that I was the villain. At some point Sherman just threw up his hands and said, 'I'm tired of this! Quarreling about this or that.' He told Marian, 'If you're unhappy, why don't we just give you your masters and you go about and do Halcyon and we'll carry on recording other people.' And that's essentially what happened."

Fate soon rendered the quarrel moot. In March 1971, Fairchild went into the hospital for routine surgery and died in recovery. Three years after they had started Halcyon, the cooperative had gone asunder. O'Neal bought out Fairchild's share and started the Chiaroscuro label, which released more than two hundred albums. Marian kept the Halcyon imprint and the masters for her two albums and her duets with Teddy Wilson.

"It really is one of my great regrets," said O'Neal, who later served on the boards of the jazz program at the New School in New York and the Jazz Gallery, Manhattan's progressive nonprofit nightclub. "Because Marian was really kind of mad, and I wasn't. We had so much fun and then there wasn't any more fun. I tried to call about this and that and the other thing . . . and it's too bad, because it was over nothing. Over misconceptions."

In fact, the quarrel was probably inevitable. O'Neal was interested in running a professional, well-distributed, independent record label; Fairchild was an extremely successful businessman and a technical genius who had impeccably high standards for quality control; and McPartland was interested primarily in releasing her own albums. Fairchild's uneasiness about quality was justified. Halcyon album sleeves failed to list crucial information, such as when and where they were recorded and the date of release, nor did they include the length of the cuts, essential for radio airplay. The cover designs lacked consistency and character, and as Fairchild had noted, the recording quality was erratic. As far as McPartland recalled, no Halcyon album ever went into a second pressing. Marian continued producing Halcyon records in her own haphazard way throughout the 1970s—eighteen in all—and musically, at least, some nice surprises lay ahead.

One of the best was *The Marian McPartland Trio Plays the Music of Alec Wilder* (Halcyon 109). Whatever spat Marian and Alec had had over Nixon and the war, it apparently evaporated when Marian went into the studio June 20 and 23, 1973, and recorded this lovely tribute to Alec's music and to their companionship. Side one featured duo tracks by Marian and Moore; side two, a trio with Rusty Gilder and Joe Corsello. The songs were short and to the point, as much a showcase for Wilder's melodies as for Marian's improvisational prowess, opening the fragile secrets of his songs like precious boxes of vintage treasure. The cover art featured another fine Joe Hendrick collage with an orange antique-store wash, including an oval-framed photo of Alec as a boy, a snippet of the manuscript on which he'd written, "Okay, school's out," roses in bloom, and a peaceful country barn.

The album was well received by *The New York Times, Playboy,* and the *Hartford Courant*'s Owen McNally, a confirmed McPartland fan, who described it as a "beautiful trip over rich hills and valleys of harmonic and melodic development." It remained one of Marian's favorite albums in her fast-growing oeuvre and was reissued twice on CD by Jazz Alliance, receiving more raves in that format from *The Sunday Times* (London) and *Jazz Journal International.*

But McPartland wasn't through with Wilder, not by half. In July, at the Newport Jazz Festival (which had moved to New York), she took part in a tribute to Wilder's book *American Popular Song,* which had been published the previous fall. In November, she and Wilder appeared together at the Bruno Walter Auditorium at Lincoln Center, on a program arranged by Marian's fan from the Cookery, Bernice MacDonald, who coordinated adult services for Manhattan's branch libraries. Harold Arlen attended and sat in the first row, wearing a red boutonniere. Wilder sat on a stool and read excerpts from the book, Marian illustrated the tunes, and Teddi King, a full-throated songstress in Mabel Mercer's style, did the vocals.

The concert honoring Wilder's book sparked a long and deep friendship between Marian and Bernice and her good friend Mary Kay Conwell, that would lead to several future collaborations as well as peaceful summer retreats at MacDonald's Connecticut lakefront cottage. Bernice and Mary Kay were part of a circle of strong, active, capable women that would gather around Marian in middle age. They would become her closest companions—confidantes, helpmates, lunch dates, holiday pals, travel buddies, and—in the later years of her life—an advanced guard against adversities that struck, though they often had to keep their inter-communication quiet, so as not to offend Marian's strong need for independence. Though Marian never quit loving the company of men, wanting to be admired and flattered and thought attractive by them, the women in her life, ever so gradually, grew even more important.

Marian reached two career milestones in 1973. The effervescent supper club singer/pianist Bobby Short asked her to sub for him for two months at the Café Carlyle during his winter vacation, a gig that would begin a long run for her at this posh East Side hotel. And Whitney Balliett, the sterling jazz writer for *The New Yorker* known for his evocative metaphors and lengthy interviews, published a major profile of McPartland, "The Key of D Is Daffodil Yellow," coinciding with the gig. The article placed Marian firmly in a small, sophisticated, elite Manhattan jazz milieu known for its dedication to—and deep knowledge of—the Great American Song-book and modern jazz.

The Carlyle gig and *New Yorker* profile coincided with a major move in Marian's personal life she had been working up to for some time. Just before Jimmy had gone to South Africa, in 1972, Marian had fallen into another deep depression. That winter, though she had officially ended her analysis, she went back for several "refreshers" with Dr. Benjamin. Her jottings in December 1971 and January 1972 revealed not only extreme anxiety, but a brave, questioning spirit, deep insights, and—as always—a stiff upper lip:

"I feel panicked," she wrote. "Just lately it is as if my whole feeling and personality is breaking apart. I have a mental picture of little chunks of glass: me, my thoughts and feelings, all my defenses—maybe that's what's breaking down. I keep it to myself. No one knows it but me and the doctor, and Jimmy and maybe Alec . . . but I'm afraid to tell him too much. I don't want him telling everybody I'm lonely or sad or something like that. No, I'd rather keep it to myself. Maybe this is how life is—are we all concealing fears and anxieties and smiling and telling each other life is great?"

It appears from her notes that Alec had encouraged Marian not only to get busy writing her own songs, but also to start an autobiography, a project she was totally unprepared for psychologically. Time and again, she found herself procrastinating, which only upset her more:

Begin. That's always been hard for me to do, whether it be starting a new composition, practicing, writing out a piece—anything to do with helping myself has always been difficult. I can take time to do a million jobs for other people, and get them executed promptly and efficiently. But when it comes to things for me, I hang back, waste time, I dawdle, and potter about. It's uncanny how much I take after my father. . . . I'm a perfectionist, nothing is too good for the other person, but I'll take what's left. . . .

How strange, just the fact of knowing that Alec was concerned enough to call me about starting to write might be the very thing to get me started. Why? Just because someone says they care? Dottie Dodgion used to say I needed love, as if I needed an inordinate amount of it. Doesn't everybody? Or does she see the need to be loved? Maybe everyone sees how I really am and I'm not concealing a thing with my flip attitude, jokes, animation. But one has to act that way. How foolish to burden friends and acquaintances with one's fears and worries. No one wants to hear that, and I don't either.

For a long time, Marian had been thinking about moving back to Long Island, partly because she was tired of apartment life (she told Blossom Dearie she was "sick of living in the same room with the piano"), but also to be closer to Jimmy. In December 1972, she bought a house at 302 Clinton Street in Bellmore, Merrick's slightly more rural south shore "sister town," and two days after her debut at the Café Carlyle, in January 1973, she moved in. It was a short hop to Jimmy's from her new house, and the Long Island Rail road station was just two blocks down the street, though Marian still often drove to the Carlyle—thirty or forty minutes away. The house was a huge rambler with several additions and two rental units, so it provided extra income as well as elbow room for the cottage industry Halcyon had become. There was a public pool within walking distance, and it wasn't long before Marian and Jimmy were going to the pool together and basking in the sun at her beloved Lookout Point. For convenience, she kept her apartment on the Upper East Side so she could stay in town when she wanted to.

In May 1973, Marian and Jimmy celebrated their renewed "propinquity" with a musical reunion at the Americana Hotel's Royal Box, with Kansas City tenor saxophonist Buddy Tate. Ironically, the huge hotel stood across the street from the defunct Hickory House. Marian seemed happy to be working with Jimmy again in New York. At the gig, looking portly in bow tie and tux, Jimmy, ever the rake, managed to get his picture snapped with the newly crowned Miss USA, Amanda Jones, for a tourist magazine.

"It's funny," observed Marian in retrospect. "I didn't even notice it my-self that things were getting better."

In years to come, Marian would often quip that "the divorce was a fail-ure," a line that might have been plucked straight from a Noel Coward play, and that she and Jimmy became even closer—and treated each other with more respect—after they were divorced than before. There was cer-tainly some truth to that. But, as always, Marian's bon mot hid as much as it revealed. The divorce, in fact, had been a spectacular success. It ignited a bonfire of creativity and originality. Without it, she never would have become the independent woman and artist who emerged after 1967. The music, the songwriting, the take-charge attitude as a leader, the career as an educator—all these blossomed after the divorce. She may have suffered while she was alone, but through the crucible of that suffering, she came out the other side as an independent, vibrant voice.

Or as Alec Wilder put it, "A kitten walked in and a tiger walked out."

Even Jimmy acknowledged the change: "Marian never knew herself. Her music was a conglomeration. Now, she has found her own identity. You hear her play something and you can say, 'That's Marian McPartland.'"

But, in a way, she was right about the "failure" part, too, because rather than drive them apart, divorce made it possible for her to come back to Jimmy on a new footing and actually enjoy life with him. There had al-ways been some part of her that ultimately did not want to leave.

"It was like getting rid of your brother," said Helen Merrill. "It's not possible. She never really abandoned him. She was always by his side, ac-tually. They really were longtime lovers. I don't know if that's the right word for married people, legal or not. . . . She loved Jimmy with all her soul and heart. She had to take care of Jimmy. And she did."

12.

The Jazz Renaissance
(1973–1978)

THE "JAZZ RENAISSANCE" is usually said to have begun around 1976, but the music had begun to seep back into American soil early in the decade. Even while the marketplace turned its back, enterprising musicians kept jazz alive, releasing their own records, working in the schools (and in Europe), developing new markets, and remaining faithful to a loyal, if diminished, audience. By the end of the decade, jazz reemerged, albeit with a different identity. Marian, with her boundless energy, actually saw a rise in income between 1973 and 1978 and a steady heightening of her profile, buoyed by the jazz education movement and feminism. On the personal front, she and Jimmy fell into a comfortable new rhythm.

Marian was already a leading figure in jazz education, having headlined the first convention of the five-year-old National Association of Jazz Educators in Chicago, in 1973. As a spokesperson for the movement, she wrote a partisan feature for *The New York Times* about her work in the schools: "I Was Indignant That Rock Reigned Supreme." In 1974, her bid to Nixon aide Len Garment bore fruit in the form of a $55,360 grant from the National Endowment for the Arts and the U.S. Department of Health, Education and Welfare to conduct demo/workshops in Washington, D.C., schools for nine weeks, staggered over several months. Billy Taylor, young trombonist Janice Robinson, saxophonist Andrew White, drummer Billy Hart, bassist Fred Williams, and—for one class—Jimmy and some of his pals taught in the program.

Most of Marian's work in the schools had been with white middle-class kids, but the D.C. project took her to poor black neighborhoods. McPartland was appalled and depressed by the children's ignorance of their musical history and their aggressive preference for disco over Duke. She was also unprepared for the noisy and physically restless black youngsters, their saturation by mass media and by music teachers, and local musicians openly hostile to her because a white person had been selected to teach black music. But, as always, she found new routes to the kids' hearts. In one class, she demonstrated how Kool & the Gang's "Jungle Boogie" was a reworking of rhythmic figures Louis Armstrong had pioneered a half century earlier and sparked their interest with the infectious, booming bass line of Herbie Hancock's Headhunters hit "Chameleon." The D.C. schools owned few musical instruments, but she made the best of what she had, bringing fifty kids onstage to ting and tang their "melody bells" (a small vibraharp used in the popular Kodály method) on Duke's "C Jam Blues," along with the United States Navy Band the Commodores, which she recruited to play a concert for thirty-five hundred students.

Marian discovered that the way she explained things sometimes went over the students' heads. A teacher counseled her to ratchet down her vocabulary.

"I took so many things for granted, until Mary Taylor suggested going right to the beginning and explaining what a bar of music was," Marian wrote. "Learning to describe musical procedures on such a basic level was hard for me, but very necessary, and I soon learned to talk about 'tone' instead of 'notes,' 'measure' instead of 'bars,' and 'counts' instead of 'beats.'"

Black parents were demanding that school districts recruit black teachers, so it was no surprise when a pianist with the local African Jazz Ensemble wrote a furious letter to the endowment, which he copied to Marian, protesting the fact that a white woman had been chosen to teach. Always the conciliator, Marian invited the pianist to perform, which he did. In her postmortem, she suggested such complaints be preempted by actively recruiting local artists, though she was still slightly contemptuous of their passivity.

"It does seem hilarious on the face of things that a white Englishwoman would be teaching these black children their own music," she wrote. "I did find myself thinking, what on earth am I doing here? But it just seems as if nobody else would come forward to do it. Not one of the local artists has made a suggestion. They're willing to work when you call them up, and all they want to know is what's the pay? But no one has ever called up to say, 'What can I do to help?'"

McPartland's impatience, though justified in principle, revealed a lack of awareness of white privilege, not to mention a sense of noblesse oblige no doubt inculcated by her family. It could easily be read—though certainly it was not meant—as moral superiority.

When Duke Ellington appeared at Georgetown University that February, Marian asked him to play at Hawthorne School. Though he was ill (he died shortly thereafter), Duke agreed. When Marian arrived at the school, she discovered to her horror that the concert was on the fourth floor.

"I heard you're going to carry me upstairs," Duke joked.

"We sat in a hallway and I held his hand," Marian said. "People were snapping pictures. . . . Duke suddenly looked very pale and disoriented. 'Christ, what am I doing here?' he asked nobody in particular. 'What am I going to do?' 'You're going to play like you always do for kids and talk to them a little,' I said."

As with all events with cameras rolling in Washington, politicians flocked to the site. President Nixon sent his daughter Julie Eisenhower to present Ellington with a letter addressing him as "His Excellency the Duke of Ellington." When pictures appeared the next day in newspapers around the country, Marian was annoyed at having been upstaged. She also sent an apologetic letter to Duke's son, Mercer, who had arranged for Duke to get upstairs.

"I really wish there were two of you so that one could stay down here and help me handle this whole damn school project," she wrote. In the end, the "whole damn school project" turned out to be a great learning experience, stoking yet higher her missionary fire to spread the gospel of jazz. In a memo, she referred to herself as a "champion, a spokesman, even a salesman for the music," noting later, "It's a crusade with me." But beyond the music itself, Marian saw a broad humanistic goal in her school-work. In the slavish narrowness of kids' musical taste, she sensed a sad repetition of the proscriptions of her own childhood, in which children were not encouraged to make decisions about who they were or what they wanted to be. In notes for an article about her experience in D.C., McPartland spelled this out: "Many of us have as children been told what to think, how to act, and especially now, with the omnipotence of TV performers and radio DJs. They tell us what to listen to in music and what we should like. . . . How can one learn taste and individuality and discernment without being afraid what others will say unless these qualities are developed in early childhood as a part of education? . . . As small children they are not afraid to offer opinions. They are honest, before the stresses of society are forced on them, when patterns are learned—anxieties grow—conformity comes over them like a blight, and instead of growing their horizons, it narrows." Karl Menninger's book about the constructive, humanizing effect of play had clearly influenced her thinking. And so had the more recent Utopianism of the 1960s. "It's more than playing jazz for them," she wrote. "It's using music as a force for good—I'd like to see them develop values other than material things—awareness of natural beauty, of nature. Do children have to develop the urge to kill, to destroy, waste, pollute? Isn't it time that all of us who can, will take time to get them involved in something of value that gives lasting pleasure, that can't be bought—to help them expand their consciousness?"

As the decade progressed, McPartland expanded her education work, doing free concerts at youth guidance centers and, eventually, at New York's infamous prisons on Rikers Island and at Attica. She was a believer.

While Marian was working in the D.C. schools, she was getting up every morning at five A.M. to practice a new, quite difficult chamber piece Wilder had written for her, *Fantasy for Piano and Wind Ensemble*. On a break between workshops, she went to Raleigh, North Carolina, for the premiere. Though Wilder admired Marian's ability to improvise, he was contemptuous of her poor sight-reading. He was annoyed to discover that she had learned the piece by listening to a cassette. He nevertheless attended an open rehearsal and the April 21 premiere at Duke University's Page Auditorium. At the rehearsal, when Marian introduced him to the students, Wilder leapt on the stage and Marian never got in another word.

"He's a closet ham," she said. "He took over the rehearsal and workshop."

The Duke University Wind Symphony ably performed Wilder's seven-minute atonal but lyrical composition. The piece floated through variations on three short, declamatory themes, drawing miraculous sonorities from the winds that included muted brass, luscious flute/brass combinations that would have fit nicely behind Frank Sinatra, and a couple of Debussy-like lone English horn passages. But most impressive was the rhapsodic piano interlude Wilder had written for Marian, which captured in written form something very much like what McPartland might have improvised herself, complete with lickety-split arpeggios up the keyboard, pounding right-hand octaves, phrases that circled back into themselves, and glittering glissandos.

The following year, Marian coaxed Wilder onto a locally produced public TV show, hosted in Rochester by their friend Tom Hampson. Called *Such Good Companions,* the program was a low-key, highbrow affair that featured Marian playing various tunes by Alec and his favorite songwriters. Marian, still blond and stunning, wore a bright blue jacket, checked blouse, scarf, and long false eyelashes. Alec was his lapsed-professorial self, wearing a sport jacket and tie, languidly intoning comments in his resonant smoker's basso, often hiding his face with his hand or leaning his chin into it, and holding a cigarette with thumb and forefinger. They both sat at the piano as Hampson moderated from the side, though neither of these "hams"—in or out of the closet—needed much prodding. The conversation was notable for its high sophistication and absolute refusal to make concessions to a general audience. It also had a slightly snarky undertone. Wilder scolded her for playing his tunes correctly the first time through, then changing them, he suggested, just to annoy him.

The TV show in Rochester led Wilder to publish a curious essay about Marian in his next book, which came out in 1975, called *Letters I Never Mailed*. *Letters* was pure Alec—facetious, witty, wry, whiny, arch, smart, sarcastic, oblique, self-pitying, and sometimes downright nasty. The premise, of course, was a conceit. He had not written most of these so-called letters. They were more like retorts he wished he had said but never had and were also, in their own way, twisted homages to the people who had been important (or annoying) to him, including Tony Bennett, Peggy Lee, and Mitch Miller, among many, many others. Some of them stung. In his letter to Marian, he accused her of "conning" him into doing the TV show.

"Why are you so determined to drag me into public life?" he demanded. "I hate to sound so damned snobbish, but who in God's name wants to be notorious in this schlock society? What possible distinction can there be in being accepted by a public you have no respect for?"

When Marian received a copy of the book, she was so furious she pretended it hadn't arrived. When Wilder sent another one, she asked him to forward it to her hotel on the road so she could pretend she hadn't received it. Finally, she wrote back, saying she felt his piece was a condescending, "fatherly put-down."

"I wash my hands of Alec," she told Jim Maher, who had helped Wilder write *American Popular Song*. "I would never, ever suggest anything for him again."

But the hand washing would not be so easily accomplished. Charlie Bourgeois had asked Marian to emcee a concert devoted to Stan Getz that summer at the Newport Jazz Festival in New York and, unaware of the friction between the two, had inadvertently paired her with Wilder.

"Don't blame me for this," she admonished the composer. "I have a damn good mind to back out and leave you with it, after all the things you said about me."

At the concert, in July 1975 at Avery Fisher Hall, Marian and Alec sat a table onstage. Whitney Balliett wrote that they "looked as if they were stuck in the library on a lovely Saturday afternoon." Marian had a troublesome Newport all around. Asked to host a solo piano concert at Carnegie Hall, she was not invited to play, which she found humiliating, not to say ridiculous. The biggest name on the program was Eubie Blake, and the concert drew only half a house. "Never again!" Marian scribbled on the program she saved. She did have one high point, a concert devoted to Bix, featuring Jimmy and Warren Vaché, during which Marian played reportedly glorious solo versions of "Candlelights" and "In a Mist." After these incidents, Alec and Marian drifted apart, though McPartland never really stopped singing Wilder's praises and even wound up writing a foreword to the second edition of *Letters I Never Mailed*.

In the 1970s, Newport Jazz Festival producer George Wein expanded his reach beyond the United States, and he took Marian along for the ride. In 1974, he revived the jazz festival in Nice, France, which had started in 1948 but had fallen on hard times. Le Grande Parade du Jazz ran July 15–21, with multiple stages and a traditional outlook, featuring Marian and Jimmy, Bud Freeman, violinist Joe Venuti, trumpeter Wild Bill Davison, guitarist George Barnes, clarinetist Kenny Davern, and a host of other old-school players.

All the musicians were housed in one hotel—Jimmy amused everyone by icing his celery and other groceries in the bidet—and one warm, summer night, when the sound of Venuti's violin came wafting through the air, Marian and Jimmy knocked on his door.

"Joe was there with two young Italian guitar students, playing *Le Tombeau de Couperin*," said Marian. "We stayed up for hours listening and watching."

Venuti was a living legend. The classically trained violinist had played with Paul Whiteman during the same era as Bix, and Venuti's recordings with guitarist Eddie Lang had laid the foundation for "string jazz," in particular the work of Django Reinhardt and Stéphane Grappelli. Listening to Venuti, Marian hatched the idea of a duo album for Halcyon, and he readily consented. She rented a local studio, and she and Joe recorded *The Maestro and Friend: Marian McPartland and Joe Venuti* (Halcyon 112). It was a relaxed, jamlike effort, and though the recording quality was brittle, it had some sweet moments. After the festival, Wein hosted the McPartlands at his villa in Vence, about twenty miles from Nice, then they headed to Perugia, Italy, for Umbria Jazz, a celebration that would become one of the greatest of all European festivals. The European circuit, which eventually extended from Norway to Istanbul, was a welcome income booster during the great jazz drought and would become a summer staple for American jazz musicians for the next quarter century.

Marian was back in New York only a few days before Wein sent her out on the road again, this time to a less traveled destination—South America. For the tour, the Boston promoter engaged four pianists—Marian, Teddy

Wilson, Earl Hines, and Ellis Larkins—and from August 8 to August 20, the quartet played eight concerts in seven countries.

"It was kind of a whirlwind," she said. "Everywhere we went people came backstage in droves. Fans thronged the halls carrying copies of our records, pictures, and programs for us to autograph."

At some of the concerts fans brought tape recorders, and Marian and her colleagues were astonished to see them playing back the tapes in the lobby at intermission. Though Marian was delighted by her stellar company, she was disappointed that Hines refused to play duets with anyone, insisted on playing last, and usually stole the show. But in Buenos Aires, local musicians hired a theater and put on a concert for the quartet, and everyone sat in. Wein agreed to let Marian record the pianists there for Halcyon, and Mickey Kappes (brother of drummer Jim Kappes), who was living in Buenos Aires, served as translator at the studio. A small audience was invited to the session, released as the double album *Concert in Argentina: Earl Hines, Teddy Wilson, Ellis Larkins, Marian McPartland* (Halcyon 113), with each pianist playing one side. On a medley of Duke's tunes, Marian's airborne right hand flew over walking bass on "It Don't Mean a Thing," and "Caravan" curled through the desert in two keys, followed by a big-tent finish. But Larkins was the prize, showing creativity in his choice of tunes, which included a mysterious and velvety "Perfidia" by Mexican composer Alberto Domínguez and an elegantly striding "Blues in My Heart" by Benny Carter. When someone in the crowd shouted, "My Mama Done Told Me," he went right into "Blues in the Night." The album received due praise, not only for Marian's playing but for documenting the historic tour.

Marian extended her international reach to yet another corner of the world in January 1976, when she was invited to Japan for a series of concerts called *Piano Playhouse,* with Ella Fitzgerald accompanist Hank Jones and John Lewis, co-founder of the Modern Jazz Quartet. Japan had a fanatically devoted jazz public willing to pay top dollar, and it was always a pleasant surprise for Americans to discover how assiduously informed—if curiously quiet—the audiences were there. In a small, obscure town near Kyoto, Lewis and McPartland trekked up a hill in the snow to a little bar to get a cup of coffee and a sandwich while waiting for a train. They were shocked to find that the proprietor and several locals owned a slew of Lewis's albums. Before they left, the owner gave Lewis a pair of straw shoes.

Marian worked on her solo playing throughout the 1970s, partly inspired by Keith Jarrett's brilliant 1971 stream-of-consciousness album,

Facing You. She loved the freedom of working alone, though in an article she also acknowledged that she used to be scared to play alone.

"The drums and bass were my security blanket," she wrote.

She recommended to young pianists that to maintain rhythmic momentum, they should either play a bass line with the left hand or "hear it in your head" and voice chords accordingly. She also recommended listening to solo records by Art Tatum, Oscar Peterson, Teddy Wilson, Mary Lou Williams, Bill Evans, Jess Stacy, Jimmy Rowles, Dave McKenna, and Jarrett. Jazz writers often pointed to these very players as influences on her, but they rarely talked about her overarching aesthetic. One exception was an unusual review in the *Village Voice* of a performance at the Cookery, which suggested that even as early as 1973, she could reach a transcendent level as a soloist. In his review, Victor Stein noted that her work reflected a concern with human relationships and the soul, implying accurately that Marian, in spite of her fondness for musical impressionism, was not at heart a romantic at all, but a classicist, for whom clarity of line, concision, and control were the ultimate ideal.

"Her music," wrote Stein, "lives in the place where we think clearly and act correctly, the place where we live when we are what we know we can become." She doesn't "wobble." Invoking Zen master Unmon, Stein then said, "When she sits, she sits, when she walks, she walks." Few writers would ever approach McPartland's work with such insight.

In November 1973, Marian played a solo concert at Haverford College in Pennsylvania, which led to her first solo album. The project reflected perfectly the classic values and breadth of scope Stein had highlighted in his review. The program was spawned by a hip white freshman with an Afro, John Schreiber, and his best friend, Bob Sherman, who had become enamored of Marian's playing at the Cookery that summer. Though they had never produced a concert in their lives, after hearing Marian, the enthusiastic pair decided they must bring her to campus. Marian not only agreed, she essentially taught them how to put on a show—explaining how to book a hall, do publicity posters, write contracts, and so forth. Schreiber got the college to chip in $2,000.

"Whether she played the music of Gershwin or the Beatles, she won Haverford over completely," wrote Schreiber, who added with a note of cultural triumph, "Carly Simon had been temporarily eclipsed!"

When Schreiber came back to see Marian at Michael's Pub, an Anglophile watering hole on the Upper East Side, she asked if she could come back to do a live solo recording at the college. Schreiber enthusiastically agreed. On April 12, 1974, between gigs in Washington, D.C., she recorded *Solo Concert at Haverford* (Halcyon 111). Though it owed nothing to the pulsing, run-on improvisations of Jarrett, Marian's playing had the clarity, poise, and transparency that would become signatures of her mature period. It was as if one were listening to someone think out loud. Emotions ranged from tender and winsome to stentorian and grand; her technique from funky blues (Ben Tucker had left his mark) to baroque, this time on Jerome Kern's "Yesterdays," melded with Paul McCartney's "Yesterday," a clever pairing she had been trying out in clubs and which would become a permanent part of her repertoire. Always alert to new tunes, she played a touching version of Stephen Sondheim's ballad "Send in the Clowns" from *A Little Night Music,* which had hit Broadway in 1973, and offered the clearest (because most direct) reading yet of her own tune, "Afterglow," as an encore. After the experiments of the late 1960s, Marian had pulled back toward a new center, from which she could reach out in multiple directions at will.

Haverford received five stars in *Down Beat* and a rave in *High Fidelity* by *New York Times* critic John S. Wilson. But nearly every reviewer lamented that McPartland had been reduced to releasing records on her own, poorly distributed label. The fact that Jimmy Rowles and Dave McKenna were on the label, too, highlighted even more dramatically how little demand there was for jazz, said the critics. An interesting spin-off of the Haverford concert was its effect on Schreiber, who took over the school concert series and, after he left school, and thanks to an introduction from Marian, went to work for George Wein himself. Schreiber was one of dozens of young people whom Marian generously took under her wing.

"Marian changed my life," said Schreiber, who later produced Marian's eightieth and eighty-fifth birthday celebrations.

Though Marian was recording often and touring the world, her profile on the West Coast of the United States had never been high. Max Cavalli set out to change that, booking her into the Playboy Club in Los Angeles in October 1974. Jimmy's grandkids, Donna and Doug, had both moved to the West Coast in 1972—Donna to Los Angeles, Doug to San Francisco—and Marian took advantage of the opportunity to renew her relationships with them, which had ebbed after Dorothy's death. Doug came down from San Francisco for the L.A. gig, and they all got together. Marian found it easy to get along with Donna. She was sunny and optimistic and full of fun, quite like her mother. Donna eventually became, for Marian, an almost eerie surrogate for Dorothy herself, someone she could cut up with privately, a respite from the formality of her public persona. They reveled in blue humor—one of their favorite photocopies was a sheet of cheeky jokes about the "magical" versatility of the word *fuck* (transitive verb: "John fucked Mary"; intransitive verb: "Mary really doesn't give a fuck")—and giggled over the off-color, off-the-wall cartoons of John Callahan, who poked genial, politically incorrect fun at the handicapped, of whom he was one.

"Marian's a really good girlfriend-type person," said Donna. "She was a girlfriend with my mother, and she's like a girlfriend with me. She'll talk about boys having nice asses or being really cute—'I would roll over for a dime anytime'—she was really cute like that. She's like all of us. No matter how old we all get, you always stay sixteen some way."

But with Doug, things were prickly. He was sardonic and dry—he had taken classes at Chicago's Second City—and his childhood had left him wounded and angry. His inability to find an even keel in life brought out a dark and not particularly attractive side of Marian, an impatience with what she perceived as his lack of ambition. This impatience was perhaps driven by Marian's having taken on a kind of oblique guilt for Jimmy's neglect of Dorothy and for the abortive year in Merrick, when she and Jimmy had unwisely attempted to help Dorothy raise her kids. Marian was prone to internalizing responsibilities for how things worked out for others; when they didn't, it sometimes resurfaced in distorted form, as anger and even contempt. She continually encouraged Doug to play drums with her and with his grandfather, but she also feared he might take her generosity for granted.

Doug's tendency to put on weight brought out an extremely unpleasant, even mean side of her, often mentioned by other friends who struggled with their weight. Marian had always worked hard at staying trim and fit. People who could not—or would not—annoyed her. After the visit in L.A., Marian sent Doug a postcard, saying it had been a "kick" seeing him after such a long time. When Doug failed to respond quickly, she fired off a nasty note, which crossed paths with a rather sweet letter from him. She responded with a humble apology, but it was the beginning of an unfortunate pattern—volleys of misunderstandings, recriminations, and apologies. If they'd been playing jazz, one might have said their sense of time never quite jelled.

In March 1975, Marian came back to Los Angeles for a prestigious Monday night solo series called *Intimate Jazz* at the Mark Taper Forum. Cavalli also snagged a week for her in a San Francisco club and got her onto a piano program at the Monterey Jazz Festival with John Lewis. In L.A., she knocked out fans and critics alike, drawing the largest crowd of a four-concert series and netting a review by the *Herald-Examiner*'s Bill

Pollock that described her as a pianist "with enough wit and charm to fill a dozen auditoriums." Leonard Feather, already a McPartland champion, said she had "progressed from a competent but derivative British import to a major artist of complete self-assurance." He was particularly taken with her ballads, to which repertoire she had now added Billy Strayhorn's haunting "Lotus Blossom." Marian returned to the coast in September for a solo gig at El Matador, a longtime jazz haunt in the once hip but by then tawdry North Beach neighborhood where the beats and the Jazz Workshop had once flourished. El Matador had a huge bullfight mural on one wall, and its pistol-packing owner was reputed to be in the Mob.

Doug, working as a drummer at the time, came by.

"It was really seedy," he said. "The waitresses all kept their trays up like this, so when they'd give you your change you'd be in the dark, feeling around, and you'd miss half of it or you wouldn't take the change, you'd just take the bills. Her dressing room was in the basement. It was really narrow and dark and foreboding."

Marian played solo at El Matador. The *San Francisco Chronicle*'s art critic, Thomas Albright, liked her playing but complained that she didn't swing hard enough, a criticism that would dog McPartland most of her career. It was not always unfair. For while Marian definitely could swing— her recordings were ample proof of that—sometimes, like Melville's Bartleby, she simply chose not to, preferring to concentrate on dreamy, rubato ballads and meandering explorations. After El Matador, Marian made her first appearance at the Monterey Jazz Festival, 120 miles south of San Francisco above foggy Monterey Bay, with its windswept cypress trees and lingering ghosts of John Steinbeck's *Tortilla Flat* and *Cannery Row*. Crowds at Monterey's outdoor arena were notoriously unruly in the 1970s, but Marian brought the audience to a hush. Wearing a floor-length brocade gown and a spiffy, layered blond do, she began and ended "Afterglow" by strumming the strings like a harp.

But the most important solo gig Max got for Marian was in New York, at Bemelmans Bar at the Carlyle, where Marian had successfully subbed for Bobby Short the last two winters. The Carlyle was the definition of Upper East Side panache and had become even more fashionable in the 1960s when it became a favorite of the Kennedys. In the 1970s, Jackie Onassis continued to come by. Named after Ludwig Bemelmans, author of the *Madeline* children's stories, Bemelmans Bar was across the hall from the main room. It was hardly ideal for music, which was probably why it had never had any. A small room with a dozen bar stools, four horseshoe-shaped booths, and walls decorated with Bemelmans's murals of New

York, it was patronized by stockbrokers, lawyers, and art dealers from across the street at Parke-Bernet, looking for a splash of Pernod, not piano. She did not get off to a good start. Right before she opened, the hotel booked the glitzy vocal quartet Manhattan Transfer in the big room, and Ahmet Ertegun, the powerful Atlantic Records producer who had made Ray Charles's career, asked Marian to "warm up" the crowd in the big room. Marian, understandably hurt, refused, and Ertegun threatened to put her piano out in the hallway if she didn't cooperate. The affair became a minor cause célèbre, with *The New York Times* chiding the management for its insensitivity. After Manhattan Transfer left, however, the hotel bought a good grand piano and sound system for Bemelmans, and Marian cultivated a devoted following there, playing extended runs until the early 1980s, when Barbara Carroll got the gig. According to Father Peter O'Brien, during the kerfuffle with Ertegun, Mary Lou Williams was helpful.

"Marian was furious that the management there had done this to her," recalled O'Brien. "Mary Lou said, 'Stay here. Make this *your* room!' And she did. She did that at Mary Lou's behest. That was one time when Mary Lou did Marian a good favor."

Though the noise in the room was often frustrating (her bass player, Frank Tate, nicknamed the place "the Dog Pound"), the Carlyle took a relaxed attitude toward musical guests, which meant Marian could hire a bass player to help anchor the crowd's attention with a stronger swing feeling. When Michael Moore came down, Whitney Balliett at *The New Yorker* said they had the "ceaseless interplay and subtle competitiveness" of "a whole band." Marian invited singers and other instrumentalists, too, including the wonderful Carol Sloane, Teddi King, the ill-fated Susannah McCorkle, Dick Sudhalter, Gerry Mulligan, and Gene Bertoncini. She even convinced Jimmy to come down and play ballads with his Harmon mute. Alec Wilder often dropped by, sometimes shushing the crowd (Marian occasionally barked at them, too) or quietly jotting down notes at a table in the corner, wearing his customary ratty sports jacket. One night Marian scolded him from the bandstand.

"I don't know which is worse, people talking or a guy writing letters while I'm playing," she said.

Alec leaned forward and said in stage whisper, "Yes, but you can't hear me."

During her first month at Bemelmans Bar, in January 1975, Marian played at a Harvard University program where a reviewer praised her for taking the time to explain who wrote the songs she was playing and where she had learned them. He was also impressed by her historical and stylistic range, from stride classics like Joe Sullivan's "Little Rock Getaway" to the "Yesterdays/Yesterday" medley. Marian had settled into the performing style that would characterize the rest of her career. Unlike so many jazz players, she did not jet onstage, give a perfunctory salutation, then disappear into a haze of sound, only to reemerge at the finale for a drenching of applause. On the contrary, her sets were more like a recital. She collegially engaged her audience as genteel equals, conveying the impression that they were as curious about the music as she was, occasionally offering a joke or anecdote, and even asking for requests. In return, she had begun to expect a level of respect she had never demanded in her "saloon" days at the Hickory House. "I am no longer content to play and be ignored," she said in a letter to Irving Townsend.

Townsend was a highly respected producer whose credits included Miles Davis's classic album *Kind of Blue*. While in California for the Monterey Jazz Festival, Marian had visited him at his Santa Barbara ranch and enlisted him to help her take another shot at writing her autobiography. Townsend was far from the stereotype of a crass record producer—a cultured gentleman who could play music (clarinet) and also had a keen ear for language. Marian told Townsend she would write her recollections on the fly if he could organize them into a coherent narrative. And write she did—on hotel and airline stationery, yellow pads, envelopes, pretty much anything to hand—as well as dictating long tape recordings, which were later transcribed and mailed to the producer.

"I had a very bad night at the club last night," she wrote of Bemelmans Bar in 1975. "Alec was there, and we had quite a discussion about why I found the noise so hard to take NOW, when years ago I put up with it. Maybe it all comes down to having a sense of my own worth and feeling that if people are going to come in the room, especially to hear me (and there is a $3.00 cover!) [and a two-drink minimum, too], they should at least not yell at the tops of their voices. . . ."

But there were good nights, too.

"Last night has to be the best night I've had there yet, in terms of good business and a listening crowd," she wrote. ". . . I was able to play quite well, and do things on a deeper level, because I felt that fine thread of sympathetic vibration held between us. It seemed that nothing could go wrong. I stretched out and played dangerously, so made a few clinkers, but I don't feel too bad about that, it's bound to happen if you take chances and go over your head and not play safe. I always feel grateful for such a good audience and want to give them everything I'm capable of—the real me, not the shallow, playing-on-the-surface person I'm forced to be on many nights."

Marian worried sometimes if that "playing-on-the-surface person" got the best of her. Was she pandering to the crowd or being true to her own standards? When Townsend pressed Marian to talk more about this, she came up with some soul-searching answers.

"I can't really play much of my jazz repertoire in that room anyway," she wrote. "No Coltrane or Monk, or any of my originals. The people's taste goes from 'Send in the Clowns' to 'Funny Valentine' to 'Satin Doll' to 'Misty' and back to 'Send in the Clowns.'"

One night, Wilder came into the bar and told her he thought she was playing quite differently from usual.

"'You're really having a party with yourself tonight, aren't you?' he said. 'And some arguments, too.' I was pleased, because I've been thinking a lot about what I said to you about honest playing, and have come to the conclusion that I don't play that way very often. Alec says, 'You're a performer as well as a pianist.' I think that gets in the way sometimes. My choice of tunes is dictated by the thought as to whether they will go over big with the audience. I do like to put on a show."

Though Marian's work with Townsend produced some excellent material, she felt Townsend wanted to work too fast, so she let him go and brought on Jim Maher as a replacement. As their work progressed, Marian began to feel uneasy about how much she wanted to reveal. Her notes show her seesawing between anxiety and abandon: "Is he understanding enough to empathise with me? . . . Still don't know how he would write my stuff. . . . Look at Bacall's book. K. Hepburn's book . . . Fonda. He confessed a lot of things. I feel like doing that, too. . . . Who decides what's interesting and what isn't? What sounds good on tape doesn't necessarily look good."

Ultimately, controlling her own narrative became more important to her than getting the book done. After a year, Marian dismissed Maher, too, though it was a friendly parting of the ways. She and Maher and his wife, Barbara, remained good friends until Maher's death in 2007. It would be one of several false starts at trying to tell her story.

As Marian thrived at Bemelmans, Jimmy moved along in fits and starts. In 1975, after playing some gigs in Scandinavia with Bud Freeman, Jimmy came home quite ill. Marian complained in one of her letters to Townsend that Jimmy seemed more in need of attention than medicine.

"A worse hypochondriac, or big baby you'll never see!!" she wrote. "Although I may be wrong, a lot of it seems to be a sort of self-pity—a need to tell someone how terrible he was feeling." As it turned out, Marian was way off the mark. In Europe, Jimmy had contracted a staph infection in his leg as well as bronchial pneumonia. It took him several weeks to recover. Marian was later chagrined by her lack of sympathy. While all this was going on, the pair did a tribute to Bix with Joe Venuti in Rochester, which was filmed at the Top of the Plaza by local station WXXI, aired nationally on PBS, and released as a spirited videocassette, *Jazz at the Top.* Marian gave resplendent readings of the Bix piano numbers, but Venuti stole the show, giving one of the last great performances of his life.

Though Marian had been wrong about Jimmy's illness, it was easy to sympathize with her perception of him as "childlike." Sometimes his combination of bluster and naiveté reminded her of Ralph Kramden, the comic character Jackie Gleason played on the TV show *The Honeymooners.* An incident at the end of November could have been scripted for the series. While Jimmy was playing at the Hilton Head Arts and Jazz Festival in South Carolina, he decided he was going to make a mint by starting a "quail farm" in Merrick. "He brought back two quails in a basket," said Marian. "He had a bag of seed in the garage. I was so upset. One of them got out and flew away, probably killed by a cat. The other one we took back to South Carolina. . . . Jimmy really didn't realize that that was an impractical thing to do!" Jimmy apparently didn't give up on the plan, either—or at least the fantasy of it. The following year, he told an interviewer he owned a "private game reserve" in South Carolina.

Despite these occasional fracases, Marian and Jimmy were getting along well. John Schreiber painted a sweet picture of the couple having dinner at his apartment above Wein's festival office on West Seventy-fourth Street, not far from where Marian and Jimmy had lived when they had first moved to Manhattan.

"I said, 'Would you like a drink? A glass of wine?'" said Schreiber. "'No, that's okay,' he said. 'Give me a glass of water.' He got an ashtray and Jimmy then got stoned. He immediately started smoking. And Jimmy was probably sixty-five years old. In my mind this was an old guy. I'd never seen anybody that old get stoned. To me, the only people who got stoned were college kids and hippies, and here's this old guy, it just seemed so silly. And she got stoned. And we had a hilarious two hours. I heard all sorts of funny stories about Bud Freeman, and she of course is such an amazing student herself, she's a great historian, you know, and I don't know how many times she had heard these stories, but it didn't matter. It was like it was all new. . . . She was his best audience."

After Marian had been playing Bemelmans Bar two years, she decided to honor this man by throwing him a surprise seventieth birthday party. Amazingly, though she invited one hundred guests, most of whom Jimmy knew—including Willis Conover, Eddie Condon, George Shearing, Roy Eldridge, John Lewis, and Mabel Mercer—Jimmy somehow didn't get wind of it. When he got to the glass door of the café at eight P.M., he peered inside, then came in, and a TV spotlight illuminated his genuinely startled face. One hundred voices sang "Happy Birthday" as Marian, in a band with Vic Dickenson and Mousie Alexander, played along. Conover made a speech, then read telegrams from Buck Clayton, Clark Terry, Benny Goodman, Harold Arlen, and Alec Wilder. As he cut the cake, Jimmy said, "I suggest that all married people get divorced and begin treating each other like human beings." He then joined his colleagues for "Rose Room." At ten P.M. nobody wanted to leave, but the club had to open for the regular night's business, and the party was over.

Neither Doug nor Donna was invited to their grandfather's seventieth birthday party. When Doug registered his disappointment, Marian wrote back, saying, "Naturally we would love to have had you come to the party, but I realize it would have been a bit impractical," implying she had not been interested in subsidizing his visit. She closed her letter by telling him he could read all about it in the next issue of *The New Yorker.* Donna felt hurt, too, but she had other things on her mind. Not long after Jimmy's birthday party, she left Los Angeles for France, where she fell in love with a prosperous industrialist, Jacques Gourdol. They later married and had twin boys and moved to a small town outside Paris. It would be several years before she saw Marian or Jimmy again.

Marian's steadily heightening public profile in the mid-1970s paralleled the rise of feminism's second wave, known popularly as "women's lib," which led the press to repeatedly present her as a paradigm of the new, liberated, successful woman. The second wave had gotten under way in the mid-1960s with Betty Friedan and Simone de Beauvoir, both of whom Marian had read, but picked up steam in the public imagination with a widely heralded 1968 event in which a group of women protested a beauty pageant by throwing their bras into a garbage can and, the following year, with the formation of the National Organization for Women and the battle for the Equal Rights Amendment. One of the first pointedly feminist articles about McPartland was written in September 1974 by Leonard Feather—ironically, the very critic who in 1951 had facetiously written that being female was one of "three strikes against her." The British émigré and jazz encyclopedist, now a columnist for the *Los Angeles Times,* previewed Marian's appearance at L.A.'s Playboy Club—of all places!—and zeroed in on Marian's gender in a piece cleverly titled "A Blow for Women's Ad Lib." Arguing that no woman had achieved as much in jazz since Mary Lou Williams, Feather let Marian explain her own solution to sexism: "I knew it was not advisable to allow any categories to be detrimental and therefore decided to ignore them," she said.

Feather's piece would become a template for journalism about McPartland. Over and over she would be asked, How did you accomplish this, *as a woman*? What was it like *being a woman*? Isn't it terrible how *women* are discriminated against? You're such an important *woman*. McPartland felt profoundly ambivalent about this gendering of her success. The attention was fine. And that women were finally getting a fair shake was even better. But she did not welcome being lumped in with other activists and resented the implication that her accomplishments were now somehow more important or valuable—or, God forbid, that they had been achieved—simply because she was female. Though she actively sought out and championed other women musicians, she was not, strictly, a feminist. On the contrary, many tenets of the movement—its characterization of housework as demeaning, its emphasis on "de-feminizing" women, its extolling of women's accomplishments as a class—were repellent to her. Marian had met Gloria Steinem socially back in the 1960s, when Steinem had been dating Brubeck saxophonist Paul Desmond. In 1974, in a more formal encounter with Steinem at DeKalb College, the *Ms.* magazine editor had said to Marian sympathetically, "Oh, what you must have gone through!" Marian had replied, "Well, I really didn't. It always seemed like an advantage to be a woman." This was precisely the tack Marian and Barbara Carroll had taken on the supper club circuit, using female glamour as an added attraction. It was one of the reasons McPartland always took such care with her appearance. (She even went so far as to have a face lift, though precisely when isn't clear.) She was not a flirt—and certainly no kitschy Eartha Kitt!—but she was a woman, and she enjoyed being, looking like, and being looked at *as* a woman. No baggy pants and braless tops for her. She was a lady. A lady who could swear like a sailor, but a lady nonetheless.

In 1975, Marian laid out her views on women and jazz in an essay titled "You've Come a Long Way, Baby" for *Esquire's World of Jazz,* a handsome, lavishly produced coffee table book featuring a reprint of the *Great Day in Harlem* photograph across two pages. A photo of Marian, wearing a flamboyantly colorful jacket and a wide, loosely tied white scarf, sitting at the keyboard with one of her young, black female students accompanied the article. In it, McPartland kept the tone light and personal, taking on stereotypes but carefully avoiding ideology. She refused to pretend that men had not been helpful to her, stating forthrightly that her first big influence had not been a woman at all, but a man—Duke Ellington—and emphasized that another man, Jimmy, had been the single most important person in her life. If things had been tough for women back in 1951, she took it not as an insult or injury, but as an "accolade" that highlighted her own determination. And thank goodness everyone had it straight now, since this whole darn sexism thing had been one colossal misunderstanding. Marian simply would not take up the torch for women as a group.

"Anything is possible if one has drive, motivation, and is willing to take trouble—to get involved—to be ready to give unlimited time, to learn by trial and error," she wrote.

Feminists call this the ideology of "the exceptional woman," an individual who has triumphed over the oppression of women as a class because of her extraordinary talent and hard work. Unfortunately, as the feminist thinker Carolyn Heilbrun has pointed out, "Exceptional women are the chief imprisoners of nonexceptional women, simultaneously proving that any woman could do it and assuring, in their uniqueness among men, that no other woman will."

In Marian's defense, it must be said that in jazz there had been a good deal of gender self-selection from the beginning.

"People are always saying, 'Why aren't there more women playing jazz?'" asked Maria Schneider, the brilliant composer and bandleader whose career took off in the 1980s. "I always say to people, 'When jazz came up, look at the environment it developed in. Out late at night, or being on the road. Most women at the time, they wanted families, or that was kind of the norm. What woman can have a life like that? Or would want to? Very few. It wouldn't be desirable to very many women. You have to be a woman that can deal with the raunch. Not only deal with it, you have to be a woman that has a bit of a raunchy side, too."

Marian, with her potty mouthy and irreverent sense of humor, certainly qualified. And while she abhorred the idea that affirmative action was improving her status, that was clearly becoming part of the truth. She cheerfully, if carefully, went along for the ride.

"I guess I was women's libbing long before there was a name for it," she told Feather diplomatically, "and I didn't think it was anything strange."

A more enduring—and endearing—part of Marian's ideology surely came from Menninger's humanism. In her *Esquire* essay, she wrote, "We are all members of the same race—the human race—and we must dig into our own heritage and bring forth the creative gift that is within each one of us." This was Marian through and through, a hardworking product of the Protestant ethic, an individualist and egalitarian, from the tip of her very grand nose to the well-worn leather of the soles of her shoes. Her constant drive to do better—and to hold herself to an impossibly high standard, to never, in fact, be satisfied—would be both a propellant as well as a powerful depressant in her emotional life. In her own eyes, she would never really be good enough.

One of the more amusing aspects of Marian's press coverage during this period was her frequent appearance in the "women's pages" of newspapers, in which Marian, who didn't mind cooking (but rarely did), was routinely asked for her favorite recipes. She finally hit upon sautéed lamb kidneys as a suitably British offering, though it's doubtful she ever really cooked them. *Parade* magazine, the national Sunday insert, managed to get a kitchen photo of her serving up kidneys with scrambled eggs and hot French bread. Later in her career, when she had had enough of this, Concord Records asked her for a favorite recipe for a company cookbook, and she cheekily gave them one for "spotted dick" (suet pudding).

As the 1970s progressed, a vogue for all things female emerged in jazz as it did in the rest of society. "All-girl" groups had been a novelty in the swing era, but the new movement stressed the serious political injustice that women musicians—no longer called "girls" (much less "chicks" or "larks"!)—had endured and demanded not only that past masters, such as Mary Lou Williams and Clora Bryant, be acknowledged, but that young women be heard and encouraged. In early 1977, Marian asked George Wein if she could bring an all-female band to Newport. When he said there weren't enough good women musicians to form such a band, she set out to prove him wrong, gathering an all-women quintet at the invitation of *Today* show host Gene Shalit, who happened to drop by the Carlyle one night. Marian called Channel 21 in Rochester and suggested the final installment of its locally produced PBS show *At the Top* feature the new quintet. She then booked the band into the Monticello Room and scheduled a live recording for Halcyon the day after the filming.

For the quintet, Marian called four women who had never played together: Dottie Dodgion, her swinging, whiskey-voiced drummer from Strollers; the soul-drenched veteran Los Angeles alto saxophonist Vi Redd; guitarist Mary Osborne, her Hickory House predecessor; and a 1968 Eastman graduate named Lynn Milano on bass. On March 31, 1977, two weeks after Jimmy's birthday party, the new all-female group appeared on the *Today* show, then in June played three nights at the Monticello Room. A live recording, *Now's the Time* (Halcyon 115), suggested it was a swinging if somewhat loose-knit outfit. Redd, who had a sour, Charlie Parker–influenced sound, played wildly out of tune. But Osborne's richly chorded feature on "Sophisticated Lady" and Marian's equally lovely "Laura" were compelling.

Just as Marian was launching her all-female quintet, two idealistic young women in Kansas City, Carol Comer and Dianne Gregg, decided to produce the first women's jazz festival. Marian had gotten to know Gregg while playing jazz education events in Kansas City, and Gregg, a deejay, often played Marian's albums on the air. Dianne called Marian for advice.

"Oh, my God, it's a beautiful idea," Marian told her. "I wish I'd thought of it myself. I'll do whatever I can."

Marian put Comer and Gregg in touch with Leonard Feather, as well as Mary Lou Williams and Toshiko Akiyoshi, and put together an expanded female group for the event. The first Women's Jazz Festival opened at Kansas City's Memorial Hall Friday, March 17, and ran through the weekend. The festival featured concerts, clinics, an impromptu exhibition hall in the lobby of the festival hotel, student bands, and professional groups. The highlight came Palm Sunday, March 19. For the afternoon concert, Williams performed *Mary Lou's Mass* at Immaculate Conception Cathedral. For the evening show, Marian's trio led off with young Chicago bassist Brian Torff, whom she had discovered working with Mary Lou at the Cookery, and left-handed Chicago drummer Rusty Jones, with whom she had just worked for the first time in February at Rick's Café Americain, on the recommendation of Chicago pianist Judy Roberts. The concert, taped and broadcast by PBS, drew two thousand people, about three-quarters of a house. Marian oriented her set around songs by women—Ann Ronell's "Willow Weep for Me," Bernice Petkere's "Close Your Eyes," and her own "Ambiance" and "Afterglow." McPartland played with crisp energy, and Torff and Jones tore up "Ambiance" at a quick tempo that took its lead from Jerry Dodgion's arrangement of the tune for the Thad Jones/Mel Lewis Jazz Orchestra. The trio was followed by Betty Carter, then Marian presented an all-star band featuring the rhythm section from Rochester—Dodgion, Osborne, and Milano—plus horn players Mary Fettig and Janice Robinson.

"It was quite a rush," recalled Fettig. "There were all these jam sessions. It was quite a festive weekend. Everyone socialized. Press from all over the world was there because it was such a big deal. It was party time."

Marian had discovered Fettig, the first woman to play in the Stan Kenton band, at a jazz education festival in Kansas City two years earlier. She knew Robinson from the 1974 D.C. schools project. Remarkably for

a first-year event, the festival broke even. Reviews were uniformly positive and perhaps best summed up by Feather's comment in the *Los Angeles
Times* that the women "gave the lie resoundingly to old critical comments
that jazz is essentially male music."

That, of course, had been part of the point, and feminist discourse
flew fast and furious all weekend. Comer and Gregg had printed up and
distributed a four-page poop sheet titled "The Times—Are They a-
Changin'?," a compilation of outrages and paeans published over the
years about women's ability—or putative lack of it—to play jazz. Before
the event, one group threatened to picket because the emcee (Feather) was
a man. Another protested that Toshiko Akiyoshi's band was all male (to
which she calmly responded there would be no music for the men to play
if she weren't the leader). But the surly Williams stirred the pot to the
boiling point. At a pre-festival news conference, the pianist said, "I'm
feminine, but I think like a man," declaring she preferred playing with
men. By contrast to Williams, Marian sounded like a die-hard feminist,
despite claims to the contrary.

"She's very much a feminist," said Comer. "She's a supportive woman
who wants talented women to have opportunities. I think she wouldn't
label herself a feminist, but she would label herself an egalitarian." Interestingly, however, after 1978, McPartland never hired a woman for her
trio again. "One woman is enough," she quipped to Annie Gottlieb in
Ms. "Maybe too much." (McPartland later told Irving Townsend she
didn't hire Dodgion again because she played too loud, though this probably said less about Dodgion's drumming than Marian's newfound subtlety
since her days at Strollers.)

Her comments may have been provoked by her experience in Rochester, where, according to Dodgion, Milano stirred up some drama that left
a bad taste. According to Dodgion, during one of the first rehearsals, Milano confided to the drummer that she felt "used" by being promoted in
an all-women format and threatened to pack up her bass and take the train
back to New York. Ultimately, Milano stayed, but not before Dottie re-
layed this confidence to Marian, who said, "Well, fuck her. We'll get a
male bass player."

In a later interview, Milano said she didn't remember threatening to
quit but admitted it was entirely possible. She was "freaked out" by the
sudden exposure of performing on television and radio, on a recording,
and for huge audiences and also felt somewhat betrayed by Marian, who
she said had promised to play one of Lynn's tunes but never did.

"I had my hopes pinned on her, that I could trust her, that she would be a mentor," said Milano. "She told me I could listen to the tapes with her. I told her I was with BMI and needed to get something on record. None of the stuff she said she was going to do—she didn't do any of it."

"I could have killed her," said Dodgion, referring to Milano. "She put me through all that. Then Marian gave me that look [as if to say]: 'What are you telling me this stuff for when there's no problem?' It really put me in the middle. [Milano] had to worry about her ego and being exploited. She couldn't concentrate on the music. So I didn't use women musicians for the same reason. Because they didn't have their mind on the right thing, most of them."

Another possible reason McPartland distanced herself from women side players is politically more delicate but should not go unmentioned. Though the players in that particular band were straight, the "women's music" scene of the 1970s and 1980s had a prominent lesbian contingent. Marian had always been comfortable around assertive, even "mannish," women—starting with her adolescent friendship with Doris Mackie. But she was decidedly heterosexual, and the backstage atmosphere around certain gigs could become oppressive.

"I remember one time we were doing a women's festival in Minnesota," said her bassist Steve LaSpina. "We were running late, so I had to change and I said, 'Marian, can I use your bathroom to change my clothes?' 'Sure.' And there were all these women in there, and a lot of them were a little on the masculine side. So I come out of the dressing room and these people are really annoying her. But she's too polite to say anything. She says, 'I'm going over the tune list. What do you think about this tune?' And I looked at it and she had written, 'There sure are a lotta dykes here.'"

"She didn't like all these lesbians that used to latch on to her," said her old friend Diana Schwartz. "There were people who tried to attach themselves to Marian because they thought maybe she was gay, or because she was feminist, or a strong woman, and maybe she would support their cause."

Notwithstanding such internal conflict within the women's movement, the Kansas City Women's Jazz Festival marked the beginning of a decade of productive activism for women in jazz. In 1978, two New York venues presented "salutes" to women, and another club offered a five-week series called *Great Women in Jazz*. Marian invited vocalist Marlene VerPlanck to the Carlyle for a program devoted to female songwriters, which included Carla Bley's "Sing Me Softly of the Blues." As the 1970s became the 1980s, Cobi Narita formed the Universal Jazz Coalition in New York, devoting programs to women; the Newport Jazz Festival presented concerts featuring female musicians; San Francisco spawned the group Alive! with the belt-'em-out singer Rhiannon; and sizzling players like Mary Fettig were joined by other remarkable musicians, such as drummer Terri Lyne Carrington, keyboardist Patrice Rushen, and, later, bandleader Maria Schneider. Marian McPartland—as with jazz education—had been in on the ground floor.

As Marian embraced her new public role as a champion of women, she also moved forward on a second front. Frustrated by the noise at Bemelmans Bar, and fed up with nightclubs in general, she turned her eye toward the symphony circuit. After speaking with her friend George Shearing, who was playing concert halls regularly, Marian called Isaiah Jackson, conductor of the Rochester Philharmonic, and inquired if he would be interested in presenting her in a program featuring the Grieg Piano Concerto in A Minor. To her great delight, he said yes, and she embarked on the ambitious—and for her, considering her limited reading skills, unlikely—project of learning to play this popular concert warhorse. Despite her background at the Guildhall, Marian had never performed a proper concerto with a symphony. It was a gig that guaranteed an attentive audience in an acoustically fine hall, and it was lucrative. In one night, she could easily earn as much as she would make in a week at the London House. The Grieg is a romantic, crowd-pleasing piece with swelling melodies, dazzling runs, and pastel harmonies that suggest the pastoral Norwegian landscape. It would also prove sympathetic to Marian's harmonic approach to jazz.

"I chose the Grieg because I thought it was the least difficult of the piano concertos," Marian said. "Little did I know how tricky and difficult it was until I was so far into it that I could not turn back."

As always, Marian began learning the piece by ear, listening to Arthur Rubinstein's recording. She bought a portable record player and took the album on the road with her everywhere she went. In New York, she rehearsed with another pianist, Joellyn Ausanka, who played a transcription of the orchestral accompaniment. Marian had met Joellyn through Alec Wilder and Jim Maher in 1970, when Joellyn was typing the manuscript of Wilder's masterpiece, *American Popular Song*. A warm, generous, heavyset woman with a sharp eye for detail, a babycakes voice, and the enduring patience required of a good editor, Joellyn lived near Bemelmans Bar and was a regular. Marian, who never learned to type, hired Ausanka to help with her correspondence, but the relationship grew until, like Bernice MacDonald, Ausanka became an important member of Marian's inner circle. She would eventually work as developmental editor on Marian's book for Oxford University Press. In the 1970s, she began spending the holidays with Marian and Jimmy, baking Christmas cookies, a tradition they maintained for life.

On July 13, 1977, Marian and Joellyn were practicing the Grieg at NOLA studios in midtown Manhattan when the lights suddenly went out. The second New York blackout had struck. Marian and Jimmy were scheduled for interviews that day with a freelance writer from South Carolina named Zane Knauss, who was working on a book called *Conversations with Jazz Musicians*. After watching Jimmy play at Jimmy Ryan's by candlelight, the three wound up sitting all night on a curbside doing the interviews in the dark by Jimmy's car. Marian told Knauss one reason she wanted to play the Grieg was to make good on a long-ago broken promise to her parents to finish at the Guildhall. Marian often repeated this story, as well as another one in which she said she decided to learn the Grieg to "prove a point" to Alec Wilder, who had laughed when she had asked him to write a symphonic piece for her and had told her to "take a course in sight-reading." Being both conscientious and competitive, Marian no doubt entertained both these thoughts as she practiced four hours a day during the summer of 1977. But it's unlikely she would have committed the time or energy the project demanded to "prove a point"—to her parents, herself, or anyone else. She was motivated by the attraction of getting onto the concert hall circuit.

By fall, however, Marian began to realize that if she wanted to learn the Grieg properly, she was going to need expert help. She found it in the person of Ada Kopetz-Korf, a pianist she had known since the Hickory House days and who taught classical piano at the Manhattan School of Music. When Ada dropped by Bemelmans Bar one night, Marian asked her if she knew someone who might "straighten her out" with the Grieg.

"Well, Marian," said Kopetz-Korf, "if you don't let me do it, I'll kill you."

For the next four months, McPartland went to Ada's apartment on East Seventy-ninth Street three or four times a week, and they practiced the piece at the two grand pianos in her living room. Ada refused to take a dime for her services. Ada was impressed by Marian's classical touch and excellent technique, which included "natural octaves."

"The most difficult thing for Marian was memorizing," said Kopetz-Korf. "And why? Because Marian harmonically hears things very differently. Her harmonic sense is incredible. So in the Grieg you have like a seven chord and she would put a ninth in. And she was so right. She was improving on it. That was the funniest thing. That was the most difficult. Just to read the score the way it was written."

"Ada showed me how to get a better sound out of the piano," Marian said, "not to bang on it, to do things with the pedal, to pace myself, not to wear myself out, to work from my back and shoulders. These were things I had never learned."

The Rochester Symphony set an April 1 date for Marian's classical debut, but she wisely scheduled a series of run-ups to get comfortable with the material. She first performed the Grieg publicly in a student lounge for 150 people in early January 1978 at Bates College in Lewiston, Maine, accompanied by a local pianist recommended by a student, Daniel Griffin. According to Griffin, a classical music buff and sometime pianist himself, she did not play the piece at all well, "but at a certain point it didn't matter," he said, "because the point was to open the door." Marian ran through the Grieg again on January 28 at Bemelmans Bar, with Ada. George Shearing, a consummate master of classical piano, was playing the big room across the hall, and he sat in for some duets, during which he tweaked Marian by mischievously playing quotes from the concerto. In a February 15 letter written on American Airlines stationery to Jim Maher, Marian sounded anxious but also cheerful about her impending debut.

"The performance last night in Potsdam was very good," she wrote, "and a nice sympathetic conductor helped me through. Actually the thing doesn't sound bad—I have it on tape, and can learn a lot . . . I'll be back Friday . . . then leave for Chicago Tuesday for 5 nights at Rick's and a date (don't laugh) with the Senior Citizens Symphony Orchestra on Friday in a new hall connected with the Chicago Public Library. This whole thing is getting to be a riot, but I love it! . . .

"Incidentally, there was an excellent girl French horn player in the orchestra, and a girl oboe player, too. Amazing, but good to hear.

"See you all soon. I'll return Led Zeppelin to you when I get back. Please tell Fred I learned 'Stairway to Heaven,' but it's a bit repetitious. (I'll fix that!!)"

After one more "preview" in Geneva, New York, Marian plunged in with the Rochester Philharmonic at the Dome Arena. Ada came up for the debut, "nervous as hell," but much to her relief, she said, "it was better than anyone expected." The leading classical music critic for the *Democrat and Chronicle,* George Murphy, begged to differ. He savaged McPartland, describing her playing as "over-cautious, and replete with stylistic mannerisms which resulted in a continual pulling and tugging at phrasing and tempo," and said her technique was "unequal to the task." Murphy drove a stake into the heart of the evening with a parting shot: "The Grieg concerto and Robert Schumann's concerto for piano and orchestra, both of which are in the same key, are sometimes referred to as the 'ham and eggs' of the romantic concerto literature. Miss McPartland's Grieg was mostly ham."

Private recordings of Marian playing the Grieg on other occasions suggest that Murphy, though harsh, was not far off the mark. Marian skated through difficult passages and conveyed that she was intimidated by the piece rather than in command of it. Though Kopetz-Korf had some reservations about Marian's phrasing, she chalked up the harsh criticism to a snobbish prejudice against jazz players invading the classical arena and described a lot of the reviews as "cheap, and very uncalled for."

Which pretty much reflected the way Marian felt. Proud, and riding on a wave of self-esteem after years of analysis, she dismissed the critics, though she acknowledged she could never play the piece well enough to record it.

"I thought it showed a lot of balls on my part," she said.

Furthermore, with the Grieg under her belt, and a growing book of orchestral arrangements—on the second half of the concert, she played a string arrangement of "Eleanor Rigby" that exotica producer Frank Hunter had made for her years earlier, as well as two charts of her own tunes, "Ambiance" and "Willow Creek," arranged by Eastman School of Music student Lance Rubin—McPartland had acquired a visa to new territory.

"Doing the Grieg changed her whole life," said Ada. "It took her out of the jazz places and took her into playing with symphony orchestras. And took her into clubs where people are quiet."

Marian's relationship with Rochester was special and enduring, but she also cultivated a following in another city in upstate New York. In the 1970s, an ambitious, jazz-loving real estate magnate in Buffalo named Bill Hassett, who owned the Statler Hilton Hotel there and opened a jazz club in it called the Downtown Room, began to book Marian and Jimmy. Like the Monticello Room in Rochester, the Downtown Room was an A-list club that hosted the likes of Bill Evans, Oscar Peterson, and Mary Lou Williams, who in 1976 recorded one of her finest albums at the club, *A Grand Night for Swinging*. Buffalo had an avid jazz crowd, and the club was quite successful. At some point, Hassett—a tall, lanky man with prematurely white hair and bushy black eyebrows—befriended Tony Bennett and they started talking about forming an independent record label. Bennett had become increasingly frustrated by Columbia's persistent requests to sing rock 'n' roll. Bennett and Hassett formed Improv Records in 1975, using the Downtown Room as a proving ground for talent. Marian released three albums on Improv, all recorded live at the club, the first with a trio, the other two with a four-horn front line featuring Jimmy and Bennett.

The first album, recorded in 1976, was a tasteful though not particularly adventurous set called *A Fine Romance* (Improv 7115), on which Marian debuted a new, impressionistic composition, "Silent Pool," inspired by childhood visits to the mystical spot in the Surrey Hills where her uncle Will and aunt Mabel had taken her. It was a symmetrical, thirty-two-bar tune with a fetching A section, pellucid harmony but, unfortunately—her nemesis as a songwriter—a rather bland bridge. The following year, Improv brought out the rambunctious *Wanted (Live)* (Improv 7122), with swashbuckling Kansas City tenor man Buddy Tate, the sparkling New Orleans clarinetist Herb Hall, and Jimmy. A mishmash that ranged from an elegant piano trio to a raunchy version of Ray Charles's "Lonely Avenue," complete with honking tenor sax, the album captured the animated and carefree mood of a live set, but the cover art was amateurish, a silly send-up of a Wild West "Wanted" poster, complete with black-and-white pictures of Marian and Jimmy wearing masks, their accomplices billed as "The All-Star Jazz Assassins." On the last night, with guitarist Charlie Byrd on hand and Alec Wilder in the audience, Bennett emceed, sang a few tunes with his own trio and with Marian, and engaged in a dialogue about American popular song with Wilder. A live set (sans the Wilder conversation) was released as *Tony Bennett, the McPartlands and Friends Make Magnificent Music* (Improv 7123). It was an odd album, particularly since Bennett's appearance—though refreshingly spontaneous and including an excruciatingly beautiful rendition of Wilder's "While We're Young"—was too short to make the album his and too long to make it a mere cameo. According to bassist Brian Torff, there had been a miscommunication.

"Bill Hassett wanted to do a double record of a live performance," said Torff. "We did a set, then Tony Bennett was going to join us and he was going to do a record. Tony came in all enthusiastic and he did about four or five songs and then somebody said, 'Okay that's it, good night.' I remember Marian and I on the stage with our mouths open. . . . So if it seems like a strange record, it was not really what we expected to happen."

Bennett had already released three albums of his own on Improv, one of which was a marvelous duet with Bill Evans. But thanks to Hassett's ignorance of the record business, the label had turned into a financial nightmare. Bennett wound up buying out his partner to the tune of $250,000 just to get out of the deal.

"It was very disappointing," said Bennett. "We started out so optimistic, doing things for the sheer love of it. But I still don't regret it. It's not a failure to me. Those were wonderful days for me."

Bennett had first met Marian through Whitney Balliett and Alec Wilder, in the 1960s. Like them, he felt rock music had destroyed the music business.

"With all due respect to Elvis Presley," said Bennett, "when he became famous, good music died. It was the beginning of mass promotion. The Rolling Stones, the Beatles, Madonna, Elton John. It's a marketing thing now. It wasn't where everybody was searching for something to do well."

Looking back, Bennett saw Wilder, McPartland, himself, and a select few others as a minority holding out against the prevailing mediocrity, like medieval monks copying out classical manuscripts, waiting for the dark ages to end.

"There was a small, very good clique of very, very influential and creative people that she was part of and so was I," said Bennett of McPartland. "Now everybody's doing the American Songbook. It's interesting to me I was there at the very beginning, when no one was even thinking about that. We were the vanguard, the first ones to realize that the American Songbook will never die. I'm absolutely convinced that thirty-five to fifty years from now it will not be regarded as light entertainment, but it's going to become the classical music of America."

Though Bennett's account conveniently omitted Norman Granz's production of songwriter-specific albums for Ella Fitzgerald in the 1950s, the crooner had a point. By the end of the decade, fans of old-school sophisticated popular music had begun to blithely refer to the Great American Songbook as if the concept had always been around, when, in fact, Wilder and others like Marian had brought the idea into the daylight. Whitney Balliett's 1974 book, *Alec Wilder and His Friends,* helped solidify the concept. In it, he reprinted his 1973 essay about Marian from *The New Yorker,* as well as articles about Bennett, Jackie and Roy, Mabel Mercer, and others, creating a loose association of artists committed to sophisticated, noncommercial, antirock, jazz-influenced popular song, which helped to establish Marian's identity during the 1970s.

Bennett's and McPartland's neoclassical appreciation for the pre-rock landscape worked hand in glove with the neoconservatism of the jazz renaissance then getting under way. After being knocked out of the popular arena, jazz had reemerged as an art music. Jazz clubs became quieter and quieter. Eventually tobacco would disappear and, sometimes, even alcohol. By the 1990s, the whole image of the bohemian basement jazz club, full of smoke and gin (and romance), had virtually disappeared. Jazz clubs had become citadels of fine art, the music enshrined as an American national treasure.

This change in the cultural positioning of jazz was spurred on by the baby boomers, weaned on the Beatles and Motown but searching for music with more heft. In September 1976, the *New York News* noted that jazz was "flourishing" again in nearly sixty clubs around town. Five years earlier, there had been only a handful. That same year, Marian discussed the jazz resurgence in a prescient interview with trumpeter, critic, and Bix biographer Richard Sudhalter, who despite his baby boomer age bracket was a "moldy fig" who preferred vintage music over new styles. He had written the liner notes for the Halcyon Venuti album, was a lifelong fan of Jimmy—whom he looked upon as a sort of father figure—and had even recruited Jimmy in 1975 for a re-creation of the old Paul Whiteman band with Bix.

"Every place I work, business has never been better," Marian told Sudhalter, adding that young people were requesting tunes at the Cookery they'd discovered in their parents' record collections. She was also encouraged by the popularity of the film *Lady Sings the Blues,* in which Diana Ross played Billie Holiday, and by the proliferation of jazz festivals around the world. Everywhere she taught, she found talented students thirsty for jazz.

"I'm hearing rock players tell me, 'There must be more to music than this,'" she said. "Guys like Blood, Sweat and Tears want jazz players in their bands and are recording tunes like 'God Bless the Child.'"

Sudhalter suggested that the future of jazz lay in the "re-creation" of past styles rather than the development of new ones.

"Jazz is a rich tradition," he said, "not a 'railroad track.'"

"I agree," said Marian. "I would love to see a concert done on that premise—taking different eras and different kinds of jazz and putting them all together."

In fact, such concerts were already under way. In 1974, George Wein had debuted the New York Jazz Repertory Orchestra on precisely this premise, and later the same year, ex–Bill Evans bassist Chuck Israels had established the National Jazz Ensemble for the same purpose. Though neither of these orchestras survived, they were an augury of what was to come when the industry shortly found a proper hero to lead the revival—the brilliant young trumpeter and composer Wynton Marsalis. Marian first heard Wynton and his brother Branford right around this time, while playing at Le Club at New Orleans's Hyatt Regency. According to Branford,

Paul Lintz, the promoter for Le Club, asked Marian to play with the Marsalis brothers and several other high school kids. Marian wasn't that eager, "but when we started playing," said Branford, "she was amazed at what she heard."

"I was absolutely knocked out," said Marian. Wynton recalled playing "Maiden Voyage" with McPartland onstage. "She always reached out like that," he said.

When Wynton Marsalis later established a resident orchestra at Jazz at Lincoln Center, the repertory movement as envisioned by Sudhalter, with its emphasis on jazz as a repository of historical treasure, would be realized.

Everything about the jazz renaissance played to Marian McPartland's strengths. She was a historian and student of the music, an educator, a spokesperson, and—like Marsalis—a public champion of jazz as a great American art form. And, also like Marsalis, she was not an innovator, but a synthesizer who kept growing and growing, incorporating new developments into her music, taking what she saw as valuable from each, and discarding the rest. She was also an entertainer who refused to show disdain for her audience, as so many jazz musicians had in the 1940s and 1950s, when a more cultish hipper-than-thou attitude had been in vogue. The only thing Marian didn't have was a stage from which to project these myriad talents. When Wilder and lyricist Loonis McGlohon were offered a radio program in 1976 in Columbia, South Carolina, based on Alec's book, the last bit of set dressing was in place for Marian's triumph.

13.

Piano Jazz
(1978~1982)

"Tea at the Plaza yesterday with some people from Harvard," Marian wrote Irving Townsend on October 9, 1975. "We are setting up a three-day tribute to Mabel Mercer in January (do I mean salute? 'tribute' is when you're dead, isn't it?). It will involve me, John Lewis, Alec, Bobby Short & possibly Stan Getz."

Marian couldn't have known, but tea would lead, albeit by a circuitous route, to *Piano Jazz*. After the Harvard show feting Mercer's seventy-fifth birthday, Wilder assisted on a 1972 TV program about her and her male supper club counterpart, Bobby Short, for South Carolina Educational Television (SCETV). The network's public relations director, Dick Phipps, was so impressed that he suggested Alec do a radio series based on *American Popular Song,* in which he would interview vocalists and invite them to sing and discuss their favorite songs and songwriters. Apparently having overcome his much vaunted aversion to publicity, Alec eagerly accepted and invited his friend Loonis McGlohon, the songwriter from Charlotte, North Carolina, to play piano with a trio for the show. Phipps offered the living room of his house on Lake Murray, outside Columbia, South Carolina, as the setting. In September 1976, the station launched the series with a party in Alec's "living room"—the Algonquin Hotel—and after the show everyone repaired to the Carlyle to listen to Marian.

Over the next two years, Tony Bennett, Johnny Hartman, Margaret Whiting, and other classic singers appeared on *American Popular Song with Alec Wilder and Friends,* a highbrow but intimate and casual affair. In 1978, however, Wilder's health had begun to fail and the network began looking for a successor. Wilder wrote a letter to the station's executive director, Bill Hay, recommending Marian. That Wilder supported her behind the scenes was significant, because their periodic spats had continued. Just that May, Marian had agreed to do a concert devoted to Wilder's tunes to christen the newly restored Rochester City Hall. Still under the influence of the Kansas City Women's Jazz Festival, perhaps, she somehow switched course midconcert and started to play a program of tunes by women composers. Wilder, in the audience, leaned over to Tom Hampson and said, "I think I would have been better off if my name had been Alice Wilder." When Marian finally did play "I'll Be Around," Wilder said— quite loudly—"Why does she always have to play that? She's a woman in her sixties, for God's sake." Alec did not show up for the after-concert party.

All this could explain why Wilder never gave Marian the satisfaction of telling her he had recommended her for the show. (She found out much later, when Hay sent her a copy of Alec's letter.) But when McGlohon seconded the recommendation, Hay called Marian to ask if she was interested. She of course said yes. Marian had met Dick Phipps at one of Alec's tapings, so it was decided Phipps would be her producer. Marian suggested they make it a two-piano show. Phipps agreed and named the program *Piano Jazz*. Nearly thirty years after swooning to Wilder's octets on the BBC, Marian was, thanks to the composer, on the brink of becoming a radio personality herself. She immediately began forming a mental list of guests to invite.

"With so many people to choose from I was like a kid in a candy store," she wrote. "I was always on the telephone, calling somebody to ask him or her to be a guest on the show."

The format was simple. Marian would set up the show with a brief introduction, welcome her guest, ask a few questions, then extend an invitation to play a few tunes. After each song, she and her guest would have a brief discussion. Sometimes the conversation would be technical, but just as often it would be an anecdote about a club or club owner, a sideman, or an amusing experience on the road. Marian would politely suggest they play a duet, sometimes joining in for two or three tunes during the hour. Toward the end, she would perform solo. The show was spontaneous and relaxed, but of course the set list was written in advance, even though listeners were led to believe tunes were chosen off the cuff (and sometimes they actually were).

Jazz listeners have been living with *Piano Jazz* so long, they may well have come to take for granted just how unusual it is. But there is nothing else quite like it. Its host—a most self-deprecating and talented interviewer—manages to draw out her guests by inviting them to play selections from their repertoire and discuss their lives. But unlike a traditional interviewer, she also performs herself, in duets and solos, improvising in real time, the devil take the hindmost. Asking someone to play improvised music is quite a different proposition from doing an interview. It's an invitation for both parties to reveal themselves, the very essence of the spirit of jazz. When McPartland asks her guests, "Shall we play that one together?" she is inviting them to perform their lives, but also inviting herself *into* their lives, in the moment. As such, unlike Wilder, who was a composer—or, say, other expert interviewers such as Bill Moyers, Terry Gross, or Charlie Rose—McPartland is both the host of the show and, in part, its subject. A more perfect vehicle for McPartland would be hard to imagine, in that it satisfied both her great desire to thrust brilliant jazz players into the limelight and to share that limelight herself. Its hybrid nature as journalism and performance was a perfect match.

It was decided there would be thirteen shows for the first season. Marian chose Mary Lou Williams, Billy Taylor, John Lewis, Bobby Short, Barbara Carroll, Teddy Wilson, Bill Evans, Dick Hyman, Ellis Larkins, Chick Corea, Tommy Flanagan, Dave McKenna, and Joanne Brackeen—a list notable not only for the extraordinary quality of every player, but for the fact that it included three women. Marian would faithfully continue to feature a high percentage of women throughout the life of the show. The Baldwin Piano Company came on as a sponsor by offering its Manhattan showroom at Fifty-ninth Street and Seventh Avenue as an on-location studio. The room had twenty or thirty pianos. Marian would come in and try them all, then pick two she liked, and someone would pull them up together side by side. The engineer drove up from South Carolina. On those first shows, you can hear the boom of the room and there are moments when Marian or her guest occasionally even moves off-mike; twittering from invited guests can be heard, too. But considering the circumstances, the shows came off rather well technically.

Marian's first *Piano Jazz* interview took place at the Baldwin showroom on October 8, 1978. Her guest was Mary Lou Williams, whom she chose quite consciously, meaning to honor her longtime idol and the most important woman in jazz. McPartland immediately regretted it. Haughty and arrogant, Williams came in with a conspicuous chip on her shoulder and sulked through most of the show. At one point, according to Marian's friend Diana Schwartz, who was at the taping, Williams turned to Dick Phipps and said outright, "I should be doing this show." Which was no doubt precisely how she felt.

Marian expressly asked Williams not to bring a bass player, so they could enjoy rhythmic freedom in their duets, but Williams brought Ronnie Boykins anyway. The show kicked off with Mary Lou playing a bright and bluesy edition of her composition "Space Playing Blues," full of percussive dissonance. Afterward, Marian ingratiatingly inquired, "How do you explain this to your kids when you play a chord"—she smashed a random illustration on the piano—"like that?"

"I didn't play a chord like that," argued Williams, adding petulantly, "I just tell them the chord: E-flat nine with a flat five."

As always, Marian glossed over Williams's contrariness with cheery élan: "I haven't even had a chance to welcome you to the show. And it's such a thrill for me."

"That's nice to know," said Williams.

And so it went, with the two women stepping on each other's lines, each trying to take the reins. At one point, when Marian asked Williams what key she preferred, she said curtly, "Depends on my mood."

"What kind of mood are you in now? A B-flat mood, a D-flat mood?"

"Oh, I could just be in a flat mood, period."

After a scintillating duo by Mary Lou and her bass player on "Caravan," Marian asked Williams to repeat the fourth-based chords she had interpolated into the piece. Williams didn't play a note. Reading her mind, McPartland said sarcastically, "I'm trying to steal it, can't you tell?"

In an attempt to establish some kind of camaraderie, Marian slipped in a reference to her and Mary Lou having played opposite each other at the Composer back in the 1950s. But Mary Lou had obviously come with her own agenda. In fact, despite the lack of civilized conversation, she delivered some wonderful music. Williams bragged she was the only piano player alive who "played all the styles," from early jazz to free, and lived up to her boast, making smooth connections between historical periods. She finally let her guard down, at least momentarily, when Marian "dared"—Marian's word—her to sing the lyric to a rock song Mary Lou had composed, "Rosa Mae." After she took up the dare, the two giggled like girls—and so did some other folks in the showroom. It was the only easygoing moment in the whole historic, hour-long program.

When she later wrote about this encounter—or talked about it in interviews—Marian was deferential to Williams, even while acknowledging that she had been "snotty." But American history and racial politics notwithstanding, she knew Mary Lou Williams could never have done a show like *Piano Jazz,* whether she felt she was somehow "entitled" to it or not. And so did everyone else.

"Mary couldn't have done it because she was too opinionated," said Dan Morgenstern. "If anybody had said anything that she didn't agree with, she would have knocked them down!"

"I just was better qualified to do it," Marian told James Williams in her oral history interview for the Smithsonian Institution. "It wasn't her style. She was very into her own thing. . . . I had to be very concerned about how I was going to present the other person and wanted them to look good. . . . So I think that's probably it, in plain language, that she was jealous of me doing it, and thinking, 'How is this white uppity person doing this?' But she cooled off afterwards."

Charlie Bourgeois supported Marian's interpretation.

"Dorothy Donegan and Mary Lou Williams envied her—not her chops, but her ability to communicate the music," said Bourgeois. "They envied her popularity."

Marian taped nine of the first thirteen programs that fall, picking up Corea, Flanagan, McKenna, and Brackeen the following March. When the season debuted April 1, 1979—on its home station, WLTR, in Columbia, South Carolina—it was offered by National Public Radio (NPR) to all 225 affiliates around the country. Though Williams had been the honorary first interview, the on-air premiere featured Billy Taylor—a good choice, as Taylor was already an established radio host, had a smooth, on-air manner, and, like Marian (and unlike Williams), put his ego aside to project an ambassadorial view. In truth, if anyone could lay claim over McPartland to hosting Piano Jazz, it was Taylor. He was not only black, male, and American, he had been doing jazz radio since the 1960s and had been hosting a show on NPR, Jazz Alive, since 1977. If Taylor felt any animosity or jealousy, he hid it well, with the exception of a gibe during the show about how Marian had "put a padlock on the door" at the Hickory House for seven years so no one else could play there. When asked in an interview if he considered it an injustice that a white Englishwoman had become the national spokesperson for American jazz, Taylor said simply, "That is the society we live in. . . . She's worked very hard and she earned the respect that she got." Taylor's guest spot was a model of everything Piano Jazz could be—an hour packed with personal reminiscences, stellar playing, sympathetic duets, and lecture/demo material for students. On Wilder's show, examples in the last category had occasionally slipped into insider's talk. But in what surely must have been one of Piano Jazz's first producer-generated inserts, Marian, after chatting merrily away with Taylor about "comping," went back and explained what "comping" meant. Then she and Billy illustrated the concept.

If all the guests had been as felicitous as Taylor and Bobby Short, hosting Piano Jazz would have been a snap. But some guests—as wonderful as they were as players—were just dull. Ellis Larkins clearly did not enjoy talking about music (and according to Marian kept a mild buzz going with steady drinks during the show). Flanagan, who nodded when Marian asked him how he was, was a close second in the radio-challenged department. Teddy Wilson started out laconic but warmed up as she drew him into a fascinating discussion of classical piano as well as his fabled left-hand tenths. When the great Boston saloon pianist Dave McKenna came into the studio, however, Marian had to draw from a whole other toolbox. She knew the hard-drinking McKenna well and had even asked Charlie Bourgeois to "babysit" him the night before the show. By the time McKenna got to the showroom, he was three sheets to the wind.

"The one that got the hangover was me," said Charlie.

When he came in, he slammed the door and said, "I'm sick of your British shit! What do you know about fish and chips?"

"He kept saying it over and over again," said Joellyn Ausanka, who was there, along with Bobby Short. "He was slurring all his words and going on and on in between what they played."

When Dave asked Short to play the bridge to "I Hear a Rhapsody," he pushed him off the piano bench as soon as he started and said, "I know that!"

"Marian, this man is drunk!" Short said. "What are you going to do?"

"I don't know," she said. "I guess we'll have to try to get through the show."

Needless to say, there wasn't much conversation, and when McKenna did speak, he was insultingly familiar and scatological, referring at one point to Cole Porter as Cole Porthole. Marian gave back as good as she got, goading him by continually tossing the "fish and chips" line back at him (which no doubt mystified the listening audience).

When Marian suggested they play "Avalon," the barn-burning 1920s favorite, McKenna said in a phlegmy Boston accent, "Of course, Marian. Whatever, babe."

"What key?"

"Whatever you want, hon."

"E-flat . . . darling?"

"Okay, love."

The resulting duet was dazzling—or as vocalist Daryl Sherman put it in her introduction to a reprise airing of excerpts from the show, "The paint never dried."

But the pièce de résistance of the first season was Marian's interview with Bill Evans, which immediately began to circulate among jazz pianists as a bootleg cassette. Evans, who had been a heroin addict early in his career, was known to be an introvert, but by the time he got to *Piano Jazz,* a year before his death, he had switched poisons—to cocaine—which may partly explain the eager and outgoing nature of his disquisitions on the show. Evans spoke eloquently about how he approached soloing, conceptualizing the form of a tune until it was something second nature, how he *planned* his solos, worked on rhythmic displacement (moving the beginnings of phrases to different beats), and preferred to "practice one tune for twenty-four hours rather than twenty-four tunes in an hour." Marian repeatedly pointed to the Evans show as one of her proudest achievements.

Phipps felt the show needed a theme song. Just as Evans arrived, he asked Marian to write one, requesting something "nervous." That was easy, since she was all nerves composing in front of one of her idols. She came up with a sparkling series of arpeggiated sharp-eleven chords over a bass line that rose in half steps, running down, then up, then down, then up, like a hamster scurrying on a ladder. She followed it with a blues line over a harmonically ambiguous walking bass and reprised the first motif. Later named "Kaleidoscope," the piece was adopted as the show's theme and Marian later used it as a vehicle for improvisation.

The first thirteen programs of *Piano Jazz* established other traditions. When Chick Corea appeared, he spontaneously composed a musical portrait of Marian (but not before she coyly begged him not to include her nose in the picture). Marian returned the favor and did a crunchy, angular "portrait" of Chick. The idea of playing a free-improv piece was in the mix from the start, too, though the results usually had more shock value than musical substance. Marian frequently disparaged musicians who looked upon music as a competition, particularly the rhythmically ferocious and technically exhibitionist Chicago pianist Dorothy Donegan, who steamrolled through her show as if no one else were there. (When McPartland offered a sarcastic, left-handed compliment at the end—"You win"— Donegan responded, "No contest.") But in fact, Marian was extremely competitive herself.

"The jazz of yesterday used to have a lot of gunslingers, and Marian is notorious for that," said Seattle club owner John Dimitriou, who booked McPartland at Jazz Alley twenty times. "I've seen it over the years when guest artists would play, she would always outplay them—any tune, any key, that was her philosophy."

As she had with Mary Lou, Marian frequently offered to "challenge" her radio guests.

(Bill Evans quietly said he would not look forward to a ballad "challenge.") When Oscar Peterson came on the show, they agreed that every night in jazz was "a threatening contest." "I love it," said Marian, who said Shearing was always trying to "waste her" when they played. "He changes key, plays some stride, he'll do some things that are really mean, but I love every minute of it."

·

And while her tone was good-natured and even facetious, she liked her guests to know she was up to their level. McPartland used her competitiveness in the best tradition of jazz, to up the ante, put an edge on things, and get the best music out of her guests—and herself. When ninety-six-year-old Eubie Blake played his sparkling jazz version of "Stars and Stripes Forever," Marian leapt to the keyboard to play the cascading trombone counterline. The result was stupendous, spine-tingling.

McPartland seems to have arrived at her famously disarming, girlishly awed radio persona before the show ever started. Sometimes she sounded as if she had stepped out of an old Judy Garland movie, saying things like "Gosh, that was great" and "Gee, that was a kick." She also began constructing a pedigree from the first show forward, making sure listeners knew she had played at the Hickory House in the 1950s, had been married to Jimmy McPartland, knew Duke Ellington and Louis Armstrong on a first-name basis, and had pretty much been around the block. It was important, not only to establish her credibility with listeners and guests, but also to create a role for herself in the historic flow of the music. The incongruity of her English accent was irresistible to the public.

"Here's this old British lady who turns out to be the hippest person in the world," said Nick Phillips, one of Marian's producers at Concord.

Marian's frequent use of self-deprecating phrases such as "Well, I'll try, I hope I don't mess this up" reflected genuine humility. At the same time, her stance served as a strategy to put guests—especially older men—at ease. The last thing she needed was to come off as some "pushy, aggressive" dame. And yet that's precisely what she was. But her good humor, self-deprecation, and civilized curiosity softened the blow. Marian's voice was much higher back in those days, and she had a girlish giggle and a hitch in her voice she could turn on at will. (You can hear this as early as 1961, in a radio interview with Studs Terkel, when she says of her love of Dizzy Gillespie, "I guess I can't get away from trumpet players, can I?") She projected the notion that she was as much an awed fan as a seasoned practitioner. This made the listener feel like a fly on the wall, privileged to be listening in on a casual conversation between peers. As relaxed and casual as it all sounded, it was, of course, partly scripted show business. The segues between songs, made to sound spontaneous, were predetermined, if not word for word, then by a prearranged set list. So when a player might say, "Hey, how about we do 'How Deep Is the Ocean,'" it wasn't a surprise to her. Nonetheless, there was plenty of room for improvisation, and Marian deliberately worked from a spare script.

Critical reaction to *Piano Jazz* was swift and enthusiastic. It had been on the air less than a month when Phil Elwood, the perceptive writer for the *San Francisco Examiner,* himself a trad pianist, described the show as a "rare treat" and "marvelously entertaining," praising Marian for letting her guests "play as they wish." Leonard Feather lauded her for "keeping everything on a light note while maintaining the sense that this is at least in part an instructional series," though he faulted the conversation for occasionally becoming too esoteric. This criticism certainly applied to the Evans interview, in which first-name references were made to Scott LaFaro and Eddie Gomez without ever explaining who they were, not to mention all the technical information—though since it turned out to be so helpful to musicians, it was hard to complain.

As Marian wrapped up the 1978 sessions for the first season of *Piano Jazz,* she flew out to California to make an album for Concord Records. It was the start of her first contract with a commercial label since her stint with Capitol in the 1950s. Concord was named for the town where it was founded, a San Francisco exurb in a hot, dry valley on the other side of Mount Diablo from Berkeley. The force behind the label was Carl Jefferson, a successful Lincoln-Mercury car dealer with a big civic spirit and a taste for jazz, particularly mainstream bop of the sort regaining momentum in the jazz renaissance. Jefferson ran a music festival, for which he had erected the lovely Concord Pavilion in 1975, surrounded by lawns and hyperactive crickets that became part of the atmosphere on warm summer evenings. When guitarists Herb Ellis and Joe Pass played the festival in 1972, they suggested Jefferson record them and the Concord label was launched. Notoriously tight with money, "Jeff," as he was known, produced LPs on a down-and-dirty budget—one session, take it or leave it— with literal cover art favoring belabored representations. He refused to buy ads, even in *Billboard,* but made a deal with a local radio station to get Concord on the air two hours a day.

"He understood sales," said Frank Dorritie, a trumpet player who helped produce Marian's early Concord albums. "He sold Lincolns. He knew about branding. He was very smart with his money."

A larger-than-life character, Jefferson had a way of making oxymoronic pronouncements, such as "I know you don't know anything about finance, but I sign the checks!" But he endeared himself to most who worked for him.

"He'd call us into his office to hear the rough mix of a new album," recalled Nick Phillips. "You'd see this little half smile come onto his face. Then he'd say, 'Well, you think we'll ever amount to anything?'"

Jefferson, who met Marian through Jake Hanna, nicknamed Marian

"George," because her chiseled face reminded him of George Washington, and it became her secret moniker around the modest Concord office and warehouse, in a building that also housed a fish market, next door to the car dealership. McPartland and Jefferson developed a close relationship, though she was constantly trying to get him to spend more money. Though he had a gruff exterior, she could usually cajole him into doing what she wanted him to, including recording the tunes of Mary Lou Williams, whom he insisted no one had ever heard of, and dueting with Benny Carter, who Jefferson complained would be too expensive. Marian thought Jefferson should advertise her albums in *The New Yorker,* a strategy that had worked for her with Halcyon; when he refused, she threatened to take out ad space herself. Jefferson relented.

"She wouldn't fume at him," said Merrilee Trost, who worked at the label. "She wouldn't threaten him. She would just work it, with her sweet voice, her genteel ways, and she got her way every time."

"They were two of a kind," said saxophonist Mary Fettig, who wound up recording with Marian on Concord. "Strong-willed, and neither of them was going to bully the other around."

Trost, who started as a receptionist at Concord and graduated to public relations, said, "Carl Jefferson loved her. He never returned Stan Getz's phone calls. He just didn't want to deal with it. He wanted to show 'em who was boss. But with Marian, he would always return her phone calls. And it was reciprocal. It was a true affection."

The Concord "brand" soon took hold. With bassist Ray Brown as musical adviser, the label became a safe haven for beboppers whose careers had been eclipsed or who had been buried in the studios. The label was a new lifeline to singers Ernestine Anderson and Rosemary Clooney, guitarist Tal Farlow, drummer Art Blakey, saxophonist Bud Shank, pianists Monty Alexander and Jimmy Rowles, and hundreds of other straight-ahead jazz musicians.

Marian recorded her first album for Concord, *From This Moment On,* in San Francisco in the fall of 1978, with Jake Hanna and Brian Torff. The LP featured a solid program of romantic standards played in Marian's sturdy, classic, harmonically mature style. It was a treat to hear her again with Hanna, particularly as he soft-shoed through a fleet rendition of "There Is No Greater Love." But the highlight of the album was her solo version of Tadd Dameron's "If You Could See Me Now," which showcased her crystalline sound and assured touch.

"Marian McPartland might well be the Bill Evans of the '80s," wrote

Terry Teachout in the *Kansas City Star,* one of a stack of uniformly excellent reviews netted by the album.

Marian recorded two more LPs for Concord over the next nine months. While she was glad to finally have someone else producing her records instead of doing them herself, in the fall of 1979 she decided to deliver one last hurrah from Halcyon. *Live at the Carlyle* was an extraordinary farewell. It featured the nimble, twenty-five-year-old bassist Steve LaSpina and drummer Mike Di Pasqua. LaSpina had grown up in Dave Tough's hometown, Oak Park, and had moved to Chicago in 1972. After playing a few gigs with Marian in Wisconsin in the spring of 1978, LaSpina joined Marian's trio when Brian Torff left in April 1979 to play with George Shearing. The new trio played a tribute to Alec Wilder with vocalist Marlene VerPlanck at Michael's Pub that spring, then worked that summer in the main room at the Carlyle, filling in for Bobby Short. By fall, Marian decided they sounded so good that she wanted to record. She wasn't wrong.

Marian's playing by this time was reflecting the profound influence of Chick Corea, most obvious in her version of Corea's "Crystal Silence," but also in her charming composition "A Delicate Balance," a forty-four-bar, AABA tune with a childlike melody and a daring pause at the end of the A section that also showed the abiding influence of Wilder. Marian's playing had a spring water clarity, a stripped-down quality that had not been evident before. Unlike Corea's ensembles, however, her trio was warmly textured and swelled with lyricism, Evans-style, for the private audience of musicians, writers, and artists invited to the session. *Live at the Carlyle* was one of the best albums she ever made.

McPartland, LaSpina, and Di Pasqua developed a hilarious camaraderie on the road. Di Pasqua, who later left music to work for his father (who started the Subway sandwich chain), had the reputation as a terrible man for the ladies. At one point, McPartland left a pair of boxer shorts on his snare drum, with the words *Home of the Whopper* printed on them.

"She was always so much fun," said LaSpina. "I remember a time I bent over to pick up something and Marian said, 'Nice view.' And I said, 'Marian, that's sexual harassment!'"

Marian was enormously generous to her young sidemen. She even paid to have LaSpina's piano moved out to New York.

"She was particularly good with mentoring young women that were trying to break in," he said. "Marian was the pioneer. I remember Susannah McCorkle saying how Marian had taught her so much about business. About booking. And really taking care of things right away. I think she really influenced a lot of women musicians. She was proof that you could do it. She was an example to everybody. She was shipping records to herself in different locations before anybody else. Even the Concord records. We'd get off the airplane and she had shipped three cartons of records. Now, that's how we all do it. Back then, nobody was doing that."

Another woman who reaped the benefits of Marian's generosity was Mary Fettig, the greased-lightning saxophonist Marian had invited to play with her at the first Women's Jazz Festival. After using reedman Jerry Dodgion on her second Concord album, a swingin' affair called *Portrait of Marian McPartland,* the pianist decided she wanted to make another disc with a horn player. She invited Fettig to make a live album with her at the 1979 Concord Festival. Fettig had grown up in Concord, where her jazz band at San Ygnacio High School had won the first Monterey Jazz Festival school competition in 1971. Mary had known Carl Jefferson since she was a teenager, when Jeff had hired her band to play the festival picnic music. Jefferson's Rotary Club philanthropy and subsidy of local jazz education was well-known around town. On the live album, Marian played gorgeous versions of "In the Days of Our Love" and "Willow Weep for Me" before introducing Mary (on the second side), who showed her stuff on "Oleo." A few years later, Jefferson invited Fettig to do her own album, and Marian graciously agreed to play piano. Ray Brown was on the session, too. As usual, studio time was kept to a minimum.

"Everybody flew in that morning," said Mary. "We didn't have a rehearsal. You just shake hands and go. All live, in one room. Ray Brown's coming straight from a month of golf in Hawaii. I kept cutting him off because I've got six hours to make a record, beginning to end. Marian was really funny. She always said, 'I just love the way you stood up to Ray Brown.'"

Down and dirty or not, *Mary Fettig Quartet: In Good Company* was a much better showcase of her talents. She soared on Charlie Parker's "Scrapple from the Apple," and Marian answered Mary's harmonic substitutions with playful, Monkish excursions.

"It was so cool for me to meet another woman who was playing jazz," said Mary. "She was very comfortable in her skin. She was extremely gracious and extremely generous. Marian was a great role model. I learned you take your dress and roll it up and carry it in a canvas bag. She was the real pro."

Mary also noticed that Marian carefully controlled her public image.

"She had final say over all photos," said Mary, "and had them touched up."

The subject of the female image (and, by inference, the male gaze) was productively discussed in a *CODA* magazine review of Marian's outstanding fourth Concord album, with LaSpina and Hanna, *Personal Choice,* by far her best effort for the label yet. In the liner notes, the respected West Coast jazz critic Doug Ramsey argued that if there were women around who played as well as Marian, gender was no longer relevant.

"While one is inclined to sympathize . . . ," wrote reviewer Julian Yarrow in response, "one need only listen to the music to continually discover a profound charm and discrimination of a distinctly feminine character. . . . But if you really think that gender is irrelevant, take a look at the record cover: here is the artist replete with eye shadow, mascara, lipstick, perm, hanging earrings, with the album title in ornate, even florid lettering, and the bulk of the cover awash in *bright pink.* Now it so happens that she looks very nice and it doesn't seem to me that she is trying to pretend that gender is irrelevant. She has more sense than that. Imagine trying to pretend that Mary Lou Williams wasn't black."

Yarrow was precisely right. Everything Marian had said about accepting the feminine side of her playing had come fully into view. The album was lyrical and gorgeous at the same time that it was sturdy and strong. It wasn't that gender was irrelevant. It had been redefined. And in jazz, Marian had played an important role in that redefinition.

Right after the Women's Jazz Festival in Kansas City, as if she didn't have enough to do—leading her own group, performing the Grieg concerto, fulfilling a new recording contract—Marian decided to write a historical reference work about women in jazz, with an accent on what had kept women out of the profession. She applied to the National Endowment for the Humanities (NEH) and received a $20,000 grant for the 1979 calendar year to write the book, with a provisional deadline of December 31, 1980. She approached Oxford University Press, where Joellyn was now working as executive assistant to Sheldon Meyer. Under the direction of Meyer, Oxford was publishing the finest jazz books in America. Meyer agreed to publish Marian's book. She focused her initial research on the legendary International Sweethearts of Rhythm, an all-women, all-black band formed in 1937 at the Piney Woods Country Life School in Piney Woods, Mississippi. The Sweethearts had been a cut above novelty all-girl swing bands, playing the Apollo Theatre and Howard Theatre, but had long since been forgotten. Marian tracked down every member of the band she could find, one by one, and recorded extensive reel-to-reel tape interviews with each one, including drummer Pauline Braddy and vocalist Evelyn McGee Stone. She then invited the nine surviving members to a "Salute to the International Sweethearts of Rhythm" at the third Women's Jazz Festival in Kansas City. (McPartland and Torff had played as a duo at the second edition, along with Carmen McRae and Joanne Brackeen.) The standing-room-only concert at the Crown Center that March was a resounding success and a profoundly emotional event for the players concerned, most of whom hadn't seen one another for three decades. They sat in the front row, watching the all-women Janofsky-Patterson big band. Leonard Feather then briefly interviewed each Sweetheart and vocalist Stone took the stage, singing "Unforgettable," accompanied by McPartland. Braddy joined in, and trumpeter Nancy Brown Pratt borrowed a horn from a band member and played "I Cried for You."

"The crowd (which included Cleo Laine, in town for the festival's main concert)," wrote *Kansas City Star* columnist Terry Teachout, "roared with delight."

In all the excitement, trumpeter Ruth Kissane, who played in the big band, fell off the bandstand and broke her arm. Marian calmed down the crowd with "Little Rock Getaway."

"I wish you could have been here today when the Sweethearts (who showed up en masse) were feted and eulogized," wrote Marian in a postcard to the Mahers. "I never got such vicarious pleasure out of anything!"

Formal writing did not come easily to Marian, and it was not until June 1980 that she finally finished a provisional version of her essay about the Sweethearts. Her publicist at the time, Betty Lee Hunt, who represented Bobby Short as well as a theater roster that at one time had included Edward Albee, suggested they pitch it to *The New York Times* to promote Marian's opening at the Carlyle. When the paper turned it down, Hunt printed up the essay anyway and passed it out to reporters as a stand-alone publicity piece. In an article by the *Post*'s Jack O'Brian, who had now been covering Marian's career for three decades (including the announcement of Marian's divorce), you could feel her excitement. The Sweethearts' history read "like an adventure story," she said, "16 young girls . . . barnstorming all over the country," touring Europe with USO camp shows, appearing in a Hollywood film and on the Armed Forces Network with Lena Horne, Jimmy Durante, and Ethel Waters. Marian's vicarious bounce clearly had brought her back to her youth. She soon set to work on an essay about Lil Armstrong and continued to interview every female musician of note she could find, sending the tapes to Joellyn.

Marian devoted a lot of her time in the early 1980s to advocacy for women, which dovetailed nicely with the research. She and Carmen McRae hosted seven half-hour TV shows for PBS called *Women in Jazz*. Marian narrated from the piano, playing from time to time to demonstrate a point. The series included archival footage of the Sweethearts and Osborne and contemporary coverage of Carla Bley rehearsing and Joanne Brackeen performing. Mary Lou Williams and Helen Humes were also featured. At Newport, now called the Kool Jazz Festival (sponsored by Brown & Williamson tobacco) and presented in New York, Marian played a well-received show at Carnegie Hall called "Women Blow Their Horns," with the great trombonist and arranger Melba Liston, Dorothy Donegan, steamy funk saxophonist Willene Barton, bassist Lucille Dixon (who had worked with Earl Hines), Osborne, and others, with assists from Dizzy Gillespie and Clark Terry. Conspicuously missing was Mary Lou Williams, who, sadly, had died just a few days earlier in Durham, North Carolina. Marian and Osborne offered a moving musical tribute to Williams on the show.

Mary Lou, who had been offered a teaching position at Duke University in 1977, had been diagnosed with cancer, which she made public not long after taping her *Piano Jazz* episode. Marian contemplated visiting her in Durham, but Jim Maher advised against it.

"She might simply explode and throw you out or walk out," Maher said.

McPartland didn't make the journey, but she started to call Mary Lou frequently, and to her delight she found the pianist far friendlier than she had ever been. Williams biographer Linda Dahl speculated the cancer had something to do with her change of heart.

"She made a lot of progress in her own spiritual life, so she let go of a lot of things at that point," said Dahl.

Marian knew Mary Lou wanted a gold medallion of St. Cecilia—the patron saint of music—and Marian scoured New York to find one. She sent the medal, and Mary Lou was charmed. Shortly thereafter, Mary Lou died. Father O'Brien invited Marian to play at Mary Lou's funeral at St. Ignatius Loyola Church in New York on June 1, 1981. Marian played "What's Your Story, Morning Glory?" in honor of the woman she had revered since she was a teenager in Bromley and with whom she had finally made peace.

Before the rapprochement with Mary Lou, Marian had begun seriously thinking about moving closer to an even more central figure in her life—Jimmy. She had been living in Bellmore now since 1973, but she and Jimmy spent so much time together, she wondered why they were still separated. One night in Rochester, she was profoundly moved when she and Zena Collier went to see the Ingmar Bergman film *Scenes from a Marriage,* which deals with a couple who have multiple affairs, get divorced, then drift back to each other.

"Marian grabbed my arm in the dark," said Zena. "'That's my story!' she said. 'They're telling my story!'"

At one point, Marian made a "for and against" chart, plotting out the pros and cons of moving back to Merrick. On the one hand, Jimmy had tenants upstairs, so if she moved in, they would have to move out, an upheaval she did want not to precipitate casually. She would have to stick with her decision, which made her apprehensive. On the other hand, she realized she was spending most of her off-road time on Webster Street anyway. After several months anxiously weighing the options, in January 1980 Marian sold the house in Bellmore and moved back to Merrick, thus ending the couple's thirteen-year separation. She kept her East Side apartment so she could stay overnight in the city when she needed to. Though she lived upstairs and Jimmy down—the place was still a duplex—Marian conceded to *JazzTimes* magazine that it had been "too late to get a divorce, really; we still needed each other."

Diana Schwartz, who occasionally came out for dinner with her husband, Jack, remembered Marian and Jimmy in this period as a happy couple.

"They were great together!" she said. "It wasn't the same electricity as when Marian was together with Joe, but it was this comfortable feeling."

Jimmy had been sober since 1968 and was working steadily. He was often showered with honors, as befitted the current revivalist spirit. George Wein engaged Harriet Choice of the *Chicago Tribune* to curate "Goin' to Chicago" for the 1980 Kool Jazz Festival, and Jimmy was noted in *The New York Times* as dependably "insouciant." He and Bud Freeman were fussed over in 1982 at the Chicago Jazz Festival. A home video shot at a family jam session with Bud and others out at Haydon McPartland's Oriental Rug Factory in St. Charles revealed Jimmy as the still ebullient front man of his youth. With sideburns and perennially reddened upper lip, Jimmy wore a scarf, loud blue shirt, and glasses and prowled the crowd, joshing good-naturedly as he lectured the kids about the sacred rituals of jazz and introduced his childhood friend Bud as "one of the greatest saxophone players who ever lived." Jimmy wailed on "Sugar," "China Boy," and "Rose Room," his chops in good shape.

As a couple, Jimmy and Marian started playing an annual gig in Freeport called "It's OK Not to Drink." They also played the Boston Globe Jazz Festival, went south for the winter holidays to the Buena Vista Lounge at Disney World, and at the Dinkler Motor Inn in Syracuse, Jimmy could be found after their gig at the motel, heating water for tea and feeding Tippy.

From time to time, they were both at home, Marian working in the garden, Jimmy watching sports on TV, cooking, drinking tea from a mug, and tending the cats, which now numbered four. It took a while getting used to each other again.

"We seemed very grumpy," Marian wrote of the first months. "And he seemed impatient with me. He loved to shop for groceries and would go over to the market with the shopping cart. I would watch him from the window. . . . Coming downstairs for meals he would cook, and I'm sure I was never grateful or appreciative for what he did. I just took it as a matter of course—yet I can think of things I did for him—always getting his stuff cleaned, changing his bed, washing out his dirty underwear at times. It seemed like something I needed to do for him, but he didn't care. He got very careless and I'd have to practically rip the undershirts and underpants off him. He'd say, 'It's not dirty,' and give me an argument.

"I did so much in the garden, and nobody really saw it but me, because Jimmy didn't really notice. One year Diana [Schwartz] and I planted a whole bed of natural flower seeds, and when they all came up it was like a nature lesson, noticing how each plant sort of depended on the others—as one grew, another went to seed. Cornflowers, daisies, a sort of Queen Anne's lace all mingled, and there were some species I couldn't name with rich colors."

In an interview for the *Daily News* at the Café Carlyle, Marian painted another picture of her daily life, one that sounded pretty similar to the way it had always been (minus the uproars over Jimmy's drinking), except there was a subtle shift in tone.

"I love the sun," she said, explaining that she would often drive back to Long Island after the Carlyle gig so she could get up at eleven, bask in the sun, and take care of business calls in the backyard, using a phone with a long cord. "If there's something I hate," she said, "it's getting calls from California or somewhere and then to have to phone them all back later." After the morning calls she would take a brisk walk to the post office to pick up records and tapes and letters, taking care to write answers immediately. "Sometimes I'll put them on a tape for the girl who works for me in town [Joellyn], or I'll call her from the backyard—'I've got a hot letter I must dictate to you right now.'"

In her free time, she would drive out to Freeport to buy fish at the dock, then freeze it, or make up a batch of hamburgers—seasoned with parsley and thyme and sage and mushrooms—and freeze them, too, so there would always be something on hand to eat for both of them. In the city, she would do something "mundane," she said, like get her hair done, but usually her "very alert press people" had some mission for her to accomplish (such as an interview). After the gig, she and the guys would go down to Bradley's or Sweet Basil or Fat Tuesday's to see who was playing. One night it was George Shearing.

For the first time, rather than apologizing for success, Marian now seemed to savor its demands—as well as its privilege and status.

Perhaps the most disruptive event on the domestic front for the reunited couple was the death of Jimmy's first cat, Tippy, on October 4, 1980. It was hard to believe, but Tippy was sixteen. Marian and Jimmy buried him in the backyard, close to the hemlock tree, and Marian planted crocuses on his grave. In some scribbles for an obituary, Marian wrote, "The cats have been one of the many bonds that kept us friends."

Jimmy's grandchildren provided another bridge, particularly Doug, with his budding career as a jazz drummer. Doug hadn't seen his grandfather in a long time. In late June 1981, in conjunction with a junket to the San Francisco Bay Area to interview women musicians for her book, Marian hired him for a gig on a KQED-TV show hosted by the legendary Broadway actress Mary Martin and Jim Hartz, who had co-hosted the *Today* show. *Over Easy* was a talk show for seniors. Marian and Jimmy now not only qualified, but their unusually happy divorce was a winning subject. Prior to the interview, the couple played a medium blues in A-flat with a trad septet featuring Doug, looking proud in his wool suit and vest as he was introduced on the air as Jimmy's grandson. Marian and Jimmy later went out to hear Doug with his regular band, a regionally successful old-timey group fronted by a trio of female vocalist/instrumentalists called Nicholas, Glover, and Wray.

"It was the only time in my life they actually came and sat and listened to me play," he noted wryly.

Obviously, the resentment was still bubbling just under the surface.

"I think he still thought of us as the kids we were in Merrick," Doug said. "I don't know if he was half serious or just out of it, but I left their hotel room and he handed me a ten-dollar bill and said, 'Here, kid, buy yourself some candy.'"

Marian and Jimmy both made a point of writing when they got home, praising Doug's feel for swing (definitely in the pocket), and Jimmy promised to look for a more substantial gig out west where they could really stretch out.

Later that year, Jimmy had a reunion with the British side of the family as well. During a tour that took in Cardiff, Derby, and various spots in and around London, he played the venerable Dixieland spot the Red

Barn. Joyce took the kids to see him there and at a club in London, where Marian's nephew Chris reintroduced himself. Jimmy didn't recognize him at first.

"He said, 'Holy shit! When I last saw you, you were about that high!'" Chris remembered. "It was lovely. Sheila was there and we sat there all afternoon chatting and catching up."

Marian subsequently joined Jimmy in London, where they played Pizza Express and Donna brought her fiancé, Jacques, from France. As always, things went more smoothly with Donna than with Doug.

"Marian thought Jacques was just the greatest," said Donna. "And Jacques just loved my family, because they're all just the opposite of how he was raised. We just had the greatest time and partied and laughed."

Not long after this, Donna and Jacques visited Marian in New York, the first of many joyful transatlantic visits.

"She found us an inexpensive hotel near Carnegie Hall," recalled Donna. "She'd play at the Carlyle and then afterwards we'd go to all the clubs. There was a big snowstorm at that time and we were roaring drunk at the end. When we went back to her apartment . . . she took a hammer to the elevator, standing on a stool. 'Marian, you're waking up the whole building!' She's laughing away, hiking her skirt up, and banging. At her apartment, Jacques and I were just rolling on the floor laughing. She was saying, 'This thing never works right!' It was three or five o'clock in the morning."

With the growing notoriety of *Piano Jazz,* Marian's career moved into high gear. She was working the Carlyle, researching the book, taping interviews for the radio show, and playing the Grieg and *Rhapsody in Blue* all over the country. The gambit in Rochester had really panned out. Thanks to Susan Pimsleur, who had served as the first booking agent for the Alvin Ailey Dance Theater, Marian had symphony engagements up to a dozen times a year; she played for George Wein on a Kool Jazz Festival tour of one-nighters and was invited to Gracie Mansion for the festival opening; and she and George Shearing began to play as a double attraction (including a stop at the Ravinia Festival outside Chicago). If an event had anything to do with women in jazz or jazz education, Marian got the call. In January 1981, Boston journalist Fred Bouchard profiled her for a cover story in *JazzTimes,* in which he accurately praised her as "more of a doer than a talker," noting she had "already packed several overlapping careers into her life." Marian told Bouchard she was reading R. D. Laing's *The Politics of the Family.*

"When you're born," she said, praising psychoanalysis as a godsend, "they put a stamp on you. When I was about 3 years old, my mother would say to me, 'You're pigheaded, just like your father.' I figured, 'Well, if they say I am, then I must be.' Then it takes you half a lifetime to think differently."

One subject she refused to talk about in interviews was her age. Had she not been so sensitive about it, she might well have boasted that her career had bloomed when most people were starting to think about applying for Social Security. Marian was sixty years old when Bill Hay offered her a radio show, sixty-three at the time of the *JazzTimes* story. But she did not wish to be thought of as a late bloomer. She worked hard at staying fit and always looked great onstage. On the TV show with Jimmy and Doug, she had worn a colorful, full-length peasant dress and light purple blouse with a scarf that was part of the collar. She was tan and trim, and her hair was done to a T. She spoke the Queen's English and held herself erect at the piano and on the interviewer's couch. She smiled frequently. She projected a sense of consummate control, even while she was relaxed and always ready for a good laugh.

But success also brought out qualities that had been muted before, in particular a certain imperiousness. She had never suffered fools gladly, but now that she had a bit more clout, she sometimes acted on her impatience. An incident involving the young student who had helped her out at Bates College in Maine, Daniel Griffin, was a good illustration. After graduation, Griffin had gotten a job as the editor of *Independent School,* a trade magazine for American private institutions. Griffin offered to profile Marian for the magazine, focusing on her work in education. She agreed. Griffin opened the piece with a crisp portrait of Marian doing a workshop for third graders in Cincinnati, then, after circling back through her life and accomplishments, addressed an obvious if perhaps impertinent question: If Marian loved kids so much, why had she never had children of her own? He quoted Marian: "An interviewer just asked me why I never had any children. I guess I'm just too busy having everyone else's." It seemed a benign enough answer and certainly was characteristic of Marian's love of a clever comeback. When Griffin, who was nervous about writing the article, sent Marian a draft manuscript, she suggested some changes, some of which he accepted, but he pushed back on her request to delete the line about children. He had apparently struck a nerve.

"Marian turned ice cold and became absolutely brutal," said Griffin. "She was excoriating. The matter turned quickly from a disagreement between friends or even colleagues or professionals about substance or approach to a personal attack. . . . To say she was 'haughty' would be a complete understatement. She was positively cruel.

"'And you think you're *a writer*?' she scoffed. Without strong confidence in myself at the time, I was humiliated and confused. Here was someone with whom I had—I thought—a good relationship . . . I was speechless."

Marian eventually demanded that Griffin transfer her to his boss, to whom she dictated the changes she wanted in the article. Griffin vowed to never write anything about her again (a vow he eventually broke), but they did remain friends. In fact, he became an important resource, frequently offering suggestions for questions to ask some of the more intellectual guests who came on the show, such as William Buckley, and also volunteering to tour with her when she wanted a companion. But Griffin had learned to tread gingerly around certain subjects and to always keep in mind that McPartland might suddenly "go off" on him without warning.

Marian certainly had lost her temper often enough over the years with Alec Wilder. But as much as she loved him, that stormy relationship had waned. As 1980 drew to a close, she was about to lose her curmudgeonly pal forever—to lung cancer. Wilder was in Gainesville, in the hospital, and Mitch Miller's wife, Fran, was looking after him. Tom Hampson went down to update Alec's will, a crumpled document Alec had stubbornly carried around in a jacket pocket for years. Wilder had few possessions—just two suitcases from the Algonquin he'd dragged everywhere—but divvying up the rights to his royalties was serious business. Hampson got there in the nick of time. A day after naming his attorney as his executor, Wilder died, on Christmas Eve.

In his probate work, Hampson discovered something that surprised everyone in Wilder's circle: He had a daughter in England.

She wasn't interested in inheritance, said Hampson.

"She just wanted to know about her father. Alec never acknowledged her. He was a damn fool. She would have been a great source of comfort to him."

Wilder's friends planned a memorial service at St. Agnes Cemetery in Avon, New York, where his friend Father Atwell had lived. Marian attended, as did Loonis McGlohon, Jackie Cain, Roy Kral, the writer Joel E. Siegel, Tom and Zena Hampson, Lou Ouzer, and the rest of the Rochester gang. Marian bought a tree to plant over his grave. As they stood around Alec's open grave, Sal Sperazza played "It's So Peaceful in the Country" on solo trumpet, and Ouzer blew bubbles over the grave. Marian read a eulogy, noting that it was ironic Alec had died on Christmas Eve, a holiday he dreaded every year.

"One Christmas he called me from Nantucket where he was staying at the Jared Coffin House," she said. "He was jubilant! He had been looking at seabirds, walking through the deserted streets, being fussed over by the owners. 'It's beautiful here,' he said. 'No tourists, just snow and natural beauty.'"

After the burial, everyone went to the Hampsons' and told stories about Alec, which, according to Cain, moved rapidly from sentimental to irreverent, including how scared everyone always was that Alec would burn their houses down with an errant cigarette. In an obituary for Wilder in the *Philadelphia Daily,* Nels Nelson recalled seeing Wilder and McPartland entering the lobby of the Algonquin one night.

"They made a handsome couple," he said, "an indelible image of Manhattan urbanity as the mind's eye would devoutly wish it to be."

McPartland, Jackie and Roy, and others kept the embers of Wilder's music and memory alive. In June, Marian and Susannah McCorkle did a tribute to the composer at Eastman; the following year, at Carnegie Hall, an ad hoc group calling itself the Friends of Alec Wilder played a concert in his honor at the Kool Jazz Festival and thereafter, from 1985 forward, played a birthday tribute to Alec every February. The first one featured Mabel Mercer, Marlene VerPlanck, Jackie and Roy, Stan Getz, Gerry Mulligan, Bob Brookmeyer, Mitch Miller, Kenny Werner, and Gunther Schuller. Marian played the first tune Alec had written for her so many years ago, "Jazz Waltz for a Friend." Marian never heard whether her old friend liked—or, for that matter, even heard—*Piano Jazz.* Nor did she ever have the opportunity to thank him for recommending her for the show.

14.

Heyday
(1982–1987)

DESPITE THE SUCCESS of its first two seasons, *Piano Jazz* was put on hold between September 1980 and June 1981, and no shows aired in 1981. It's not clear why 1981 was a "by" year, though Marian did allude in one interview to having had a brief falling-out with her producer, Dick Phipps. Shari Craighead (later Hutchinson), who ultimately became the show's producer, confirmed that Marian mentioned this. It was no secret that McPartland and Phipps did not get along. She found Phipps "authoritarian," "difficult," and narrow in his musical taste.

"He was sort of condescending to Marian," recalled her friend Diana Schwartz, who often came to the tapings. "I think Marian was very unsure of herself, doing that show, and I think in the beginning they just clashed about everything and it was very unpleasant for her."

Phipps's taste was indeed conservative and fussy.

"There were a lot of people he really didn't want me to have," Marian said, referring to more adventurous players such as Herbie Hancock, Chick Corea, and Cecil Taylor. "I went ahead and got them anyway. He used to be trying to get me to have certain friends of his which were not necessarily name people or people I was particularly interested in."

"Dick Phipps was more from the Alec Wilder milieu—gay fans of popular songs," said Schwartz. "[He] was this big guy with a bald head and he had these gorgeous young men hanging around him. It pissed Marian off. [She'd shout,] 'I'm trying to do this show, I can't concentrate!' And it was true. I remember Marian really going off on him. She could really go off on people. She'll fight with anybody. She's always run her own show. She doesn't like to be told what to do. And she won't listen. If she doesn't want to do it, she doesn't do it."

In Phipps's defense, it must be said that *Piano Jazz* would not have existed without him. And with his deep background in American popular song—his lakeside home was lined floor to ceiling with LPs—he was supremely qualified to produce the show.

"He should be credited for what he did do," said Polly Kosko, who worked in development at the station and, early on, recruited Exxon as a sponsor. "This was a coup for South Carolina to be doing this. It was way ahead of its time, very sophisticated."

Phipps also knew where to look for money—the National Endowment for the Arts, for instance—and was an enthusiastic promoter of the series. Before *Piano Jazz,* he had been the head of promotion for SCETV.

"He was a public relations master," said Hutchinson. "All of the press kits were written by Dick."

Whatever their differences, Marian and Phipps must have resolved them. When *Piano Jazz* tapings resumed, Marian threw herself into the show, doing thirteen segments a year between 1981 and 1985 and twenty-six shows in 1986, sometimes traveling to new locations to record the interviews. Two thousand people came out to hear a live show with Teddy Wilson at Davies Symphony Hall in San Francisco in 1983. Listenership grew, especially when the show got picked up by the New York area's prime jazz station (located in Newark, New Jersey) WBGO. Critics fell all over themselves writing about it.

"I suggest you could learn more about jazz piano here than anywhere," wrote Steve Voce in *Jazz Journal International.*

Nels Nelson of the *Philadelphia Daily News* said, "Maid Marian's weekly pianologue is one of the fastest hours in broadcasting, an absorbing amalgam of chitchat, shop talk and keyboarding."

Longtime champion Leonard Feather, usually wary of blanket pronouncements, ventured to say that *Piano Jazz* was probably the best jazz radio show ever produced. It was hard to argue, as the next few seasons yielded one remarkable program after another, with marquee names like Dizzy Gillespie, Steve Allen, Oscar Peterson, Dave Brubeck, and George Shearing, as well as lesser-known but often equally or more engaging figures such as Jess Stacy, Cy Coleman, Hazel Scott, and Cleo Brown. One of the hallmarks of the show was McPartland's great flexibility. Though naturally she and her guests came into the studio with a list of tunes, Marian seemed to have a near telepathic empathy for where her subjects wished to roam. The result was that each show had a different atmosphere and mood, depending on the guest. There was no cookie-cutter formula. Often Marian, ever an avid student, simply used the show as an excuse to get a free lesson. Gillespie, who came on in January 1985, delivered what was probably the most notorious of those tutorials.

Marian's weak point had always been rhythm, so when she broached the subject of Afro-Cuban jazz, which Gillespie and Cuban conguero

Chano Pozo had pioneered in the 1940s, and Dizzy assigned Marian half of the polyrhythmic vamp to his tune "Manteca," Gillespie ever so gently but firmly took it upon himself to teach Marian something about swing time.

"I notice sometimes certain people can get a stiffness that has nothing to do with gospel and blues," he said, clearly meaning the certain person he was talking to.

Gillespie then clapped out the rhythm, with its triplet underpinnings, asking Marian to clap along, which she did.

"Boy, that's hard!" she said, getting it wrong.

"Yes, it's hard," said Gillespie. "The reason I can do it so easily is that I play conga. But piano players should do it, too."

Cynics might easily have taken this incident as a public chastening with the kind of racial overtones Mary Lou Williams brought to the music. But Dizzy wasn't saying, "I'll show everybody this 'uppity white woman' doesn't know how to swing." He didn't think like that.

"He was saying, 'You sure can play,'" explained Billy Taylor. "Dizzy didn't offer that to a lot of people. He didn't have to. And she knew that. [So] if he's going to take that time with me[, she thought], I'll take a look."

Gillespie's generosity was on display the whole hour. The man who had taught his contemporaries how the new, chromatic chords of bebop lay on the piano patiently demonstrated each chord to the intro and outro he had written to Thelonious Monk's "'Round Midnight," with the transparent clarity of a piano professor. Dizzy also demonstrated his compositional device of using a minor sixth as a substitute for the more final-sounding major seventh at the end of the phrase. Marian entered the mood, magically composing a piece in the moment she named "For Dizzy," which was later set to an orchestral arrangement. Gillespie was convinced she had come into the studio with it prepared.

The session with George Shearing (who appeared on the second season and would return many times) was stunning in an entirely different way. Like Marian, Shearing was a show-off, and the competitive edge between the two Brits bubbled to the surface, where they both splashed around playfully. Shearing's inner-city London accent, with a trace of Cockney made more abrasive by its Americanization, contrasted with Marian's royal vowels, which had also begun to shorten with her own time in the United States. At first, he sounded more prim and proper than street, but when Marian asked him to play his tune "Lullaby of Birdland" in a sequence of classical styles, he produced an eruption of pianism from Brahms to Stravinsky. "Oh, you stinker," Marian said when he had finished, sounding ever so much like the younger sister in that Judy Garland movie she could conjure so well. They both then confessed to a mutual love of Delius, and Shearing made a wonderful pun on one of Delius's compositions, calling it "On cooking the first hero in spring." Marian could often put forward a formal, show business cordiality, but on this show, she and George sounded like real, old friends who shared a special secret.

"Marian is a wonderful interviewer," said Shearing. "Since both of us are from England—we understood each other's innate English sense of humor. I always felt very relaxed talking to a fellow 'landsman.'"

The program with Dave Brubeck was one of the warmest and most charming of all. Marian and Dave had known each other for thirty years. They reminisced about some of their history, including their first meeting in Boston, when Dave and Paul Desmond had played their famous ad hoc duet on "Over the Rainbow." Yet for all their time in "the business," they came off not like jaded professionals, but more like eager young students feeding off each other's ideas. Hearing their exchange was like a youth tonic. Surprisingly, Brubeck had to be coaxed to appear on *Piano Jazz* and didn't make it until 1984.

"I told her I wouldn't play unless I brought my son to play bass," said Dave. "I rarely play solo piano. I wanted the anchor."

Marian allowed Brubeck to bring his son, Chris, but he never played a note.

Brubeck and McPartland really hit it off on their free-improv piece, with Brubeck driving the train, adding rhythmic verve to Marian's harmonies. On Dave's brilliant melody "In Your Own Sweet Way," Marian caught a bittersweet wave. She noted that the tempo Dave set was slower than people usually played it, then went back to the keyboard and laid out the melody again in the "correct" tempo, as if thinking out loud, reharmonizing the tune while she was at it.

"Whoa!" said Brubeck. "What was that? Play that again."

"Oh, I don't know," Marian said offhandedly, her chording having now become a matter of finger instinct rather than analysis.

"Boy, your inner voices are great!" Dave said.

Brubeck felt that Marian's musical self-confidence had a lot to do with her being such a good radio host.

"When you've got everything going for you like she had, there's nothing you fear," he said. "That's one of the first times anybody ever asked me to play free. Marian is up to any idea or challenge."

Per Brubeck's observations, the session with singer-pianist Shirley Horn had a risky feel, with McPartland occasionally urging Horn on to extra choruses and the two almost having a train wreck on the bridge of the 1928 Don Redman classic, "Cherry." But they were having so much fun, who cared? By the end of Charlie Parker's bebop blues "Billie's Bounce," both women were laughing out loud. Horn brought a sense of childlike wonder to the Tom Adair–Matt Dennis ballad "Violets for Your Furs," gliding over cushiony chords, then suddenly shifted from the key of B-flat to A at the end.

"My goodness, Shirley Horn," said McPartland, "that is some modulation!"

Marian added a similarly odd ending to "Guess I'll Hang My Tears Out to Dry" and told her guest, "I was trying to pull a Shirley Horn!"

Marian established the same kind of relaxed, girlfriend-to-girlfriend rapport with Carmen McRae, who bravely agreed to accompany herself on piano, something she had done early in her career. When Marian suggested "I'll Guess I'll Hang My tears Out to Dry" on this show, too, Carmen agreed to sing the verse a cappella.

"How did I get into this, Marian McPartland?" Carmen asked good-naturedly.

"I've got a lot of nerve," replied Marian.

Marian tracked down one of her childhood boogie-woogie idols, Cleo Brown, in Denver and convinced her to come on the show, even though she'd given up jazz for Jesus. On the program, Marian thanked Cleo for giving her a window on American swing she never could have gotten firsthand in England. Cleo answered by singing "hallelujah" lyrics to "Pinetop's Boogie." Years later, Marian told Lloyd Sachs of the *Chicago Sun-Times,* "If jazz is really sinful, then I hate to think of where she's going. She still swings like crazy." Other guests included Cy Coleman and Henry Mancini, who brought crisp insights into the world of commercial songwriting; Roy Eldridge, who reminisced about the Embers and his Long Island "club dates" with Marian; and Gerry Mulligan, who played piano, not baritone saxophone, and offered a glimpse of how an arranger hears the piano.

All this work did not fall on deaf ears. In 1984, the University of Georgia's Grady College of Journalism awarded *Piano Jazz* the George Foster Peabody Award for excellence in broadcasting for the 1983 season. Winning a Peabody, the equivalent of a Pulitzer Prize, put McPartland in the company of Edward R. Murrow, Jim Lehrer of *The NewsHour* (PBS), and Julia Child. The producers of *Piano Jazz* in Columbia, South Carolina, soon realized that the accumulation of Marian's interviews with jazz musicians was a treasure trove that needed to be safeguarded. In 1985, it was arranged through Marian's friend Bernice MacDonald at the New York Public Library that tapes of seventy-eight shows be donated to the Rodgers and Hammerstein Archives of Recorded Sound at Lincoln Center. Subsequent tapes (and, later, CDs and digitized versions of the original 278 tapes) were also donated to the library, as well as to the Smithsonian Institution. On October 28, 1985, a gallery of pianists including Dick Hyman, Duke Jordan, Shirley Horn, Roger Kellaway, Patti Bown, Ellis Larkins, and George Wallington came to the library for a formal presentation of the tapes. Marian and Shearing performed.

Right about this time, Marian's producer, Dick Phipps, became seriously ill and his assistant, Shari, took over production of the show. Hutchinson, a Columbia, South Carolina, native, had been working as a recording engineering for *Piano Jazz* and as a producer for classical music. As an engineer, she had substantially improved the sound quality of the program, which had not always been top-notch at the start. (The Shearing interview had been particularly plagued by room sound, including people walking across the floor.) Hutchinson was instrumental in moving *Piano Jazz* out of the Baldwin showroom and into the RCA studios.

Hutchinson had played classical piano for ten years but had no background in jazz. In some ways this was good, since she came to the show without prejudices and was willing to let Marian take the artistic reins. After Phipps's departure, the ironclad rule against having guests who didn't play piano was finally relaxed. (Before, even horn players like Eldridge and Gillespie had been asked to play piano.) Hutchinson also let Marian stretch her wings stylistically. Jazz/rock fusion musicians such as Hancock and avant-gardists Cecil Taylor and Jaki Byard were welcomed. Hutchinson improved the program's listener friendliness. Once she was in the driver's seat—starting with the January 1986 taping of Sarah Vaughan—Marian was no longer able to get by with inside-baseball references to jazz musicians without explaining whom she was talking about. Never again would names like "Eddie" and "Scotty" be uttered without explaining that this meant Eddie Gomez and Scotty LaFaro. Hutchinson brought a quicker tempo to the show, too, emphasizing music over conversation and insisting that conversations be relatively brief, moving *Piano Jazz* even further away from the languid parlor atmosphere Wilder had established years before. All that said, Hutchinson still maintained the casual and intimate feel of the show. Marian later acknowledged this change of pace, though she took credit for it herself.

"We were trying to be so educational that my guests and I talked a lot more between tunes than we do now," she told Robert Doerschuk in an article in the *San Francisco Chronicle*. "Eventually, I listened to some of the tapes and decided it wasn't the way to go. We should have more music and less talk, unless it works out that what is being said is so interesting that you just have to leave it in."

Hutchinson, a short, pert blonde who wore low heels and no-nonsense business suits and made no secret of who was in charge in the control booth, said she never had to teach Marian anything about radio interviewing—"she's a natural"—but that Marian was, at bottom, not really a radio person.

"A typical radio person will know that you've got thirty seconds before you need to hit that spot," said Hutchinson. "She just doesn't think about hitting fifteen and thirty-five."

Hutchinson's reference to Marian's lack of an "internal clock"—as natural to radio folks as metronomic time is to a jazz musician—was, of course, part of Marian's charm. If she had to be reminded again and again that station IDs were coming—and she often got cranky with Hutchinson for doing so—she made up for it with total immersion in her subject. The listener could feel how involved she was, and the fascination was contagious. Though Hutchinson's obsession with clarity and time could become frustrating, there's no doubt she made *Piano Jazz* a much better show—crisper, cleaner, and more accessible, without sacrificing its heart.

"Marian was fortunate enough to have good people around," said Billy Taylor, who understood from experience the importance of production values. Taylor added that Hutchinson "kept up with the times" and "made sure that Marian stayed up-to-date and that she was never put into a position where she was embarrassed. She knows what's right for Marian and what Marian won't have a problem with. There have been times when things fell apart . . . but you never got the feeling it was [Shari's] fault. Would that everybody could have that."

Marian was "terrified" of playing with virtuoso technician Oscar Peterson, who appeared on the second season, recording his session on a rented Bösendorfer at a daytime session at Rick's Café Americain in Chicago. She needn't have worried; her ear was keen. When Oscar added a delicious B-natural against a C to fatten a chord on his Tatumesque opener, "Old Folks," Marian pointed it out. Though clearly his technique was superior, they got along famously in duets.

"I had to remind myself not to be nervous and get off my arse and play," Marian told Bouchard at *JazzTimes.* "We'd never played together before, and he was very kind; he didn't waste me. He just played along gently."

When Marian reminded Oscar that she and Jimmy had played opposite him at the Colonial Tavern in Toronto some thirty years earlier, she seemed to have the whole history of jazz at her fingertips. Who was this Forrest Gump–like character who seemed to have been everywhere and heard and met everyone—albeit sometimes secondhand, through Jimmy—from Bix to Bird? It was hard to believe it was all true. But it was. And it was absolutely delightful.

McPartland was equally intimidated by Hancock, who appeared on the eighth season, in 1987. Hancock had just played himself in the 1986 jazz film, *'Round Midnight,* which told the story of Bud Powell's (conflated with Lester Young's) years in Paris. Its success was yet another indication of America's rediscovery of jazz. There was not a lot of conversation on the show—per Hutchinson's new regime—but Hancock's explanation of how he wrote a takeoff on Powell's "Time Waits" for the film—because there were copyright issues with the original—was priceless. Hancock complimented Marian's gorgeous textures on her solo version of "It Never Entered My Mind."

"I get kind of nervous with you watching me," she said.

"I have no idea what you're doing," Herbie replied. "It just sounds great."

By the time Hancock appeared on *Piano Jazz,* musicians were avidly circulating tapes of the show, even in Britain, according to British jazz writer Steve Voce, who lamented the BBC had not picked up the program.

While England may have ignored *Piano Jazz,* in the United States it became Marian's brand, with her performance reviews now routinely beginning with a reference to the show. Her new status also gave her access to places with more respectful and attentive crowds. During a stunning solo stint in Seattle in November 1982 at Parnell's, McPartland told the crowd, "I can't get over how quiet you people are. It's fabulous." McPartland was so impressed, she mentioned it a few days later in an interview for the Yale Oral History of American Music. The frequency of such topnotch engagements kept increasing, and so did her fees. Playing in Baltimore earlier that year, she told a reporter she was doing very well—"not rich," she said, "but well-off." Throughout the decade, things would get better and better, until McPartland became one of perhaps fifty (if that) marquee jazz musicians in America who could always depend on finding work in A-list rooms—and beyond. Under the auspices of the nonprofit organization Meet the Composer, dedicated to putting composers of all kinds in the limelight, McPartland played a concert in Puerto Rico that showcased her own tunes as well as her astonishingly eclectic repertoire, from John Coltrane's "Giant Steps" and Chick Corea's "Windows" to Joe Sullivan's "Little Rock Getaway" and Bix's "In a Mist." In 1983, she played the first Mary Lou Williams Jazz Festival at Duke University and also got on the high-paying summer "sheds" circuit—including Wolf Trap, outside Washington, D.C.—amusingly, on a double bill with comedian Phyllis Diller. Four years later, she returned, in somewhat more esteemed company, for a gala celebration of ASCAP songwriters that included Henry Mancini, Tony Bennett, Bernadette Peters, Roberta Flack, Patti Austin, Sweet Honey in the Rock, Bobby McFerrin, the Oak Ridge Boys, and Judy Collins—rare company for a jazz musician. At a 1987 "Evening with the Lions of the Performing Arts" at the New York Public Library, Marian sat listening to Isaac Stern in a crowd of honorees that included Vladimir Horowitz, Philip Glass, James Levine, and Joseph Papp.

Marian's close friends often found themselves beneficiaries of her new-found status, which she expressed with tasteful generosity.

"We flew out to East Lansing, Michigan, and she played the beginning of a gig where Dave Brubeck was the second part," recalled Dan Griffin. "I just did it for the hell of it. I had zero to do except walk around East Lansing and make sure she got to the gig, and that was it. When I got home, she sent me this $600 ice bucket from Tiffany's."

Jackie Cain received a Steuben glass vase.

"When my father died," said Griffin, "there were flowers for him."

"She sends flowers all the time," said Diana Schwartz. "I remember once when I was just traveling somewhere, I was going to someplace, for business, she sent this big bouquet of flowers."

Yet habits of thrift, ingrained by a British upbringing, also never quite died. Judy Roberts recalled having dinner with Marian one night in Chicago and watching her pocket the crackers and pats of butter from the table.

"She put it in her purse to take it up to her room, so she could have it later," said Roberts. "Made sense to me! She was thrifty and sensible—she was British!—and not flamboyant. And the most generous person ever."

With her elevated status, McPartland occasionally found herself onstage with scene-stealing entertainers, to which she did not respond kindly. On a May 1985 triple bill at the State Theater in Kalamazoo, Michigan, with George Shearing and Steve Allen—a passable pianist but certainly not in her or Shearing's league—Marian and George did to Allen what Oscar Peterson had so graciously declined to do to Marian: They "wasted" him. Allen gave them reasonable cause, disrespectfully going a half hour overtime, telling jokes to the crowd, while George and Marian waited in the wings for a three-piano finale.

"They didn't say anything," said drummer Rusty Jones, who played the gig with Marian. "It was unspoken. It was, 'Let's get this motherfucker.' Whereas if he had been kind of deferent, they would have been very cooperative and not tried to bury him. They went out there and went way above his head. It was just wonderful to watch. He didn't know what was going on. Marian, I'm telling you."

That summer, in July, Marian and Jimmy played for a sad occasion— the final curtain on the club Marian had played on her first trip to New York in 1946—Eddie Condon's. The club had been open in various locations since 1945 and had been kept alive even after Condon's death in 1973. Shortly thereafter, Marian was invited back to the European festival circuit, where she played, among other places, the North Sea Jazz Festival in The Hague; Tivoli Gardens in Copenhagen; and a return engagement with Jimmy at the Grande Parade du Jazz in Nice. The trip to France gave her an opportunity to see Donna and Jacques, who had gotten married right before the festival, though Marian's schedule prevented her from attending the wedding. There was talk of Jimmy flying over on his own, but Marian fretted in a letter to Donna that "the old man" was getting so forgetful, she was afraid to send him over unless they could pick him up and find a place for him to stay. He decided not to go, but he did play the festival, which Donna and Jacques attended.

Donna recalled listening to Jimmy while she hung out with Dizzy Gillespie at a Creole restaurant in the middle of the grounds. Dizzy was folksy and accessible, but when Miles rolled up, he was in a "limousine with four bodyguards." Miles told Marian he wanted to speak with Jimmy, who went backstage to pay his respects. When he came back, he said, "Yeah, I told him, 'Kid, you're going to be all right! You sound really good. If you keep playing like that, you'll go somewhere someday.'"

Marian went back to Nice in 1986, this time on her own. On the same trip she played for the first time at the Barbican Centre, in London, with the great British reedmen John Dankworth and Ronnie Scott. Marian had known Dankworth casually since 1952, when they had been photographed under the mistletoe at a BBC party. They had crossed paths again in Cleveland in the early 1970s, when John and his wife, vocalist Cleo Laine, began to tour the United States regularly. In the 1980s, however,

John and Marian became friends and staunch supporters of each other's work. In the spring of 1987, Dankworth invited Marian to perform under his baton with the London Symphony at Royal Albert Hall, and she in turn hosted him on *Piano Jazz* the following fall. The same year, she performed for the first time at the sprawling and magnificent Montreal Jazz Festival. In Nice for the third year running, Marian matched wits with Earl "Fatha" Hines for a crowd of thirty thousand that included Princess Grace of Monaco, Josephine Baker, and James Baldwin. Hines had played the first Nice festival in 1948 and was the hero of the night, but Marian held her own and finally—after the frustration of South America—got to duet with him.

"It was fascinating to compare their approaches to 'Tea for Two' 'Rosetta' and 'Mood Indigo,'" wrote Leonard Feather, "the Father incisive and rhythmically ingenious, the lady reflective and harmonically subtle. For a finale they got together for some happily interlocking four-handed blues."

Critics nearly always heaped praise on McPartland in the 1980s, lauding her rich and subtle harmonies, vast repertoire, and luminous ballads. But there were exceptions. Her longtime supporter in Cleveland, Dale Stevens, so enamored of her work in the 1960s with Swallow and LaRoca, disliked the prim, popular, middle-of-the-road persona Marian adopted in the 1980s and made no secret of it. In a January 1982 review in the *Cincinnati Post* of an underattended solo show at Xavier University (it was Super Bowl Sunday), Stevens called her a "female George Shearing," and he didn't mean it kindly, finding her facile and decorative.

"She tells nice, fussy little stories between songs, and you accept her as the pretty lady in the lovely bronze gown who obviously is a very nice person," wrote Stevens. "The result is 80 percent fun, 20 percent jazz." Stevens called Marian's Mozartizing of "I Could Have Danced All Night" "a Shearing trick" and described her as merely "a pleasant institution" who did not measure up to greats like Tatum or McCoy Tyner.

Alex Cirin, who had played bass with Marian and Jake Hanna in Palm Beach back in the early 1960s and was now playing symphonic bass locally, happened to see Stevens's review and fired off an unusual response—a long, stream-of-consciousness poem defending Marian's honor. Stevens published the entire poem in his column. In his ode, Cirin described stopping by Marian's dressing room before the concert, where he watched her warming her hands in gloves to get ready for the show.

He wondered aloud if she later played "Where or When" for him, because she used two of his favorite chords in the fourth bar. After comparing her to Django Reinhardt, George Shearing, Charlie Parker, and Dizzy Gillespie, he closed his paean with a sweet bit of wit:

> *It was an outstanding concert that Sunday evening*
> *The Bengals lost*
> *Sorry*
> *I won.*

Cirin later mailed a copy of the review and his poem to Marian. She was quite touched. As for the review itself, it stung. Though Marian dismissed it curtly by saying she "didn't think too many people would take notice of that," adding, "I don't think people really read writers," she knew very well that they did. She had spent a lifetime courting the press. Marian had occasion to be compared with George Shearing again in another 1982 review, this time more favorably. After a performance in Troy, New York, *Schenectady Gazette* reviewer John A. Marcille ventured to say that while Shearing had become bland and predictable, Marian had ventured into new territory, exploring areas pioneered by Evans, Hancock, and Corea. Noting that McPartland had perhaps a less "personal sound" than Shearing, she was nonetheless "secure in her position as a kind of jazz matriarch."

Critical use of gender-specific terms like "matriarch," "queen," "lady," and "grande dame" became more and more frequent in Marian's write-ups in the 1980s, and while this could be easily read as a genteel update on the left-handed compliment of yore—"plays good for a girl"—it also reflected an elevated status in the jazz hierarchy. Now that Mary Lou Williams was gone, there was no one else to challenge her, wildly talented players such as Joanne Brackeen notwithstanding. Marian's status was reflected in the floods of praise that routinely poured in not only from the older generation of critics—Hentoff, Feather, Balliett, Elwood, and Wilson—but also from the next generation. *The New York Times'* Stephen Holden, surely one of the most perceptive of that cohort, said of McPartland's 1985 Kool Jazz Festival solo program: "An expressive serenity and a classical sense of how the elements of jazz pianism ought to be balanced are the artistic hallmarks of Marian McPartland who, at 65, remains a pillar of genteel jazz taste." Movie critic and jazz-loving columnist Rex Reed also gushed over McPartland and even went so far as to send her a personal note in 1982, praising the Concord album *Portrait of Marian McPartland*.

Reed wrote that while he feared he had run out of "laudatory adjectives" for her "infinite gifts," the new record was "sublimely swinging" and "passionately felt." He hadn't stopped playing it since it arrived and the music was his constant companion, "drifting through the summer air into the garden."

Marian's recorded output for Concord in the 1980s for the most part received equally loud—and well-deserved—rounds of applause. A 1981 album of duets with Shearing featured the most gorgeous recording ever—by Shearing, who loved the tune—of Marian's ballad for Joe, "There'll Be Other Times," as well as a cute liner note documenting their sparring over tea and biscuits before and after the date. Their collaboration on Shearing's "For Bill Evans" drew out the best of both of them. But 1982's *Personal Choice* marked the beginning of McPartland's peak as a recording artist, though she crustily noted in a quote on the jacket liner that she was irked when an interviewer had asked what she considered to be the peak of her career. "It hasn't happened yet," she said, "but I'm working on it." In fact, it had most certainly begun. Warm, rich, inventive, and absolutely commanding, Marian reached a level of confidence and poise on this album that allowed her to suddenly strike out in new directions without ever losing her balance, as she demonstrated on an effervescent pas de deux with LaSpina on Oscar Pettiford's "Tricotism." And if there was still any question that the girl could swing, the album's opener, "I Hear a Rhapsody," put the issue to rest for good. The critics noticed. "Pianist Marian McPartland just gets better with age," wrote Owen McNally in the *Hartford Courant*. Phil Elwood said, "McPartland has a crispness in her attack and a rhythmic awareness that few jazz pianists can match. She carves away at melodic lines as she enhances the supporting harmonies." *Stereo Review* compared her to Glenn Gould, and *Down Beat* awarded the album four stars.

Marian followed *Personal Choice* in 1985 with a solo album, *Willow Creek and Other Ballads,* named for a tune she had been performing since 1970 and to which Wilder's old friend Loonis McGlohon had provided a lyric—and the title. It was a pretty LP, to be sure, but overall rather tepid, and in a review for *Down Beat,* Jon Balleras hit the nail on the head when he lamented that the "experimental, expansive air" of the Marian he'd known on Halcyon had been replaced by something like a "Bill Evans-in-slow-motion sort of impressionism, melancholic and bittersweet, tinged with introspection and carried on with iridescent, yet somehow static harmonies." On the plus side, Marian penetrated deeply into the unutterable sadness of Billy Strayhorn's "Blood Count," one of the last tunes he wrote, as he was dying in the hospital of lung cancer. Perhaps that's why she dedicated her next album to the great songwriter and Ellington collaborator. On *Marian McPartland Plays the Music of Billy Strayhorn*, it was if Marian had invited "Sweetpea" himself, as Ellington used to call him, into the studio, challenging him to "play that one together." Applying a light touch and tasty, Basie-like sense of swing—no one could accuse her of playing "too many notes" this time!—Marian invited alto saxophonist Jerry Dodgion to join her; drummer Joey Baron gave a lift to the proceedings, especially with his brushes. Smartly and simply arranged, with piano and alto sax occasionally carrying the melody together with a twist, Marian got down on "Intimacy of the Blues," unspooled clean sixteenth-note runs on "Isfahan" (on which Dodgion captured the original Johnny Hodges attack beautifully), and laced a sprightly "Rain Check" with mischievous substitute chords. Leonard Feather wrote perceptively that Marian "submerged" her own personality into Strayhorn's. This was part of her gift, a selflessness that exhibited mastery and confidence.

The language used by reviewers to describe McPartland almost always included some combination of "graceful," "civilized," "genteel," "balanced," and "elegant"—all words that, while complimentary, unwittingly implied a class basis for the quality of her music, as if gentility and civilization were somehow the equivalent of good art. These reviews were correct in identifying qualities of classicism in her playing—balance, skepticism, control, artifice, formal integrity, and poise. The implication was of a world in which, as the *Village Voice* reviewer had said so many years ago, everything was in its place. But reviewers often seemed to conflate McPartland's upper-middle-class English persona with her music. Was her playing really all that "genteel"? Certainly not always. She could be eruptive, dissonant, and ferocious as well as "tender," "delicate," and "gossamer"—another set of gender-based words. Unpacking the critical vocabulary that swirled around McPartland was a full-time job.

That is one reason why reviews of her classical concerts were so markedly different from her jazz reviews. Elegance and gentility were a given in that world—no brownie points for good vocabulary—and most serious classical reviewers could easily hear the deficiencies in Marian's technique and, as had been the case in Rochester, found it hard to resist pointing out her flaws to adoring crowds who could rarely tell the difference. In Scranton, reviewer Jane Krupa (one assumes no relation to Gene) called Marian's performance of the Grieg "lifeless" and lacking in rapport with the orchestra. In Oklahoma, W. U. McCoy said with damningly faint praise that "it was an increasingly respectable performance." But as Marian had suspected, the second half of her concert hall gigs—when she played orchestral arrangements of "Ambiance" and "Willow Creek"—nearly always won people over, even the critics.

But the whole notion of classical music as serious and jazz as recreational was about to get a makeover anyway, thanks to Wynton Marsalis, who was indeed a master of both crafts. Marsalis looked upon jazz in much the same way Tony Bennett saw the Great American Songbook—as America's classical music. This concept was not original to them, but no one had acted upon it with quite so structured and thorough a program. Holding up European classical music as a model, Marsalis proposed that certain jazz repertoire and composers—starting with Louis Armstrong and Duke Ellington—be canonized as "classic" and that jazz methodology be codified and taught. Unlike "third streamers" such as Brubeck and Shearing, Marsalis didn't want to merge baroque music and jazz. He wanted to apply the methodology of classical music to jazz—its rigorous standards, historical perspective, and respect for repertoire. To do this, he created an orchestra, a teaching institution, a jazz concert hall, and a comprehensive program, Jazz at Lincoln Center. Marsalis's approach was dubbed by jazz critic Gary Giddins as "neoclassicism."

Though it's rarely pointed out, Marian McPartland played on the first of the three seminal 1987 concerts at Alice Tully Hall, tellingly titled *Classical Jazz,* that led to the formation of the Jazz at Lincoln Center leviathan. Titled "Ladies First: A Tribute to the Great Women of Jazz," the concert featured Marian (with LaSpina and drummer Joey Baron) playing Williams's repertoire, plus Betty Carter, Janis Siegel, and Sasha Dalton paying tribute to Bessie Smith and Dinah Washington. The next two concerts were devoted to the music of Thelonious Monk and Charlie Parker. Though Stephen Holden found "Ladies First" lackluster and Marian's performance "sedate," the concert nevertheless marked a turning point in the evolution of jazz from its status as a challenging, bohemian outsider, wedded to innovation and, what was ultimately a critique of the status quo, to mainstream high culture. That Marian was there from the beginning was no surprise. Though she valued innovation and was far more open-minded than Marsalis—she did not, as he did, reject the avant-garde or jazz/rock fusion—she had been saying pretty much the same thing for fifty years. Jazz was an American art form with a long history, from Eubie Blake to Cecil Taylor. All of it was important and valuable, not just the latest style, and it should be taught and shared. She was doing that—in fact, performing the idea—with her radio show. Though it had taken a while for the world to catch up, Marian was in tune with history and it with her. That her success coincided with the flowering of jazz's neoclassical period made perfect sense.

But Marsalis was a divisive figure with whom Marian also often disagreed. Opinionated and never shy to share his views, Marsalis alienated many fans, critics, and musicians, including Keith Jarrett, who wrote a letter to *The New York Times* denouncing the trumpeter as a dangerous reactionary. When Marsalis appeared in a cover story in *JazzTimes* and not only voiced his trenchant opinions of other players but laced his language with profanity, Marian, in a tone worthy of Miss Wilkinson at Stratford House, wrote a letter scolding him for his poor comportment.

"I have just finished Hollie West's article on Wynton Marsalis," wrote McPartland. "Wynton is a fine young man and a brilliant musician, so I am concerned by this display of hostility and arrogance. Denigrating other musicians and business associates is unprofessional. Wynton's extraordinary talent is setting a new level of excellence in music. One would hope that the image he presents to the public will in future be more in keeping with his musicianship."

McPartland's was one of several letters to the magazine protesting Marsalis's interview. Chastened, he responded in print, saying he had learned a "very painful lesson" about humility. But the important point for Marian's career was that she was playing a public role in what was becoming a very noisy dialogue about jazz, a role she had adopted as early as the 1950s but which now had substance to back it up. When she spoke, she was heard. Along with that status began a string of public honors that continued to roll in for the rest of her life. She had already won the Peabody Award, and the Yale Oral History of American Music had considered her important enough to interview for posterity. In 1983, an interview with McPartland appeared in a scholarly study, *Jazz Women at the Keyboard,* by one Mary Unterbrink, who conveniently had alerted Marian to the fact that Cleo Brown—whom Marian thought had passed—was still alive. In her introduction, Unterbrink referred to McPartland as the "godmother" of jazz, yet another gender-based encomium in a long list. In 1986, the National Association of Jazz Educators named Marian Jazz Educator of the Year at its convention, the first time a woman had been so recognized. *Piano Jazz* also won the International Radio Festival of New York Gold Medal Award, and the Gabriel Award, presented by the Catholic Academy for Communication Arts Professionals. Universities stepped forward to offer McPartland honorary degrees, too. In 1981, the Stratford House and Guildhall dropout (who married an Austin High dropout) was given a doctorate from Ithaca College in New York. In 1986, Union College in Schenectady offered her a second degree—"Just call me doc," quipped the obviously proud McPartland at a club date at Schenectady's Van Dyck Lounge—and in 1989, Bates College, where she had first unveiled the Grieg, joined the throng.

Marian was so busy during this period, it's surprising she had time to pick up her awards. A genuine workaholic, she never took vacations (though she did always find a warm place to work in the winter, where she could lie in the sun) and always drove herself to do more and more—conducting interviews for the book about women in jazz, preparing for *Piano Jazz,* recording shows in the studio, composing, making albums, performing, and learning new pieces. "Work," she wrote in a somewhat self-pitying mood in her random journals, "is something that never lets you down." What "leisure" time she had was spent on the phone talking to business associates or scouting musicians in clubs.

"She's on the phone twenty-four hours a day," said Glenn Davis, Marian's East Coast drummer of choice in the 1990s. "On the road that's all she does. She doesn't know anything except this business."

"She's all about music," said Diana Schwartz, who often went on prowls with Marian to Knickerbocker's and other Manhattan clubs, then finished off the evening at Bradley's. "She's not interested in anything else, which used to really irritate my husband to death. He would give her books and say, 'You know, I love Marian, but you can only talk about one subject with her.'"

In her *Piano Jazz* session with Oscar Peterson—another driven performer—Oscar had declared, "My profession is music and my hobby is music." Marian had heartily agreed. "It becomes your whole life," she said.

There were exceptions. Diana's husband was a computer science mathematician whose sister happened to be married to the great literary critic Alfred Kazin. Oddly, Diana said, Alfred and Marian got on famously.

"He was a very defensive, prickly guy—exactly like Marian. When we had dinner parties with Judy, my sister-in-law, the two of them together were really vivid. It was an amazing friendship. Alfred wasn't really into jazz, and Marian was not into reading. But they got along great. They talked about the war, they talked about the hardships in England after the war. I had never seen Marian connect with anybody that way who wasn't in the music business."

Marian played at Kazin's funeral at the Ninety-second Street Y in 1998.

Marian was a delightful companion, said Schwartz, even if she always had business on her mind. And she was an irrepressible cutup.

"I remember drinking with Marian," said Diana. "We never drank that much, but this one night we had just come out of Bradley's and we were walking and it was cold, it was wintertime, and we were walking in Washington Square Park and giggling like two girls in the snow. Then we got a cab. She's so much fun!"

Another night, at Knickerbocker's, listening to Joanne Brackeen, Schwartz remembered Marian "going off" on a couple sitting in front of them. "They were just kissing, passionately, totally out of place. Marian felt they should be paying attention to the music. So she took her roll and wadded it up and flung it over there and hit those guys in the face! I thought this would be World War Three. And she said, 'Shut the fuck up! I'm trying to hear the music!'"

Schwartz came to see, through Marian, that going out to hear other musicians was not just recreational, it was a form of work.

"We were out in those clubs and I would go with her and they'd say, 'Marian McPartland is in the audience,' and she'd stand up and she'd come up and play," said Diana. "That's part of the scene. You had to be seen to advance yourself. You had to be in New York and you had to be out there doing it."

The occasional, inevitable hypocrisy that crept into such show business relationships rubbed Schwartz the wrong way, turning her away from the idea of being a player herself, though for a while she studied informally with Marian.

"Tony Bennett would be singing and we'd go backstage and get to meet Tony Bennett, and he'd be hugging her and they'd be taking photographs of her and everything," she said. "There was a lot of that. You'd be sitting there and somebody's playing on the stage and Marian's like 'They missed that change,' or 'That sucked,' or 'I hate this,' and then you go backstage and [she says,] 'That was great!'"

But if it was all part of the job, that was good, because Marian adored nothing more than being out on the town. She loved the frisson of Manhattan, where one night she might be backstage talking to Horowitz, the next night having Frank Sinatra drop by the Carlyle. She adored meeting celebrities, as much as she might pooh-pooh the experience later. In 1981, Katharine Hepburn was cast on Broadway in the role of Margaret Mary Elderdice in the play *The West Side Waltz,* in which she had to appear to know how to play the piano. Marian thought this might be a good time to meet Hepburn, so she wrote her a letter, offering to come backstage to talk piano. Hepburn invited her to the show. Marian took Charlie Bourgeois backstage to meet the great lady.

"I was able to ask her how she got to look so elegant at the piano when she couldn't really play it," said Marian, whose backstage tête-à-tête with Hepburn made Liz Smith's gossip column in the *Daily News*. "She didn't know much about jazz, but she was very nice. Charlie thought the whole thing was great."

When Hepburn's memoir *The Making of The African Queen* came out in 1987, Marian sent her a copy of the book with a return envelope and asked her to autograph it.

"She said, 'I'm sorry, I can't start autographing things,' but meanwhile she signed the letter," said Marian. "I thought that was cute."

Marian had moved back to Merrick in 1980, but it wasn't long before she began to regret it. She didn't really like the house anymore and found the south shore's blue-collar environment tedious. Particularly now that she was traveling in such different circles, she didn't feel the house was appropriate to her station, though it was hard for her to admit to such feelings.

"Why am I so ashamed of being in Merrick?" she asked in one of her agonized notes to herself. "Because someone like me, with my ability, because (I keep thinking) 'because of my position,' I should be somewhere nicer. I like a quiet place, being anonymous, not opposite a parking lot! Yet two years ago I couldn't wait to be here."

Whenever Marian brought up the idea with Jimmy of moving to a nicer place, he was indifferent. He was also becoming tiresome. Though he had stayed sober, he often dragged his feet about going to AA meetings and increasingly showed the characteristics of a "dry alcoholic."

"Dashing around, eats at midnight—can't sleep—then talks about 'my routine,'" wrote Marian. "Next day looking glum refuses to go to meeting but fritzes about all day, shopping & watching TV, then says he can't go to meeting, always in a lofty tone. . . . Right now can I say it's the disease talking? Like he's drinking—a Jekyll & Hyde—starts talking with a pompous air. . . . Tried to get over it, went upstairs & got busy. Kept wondering if he was acting like this for me to make a fuss of him. I wanted to but couldn't bring myself to. Guilt? More involved with him; just like I used to be."

As early as 1982, Marian also noticed that Jimmy's memory was failing.

"Not about things past," she wrote in a letter to Don Kassel in advance of Jimmy's appearance that year at the Chicago Jazz Festival, "but he'll ask you the same question over and over. I guess it's natural, all things considered."

Those "things" considered being Jimmy's advancing age—he was now seventy-five—but also the years he had abused his system with alcohol, not to mention tobacco, which he still used, smoking nearly a pack a day. When the Yale Oral History folks decided to interview Jimmy in 1985 for the series that had included Marian, she sat beside him at the house in Merrick, coaching him on the facts of his own life, and very nearly took over the interview. Jimmy was his usual bloviating self, embellishing stories with abandon.

In 1986, Marian decided she needed to make a move, even if Jimmy would not. Diana took her house hunting on the north shore. Jimmy could stay on Webster Street if he wanted to. She was going to move. After considering houses in what Schwartz described as bland suburban developments, Marian and Diana eventually found a cozy, split-level home in Port Washington nestled between a gently curving street and a three-hundred-yard greenbelt with hickory and sweet gum trees that separated the neighborhood of New Salem from the Port Washington line of the Long Island Rail Road. The house had a wood-paneled den and bright, sunlit kitchen with a view onto the woods.

The street that led from Port Washington Boulevard to the neighborhood had the perfect name—"Derby," which Marian pronounced the English way, "Darby."

"She liked that," said Diana.

Another plus was that it was only a fifteen-to-twenty minute drive from Merrick.

Port Washington is an upscale town with a magnificent marina, seafood restaurants, antique stores, and, on clear days, peekaboo views of the Empire State Building. Marian's new home was about a mile from the quaint main drag. She bought the house in 1986 and remained there, gardening, taking vigorous walks to the post office, and feeding the birds on the back deck. She installed an enormous feeder raised by a pulley into one of the sweet gum trees, and she replenished it every day. Fat red cardinals often perched on the railing of the deck. Marian grew to love sitting at the white-laminate-topped kitchen table, staring out the window at the trees and birds.

For a while, Marian shuttled between Merrick and Port Washington, using the new home, she said, almost as a "toy" or "playhouse." But not long after she bought the house, she fell and broke her hip and had to be hospitalized. When she got out, she realized she could not go back to Webster Street.

"There was no way I could recuperate in Merrick," she said. "There was no way I could climb the stairs. Jimmy said to me in the hospital, 'Of course, as soon as you get out of here you'll come back home,' and I said,

'I can't. There's no way. I just have to go to Port Washington.' Jimmy was sort of appalled, like 'What? You're not going to come home with me?' So now I really moved into the Port Washington house. I had a wonderful nurse, Teresa, and between her and Jimmy I soon recovered."

Marian's hip fracture was the first of several signs that she had inherited her mother's osteoporosis—which causes bones to become brittle—as well as severe arthritis. As early as 1983, she had slipped on the sidewalk in Merrick while walking to the cleaner's and broken her kneecap. Over the next fifteen years, Marian would break both hips (eventually having one replaced), her left wrist (requiring a pin to be inserted), and, in a near tragedy that almost ended her career, her left elbow. She also experienced several collapsed spinal disks, which over the years reduced her height by nearly three inches.

"I'm broken all over," said Marian, who somehow managed to keep a cheerful demeanor and stiff upper lip through all the fractures. Her closest friends and family all attested that she rarely, if ever, complained. On the contrary, she always pushed forward, anxious to get to the next project.

"I guess you heard about my accident from the old man," she wrote in a 1985 letter to Doug Kassel, referring to her wrist. "Well, I'm doing fine now, & getting ready to start taping for NPR April 20th. We have twenty-six new shows."

McPartland's letter was typical—cheerful, full of career information and a supportive compliment or two about Doug's endeavors. But she could become impatient if he didn't reply promptly.

"Don't you ever write?" she asked in January 1986. "Are you okay? (Not ill I guess, or I'd have heard about it from Donna.) Did you get our Xmas card? Did you get my record, *Willow Creek*? You really are an asshole for never writing."

Doug had moved away from jazz, into acting (with a Bay Area improv group called the Flash Family), but he occasionally worked with Marian and/or Jimmy. In the summer of 1983, Jimmy asked Doug to sit in at their gig at the biggest trad festival in the country, the Dixieland Jazz Jubilee in Sacramento. At the hotel one afternoon, sitting on the bed with his shirt off, Jimmy turned to Doug and, out of the blue, asked, "Why'd she do it?"

Doug was caught off guard. For years, he had wanted to talk to his grandfather about his mother's suicide, but he had never known how. Jimmy had always put on a front of bluff bravado. But now he really seemed to want to talk.

"It was the first time I ever heard him say anything about it," said Doug. "Marian kind of blanched. I said [to myself,] 'I'm not going to blow this off.' And so I said, 'I don't know, my feeling is I think she felt trapped, that she had made a mistake, that she felt isolated, I think she felt guilty about leaving me, and all of her friends. Nobody thought this was a good idea for her to go. She just wound up in a dead end and couldn't get out of it.'"

What Doug didn't say was that his mother had told him she felt her father didn't love her, which Doug surmised had played as big a role in Dorothy's suicide as anything else. But even if he had wanted to say something so devastating to his grandfather, he never got the chance. The moment was over as fast as it came. Suddenly they were talking about something else.

Doug played with Marian again that fall, for a school broadcast sponsored by Chevron called "Jazz Makers." To a TV studio audience of children sitting on bleachers, Marian demonstrated the various styles of jazz, from ragtime to free. A couple of years later, in a sweet gesture, Marian sent Doug one of Jimmy's cornets and had Jimmy's name engraved on it. Marian secretly hoped it might inspire Doug to take up jazz again, but it would be many years before that happened.

After the TV show in San Francisco, Marian sent an aerogram to Donna in Paris.

"Grandpa played very well," she said of the Sacramento gig. "We were all delighted because I don't think anyone was expecting him to be that strong! I wish Doug would play more, he's an excellent drummer, but he doesn't seem to have any drive for that sort of activity. He does seem happy, though. We were grateful that he took the time to make the two-hour drive to be with us. It gave us a chance to catch up on things—we talked for hours."

Amid all this traveling and performing and radio hosting and gadding about Manhattan, Marian McPartland was also supposed to be finishing her book about women in jazz for Oxford University Press. But as the reels and reels of interview tapes accumulated, and Joellyn Ausanka dutifully typed them up, Marian began to realize that writing a book was not something she could accomplish between gigs. Worse, she found herself procrastinating. Though she had written record reviews and profiles for *Down Beat,* compiling a comprehensive book based on primary research was a far vaster undertaking. In her final report to the National Endowment for the Humanities, she found herself blushingly inflating what little progress she had made. For an answer, she received a rather scolding letter from the NEH program officer, pointing out that it was "unusual" for fellows to pursue regular work during the grant period but that the endowment had made an exception for her, so as not to negatively impact her career. Could she please itemize all the gigs she had taken and explain why she had taken them? In the meantime, Marian received yet another fellowship from the Guggenheim Foundation in 1980. As the book project dragged on, she began to feel a great burden of guilt—for not meeting her obligations to the granting agencies and the publisher, much less the women she had interviewed. Years before, she had told an English reporter that, somehow, the more work she did, the more she was able to do. Now that she was so much in demand, however, that formula had finally reached a point of diminishing returns. Her great appetite for work had turned around to bite her.

"What is it that keeps me from doing the book?" she wrote to herself in May 1982. "I know I'm allowing myself to drift away from it. Is it enough to say I don't feel like it? There has to be a guilty feeling down inside. Surely I've learned enough about myself to know that I can get in my own way."

It didn't help that everywhere she went, reporters asked her how the book was coming.

"My difficulty these days is time," she told Phil Elwood in San Francisco. "I am doing so many things that I have trouble getting on with some projects."

Yet in the same interview, she told Elwood she was interested in starting a TV show! Marian agonized about the book throughout the rest of the year. In notes to herself, she sometimes lashed out, blaming others—living with Jimmy was dragging her down, Jim Maher had "misled" her into thinking he would help her more than he had, Alec had made her think she was a better writer than she was. By October, she was "feeling hopeless. That book is too much for me." In November came a crushing—if entirely predictable—surprise. Sally Placksin published *American Women in Jazz,* the first book of its kind. It included interviews with many of the same women Marian had spoken with. Worse, Placksin did not mention Marian.

Disconsolately, Marian wrote, "Feel all my research is a waste. She talked to all the Sweethearts girls. I was responsible for getting them to the festival. But I must forget all that."

Placksin had begun *American Women in Jazz* in 1978 and was aware that Marian, too, was researching some of the same folks, but she did not feel particularly pressured that Marian would finish first.

"I was too young and madly obsessed to think about getting paranoid," said Placksin.

Placksin offered profiles and oral histories of major figures by decade, starting with Bessie Smith and Ethel Waters in the 1920s and working up to Joanne Brackeen and Jane Ira Bloom in the 1970s. She was aware of *Piano Jazz,* of course, and her knowledge of Marian even predated her interest in jazz. But the reason she didn't include Marian, she said, was that Marian was British. The publisher had asked Placksin to limit herself to American players, just as the title said. Placksin herself also wanted to focus more on instrumentalists other than pianists, who, like female vocalists, had always gotten the lion's share of attention. Placksin wanted to shed light on lesser-known women, too, such as trumpeter Jean Davis and bassist Carline Ray. In fact, she said her publisher ultimately had to cut her off, telling her to stop doing interviews because the book was getting too long.

Three more books about women in jazz came out in the 1980s. Antoinette Handy wrote two of them: *Black Women in American Bands and Orchestras* and *The International Sweethearts of Rhythm,* which was released in 1983. In 1984, Linda Dahl published *Stormy Weather: The Music and Lives of a Century of Jazzwomen.* Dahl's book was theoretically heftier than the others; her essays about the way bias had played out against women in jazz were thorough and thoughtful. Curiously, however, she did not choose Marian as one of her ten profile subjects, preferring instead, as did Placksin, to concentrate on lesser-known players such as Dottie Dodgion and guitarist Mary Osborne—ironically, women who had been side players for Marian. Dahl devoted exactly a page and a half to McPartland, in a section titled "The Ladies of the Keyboard"; *Piano Jazz,* a major force in exposing women players, was not even mentioned. Dahl explained that although *Stormy Weather* was written in 1981, her omission of *Piano Jazz* "could have been an oversight." The program, she said, had not yet made a huge impact. Dahl was far more interested in Mary Lou Williams, whose biography she would eventually write.

With a flood of books about women in jazz upstaging her idea, and in a funk about writing the book, Marian began to rethink the project. She sat down for a powwow with Sheldon Meyer at Oxford. They agreed Marian could fulfill her contract by publishing the Sweethearts piece as part of a compendium of articles she had already written for various magazines, starting with the autobiographical one she had done for the *Esquire* yearbook, "You've Come a Long Way, Baby." Joellyn stepped in, helping Marian shape the Sweethearts essay and trim and update everything else. On September 7, 1987, nearly a decade after the Women's Jazz Festival had inspired Marian to write a book about female jazz musicians, Oxford published *All in Good Time,* with a lovely foreword by Jim Maher. The book featured thirteen essays, including Marian's profiles for *Down Beat* of Alec Wilder, Mary Lou Williams, Jake Hanna, Benny Goodman, Paul Desmond, Joe Morello (who got two essays), and the pairing of Eddie Gomez and Ron McClure; the *Esquire* piece; a vivid reminiscence about the Hickory House, which also served as the liner note for a CD reissue of her Savoy recordings; the essay about the International Sweethearts; an essay about Bill Evans done in 1968 for *Melody Maker;* and a piece about British actor and sometime pianist Dudley Moore written for *Keyboard* magazine in 1983.

It was a miscellany, to be sure, but in its own haphazard way the book managed to communicate a sense of the remarkable range of Marian's career; her witty, urbane, sometimes salty point of view; and a feeling for the jazz life, lived. The book sold out its run of five thousand and by and large received good reviews. Whitney Balliett called McPartland an "English-born Renaissance person" and praised her as a writer for keeping herself "out of the way" most of the time, while noting nevertheless she was "a born self-publicizer, an ability few jazz musicians have (and all need)." Leonard Reed, in the *Record,* noted the book lacked an overall focus but nevertheless brought forward a vivid sense of a woman struggling to find her individual style. Peter Keepnews of *The New York Times* found Marian at her best when championing women and detailing the travails of the working musician—particularly dealing with patrons who talk too much in clubs. He found her wanting as a critic, however, writing only about musicians she liked, and he questioned why Moore had been included in a book that also dealt with Evans and Williams. *All in Good Time* was still netting reviews in the winter of 1988 and, like *Piano Jazz,* became another calling card for Marian on the road.

The year *All in Good Time* came out, twenty-six new episodes of *Piano Jazz* aired on nearly two hundred stations across the country. McPartland continued to top herself on the show, bringing in Michel Petrucciani, the three-foot-tall French pianist with glass bone disease, for an effervescent hour and coaxing the grandfather of the avant-garde, Cecil Taylor, to explain his unorthodox approach to the piano. McPartland and Petrucciani really hit it off. Michel confessed he had always been intimidated by the complicated, lickety-split chord progression of Coltrane's "Giant Steps," then showed her the arpeggios he had practiced to get the tune under his fingers. "That's pretty hip practicing," Marian said, then suggested she play the chords very slowly while he improvised over them, so she could watch what he was doing. The mood was suddenly intimate—total absorption in pianoland. It was very much a part of her genius that they arrived at this level in a half hour. Eventually, they tore into the tune's real tempo, glancing off each other like diving ospreys.

"I'm speechless," McPartland said when they finished. "You are such an interesting and fabulous player."

Petrucciani also turned Marian on to Ornette Coleman's blues "Turnaround," which henceforth became part of her repertoire.

McPartland never once stooped to the obvious by asking Petrucciani about the bone disease that had made him such a physical anomaly. Likewise, with Taylor, though she cheekily said in her introduction that his music was "difficult," she avoided the critical rhetoric that had jangled around Taylor's music, expressing nothing but avid curiosity. Did he really play compositions? If so, where were they? He'd brought no written music into the studio, so what did he mean? In some ways, the show was amusing; because McPartland came from such a literate, formal background and Taylor derived his music from a well of spiritual and aural knowledge, it sometimes sounded as if they were speaking two different languages. After Cecil played the first part of a new piece he'd written in Banff called "Mountain Eyes," Marian asked, "Is that a total improvisation with a little idea in your mind? How much of it is preconceived?" Taylor played the kernel of the composition.

"How do you practice?" Marian asked.

"Practicing is key," answered Taylor. "I think of it as finding the joy."

"Do you have a mind picture when you do these things?"

Taylor described the landscape of the Canadian Rockies.

Marian's free improvisations usually tended toward the flaccid, but Taylor spurred her to vivid contrasts and punchy rhythms. Cecil answered her gorgeous edition of "Chelsea Bridge" with an abstract but hymnlike ballad that had a winsome melody. In retrospect, Marian told a reporter she felt Taylor had "dodged" her questions and that she still found him to be "an enigma." But if hipster fans of Taylor were secretly chuckling over his appearance on a show conducted by this prim and proper lady who went to the Guildhall and played the Carlyle, Taylor felt no such condescension. At the end of the program, in his inimitably warm, caressing whisper, Taylor unleashed an astonishing, graceful encomium.

"I think that it must be said one of the things I've learned from Billie Holiday, Mary Lou Williams, Helen Humes, and certainly Lena Horne has been exemplified by the generosity of your spirit and your cordiality in making me feel at home here. Your taste of colors I have always admired. And you are one of the most elegant women I have ever met in this business. And I thank you."

"You just made my day," said Marian, who had just been assigned a place in the highest pantheon of female jazz performers—and by one of the most creative, innovative avatars in the music. From here on out, it was going to become more and more difficult to go herself one better.

15.

Exit Jimmy
(1987~1994)

WHEN MARIAN MOVED TO PORT WASHINGTON, she thought she might be seeing less of Jimmy, but the eccentrically "divorced" couple soon established a routine that was not all that different from the one they had enjoyed in Merrick. Around five o'clock, Jimmy would come over to Port Washington with food for dinner—rye bread, grated Romano cheese, fish or chicken, and—his favorite—ice cream and cookies. After dinner, he would retire to the den, a few steps down from the kitchen, where he'd turn on the TV, light a cigarette (or a joint), and "relax," drinking his coffee or tea from a mug Marian gave him with "Old Fart" written on it. The den was a rustic, masculine room, with a fireplace, knotty wood paneling, and a hardwood floor fastened by three-pronged black nails; a piece of driftwood facetiously suggesting antlers was mounted above the fireplace. A small impressionist oil painting by the jazz bassist Bob Haggart of a Parisian street scene, with Sacré-Coeur in the background, hung over a counter where Jimmy's collection of meticulously accurate miniature toy cars was displayed. Jimmy would stay overnight upstairs in what came to be called "Jimmy's room." In the morning, he would have breakfast, then drive back to Merrick with his thermos full of tea to his house and the cats, as if he were going off to work.

"Although I was always kind of glad to see him go," Marian wrote, "I always looked for his return about five or six, brimming with good humor and anxious to show and tell about all the groceries he had bought."

When Marian came home from the road, she would call Jimmy—"I'm back!"—he would drive over, and the routine would start all over again. When Marian noticed Jimmy's attention span getting short, she brought a cassette player to the table, and as they talked, she played some of his records, including *Shades of Bix* and *The Music Man Goes Dixieland.*

"Jimmy became a fixture in the new house," said Diana Schwartz. "He was only allowed to smoke down there in the den. He was there more often than not. He used to say, 'I love having a rich wife! I'll just sit down here.'"

Jimmy was joking, of course, but in fact he was no longer pulling his weight. His attitude was that he was eighty-two years old and had paid his dues.

When a reporter from the Long Island weekly desk of *The New York Times* came out to the house, Jimmy proudly declared he had been playing gigs since he was fifteen and didn't miss it. He was "enjoying life" now. Marian good-naturedly responded by calling him a "couch potato," reminding him how much he loved being out on the town, playing and hanging out, once he got his chops back in shape.

The gentle tenor of their banter suggested they were still both quite comfortable with each other. When the subject of their divorce came up, Jimmy boasted that Marian "couldn't find anyone as interesting as I am."

"I'm just used to your type."

"I always said you had good taste."

In fact, Jimmy still performed from time to time. In December 1987, he and Marian and Bud Freeman delivered a spirited set at Fermilab, the physics research center outside Chicago. Haydon McPartland brought his son, Josh, who had taken up the cornet, and Jimmy gave Josh one of his horns. Jimmy was now a great-grandfather, but he had never seen Donna's twins, Alexandre and Benjamin. In August 1988, Donna and Jacques made the trip to Chicago to show off the eighteen-month-old boys. In a home movie of an outing to the Chicago Zoo, Jimmy clowned for the boys in their double stroller, chasing squirrels, mugging, and making a buzzing sound with his lips, as if he were warming up to play. Marian, wearing Keds (her preferred casual footwear) and sitting on a park bench, stiffly bounced Alexandre on her knee.

"That's about as motherly as she ever got," said Donna, watching the film years later. "That was a big trip."

Jimmy was feted on his eighty-first birthday at a private party in Garden City, a few miles from Port Washington, thrown by Argentine orthopedic surgeon Jorge Cerruti, whom the McPartlands had met in the Hamptons. Cerruti had grown up in Buenos Aires playing cornet and adoring Chicago jazz. When he saw Jimmy and Marian playing on a flatbed truck— Jimmy looking debonair with a white scarf—he was overjoyed. Cerruti assumed Jimmy had long since passed. The doctor introduced himself after the show, and Jimmy shouted, "Hey, Marian, come here. There's a guy from Argentina who knows me!"

Dr. Cerruti's suburban home had a piano in the basement, which was decorated like a medieval cellar, with portal archways and oversize Spanish furniture. He invited the McPartlands over for a jam. When Marian sat down to play "In a Mist," he was incredulous at his good fortune. Soon, the sessions became a quasi-regular thing, with Richard Sudhalter occasionally joining in. Ever alert to a good bone specialist, Marian went to Cerruti when she sprained her ankle in 1988. Along with Dr. Oshrain in Rochester, Cerruti became Marian's other first-call, jazz-loving, jazz-playing physician—and a close friend.

By this time, said Cerruti, Jimmy already had dementia, but "what amazed me was that even at that very late stage . . . his tempo was exact when he sang or when he played the cornet." Cerruti's description proved accurate on a December 1989 edition of *Piano Jazz* featuring Jimmy with a trad outfit, though his tone and intonation were iffy. In their interview, Marian fed him lines, seemingly worried he might forget his own life story, but even though Jimmy had trouble focusing ("he didn't have much of an attention span," said Shari), the tales rolled off his tongue with mellifluous ease. In a sweet moment, after Marian played a lovely piano solo on "Struttin' with Some Barbecue," Jimmy said, "Swingin' there, kid." Jimmy really came alive on a Harmon-muted solo on Charlie Shavers's "Undecided."

"Thanks, James, for coming down to do the show," Marian said. "All I can say is just keep doing what you're doing."

"Well, breathing is the most important," he quipped. "Breathing and drinking my tea."

As Jimmy wound down his career, Marian continued to pile on more and more work, in spite of repeated physical injuries and an exhausting radio schedule that now involved the production of thirty-nine shows per year—three seasons with thirteen artists each (with occasional repeats). One of her guests in 1985 was pianist Carol Britto, who had been married to Marian's bassist Bill. When Carol fell ill two years later, Marian, Dave McKenna, and others played a benefit at St. Peter's Church at Fifty-fourth and Lexington. St. Peter's was—and is—a focal point in the Manhattan jazz community, a Lutheran "jazz ministry" established in 1965 by Reverend Peter Gensel. Marian had attended Thelonious Monk's funeral there a few years earlier and, over the years, had become friendly with Gensel. That fall, just a few blocks away from St. Peter's, Marian and George Shearing inaugurated the newly redesigned Donnell Center of the New York Public Library on Fifty-third Street, at the behest of Bernice MacDonald.

"She called me in the morning as we were setting up the stage," said Bernice. "She said, 'I'm going to be there, but I just want you to know I broke my ankle this morning, so I'll be on crutches.' And I said to myself,

'Other people would say, "I broke my ankle, I can't come."' She came, on those crutches."

Having not checked in with family for some time, Marian made a trip to England in June 1988, where she had a pleasant visit with Joyce and the kids, then played a solo concert at Eastbourne's Towner Art Gallery and a gala date with John Dankworth and Cleo Laine at the Stables, their bucolic venue north of London. Marian stayed with John and Cleo in their home at the back of the property, an enormous stone rectory with a sun-drenched conservatory and rolling green garden. John and Cleo had established the Stables in 1970 with the help of Princess Margaret, who had a soft spot for jazz and American popular song. In 1997, the princess hosted a pre-concert reception and dinner at New York's Town Hall to raise money for the Stables music education program, a concert that also celebrated Cleo's seventieth birthday. Marian performed. Though it was a stiff affair, she was honored to meet Princess Margaret backstage in a formal reception line.

In England, Marian also promoted the upcoming British publication of *All in Good Time.* She took particular delight in being celebrated as a literary figure. Back on Long Island, she appeared at the Swan Club, across Hempstead Harbor from Port Washington, on a program sponsored by the Port Washington Public Library, with former diplomat E. R. Braithwaite, author of *To Sir, with Love,* and Thomas Flanagan, on the best-seller list with *The Tenants of Time.* The Swan Club, with its whitewashed façade and uniformed parking attendant, was just the sort of posh, suburban redoubt where she and Roy Eldridge had been asked to eat in the kitchen when they played club dates.

In the late 1980s and early 1990s, Marian continued to play jazz events highlighting women, but such concerts became scarcer as women entered the mainstream. Carol Comer had said of the Kansas City Women's Jazz Festival, "Our objective was to go out of business," which it did in 1985, thanks to poor attendance, though it was debatable whether her larger goal of eliminating the need for affirmative action had been met. In 1988, Marian played the Women in the Arts Festival in Winnipeg, Manitoba, and headlined a "Women in Jazz" program in Atlanta, presenting a two-piano concert with Joanne Brackeen in Piedmont Park. During the first song, Marian and Joanne donned bizarre "antennas" made from brightly colored balloons Brackeen facetiously explained were meant to facilitate communication. Presumably they did not wear these bizarre headdresses at the lecture demo they presented at Agnes Scott College.

Thanks to *Piano Jazz,* Marian was drawing an audience that didn't normally come out to jazz clubs. (Joe Segal, the notoriously grouchy owner of Chicago's Jazz Showcase, grumbled that McPartland's fans never came out for *any* other jazz acts.) It was a well-heeled, middle-aged crowd that usually included more women than men. The existence of new, upscale, nonsmoking listening venues like Birdland, Jazz Alley, and the Jazz Bakery helped this transition. Phil Elwood, in a rave review in July 1989, noted the change.

"The second nicest aspect of pianist Marian McPartland's opening night at Yoshi's," wrote Elwood, "was the friendly feeling, the ambiance; folks who had never ventured into a jazz club—most of them National Public Radio listeners to McPartland's *Piano Jazz* show—sat there, all ears, all eyes, with a reverential attitude as McPartland laid down a perfectly structured recital.

"The nicest part of the 70-minute, 13-tune set was—of course—her interpretation, her performance of those compositions."

Marian performed at Yoshi's with bassist Bill Douglass, who had hooked up with her in Sacramento in 1986. A rhythmically limber player with a rich, warm sound, Douglass would henceforth become her bassist of choice on the West Coast. Of Marian, Elwood wrote, "She is the perfect example of the musician who does not allow herself to be caught in clichés." On the same tour came an equally perceptive review from another western outpost—Eugene, Oregon. Marian's melodic lyricism and implicit knowledge of the lyrics to songs, wrote Mike Heffley, "seemed informed by a feminist aesthetic that was unmistakable, though understated. You hear the frustrated singer in her touch. In a genre notorious for its (overwhelmingly male) virtuosity and competitiveness, she plays more like one with a story to tell than with something to prove."

Marian toured Japan for ten days in May 1989, but when she was invited back twelve months later after a breakneck northwest tour, fatigue caught up with her. She asked the Japanese promoter of the program—called "100 Golden Fingers" because it featured ten pianists—if he could find a sub. Harold Mabern recommended a young pianist out of Milwaukee named Lynne Arriale, a lovely player with an affinity for Bill Evans. When Arriale got back to the States, Marian hosted her on *Piano Jazz*.

McPartland regularly championed young female players, among them Ellen Rowe, a pianist from Connecticut who, ironically, had studied with John Mehegan (of the infamously grumpy Brubeck critique in *Down Beat* back in the 1950s) when she was in high school. In 1981, when Rowe was a graduate student at Eastman, she was introduced to Marian by Rayburn Wright, director of the school's famously productive "Arranger's Holiday" summer workshop. The concert featured Alec Wilder's music. Rowe arranged "Where Are the Good Companions?" for Marian's trio and orchestra, which she performed on a concert that also included Manny Albam's setting of Alec's tune for Marian, "Jazz Waltz for a Friend." Susannah McCorkle, whom Marian had taken under her wing at the Carlyle, was also on the program. The evening was telecast on Rochester public TV.

Rowe said things didn't go quite as well as planned.

"I accidentally turned two pages at once while Manny Albam was conducting and things fell apart in front of my eyes," she said. "The lead trumpet player shouted out, 'Letter C!' But Marian liked the arrangement."

She must have. She asked Rowe to transcribe her solos on eight tunes, the result being the 1985 publication of *Willow Creek and Other Ballads,* which came out the same year as another book of six tunes transcribed by John Oddo and Don Sickler, *The Artistry of Marian McPartland.* Seeing these notations of Marian's stormy flourishes, relentlessly complex chords, and stacked alterations of sharp elevens and flatted thirteenths must have been enlightening for pianists who had been wondering what in the world Marian had been up to all these years. Rowe, who has a tremendous ear, was surprised by what she discovered.

"I would listen over and over again and there were always fewer notes than I thought," she said. "One of the unique gifts she has is being able to make a six-note chord sound like it has ten notes in it. Whether she realizes it or not, she's utilizing the overtone qualities."

This was, of course, precisely the approach taken by Marian's primary inspiration, Duke Ellington. Rowe noted McPartland also "had this gift of voicing the chords so that the top notes make the other chords below it sound better. She gets the top note to sing, through her attack and touch."

Rowe appeared on *Piano Jazz* in 1990 and again in 2002, transcribed another book of solos, *Piano Jazz, Volume 1,* and wrote orchestral arrangements of Marian's spur-of-the-moment improvisation done for Dizzy Gillespie, "For Dizzy," and "I Hear a Rhapsody." Rowe's transcription of Marian's spontaneous portrait on *Piano Jazz* of conservative political commentator William F. Buckley (who played a bit of piano) led to a humorous incident.

"I got the tape from the show, put it in the cassette player, and I thought, 'This is amazing!' It was in C-sharp minor. Just incredible! I sent it off to her. Her first response was, 'I couldn't have possibly played this.' It turned out my cassette player was running fast. It was really in C minor. She was upset with me."

Marian got over it, said Rowe, noting that, ultimately, she was "a good sport with a great sense of humor," which she proved again in 2000, when Rowe, who by then had become head of the jazz department at the University of Michigan, invited Marian out to help raise money for a scholarship in Marian's name.

"We put on a dinner at the nicest place in town," said Rowe. "They said they'd print up a special menu with her name. All the highfalutin donors came, dressed to the nines. I get Marian there on time. I pick up the menu and it says, 'School of Music Honors Marian McPratland.' I was mortified She just laughed. She said, 'Well, at least it doesn't say "McPhartland."'"

McPartland's endowment to the Michigan program was becoming more and more typical. In November 1991, she made a donation to Port Washington's Schreiber High School to enable the creation of a library of jazz recordings. In 1994, she put up $2,500 administered by Concord toward a Marian McPartland scholarship.

In November 1993, while serving as a judge for the Thelonious Monk piano competition in Washington, D.C., Marian adopted another young pianist named Roberta Piket, whom Marian began formally calling a "protégée." Piket was from Queens, and her father, Frederick Piket, was a modern classical composer who taught at New York University. Roberta had studied both music and computer science. Though the French tyro Jacky Terrasson was the unanimous favorite at the Monk competition that year, Piket's spiky, experimental style caught Marian's ear. She invited her to appear on *Piano Jazz*.

When Marian told Roberta the show paid $500, she replied, "I don't care about the money."

"You should never say that," Marian scolded.

That was just one of the many bits of career advice Marian proffered. She also instructed Piket to take her age out of her press biography.

"When you get older," said Marian, "you're going to want to be younger."

Later, when Piket got a good gig in the Delaware Water Gap, Pennsylvania, Marian advised her to call the local papers and the local radio station.

"I was so naive, it hadn't even occurred to me to do that," she said. "And I did get a nice write-up in the *Allentown Morning Call*. Marian was really supportive. I would send her information about my gigs and she would always write back a nice note. Sometimes she'd even call me."

Marian also rallied to the support of Noreen Leinhard, one of the high school students she had inspired at the National Stage Band Camps. When

Noreen wrote Marian that she was going to move to New York to play with Joe Morello, Marian sent her a list of venues to check out, helped her find a place to live, and sent her a composition Joe had written, "Lost Island."

When it came to up-and-coming talent, not much escaped Marian's ear. Part of the reason for this was that she continued to travel to competitions and festivals featuring youngsters. She performed four years in a row at the Lionel Hampton Jazz Festival in Moscow, Idaho, a mammoth student competition featuring nearly one thousand bands, four nights of concerts, and marvelous up-close-and-personal clinics with the stars. At her 1993 clinic, she told the students, "It's a great life. Never mind what your parents say. My parents were mad as hell."

Over the years, Marian extended her support to scores of young players, including Eldar Djangirov, Helen Sung, Aaron Parks, Grace Kelly, Julian Waterfall Pollack, and Taylor Eigsti. Spotting new talent became one of her public signatures. When *The New York Times* ran a feature in 1994 on the new crop of jazz players, she pointed out in a letter to the editor that Geri Allen, Benny Green, and Geoff Keezer had been omitted.

Though Diana Schwartz was not strictly a musical disciple, Marian had taken Diana under her wing, too. Diana and Marian had met in 1977 through Alec Wilder, while Diana was getting a music education degree at the University of Ohio in Athens. Wilder had come out to the school for a festival celebrating his music. When he heard Diana play—she was a huge fan of Marian's album *Ambiance*—he called Marian and said, "You've got to talk to this girl. You've got to take care of her." When Diana moved to New York, Marian helped her find a place to live and they had been buddies ever since. Like Roberta, Diana was interested in computers, but more for their practical application through MIDI (musical instrument digital interface), which among other things allowed players to sequence and coordinate music played at different times and to input sound and get sheet music out. Diana's husband, Jack, had worked on the first generation of MIDI at New York University, and he and Diana had a Kurzweil 250 synthesizer in their apartment in Greenwich Village. Marian and Jimmy often came for dinner, particularly when Jack's famous spaghetti sauce was on the menu. Marian loved to play the Kurzweil, and she invited Diana to play it on the show in December 1990. One night, after dinner at one of their parties, she and Marian had a glass of wine and Marian sat down and—seemingly out of the blue—improvised two movements of a long-form classical work. Diana was floored.

"That's where she wrote the Rachel Carson thing—at my apartment," said Diana. "I said, 'Okay, I'm going to record this now.' She did it on MIDI, so there was an electronic file I could get back to her. She must have had it all composed in her head, because she played it through twice and it was the same. I said, 'Marian you have to do something with this!'"

A Portrait of Rachel Carson, as the piece came to be known, would not see its world premiere until 2007. Marian had given Diana a copy of Carson's *Silent Spring* shortly after they met, and they shared a concern for the environment. During the 1970s, Marian had rarely spoken out in public about environmental issues, but when Ronald Reagan appointed the anti-environmentalist James Watt as secretary of the interior, Marian ended her own "silent spring."

"I can't stand James Watt," she boldly told a reporter in Baltimore. "He's holding us up."

On a visit to Juneau, Alaska, for the city's Jazz & Classics Festival, Marian told a local reporter she had considered canceling the gig as a protest against Alaska governor Walter J. Hickel's policy toward wolves.

Ultimately, however, Marian pulled back from public comments, though she occasionally made offhand remarks during her concerts that made it clear where she stood. She also continued to make substantial financial donations to the Sierra Club, the Cousteau Society, the Nature Conservancy, and author Cleveland Amory's Fund for Animals.

"I could get up on a soapbox and talk of all the things that are not good, all the environmental changes that I do not like, animals becoming extinct because people are taking away their habitat," she told the paper in Utica, New York, in 1997. "But I don't want to get on the soapbox."

McPartland's abiding concern for the welfare of animals stood in marked contrast with her profound resistance to intimacy with people. (She adored Dr. Oshrain's Welsh corgis and at one point in her journals jotted a riff on a famous bon mot: "The more of men I see, the more do dogs appeal to me.")

"The seals, the stallions, the wolves . . . ," exclaimed Patti Sarka, privy to Marian's array of causes when she served as temporary executrix during one of Marian's European jaunts. "But she doesn't trust people."

Indeed. Though gregarious and delighted to be admired from a distance, privately Marian held people at bay. She particularly recoiled, said Donna, from the kind of unsolicited intimacy that became so common in the 1970s, when people she hardly knew would run up to her and say, "I love you."

"She's like 'Wait a minute. I don't know you. How can you love me?'" Donna recalled.

But even with Donna, her best friend, Marian shrank from uttering those words, asking her at one point on the phone, "Why do people say, 'I love you'? Why do you love me? What do you mean?"

"She's an extremely private person," Donna said. "That's why she moved off into the country. She likes animals and birds."

And yet from a distance, Marian was always there for friends and colleagues. In the mid-1980s, when Shari was going through a divorce, Marian made a point of talking to her over dinner about what she had gone through with Jimmy.

"There have also been times that I have had difficulty in my work because I am a woman, and she's definitely appreciated that and been very supportive," said Hutchinson.

Over the years, McPartland and Hutchinson naturally developed a close—and at times contentious—relationship. Sometimes this played out as a simple power struggle over who might make a good guest on the show. But in the studio, more subtle conflicts simmered. From childhood, Marian had despised being told what to do; Shari was not shy about asserting her authority.

"In the beginning," said Diana Schwartz, "Marian was so pissed because they'd be in the middle of a conversation that Marian thought was going really well and Shari would interrupt her and Marian would say [imitates indignant English voice], 'I cawrn't keep my train of thought if you keep interrupting me!' She'd call me up and say, 'How am I going to tell her to stop interrupting me?' I said, 'Marian, just tell her! I'm sure she'll be fine.' They had that running battle for years."

Shari soon learned to work around rather than confront Marian, or to simply make decisions in postproduction, deleting certain pieces of music or conversation. Marian rarely noticed or, if she did, only occasionally made a fuss. But Shari nevertheless found it necessary in the studio to guide the flow of the show, reminding Marian to do station IDs, make smoother transitions, or clue listeners in about who was being discussed. Not once in thirty years did their tiffs spill over into tantrums. There were no histrionics, no walkouts.

"Whenever there was any kind of disagreement, it was very short-lived," Hutchinson said.

When their conflicts touched Marian's hot buttons, however, such as trust and loyalty, the rifts were patched over less easily.

"I would say the most upset she was with me was when I was working on another show. She felt that I abandoned her."

McPartland was a possessive friend, always wary of betrayal.

"It took Marian twenty years to trust me," said Hutchinson. "That's an exaggeration. But she is very tough."

Ultimately, trust did develop. McPartland and Hutchinson became not only a well-oiled team but the best of friends.

By the late 1980s and early 1990s, the show had become a fixture in American cultural life, supported by an annual grant from the National Endowment for the Arts to the tune of $50,000 to $60,000 and pushing toward a yearly budget of $375,000. A show Marian thought might squeak by for one or two seasons had now been running fifteen years and become the centerpiece of her career. In 1993, at Tavern on the Green, a Central Park restaurant where Marian was playing her first Manhattan gig in many years, her associates presented her with a surprise birthday cake to celebrate the show's decade-and-a-half milestone. Readers of *JazzTimes* magazine voted it the Best Syndicated Jazz Program.

Marian continued to draw from a wide-ranging palette for the show. In October 1989, in hopes of finally breaking into the British market, she flew to England to record four U.K. pianists—Alan Clare, Dave Lee, Brian Lemon, and Stan Tracy—but, alas, there was still no interest in broadcasting there. A year later, she reunited the old Hickory House trio for a program. From the moment they hit the first tune, "I'm Beginning to See the Light," a buoyancy coursed through Marian's fingers that made it obvious how delighted she was to be playing with Joe Morello again. When they traded eights, you could feel the electricity.

"Oh, but there were sparks with those two!" said Schwartz. "I remember when Joe was playing in '92 or '93 with a quartet at a place on Eighteenth and Third, Fat Tuesday's, downstairs. Marian was like this blushing seventeen-year-old, the two of them in this room, and Joe's half-blind by then, and they're sitting at a table, they were flirting outrageously. Then they played together and you could see it, you could see what it must have been like for her. That was her great passion."

In 1994, the new singing sensation Diana Krall, perched on the brink of success with the incipient release of her first American CD, *Only Trust Your Heart,* offered another scintillating hour on *Piano Jazz*. Marian had been well aware of Krall for years, as the young Canadian had made a cold call to Marian when she was a teenager, asking her advice about her career. Sometimes duets on *Piano Jazz* tended to get muddied and jumbled, but as the two of them jousted on "Broadway" and "Surrey with the Fringe on Top," you could hear every note, punched with clarity and rhythmic drive. This was all the more remarkable considering Marian had fallen in the garden and broken her left thumb a few days before the show and had to hire a second pianist play her left-hand part. The pair shared a touching moment when Krall recounted how supportive her family had been regarding her choice of career. Marian confessed her parents had never heard her play jazz.

Krall's precursor, Rosemary Clooney, who had hit big with "Come On-a My House" back when Marian was at the Hickory House, also made a sizzling appearance. Rosie was in great voice and was also a great talker. She painted a vivid portrayal of Mitch Miller's once powerful position in American popular music, and her folksy tales of living next door to Ira Gershwin brought the pantheon of the Great American Songbook down to earth. She and Marian were perfectly in sync.

Ever since her days with Carroll Levis, Marian had had good show business sense, so she knew that snagging mainstream celebrities like Ray Charles would expand the show's listenership. She was not above wearing out a little shoe leather to land her prey. One night, she and Shari stood outside on the sidewalk, waiting in line to see Charles at the Blue Note in New York, then at intermission Marian raced upstairs to waylay Charles and slip him a cassette of the show she'd done with George Shearing (good choice!).

Though it was a smart move, in truth, the show with Charles felt slightly awkward. Marian had little understanding of—or, for that matter, interest in—the expressive, slow drag sexuality and gospel inspiration that flowed into Charles's unique, hybrid style, much less the kind of cultural envy—or perhaps awe—a white American jazz musician might have experienced sitting in a studio with him. Indeed, Marian's focus was song, not soul. In an acid quote in a 1981 *New York Times* article heralding the return of the Great American Songbook to the popular scene, and its putative retaking of the ground rock had usurped in 1950s and 1960s, Charles's onetime producer Ahmet Ertegun—Marian's old adversary from the Carlyle incident with Manhattan Transfer—dismissed Harold Arlen, Jerome Kern, and George Gershwin as "a claque of publishers and songwriters from Tin Pan Alley and Hollywood, European in origin, feeding foreign music to the American people." Real American music, he said, was derived from the blues.

This was divisive hyperbole—Gershwin surely was as American as Robert Johnson, and vice versa—but there was no question Marian's biases ultimately leaned toward the "European," if that meant melody and harmony over rhythm—and blues, her wonderful version of "Willow Weep for Me" notwithstanding. Her presence in the studio with Charles reflected that divide. After he sang an absolutely heartbreaking, moaning rendition of "Summertime," she didn't seem to know what to make of it and promptly changed the subject to his version of "Rudolph the Red-Nosed Reindeer." But hey, you had to give her credit. She was fearless. And certainly no one was embarrassed. Even better, Charles sounded happy as could be, rattling off stories about his musical upbringing and outlook, including a particularly poignant moment when he said he liked "Rudolph" because he identified with that outsider reindeer.

In England, Marian had discovered a brisk underground trade in cassettes of *Piano Jazz*. It occurred to her—and her assistant producer at Concord, Frank Dorritie—that it might be a good idea to issue selected shows on CD. Marian suggested the idea to Carl Jefferson, and in 1992 he hired Canadian engineer Phil Sheridan to head up a dedicated subsidiary, Jazz Alliance. The label released thirty-two CDs, including classics by Brubeck, Clooney, Bill Evans, Dizzy Gillespie, Oscar Peterson, and Mary Lou Williams. Critical reception was enthusiastic, but sales were slack—two to three thousand, if that—and after Jefferson died in 1995, Jazz Alliance flagged. The label was revived in 2002, but it soon became clear that the Internet was a better platform for the project and it was taken over by NPR.

In the summer of 1990, Marian began to notice Jimmy was "tired all the time," having trouble staying alert. Only a few months earlier, in the spring, they had played a lively gig at West Babylon High School on Long Island, with the same band they'd used on *Piano Jazz*. Jimmy had played well and had talked about it for days afterward, vowing to stay in shape. It would be the last time he played his horn with Marian. In September, Jimmy went into the hospital for tests. Marian's worst fears were confirmed: A lifelong smoker, Jimmy had lung cancer. Doctors determined surgery wasn't an option, so Jimmy went for radiation at Long Island Jewish Hospital. Marian's reaction was curiously matter-of-fact, almost as if she could not face the reality of Jimmy actually dying—not to mention the deep well of emotion it called up in her.

"I guess a person who smokes for 65 years is bound to get something, & he got it," she wrote to Dan Griffin, then quickly changed the subject to her touring schedule. That included a fund-raiser in Chicago for the newly created Chicago Jazz Archive (CJA), which Dick Wang, their old friend from the Rose Bowl days, had helped to create. Wang was teaching jazz at the University of Chicago now, and he invited Marian and Jimmy to play on campus at Mandel Hall on October 27, 1990. Though the bulk of Marian's archive was already earmarked for Eastman, she and Jimmy made a selective donation to the CJA of photographs, programs, and other memorabilia, as well as a nearly comprehensive run of Jimmy's recordings.

The first-rate band at the show included clarinetist and jazz historian Franz Jackson, trombonists Jim Beebe and Russ Phillips, bassist Truck Parham, and drummer Kansas Fields. Jimmy could no longer blow his horn, but he sang with verve and élan.

"He was in the front line," said Wang, "mugging, urging the band and Marian, and complimenting her regularly. He was in great form. All the relatives from the far west suburbs were there to meet and greet and celebrate. We had some champagne ready to pop backstage, and Kansas Fields and Truck managed to polish off a good deal of that during intermission, so they weren't in such great shape in the second half." Somehow that seemed fitting. The concert raised $6,000, and Jimmy was presented with an award. In November, Marian was scheduled to play Jazz Alley in Seattle with Mary Fettig and her husband, drummer Eric Thompson, but she was ambivalent about leaving Jimmy over the Thanksgiving holiday. Diana encouraged her to go, offering to come out to the house with Jack and fix dinner with all the trimmings.

"[I said,] 'Don't feel guilty,'" said Diana. "'You have to work. We'll come out.' My husband and I went out there and we made a whole Thanksgiving thing and he ate really well. That's the last time I remember Jimmy being really well. He ate this big plate of turkey, stuffing, mashed potatoes, cranberry sauce. We ate down in the den, in front of the TV. I said to Marian, 'I never saw Jimmy eat that much.'"

When Marian got home, she hired a nurse and moved Jimmy onto a hospital bed in the guest room a few steps down from the den. On December 20, she wrote to Donna: "Grandpa may not be here for too much longer—maybe a month or two. If you want to come over, it should be soon."

In January, Doug flew out from California. While he was helping Marian move Jimmy's things from the house in Merrick, they made an interesting discovery.

"I hadn't been there since I was little," recalled Doug. "We went in and gathered up his clothes and there was a little flask. She just kind of shook her head. I made a Chinese dinner—I had gotten into wok cooking—and Marian got up to get something or go answer the phone or something and he reached over and grabbed my wineglass and I went, 'Grandpa, that's wine,' because I thought maybe he just wasn't being clear. But he was."

Marian had to fly west again in January, this time to record a live solo album before an audience at Berkeley's acoustic jewel box, the rustically wood-framed Maybeck Recital Hall. Marian's set was, not surprisingly, a probing study—earnest, deep, and absolutely translucent, especially on

"Easy Living," "Willow Weep for Me," and "Twilight World." Her crisp ramble through the theme from *Piano Jazz,* "Kaleidoscope," was dazzling as she clambered over the keyboard in ascending and descending whole tones, returning to the agitated theme several times. Maybeck would become Marian's second-best-selling disc of all time (the first had yet to be recorded), a sweet reflection on the discerning sophistication of her audience. On February 13, Marian flew to Rochester, where she, Loonis McGlohon, and Marlene VerPlanck performed a concert of Wilder's music in the Eastman Theatre to mark the dedication of the Sibley Music Library's Alec Wilder Reading Room. On February 24, she was honored by the New Jersey Jazz Society at the twenty-second annual Pee Wee Russell Memorial in New Brunswick, New Jersey, along with her archnemesis from Halcyon days, Hank O'Neal. Three days later, Marian McPartland did a very curious thing. She remarried the man she had divorced twenty-four years earlier.

Marian had given this idea a great deal of thought. She knew Jimmy had been hurt by the divorce, that he had never accepted it, and that in the end she hadn't, either. Why not give him the satisfaction of going out with their marriage intact? It somehow seemed like the right thing to do. There was a practical consideration, too. The funeral parlor had told Marian that if Jimmy died at home—which they intended for him to do—an inquest might delay his burial for days. Furthermore, as his ex-wife, Marian would have no say in where or how he was buried, which could lead to a dispute with the Chicago McPartlands, something she wanted to avoid. "When I heard that from the undertaker, that just tipped me over the edge," Marian wrote. Marian called Father Gensel at St. Peter's. A few weeks shy of his eighty-fourth birthday, Jimmy, sitting in his big chair, renewed his marriage vows with Marian. Father Gensel's wife, Audrey, and the nurse were the other witnesses. After the ceremony, the party went out for lunch in Port Washington. When the Gensels went back to the city, Marian told Jimmy she had some errands to run.

"Would you like some company?" he asked.

Marian was surprised. She had never been able to get Jimmy to go anywhere with her, even when he was well. She helped him on with his hat and coat, then they got in the car and made the rounds of Port Washington, stopping first at the post office, where everyone knew Jimmy because he had picked up Marian's mail when she was recovering from her broken hip. They stopped at the beauty parlor, and the hairdresser came out and spoke to Jimmy. All over town, people said hello as they passed the couple on the street. It was Jimmy's last outing.

Had Marian read Carolyn Heilbrun's book *Writing a Woman's Life*? If she had, she most certainly would have agreed with these words: "Most of us begin, aided by almost every aspect of our culture, hoping for a perfect marriage. . . . It almost never is. . . . But the dream lives on that this time will be different. Perhaps the reason the truth is so little told is that it sounds quotidian, bourgeois, even like advocating proportion, that most unappealing of all virtues. But . . . proportion is the final secret, and that is why all good marriages are what Stanley Cavell calls remarriages, and not lust masquerading as passion. Only those who remarry are married."

Donna arrived from France a few days later. A steady stream of visitors came by to make their farewells. Marian even called Hank O'Neal and asked Jimmy to say hello, which he did. Toward the end, Jimmy began to feel some pain, and the nurse administered modest injections of morphine. On the evening of March 13, Donna and Marian and Jimmy spent the evening listening to *Shades of Bix*.

"That's a good album, isn't it?" Jimmy whispered.

"Would you like some ice cream?" Marian asked.

"Oh, boy! Yeah!" he said.

Jimmy died that night.

Jimmy McPartland was hailed as a hero in obituaries all over the world. If he was listening, he surely would have been tickled to hear his tales of the Spoon and Straw, Al Capone, Bix Beiderbecke, Benny Goodman, Ben Pollack, the Battle of Saint-Lô, the Chicago revival, and—most of all—his two weddings to Marian Page regaled in the press. Two days after Jimmy passed, his old friend from Austin, Bud Freeman, died as well. Richard Sudhalter was convinced Freeman had been waiting for Jimmy.

"Between these two boyhood chums it was in the actual order of things that Jimmy should go first . . . ," wrote Sudhalter. "Think of it. Big, jovial Jimmy McPartland, the tough street kid who took up the cornet because with it he'd always be the leader; Bud the dandy, the self-conscious 'artist,' content to follow. Who else to lay the gentle hand on Bud's arm, to say softly but firmly, 'Okay, pal, it's all over. Let's go.'"

Five days after Jimmy died, Marian performed with the Schreiber High School Jazz Band. Ellen Rowe, then teaching in Storrs, Connecticut, came down to conduct her arrangement of "Cross-Currents."

"I don't think I was even aware that Jimmy had just died until afterwards," said Rowe. "I think she kept it from us. Trouper. The absolute meaning of the word."

Jimmy was cremated, his ashes buried in Elmhurst, the Chicago suburb where he and Marian had helped his brother Richard dig the foundation of their house so many years ago. On the weekend of March 30, a small group of family and friends gathered at his graveside. Marian flew Reverend Gensel out to conduct the service, mostly to make sure Richard's son, Haydon, who had become an assertive born-again, didn't take over the ceremony. Haydon's son Josh played "Blue Bells of Scotland" on Jimmy's horn. "It was a windswept March day, I remember, and it was cold out there," said Dick Wang. Jimmy's gravestone was simple, a flat square in the grass. Marian planted a tree just behind it. Whenever she or anyone else in the family visited, they tossed pennies on the stone, as an homage to the days when Jimmy used to pick up pennies he found on the sidewalk. "It became sort of a joke," said Marian, "because they would always be gone when we came back. We would always say, 'Jimmy took it.'" On Tuesday, Marian opened at the Palmer Hotel's Empire Room with Steve LaSpina and Charlie Braugham. Mayor Richard M. Daley proclaimed it Marian McPartland Day. Howard Reich of the *Chicago Tribune* reported that her set was notable for its quiet lyricism.

The New York memorial for Jimmy was held at St. Peter's on May 23. Reverend Gensel opened and closed the service, explaining how he had remarried Marian and Jimmy. Dick Sudhalter emceed and presided over a musical tribute featuring a variety of players, from Clark Terry and Ruby Braff to John Bunch and Marian, who bade Jimmy farewell with a tender, andante "Singin' the Blues" on solo piano. Studs Terkel delivered a conversational, off-the-cuff eulogy, capturing Jimmy as the dashing, archetypal "young man with a horn" from Chicago. Josh McPartland played "Blue Bells of Scotland" again. The whole thing felt a bit stiff and formal—until Donna took the lectern.

"When I was a little girl," she began, "I just remember my grandfather was sort of a strong, athletic man, and always telling us stories I didn't quite understand. Then when I met him again when I was much older, he was still telling me stories and he was still strong and athletic, but then I did notice that he was a great bullshitter." The crowd exploded into laughter. "But as Grandpa would say, a sincere one," she added.

"She said it so sweetly, so fondly," said Zena Collier. "It was a very good note, after all the praise."

Donna got a laugh, but deep down she and Doug both felt as though their grandfather had been hijacked by the jazz world.

"We were a little jealous," said Donna, "seeing all these people that had lots of stories to tell about all those years we were all alone. And how he took their children fishing. That really hurt Doug. Jazz musicians were their family. . . . Everything that was given to my grandfather at his funeral was given to the Cousteau Society or something. Doug said, 'Everything is going to these fish!' "

Donna had a knack for getting past the hurt. With Doug, the bitterness festered. Not long after Jimmy died, he lost his job. When Marian sent him a substantial subsidy to tide him over and he failed to thank her promptly, an angry exchange ensued. The air never quite cleared.

"I guess you don't realize that if someone sends you a gift (like a thousand dollars) they do expect at least a phone call, or card or something to at least say you GOT IT!!" Marian wrote.

"It was always an awkward thing to talk about money with Marian because everybody always assumed she had lots of money because she paid for everything," said Donna. "She'd pay for dinner when you'd go to restaurants and she'd fly us in and out because they had more money."

This generosity notwithstanding, Marian also clearly was wary of being used.

Doug did finally write, but he asked Marian why they did not have a closer relationship.

"As far as needing to talk to anyone about my problems," Marian answered, "I have several women friends who have lost their husbands, & we all commiserate with each other. As far as that particular problem is concerned, I'm sure it will never go away, but I'm dealing with it. As to other things, well, I deal with those, too! I'm lucky to have my health, work, friends, new projects, & enough money so no one has to give a benefit for me!! I'll look forward to seeing you when I get to Yoshi's. I'll be at the Shattuck again."

But Doug was never quite sure how to read such invitations.

"We learned a long time ago when she comes to town, just don't make any plans," he said. "You don't know if you're going to get to see a lot of her or you're going to see any of her. And every time we tried to figure out what she might want, we were wrong. One time she got ticked off because she didn't think I was coming enough. 'I'm here all week, I'm just sitting in the hotel.' So the next time she came I said, 'Okay, I cleared my calendar, I can do Wednesday through Saturday, and she said, 'Oh, that's too much.' "

And so it went, Doug complaining, Marian chastising—or nagging, again and again, to call her old friend Norton Wright in Hollywood, who could help Doug with his career. At one point, she offered some "tough love."

"I feel . . . frustration at seeing you wasting your life," she wrote, "and knowing how very talented you are, & that you could be making a good living. Obviously, I can't help, no matter what I do or say, but I do care about what happens to you, and I'd be the first one to cheer you on, if you got a good gig, or really get yourself together, or both. Anyway I hope you do decide to go to Chicago, but can't you stop expecting a certain type of behavior from your old man? He isn't going to give you help & support. You have to do it yourself. Anyway I hope to talk to you soon.

"Love, Mag."

Even more dramatic misunderstandings lay ahead.

After Jimmy passed, one of Marian's first orders of business was to dedicate an album to his memory. To leaven what might have been an occasion for nostalgia and mourning only, she invited Chris Potter, a vigorous young player with a muscular, Coltrane approach who may well have represented to her the spirit of a new Jimmy McPartland. Marian had run across Potter in 1986 when he was a fifteen-year-old student at Columbia, South Carolina's Dreher High School, at the memorial party for Dick Phipps. Marian had been so impressed, she told Chris's father the boy should go out on the road with Woody Herman. Chris had finished school, however, and was now on the New York scene. He shared six tracks with Marian on *In My Life* and, thanks to Marian, was signed to Concord.

"That was my introduction into the fold," said Potter, who later played with Dave Holland and became a poll-winning leader in his own right. "She went to bat for me, and I'm extremely grateful for it. She encouraged me to go to New York. She's extremely generous."

The album turned out well. Marian played with spare clarity and Potter sounded way beyond his years on Coltrane's ineffable "Naima." To honor Jimmy, Marian closed the album with the Bix specialty "Singin' the Blues." Later that year, she invited Potter to perform with her at the Concord Jazz Festival. The performance was recorded and released on the compilation *Silver Anniversary Set: Fujitsu-Concord 25th Jazz Festival*. The years from 1987 to 1994 were a strong period for Marian in the studio. She had long wanted to do an album of Mary Lou Williams's songs, and in 1994 she finally convinced Carl Jefferson it was a viable project. Marian was lucky to have the services of recording engineer Phil Edwards, who knew how to pull a robust, ringing sound from the piano. Marian delivered the opener, the catchy riff "Scratchin' in the Gravel," with such tart spareness, slyly laying behind the beat, it felt as if she had written the tune herself. On "What's Your Story, Morning Glory?" she took an Ellingtonian approach, scampered through "Easy Blues," then offered a brilliant new tune written for Mary Lou. "Threnody," named for the poetic form meaning "memorial," ranked with "Twilight World" and "Ambiance" as one of Marian's best tunes. It was a thirty-two-bar waltz composed of a sixteen-bar melody played twice at a medium tempo. The harmonic movement combined a melancholy D minor that moved to its tritone cousin A-flat, then made a startling jump to four bright major chords out of the key, descending in parallel—D, C, B, A—in a jauntily syncopated, quarter-note/half-note rhythm, then moved to an E tonality, completing its "Giant Steps"–like path from C to A to E. The tune was very much in Mary Lou's spirit with its ragged rhythmic interest, harmonic insouciance, and under-tone of melancholy. "Threnody" was a fitting cap to the forty years Marian had spent singing Williams's praises.

In keeping with Marian's sense of jazz as a collaborative effort, she would ultimately record six composer tributes. She had already covered Leonard Bernstein, Alec Wilder, and Billy Strayhorn; Duke Ellington and Mary Lou Williams would follow. Before Jimmy died, she recorded an album dedicated to the songs of the veteran bandleader, arranger, saxo-phonist, trumpeter, songwriter, and film composer Benny Carter. Carter had participated in the formative years of the swing era but had always been a bit under the radar for the average jazz fan. Few knew he had writ-ten "When Lights Are Low," much less "Only Trust Your Heart," which Astrud Gilberto and Stan Getz had popularized and Krall would ride to stardom. But it was just that kind of slightly obscure material Marian thrived on.

The project grew out of a meeting Marian and Benny had at his home in Los Angeles before his appearance on *Piano Jazz* in 1989. Carter was a stern, sometimes touchy taskmaster. (During the *Piano Jazz* taping, Shari inadvertently offended him—easy to do—and according to Marian, he became "quite snotty.") But he was still game for the album. In January 1990, she went back out to Hollywood to record *Marian McPartland Plays the Benny Carter Songbook,* with John Clayton on bass and Harold Jones on drums. It was an elegant, genteel affair—as befitted two such stalwart veterans—played with classical grace and aplomb, though Carter's pre-bop articulation on his "jolly riff tunes," as Marian called them, sounded a bit dated with Marian's expansive harmonies. The high points of the disc were actually Marian's trio versions of the haunting, impressionist ballad "Key Largo" (unrelated to the film) and the ruminative "Lonely Woman." Marian convinced Carter to let photographer Wayne Seidel shoot the cover at Carter's house. Marian sat at the piano bench in a white skirt cut at the knee and one of her custom-made print blouses with a wide collar; Benny, in a gray V-neck sweater, stood behind her, his right hand resting easily on her right shoulder, his left hand on the piano. Behind them, on the wall, hung a dramatically lit still life of fruit in a basket that screamed "old masters." Which indeed they both were. Marian was at the pinnacle of her powers.

Benny must have been happy with the date. The following year, he recruited Marian for a whirlwind two-week European tour called "Benny Carter's Swing America." The trip kicked off June 29, 1992, at Jazz à Liège in Belgium and continued through Denmark, France, Turkey, Italy, England, and Holland. It was another "old masters" band, with Milt Hinton (bass), Louie Belleson (drums), Harry "Sweets" Edison (trumpet), and Al Grey (trombone). The tour was good medicine, coming right after the memorial, as Marian could throw herself into work to keep her spirits up. Belleson's wife, Pearl Bailey, had just died, too, so she had someone to commiserate with.

"Benny was wonderful," said Marian, "but he was getting on in years and he didn't hang out much. He and [his wife] Hilma would get off the plane and they would disappear. Sweets was a character, a sort of would-be womanizer. Milt Hinton spent every available moment taking pictures."

Reviews were strong.

"It is easy to get old, anyone can do that, if you live long enough," wrote a Danish critic of the performance at Tivoli Gardens. "The remarkable thing was the excellence these musicians still possess."

Marian came in for particular praise for the way she "unfolded" "Willow Weep for Me." Donna came down to Juan-les-Pins, where she remembered Marian warning Herbie Hancock, "You stay away from her. She's married to a wonderful guy!" Marian went back to Europe in May 1992, appearing at the International Jazz Festival in Bern on a "Super Piano Night" with Shearing, Billy Taylor, Junior Mance, and the Ray Brown Trio. After visiting family in England, she came home, then flew directly to Chicago to do another benefit for the Jazz Institute of Chicago at Mandel Hall, a memorial concert for Jimmy arranged by Dick Wang and the university music department. Donna came out for the show, and she and Marian made a pilgrimage to Elmhurst, where they tossed pennies on Jimmy's grave.

"It was sad," Marian wrote in a postcard to Diana and Jack, "but good to see this nice tree & we planted Forget-Me-Not seeds."

In the fall, Marian sent a picture postcard of the redwoods to the Schwartzes after performing at Humboldt State College. She was duly impressed by her first glimpse of those enormous, stately trees, which Ronald

Reagan, as California governor, had been willing to cede to loggers. Under the space on the card where it said, "Do Not Write Below This Line," Marian, ever the class cutup, scribbled, "Why not?" At Christmas, she went back to England to visit Joyce, who had begun to suffer from the debilitating arthritis that had killed their mother. Marian also visited her mother's birthplace, Tunbridge Wells. She returned to New York just in time for a January 12 memorial to Dizzy Gillespie, who had died on January 6. Marian and Clark Terry opened the musical tribute with "I Can't Get Started." In May 1993, it was back to Japan for "100 Golden Fingers"—this time, she made it—with John Lewis and eight other pianists. Marian hung out with Tommy Flanagan. They both found Lewis to be a bit of a stuffed shirt.

"John Lewis was a real martinet," said Marian. "Like a bloody old schoolmistress. We were doing a TV show or something and Tommy and I were playing a duet, and John said, 'You can only play one tune.' So we picked the longest tune we could find, verse and all."

Back in the States, McPartland continued to snag high-end engagements in the summer "shed" circuit, including the summer festival at Ravinia outside Chicago and, for the first time, the prestigious outdoor venue at Tanglewood, summer home of the Boston Philharmonic, in western Massachusetts. The Tanglewood connection came about because of a switch in booking agents. Since Marian's album with Shearing, *Alone Together,* she had been playing dates with George that were often booked by a young classical agent named Pam Parsons. When Marian's agent, Susan Pimsleur, suddenly died, George's manager had encouraged Pam to take Marian on as a client. Parsons made Marian a sort of project, regarding herself as more of a manager than a booking agent—which rankled Marian, who liked to be in control herself—creating a formal press kit for her, which, according to Parsons, Marian had never had.

"We marketed her in a different way than she had ever been marketed," said Parsons. "We cleaned up a lot of stuff. We had a very strong presence in the orchestra world. We raised her fee. She was happy about that. We started maybe at $3,000 to $4,000, and I would raise it every year. It needed to be raised. We eventually got it up to around $10,000 in the concert hall. Clubs? I'm going to say $7,500."

Parsons also arranged for a little more "care and feeding" on the road. Marian was breaking bones with such shocking regularity now that it was not uncommon for her to need a wheelchair and/or some extra attention from a student or intern at the business end of a flight. Marian often enlisted friends such as Diana, Bernice, Merrilee Trost, or Dan Griffin to travel with her, not only for the company, but as a helpmate who could fetch things she needed, whether it was her favorite road food (bananas), tea (she carried a tea ball and a china cup with her), flowers for the dressing room, a gift for someone special, or a snack of cookies and crackers and cheese. Parsons soon became aware that Marian's often constant pain—and perhaps her enhanced status, though who can say; she was in no way a pretentious woman—had begun to make her cranky on the road. She could be very demanding.

"She liked nothing better than to have someone run errands for her, even if she didn't need anything," said Parsons. "I remember there had been a student assigned to her and she was standing outside the door. 'Is there anything I can get you?' She said, 'I don't like the look of this plate. Can you get me something else? Strawberries would be really nice.' She got kind of nasty about it and the student started to tear up. 'I'll do it. I will.' She ran several blocks in the snow and used her own money and went to a 7-Eleven and had them make up a little tray. Before Marian went on-stage, she arrived with it. It was rather beautiful. And Marian said, 'What's this?' At that point the student started to sob."

Asking questions as a form of implied criticism—"When do you suppose that will be finished?"—was one of McPartland's specialties, said Parsons. She found Marian to be a "tremendous bully. She loved to ask somebody to do something, knowing she'd already done it or she was going to do it that second. So when you got the information, she could always say, 'I already did it.' She loved to set people up that way. She did it with everybody. I'd call her and I would say, 'Marian you already knew this.' She would say, 'The only way to get something done right is to do it yourself.'"

"Nothing can ever be done well by another person," said Griffin of Marian's attitude. "Because she's extremely hard on herself."

Merrilee Trost, too, inadvertently confirmed this syndrome.

"Marian would call," said Merrilee, "and say, 'Okay, let's start talking to Yoshi's again, because Pam's not doing anything.'"

Some of this behavior no doubt related to the increasing anxiety that naturally comes with age.

"She got her undies in a bundle about every trip," complained Pam. "No matter how simple it was, she spent so much time with all this anxiety about every single thing. If there wasn't something obvious, she would find something to worry about."

Before the flight to Europe with Benny Carter, Marian was so convinced the plane would never leave, she paid for Pam to come to New York and sit with her at the airport until the plane left.

"Here's everybody sitting at the gate and damn if the flight wasn't delayed," she said. "In Marian's mind, that means she shouldn't be going. I watched her work on every musician there: 'This itinerary doesn't look right to me.' 'I understand this hotel is just awful.' And 'what if' and 'what if.' Finally, somebody said, 'Marian, just shut up! You're making us all miserable.' And she was quiet for quite a while, then she started up again."

Pam said Marian also worried about not getting paid. To be fair, this was not an uncommon, or unwarranted, anxiety among jazz musicians who had come up in the trenches, but it was a new twist in Parsons's genteel world. Shortly after Marian fractured her other hip in 1992, Parsons got her a gig at a small Christian school outside Nashville, Tennessee, David Lipscomb University. Both Parsons and Marian's friend Daniel Griffin accompanied her. Marian was worried sick her wheelchair would not be loaded on the plane. When they arrived, there was no chair.

"I told you that wheelchair wasn't going to get on the plane!" Marian said.

It was a hectic trip with a lot on the agenda, with solo and symphony concerts and a meeting with a conductor from Florida flying in to decide if he wanted to invite her to play with his orchestra. Marian was impatient.

"You couldn't order a hamburger with Marian," said Griffin. "It couldn't come fast enough. In the hotel room, if the phone rang, after the first ring, she'd bang her feet. 'Answer the phone!' The cab couldn't come fast enough."

Griffin said this wasn't so much crankiness—he enjoyed her company—as Marian in work mode: "driven, focused, intense, and amiably but forcefully demanding about everything. When she was working, things needed to *happen*—and nothing happened fast enough." He seems to have been more forgiving and understanding than others. But he also acknowledged Marian's tremendous need for control.

"People who have issues with self-esteem—and at one time I counted myself among them—want total control," said Griffin. "They feel a great need to manage their environment to reassure them that everything is okay."

Griffin's understanding of his longtime friend was invaluable. For while he agreed she could be imperious, demanding, critical, impatient, and even mean, he also said, "She is one of the smartest, most generous people, with a rapacious sense of humor, great intellectual curiosity."

He managed to keep his sense of humor about her faults.

"She's one of the most difficult people I've ever known," said Griffin. "She is a hypercritical person. Once I said to her—I was joking—'If there was a national association of difficult people, Marian and I could have been members of it.' She looked at me and she was angry. 'I'm not difficult!' Then I realized that the moment you realize you could be a member you could no longer belong."

In a droll, English way, John Dankworth offered another anecdote that spoke to the same notion. In May 1996, John and Cleo had Marian back to the Stables and arranged for her to play several dates in the Midlands, as well as London's Wigmore Hall.

"Driving back one night from Nottingham," said Dankworth, "I found out the other side of Marian, that she can be a bit . . . sort of—anything but optimistic. Marian said, 'That's a long journey to Nottingham, longer than I care to take.' And I said, 'Marian, it's only an hour. You can be in a cab in New York that long.' She said, 'I don't think I want to do it.' If she'd known me a bit better, she might have complained. On the way back, we encountered some traffic, so it was more than an hour. It happened to be slightly raining. I was doing sort of ninety, I suppose, which to an American seems very fast, but on English motorways everybody does that fast. She was sitting next to me. I didn't detect she was very uncomfortable about the speed. It was stupid of me not to have seen it, and it was impertinent of me not to have slowed down, even if I suspected it. Anyway, she said, 'John, you're sure you're not going too fast?' So I said, 'It's all right, it's very safe here. There's no one pressing my tail.' So Marian said the first thing she'd ever said that amounted to criticism. She said, 'Don't you think eighty would be better?' It was a constructive criticism, suggesting an alternative! It was funny. Because she was probably right."

Marian and Pam Parsons eventually fell out, and in 2003, Ted Kurland Associates, a large, jazz-focused business based in Boston, took over her booking. Marian had long been dissatisfied with Pam, feeling she was not aggressive enough and not a real jazz insider. She also felt Pam didn't haggle hard enough.

"Pam was a nice person, but couldn't get any real money [for me]," said Marian. "I did a lot of things myself and let her take the credit. I think she was too shy. An agent is supposed to be full of piss and vinegar. She didn't know how to handle a person like me."

Manager-artist relations are almost as volatile—and personal—as marriages, so it's hard to know where the truth lay. Having had rough-and-tumble characters like Joe Glaser and Max Cavalli working for her, Marian no doubt believed that Parsons seemed "shy." But given Marian's often observed need for control, her comment about Parsons not knowing how to handle her is probably the most accurate—and fair—of all Marian's criticisms. Whatever her complaints, when Parsons booked McPartland, she was one of the better-paid figures in jazz, not to mention a regular at prestige venues like Tanglewood and Ravinia. She may not have been making as much money as Shearing and Brubeck, but then she wasn't as popular as they were, either.

By the time of their falling-out, Parsons, aware that Marian was being courted by Kurland, had backed off booking a lot of engagements anyway.

"I was just as happy to let her go," said Parsons. "In fourteen years, she never said thank you to anything. Ever. *Ever.*"

There was no love lost between the two.

"I was quite happy to tell Pam to take a walk," Marian said, "and we haven't spoken since."

Marian's heightened profile in the 1990s led *Down Beat* to give her its highest honor, the Lifetime Achievement Award, in September 1994 at the Chicago Jazz Festival. This happened right after she had broken her thumb. Marian received a standing ovation for a crisp, nine-digit performance with Chicagoans Jim Cox and Charlie Braugham that included a decidedly Monkish "Sweet and Lovely" and also featured Mary Fettig. The magazine's editor, John Ephland, presented the award onstage. *Down Beat* ran a major feature on Marian that month by Michael Bourne titled "Our Dame of Jazz," in which he suggested the queen honor this daughter of Albion with the title of "Dame."

Marian, too, had begun to look back at her life and career and, once again, had taken up the idea of writing an autobiography. As always with writing, however, she was having a devil of a time getting started. After a particularly wonderful and well-received solo performance at San Francisco's Herbst Theatre in November 1991, Robert Doerschuk, editor of *Keyboard* magazine, broached the idea of doing an "as told to" biography. Doerschuk came out to Port Washington to begin the interview process. What happened next could have been scripted by Oscar Wilde.

"We spoke for several hours with the tape running, and when she excused herself for a short break, leaving me alone in her living room, someone knocked at her door," said Doerschuk. "I opened it, and a guy I didn't know asked if Marian was in. I told him she would be out shortly. He asked about me, I told him what I was doing, and he looked surprised and a little hurt."

When Marian came back, she discovered to her chagrin that the visitor was Richard Sudhalter, whom she had invited to help her write her book a few months earlier. After an awkward interval, Sudhalter dismissed himself and Doerschuk and Marian resumed the interview, albeit with a good deal less enthusiasm. A few days later, Marian called off the project, with the excuse that it would be impractical, as Doerschuk lived on the West Coast. Sudhalter, meanwhile, telephoned. When she tried to bring up what had happened, he stopped her cold.

"We shall never speak of it again," he said.

Marian the autobiographer was on her own again. To try to inspire her to write, Diana gave Marian a copy of Mary Catherine Bateson's *Composing a Life* for her seventy-fourth birthday. It was a perceptive choice. Hailed by feminists, Bateson's autobiography stressed the interdependence of four other women in her life, rather than putting herself at the center of a heroic quest, as a traditional male autobiographer might have done. She also characterized women's lives as "improvisations," which of course appealed to Marian. Particularly at this phase in her life, and especially after Jimmy's death, Marian had begun to position herself within a close web of mostly female friends. Years ago, she had even thought herself of structuring an autobiography as a tale of how other women, such as Cleo Brown and Mary Lou Williams and Joanne Brackeen, had influenced her. The idea of a communitarian narrative was right up her alley. And yet. And yet. There was also Marian the diva, the performer who needed control and to be at the center of that same circle. By February 1993, she was back at work with Jim Maher on a more traditional story of her life.

Maher and Marian never finished their book. Did they quarrel? Did she—or he—lose interest? Was it a matter of money? She never would say. Whatever happened, it's clear that in the mid-1990s, Marian's focus shifted away from writing about herself to writing about Jimmy. Starting in 1992, she began to make notes for what she eventually called a book—a book that, like the one about herself, never got written, but which generated mountains of notes. The genesis of it, quite simply, was missing him terribly.

"I miss Grandpa a lot," she wrote to Donna and Jacques the year after he died. "It's funny. I can go for a while, being occupied with whatever I'm doing, and then suddenly I see him sitting in the chair in the den, kind of smiling, and talking about feeding the birds, or one of the other little things he loved doing, and I feel a real agonizing stab of pain . . . mental and physical, and tears come . . . boy, I never felt anything like this before!"

Marian's other impetus was regret. Over and over, in her notes and letters, she chastised herself for not having treated Jimmy better and somehow even blamed herself for the fact that his career never took off. How was it that she had "made it" and he hadn't? She felt particularly guilty for having left him alone so often toward the end.

"I wish I had taken time off and stayed with him, instead of doing all those dates," she wrote Dan Griffin.

He was always so good about it, although he always asked how long I'd be gone, and then when I'd got to where I was going and called him up, his first words were always, "When will you be back? I miss you." He hated having the nurse there, although she just cooked for him. He was able to walk around and go upstairs, and he pretty much ignored her. I was just afraid he'd set the house on fire. He always put on the kettle for tea and then forgot about it! We threw out more burnt-out kettles. I was always in the store buying new ones, and finally got a really good electric one, which cut itself off when the water boiled.

I was always so impatient with him about all these little things, but he accepted it like he did everything else. He used to run the water like crazy in the sink (he seemed to like doing dishes—he'd never put them in the dishwasher) and I'd say (or scream!) "Don't run the water like that! We won't have any hot water left!" and he'd always make the same reply. "It's gotta be HOT." Funny, isn't it? Now I'm rinsing dishes and saying to myself, "It's gotta be hot."

In her ruminations—sometimes taped and then transcribed by Joellyn or scribbled out on various scraps of paper, as was her wont, she wrote:

Jimmy never seemed to grumble or bitch like I did, and I was very critical, too. Jimmy would say, "You shouldn't tear people down. Everyone needs encouragement." And he certainly put this into practice where I was concerned. Always telling me I sounded great or looked good, or praised my figure or my clothes. I never realized how lucky I was to always have these warm words, and now I feel a great emptiness, a hollow feeling, and I strive to be more like Jimmy in my dealings with other people.

I think drinking was the thing that kept him from being a real star. He had great looks & charm & he could play but maybe (I'm just surmising) he was too much into drinking, & of course that always was known to everyone. It's a shame even after he joined AA, he never really lost that reputation as a drinker, & of course he always liked to smoke pot. Some people "made it" in spite of that but somehow he didn't.

The worst times we had were when I moved back to Merrick. My mind always seemed preoccupied—work and the many phone calls and jobs. Coming downstairs for meals he would cook, and I'm sure I was never grateful or appreciative for what he did. . . . It's funny, but in looking back, I think I cared more deeply for Jimmy in our last years together in spite of the insane, besotted kind of love or lust I had for Joe.

Now that Jimmy is gone, it's like a searing pain whenever I think of him—a guilt and/or remorse thing. Why didn't I appreciate him more? I took him completely for granted yet always wanted him around. I guess he wanted to be around, else he would have found somebody else.

Ultimately, the house in Port Washington became, in part, a sort of shrine to Jimmy McPartland. When visitors walked into the kitchen, a genial photograph on the refrigerator greeted them of Jimmy blowing cornet, with Tippy perched on his shoulder. (Above, a sign encouraged people to "Have a Weird Day," a catchphrase Marian and Donna enjoyed sharing.) In the cupboard, his "Old Fart" mug still sat on the shelf. Downstairs in the den hung the poster from the 1949 jazz festival he'd played in Paris, which Marian had reviewed for *Down Beat*. On her 1999 album of collaborations with various pianists, *Just Friends,* Marian ended the program with a solo track tailor-made for James, which began with a dirge-like version of "When the Saints Go Marching In" followed by "Blue Bells of Scotland." It became a standard closer for her show. Sometimes in the evenings, sitting alone at the kitchen table after her housekeeper, Gosia Gil, had left, Marian would listen to that track and—in spite of her determined unsentimentality—quietly tear up.

Sweet Times
(1995–2003)

MARIAN HAD A LONGTIME CHAMPION in Howard Reich at the *Chicago Tribune*. In May 1995, Reich wrote a handsome advance of McPartland's upcoming appearance at the Jazz Showcase, in which he said these were "sweet times" for the pianist. He was right. *Piano Jazz* was now broadcast on more than two hundred stations and issued on CD, *Down Beat* had given Marian the Lifetime Achievement Award, and she was playing at the top of her game, "one of the more adventurous pianists in jazz."

"I hardly can believe my good fortune," she said to Reich. "There always seems to be something new and exciting around the corner, so I feel like a kid."

One of the new and exciting things that year was a documentary film produced by Jean Bach about the 1958 photograph *A Great Day in Harlem*. Bach, who had dated Squirrel Ashcraft back in the day, had hung out with Jimmy one night in Chicago in the late 1930s when he sat in with Duke Ellington. She had married the swing-era trumpeter Shorty Sherock and was a radio producer famous for her Manhattan jazz parties. But she had never made a film in her life. Nevertheless, when she heard live footage existed from that famous day, she got it in her head that she wanted to make a documentary. She recruited Marian and Nat Hentoff as voice-over commentators. Marian also came to Jean's two-hundred-year-old house on a cobblestone street in one of the Greenwich Village mews for an interview proper, where she chatted amiably at the piano about her admiration for Mary Lou Williams and how Jimmy had missed the shoot. As she talked, the camera panned over Marian and Mary Lou, caught in midsentence in the photo, Marian in her famously flattering sundress. The film was a kind of meditation on memory, wrote Peter Watrous in *The New York Times*—poignant, but also sad in the way it conjured absence, reinforced by an unfortunate stunt pulled by *Life* magazine, which staged a redo of the photo on the same stoop featuring the survivors, standing in the same spots they had taken in the original. There were only eleven people in the photo. Marian was delighted she could still fit into the same dress she'd worn in 1958. But for the new picture she wore a red wool dress with bright buttons, an overcoat, a colorful scarf, and low heels. She was surrounded by empty space. That era may have been golden, but it was history.

On July 30, the Long Island Jazz Festival made the film the centerpiece of a program and Nassau County declared Marian McPartland Day. Marian had broken her wrist on a jazz cruise just before the show, so she enlisted Janice Friedman to help her out with left-hand parts on another piano. The cruise had been an Atlantic crossing from Southampton to New York on the *Queen Elizabeth II*. The English class system had apparently boarded with the passengers, as Marian's East Coast rhythm section—bassist Gary Mazzaroppi, whom Marian had met in 1982 through Dick Sudhalter, and Massachusetts-bred drummer Glenn Davis—and her nephew Mark, who had come along for the ride, were told they would not be allowed to eat with Marian, because they had second-class cabins. Marian made a huge stink.

"She was not having any of this shit," Mark remembered. "Eventually, the Cunard people said you can all eat first class and we had a really nice time."

Getting summoned to appear before the Supreme Court would give most people pause, but when Marian got the call in 1997, she did not have to plead her case—except from the piano bench. Sandra Day O'Connor, a fan of Marian's show, suggested they invite her for one of the Court's "musical afternoons." On April 17, Marian presented a solo recital in the East Conference Room of the Supreme Court Building on a program that also featured mezzo-soprano Denyce Graves. "That was the best gig I ever got for her," said Pam Parsons. But Marian was nervous and a bit out of sorts. Pam made her a "cheat sheet" in advance so she could identify all the justices at the reception. Marian threw it on the floor of the hotel lobby, saying, "What the fuck do I want this for?" The night before the concert, Marian called Dan Griffin from the Willard Hotel in D.C., in a bit of a panic.

"What should I open with?" she asked.

"'Take Five,'" Griffin answered.

"Why?"

"Because it takes five votes to get anything out of there."

Indeed, Marian opened with the Brubeck tune and got a good laugh by refining the quip, explaining she was doing it because so many of the Court's decisions were coming in 5–4!

Bernice MacDonald remembered it as a delightfully intimate afternoon.

"It was a lovely, lovely room, just down the hall from where the justices sit," she said. "There were no more than about forty people there—only the supremes and their spouses and one or two of their relatives. Sitting right in back of me was Clarence Thomas. I got myself a wonderful seat, with a great view of this gorgeous Steinway and this picture window looking out over the courtyard. It was a rainy day. Afterwards, there was a reception in an adjoining room with a big round table with all kinds of hors d'oeuvres and waiters taking around champagne." Marian had dinner with O'Connor and her husband after the performance. When she got home, she mailed copies of her latest CD to all the justices. In her thank-you note, O'Connor sounded genuinely pleased: "A glorious treat," she said. Justice David Souter wrote, "It was one of the happiest afternoons I've spent in this building."

In the fall of 1997, Marian snagged a two-week spot at the smart London jazz club Pizza on the Park, with John Dankworth's son, Alec, on bass, and drummer Ralph Salmins. *The Guardian* averred that she had "lost none of the graceful precision, infectious bounce and eager adventurousness of earlier times." At the gig, when a patron requested "All the Things You Are," Marian protested, "I made that record forty years ago."

"That's when we bought it," was the reply.

Marian and her niece Sheila had lunch the next day. Walking back to the hotel, Marian tripped on the curb, fell, and broke her elbow. She checked herself into Chelsea Health Care. It was a serious, painful, and complicated fracture, a potentially career-ending disaster. Desperate, she called Dr. Cerruti and they agreed she should fly home. Mark came up to help her pack (as did Eleanor Bron), and she left as soon as she could get a flight. She would never return to England again.

"It was too late to do surgery," said Cerruti. "But the recovery was amazing. I never thought she would have such a good result. She is a very good patient."

Though Marian had long abandoned the Grieg concerto, from 1995 to 2002 she toured in a unique format featuring classical pianist Ruth Laredo, known for her interpretations of Stravinsky, Mozart, and Beethoven, and Dick Hyman, who could play anything in the pre-bop piano literature from Scott Joplin to Art Tatum. "Three Piano Crossover" was the brainchild of Hadassah Markson, who booked Manhattan's Ninety-second Street Y. A typical program might include Laredo playing Albéniz's *Tango in D,* Hyman doing Zez Confrey's "Dizzy Fingers," and Marian playing the Jobim bossa nova "Wave." When Laredo played Chopin's Prelude in E Minor, Marian pointed out it was the basis for Jobim's "How Insensitive." The show ended with a blowout on Juan Tizol's "Caravan." The program was a highbrow crowd-pleaser that appealed, as did *Piano Jazz,* to one of Marian's core constituencies—that huge cohort of people who at one point or another in their lives had taken a few piano lessons. That audience constituted the core of a large crowd that made McPartland an attractive subject for general-interest media, in a way that other jazz players usually were not. What other jazz musician, after all, was interviewed by James Brady in *Parade* magazine, the Sunday supplement that went out to thirty-two million readers? But there she was, in the August 6, 1995, issue, wearing a silk dress, gold earrings, and necklace (with a sling on her left arm), having just chatted with Brady in the lobby of the Algonquin Hotel. The "culture wars," sparked in 1989 by the provocative work of Andres Serrano and Robert Mapplethorpe, were still seriously in play, and public arts agencies such as NEA, PBS, and NPR, so important to Marian's career, were under fire.

"They just want a blue-collar world, it seems to me," she said of the congressional backlash.

Recognition flowed from more serious quarters, too. Author Wayne Enstice came out to the house in November 1996 to conduct a substantial interview for a book called *Jazzwomen: Conversations with Twenty-one Musicians* that would be published in 2004. Marian had told her story many times, but she slipped in a few new insights and nuances, particularly her lingering regrets about Jimmy.

"I feel that I was so unfair to him a lot of times," she said.

Marian's attitude toward the avant-garde, diplomatic in her *Down Beat* days, had apparently hardened. When she first heard Cecil Taylor, she said, she ran for the door, "falling over people" to get out of the club. Enstice pressed her, asking why she couldn't appreciate the music on an intellectual level.

"Oh, that's ridiculous!" Marian replied. "To be sitting in a nightclub, hearing a lot of honking and total cacophony. To me, that's not music, and I certainly wouldn't expect to have to stay there and have my ears assaulted. . . . I don't think I should be judged as an intolerant person because I didn't appreciate what was going on. I sometimes think people in the audience pretend to like it because they think it's the thing to do."

Her comments echoed something she had said a few years earlier in Chattanooga, Tennessee, when Wynton Marsalis was criticized as too conservative.

"I don't know that jazz has to be pushed to the boundaries," she said. "What are the boundaries? I mean, Coltrane pushed his music to that boundary, but as far as I'm concerned it just gets . . . I don't know, some people just get too far out for me."

Inevitably, a bit of the "good old days" sensibility had snuck in.

"You know what?" she told Enstice. "I have a real feeling of regret. Of course, you've seen that movie *A Great Day in Harlem*? At that particular time, it seemed to me that jazz was in a good position, that there was a lot happening, and people were very enthusiastic. There was a lot more of a general good spirit."

Marian echoed the same sentiment in a *Down Beat* "Blindfold Test" that year, her first in fifteen years. Upon hearing the Erroll Garner cut "Gemini," she said Garner had that "cheerfulness that you miss in some of the people playing nowadays."

Kudos continued to come Marian's way. In November 1997, along with Chaka Khan and James Moody, she was inducted into the International Jazz Hall of Fame, which celebrated its inductees at a concert in Tampa, Florida. Marian deposited her trophy from the event, a tall, abstract obelisk on a glass pedestal, among the growing forest of plaques and awards in the den. The same month, *JazzTimes* magazine saluted her as a guest of honor at its annual convention—held in Meadowlands, New Jersey—and ran a Festschrift cover story written by seventeen colleagues, from Joanne Brackeen to George Shearing. Marian reunited at the convention with Joe Morello and Bill Crow for a panel discussion moderated by Dan Morgenstern. A representative from the Baldwin Piano Company gave her a crystal bowl from Tiffany's, and *Piano Jazz* producer Tom Clark presented her with a silver-framed photo.

"Does it have a picture of Kenny G in it?" she asked.

In the *JazzTimes* article, Marian's age was listed as seventy-seven. But ever since Leonard Feather had mistakenly listed her birth date as 1920 in his encyclopedia, she had been lying about her age. At the convention, she decided it was time to 'fess up. Explaining the story with droll good humor, she announced that she would be celebrating her eightieth birthday on March 21 at a gala party at Town Hall.

"Cleo Laine had her 70th at Town Hall," she told the *Herald-Sun* in Raleigh, North Carolina. "Lena Horne had just had a big shindig for her 80th. I thought what the hell does it matter?"

Indeed. She had been a late bloomer. So what. She was on top of the heap now, and she still looked good, too, certainly nowhere near eighty. In typical Marian fashion, she turned a disadvantage into an advantage, making news out of something she had formerly hidden. John Schreiber, who had produced the *Concert at Haverford* and was still working for George Wein, produced the party and it was broadcast live as a benefit for NPR and the S.L.E. Lupus Foundation. Billy Taylor emceed. On the bill were the old Hickory House trio, Kenny Burrell, Tommy Flanagan, Jacky Terrasson, Christian McBride, Ray Bryant, Harry "Sweets" Edison, Barbara Carroll, Bill Crow, Joe Morello, Benny Green, Herbie Mann, Lewis Nash, Renee Rosnes, Jackie Cain and Roy Kral, Norman Simmons, Grady Tate, and James Williams. A preview in the *New York Observer* cleverly dubbed her "jazz piano's answer to Julia Child."

The birthday party was a smashing success, selling out and garnering great reviews. Ira Gitler, writing in *JazzTimes,* said the old trio "sounded like they had just come over between sets at the Hickory House," evincing "effortless perfection." Marian played a dashing duet on "Caravan" with Monk competition winner Terrasson and a flashy four-handed "Jeepers Creepers" with Flanagan. Concord presented Marian with a plaque and the whole cast came out to sing "Happy Birthday" at the end.

Though Marian told the press she had now "gotten age out of her system," she continued to be sensitive about it. Doug often told friends he had a "jazz-piano-playing grandmother" and would then put on a record of her playing the hell out of Monk's "Straight, No Chaser" to shatter their expectations. For years after he unwisely told Marian this, she sarcastically signed cards and letters to him, "Your piano playing grandmother."

Much more to her liking was the kind of humorous birthday card John Bunch sent of a granny sitting in front of her house.

"You're not one to sit on the porch and watch the world go by," it said on the front. "You're one to yell stuff and make rude gestures."

That image, she could laugh at.

The image Marian put forward to the world was dignified and elegant. Right into her sixties, she had maintained herself so well that she radiated the kind of healthy sexuality projected by actresses such as Betty Grable, Rita Hayworth, and Eve Arden (particularly the sarcasm!)—big-boned, full-figured, and poised, but never steamy or cheap. In her seventies, she pulled back to the genteel style of a patrician, reflected in her album covers for *In My Life* and *Plays the Music of Mary Lou Williams,* both oil paintings by Sylvia Rogers that lent her an upper-class aura, feminine but with dalliance more a delicious memory than an actual possibility. Like all entertainers, Marian paid attention to her wardrobe, much of which was designed by dressmaker Catherine Heiser. Periodically, Heiser would send swatches of material and Marian would suggest designs for what she wanted in the way of full-length gowns, slacks, jackets, suits, and comfortable blouses. Marian loved boldly designed prints, floral ones with curling tendrils, as well as checks, stripes, and other symmetrically designed patterns. With her watercolorist's eye, she took particular delight in subtle colors. She adored brocade and embroidery; one of Heiser's dresses was heavy with beads; another, sequins. They designed a fancy vest that could show gold one way and red the other. Her walk-in closet was full of such treasures.

"She always knew how to dress right," Pam Parsons observed. "Every other woman working with her would ask, 'What's Marian wearing?'"

Marian also used a makeup artist, Elena Giannini, who occasionally traveled with her. Once, at the house, Elena told Marian she was her favorite person to make up.

"Why?" asked Marian.

"Because you have so much character and personality."

"I really meant it," Giannini said later. "And I was so impressed that she didn't just take the compliment, but asked, 'Why?'"

Later that day, told how good she looked, Marian replied, "Slight improvement."

Attentive, yes; vain, no.

Age, arthritis, and osteoporosis began to seriously affect Marian's mobility. Her knees, in particular, were badly worn. Her doctors considered knee replacement but ruled it out as too dangerous. The Port Washington house was a virtual stepladder of levels, impossible to go from one room to another without negotiating several stairs. So in 1996, Marian hired a housekeeper to come on Saturdays. Gradually, Gosia's responsibilities widened until she was coming to the house six days a week. Gosia—who came to Marian loving Chopin and ended up, inevitably, adoring jazz—learned to work around Marian's moods, as she sat in the kitchen, listening to WBGO or CDs by potential guests on *Piano Jazz,* reading faxes from Shari that erupted in the den, or answering her mail. Over the years, they became close friends.

Piano Jazz, which won the ASCAP Deems Taylor Broadcast Award in 1992, continued to keep Marian in the limelight, and she shrewdly did live tapings in various locales where she was playing whenever she could. In October 1996, she invited Brubeck for a live show at Borders Books & Music in Washington, D.C. (The store was now a sponsor.) On the plane coming in, Brubeck wrote a song for Marian.

"Shall we play it?" asked Marian.

"I don't know," Dave said. "I've never played it. I'll give it a try."

Brubeck urged her to join him.

"It's easy," he said. "It's the syllables in your name [sings]: "Mar-*i*-an . . . Mc-*Part*-land.""

She laughed, protesting, "I don't know anything about it."

"Well, you know your own name, don'tcha?"

It was a cute tune. When Dave had finished, she exclaimed, quite delighted, "You made me into a jolly-sounding female!"

It was a jolly show all around. Before they played Dave's "In Your Own Sweet Way," Marian suggested they decide whether they were going to play it the way Miles did—with an E-flat—or the way Dave had written it—with E-natural. Dave just plunged ahead, playing E-natural the first time through, then puckishly tossing in an E-flat the next time, which got a giggle out of Marian and a laugh from the cognoscenti in the crowd.

Marian did another live *Piano Jazz* with Cleo Laine and John Dankworth in Kilbourn Hall at Eastman right before the *JazzTimes* convention, then hooked up with her old friend Helen Merrill, who sang a wonderfully elastic version of Sy Oliver's "Dream of You," with Marian improvising a bass line.

Bassist Steve Swallow, who had had such an influence on Marian in the 1960s, came in for a show with his wife, Carla Bley. Carla and Steve were a dry, sardonic couple and at first Marian didn't sound at ease. But Carla eventually warmed up. When Marian told her how her father had always made her furious by asking her why she couldn't play more like Winifred Atwell, Carla said, "When I was a kid somebody asked me, 'Why can't you play like Marian McPartland?'"

"I'm glad you didn't follow their advice," Marian shot back.

A lovely version of Bley's ballad "Ida Lupino" played by all three gave rise to a fascinating discussion about women in jazz.

"That really is a wistful, pretty piece," Marian said.

"I wanted it to be fiery and angry and dissonant, and this awful pretty thing came out of me," said Carla.

"The soft and pretty things are in the minority," commented Marian about Bley's composing.

"I try to keep it that way."

"Why?"

"Well, because people think girls write soft and pretty things and boys write interesting music. I would rather write like a boy than a girl."

"Male chauvinism is alive and well. Nobody can accuse you of writing like a girl."

An invitation to Bud Powell's daughter, Celia, gave Marian an excuse to play the reel-to-reel tapes she'd made with Bud in Sherman Fairchild's home studio back in 1955. Celia talked about being on the set in Paris for the filming of *'Round Midnight*. But Marian continued to look forward, too, despite her private reservations about the avant-garde. Free improvisers Marilyn Crispell and Paul Bley, as well as Brad Mehldau, more from the Keith Jarrett/Bill Evans school, appeared on the show. In her questions to Crispell and Bley about how free improvisation worked, it gradually became clear—as it had with Cecil Taylor—that McPartland's notion of free playing had very little to do with the procedures as actually practiced by its adherents. "It's hard to believe that you're not thinking very hard when you're playing," she said to Bley, as if playing free were an egoless draw on the unconscious and thinking somehow broke the rules. But in fact Crispell, Bley, and Taylor approached improvisation quite consciously and with a keen ear for structure. It was just that the structures they were hearing had nothing to do with harmonic progressions or bar lines.

"I have to confess I don't always know what you're doing," Marian said to Crispell with refreshing honesty.

One of the sweetest moments of the Crispell show came when they played a duet on "Twilight World." Marian wondered how Marilyn could shift from being so "out" to so far in.

"I feel like it all flows together," she said. "I'm very romantic and I love beautiful melodies. I hear the 'out there' stuff being rooted in blues."

Mehldau was more up Marian's alley. After the eager, then boyish-sounding Mehldau tore hell out of Cole Porter's "From This Moment On," Marian drew him out about his method, how he concentrated on one bit of the melody, then sliced it into different voices for a sort of contrapuntal, classical feeling. "Exactly," he said, seemingly delighted that she had figured him out. Brad told her his parents had gone to see her at the Hickory House on their first date in June 1958.

"All my Hickory House couples stayed married!" she said. "I have so many people come up to me and tell me they met there."

"You're a musical matchmaker," Brad said, which prompted a girlish giggle.

The show was as perfect a model as one was likely to find for how jazz lore and technique were passed from one generation to the next. Yet it was all relaxed and never didactic.

Marian made four albums for Concord between 1995 and 1998. *Live at Yoshi's Nitespot*, recorded in November 1995 with Bill Douglass and Glenn Davis, was subdued, crystalline, and concise. She set the tone with the opener, "Like Someone in Love," gliding with an insouciance tinged with regret. The album was a particularly brilliant showcase for Douglass, who swooped under McPartland with just the right supportive note without ever drawing needless attention to himself. On Monk's "Bemsha Swing," he echoed the lines of the melody, creating a canonlike feel. Marian, in turn, comped energetically behind Douglass's warm, melodic solos instead of laying back the way so many pianists do when the bass player steps out.

"There's always this dialogue going on with her," said Douglass. "There's this sense of play. There are some piano players I've played with and it's fun but there's no air in it. You're just playing to accompany them. But with Marian there's the idea of dialogue, of throwing it back and forth."

Art Lange, former editor of *Down Beat,* caught the mood perfectly in *Pulse* magazine when he wrote, "She's a watercolorist, daubing and bleeding harmonies with a light, transparent touch."

Marian reprised her composition, "Silent Pool," on *Live at Yoshi's,* and decided for her next album, *Marian McPartland with Strings: Silent Pool* (CCD-4745-2)—for the first and only time in her career—to record only songs she had written herself. That she decided to do this now may have indicated the reflective, introspective mood she had fallen into since Jimmy died. It was a plush production. Concord sprang for a big budget for twenty string players, as well as arrangements by Los Angeles pianist Alan Broadbent. Marian flew to Los Angeles June 11 and 12 to record the album at O'Henry Studios in North Hollywood, with Nick Phillips producing.

As Richard Sudhalter pointed out in his liner notes, jazz musicians have a love-hate relationship with strings, considering them on the one hand unabashed treacle and, on the other, a dream environment of softly contoured sound. Though some of the arrangements were indeed slightly saccharine, Broadbent also composed some beautiful, challenging passages. The opening of "Ambiance" evoked the distilled, pastel pools of Fauré, and a cello counterline on "Threnody" let the strings poke and push with rhythmic interest. Sans strings, Marian's trio—with L.A. players Andy Simpkins (bass) and Harold Jones (drums)—delivered Marian's best recorded version ever of her song for Joe, "There'll Be Other Times." The overall impression was of a mood—not so much the actual, pastoral tranquillity of the Silent Pool itself, but the act of looking back and feeling full, possibly a little sad, but also at peace—a fine example of Wordsworth's description of poetry as "emotion recollected in tranquility."

That mood, coupled with the album's unabashed *prettiness,* made it one of her best sellers. John McDonough summed it up nicely for *Down Beat* when he said the album might be "mood music," but it was "*her* mood music."

But the album that really floored McPartland fans didn't come out until 1997, when she released *Just Friends,* arguably the quintessential Marian McPartland album. Why quintessential? Because it was an album of duets showcasing the talents of others in tandem with her own—Geri Allen, Dave Brubeck, George Shearing, Tommy Flanagan, Gene Harris, and Renee Rosnes. But beyond that, the record embraced the wide range of styles that reflected Marian's eclecticism, from a gorgeous, creative free improvisation with Allen, "Chrysalis," to the two-hanky closer, a quiet, hymnlike rendition of "When the Saints Go Marching In" crossed with "Blue Bells of Scotland," played in Jimmy's memory. It was also the perfect Marian album because it was so civilized and sunny, as if it had been made in some fantasy jazz salon where the best and the brightest came to share their ideas with collegial glee, egos laid aside. It was no wonder that *Just Friends* would become the biggest seller in Marian's catalog, at last count pushing twenty thousand.

Marian had reconvened the Hickory House trio for *Piano Jazz* back in 1990, again for a conversation at the *JazzTimes* convention, and a third time at the eightieth birthday party at Town Hall. In 1998, she suggested they reunite one more time for a live album at Birdland, which was thriving again on Forty-fourth Street, just west of Eighth Avenue. Concord said yes; so did Morello and Crow. Bill came out to Port Washington and talked over keys and chords, and on September 16 the trio hit for a two-day gig, drawing a full house both nights. Within moments of the downbeat, said Marian, it felt as if the forty-four-year hiatus between Fifty-second Street and Forty-fourth Street had been but a wrinkle in time. With a nod to their 1954 album for Capitol, they kicked off *Marian McPartland's Hickory House Trio: Reprise* with "I Hear Music" and revisited several others they had recorded so many years ago, including "Street of Dreams," "Tickle Toe," and, from their second Capitol album, that odd tune she and Jimmy had loved so much in Europe, "Symphony." They were all much different players now—more versatile, more mature—Marian was eighty years old, and Morello and Crow were seventy. The whole thing felt warm and relaxed, a conversation among old friends. On "Falling in Love with Love," trading fours, some of those sexy sparks Diana had witnessed at Fat Tuesday's started glancing off Joe's ride cymbal. Marian and Joe indulged in a free-improv piece they dubbed "Cymbalism" that gave them a chance to blow a few more (albeit abstract) kisses. The trio closed with a wink, playing "Things Ain't What They Used to Be."

With fame having come her way, Marian found herself spending more and more time in Washington, D.C., but recognition in high places apparently did not make her any less irreverent. In September 1998, just as President Clinton was going through his troubles with Monica Lewinsky, he invited Wynton Marsalis to program an evening of jazz as part of a series called *Millennium Evenings,* telecast by PBS.

"There was a rehearsal in the afternoon," said Helene Greece, who was working as Marian's publicist at the time. "We had lunch in the small dining room in the West Wing and we had to pass by the Oval Office. As we passed by a bathroom, Marian said, 'I wonder if that's where she washed out the dress.'"

The following year, in March, Marian mounted a concert in the Washington National Cathedral, a full-out performance of Mary Lou Williams's ambitious sacred work, *Mary Lou's Mass.* NPR broadcast the program in May as part of a birthday celebration for Mary Lou. The performance received mixed reviews, though everyone was delighted the piece had finally been performed in its entirety. Some of the piano parts were difficult, so Marian improvised in some sections, to which Mary Lou's longtime manager, Father O'Brien, objected.

"Every note is written," he said.

The Capitol came calling again in 2000, when Marian was awarded the National Endowment for the Arts Jazz Masters Award. The Jazz Masters program had started in 1982; since then, fifty-four jazz artists had been inducted, including Brubeck, Art Farmer, and Joe Henderson the year before. The Jazz Masters Fellowship came with a $20,000 cash award, which Marian donated to SCETV to help pay for two *Piano Jazz* tapings in the Crescent City, one with Wynton's father, Ellis Marsalis, and a second with NOLA trumpeter Nicholas Payton.

In May, it was back to D.C. again with her regular trio with Gary Mazzaroppi and Glenn Davis for the Mary Lou Williams Women in Jazz Festival at the Kennedy Center, where Marian was honored with the festival's Lifetime Achievement Award. Flutist Jamie Baum, drummers Sylvia Cuenca and Sherri Maricle (with Five Play, featuring clarinetist Anat Cohen), baritone saxophonist Claire Daly, Joanne Brackeen, soprano saxophonist Jane Ira Bloom, and organist Trudy Pitts were all on the bill. This array of female jazz instrumentalists was heartening, particularly considering what an anomaly Marian's sidewomen Dottie Dodgion and Mary Osborne had been just two decades earlier.

On more humble ground, McPartland frequently visited Chicago during the years leading up to and after the millennium. Beginning in 1998, she and Joe Segal arranged for her to play the Jazz Showcase every Christmas, which she did for nearly a decade. It was a good opportunity to visit friends and family, as was her August 1999 appearance with the Chicago Symphony in Grant Park, around which Haydon McPartland built a gathering of the clans in St. Charles, west of the city. Donna and her family, as well as Mark, came for the party. The concert was rained out, but that didn't deter Marian's trio from playing.

"She'd rehearsed all day in the heat," said Mark, "and then the heavens opened and there was a terrible thunderstorm. She was just so cool about it. A lot of people hung on and she gathered everybody back on the stage and played trio and it was just magical. The storm was gone and things were dripping and we were all onstage gathered round. I thought it was just great. She gave this fantastic show."

Mark brought beer and Jacques, wine, to the "yard party" at Haydon's. The teetotaling Christian at first frowned but then loosened up and decided a couple of bottles of champagne wouldn't bring on the Apocalypse.

In September, Marian came back for the Chicago Jazz Festival, where she hosted a *Piano Jazz*–like segment during which she presented three pianists from the Windy City—Willie Pickens, Judy Roberts, and Jodie Christian. For the finale, all four musicians played a round robin of four-handed piano on "C Jam Blues," successively nudging one another off the bench. The situation ignited Marian's competitive side.

"It was two old white broads and two virile black guys," remembered Roberts, a two-time guest on *Piano Jazz* and no slacker herself. "We just completely kicked their asses. It got to the point where we started to feel sorry for them. We had no inhibitions at all and they were being very academic, just the opposite of what you'd think. . . . We were relentless. We were not ladylike in our pursuit of winning, let's put it that way."

The next summer, in June, Marian and Dave Brubeck shared the stage at the nearby Ravinia Festival. When Dave praised her for her generosity in playing one of his songs, Marian cracked, "You chose the tunes. I know you need the money." Marian came back to Chicago in 2001 for another tribute to Jimmy, again organized by Dick Wang. Marian at this point decided she wanted to do something long term in Jimmy's memory. She and Dick came up with the Jimmy and Marian McPartland Fellowship in American Music, a $100,000 endowment that would fund, after her death, a graduate fellowship for a musician attending the University of Chicago. Marian's philanthropy extended to her other "home away from home,"

Rochester, where she sponsored the Marian McPartland/Eastman Jazz Series in Kilbourn Hall as a vehicle for exposing young talent. In April 2000, she hosted a concert there by thirteen-year-old Kyrgystani piano prodigy Eldar Djangirov.

"Eldar looked as if he were wearing his father's Sunday best suit cut down for him," said Tom Hampson. "Then he'd rip off one of those Oscar Peterson things and look at the audience as if to say, 'How'd you like that one?'"

Hampson told an amusing story about how Marian's goals occasionally came into conflict with one another.

"She's been so determined about getting paid for what she does," he said. "She came to me afterward and said, 'How come I'm not getting paid for this gig?' 'But Marian,' I said, 'it's your own money!'"

Of course, Marian kept busy on the home front, too. At the 1998 JVC Festival, she presented a tribute concert to Jimmy at the Kaye Playhouse at Hunter College. She also continued to hold writers' feet to the fire at *The New York Times*. When David Yaffe wrote that fans would have difficulty naming any female jazz drummers besides Susie Ibarra, Marian retorted, "Mr. Yaffe evidently has not heard, or heard of, Terri Lyne Carrington or Cindy Blackman," not to mention Allison Miller, she added. She also took Yaffe to task for his erroneous assertion that the International Sweethearts of Rhythm had trouble finding a drummer, pointing out that Pauline Braddy had done a splendid job and "helped pave the way for other women players."

Such steadfast public support of female players notwithstanding, Marian remained firmly exceptionalist in outlook. In an interview for a feminist Ph.D. thesis by Rutgers graduate student Michelle Labieniec-Despard, Marian told her interlocutor that the idea of being asked about women in jazz "always sounds ridiculous to me" and maintained that men were never patronizing toward women "when they were good," citing Mary Lou and Melba Liston as examples, seeming to have forgotten that both women were on the record about the discrimination they had experienced.

But Marian's record of advocating other musicians, male or female, was unassailable. In fact, she was becoming an institution. In December 2000, she was presented with the ASCAP Lifetime Achievement Award at the Stanley H. Kaplan Penthouse at Lincoln Center and the same year launched a TV advertising campaign, with pianist Eric Reed, for Verizon Wireless. Such exposure and status were not always healthy, as Peter Dobrin, writing for the *Philadelphia Inquirer,* pointed out in a review.

"The trouble with becoming an institution," he wrote, "as Marian

McPartland surely has, is that people stop listening to who you are as an artist . . . but when it comes right down to it, McPartland remains one of the most strongly-defined pianists of our time."

Thank goodness some people were still listening, instead of just listing her accomplishments and awards. Dan Morgenstern still had his ears open. Nine years after the fact, he recalled hearing Marian on the 2000 "Jazz in July" program at the Ninety-second Street Y: "Bill Charlap was the new glamour boy and of course Dick Hyman was all over the piano. Then Marian played. She came on late. She played 'Darn That Dream' and I gotta tell you I'll never forget that. It was one of the most beautiful piano solo versions of a ballad that I've ever heard. Her voicings, which she does wonderful harmonic things with, blew me away. Just perfect. I wish somebody had recorded that." All over the country, such memories lingered. If one had the right machinery, no doubt a virtual cloud of Marian McPartland ballad voicings could be seen, floating over every American city. Her music was, literally, in the ether.

But in England, not so much. Yet that didn't prevent the Worshipful Company of Musicians—the London livery company that had subsidized her schooling at the Guildhall some sixty-three years earlier—from awarding Marian its Jazz Silver Medal in 2000. Marian booked a ticket to London but at the last minute canceled, as her hip had become excruciatingly painful. Marian asked Bernice, who had been planning to go with her, to pick up the award. In August, Dr. Cerruti performed a hip replacement.

While she was in England, Bernice tried to call Marian's sister, Joyce, who had been in a nursing home since 1997, but she couldn't get through. Joyce died in November. Though Marian had kept in close touch, she had not seen Joyce since the 1997 visit that had ended with Marian in the hospital. It was a great loss. Joyce—warm, family-oriented, unpretentious—had served as a kind of alter ego for Marian, remembering the little things about their childhood and family that Marian always seemed to forget. Doug sent Marian a condolence note via fax—she refused to buy a computer—and Marian replied with a funny note.

"I'm sorry you never got to meet Joyce, but your old man became quite friendly with her when she came to visit me in Chicago, even though she was quite pregnant at the time," she wrote. "I think some people thought he was going to be the father. [!!!] I'm glad they were able to correspond all these years, and she had a couple of his paintings in her room, which she liked a lot."

As always when she was grieving, Marian put up a good front and buried herself in work. She loved taping *Piano Jazz* live. Something about doing the show before an audience brought out the "ham" in her. In June 2000, she invited the clever songwriter and bop pianist Dave Frishberg, who wrote "Peel Me a Grape," a hit for both Blossom Dearie and Diana Krall, to do a show live at Seattle's King Cat Theater—an old movie house converted into a concert hall. Marian created a deliciously intimate atmosphere. The setting was simple: two pianos rolled side by side, with a water glass perched on a music stand flipped horizontally between the two piano benches. After a duet on "Sweet and Lovely," McPartland said, "Oh, I love how you use those little Thelonious Monk changes in the bridge. That's so clever." Then she played through the juicy chords again, just to please herself. "I'm getting a piano lesson here," she said. "You must be raking in the money on that 'Peel Me a Grape.'"

"I'd have to buy a couple of new rakes first," Frishberg replied dryly.

Later that week, at Jazz Alley, with Douglass and the late drummer Scotty Morris, she showed the same active curiosity, caressing and recaressing the melody of Billy Strayhorn's "Isfahan," reveling in its beauty and structure, and skittering over the keys with lively ideas on "Rain Check."

In August 2002, Marian started doing live *Piano Jazz* sessions at Tanglewood. The first featured Sir Roland Hanna, not particularly inspiring, but subsequent sessions with Norah Jones, Taylor Eigsti, Madeleine Peyroux, Elvis Costello, and Renee Rosnes came off beautifully. Marian scored another *Piano Jazz* coup when she snagged the great songwriter Willie Nelson with his longtime guitar player, Jackie King. Willie had proven his love for the Great American Songbook with his wildly successful album *Stardust Memories*. On the show, he soloed on his little acoustic guitar and Jackie sounded terrific on electric. When they played Nelson's classic hit for Patsy Cline, "Crazy," Marian got into the spirit of Nelson's style, playing single-note lines that, like Willie, sounded laid-back at the same time they were right on top of the beat.

"Did it take you a long time to write that?" she asked.

"No, it was one of those easy ones that just fell out of there," Willie replied.

"Do you ever struggle with one?"

"Usually if they don't work out, I throw them away."

"I write on the backs of matchbooks and keep every little scrap and sometimes you find one that works . . . but maybe I should throw one out."

Willie was so charmed by his experience on the show, he lingered in the studio an extra hour, then invited Marian to sit in with him at Irving Plaza.

Adam Gopnik, writing in *The New Yorker,* said the crowd was stunned: "An elegant elderly woman in a sequined gown comes out, and slips in at the piano bench—the grande dame of jazz piano. She and Willie duet on three liquid numbers, 'Sweet Georgia Brown,' a slow version of 'The Gypsy,' and 'The Heart of a Clown.' Her lilting, dreamy piano complements Willie's voice as he carefully negotiates the complicated chord structures of the jazz songs, like a man climbing down from a high roof on a homemade ladder. The crowd listens, a little baffled—the band listens, a little baffled—and then she leaves in a shimmer of sequins and high, lacquered hair."

Gopnik wondered out loud if Nelson had been trying to tweak his fans. But if he had listened to *Piano Jazz,* he would have realized Willie just liked Marian's love of song and honest attitude. He had found a kindred spirit.

Norah Jones was the big sensation in 2002, with her surprise debut megahit, *Come Away with Me,* and Marian decided she had to have her on the show. Considering how quickly Jones was devoured by the media, it was remarkable that Marian was able to get her so quickly. But Norah—even though she had taken a turn into softly countrified singer/songwriter territory—was actually a jazz baby, having studied for two years at North Texas State. She had listened to tapes of Marian's show during long car trips from Dallas to Florida, courtesy of her high school music teacher in Dallas, and had seen Marian perform at the Dallas Museum of Art. She knew perfectly well who Marian was and what a compliment it was to be invited on the show. The pair hit it off from the get-go, with Norah launching into "September in the Rain," infusing the song with forward motion even as she ornamented it with idiosyncratic sighs and whispers. In just one more indication of how Marian subtly adapted herself to her guests, she lowered the volume of her voice to Norah's, taking the edge off, which gave their encounter even more intimacy. Before Marian played "For All We Know," the young singer recounted how the song had special meaning for her, because it was the first one she'd ever played in front of a band. Marian said the song had special meaning for her, too, because of its lyric "We come and go, like ripples on a stream."

"When Jimmy, my husband, died," Marian told her, "a musician we know sent me a card with those words on it."

The most daring—and productive—of all Marian's nonjazz bookings was Elvis Costello. When he came into the Avatar studio in May 2003, the English rocker was already dating Diana Krall (they would marry that December), but it was not public knowledge. In the late 1970s, Costello had pioneered and perfected a new form—the crisp, new wave, three-minute rock song—but he came from a jazz background. His dad had sung with swing bandleader Joe Loss, and Elvis himself was an avid student of the American Songbook, as familiar with Cole Porter and George Gershwin as he was with Leiber and Stoller and Paul McCartney. McPartland and Costello struck up an easy rapport. When Elvis offered to sing "Gloomy Sunday," the morose song made famous by Billie Holiday, Marian responded, "I promise not to kill myself," and the two Brits hit their stride as Costello crooned another mournful plaint, "You Don't Know What Love Is." Costello would later write and record lyrics to "Threnody," Marian's song for Mary Lou. An excellent interviewer himself, he would also host two well-prepared sessions of *Piano Jazz* in which he turned the tables on Marian, interviewing her, a pair of shows that became extremely popular.

In 1999, National Public Radio released an album of twenty of the spontaneous musical portraits Marian had composed on the air, with proceeds folded back into the show. The album was called, simply enough, *Portraits* and pictured an elegant Al Hirschfeld line drawing of Marian at the keyboard on the cover. Some, like the one for Dizzy Gillespie, were nothing short of magical—and mysterious, too, in the way this structured song had come into Marian's head in a rush. Other subjects illuminated well included Tony Bennett, who got a treatment appropriately both tender and grand; Paul Shaffer, whose puckish humor came through in a fanciful blues; Helen Merrill, sad and misty, projecting inner strength; Randy Weston, with dignity in the bass and irreverent dissonance up top; Judy Collins, gauzy and romantic; and Bud Powell, brooding yet lyrical, too. Many of the other portraits were puzzling, possibly having more to do with Marian's feelings about the guests than their personalities.

One of the remarkable features of these late *Piano Jazz* sessions is how crisp and tart Marian's voice remained—there was no frogginess, no hesitation—and how sharp her wit remained. Right up to her eighty-fifth birthday—and beyond—she was pert and alert. And though she had slowed down a bit at the keyboard and occasionally muffed a note or two, she had no trouble keeping up with anybody who came into the studio, whether they played stride, swing, bop, or free.

Piano Jazz had now been on the air for more than two decades. Many of the early shows had been recorded on reel-to-reel tape, which would eventually deteriorate. In 2002, SCETV applied for federal money from a program called Saving America's Treasures and received $81,100 to preserve the first 279 tapes, which were baked in an oven, then transferred electronically. This was the beginning of a digital archive that would eventually include more than seven hundred shows, which the station planned to use as an educational resource.

Marian was always happiest when she was working. Despite the pain she experienced every day from physical deterioration, it was difficult for her to slow down. Toward the end of the 1990s, however, she began to learn to take time out, falling into a relaxing seasonal rhythm with her friend Bernice, who lived in a rustic, one-story rambler in Hartsdale, Westchester County, with old farm tools hanging in the workshop and a well-outfitted kitchen. At Christmas, Marian would hire a car service— one of two extravagances in an otherwise frugal, unflashy life (the other was the telephone)—and come to the house to hang out and relax. The women began a tradition of cooking a holiday meal together.

"I always cooked up a storm," said Bernice. "She just likes to sit and talk and listen to music and talk about music, and that's what we do. I love looking at her when she's listening to music. It's almost as if you can read her critiquing it. She's always been interested in what everybody else has to say about the music, too. We love many of the same songs very, very, very much, like 'Last Night When We Were Young,' 'The Wee Small Hours.' In fact, for two or three or four years we used to put [the album *In the Wee Small Hours*] on when we went to sleep. We have had some of our happiest moments just talking about individual songs and how great they were. . . ."

Summers, Marian began visiting Bernice and her friend Mary Kay at Bernice's lakefront cottage near Litchfield, Connecticut. There was a boat there and the place was just a stone's throw from Tyler Lake.

"We'd go out on the boat, a party boat, with pontoons," said Bernice. "You can take six people out on it. Marian would feed the geese. She really relates to being outside. She just loves it up there. She'd sit on the steps on the front porch, looking at the water, and then she'd pick up these toads— she thought they were so cute—and then she'd let them go very gently. She loves nature."

Being a librarian, Bernice was a great resource. She consistently recommended new reading material.

"Even though she doesn't have time to read the way I read, she is a good reader," said Bernice. "She is sensitive and picks up things in the air. She likes biographies. She's not a deep history reader, but light stuff doesn't appeal to her, either. Not thrillers or mysteries. She likes strong stories. And she likes humor."

Bernice lent Marian *Suite Française,* the pre–World War II Jewish saga by Irene Nemirovsky, who was killed at Auschwitz.

"Marian loved that book," Bernice said. "I couldn't get it away from her."

Over the years, Bernice recommended—with success—the charming long-distance romance centered on a London antiquarian bookshop, *84, Charing Cross Road, My Life in France, The Girl with the Pearl Earring, The Year of Magical Thinking,* and *Two-Part Invention,* Madeleine L'Engle's book about her forty-year marriage and the death of her husband.

"She's always been aghast that I, being who I am, don't have a subscription to *The New Yorker.* We traveled a lot and we've talked a lot. I feel I know her very well. There aren't more than one or two other people in my life that I think of as so nice and honest and trustworthy and intelligent."

Marian's gal pal on the West Coast, Merrilee Trost, also served as a travel companion. Merrilee was in the business and for a while booked the beautiful outdoor venue Filoli in Woodside on the San Francisco peninsula, bringing Marian in for a 2000 show. Merrilee usually traveled up to Seattle if Marian was playing Jazz Alley or down to Los Angeles if she was at the Jazz Bakery. They would visit, and Merrilee would help out with various things, including selling albums after the gig.

"She was always so gracious," said Merrilee. "I went out with a lot of different artists [on the road] and I have never seen anyone, after doing two sets at a club, go out afterwards and sit for an hour while this long line of people went past her saying all the things people say: 'Oh, I saw you at the Hickory House in nineteen fifty whatever.' 'I'm so glad you came to that. What is your name?' And she would have a private conversation with everyone. She would write their name and autograph. Everybody felt like they had sat down and had a private thing with Marian McPartland."

One year, before Marian was scheduled to come out to play Yoshi's in Oakland, she confided to Merrilee that she had heard something disturbing. A friend had called to say that she'd seen Joe Morello's drums advertised on eBay. Marian knew Doug enjoyed hunting for vintage memorabilia online, and she had often enlisted him to find things for her. He had come up with some of Jimmy's most obscure albums, as well as recordings of Jimmy's first wife, Dorothy Williams. He was also hard up for money. Marian called him immediately. It turned out that Doug, who was having trouble paying the rent, had indeed put Morello's practice pad up for bid—"I would never sell the drums"—but had taken it down as soon as he'd found the money elsewhere. But Marian feared the worst. She told Doug she wanted Jimmy's horn back.

"I'm gonna be at Yoshi's," she said. "I want you to bring it to me."

Feeling bad at the same time she felt anxious, Marian paid Doug $1,000 for the horn. Doug was enormously hurt by Marian's suspicions, though later in life, they finally established a more trusting relationship. Marian kept the horn and later sent it to Donna's sons. Anything associated with Jimmy was bound to evoke strong reactions in Marian. Though it had been nine years since his death, she continued to brood about him. Bernice recalled one night in April 2001, when she stayed overnight at Marian's house after helping out with a live recording session in New Jersey, Marian "got real nostalgic and started talking about him. She pulled open one of her bureau drawers and out came these pictures."

Some of the pictures were also of Joe. That made sense. She had been working with Joe that night, recording an album titled *Live at Shanghai Jazz,* in a trio with bassist Rufus Reid. It was a good album. With the aid of Reid's booming sound, which had a long, rich sustain, and spurred by the live audience, Marian played with robust, muscular abandon, especially on the memorable opener, Mary Lou's "Scratchin' in the Gravel," and an expressive rendition of Duke's "Prelude to a Kiss." Marian usually liked to record new tunes, but this record featured almost all songs she had recorded before. It was hard to resist reading secret meanings into the program. Marian and Joe had recorded "For All We Know"—with the lyric Marian had discussed with Norah Jones, "We come and go, like ripples on a stream"—on her Capitol album with Joe, *After Dark.* "Black Is the Color of My True Love's Hair" had appeared on *With You in Mind,* the soporific strings album Marian had recorded right after breaking up with Joe—the first time. And was there a reason for playing "You'd Be So Nice to Come Home To"? Perhaps. Perhaps not. But there could be no mistaking the irony in the clever title Marian picked for the effective, expressive free-improv piece they played that night: "A Snare and a Delusion." Marian didn't really want to "come home to" Joe—she knew that never would have worked out—but she liked musing about their long affair and, as devoted as she was to the memory and legacy of Jimmy, she never forgot the "besotted" love she had had for Joe. It was nice to be working with him again.

When Bernice came back to the house with Marian after the gig, she was impressed by Marian's stamina, working till three A.M.—"I wasn't used to those kinds of hours!"—but also saw that Marian was having trouble getting around. At home, she had begun to use a walker and would eventually have chairs on electric runners installed on all the stairways. Nevertheless, Marian continued to work. On September 7 and 8, she flew to Boston with her regular East Coast trio—Gary Mazzaroppi and Glenn

Davis—and played at Scullers, where jazz critic Bob Blumenthal noted her style had become "leaner" than in the old days, with the "dark under-currents" and "haunted voicings" of Bud Powell and Bill Evans.

On the morning of September 11, Marian was home, sitting at the kitchen table, watching the TV mounted above the table, when the two hijacked planes assaulted the World Trade Center.

"That all those people on the airplane had to die, to further their plans," she said. "I couldn't believe that they were able to do such a thing. I'm sure they have been planning for something else, you know they are."

As with the London Blitz, however, Marian shrugged and said, "You can't be shuddering and looking around corners and worrying. You just have to go on with life and hope that it won't happen or just have to not think about it every day."

In addition to *Live at Shanghai Jazz,* Marian made two more excellent live recordings in this period, starting with a tribute to Duke Ellington recorded April 17, 2000, at Maybeck Hall, *The Single Petal of a Rose.* The original idea, said producer Nick Phillips, was to do another solo album, but Marian ultimately decided to recruit Bill Douglass for support. "The Single Petal of a Rose" was a gorgeous, little-known tune—Marian was always so good at finding them—from Duke's *Queen's Suite,* written for Queen Elizabeth II. It was less of a tune than a melodic idea repeated over and over, like waves washing on the shore, creating a dreamy mood with layers of overtones. For the cover art, Marian selected the watercolor of a rose she had painted herself at Stratford House. Like the album, it was el-egant, precise, simple, and to the point. As with the first Maybeck album, she performed for a live audience, but this time it was a select crowd of about fifty invited guests. It was a quiet set, more like a prayerful meditation than a celebration, with her version of "Mood Indigo" sounding like a hymn. In the spirit of Ellington's "blue period," Marian contributed a moody tune of her own, "Cerulescence," the title referring to a shade of blue. Of all her recordings, this one most reflected a feeling of repose.

By contrast, Marian's next record, a duet album with Chicago pianist Willie Pickens, really strutted. Here was a pianist in complete control of her craft, someone who could swing at will and knew when to leave notes out and when to smash a chord so thick that it rang the soundboard. Pick-ens was an unlikely partner, a rambunctious, bluesy, color-outside-the-lines swinger in the best Chicago tradition. But when they got together, something clicked. Marian had known Willie for some time. He'd done *Piano Jazz* in Pittsburgh in 1997, and in 2000 they'd done some dates together in San Francisco and Montana. Pickens had also played on the wonderful "round robin" with four pianists at the Chicago Jazz Festival. Evidently, the idea for making the album was a spur-of-the-moment decision. In a November letter, Marian wrote Doug that she would be at the Jazz Showcase for Christmas with Willie.

"I know he doesn't give me all that much space," she said, "but it doesn't bother me. I really enjoy playing with him and I thought it would be a change from the same old trio format. In fact, we might even record it—what do you think?"

Pickens brought out the competitive, rhythmic edge in Marian; she brought out his dissonant, daring side; and from there it was just, as Marian might say, 'hev at it!" "It Don't Mean a Thing (If It Ain't Got That Swing)" was a playful, tumbling romp, like two kids in the candy store of swing. "Spring Is Here" was not just gossamer, but firm and deliberate. "(It's Only a) Paper Moon" might legitimately have caused Tatum O'Neal to shake her head and say, "But where's the melody?" On "Just One of Those Things," Marian exploded into stride.

With a suitcase full of new albums to autograph, Marian set out for Toronto in January 2003 for the IAJE convention, where she was to be honored for her eighty-fifth birthday by the premiere of two new works commissioned by ASCAP, Robin Eubanks's "Full Circle" and John Hollenbeck's "Folkmoot." It was a bitterly cold winter weekend, with heavy snow falling in broad, wet flakes, making the short walk between the grand old Fairmont Royal York Hotel and the modern Toronto Convention Centre quite an adventure, even for able-bodied folks. In addition to attending the premieres, Marian performed with Canadians Don Thompson (bass) and Barry Elmes (drums). Marian's set ran overtime and "she could have easily held her Bassett Theatre audience in place another hour," wrote Ken Dryden. Oscar Peterson was also at IAJE that year, promoting his fascinating autobiography, *A Jazz Odyssey*. He was just a step ahead of Marian. The following month, the University of Illinois released an updated version of her book under the new title, *Marian McPartland's Jazz World*. Marian had been working on the revision for more than a year, writing postscripts to the original chapters and—most important to her—a new preface that included a segment about Jimmy. Joellyn and Bernice both helped her with the essay.

"She *agonized* over it," said Bernice. "Whenever she was writing anything, she was stressed about it, and talked a lot about it. Writing for her is one of the hardest things in her life."

Only three pages of the new preface dealt with Jimmy—she had tried to write a whole essay but felt she could never quite get it right—but they were heartfelt, hard-won pages. In them, she confessed what she had been writing to herself all these years, that she wished she had treated him better and "not been so controlling . . . I always wanted to have things my own way. Being with him changed my life in ways I never would have thought of. I don't think I would be playing today if it were not for his encouragement and support. . . . I discovered that dreams can become a reality. Anything can happen if you work, plan, and keep dreaming. Jimmy did this for me."

It was a lovely tribute.

In Marian's postscript to her essay "You've Come a Long Way Baby," she went after Ken Burns's PBS documentary *Jazz,* which had been released in 2001, noting that Mary Lou Williams—much less other women (such as herself, though she was too polite to say so)—was barely mentioned and that, overall, the film was "narrow and somewhat limited in scope. . . ."

"There are many different cultures in jazz, but the Burns series, for whatever reason, omitted Europeans and almost all women," she continued. "To me, the Burns series didn't bring out the richness of jazz, its global impact, and its ability to cross barriers of gender, age, and race. Rather, it described a period in American history, using jazz as a background instead of putting it in the forefront."

It was a calm but firmly damning critique.

Two months after IAJE, Marian celebrated her eighty-fifth birthday at Birdland in a gala, four-hour gathering (again produced by John Schreiber) that would become typical of her New York engagements, more a group celebration than a trio gig. The lineup included vocalists Tony Bennett, Jackie Cain, Nnenna Freelon, Karrin Allyson, Norah Jones, Curtis Stigers, and Barbara Carroll; pianists Billy Taylor, James Williams, George Wein, Jason Moran, and Bill Charlap; bassists Bill Crow and Gary Mazzaroppi; violinist Regina Carter; guitarists Jim Hall and Jackie King; saxophonists Phil Woods, Ravi Coltrane, Chris Potter, and Loren Schoenberg; trumpeters Jon Faddis, Roy Hargrove, and Dave Douglas; flugelhornist Clark Terry; and drummers Joe Morello and Glenn Davis. Carroll set the tone by singing and accompanying herself on Stephen Sondheim's chipper salute "Old Friends": "Here's to us / Who's like us? Damn few!" Roy Hargrove silenced the crowd with beyond-his-years sensitivity, with Marian accompanying, on "My Foolish Heart." Marian and Bennett swung through Duke's "In a Mellow Tone." And Allyson delivered a silvery version of "Twilight World" that penetrated the aching heart of Marian's song in a way no one else ever had, including Bennett. Terry added his usual lick of humor by saying, "The golden years suck!" then played a stirring duet with Marian on Duke's "Come Sunday." The Hickory House trio was slated to perform, but for some reason that he has never been explained, Morello asked Glenn Davis to play, saying, "I'll be right back," then disappeared. Marian speculated Morello had been drinking and had gotten jealous that another drummer was there.

NPR broadcast the occasion and Concord released a wonderful two-disc set titled *85 Candles—Live in New York,* which happily included both Carroll's and Allyson's numbers, as well as Jones whispering a fetching version of "The Nearness of You" with Marian's trio. When they finished, emcee Murray Horowitz declared, "The winner—and still champions!"

As Dan Ouellette said in the liner notes to the album, it was a "one of a kind event that could only have happened in New York."

He was right. This "snapshot of the Manhattan jazz community," as *The Guardian* called it, was in spirit very much like the photograph, *A Great Day in Harlem*—but better, because the gathering not only brought together old friends who were usually on the road but made it possible for them to play together, too. Marian, at the center of it all—headmistress, den mother, queen bee, grande dame, call her what you like—was in her ideal element, in the middle of the action, sharing the limelight, with the people she loved and admired, making music together. But in this case, though Marian would never have taken the credit for it, one of the reasons the New York jazz community was so tightly woven was Marian herself. She was like a switch, through which every wire in the community had somehow passed at one time or another.

The *Wall Street Journal* ran a long feature about Marian after the show, celebrating her many accomplishments. Noting she had osteoporosis, arthritis—"everything," as Marian put it—the paper wondered if she might retire sometime soon. "Retire?" Marian asked another reporter later that year, when he brought up the same impertinence. "Should I give up hanging out with musicians, making money, playing for an audience, the applause? What am I gonna do? Sit at home looking over the fence at the neighbors? Get a Winnebago and drive around? I can't die, I've got stuff worked out to do until next year."

And several years beyond. Indeed, Marian's sarcastic remarks about "retiring" would become an annual refrain. Though she no doubt reached her peak in 2003, she was remarkably productive even as she slowed down. She continued to tour until 2008, striking out in various years for the West Coast, Southwest, Northeast, eastern seaboard, Midwest, Florida, and her beloved Rochester. In 2007, she finally premiered the piece she had improvised one night at Diana Schwartz's, *A Portrait of Rachel Carson,* in Columbia, South Carolina, with the University of South Carolina Symphony Orchestra, Donald Portnoy conducting. She performed it again in 2009 at New York's Trinity Church. In 2004, she received a Grammy, a Trustees Lifetime Achievement Award celebrating her work as an educator, writer, and radio host. Marian released her last album for Concord, *Twilight World,* in 2008. Her hands had slowed down, but by carefully and creatively playing within her means, she, Bill Douglass, and Charlie Braugham delivered a gorgeous, passionate, translucent farewell that carried the mood of its title with dignity and perfection.

In the summer of 2008, at age ninety, Marian was still churning out four *Piano Jazz* shows a month, keeping up with new artists such as Robert Glasper and Grace Kelly, visiting ones she had somehow overlooked, such as Sheila Jordan, and revisiting old friends like Hank Jones and Renee Rosnes. Marian hosted *Piano Jazz* until the spring of 2009, at which point she remained as artistic director, designating guest hosts such as Bill Charlap and Jon Weber. She also did live tapings at Tanglewood every summer through 2008, including a fabulous afternoon with Elvis Costello that featured a cameo appearance by Diana Krall. In 2004, at the Monterey Jazz Festival, she did an amusing live show with festival board member Clint Eastwood. Two years later, she finally convinced Keith Jarrett to do the show, a dream of hers for years. *Piano Jazz* celebrated its twenty-fifth anniversary with a gala concert at the Kennedy Center and its thirtieth at Dizzy's Club Coca-Cola in Manhattan. Marian also threw a party for her own ninetieth birthday in March 2008 at Dizzy's and continued to preside over similar programs at the club through October 2010. As with her eighty-fifth birthday party, all of these concerts served as a toast to the community as well as her own accomplishments, with dozens of guests joining in.

On June 6, 2010, at a ceremony held at the British consulate in Manhattan, Margaret Marian McPartland was named by Queen Elizabeth II (in absentia) an Officer of the Most Excellent Order of the British Empire (OBE). The twenty-six-year-old girl who had stood in a British Army uniform on the shores of Britain in July 1944, staring across the English Channel, wondering what lay ahead, could never have dreamed of such an outcome. Marian had crossed not only the English Channel, but the

Atlantic Ocean, not to mention any number of social barriers that might have daunted lesser mortals along the way. At each point along the road, she had asked, "Shall we play that one together?" First, she had asked Jimmy, then Mary Lou, then Joe, then Alec, then every jazz musician she met in New York, from Duke Ellington to Jason Moran. Each time, the answer had been a genial, if sometimes curious, "Yes." Finally, now, she had asked the world at large, "Shall we play that one together?" Again, the answer had been a resounding, "Yes."

Notes

Abbreviated citations such as "Marian McPartland (1972)" or "Irving Townsend material, Marian McPartland Personal Archive (MMPA)" refer to sources listed in detail in the bibliography. Unless otherwise cited, quotations in the text from sources interviewed by the author were drawn from the author interviews listed in the bibliography. Citations are as complete as possible, but in some cases newspaper articles cited are photocopies in the Marian McPartland personal archive, sometimes without identification of the publication or the date.

Chapter One: "What Shall We Do with Her?"

1 "July 23, 1944": In her 2006 Ph.D. thesis, Clare Hansson gives this as the date of Marian's arrival in France. In an e-mail (February 8, 2012), Hansson explained that her source for the date was an unidentified newspaper clipping in the Marian McPartland file at the Institute of Jazz Studies, in Rutgers, N.J. The article very likely comes from a Chicago newspaper published between June 10 and June 15, 1946, as it also refers to Marian's June 9, 1946, performance at the Hot Club of Chicago as having happened the previous Sunday. It is unclear where the reporter got the date, but it is certainly plausible. Hostilities in St. Lô ended July 20, 1944, and Marian's account of traveling through France suggests that the battlefields were still fresh when she arrived. She traveled several weeks through France before attending a concert in Paris on September 24, 1944, the first firm date for this period of her life.

3 "arsenal was a dangerous place": Hogg, p. 916.

3 Dyson family history: Kelda Roe, assistant archivist at St. George's College, to author, e-mail, September 15, 2009.

3 Frederick Dyson: It's possible Frederick also sang in St. George's Choir, though the archives of St. George's College, which administers the choir, are somewhat confusing on the point. Frederick is listed as a "boy chorister" in 1872, when he would have been seventeen years old. (The choir's angelic boy sopranos are generally far younger.) Marian, on the other hand, says she definitely remembers being told that Frederick sang in the choir.

3 Dyson piano shop: See: www.thamesweb.co.uk.Windsor/windsorhistory/scheme61.html

4 Eggcup story: Marian McPartland interview with author, July 10, 2008.

4 Frederick knighted: Unidentified newspaper obituary for Sir Frederick, 1932, MMPA.

5 Slough: Slough has not always been so reviled. In the early twentieth century, it had the reputation as a pastoral area of Buckinghamshire with several wonderful estates, including that of the Astors. Slough was also the site where Sir William Herschel built his famous giant telescope in the nineteenth century.

5 Marian's homes in Woolwich: The house at Wrottesley Road is the only one left of the three homes Marian lived in. The house at Eglinton Road was torn down and replaced by a large, ugly apartment block. The site of the Eglinton Hill home is covered by a huge complex of council housing.

6 Royal Arsenal statistics: Hogg, p. 911.

6 "heavy chuff chuff" and memories of first homes: Autobiographical notes and sketches, MMPA.

7 "it was like a vision": Notes and sketches, MMPA.

8 household help: Notes and sketches, MMPA.

8 "I really have few memories of Mummy": Letters to Irving Townsend, MMPA.

9 "Little Doris," other Marian's childhood stories: MMPA.

9 "She was overstrict": Armitage, n.d., MMPA.

9 "They never heated the house": Ibid.

10 Marian's relationships with her mother and father: Adrienne Rich, quoted in Carolyn Heilbrun's *Writing a Woman's Life*, observed, "It is a painful fact that a nurturing father, who replaces rather than complements a mother, *must be loved at the mother's expense* [italics in original], whatever the reasons for the mother's absence."

11 Car ownership in Britain: The Turners were not unusual. In 1928, there was only one automobile for every forty-four people in England (B. R. Mitchel, *British Historical Statistics*, Cambridge, New York: Cambridge University Press, 1988); in the United States that figure was one in 5.6 (Susan B. Carter, Scott Sigmund Gartner,

Michael R. Haines, Alan L. Olmstead, Richard Sutch, and Gavin Wright, eds., *Historical Statistics of the United States: Earliest Times to the Present, Millennial Edition*, Cambridge, England: Cambridge University Press, 2006).

12 Miss Hammond's School: The formal name of the school as listed in city directories was the Minster Road School. "Miss Hammond's" was a colloquial name.

13 "Where the flowers grow the sweetest": Frank Turner may have written these verses, but Marian does not think so.

14 "I don't remember there being a Depression": Notes and sketches, MMPA.

14 "It was a very long way": Armitage, MMPA.

14 "When Mother wanted to move." Ibid.

15 "I was a dreamy sort of child.": Notes and sketches, MMPA.

15 "Being ill, I felt": Armitage, MMPA.

16 "It was in some parochial": Notes and sketches, MMPA.

17 Fashions in the summer of 1928: Graves, p. 142.

17 "What are you wearing?": Armitage, MMPA.

17 "He would take a foot rule": Smithsonian Institution (1997), p. 27.

19 "Life of crime": Armitage, MMPA.

19 "Lots of throwing up": Notes and sketches, MMPA.

19 "every inch a headmistress": Pittman, p. 45.

20 "well-spoken and well-bred girls. . . began with a prayer" Ibid, pp. 21–23.

20 "I feel sure": Ibid, p. 61.

20 "Being trained not for university": Only fifteen percent of girls in Britain in the 1930s pursued education past age fourteen (Virden, p. 39). Though Oxford began granting degrees to women in 1920, Cambridge would not follow suit until 1948. No girls' school equivalent of Eton or Harrow existed that could prepare them for entrance to those universities. Despite suffrage, the proportion of women in the higher professions in 1935 in England was no higher than it had been in 1914.

20 "Handily carrying": Doris Kidney to Marian McPartland, letter, December 16, 1976, MMPA.

21 "Margaret has good ability": Spring, 1934 report card, MMPA.

21 May 1934 concert: Concert program, MMPA; unidentified newspaper clipping, n.d., MMPA.

22 "Very keen": Notes and sketches, MMPA.

22 "[Ken] made me really listen": McPartland (1987), p. 4.

22 "I always felt like": Notes and sketches, MMPA.

23 "Sophisticated syncopation": There can be no doubt that there was a racial element to this nomenclature. In Britain in the 1920s, jazz was considered "sensual, noisy, stupid and grotesque" (Parsonage, p. 174) and associated with negative stereotypes of blacks. Appearances by black revues were even protested and restricted by the British musicians union. (Whiteman, by contrast, on close personal terms with Lord Mountbatten, was allowed to come into the country and play pretty much when and where he pleased.)

23 "I didn't know what was pop": McPartland, *International Musician,* September 1969.

24 "we can't keep you": Notes and sketches, MMPA.

25 "shaking in my boots": Notes and sketches, MMPA.

25 "sadly lacking in technique": *Family Circle,* 1952, MMPA.

Chapter Two: London

27 Guildhall School history and location: Barty-King, p. 21 and 67 ff. The Guildhall School is now part of the architecturally monstrous arts complex called the Barbican Centre.

27 "When bass singer Norman Walker": Ibid, p. 91.

27 Dropping out of Stratford House: Marian would later take a school equivalency exam to matriculate.

28 "He showed me some things": Smithsonian Institution (1997), p. 23.

28 The Worshipful Company of Musicians was a London "livery company"—like a guild—formed in the sixteenth century to protect and promote the rights of musicians.

29 "He was a dirty old man": Smithsonian Institution (1997), p. 16

29 "That guy used to chase": Notes and sketches, MMPA.

29 "Father said": Armitage, MMPA.

29 "no teenage life at all": Hansson (2006), p. 423.

30 "duplicate Bob Zurke choruses": Mark Gardner, "The Jazz Journal Interview: Marian McPartland Talks to Mark Gardner," *Jazz Journal* (1973), in Hansson (2006).

30 "discordant trash": *Family Circle*, 1952, MMPA.

31 "by this time we were just friends": Smithsonian Institution (1997), p. 27.

31 "I don't know why": Irving Townsend material, MMPA.

31 Billy Mayerl school: http://www.musicwebinternational.com/Rev/2002/May02/Mayerl.htm

32 Multi-Tone pedal: The Multi-Tone device was designed, coincidentally, by an Englishman who had the same name as the great American jazz pianist who would later have such an impact on Marian—Bill Evans.

32 "He showed me . . . flabbergasted": Manuscripts and interviews with Maher, MMPA.

32 "It is a stupid choice": Notes and sketches, MMPA.

33 "You'll come to no good": Smithsonian Institution (1997), p. 18.

33 "Don't throw your talent away": Manuscripts and interviews with Maher, MMPA.

33 "He asked him all kinds of questions": Notes and sketches, MMPA.

33 "In spite of my image": Ibid.

34 Marian Page spelling: Marian's name was variously misspelled in both the American and the British press over the years, her first name often appearing as "Marion" or even "Marilyn" and her last name as "Paige." But Marian Page was her spelling of choice.

34 Billy Mayerl reviews and itinerary: John Watson to author, e-mail, October 9, 2009.

35 Pathé newsreel: See: http://www.britishpathe.com/record.php?id=11259

36–37 "All these landladies . . . some kind of junk . . . pass at Dorothy . . . couple of virgins . . . naïve young chick": Notes and sketches, MMPA.

37 "Mother's arthritis": Armitage, MMPA.

39 "I was at loose ends": Maher material, MMPA.

39 Ivy Benson audition: Marian could be wrong about being glad she failed the audition. If Benson had hired her, it's likely Marian would have found her way into the London jazz scene and thereby put her development on a faster track. On the other hand, as Sherrie Tucker points out in *Swing Shift*, playing in an all-girl band rarely led to a strong career. They were "marketed as spectacles; they were rarely recorded. If their performances were reviewed, it was often as though their medium was inherently visual rather than auditory, frivolous rather than serious" (Tucker, p. 27).

39 "I really didn't know": Smithsonian Institution (1997), p. 20.

40 "blush with shame": Irving Townsend material, MMPA.

40 Reginald Foresythe: Foresythe's composition "Deep Forest" also became a staple in the repertoire of jazz pianist Earl Hines.

40 Leslie Hutchinson: Born in Grenada and raised in New York, "Hutch" was a favorite at black-tie café society venues such as the Café Malmaison and is satirized in openly racist language as "Chokey" in Evelyn Waugh's novel *Decline and Fall*. Flamboyant and extravagant—he owned a Rolls-Royce and bragged about his sexual prowess—"Hutch" was constantly embroiled in society scandals, among them the still persistent rumor that he fathered an illegitimate child with Lady Mountbatten. He made women swoon. McPartland, in her youthful naïveté, says she had a "crush" on him. (She was surprised to be told later that he was gay—in fact, he was bisexual.)

41 "get a style like Winifred Atwell": Maher material, MMPA.

42 "There was a mystique": Rusty Jones, 2008.

42 "One day men started putting up": Maher material, MMPA.

42 "The weather was lovely": Armitage, MMPA.

43 Terry-Thomas: Terry-Thomas appeared in Levis's rather entertaining 1948 comic film *Brass Monkey*, which offered a humorous parody of variety, complete with female contortionist, comb-and-tissue-paper busker, William Tell act (with head bandage), and "Hutch" doing an excellent vocal turn.

43 National Service: The National Service Act No. 2 of December 1941 called for conscription or "liability for service" of single women ages twenty to thirty to begin in January 1942.

43 "They had a bunch": Smithsonian Institution (1997), p. 32.

44 bombing of Royal Arsenal: Hogg, p. 1024.

45 "I never knew": Maher material, MMPA.

46 Wrote Joyce of her mother and father: Armitage, MMPA.

46 "I was so afraid of sex": Notes and sketches, MMPA.

46 "One day": Conversation with author, April 19, 2009.

47 "We would go to bed": Notes and sketches, MMPA.

48 "David was my first real affair": Ibid.

48 "You ought to go with USO": Smithsonian Institution (1997), p. 33.

48 "Dying to meet Cagney": Ibid, p. 38.

49 50,000 English war brides: Virden, p. 73.

49 "We all thought anything American": Smithsonian Institution (1997), p. 33.

49 "It was all very secret": Knauss, MMPA.

49 Band Wagon embarked across the Channel: McPartland often said in interviews she was the first English female entertainer to play in wartime France. While it's true USO entertainers arrived in France a month before those of ENSA, according to Richard Fawkes's *Fighting for a Laugh*, the first English entertainers to officially reach Normandy were members of the Stars in Battledress. Five parties, serving under Sergeants Rudy Jess, Bif Byfield, Sid Millward, Arthur Haynes, and Harold Childs, made the crossing on June 14. Marian went over in July.

Chapter Three: "Oh, No! A Girl Piano Player!"

51 "Dearest Da": Marian McPartland to Frank Turner, letter, October 19, 1944, MMPA.

52 "You knew that behind the hedge": Enstice and Stockhouse, p. 236.

53 "It happened so fast": Ibid.

53 "flock of razor blades": Unidentified newspaper clipping, December 5, 1952, MMPA.

53 "It's not that we were so good": Smithsonian Institution (1997), p. 34.

53 Willie Shore: See: http://www.schroon.net/Scaroon%20Manor/loves.htm. Shore also collaborated with Fred Astaire and Morey Amsterdam on the song "Oh! My Achin' Back."

54 Olympia Theatre Gala: Shore is the only Band Wagon member whose name appears on the Olympia Theatre program, but *Melody Maker* reported that Marian played the show. A program from the evening turned up in her archive—so she likely was there—but she had no recollection of performing.

54 "explode with wonder": Unidentified newspaper clipping, December 5, 1952, MMPA.

55 "Oh, no, a girl": Jimmy McPartland (1972), p. 3.

55 "I do remember": Notes for Jimmy McPartland essay, MMPA.

56 "small arms firing": Jimmy McPartland (1972), p. 4.

56 "Just play organ": Smithsonian Institution (1997), p. 40.

57 "I just kept telling her": Jimmy McPartland (1972), p. 5.

57 "I went to the house": Ibid, p. 5.

57 "Having lunch in the mess hall": Notes for Jimmy McPartland essay, MMPA.

58 "I drink like a gentleman": Smithsonian Institution (1997), p. 42.

58 "Look, honey": Jimmy McPartland (1972), p. 5.

60 "Is he badly hurt": Unidentified newspaper clipping, December 5, 1952, MMPA.

60 "I was down on the ground": Jimmy McPartland (1972), p. 5. Jimmy McPartland notoriously embellished his war stories, but Marian noted wryly that "if he said he *didn't* shoot it down all by himself" what he said in this story "is probably true" (interview with author, July 8, 2008).

61 "I thought, well, if I tell them": Smithsonian Institution (1997), p. 42.

61 "I suppose unconsciously": Notes and sketches, MMPA.

63 "Dearest Da, Mummy and Joyce": MMPA.

65 "like you see on *M*A*S*H*": Smithsonian (1997), p. 41.

65 "I used to say": McPartland, 1972, p. 109. Amid all this air traffic, Jimmy somehow managed to find time to record. On May 1, the cornetist went into a Brussels studio with clarinetist Tony Barbero and pianist Charles Patrick, with whom he had been jamming earlier, plus alto saxophonist Johnny Savira, bassist Johnny McKenna, and drummer Tommy Hubbard. Billed as Jimmy McPartland and His V Corps Sextette, they recorded "Basin Street Blues," "Georgia on My Mind," "Jazz Me Blues," and "Blues." The sides were not released commercially, but Jimmy gave Marian copies of the resulting two 78 records.

68 "I was flabbergasted": Smithsonian Institution (1997), p. 47.

68 "It was silly advice . . . just so in love with him": Notes for Jimmy McPartland essay, MMPA.

68 "How do you like the pictures": Marian McPartland to Janet Turner, letter, May 23, 1945, MMPA.

69 "I was like something blown about": In *Writing a Woman's Life,* Carolyn Heilbrun says the two most vigorously prohibited prerogatives for women in pre-feminist days were ambition and anger. Female autobiographies typically exploited—as does Marian in her claim to have been "blown about by the wind"—just such a "rhetoric of uncertainty," avoiding "an open admission of the desire for power and control over one's life" (Heilbrun, p. 23).

70 "Some people think": Smithsonian Institution (1997), p. 25.

71 "I am afraid I'm not": Jimmy McPartland to Frank Turner, letter, April 29, 1946, MMPA.

71 "He had the drinking thing . . . polite": Smithsonian Institution (1997), p. 42.

72 "Visiting Marian's parents": Balliett, 1973.

72 Vic Lewis recording: These recordings were not released until 1986. Some of the sidemen on the session—bassist Ken Batchelder, pianist Jerry Schwartz, and drummer Tony Vitale—were Americans who had been playing in the Army Air Force Band in London. Batchelder, who would later work with Marian and Jimmy in the States, married New York vocalist Gracie Scott, who had been working with Jimmy in USO shows. Scott sings a mannered version of "Sweet Lorraine" on the session.

73 "Barnstorming the British Isles": *Down Beat,* February 11, 1946. It's not clear if Marian and Jimmy returned to the continent in December or if they stayed in England through the holiday season. It's quite possible they stayed, even doing some shows in England with Celeste Holm. A *Melody Maker* article from October 12, 1946, says they were in England "last Christmas" and that while they were there, they were in "camp shows" that season.

73 "Statue of Liberty . . . in my life": Townsend material, MMPA.

Chapter Four: Jimmy: "I Like You, Kid"
76 "But he paid me": Balliett, 1977.

76 "I really felt left alone": McPartland (1972), p. 11.

77 "a sleepy-time neighborhood": Mezzrow, in Kenney, p. 95.

77 "Everybody flipped": Max Jones, p. 152. Dick McPartland told this tale somewhat differently, saying Bud Freeman, who had dropped out of school to work at Sears, Roebuck, spent his first paycheck on the New Orleans Rhythm Kings' "Panama," backed with "Tiger Rag," and shared it with his pals.

78 "We were ruffians": Jimmy McPartland, interview by Squirrel Ashcraft, 1966.

78 Dave Tough and jazz as antibourgeois art music: It's important to understand that for the black musicians these white youngsters admired, jazz held no so such meanings. Far from being an act of rebellion against middle-class values, jazz was often a way of accessing respectability and a dependable income in a world that barred African Americans from almost every trade.

79 "It was hypnosis": Condon, p. 107.

80 "We knew that we were hearing": Freeman, p. 6.

80 Jimmy's friendship with Armstrong: McPartland often told an entertaining—but possibly apocryphal—story about picking up Armstrong in a new car he had bought, a Rio, and bringing him to his mother's house for dinner. Mezz Mezzrow, said Jimmy, had recently sailed for Paris, leaving behind a cigar box full of marijuana, and Jimmy had promised it to Louis, a lifelong marijuana smoker. When they got to the house, Jimmy's mother said, "My boys really think you are the greatest thing that ever lived. Won't you come in and have some tea?" "Tea" was a slang word for marijuana. Louis gave Mrs. McPartland a quizzical look. Just as Louis was about to answer, McPartland whispered to Armstrong, "She means hot Lipton's, Jack!"

80 Jimmy first hearing Beiderbecke: In the hundreds of interviews Jimmy and Marian McPartland gave over the years, they offered multiple versions of when Jimmy first heard Beiderbecke. Sometimes he said it was on a steamship crossing Lake Michigan, a gig that Goodman, but not McPartland, played in the summer of 1923. (Jimmy did work on Lake Michigan on a different boat that summer with bandleader Murph Podolsky.) McPartland specifically said in his interview for the Yale Oral History of American Music that he did not hear Beiderbecke in Chicago in those days. And in an interview with Nat Hentoff in the January 13, 1954, *Down Beat,* McPartland said, "The first time I heard him was by way of the Wolverine records on Gennett— 'Copenhagen,' 'Oh Baby,' Riverboat Shuffle,' and the others." These sides were recorded May 6, 1924. So in spite of the fact that Beiderbecke and McPartland were playing in Chicago in 1922 and 1923, sometimes with the same sidemen, they did not play together and had not heard each other play before McPartland's audition with the Wolverines in New York.

80 "I was always a cocky guy": McPartland (1985), p. 21.

80 "One day he passed": Freeman, p. 4.

81 Vic Moore recommendation: Jimmy was not the group's first choice. They had already asked the New Orleans Rhythm Kings' Paul Mares, Joseph "Sharkey" Bonano, and Fred Rollison. Mares turned them down, they rejected Bonano, and Rollison couldn't play the music.

82 Riverview Park: Many sources date this engagement in 1926 but Bill Kooker, curator of the Riverview Park Web site (www.riverviewparkdsm.com), confirms that the Wolverines first played Riverview in the summer of 1925.

83 Maurice Ravel at the Nest: Other raconteurs have included Louis Armstrong in this gathering at the Nest, but no sources back this up. Jimmy did say that when Ravel heard Jimmy Noone, he tried to notate what the clarinetist was doing but eventually gave up, saying, "Impossible!"

83 "the air would play it": Condon, p. 133.

83 "It really got me floating": Stegner, MMPA. This quote and many that follow come from an unpublished biography of Jimmy written c. 1946 by Bentley Stegner, a *Chicago Sun-Times* reporter. Stegner came from the hard-boiled, if sentimental city desk school, but his careful research, in-depth interviews, and familiarity with Chicago resulted in what is probably the most accurate record extant of McPartland's early life, particularly since Jimmy himself so often embellished his stories. (He once told a reporter in Peru, Illinois, that he had met Marian "in a foxhole.")

83 "I happened to know": Max Jones, 160.

84 New version of the Wolverines: Voynow's October 12, 1927, recording session billed the band as the Original Wolverines and featured "Royal Garden Blues," "Shim-Me-Sha-Wabble," "A Good Man Is Hard to Find," and "The New Twister."

85 "These players are young men": Sudhalter (1999), p. 202.

86 Jimmy's courtship of Dorothy: Stegner.

87 "It meant starting": Max Jones, p. 164.

87 Jimmy's freelance recording sessions in New York: One of the highlights of these recordings is the revelation of just how good Benny Goodman was as a young man. "Jungle Blues" featured his only recorded cornet solo. Another amusing point of interest is that "Shirt Tail Stomp" was played as a purposely corny send-up in reaction to a producer's complaint that these young jazz musicians were too esoteric. It wound up being more popular than most of the other sides they recorded.

87 "soft-centered. . . . more aggressive": Sudhalter (1999), p. 203.

88 Broadway pit work: Many jazz musicians waited out the Depression working in Broadway shows. Pee Wee Russell played in *Strike Up the Band* by the Gershwins; Glenn Miller and Benny Goodman were also in the pit orchestra.

88 Wedding to Dorothy: There is no reason to doubt Bentley Stegner's assertion in his unpublished biography of Jimmy McPartland that Jimmy and Dorothy Williams married in New York in February 1930. But no public record of their marriage exists on file with the city of New York or with the city of Scranton, Pennsylvania, Dorothy's hometown. Nor does a marriage certificate survive in Jimmy's papers. It's possible the couple married in Nassau County on Long Island, in Connecticut, New Jersey, or perhaps in upstate New York.

89 *Crazy Quilt*: Coincidentally, the bandleader Marian first sat in with in London, Carroll Gibbons, cowrote the music for this show, with Harry Warren and Richard Rodgers.

89 "He was all run down and miserable": Max Jones, p. 166.

89 "I had a nervous breakdown": Ashcraft.

90 Triangle Jazz Band: This group recorded for Columbia in 1926, 1927, and 1928. Ashcraft played accordion.

90 Concert at the Pershing Hotel: Jimmy's band featured two musicians from the Ted Weems band—Rosy McHargue (clarinet) and Country Ashburn (bass)—as well as Jimmy's brother Dick (guitar), Jack Gardner (piano), and George Wettling (drums).

91 *The Chicago Jazz Album*: This landmark project was the first jazz album of original material ever released and also featured the first extensive liner note written for a jazz album. (Reissue sets of Beiderbecke and Bessie Smith, part of the new mania for old jazz, had preceded them.) For his own band, Jimmy chose his brother Dick; his brother-in-law Jim Lanigan, who by this time had "gone legit" with the Chicago Symphony; Teschemacher disciple Bud Jacobson on clarinet; a sensitive, nearly blind young alto saxophonist named Boyce Brown, who later entered a monastery and became Brother Matthew; and two musicians Jimmy was working with locally, trombonist Floyd Bean and drummer Hank Isaacs. The other musicians on the album were Jess Stacy and Joe Sullivan (piano), Bud Freeman and Joe Marsala (saxophone), Danny Polo and Pee Wee Russell (clarinet), Max Kaminsky and Charlie Teagarden (trumpet), Floyd O'Brien (trombone), Dave Tough and George Wettling (drums), Clyde Newcomb and Artie Shapiro (bass), Jack Bland and Eddie Condon (guitar), and Brad Gowans (valve trombone).

93 "Jimmy Darling": Dorothy McPartland to Jimmy McPartland, letter, January 28, 1937.

94 "The Chicago jazz style": *Time* magazine, July 21, 1941.

95 "not one of the Austin High Gang": *Chicago Tribune*, June 19, 1942.

95 "How are you going to win the war": Max Jones, p. 168.

96 "It was so quiet in this bay": Jimmy McPartland (1972), p. 76.

96 "like pesky insects": Barry Ulanov, "A Classical Jazz Story," *Metronome,* February, 1954.

97 "A lot of guys got it": Jimmy McPartland (1985), p. 98.

97 "My fingers were sticking": Irving Townsend material, MMPA.

98 "I'll never forget": Stegner, MMPA.

98 "I was thrilled": Schomburg.

98 Visiting Dorothy in New York: Little Dorothy was now fifteen and had not seen her father in three years. Marian said in a 1975 letter to Irving Townsend that Dorothy was living at that time with her mother on West Sixty-fifth Street, which suggests that Marian may have met her there, but neither Jimmy nor Marian ever mentioned her in connection with their 1946 visit. If Little Dorothy had been in New York, one would think Marian might have shown some interest in meeting her new stepdaughter. Given Jimmy's track record as a father, however, it's most likely he simply wanted to let his ex-wife know that his prewar vow about getting back together was now moot.

99 "He wasn't very bright": Telephone conversation with author, January 19, 2011.

99 "I just got out of the Army": Marian McPartland, notes for essay on Jimmy, MMPA.

Chapter Five: Windy City Apprentice

101 "It was not a nice thing to do": Jimmy McPartland (1972), p. 112.

102 "Jimmy always talked about 'relaxing'" : Irving Townsend material, MMPA.

102 "I was thrilled": Smithsonian Institution (1997), p. 46.

103 "Jimmy would very proudly": Ibid, p. 45.

103 Rose Bowl personnel: Jimmy's combo also included drummer Lou Finnerty, who had been working around Chicago throughout the 1940s. He was replaced by Chick Evans, who would go on to develop and market the first synthetic drumheads.

103 Django Reinhardt: According to Carlton's son Jim and Chicago guitarist Andy Nelson, at the club where Django saw Wiggins, Carlton and Nelson told an unsuspecting female bartender that the proper way to greet a Frenchman was to say, "*Voulez-vous couchez avec moi?*" At the end of the night, Reinhardt had to be dragged out, crying, "No, no, the lady wants me!"

103 "playing the greatest trumpet": *Down Beat*, February 26, 1947.

104 "People started to notice me": Maher material, MMPA.

104 chord voicings for *Down Beat*: *Down Beat,* June 4, 1947. The voicings Marian wrote out were surprisingly muddy. Marian later confessed she had asked someone else to write them and that she probably would not have played the chords as written.

106 "I drank down a pint": Maher, MMPA.

106 "It was five A.M.": Townsend, MMPA.

107 "I wanted to keep": Maher, MMPA.

107 "My mother's dire prediction": Notes for Jimmy essay, MMPA.

107 Decision to go back to England: Marian might well have considered going home even if her sister hadn't come to Chicago and/or Jimmy hadn't been an alcoholic. Having been in the States just over a year, Marian was undoubtedly experiencing culture shock as well as the depression common to new immigrants. Because of our historical connection to England and a common language, Americans often underestimate the profound cultural differences between the two countries. But as Jenel Virden's study of English war brides, "Good-bye Piccadilly," points out, "Assimilation is as traumatic for British immigrants as for any other immigrant group. The fact is that the overwhelming majority of British war brides see themselves as hyphenated Americans."

107 "Let his sister": Marian McPartland interview by Kathy Hart, October 20, 2006.

108 "it was obvious": Maher, MMPA.

108 "sit there by some lake": Balliett, 1973.

108 Squirrel Ashcraft: At one point, according to the February 27, 1947, *Down Beat*, Jimmy and Marian also made a trip to Squirrel's together, to record. Interestingly, Jack LeMaire, the guitarist who had emceed Marian's USO show in Germany, was on the date. The tapes were not issued.

108 "He went to Wisconsin": Maher, MMPA.

108 Jimmy's sober periods: Marian says Jimmy may have stayed sober for as long as six months running, but anecdotes from Jimmy's acquaintances and colleagues suggest he drank on the road when she wasn't around.

108 "Joyce sailed home": When Joyce got back to England, she lived for several months with Doris Mackie, Marian's old elocution teacher from Stratford House. Mac helped Joyce have the baby in secret. Joyce's daughter, Sheila, was born December 29, 1947. For the next three months, whenever she visited her parents, Joyce stuffed a pillow up under her dress, pretending she was still pregnant, so her parents wouldn't know she had gotten pregnant before she and Tony were married. For years, no one in the family but Marian knew. After the truth finally came out, it became a treasured and amusing family story, rather than the moral embarrassment it might have felt like in an earlier era. "I thought I was born the fourth of March, 1948," said Sheila, laughing, in 2009. "When I was thirteen and had to get my own passport, I asked my mother. That's when they told me." Joyce never did know if her father found out. Though getting pregnant before marriage was shocking to upper-middle-class folks, in the working class and titled upper class, it was quite common. "In 1938–39 no less than 42 percent of women under 20 were pregnant at marriage" (McKibbin, p. 297).

109 "just plain bossy": Maher, MMPA.

110 Lennie Tristano: Tristano, who would help spawn "cool jazz," left Chicago for New York just about the time Marian and Jimmy arrived, but they heard him live when he came back to play Symphony Hall.

110 "Jazz education consisted": G. Shaw, p. 698.

110 Joe Glaser: Glaser was a rough character, but Marian found ways to charm him. She often asked him for the stamps from Louis Armstrong's letters from around the world to give to kids in the McPartland clan.

110 "She would start a tune": *Cadence,* May 2003.

111 "His main thing": Scott Black to Marian McPartland, letter, n.d., MMPA.

111 "The first time I tried this": Maher, MMPA.

112 "shocked to have it come": *Chicago Sun-Times,* June 10, 1948.

113 "away from home and not knowing anyone": Ben Carlton, journal, 1948–49, unpublished, courtesy of Jim Carlton.

114 "She had a soft spot for him": Townsend, MMPA.

114 Dave Tough Blindfold Test: *Down Beat,* December 1946.

115 "There are only": *Chicago News,* July 28, 1948.

115 "Easy now, Marian": Marian McPartland interviewed by Studs Terkel, WFMT 98.7, May 1982. Chicago History Museum.

115 "Marian, there's nothing I can do": Maher, MMPA.

115 Early history of the Blue Note and Billie Holiday at the club: Recollections of Blue Note owner Frank Holzfiend, *Chicago Tribune,* December 15, 1974.

118 "I am having a ball": Jimmy McPartland to Ben Carlton, letter, June 7, 1949.

118 "required minimal editing": According to her editor at the time, Dan Morgenstern (interview with author).

120 "Dearest Dorie": Dorothy Kassel to Marian McPartland, letter, October 10, 1949, courtesy of Doug Kassel.

121 Recordings with Red Norvo: Guitarist George Barnes, bassist Kenny Buchanan, and drummer Mousie Alexander played on this November 9, 1949, session. The recording executive who refused to release the tapes was Bill Putnam, who would later become an innovative studio legend at his company, Universal Audio. The tapes were never issued and have apparently been lost. Ditto for four sides waxed December 7, 1949, with Mousie Alexander, Ben Carlton, and the excellent Chicago guitarist Fred Rundquist, who was working with accordion player Art Van Damme.

121 Date of move to New York: Exactly when Marian and Jimmy moved to New York is a jumble of conflicting information. Most sources—including Marian, in her own book—give the year as 1949, but this is clearly wrong, as Marian and Jimmy were playing regularly in Chicago throughout the first half of 1950. Marian has always said that on the way to New York they stopped in Philadelphia, where they played October 4, 1950, with the great clarinetist Omer Simeon at the Rendezvous. That would put the move in October 1950. However, Jimmy's name had already started to show up at the New York Dixieland hall, the Stuyvesant Casino, a month earlier, in September 1950. To make matters more confusing, Marian said that when the couple played opposite Sarah Vaughan at the Blue Note, in Chicago, on June 1, 1950, they had already moved to New York. But she told Leonard Feather in a July 1, 1951, article for *Down Beat* that she and Jimmy had made the decision to move to New York "last February," while playing at the Colonial Tavern in Toronto (they did indeed play at the Colonial that February). However, Jimmy was playing regularly at the Stuyvesant Casino throughout the fall of 1950, including a December 30, 1950, date listed in *The New Yorker* magazine. Given Marian's vivid recollection of strolling down the boardwalk in Long Beach on Christmas Day, 1950 and the confirmed date of their appearance with Simeon in Philadelphia, it's a safe bet that the couple moved to Long Beach sometime around October 1950.

Chapter Six: Getting to First Base with Three Strikes

124 "I'd heard that Bud Freeman": Smithsonian Institution (1997), p. 80.

124 Marian playing with Jimmy: Such eclecticism was not uncommon in the 1950s. Lots of modernists still played traditional jazz from time to time. Even pianist Billy

Taylor, a modernist, remembered playing with Jimmy McPartland (interview with author, 2009).

124 Jack Crystal: Jack Crystal also lived in Long Beach, a famously Jewish enclave, where he was raising a family that included his son, Billy, who would later become the well-known wisecracking comedian and advocate for jazz.

125 "the best drummer you ever worked with": Bob Hammer, interview with author. Vibes player Hammer added: "I loved George Wettling. George was a very funny guy. He was a great natural primitive painter in the line of Grandma Moses. He was quite a wit. He said he always wanted to make an album called *Suite for Swinging Nuns, I'd Like to Get in the Habit with You, You're Telling Your Beads More Than You're Telling Me,* or *Rock Around the Cross.*"

125 "whiskey out of a bottle": Smithsonian Institution (1997), p. 54.

125 Prestige recordings: Marian said these recordings were made in Boston, but the Prestige discography and the Tom Lord discography both say they were made in Chicago. Marian implied in some interviews that the session was intended for release on Unison but later licensed to Prestige. This would make sense, since the first four Unison sides were licensed to Prestige, as well, and the rights to those and the subsequent Prestige recordings reverted to McPartland and were ultimately released by McPartland on her own label, Halcyon. However, since Marian was in Boston around the time of the recordings, it would appear that the session indeed took place there, not in Chicago.

126 Hank Harding: Unidentified newspaper clip, Columbus, Ohio, October 29, 1989, MMPA.

126 "Someone with a Chopin complex": Unidentified newspaper clipping, signed L.E.L., MMPA.

127 Bob Carter: Carter, who was of Hawaiian extraction and whose given name was Robert Kahakalau, had been working in New York with Dizzy Gillespie, Charlie Parker, Dexter Gordon, and other topflight boppers since 1945. When he came into Marian's trio, Carter had been recording with accordionist Joe Mooney and guitarist Johnny Smith. Carter relocated to Honolulu in the 1950s and began working with Hawaiian bands as well as groups that played in styles from Japan, Korea, and the Philippines.

128 Ulanov review: *Metronome,* August 1951.

129 "I never went through": Townsend, MMPA.

129 "I used to be a nervous wreck": Smithsonian (1997), p. 48.

129 "I was quite nervous. . . . a favor": Notes and sketches, MMPA.

129 "flirting with the audience": Shipton, *Handful of Keys,* p. 116.

129 Piano trio instrumentation: The first trio recording featuring piano, bass, and drums was made in 1935 by Jess Stacy; Mary Lou Williams also recorded several sides with piano, bass, and drums in 1938. Drummer Lee Young, Lester's brother, said that the piano, bass, and guitar format adopted by Nat Cole in 1939 was determined by a practical circumstance, when a club they were playing cramped his drum set so badly that Lee quit. Cole continued with the guitar functioning in the rhythm role in place of the drums. Notwithstanding these early examples, the piano trio did not catch on as a popular format—with guitar or drums—until 1944–1945, when Erroll Garner began to record and perform regularly with a drummer and Cole's trio spawned imitators in cocktail lounges all over America. Bud Powell recorded bebop piano with bass and drums in 1947; Oscar Peterson continued the guitar line of the trio well into the 1950s. Gradually, the piano-bass-drums format won out as the standard form, probably for its greater flexibility.

129 "The only person I, as a trio pianist": *Record Whirl,* February 1956.

130 "Hiring and firing": Jimmy wasn't kidding. When that same bass player turned up on an afternoon gig with Jimmy and Marian, he lasted ten minutes. Jimmy said, "Take your fucking bass and get the fuck out of here" (Enstice and Stockhouse, p. 239).

130 "I know I was a pretty inept": Townsend, MMPA.

130 "Gal handles the 88": *Variety,* May 16, 1951.

130 Savoy recordings: Though she was paid a flat fee for the sessions, McPartland says she never received a penny of royalties—not unusual for the era. Her lawyer once tried to sue, but finding all the old documents proved too cumbersome to be worth the trouble.

131 "Three hopeless strikes": *Down Beat,* July 13, 1951.

131 *Down Beat* photos: The only other photograph on the page featured guitarist Perry Botkin, fully clothed, holding a lute, apparently having had his hair and makeup done earlier.

132 "Nobody spoke to me": Smithsonian Institution (1997), p. 59.

133 "Six months ago": *Down Beat,* July 2, 1952.

134 "I was pleased to be written about": Enstice and Stockhouse, p. 243.

134 "I know any number of": New York *Daily News,* July 19, 1952.

135 "male chauvinism": *Down Beat,* December 3, 1952. A survey of *The New York Times* by Jane Mansbridge and Katherine Flaster discovered the first use of this term in that newspaper in a 1934 book review by John Chamberlain. It was also used, they report, in Clifford Odets's 1935 play, *Till the Day I Die.* The authors note, however, that between 1935 and 1968 the paper used the term "male chauvinism" in less than one article every three years, so Hentoff was clearly in the vanguard. ("*Male Chauvinist, Feminist, Sexist,* and *Sexual Harassment*: Trajectories in Feminist Linguistic Innovation," *American Speech,* Fall 2005, p. 261.)

135 "playing second fiddle . . . catch up": Townsend, MMPA.

136 Le Down Beat club: Not to be confused with the Down Beat, which closed in the 1940s.

137 Garroway comments: MMPA.

138 "The food was terrific": McPartland (1987), p. 21.

138 "Broadway pinball parlor": Marian McPartland and Irving Townsend, "The Story of a Lady in Jazz," MMPA.

139 "At times I felt like": McPartland (1987), p. 20.

139 "John would bet you": Arnold Shaw, p. 142.

139 "When he was feeling good": Ibid, p. 166.

140 "The whole family": McPartland (1987), p. 22.

140 *Guys and Dolls*: Hajdu, David, *Lush Life,* New York: Farrar, Straus and Giroux, 1996, p. 166.

140 Joe Morgen's publicity plants: One of Morgen's fake stories claimed Marian and Jimmy were writing the score for a new Bing Crosby film. This and many other squibs he wrote have been repeated as gospel in writings about McPartland.

140 "Tallulah Bankhead": *Daily Mirror,* March 20, 1952.

141 "He had so much sex appeal": Marian McPartland, draft of essay about Duke Ellington, June 1974, MMPA.

141 "You play so many": Smithsonian Institution (1997), p. 57.

141 "Wig-flipping rhythm": *Time* magazine, June 2, 1952.

142 "sober up in the bathtub": The bassist was Wyatt Ruther.

143 "In spite of the defective keys": Paudras, pp. 3–4. Francis Paudras, in *Dance of the Infidels*, and Clare Hansson, in her Ph.D., imply that McPartland's visit to Bud Powell took place in the 1940s. Powell was indeed at Creedmoor from November 1947 to October 1948. But Marian was living and working steadily in Chicago at that time, and while she may have stopped to see Powell on her way to England in the spring of 1948, it seems more likely that she visited him at Creedmoor in January or February 1953, particularly in light of Powell's question about whether people had forgotten him. (In 1948, hardly anybody outside the hippest jazz circles knew who he was, so they could hardly have "forgotten" him.) Powell's playing was not central to McPartland in 1948, nor did she mention visiting Powell to reporters when she got back to Chicago from England. Paudras is no help on this score, as he elides events that happened in 1945 with ones that happened in the early 1950s, which may have led Hansson astray. According to Alyn Shipton's biography of Powell, the pianist was sent to Pilgrim State Hospital, a mental institution on Long Island, in September 1952, was released for 2 one-night passes to see how he would deal with an upcoming residency at Birdland, and then, when he did well, was sent to Creedmoor until February 5, 1953, when he was released. This is more likely the window in which McPartland visited him there.

144 Bud Powell recordings with Marian: South Carolina Educational Television, which produces *Piano Jazz,* dated the reel-to-reel tape from this session as September 21, 1951, a date that presumably came from McPartland. However, Shipton writes that Powell was arrested in June 1951 and *Down Beat* reported that Powell was "in an asylum" in October 1951, so the 1951 date seems unlikely. The tapes also feature trio performances by Powell, Ed Thigpen, and bassist John Orr. In a letter to McPartland (MMPA), Thigpen recalled the year as 1955. Thigpen also says it was his friend Dee Dee Emerson, Fairchild's secretary, who invited Thigpen to play with Powell.

144 "He looked more like a chemist": McPartland and Townsend, MMPA.

145 "With a good drummer": Ibid.

145 "Within a matter of seconds": *Down Beat,* March 3, 1960.

145 "They would play against the beat": McPartland (1987), p. 26.

146 *The Magnificent Marian McPartland at the Piano*: Both the Savoy and Tom Lord discographies date this session as December 12, 1952. Since Marian left for England December 8, this is clearly an error. Savoy and Lord also list an additional session for Savoy on December 22, 1952. Both sessions were probably done earlier in the year.

146 *Time* magazine record review: *Time* magazine, May 18, 1953.

147 New jazz history: Ulanov, p. 325.

147 "That's where I really got started": Knauss, MMPA.

147 Fred Reynolds review of *The Magnificent Marian McPartland*, *Chicago Tribune*, April 13, 1953.

Chapter Seven: New York's Golden Age of Jazz, Part I

150 "Respectability has indeed come": *Mayfair,* April 1956.

151 "I remember once I was driving": *Vintage Drummer*, n.d., MMPA.

151 "really wild, drunk": Smithsonian Institution (1997), p. 52.

151 "He was a jerk": Jim Maher material, MMPA. Had she asked around, Marian might have discovered that stories about Vinnie Burke were legion in the New York jazz community. He was a notorious "tempo Nazi," refusing to slow down or speed up if anyone dragged or rushed. According to bassist Ed Fuqua, while playing with pianist John Mehegan (an inveterate rusher) Burke decided that instead of "holding the fort," he would let Mehegan fly into oblivion. "Every time Mehegan would push the tempo, Vinnie would push it even more," remembered Fuqua. "By the time they got to the head out, it's getting too fast for Mehegan to play, so he turns over his shoulder and hisses sternly 'You're rushing!' To which Vinnie, with a huge grin plastered on his face, replies, 'Yeah. How do you like it?'" (http://www.talkbass .com/forum/f29/vinnie-burke-192762/). According to Crow, Burke was into yoga and would sometimes go into a trance—on the gig.

152 "enthusiasm, optimism and mischief": Marc Myers, "JazzWax" blog, www .jazzwax.com.

152 "It's so realistic": *New York Herald Tribune*, February 24, 1954.

153 "He would always have these terrible excuses": *Vintage Drummer*, n.d., MMPA.

154 "When his foot came down": Crow (1992), p. 118.

154 "the chicken": Many years later, when McPartland reconvened the trio for an episode of *Piano Jazz*, she asked Morello to play "the chicken" to see if she might not, after all these years, finally be able to get it right. She and Joe and Bill broke up into hysterical laugher when, indeed, she still missed the "one" (though she probably was faking it).

155 "Did I do anything bad last night?": Maher, MMPA.

155 Scandalizing the Dysons: Marian delighted in scandalizing the stuffy Windsor side of the family and would often send black musician friends to say hello at the shop on Thames Street.

155 "The waiters thought": Townsend, MMPA.

157 "I just played a couple of tunes": Conversation with author, May 15, 2009.

157 Nat Hentoff review: *Down Beat,* April 1954.

157 Bud Powell and Art Tatum: Art Tatum was reported to have made his own commentary on the Powell approach one night at Birdland. Performing with Charlie Parker, Tatum played the whole set sitting on his left hand.

157 Metropole: Veterans of this bandstand said the only way to keep good time was to watch the drummer in the mirror on the wall because you couldn't see the rhythm section and there was so much noise the sound echoed and bounced everywhere. Sometimes, reported Nat Hentoff, musicians at one end of the "stage" communicated with those at the other by semaphore. Jimmy started a long stint there in March 1954 with Bud Freeman and later traded sets with Henry "Red" Allen.

157 "They marched around the bar": Townsend, MMPA.

158 *Jazz Dance* review: *The New York Times,* September 21, 1954.

158 "We were both working": Townsend material, MMPA.

159 "That was sort of a shocker": McPartland and Townsend, MMPA.

159 "This was when the rot set in": Maher, MMPA.

160 Cello and harp parts: George Koutzen, who played the cello parts, was a member of the NBC Orchestra and had recorded with Lee Wiley and Charles Mingus.

161 George T. Simon review: *Metronome,* August 1954.

161 "as a wedge": *Record Whirl*, February 1956.

161 *After Dark* review, *Billboard*, April 14, 1956.

162 Doug Watt article: *The New Yorker*, November 20, 1954.

162 Charlie's Tavern, musicians' hangouts: According to bassist and later talent manager John Levy, "The studio musicians and players, the white musicians, used to go to Charlie's, next to the Ed Sullivan Theater, which was on Fifty-second Street and Broadway. The black musicians would hang out at the White Rose a couple of blocks away on Fifty-second Street and Sixth Avenue." Other musicians' hangouts, according to vibes player Bob Hammer, who worked with Bill Britto, included Junior's, at Fifty-second Street; Joe Harbor's Spotlite on Broadway; Jim and Andy's, Beefsteak Charlie's (primarily black); and the Copper Rail, across the street from the Metropole.

163 "He said I was like Carole Lombard": Notes and sketches, MMPA.

163 "At first it was a kind of": Maher, MMPA.

164 "One of his characteristics": Townsend, MMPA.

164 Bix's horn: Doug Kassel recalled that the bell of this horn "was all battered up so it obviously couldn't be played anymore. The story I heard was that my actual grandmother, Dorothy Williams, got into a fight with Jimmy and took the horn into the bathroom and beat the horn on the floor and the sink" (interview with author).

166 "I enjoyed the playing": Maher, MMPA.

166 "Ecstasy . . . worth it.": Notes and sketches, MMPA.

169 Margaret Jones: Jones does not appear to have published any other songs. She died in the 1990s.

169 Marian's complaints about Jimmy: *Record Mirror,* August 18, 1956.

169 Interview with Max Jones: *Melody Maker,* September 1, 1956.

Chapter Eight: New York's Golden Age of Jazz, Part II

171 "I never dreamed . . . Gee . . . out of the whole world": Maher, MMPA.

171 "My last week with Joe": Diary, 1956, MMPA.

172 "Oh, you don't have to tell me": Maher, MMPA.

172 "He had a nice": Ibid.

172 "I was really hurting inside . . . continuing the affair . . . where Brubeck was": Maher, MMPA.

173 "Part of me clings": Diary, 1957, MMPA.

174 "There were periods": Maher, MMPA.

175 "Jimmy always said . . . I kind of let it go.": Maher, MMPA.

175 "Gone was the slightly bored": McPartland (1959), p. 57.

177 "I'd rather feel that I'm": Smithsonian Institution (1997), p. 141.

177 "With one voice": Ibid,. p. 85.

178 "I wasn't a hot property": Maher, MMPA.

178 "takes Miss McPartland further": *Billboard*, October 28, 1957.

179 Mehegan article: The Mehegan article on Brubeck appeared in *Down Beat,* June 27, 1957. Marian's response in the letters column appeared July 25. In that same issue, Billy Taylor complained in a letter of his own about what he considered to be another Mehegan writing gaffe, in which Mehegan had called Taylor an "[Oscar] Peterson–style pianist." Mehegan played intermission piano for Taylor at the Composer, a room where Marian would soon be working. Had Mehegan really been listening? asked Taylor.

180 The Composer: The Composer was coincidentally co-owned by a man named Willie Shore, who, according to Marian, was not the same Willie Shore who was the vaudeville comedian she had worked with more than a decade earlier on the continental front. The more high-profile partner at the Composer was Cy Baron, a Fifty-second Street veteran who had run the Onyx Club and for whom Marian had named Bill Britto's tune "The Baron." Marian's trio at the Composer included Bill Crow (bass) and Dick Scott (drums), about whom little is known.

180 Dom Cerulli article in *Down Beat*: Marian's photo had appeared on the cover of *Down Beat* before, for the July 13, 1951, feature titled "Girls in Jazz." But the September 5, 1957, issue was her first bona fide cover story. The two-part article was curiously played, however. The first installment was very short, thanks, apparently, to yet another story about Brubeck, who had been featured in a cover story just two months before.

182 "I've never had a home": *New York Mirror,* June 29, 1958.

182 "There were good times": Notes and sketches, MMPA.

185 Q & A: *Down Beat* 24, November 28, 1957.

185 "Clean and Cool": *Newsweek,* December 30, 1957.

186 Blindfold Test: *Down Beat,* April 18, 1952.

186 "It was a dumb thing to do": Smithsonian Institution (1997), p. 58.

187 "This lesser known group": *Christian Science Monitor,* July 8, 1958.

187 A Cold War note: *Providence Journal,* July 4, 1958.

188 "I hadn't seen Mary Lou": *Newsday,* April 6, 1995.

Chapter Nine: Loss

192 "He wanted to marry me": Maher, MMPA.

193 "Sweet and Lovely" harmony: Marian reversed the song's ordinary-sounding pattern of G-minor seventh to C seventh, changing it to C seventh to G seventh, adding a thirteenth to the C and a raised ninth to the G.

193 "So Many Things": Morello would shortly record the tune himself with vibra- phonist Gary Burton on Burton's debut LP, *New Vibe Man in Town,* a version that actually highlighted the melody better than Marian's did.

194 Sinatra and Norvo: This remarkable ensemble made one of the finest albums Sinatra ever recorded, the posthumously released *Frank Sinatra with the Red Norvo Quintet: Live in Australia, 1959* (Blue Note).

194 "Jazz demands a strong, aggressive": Photocopied excerpt of UPI clip, June 20, 1961, MMPA.

194 "Can't we women": McPartland (1959), p. 59.

195 "I don't want a woman pianist": *New York Journal American,* 1959, in Hansson (2006).

195 "still something or other": *Melody Maker,* August 8, 1959.

196 "You can't get a decent kipper here": *Down Beat,* March 19, 1959.

196 "Somebody told me": Smithsonian Institution (1997), p. 126.

197 "Dizzy, wearing bathing trunks": Crow (1990), pp. 142–43.

198 First West Coast gig: The pianist had been to the San Francisco Bay Area once before, where she had played in a restaurant in the sunbaked suburb of Walnut Creek, east of the Berkeley hills, where she had probably been visiting Doris Mackie at Doris's son's house. But the Blackhawk was her first West Coast gig in a well-known club.

198 "There is an easy flow": *Down Beat*, October 10, 1963.

198 Warne Marsh: Ben Tucker appeared on Marsh's legendary *Jazz of Two Cities* LP.

199 Frank Kofsky review, "bland": *Down Beat,* February 2, 1961.

199 "Comin' Home, Baby": Tucker once estimated the song had earned him nearly $100,000 a year.

200 Royalties: Other record companies apparently stiffed McPartland, as well. In 2004, she received $3,079 in a New York State settlement that awarded $50 million to artists in unpaid royalties.

200 "Some people have an insatiable": Unpublished interview about jazz education, MMPA.

201 *Jimmy and Marian McPartland Play TV Themes*: The album bore little relevance to Marian's development as a modern pianist, save for her feature on a lovely ballad, the theme from another detective show, *Mr. Lucky*. Jimmy played with sparkling buoyancy throughout and Ben Tucker and Mousie Alexander rolled with a solid groove. The subtle arrangements probably came from the pen of Dick Cary, who played mellophone on the album, though the arranging credits said, "Aul Hedd," surely a pun on "all head" arrangements, meaning—facetiously—they were not written down. The tune choices were clever. They included "I-M-4-U" (the theme from *The Tonight Show*, hosted by Jack Paar, who would later walk off the set in a huff), and a barely recognizable version of the theme from *The Alfred Hitchcock Hour*, "Funeral March of a Marionette." Soloing was uniformly strong, including several trombone outings Marian says were played by none other than Jack Teagarden, though discographies credit Urbie Green.

201 "sporadic recordings" of the 1960s: Marian did make a record in January 1964 for a label called SESAC (Society of European Stage Authors and Composers) that has become a collector's item. SESAC today is a powerful player in music publishing that represents Bob Dylan and Neil Diamond. In the 1950s, however, it was a minor competitor to ASCAP and BMI, though it had a strong roster that included Duke Ellington and Coleman Hawkins. SESAC had recently begun an "electronic transcription" service of recordings delivered directly to radio stations but not sold in stores (hence their scarcity and later value to collectors). Marian's recording for the company, *She Swings with Strings* (SESAC N6501/2), was strictly cocktail mood fare. It featured arrangements (and conducting) by Frank Hunter, a guru of "exotica" who had also produced records by Carmen McRae and Johnny Hartman. Marian probably met Hunter through Bob Shad, who had also been involved in the "mood music" world. The rhythm section on the album was great, but the music was pretty awful— dumbed down and sweetened up. One high point was Phil Bodner's flute solo on the opener, "Y'Know What I Mean"—a medium finger-popper with a "Swingin' Shepherd Blues" feel. Two tunes were credited to Coleman Hawkins—"Hawk Talk" and "Lonely"—which made sense, since Hawkins was a sometime SESAC artist—but, overall, as reviewer David Badam wrote of a British reissue of the album on the Jazz Vault label, some seventeen years later, this was what the industry called "Eeeeasy Listening"—well played but nonetheless "flaccid and insipid." Needless to say, *She Swings with Strings* did McPartland's career no favors, though it probably did it no harm, either, since it's likely few people ever heard it.

201 "What Bill was doing": Interview with Studs Terkel, 98.7 WFMT, Chicago (1961), Chicago History Museum.

201 Bill Evans influence: McPartland has often been described inaccurately as a "Bill Evans disciple." However, jazz pianist and historian Lewis Porter points out that Marian's 1953 recording of "Laura" on Savoy employed complex harmonies such as a whole-tone transition after the first chorus, a G/C cadence interrupted by "a chromatic excursion up to A flat and D flat" and an eventual landing on a C chord with a ninth, raised eleventh, and sixth, "in effect a D chord superimposed on the C. "Recordings such as this reveal that McPartland was experimenting with modern harmonies before she, like most contemporary pianists, came under the influence of Bill Evans's early 1960s work" (*Music Educators Journal*, September 1984).

202 "La Roca and Swallow": *Cincinnati Post & Times-Star*, November 29, 1962.

203 "I'm interested in absorbing parts": *Cincinnati Post & Times-Star*, July 15, 1963.

203 Lack of recordings with Swallow and La Roca: Swallow recalled that he and La Roca and McPartland actually did record together for a background music service that may have been Muzak. Marian, in an undated transcribed interview in her files, confirmed the existence of these recordings, saying she sometimes took pleasure hearing them in airports, though she later denied they were made at all.

204 "I found him in another room . . . like that for free": Townsend, MMPA.

204 New York show with Goodman: Goodman's band featured Bobby Donaldson (drums), Gene Cherico (bass), Red Norvo (vibes), Jim Wyble (guitar), Modesto Briseno (saxophone), and Goodman himself.

204–05 "It was unnerving . . . hurt your feelings . . . that would be great.": Townsend, MMPA.

206 "I could no longer cope": Townsend, MMPA.

206 "a failure in life": Maher, MMPA.

206 "This was amazing to me": Townsend, MMPA.

207 "You have a way of": Ibid.

207 "I'd avoid talking about": Maher, MMPA.

207 "I went to see": Ibid.

208 "I was doing anything I could": Ibid.

208 "he looked like a rabbi": Notes and sketches, MMPA.

210 "Joe had been calling for days . . . that couldn't": Maher, MMPA.

210 "It's a good job": Conversation with author, April 24, 2009.

211 "Maggie dear": Joyce Armitage to Marian McPartland, letter, n.d., MMPA.

212 "She was the wittiest . . . perfectly.": Ted Turner to Marian McPartland, letter, December 20, 1964, MMPA.

212 "They say he writes a tune a day": *Melody Maker*, May 30, 1964.

Chapter Ten: Long Island Retreat

216 "buzzing back and forth": *Newsday*, November 28, 1964.

219 Benny Goodman article: *Down Beat*, April 9, 1964.

219 "Native costume": Program note, c. 1956, MMPA.

220 "I am amazed at her story . . . so many years": Toshiko Akiyoshi to author, letter, January 7, 2010.

221 "This was the start": Maher, MMPA.

221 Mary Lou Williams article: *Down Beat,* August 27, 1964.

222 Record reviews for *Down Beat*: Marian reviewed albums for *Down Beat* from March 24, 1966 (Earl Hines), to September 5, 1968 (Joe Zawinul).

222 *Intermodulation* review: *Down Beat,* November 17, 1966.

225 Archie Shepp review: *Down Beat,* April 21, 1966.

225 Last review for *Down Beat*: Marian may have misremembered the chain of events. Bassist Linc Milliman says it was an album by Dave Brubeck, not Coltrane, that put an end to her reviewing career. Recalled Milliman: "While I was working for her at the Apartment, she said, 'Linc, guess what? Dave Brubeck has asked me to review his latest album.' I said, 'Marian, what if you don't like it?' 'How can I not like it?' She came in a couple of nights later: 'I listened to the album. I absolutely hated it. What should I do?' 'That's easy, you lie. Pick out everything you like about it. The melodies, the liner notes, chords' . . . To this day [I don't know] if she wrote the review." In fact, Marian gave three stars to Brubeck's album *Time In* which may have been the disc in question. On the other hand, she obviously agonized over her review of the Shepp/Coltrane album, so a posthumous Coltrane album may just as easily have convinced her to stop reviewing.

225 Jerry Dodgion arrangement: In 1974, the Thad Jones/Mel Lewis Orchestra recorded Dodgion's arrangement of "Ambiance" on Thad Jones & Mel Lewis, *Potpourri* (Philadelphia International Records PIR KZ 33152).

226 "I had this slot open": In Marian's recollection, it was she who called Albertson, not the other way around. According to Billy Taylor, Marian had heard him on WLIB and was so "fascinated" by the visibility he got from the show, she decided she wanted to do radio, too.

227 "We'd have to play for cocktails": Smithsonian Institution (1997), p. 87.

227 "We called him Max the Mayor": Maher, MMPA.

228 "Marian's not just a fine": *World Journal Tribune,* October 6, 1966.

228 "All hail": *World Journal Tribune,* December 25, 1966.

228 "Sang and sang": *New York Post,* n.d., MMPA.

228 "Alec Wilder came prowling around": Notes and sketches, MMPA.

229 Don DeMichael review: *Down Beat,* July 25, 1968.

229 "Both of us wanted to be educated": Smithsonian Institution (1997), p. 79.

230 "I would say": Smithsonian Institution (1997), p. 78.

231 "I was so positive": Notes and sketches, MMPA.

231 "Dr. Benjamin asked": Maher, MMPA.

231–32 "I wanted to move . . . in the tube . . . I froze . . . either of us": Ibid.

233 "Dr. Benjamin asked . . . under my feet": Maher, MMPA.

233 "I never realized": Maher, MMPA.

234 "Analysis changed my life": Ibid.

Chapter Eleven: Lost . . . and Found

235 Hank O'Neal's Washington, D.C., parties: Marian and Jimmy played at one of O'Neal's parties in Washington, D.C., on May 1, 1966, while tape was running. It was later released in a limited edition as *More Informal Sessions No. 1*. The personnel included Tommy Gwaltney (clarinet), Squirrel Ashcraft (piano), Dick Barrett (guitar, vocal), Ski Arnold (beating guitar case), and Anne Read, Joyce Barrett, Jack Nevius, and Sheila Nevius (vocals).

235 Fairchild and sound reproduction: In the early 1930s, Fairchild started a small company called Fairchild Recording Products that, according to O'Neal, developed equipment superior to that of Ampex but failed because the gear was so expensive.

236 Dot Records: Dot's catalog included Lalo Schifrin's wildly popular theme for the TV show *Mission Impossible*, but its biggest success was with the vanilla crooning of Pat Boone.

237 *Interplay* review: *High Fidelity*, April 1970.

237 "should wish for": *CODA*, n.d., photocopy, MMPA.

238 "I feel like a kid again": Notes and sketches, MMPA.

238 "He taught me the fun": Ibid.

238 Title track of *Ambiance:* Marian wrote out the tune, with some suggested chord voicings, for the April 1971 edition of *Down Beat*.

239 "It looks as if": *Coda*, November/December 1971.

239 "To play a piano": Notes and sketches, MMPA.

241 "Marian's driving a yellow Pinto": *Newsday*, June 4, 1972.

242 "Should I have gone ahead?": Notes and sketches, MMPA.

242 "Gee, I feel . . . live with him": Maher, MMPA.

242 "Music takes up your": Notes and sketches, MMPA.

243 "I'm lonely": Ibid.

248 "I felt so sad": Arnold Shaw (1977), p. 169. History books generally cite 1968 as the year the Hickory House closed, with Billy Taylor on the stand. Taylor started his last week at the club December 23, 1967, but according to listings in *The New Yorker,* when the club closed in January 1968, Eddie Thompson was playing.

248 The Jazz Suite: The Jazz Suite closed after a year.

250 "I suppose you want to play . . . at the White House!": Maher, MMPA.

250 Alec Wilder's trust fund: Desmond Stone, in his biography, *Alec Wilder in Spite of Himself,* says Wilder burned through his trust fund by the late 1930s, at which point he went to work for CBS. However, it seems implausible that Wilder could afford to keep a room at the Algonquin his entire adult life without some sort of steady income. Tom Hampson, who probated Wilder's will, says Wilder lived on advances from the Richmond publishing house.

251 "In three unplanned minutes": Liner note, *A Delicate Balance* (Halcyon 105).

251 "I'm going to write a piece for you": McPartland (2005), p. ix.

251 "He often made gifts of his compositions": Wilder wrote dozens of pieces for specific people, including Clark Terry, Stan Getz, Zoot Sims, Gerry Mulligan, Bob Brookmeyer, and Roland Hanna.

251 "These poor American children": *Evening Star and Daily News*, March 12, 1973.

252 "not cut from common cloth": Stone, p. 63.

253 Correct grammar: Even in her nineties, Marian sometimes corrected herself midsentence if she said, for example, "slow" when the more adverbially correct "slowly" had been called for. She would then blame this "sloppiness" on having spent too much time in America! "For years, I thought the man's name was 'Lederman,'" she once said of TV talk show host David Letterman. "Why cahrn't Americans pronounce the letter T?"

253–54 1971 trip to Rochester: Marian took bassist Jay Leonhart and drummer Jimmy Madison to Rochester. At the workshop, Manny Albam put his stamp on Marian's ravishing new tune, *Willow Creek*, which she had begun to perform but would not record until much later. Student arrangers also presented a "Salute to Alec Wilder," which Wilder attended, graciously praising the youngsters on stage. On August 8 and 9, 1971, also with Leonhart and Madison, Marian recorded her second trio album for Halcyon, *A Delicate Balance*, which would appear the following year. By comparison with the first two, it was a disappointingly tepid affair that felt like backtracking after the forward thrust of the past two years. As she had on *Bossa Nova + Soul*, Marian played the Wurlitzer keyboard on some of the tracks and included several popular songs of the day, including "El Condor Pasa" and George Harrison's "Something." Her title tune was bland. McPartland played with compelling modernity, however, on Eddie Harris's "Freedom Jazz Dance," with Leonhart's bass lines adding a special splash. Her solo acoustic piano rendition of Billie Holiday's "God Bless the Child" was exquisite. The album also featured Marian's first recording of Wilder's "Jazz Waltz for a Friend," a tune as clever and ultimately compelling as she had described it. The trio gave it a bouncy, airy feel, with brushes, but the Wurlitzer sounded like it was on a "harp" effect that did not wear well with time. The album got so-so reviews.

255 "Dear Marian, in the event": Alec Wilder to Marian McPartland, letter (MMPA, courtesy of Alec Wilder Estate), n.d.

256 "It was a very dull gig": Maher, MMPA.

256 Jimmy and South Africa: To his credit, when Jimmy went back to Durban, he insisted on giving a tribute concert to Louis Armstrong in the black township of Kwamashu. According to a 1975 radio interview with Studs Terkel, McPartland introduced the concert in Zulu. By 1976, he told a reporter he would never go back to South Africa "without my own Army."

257 "She was very terse": Smithsonian Institution (1997), p. 68.

258 Bobby Henderson: Henderson was in Albany, dying of lung cancer, but he came down to Manhattan for Halcyon's first official recording session in March 1969 at Sherman Fairchild's home studio. Henderson died six months later.

258 "This is a real emergency": Sherman Fairchild to Marian McPartland, letter, November 30, 1970, MMPA.

259 "It's extremely unfortunate . . . over misconceptions" and Halcyon split: McPartland and Halcyon eventually wound up owning the rights to the Bobby Henderson, Earl Hines, and Willie "the Lion" Smith albums, much to O'Neal's chagrin. In 1975, O'Neal sold Chiaroscuro to AudioFidelity, which sold the masters of the three albums back to McPartland.

260 Halcyon sales: How many Halcyon albums were sold is impossible to know, because all the business dealings—contracts, orders, sales—were carried out at Fairchild's offices and the paperwork—a blip in his vast holdings—was apparently discarded.

260 McNally review: *Hartford Courant*, May 1975.

260 Concert with Teddi King: A recording of the concert—without the talking—was released on a twofer LP, *Marian Remembers Teddi* (Halcyon 118), after King had passed. (King would unfortunately die young, of lupus, in 1977.) The album nicely captured the frisson of the evening, complete with spirited applause. Though McPartland soared occasionally on short solos (Hoagy Carmichael's "Skylark" and Jimmy Van Heusen's "It Could Happen to You"), she and King modestly moved out of the spotlight and let the melodies—and lyrics—bask in its glow. The evening was all about the beautiful architecture of American melodies, such as Harry Warren's "There Will Never Be Another You," about which Wilder said, "There's not a poorly chosen note," and their cunning lyrics, with rhymes like "nestle" and "wrestle," from Jerome Kern's "A Fine Romance." King dug deeply into the pathos of Rodgers and Hart's "Little Girl Blue," with its internal rhyme and unpredictable melody. Though Wilder no doubt protested at first, King insisted on singing Wilder's "While We're Young" as an encore.

261 I feel panicked": Diary-like memoranda, MMPA.

261 "Begin. That's always been hard": Notes and sketches, MMPA.

262 Show at the Americana Hotel: In June, a slightly different lineup was recorded at the Band Box and released much later by Halcyon as *Swingin': Marian and Jimmy McPartland and Guests* (Halcyon 114).

263 "A kitten walked in": *Newsday*, June 4, 1972.

263 "Marian never knew herself": Ibid.

Chapter Twelve: The Jazz Renaissance

265 National Association of Jazz Educators: The National Association of Jazz Educators (NAJE) had organized formally five years earlier (Clem De Rosa was a founding member), and in 1971 Marian had been selected as its first "invitational member." The annual convention of NAJE—later called the International Association for Jazz Education (IAJE)—would ultimately become the most important jazz gathering in America. McPartland was regularly featured at the convention until the organization went bankrupt in 2008.

266 "I took so many things for granted": Reports on Jazz in the Schools, MMPA.

266 "It does seem hilarious": Ibid.

267 "I heard you're going to carry me": Notes and sketches, MMPA.

267 "We sat in a hallway": Ibid.

267 "I really wish": Marian McPartland to Mercer Ellington, letter, February 15, 1974, MMPA.

267 "a champion, a spokesman": Diary-like memoranda, MMPA.

267–68 "Many of us . . . consciousness": Untitled essay about jazz education, n.d., MMPA.

268 "She was a believer": In January 1983, when McPartland's trio played the Bedford Hills correctional facility for women, she was curious to meet one of the inmates, a former nightclub singer who said she had often seen Marian at the Carlyle and was now serving a life sentence for plotting the murder of her husband. The woman didn't show up, however. "I think she was afraid I'd ask her to sing," McPartland told *The New York Times*. "I wouldn't have" (*The New York Times*, January 10, 1983).

268 "He's a closet ham": Maher, MMPA.

269 "Why are you so determined": Wilder, Alec, *Letters I Never Mailed*, Rochester, N.Y.: University of Rochester Press, 2005, p. 230.

269 "I wash my hands of Alec": Maher, MMPA.

269 "Don't blame me for this": Ibid.

269 "stuck in the library": Balliett (2000), p. 449.

270 "Joe was there": Richard Sudhalter, liner note, *The Maestro and Friend* (Halcyon 112). On the back of the album jacket, Marian incorrectly wrote that it was recorded in Nice in July 1973. There was no jazz festival in Nice in 1973, nor was Marian in France that year. The album was recorded in July 1974.

271 Japanese tour: A Japanese label issued an album featuring McPartland and Jones, recorded live in Tokyo's Yugbin Chokin Hall: *Live In Tokyo: Marian McPartland and Hank Jones* (TDK Records TDCN 5141). Marian's robust, orchestral disquisition on Ellington's "Rockin' in Rhythm" was an extraordinary display of virtuosity and imagination.

272 "The drums and bass": Unidentified publication, January 1977, MMPA.

272 Victor Stein article: *Village Voice*, August 9, 1973.

272 "Whether she played": John Schreiber, liner note, *Solo Concert at Haverford* (Halcyon 111).

273 Though Marian was recording often: Marian made a record in 1974 for RCA-Victor, *Let It Happen* (LSA 3304), that was deleted from the company's catalogue almost as soon as it was released. The label invited her to record a piano quartet set—Billy Mayerl redux!—with Hank Jones, Roland Hanna, and Dick Hyman (who did the arrangements) in quadrophonic sound. Each pianist was assigned a separate channel. The idea was to sell consumers a new sound system with speakers set up in all four corners of the room. The producer was Ettore Stratta, who would go on to an illustrious concert production career in New York, and who, naturally, insisted his title tune, "Let It Happen," be played on the album. Designer Barbara Bergman's cover art was pure '70s surrealism—four grand pianos tiled in succession, with Mt. Rushmore–like profiles of each pianist carved into their left sides, floating above a green seascape. The repertoire was hip, from Herbie Hancock's "Maiden Voyage" and Ellington's "Warm Valley" to variations on Erik Satie and Scott Joplin. Jimmy Van Heusen's "Here's That Rainy Day" got a swinging reading and Marian got off a flowing solo on Herbie's tune. But without hearing the album in quad, it was hard to assess, as the sound came across as mostly muddled, which was apparently the opinion of RCA execs, as they pulled the album from the catalogue when it became clear that quad was a nonstarter with the public.

274–75 Bill Pollock article: *Los Angeles Herald-Examiner*, March 27, 1975.

275 Monterey Jazz Festival appearance: See http://www.youtube.com/watch?v=Xhtzz8vaar4

276 "I don't know which is worse": McPartland (2005), p. 10.

277–78 "I had a very bad night . . . put on a show": Townsend, MMPA.

278 "Is he understanding": Diary-like memoranda, MMPA.

278 "A worse hypochondriac": Townsend, MMPA.

280 "I suggest that all married people": Balliett, 1977.

280 "Naturally we would love": Marian McPartland to Doug Kassel, letter, March 22, 1977.

281 "I knew it was not advisable . . . an advantage to be a woman.": *Los Angeles Times*, September 1, 1974.

281 *Esquire* essay: McPartland, 1975.

282 "Exceptional women": Heilbrun, p. 81.

285 "gave the lie": *Los Angeles Times,* March 21, 1978.

285 Women's Jazz Festival publication: The quotations included this one, by critic George Simon: "Only God can make a tree, and only men can play good jazz." Bandleader Buddy Rich was represented by, "I'd never hire a chick to play in my band."

285 "One woman is enough": *Ms.*, March, 1978.

287 "had never performed a proper concerto": Marian's first appearance as a jazz musician with a symphony orchestra appears to have been in 1971, with Phil Wilson, performing a composition written by him for her with the ungainly title "The Left and the Right—Lord Buckley and Myra B," with the Westchester Symphony.

287 "I chose the Grieg": Typescript of essay by Ada Kopetz-Korf, MMPA.

288 Knauss interview: This interview was never published, though the transcript survived. Knauss sent Marian a copy, but he said she was late getting it back with corrections, so it could not be included in his book. Jimmy's interview was.

289 "Ada showed me": G. Shaw (1979), p. 713.

289 Daniel Griffin: Griffin had been introduced to Marian's music through her Halcyon album of duets with Teddy Wilson, though he confessed that until he heard her live at the Merry Go Round in Boston, he had mistakenly thought the "boring" player on the album was Marian, not Teddy!

289 George Murphy review: *Democrat and Chronicle*, April 2, 1978.

291 *Wanted (Live)*, aka *Marian and Jimmy McPartland and the All-Star Jazz Assassins*: Torff thinks this album was composed of outtakes not meant for release. "*Jimmy McPartland and the Jazz Assassins* was not a record," said Torff. "I never got paid for that date . . . I was not very happy about that. I wrote Bill Hassett an angry letter. Marian stayed out of it" (interview with author).

291 Tony Bennett and Bill Evans: Bennett and Evans also recorded for Fantasy, but Hassett made a deal with Evans's manager, Helen Keane, to allow the Improv session to be released as well.

293 "Every place I work . . . putting them all together": Marian McPartland, unpublished interview with Richard Sudhalter, MMPA.

293 New Orleans gig at Le Club: Drummer Rusty Jones, who was with McPartland on the New Orleans gig, recounted this amusing story from their three weeks in the Crescent City: "New Orleans had a basketball team called New Orleans Jazz, and the auditorium was right across from the Hyatt. They hired us to play for halftime, Marian playing electric piano and Brian Torff playing electric bass. They put us on a wheeled platform about this far off the ground, and they wheeled us out on the middle of the basketball floor at halftime. And they had our name up on the scoreboard: Marian McPartland Trio. We were playing along and fifteen minutes later, all of a sudden, Boom! Boom! Boom! Boom! What's that? And both sides, it's time for both the teams to come out and do their pre-second-half warm-up . . . and these guys from a distance they look big, but when you're sitting there and those guys and balls were whizzing by the little bandstand and damn near hit us, they were going all over, these guys shooting baskets, and man, these guys are big!"

293 According to Branford: Branford Marsalis to Mary Fiance Fuss, e-mail, April 4, 2012.

294 "I was absolutely knocked out": Smithsonian Institution (1997), p. 112.

Chapter Thirteen: *Piano Jazz*
296 "With so many people to choose from": McPartland (1996).

299 "I was just better qualified to do it": Smithsonian Institution (1997), p. 106.

299 225 stations: The number of stations on National Public Radio that carry a program generated by an individual member station has nothing to do with funding. The programs are free to all members. Funds are raised through grants, individual memberships, donations, and an annual subsidy by the Corporation for Public Broadcasting.

302 Studs Terkel interview: 98.7 WFMT, Chicago, 1961, Chicago History Museum.

303 Phil Elwood review: *San Francisco Examiner*, April 13, 1979.

303 Leonard Feather review: *Los Angeles Times,* May 7, 1979.

304 *From This Moment On*: Both the Lord discography and the sleeve for this album say it was recorded on an unspecified date in December. It seems far more likely that it was made in September, when Marian was touring in the West. Marian performed at the University of California at Berkeley on September 27 and at UCLA's Schoenberg Hall September 28. In early December, however, she played New Orleans, Baltimore, and Syracuse and was in Florida with Jimmy December 18–31.

304–05 Terry Teachout review: *The Kansas City Star*, June 24, 1979.

305 "last hurrah from Halcyon": Technically, the last album in the Halcyon catalog was *Marian Remembers Teddi*, but it had been recorded in 1973 and was released as a posthumous tribute.

307 Yarrow review: *CODA*, August 8, 1983.

308 "The crowd": *The Kansas City Star*, March 24, 1980.

308 "I wish": Marian McPartland to Jim and Barbara Maher, postcard, March 4, 1980.

308 O'Brian article: *New York Post*, n.d. photocopy, MMPA.

309 "She might simply explode": Maher, MMPA.

310 "too late to get a divorce": *JazzTimes,* January 1981.

311 "We seemed very grumpy": Notes and sketches, MMPA.

311 "I love the sun": *Daily News,* August 4, 1981.

312 "The cats have been": Diary-like memoranda, MMPA.

313 Bouchard article: *JazzTimes*, January 1981.

314 Griffin profile: *Independent School*, Spring 1982.

315 "One Christmas": Notes and sketches, MMPA.

316 "They made a handsome couple": *Philadelphia Daily News,* January 9, 1981.

Chapter Fourteen: Heyday

318 "I suggest": *Jazz Journal International*, April 1983.

318 "Best jazz radio show": *Los Angeles Times*, February 16, 1986.

319 "I notice": *Piano Jazz* taping, January 29, 1985.

320 "Marian is a wonderful interviewer": E-mail from George Shearing to author, June 2009.

320 "Whoa, play that again": *Piano Jazz* taping, March 23, 1984.

321 "My goodness": *Piano Jazz* taping, December 11, 1984.

321 "How did I get into this": *Piano Jazz* taping, March 11, 1985.

321 "If jazz is really sinful": *Chicago Sun-Times,* October 1, 1987.

321 Peabody Award: Hansson (2006) writes that McPartland won the Peabody Award for her interview with British actor and sometime pianist Dudley Moore. However, the award honored the program as a whole, not the Moore interview specifically. But because the Peabody Awards are selected via application, SCETV applied that year by sending in the Moore episode as a sample. The station had applied several times before, ironically sending in tapes of much more representative (and better) shows with Bill Evans, Oscar Peterson, and Eubie Blake. It's possible, however, that the general-interest nature of the Dudley Moore interview was more appealing to the Peabody board or that the cumulative effect of several applications finally won them over. A representative of the Peabody Awards, Noel Holston, stated unequivocally, however, that "it was the series as a whole, not the Moore episode, to which the Board members awarded a Peabody" (e-mail to author, December 21, 2010). The text of the citation does not mention Moore.

322 "We were trying": *San Francisco Chronicle,* November 3, 1991.

324 "I get kind of nervous": *Piano Jazz* taping, January 3, 1987.

324 "Not rich": *Baltimore Evening Sun*, August 20, 1982.

325 Mary Lou Williams Jazz Festival: This festival preceded the later successful Mary Lou Williams Women in Jazz Festival at the Kennedy Center, started by Billy Taylor in 1996.

327 "It was fascinating": Unidentified publication, n.d., MMPA.

327 "She tells nice": *Cincinnati Post,* January 25, 1982.

327 Alex Cirin poem: *Cincinnati Post*, February 11, 1982.

328 Marcille review: *Schenectady Gazette*, March 29, 1982.

328 "An expressive serenity": *The New York Times*, June 23, 1985.

328 Rex Reed letter: August 19, 1982, MMPA.

329 McNally review: *Hartford Courant*, June 5, 1983.

329 Elwood review: *San Francisco Examiner,* May 11, 1983.

329 Balleras review: *Down Beat,* January 1986.

330 Feather review: *Los Angeles Times,* August 16, 1987.

330 Jane Krupa review: *The Scranton Times,* February 2, 1981.

330 W. U. McCoy review: *The Daily Oklahoman,* February 18, 1980.

331 "sedate": *The New York Times,* August 5, 1987.

332 "I have just finished": *JazzTimes,* September 1983.

335 "Why am I so ashamed . . . just like I used to be.": Diary-like memoranda, MMPA.

335 "Not about things past": Marian McPartland to Don Kassel, letter, August 4, 1982.

336 "There was no way": Notes and sketches, MMPA.

337 "I guess you heard": Marian McPartland to Doug Kassel, letter, March 25, 1985.

338 "Grandpa played very well": Marian McPartland to Donna Gourdol, letter, August 17, 1983.

339 "What is it": Diary-like memoranda, MMPA.

339 "My difficulty these days": *San Francisco Examiner,* June 11, 1982.

341 Balliett review: Balliett (2000), p. 708.

341 Leonard Reed review: *The Record,* September 6, 1987.

341 Peter Keepnews review: *The New York Times,* October 25, 1987.

341 "That's pretty hip practicing": *Piano Jazz* taping, August 21, 1986.

342 Cecil Taylor quotes: *Piano Jazz,* September 9, 1986.

Chapter Fifteen: Exit Jimmy

345 "Although I was always": Notes and sketches, MMPA.

346 "When a reporter": *The New York Times,* February 19, 1989.

348 Donnell Library: The auditorium is no longer there.

349 Elwood review: *San Francisco Examiner,* August 3, 1989.

349 Heffley review: *The Register-Guard* (Eugene, Oregon), June 29, 1990.

349 Japan tour: A live recording was produced at one of the concerts in Japan and released in 2003 as *100 Golden Fingers: Piano Playhouse 1993* (Absord Japan ABCS81). Marian played Carter's "When Lights Are Low," Johnny Mercer's "Emily," and Ned Washington's "My Foolish Heart."

352 "It's a great life": *The Tribune* (Lewiston, Idaho), February 26, 1993.

352 Letter about Geri Allen, et al.: *The New York Times*, May 1, 1994.

353 James Watt: *Baltimore Evening Sun,* August 20, 1982.

353 "I could get up on a soapbox": *Utica Observer-Dispatch,* April 26, 1997.

355 Diana Krall *Piano Jazz* taping: July 24, 1994.

356 Rosemary Clooney *Piano Jazz* taping: October 14, 1991.

356 Ray Charles *Piano Jazz* taping: January 1, 1990.

356 Ahmet Ertugun comment about "foreign music": *The New York Times*, June 21, 1981.

357 Jazz Alliance label: One fringe benefit of having what was effectively her own subsidiary on the Concord label was that Marian periodically could talk Jefferson into releasing CDs from the Halcyon catalog. Jazz Alliance released *Concert in Argentina,* the Alec Wilder album, and Marian and Jimmy's trad collaborations, *Live at the Monticello* and *Swingin'.*

357 Jazz Alliance sales numbers: Nick Phillips, interview with author.

357 "I guess a person": Marian McPartland to Daniel Griffin, letter, January 19, 1991.

359 Remarriage to Jimmy: Just before Jimmy died, Marian invited a fan of Jimmy's, Paul White, to the house. White's 1990 appreciation of Jimmy in *CODA* magazine had impressed her and she thought Jimmy might take some comfort in meeting White. In a January 2011 interview with the author in Seattle, White said he thought Marian remarried Jimmy for three reasons: "1) Jimmy wanted her to. He loved her. And she loved him; 2) they had some business interests together that would be simplified if they were married; and the third reason was that a divorced wife has no say in where her husband gets buried." White said Marian called him again after Jimmy's death, asking him to "fend off the McPartland retinue" at a Milwaukee concert, just before the Chicago memorial, in May. White, who was Canadian and died in 2011, subsequently became a close friend of Marian's, booking her for shows in Calgary and Vancouver, B.C.

359 "Would you like some company": Notes and sketches, MMPA.

360 "Most of us begin": Heilbrun, p. 92.

360 "That's a good album, isn't it": Donna Gourdol, interview with author; Notes and sketches, MMPA.

360 "Between these two boyhood": Sudhalter (1999), pp. 272–73.

361 "When I was a little girl": Tape recording of Jimmy McPartland memorial service, courtesy of Doug Kassel.

362 "I guess you don't realize": Marian McPartland to Doug Kassel, letter, July 27, 1992.

362 "As far as needing": Marian McPartland to Doug Kassel, letter, July 27, 1992.

362 "I feel frustration": Marian McPartland to Doug Kassel, letter, January 5, 1993.

365 "It is easy to get old": Unidentified publication, n.d. photocopied clip, MMPA.

365 "It was sad": Marian McPartland to Jack and Diana Schwartz, postcard, May 26, 1992.

366 "Why not?: Marian McPartland to Jack and Diana Schwartz, postcard.

369 "Did not haggle hard enough": According to a fax dated December 6, 2001, from Pam Parsons to McPartland, the pianist's "full fee" was $12,000, though Parsons was negotiating for a price of $6,000 with Jim Luce. In discussing several gigs, the fax makes clear Parsons has been bargaining for the highest fees she can secure from a variety of presenters and that she is savvy.

370 "We spoke for several hours": Robert Doerschuk to author, e-mail, January 10, 2009.

371 "We shall never speak of it again": Marian McPartland, interview with author.

371 "I miss Grandpa": Marian McPartland to Donna and Jacques Gourdol, letter, January 27, 1992.

372 "I wish I had taken time off": Marian McPartland to Dan Griffin, letter, n.d.

372–73 "Jimmy never seemed to grumble . . . have found somebody else." Notes for an essay about Jimmy McPartland by Marian McPartland, MMPA.

Chapter Sixteen: Sweet Times

375 "I hardly can believe": *Chicago Tribune*, May 4, 1995.

376 Peter Watrous review: *The New York Times*, February 12, 1995.

377 "A glorious treat": Sandra Day O'Connor to Marian McPartland, letter, n.d., MMPA.

377 "It was one of the happiest afternoons": David Souter to Marian McPartland, letter, n.d., MMPA.

377 "lost none of the graceful precision . . . bought it": *The Guardian*, n.d., MMPA.

378 "I feel that I was so unfair": Enstice and Stockhouse, p. 237.

378 "Oh, that's ridiculous!": Ibid.

379 "I don't know that jazz": Unidentified Chattanooga newspaper, April 15, 1990, MMPA.

379 "cheerfulness that you miss": *Down Beat*, September 1996.

379 "Does it have a picture of Kenny G in it?": Author's notes from *JazzTimes* convention, November 5–8, 1997.

379 "What the hell does it matter?": (Raleigh, NC) *Herald-Sun*, August 21, 1998.

380 "jazz piano's answer to Julia Child": *New York Observer*, March 23, 1998.

380 Ira Gitler review: *JazzTimes*, July/August 1998.

380 "gotten age out of her system": *The Philadelphia Inquirer,* March 23, 1998.

381 Makeup artist anecdote: Conversation with author, April 14, 2009.

381–82 "Shall we play it . . . female!": Dave Brubeck *Piano Jazz* taping, October 4, 1996.

382 "When I was a kid . . . like a girl": Carla Bley/Steve Swallow *Piano Jazz* taping, August 15, 1995.

383 "I have to confess": Marilyn Crispell *Piano Jazz* taping, March 5, 1998.

383 Brad Mehldau *Piano Jazz* taping: September 12, 1996.

384 "She's a watercolorist": *Pulse!*, October 1996.

385 "Mood music": *Down Beat*, October 1997.

387 "You chose the tunes": *Chicago Sun-Times*, June 17, 2000.

388 Letter about female jazz drummers: *The New York Times*, June 20, 1999.

388 "always sound ridiculous to me": Marian McPartland, interview with Michelle Labieniec-Despard, November 29, 2000, in Labieniec-Despard.

388 "The trouble with becoming": *The Philadelphia Inquirer*, November 30, 2001.

389 "I'm sorry you never": Marian McPartland to Doug Kassel, letter, November 25, 2000.

390 *Piano Jazz* taping in Seattle and Jazz Alley show, Seattle: *Seattle Times*, June 9, 2000.

390 Willie Nelson interview: *Piano Jazz* taping: July 23, 2001.

391 "An elegant elderly woman": *The New Yorker*, October 7, 2002.

391 Norah Jones: Norah Jones *Piano Jazz* taping: July 24, 2002.

391 Elvis Costello: Elvis Costello *Piano Jazz* taping, May 6, 2003.

394 Joe Morello's drums on eBay: Donna Gourdol says her brother Doug told her it was a signed snare drum he put up for sale on eBay, not a practice pad.

396 Bob Blumenthal review: *Boston Globe*, September 9, 2001.

397 "I know he doesn't": Marian McPartland to Doug Kassel, letter, November 25, 2000.

397 "She could easily have": *All About Jazz,* January 28, 2003.

398 "Not been so controlling . . . did this for me": Marian McPartland (2003), pp. xxvii–xxviii.

398 "There are many different cultures in jazz": Ibid, p. 16.

398–99 Morello at 85th birthday party at Birdland: This would be one of the last times Marian saw Joe Morello, though they stayed in touch periodically on the telephone. Morello died in March 2011.

399 "snapshot of the Manhattan jazz community": *The Guardian*, May 27, 2005.

399 "Retire? Should I give up hanging out": *The Chicago Tribune,* September 21, 2003.

Bibliography

For one-time citations of periodicals, newspapers articles, and other sources, please see the notes section.

Large sections of Marian McPartland's personal archive (MMPA)–including an unpublished biography of Jimmy McPartland by Bentley Stegner; a memoir by McPartland's sister, Joyce; and notes and transcribed interviews for various unfinished as-told-to autobiographies done with the assistance of James T. Maher, Irving Townsend, and Marian McPartland herself—are listed here. For references to other items in the MMPA, please see the notes.

Books

Balliett, Whitney. *Alec Wilder and His Friends*. Boston: 1974. Houghton Mifflin.
———. *Collected Works*. New York: St. Martin's Press, 2000.
Barty-King, Hugh. *GSMD: A Hundred Years' Performance*. London: Stainer & Bell, 1980.
Berendt, Joachim. *The Jazz Book*. New York: Lawrence Hill, 1975.
Berton, Ralph. *Remembering Bix: A Memoir of the Jazz Age*. New York: Harper & Row, 1974.
Bennett, Tony, and Will Friedwald. *The Good Life*. London and New York: Pocket Books, 1999.
Bron, Eleanor. *The Pillow Book of Eleanor Bron: Or An Actress Despairs*. London: Methuen, 1987.
Carmichael, Hoagy. *The Stardust Road* and *Sometimes I Wonder: The Autobiographies of Hoagy Carmichael*. New York: Da Capo, 1999.
Charters, Samuel B., and Leonard Kunstadt. *Jazz: A History of the New York Scene*. New York: Da Capo, 1962.
Chilton, John. *Sidney Bechet: The Wizard of Jazz*. New York: Oxford, 1987.
Clayton, Buck, and Nancy Miller Elliott. *Buck Clayton's Jazz World*. New York: Oxford University Press, 1987.
Collier, James Lincoln. *Benny Goodman and the Swing Era*. New York, Oxford: Oxford University Press, 1989.
Condon, Eddie. *We Called it Music*. New York: Da Capo, 1992.
Crow, Bill. *From Birdland to Broadway*. New York: Oxford University Press, 1992.
———. *Jazz Anecdotes*. New York: Oxford University Press, 1990.
Crowther, Bruce. *Gene Krupa: Life and Times*. New York: Universe Books, 1987.

Dahl, Linda. *Stormy Weather*. New York: Limelight, 1984.

———. *Morning Glory: A Biography of Mary Lou Williams*. New York: Pantheon, 1999.

———. *Haunted Heart: A Biography of Susannah McCorkle*. Ann Arbor: University of Michigan Press, 2006.

Dankworth, John. *Jazz in Revolution*. London: Constable, 1998.

Davies, Andrew, "Cinema and Broadcasting." In *Twentieth Century Britain*. London and New York: Longman, 1994.

Day, Gary, ed., *Literature and Culture in Modern Britain 1930–1955,* vol. 2 of *Literature and Culture in Modern Britain*. London and New York: Longman, 1997.

Deffaa, Chip. *Voices of the Jazz Age: Profiles of Eight Vintage Jazzmen*. Chicago: University of Illinois Press, 1990.

Dickinson, Peter. *Marigold: The Music of Billy Mayerl*. London: Oxford University Press, 1999.

Doerschuk, Robert L. *88: The Giants of Jazz Piano*. San Francisco: Backbeat Books, 2001.

Enstice, Wayne, and Janis Stockhouse. *Jazzwomen: Conversations with Twenty-one Musicians*. Bloomington: Indiana University Press, 2004.

Fawkes, Richard. *Fighting for a Laugh*. London: MacDonald and Janes, 1978.

Feldman, David, "Nationality and Ethnicity." In *Twentieth Century Britain*. London and New York: Longman, 1994.

Freeman, Bud. *Crazeology*. Chicago: University of Illinois Press, 1989.

Friedan, Betty. *The Feminine Mystique*. New York: W. W. Norton, 1963.

Giddins, Gary. *Weather Bird: Jazz at the Dawn of Its Second Century*. New York: Oxford, 2004.

Gilbert, Bentley B. *Britain Since 1918*. London: Batsford Academic and Educational, 1967.

Godbolt, Jim. *A History of Jazz in Britain 1919–1950*. London: Quartet Books, 1984.

———. *A History of Jazz in Britain 1950–70*. London: Quartet Books, 1989.

Goodman, Benny, and Irving Kolodin, *Kingdom of Swing*. New York: Frederick Ungar, 1961.

Gourse, Leslie. *Madame Jazz*. New York: Oxford University Press, 1995.

Graham, Charles, and Dan Morgenstern. *The Great Jazz Day*. Emeryville, Calif.: Woodford Press, 1999.

Graves, Robert, and Alan Hodge. *The Long Week End: A Social History of Great Britain 1918–1939*. New York: Macmillan, 1941.

Grein, Paul. *Capitol Records: Fiftieth Anniversary (1942–1992)*. Hollywood: Limited Edition, 1992.

Groves, Alan, and Alyn Shipton. *The Glass Enclosure*. New York: Continuum, 2001.

Hadlock, Richard. *Jazz Masters of the Twenties*. New York: Collier Books, 1965.

Hajdu, David. *Lush Life*. New York: Farrar, Straus and Giroux, 1996.

Hansson, Clare, "Marian McPartland's Piano Jazz: A Model for Jazz Education." In *Jazz Research Proceedings Yearbook*. New York: International Association of Jazz Educators Conference, 2001.

Harthy, Michel, ed. *Lightning Fingers.* London: Paradise Press, 1995.

Hasse, John Edward. *Jazz: The First Century.* New York: William Morrow, 2000.

Heilbrun, Carolyn. *Writing a Woman's Life.* New York: Ballantine, 1988.

Hillman, Christopher. *Bunk Johnson.* New York: Universe Books, 1988.

Hentoff, Nat, and Nat Shapiro. *Hear Me Talkin' to Ya.* New York: Dover, 1966.

Hilbert, Robert. *Pee Wee Russell: The Life of a Jazzman.* New York: Oxford University Press, 1993.

Hobsbawm Eric. *The Jazz Scene.* New York: Pantheon, 1993.

Hogg, O. F. G. *The Royal Arsenal: Its Background, Origin and Subsequent History.* London: Oxford University Press, 1963.

Horsburgh, E. L. S., *Bromley, Kent, from the Earliest Times to the Present Century.* Bankhouse, Summerill, Chiselhurst, Kent: Lodgemark Press, 1980.

Jones, Max. *Talking Jazz.* New York: W. W. Norton, 1988.

Kaminsky, Max, with V. E. Hughes. *My Life in Jazz.* New York: Harper & Row, 1963.

Kenny, William Howland. *Chicago Jazz.* New York: Oxford University Press, 1993.

Knauss, Zane, ed. *Conversations with Jazz Musicians.* Detroit: Bruccoli Clark/Gale Research Company, 1977.

Korall, Burt. *Drummin' Men: The Heartbeat of Jazz: The Swing Years.* New York: Schirmer, 1990.

Lester, James. *Too Marvelous for Words: The Life and Genius of Art Tatum.* New York: Oxford, 1994.

Levinson, Peter. *Puttin' on the Ritz.* New York: St. Martin's, 2009.

———. *Tommy Dorsey: Livin' in a Great Big Way.* Cambridge, Mass.: Da Capo, 2005.

Levy, John, with Devra Hall. *Men, Women and Girl Singers.* Silver Springs, Maryland: Beckham, 2000.

Mackintosh, Iain, and Michael Sell, eds. *Curtains!!! Or a New Life for Old Theatres.* London: John Offord, 1982.

Maher, James T., foreword to *All in Good Time,* by Marian McPartland. New York: Oxford University Press, 1987.

McKibbin, R. *Classes and Cultures: England 1918–1951.* London: Oxford University Press, 1998.

McPartland, Marian. *All in Good Time.* New York: Oxford University Press, 1987.

———. *Marian McPartland's Jazz World: All in Good Time.* Chicago: University of Illinois Press, 2003.

———, foreword to *Letters I Never Mailed,* by Alec Wilder. Rochester, N.Y.: University of Rochester Press, 2005.

———, "Playing Like a Man." In *Just Jazz 3.* London: Four Square, 1959.

———, "The Untold Story of the International Sweethearts of Rhythm." In *Reading Jazz: A Gathering of Autobiography, Reportage, and Criticism from 1919 to Now.* New York: Pantheon, 1996.

———, "You've Come a Long Way Baby." In *Esquire's World of Jazz.* New York: Thomas Y. Crowell, 1975.

Menninger, Karl. *Love Against Hate.* New York: Harcourt, Brace and Company, 1942.

Mezzrow, Mezz. *Really the Blues.* London: Flamingo, 1993.

Miller, Mark. *A Certain Respect for Tradition.* Toronto: Mercury Press, 2006.

Moore, Hilary. *Inside British Jazz.* Hampshire, UK: Ashgate, 2007.

Morgenstern, Dan. *Living with Jazz.* New York: Pantheon, 2004.

O'Day, Anita, and George Eells. *High Times Hard Times.* New York: Limelight, 1988.

Ogren, Kathy J. *The Jazz Revolution: Twenties America and the Meaning of Jazz.* New York: Oxford University Press, 1989.

Panassie, Hugues. *The Guide to Swing Music.* New York: M. Witmark & Sons, 1936.

Parsonage, Catherine. *The Evolution of Jazz in Britain 1880–1935.* Burlington, Vermont: Ashgate, 2005.

Paudras, Francis. *Dance of the Infidels.* New York: Da Capo, 1998.

Peterson, Oscar. *Jazz Odyssey: The Life of Oscar Peterson.* New York: Continuum, 2002.

Pettinger, Peter. *Bill Evans: How My Heart Sings.* New Haven: Yale University Press, 1998.

Pittman, Susan. *Stratford House School 1912–1987.* Kent, UK: Meresborough Books, 1987.

Placksin, Sally. *American Women in Jazz.* New York: Wideview Books, 1982.

Ramsey, Doug. *Take Five: The Public and Private Lives of Paul Desmond.* Seattle: Parkside Publications, 2005.

Ramsey, Frederic, Jr., and Charles Edward Smith. *Jazzmen.* New York: Harcourt, Brace and Company, 1939.

Reynolds, E. E., and N. H. Brasher. *Britain in the Twentieth Century.* Cambridge, UK: Cambridge University Press, 1966.

Richmond, Peter. *The Life and Music of Peggy Lee.* New York: Henry Holt, 2006.

Schuller, Gunther. *Early Jazz.* New York: Oxford University Press, 1986.

Shaw, Arnold. *52nd Street: The Street of Jazz.* New York: Da Capo, 1977.

Shearing, George, and Alyn Shipton. *Lullaby of Birdland.* New York, London: Continuum, 2004.

Shipton, Alyn. *Handful of Keys.* New York: Routledge, 2004.

Stephenson, Sam. *The Jazz Loft Project.* New York: Knopf, 2009.

Stone, Desmond. *Alec Wilder in Spite of Himself.* New York: Oxford University Press, 1996.

Sudhalter, Richard. *Lost Chords.* Chicago: Oxford University Press, 1999.

Sudhalter, Richard, and Philip R. Evans. *Bix: Man & Legend.* New Rochelle, N.Y.: Arlington House, 1974.

Talbot, Bruce. *Tom Talbert—His Life and Times.* Lanham, Maryland, and Oxford: Scarecrow Press, 2004.

Taylor, Billy. *Taylor Made Piano.* Boston: McGraw-Hill, 1982.

Terkel, Studs. *Hard Times: An Oral History of the Great Depression.* New York: Pantheon, 1970.

Thane, Pat, "The Social, Economic and Political Status of Women." In *Twentieth-Century Britain*. London and New York: Longman, 1994.

Tirro, Frank. *Jazz: A History*. New York: Norton, 1977.

Traill, Sinclair, and Gerald Lascelles, ed. *Just Jazz*. London: Peter Davies, 1957.

Shim, Eunmi. *Lennie Tristano: His Life in Music*. Ann Arbor: University of Michigan Press, 2007.

Tucker, Sherrie. *Swing Shift*. Durham: Duke University Press, 2000.

Ulanov, Barry. *A History of Jazz in America*. New York: Viking, 1952.

Ullman, Michael. *Jazz Lives: Portraits in Words and Pictures*. Washington, D.C.: New Republic Books, 1980.

Unterbrink, Mary. *Jazz Women at the Keyboard*. Jefferson, N.C., and London: McFarland, 1983.

Wein, George, and Nate Chinen. *Myself Among Others*. Cambridge, Mass.: Da Capo, 2003.

Wilmut, Roger. *Kindly Leave the Stage! The Story of Variety 1919–1960*. London: Methuen, 1985.

Wilson, Teddy, Arie Lithgart, and Humphrey van Loo. *Teddy Wilson Talks*. London and New York: Cassell, 1996.

Periodicals—multiple references

Down Beat, 1945–2010.

Melody Maker, 1928–1975.

Billboard, 1955–1987

The New Yorker, 1950–2002.

Balliett, Whitney, "I Like You, Kid." *The New Yorker*, September 5, 1977: 80–86.

Balliett, Whitney, "The Key of D Is Daffodil Yellow." *The New Yorker*, January 20, 1973: 43–57.

McPartland, Marian, "Music in My Life." *International Musician*, September 1969: 6–8.

Newspapers—multiple references

The New York Times, 1950–2010.

Chicago Tribune, 1928–2006.

Ph.D. Theses

Hansson, Clare. "Marian McPartland: Jazz Pianist: An Overview of a Musical Career." Ph.D. diss., Queensland University of Technology, Australia, 2006.

Labieniec-Despard, Michelle. "Women in Jazz." Ph.D. diss., State University of New Jersey, Rutgers, 2001.

Shaw, G. "Relationships Between Experiential Factors and Percepts of Selected Professional Musicians in the United States Who Are Adept at Jazz Improvisation." Ph.D. diss., University of Oklahoma, 1979.

Virden, Jenel. "Good-bye, Piccadilly: The American Immigrant Experience of British War Brides of World War II." Ph.D. diss., University of Washington, 1992.

Other unpublished material

Armitage, Joyce. "For Maggie, Who Would Not Remember How Things Were When We Were Young," n.d. Marian McPartland Personal Archive (MMPA).

Autobiographical notes and sketches by Marian McPartland, n.d. MMPA.

Autobiographical manuscript and interviews by Marian McPartland, with James T. Maher, n.d. MMPA.

Diary. Janet Turner. 1959. MMPA.

Diary. Marian McPartland. June–August, 1968. MMPA.

Diary. Marian McPartland. August–October, 1968. MMPA.

Diary. Marian McPartland. September, 1956–February, 1957. MMPA.

Compendium of diary-like memoranda by Marian McPartland, n.d. MMPA.

Letters to Irving Townsend by Marian McPartland and interviews by Irving Townsend for a biography, n.d. MMPA.

Notes and outline for a biography of Marian McPartland by James T. Maher, c. 1975. MMPA

McPartland, Marian. "Jimmy McPartland." Manuscript. MMPA.

Notes for an essay about Jimmy McPartland by Marian McPartland. MMPA.

McPartland, Marian. Untitled essay about jazz education, n.d. MMPA.

McPartland, Marian. Reports on Jazz in the Schools, Washington, D.C., January 1–29, 1974. MMPA.

McPartland, Marian, and Irving Townsend, "The Story of a Lady in Jazz." MMPA.

Stegner, Bentley. "Biography of Jimmy McPartland," n.d. MMPA.

Wilder, Alec. "Marian McPartland: An Appreciation," n.d. MMPA.

Unpublished interviews

Jimmy McPartland, interview by Helen Armstead Johnston, Jazz Interaction, for the Smithsonian Institute, 1972, Institute for Jazz Studies, Rutgers, N.J.

Jimmy McPartland, interview by Mark Tucker, *Oral History of American Music*, March 20 and May 9, 1985, Music Library, Yale University.

Jimmy McPartland, interview by Squirrel Ashcraft, 1966. Privately issued CDS.

Marian McPartland, interview by James Williams, *Smithsonian Institution and National Endowment for the Arts Jazz Masters Initiative Jazz Oral History Program Collection*, January 3–4, 1997, and May 26, 1998, Archives Center, National Museum of American History, Smithsonian Institution. (Also online www .smithsonianjazz.org.)

Marian McPartland, interview by Zane Knauss. MMPA.

Marian McPartland, interview by Janice Okoomian, *Oral History of American Music*, November 27, 1982, and August 6, 1983, Music Library, Yale University.

Marian McPartland, interview by James Briggs Murray, Louis Armstrong Jazz Oral History Project, August 16, 1996, Schomburg Center for Research in Black Culture, New York Public Library. Videocassette.

Interviews with Marian McPartland by author
Fifty-one interviews between May 2006 and January 2011.

Other interviews by author
Chris Albertson (August 2008), Mark Armitage (August 2006), Chris Armitage (April 2009), Chris Armitage and Sheila Prophet (May 2009), Lynne Arriale (January 2011), Joellyn Ausanka (July 2008), Jean Bach (May 2009), Tony Bennett (November 2009), Charlie Bourgeois (July 2008), Joanne Brackeen (February 2009), Charlie Braugham (November 2008), Eleanor Bron (July 2010), Dave Brubeck (September 2009), John Bunch (October 2009), Jon Burr (June 2010), Jackie Cain (August 2008), Eileen Carlton (October 2008), Barbara Carroll (February, March, 2009), Regina Carter (May 2010), Jorge Cerruti (May 2009), Bill Charlap (February 2009), Nancy Christiansen (June 2009), Carol Comer (September 2010), Jim Cox (February 2009), Marilyn Crispell (January 2011), Bill Crow (July 2008), Linda Dahl (March 2010), John Dankworth (May 2009), John Dankworth and Cleo Laine (September 2009), Glenn Davis (June 2009), Clem De Rosa (August 2008), Dottie Dodgion (September 2008), Frank Dorritie (July 2009), Bill Douglass (September 2006), Mary Fettig (November 2009), Elaine Freeman (September 2010), Lenore Gibbs (November 2008), Eddie Gomez (April 2009), Donna Gourdol (December 2006), Helene Greece (January 2011), Daniel Griffin (October 2009), Bob Hammer (June 2010), Tom Hampson (December 2009), Zena Hampson (December 2009), Celeste Holm (July 2008), Shari Hutchinson (January 2006, August 2008, June 2009, January 2011), Dick Hyman (April 2010), Rusty Jones (November 2008), Don Kassel (October 2006, November 2008), Doug Kassel (November 2006, September, 2008), Zane Knauss (September 2010), Ada Kopetz-Korf (May 2009), Diane Lanigan (November 2008), John Lanigan (December 2008), Richard Lanigan (February 2010), Steve LaSpina (May 2009), Jack LeMaire (September 2009), Harry Lepp (December 2008), John Levy (March 2010), Noreen Lienhard (January 2009), Bernice MacDonald (June 2009, August, 2010), Duke Marcos (June 2009), Wynton Marsalis (May 2011), Debbie Marzigliano (May 2010), Gary Mazzaroppi (July 2009), Ron McClure (August 2010), Haydon McPartland (November 2008), Helen Merrill (March 2009), Lynn Milano (December 2010), Linc Milliman (August 2008), Michael Moore (September 2009), Joe Morello (July 2008, May 2009, June 2010), Dan Morgenstern (June 2009), Audrey Morris (December 2008), Dorothy Nash (September 2009), Eric Nebbia (November 2010), Peter O'Brien (April 2010), Frank O'Connell (November 2006), Hank O'Neal (February 2009), Carl Oshrain (August 2010), Pam Parsons (November 2009), Nick Phillips (December 2010), Roberta Piket (May 2010), Sally Placksin (February 2010), Chris Potter (January 2011), Charlie Rex (December 2008), Judy Roberts (September 2011), Ellen Rowe (May 2010), Fred Rundquist (November 2008), Patti Sarka (July 2008), Maria Schneider (September 2008),

John Schreiber (May 2009), Diana Schwartz (November 2009), Joe Segal (November 2008), Daryl Sherman (June 2009), Jeff Simon (August 2011), Polly Sosko (January 2011), Barbara Strudwick (May 2009), Carol Sudhalter (July 2010), Steve Swallow (June 2010), Frank Tate (October 2008), Billy Taylor (February 2009), Brian Torff (September 2009), Merrilee Trost (August 2006), Ben Tucker (November 2009), Dick Wang (December 2008), George Wein (July 2008), Paul White (January 2011), Phil Wilson (November 2009), Norton Wright (January 2011), Bill Zimmerman (October 2009).

Web sites

"Afterglow." Marian McPartland playing at the 1975 Monterey Jazz Festival. www
.youtube.com/watch?v=Xhtzz8vaar4.

"The Billy Mayerl Society," www.billymayerlsociety.co.uk/.

"Jazz.com," www.jazz.com/features-and-interviews/2008/5/2/octojazzarian-profile
-marian-mcpartland.

"The Multimedia Library," www.multimedialibrary.com/music/AboutJimmy.asp.

"The Red Hot Jazz Archive," www.redhotjazz.com/McPartland.html.

"Wilderworld," wilderworld.podomatic.com/.

"The Wolverines," www.starrgennett.org/stories/profiles/wolverines.htm
("starrgennett").

Video

Bach, Jean. *A Great Day in Harlem*. Chatsworth, Calif.: Image/Home Vision
Entertainment, 2005.

Brass Monkey. Studio City, Calif.: Televista, 2007 (Diadem, 1948).

Huey, *In Good Time: The Piano Jazz of Marian McPartland*. Portland, Maine: Films
By Huey, 2011.

Jazz at the Top: Remembering Bix Beiderbecke. Produced by Jim Dauphinee.
WXXI-TV, Rochester Area Education TV Association, 1976.

Tilton, Roger. *Jazz Dance*. Andorra: Efor Films, n.d.

Selected Recordings

This is not a comprehensive discography. It is a list of recordings referred to in the text (or notes). A notation of "o.p." means the recording is out of print. Dates in parentheses refer to release dates, when known, not recording dates.

Early (1937–1951)

Marian's first two recordings were 78 rpm discs made with Billy Mayerl, in London, just before she went on tour with him:

Billy Mayerl and His Claviers (1937). "Sweet William," "Green Tulips," "Marigold," "Chopsticks," "Ace of Spades," "Ace of Diamonds," "Bats in the Belfry." Columbia Records 16920 and 16921. (o.p.)
————. "The Toy Trumpet," "Clavierhapsody." Columbia Records 16922 and 16923. (o.p.)

In 1946, in London, Marian and Jimmy recorded with guitarist Vic Lewis. These sessions were not released until forty years later:

Vic Lewis Jam Sessions, Volume 3: 1945–1946, The Jimmy and Marian McPartland Sessions and the 1946 Jazzmen (1986). Harlequin Records HQ 3010. (o.p.)

Marian and Jimmy started their own record company, Unison, in Chicago in 1948. They recorded four sides, simultaneously released in England on the Harmony label and later picked up by Prestige Records. Prestige also released four tracks in 1950 that may originally have been intended for release on Unison. Marian reissued the first four Unison tracks on her own label, Halcyon:

Jimmy McPartland Band (1949). "Royal Garden Blues," "Daughter of Sister Kate," "Singin' the Blues," "In a Mist." Unison Records UR8815–UR8818. (o.p.). Issued (1949) in England as Harmony A 1002 and 1007. (o.p.). Reissued on Prestige Records PR 301 and PR 302 and as *Marian and Jimmy McPartland: Goin' Back a Ways* (1972). Halcyon Records HAL-116. (o.p.)
Jimmy McPartland (1950). "Come Back Sweet Papa," "Manhattan," "Use Your Imagination," "Davenport Blues." Prestige Records 303 and 304. (o.p.)

The two 78s listed below are Marian's first recordings as a leader, made in New York, to promote her gig at the Embers:

The Marian McPartland Quintet (1951). Federal Records F132 and F133.
————. Federal Records F134 and F135.

Savoy (1951–1953)

Marian recorded thirty-seven sides for Savoy between 1951 and 1953, issued in various combinations on 78s, seven-inch EPs, ten-inch EPs, and twelve-inch LPs. The only album currently in print featuring material from this period (thirteen tracks) is *Timeless* (2002) Savoy Jazz SVY-17117. A twenty-two-track compilation, *Marian McPartland at the Hickory House* (1980) Savoy Jazz ZDS 4404; a seventeen-track compilation, *Marian McPartland on 52nd Street* (2000) Savoy Jazz 92880-2; and a CD with eight tracks by Marian, *Great Britain's* (2003), also featuring George Shearing, Savoy Jazz SVY-160, are all out of print, as are the original Savoy 78s, EPs, and LPs. The following is a list of the original Savoy recordings cited in the text with corresponding reissue information:

Jazz at Storyville Vol. 1. (1951). "The Gypsy in My Soul," "Strike Up the Band." Savoy XP 8104. (o.p.)

Jazz at Storyville Vol. 2. (1951). "These Foolish Things," "Get Happy." Savoy XP 8105. (o.p.)

Marian McPartland Trio. "Strike Up the Band," "Our Love Is Here to Stay" (1952). Savoy 846. (o.p.) Also on *Moods Vol. 4* (1952) Savoy XP 8106 (o.p.); reissued on *Great Britain's,* Savoy Jazz SVY-160 and *Timeless* Savoy Jazz SVY-17117. "Our Love Is Here to Stay" also on *Marian McPartland at the Hickory House,* Savoy Jazz ZDS 4404. (o.p.)

The Magnificent Marian McPartland at the Piano (1952). "Lullaby of Birdland," "Nightingale Sang in Berkeley Square," "(It's Only a) Paper Moon," "Moonlight in Vermont," "Limehouse Blues," "Hallelujah," Savoy MG 15021. (o.p.) All tracks reissued on *Marian McPartland at the Hickory House,* Savoy Jazz ZDS 4404. (o.p.)

Moods (1953). "What Is This Thing Called Love?" "All My Life," "A Fine Romance," "Willow Weep for Me," "Lullaby in Rhythm," "There Will Never Be Another You." Savoy MG 15022. (o.p.) All tracks except "All My Life" reissued on *Marian McPartland at the Hickory House,* Savoy Jazz ZDS 4404 (o.p.) and *Marian McPartland on 52nd Street* (Savoy Jazz 92880-2). (o.p.)

Jazz at the Hickory House (1953). "A Foggy Day," "The Lady Is a Tramp," "I've Got the World on a String," "Manhattan," "Aunt Hagar's Blues," "Four Brothers." Savoy MG 15032. All tracks reissued on *Marian McPartland on 52nd Street* (Savoy Jazz 92880-2). "A Foggy Day," "Manhattan," and "Aunt Hagar's Blues" also on *Marian McPartland at the Hickory House,* Savoy Jazz ZDS 4404. All tracks but "Aunt Hagar's Blues" and "Four Brothers" on *Timeless* Savoy Jazz SVY-17117.

Capitol (1953–1957)

Marian made four albums for Capitol Records. They are all out of print:

Marian McPartland at the Hickory House (1954). Capitol Records CAP T574.
After Dark aka *Marian McPartland Trio with Strings: After Dark* (1956). Capitol Records CAP T699.
The Marian McPartland Trio (1956). Capitol Records CAP T785.
Marian McPartland Trio with Strings: With You in Mind (1957). Capitol Records CAP T895.

Various (1956–1968)

Unsigned after her stint at Capitol, Marian recorded as a leader and with Jimmy, Helen Merrill, and Gerry Mulligan for a variety of companies during the 1950s and 1960s:

Jimmy McPartland. *After Hours* (1956). Grand Award 33-334. (o.p.)
Jimmy McPartland's Chicago Rompers. *The Middle Road* (1956). Jazztone J1227. (o.p.)
Helen Merrill. *Helen Merrill with The Hal Mooney Orchestra* (1957). EmArcy Records MG 36107. (o.p.)
Marian McPartland Trio: At The London House Argo (1958). Argo LP S640. (o.p.)
Newport Jazz Festival July 3–6 (1958). With Gerry Mulligan: "Don't Get Around Much Anymore," "C Jam Blues." Phontastic Records NCD 8814. (o.p.)
Marian McPartland Plays the Music of Leonard Bernstein (1960). Time Records Time LP 52013. (o.p.)
Jimmy and Marian McPartland Play TV Themes (1960). Design DLP-144. (o.p.)
Marian McPartland: Bossa Nova + Soul (1963). Time Records LP S-2073. (o.p.)
She Swings with Strings (Marian McPartland with the Frank Hunter Orchestra) (1964). Sesac Records N6501/2. (o.p.) Reissued on Jazz Vault JV 113. (o.p.)
My Old Flame: Marian McPartland Performs the Classic Hits of Sam Coslow (1968). Dot DLP 25906. (o.p.)

Halcyon Period (1969–1979)

Frustrated by the lack of interest in jazz by major labels, Marian started her own company, Halcyon, in 1968. With the exception of an album for RCA and two for Tony Bennett's short-lived Improv label, she recorded exclusively for Halcyon during this period. She continued to release albums on Halcyon occasionally after she signed with Concord in 1979:

Interplay: Marian McPartland (1969). Halcyon Records HAL 100. (o.p.)
Marian McPartland: A Delicate Balance (1972). Halcyon Records HAL 105. (o.p.)
Elegant Piano: Solos and Duets by Teddy Wilson and Marian McPartland (1970). Halcyon Records HAL 106. (o.p.)
Live at the Monticello: Jimmy and Marian McPartland (1972). Halcyon Records HAL 107 (1972). (o.p.) Reissued (partially) on *Marian and Jimmy McPartland:*

A Sentimental Journey (with Special Guests Vic Dickenson, Gus Johnson, and Buddy Tate) (1994). Jazz Alliance TJA-10025.

Marian McPartland: Plays the Music of Alec Wilder (1973). Halcyon Records HAL 109. (o.p.) Reissued on *Contrasts* (2003). Jazz Alliance TJA-10016.

Marian McPartland: Solo Concert at Haverford (1974). Halcyon Records HAL 111. (o.p.)

Swingin': Marian and Jimmy McPartland and Guests (1973). Halcyon Records HAL 114. (o.p.) Reissued on *Contrasts* (2003). Jazz Alliance TJA-10016. Also reissued (partially) on *Marian and Jimmy McPartland: A Sentimental Journey (with Special Guests Vic Dickenson, Gus Johnson, and Buddy Tate)* (1994). TJA-10025.

Let It Happen (1974). RCA Records LSA 3304. (o.p.)

The Maestro and Friend: Marian McPartland and Joe Venuti (1974). Halcyon Records HAL 112. (o.p.)

Concert in Argentina: Earl Hines, Teddy Wilson, Marian McPartland, Ellis Larkins (1974). Halcyon Records HAL 113. (o.p.)

Live in Tokyo: Marian McPartland and Hank Jones (1976). TDK Records TDCN 5141. (o.p.)

A Fine Romance aka *Send in the Clowns* (1976). Improv Records IMP 7115 (o.p.)

Now's the Time (1977). Halcyon Records HAL 114. (o.p.)

Wanted (Live) aka *Marian and Jimmy McPartland and the All-Star Jazz Assassins* (1977). Improv Records IMP 7122. (o.p.)

Tony Bennett, the McPartlands, and Friends Make Magnificent Music (1977). Improv Records IMP 7123. (o.p.) Reissued on *The Complete Improv Recordings* (2004). Concord Records CCD4-2255-25.

Marian McPartland: Live at the Carlyle (1979). Halcyon Records HAL 117. (o.p.) Reissued on Prevue CD PR 25 (o.p.)

Concord period (1979–present)

Marian McPartland: From This Moment On (1979). Concord Jazz CCD-4086-2.

Portrait of Marian McPartland (1980). Concord Jazz CCD-4101-2. Reissued on *Windows* (2004), Concord Jazz CCD2-2233-2.

Marian McPartland: At the Festival (1980). Concord Jazz CJ-118. Reissued on *Windows* (2004), Concord Jazz CCD2-2233-2.

Marian Remembers Teddi (1981). Halcyon Records HAL 118. (o.p.)

George Shearing and Marian McPartland: Alone Together (1982). Concord Jazz CCD-4171-2.

Marian McPartland: Personal Choice (1982). Concord Jazz CCD-4202-2.

Marian McPartland: Willow Creek and Other Ballads (1985). Concord Jazz CCD-4272-2.

Mary Fettig. *Mary Fettig Quartet: In Good Company* (1985). Concord Jazz CJ 273. (o.p.)

Marian McPartland: Plays the Music of Billy Strayhorn (1987). Concord Jazz CCD-4326-2.

Marian McPartland: Plays the Benny Carter Songbook (1990). Concord Jazz. CCD-4412-2 (1990).

Marian McPartland: Live at the Maybeck Recital Hall Volume Nine (1991). Concord Jazz CCD-4460-2.

Marian McPartland: In My Life (1993). Concord Jazz CCD-4561-2.

Fujitsu 25th Concord Jazz Festival—Silver Anniversary (1993). Concord Jazz CCD2-7002-2.

Marian McPartland: Plays the Music of Mary Lou Williams (1994). Concord Jazz CCD-4605-2.

Live in Tokyo: Marian McPartland and Hank Jones (1994). TDK Records TDCN 5141.

The Marian McPartland Trio: Live at Yoshi's Nitespot (1996). Concord Jazz CCD-4712-2.

Marian McPartland with Strings: Silent Pool (1997). Concord Jazz CCD-4745-2. Also on SACD-1023-6.

Marian McPartland's Hickory House Trio: Reprise (1999). Concord Jazz CCD-4853-2.

Marian McPartland: Just Friends (1999). Concord Jazz CCD-4805-2.

Marian McPartland: Portraits (1999). NPR Classics CD 0010.

Marian McPartland: The Single Petal of a Rose, The Essence of Duke Ellington (2000). Concord Jazz CCD-4895-2.

Marian McPartland and Willie Pickens: Ain't Misbehavin'—Live at the Jazz Showcase (2001). Concord Jazz CCD-4968-2.

Marian McPartland Trio with Joe Morello and Rufus Reid: Live at Shanghai Jazz (2002). Concord Jazz CCD-4991-2.

Marian McPartland & Friends: 85 Candles—Live in New York (2005). Concord Jazz CCD2-2218-2.

Twilight World (2008). Concord Jazz CCD-30528.

Marian McPartland's Piano Jazz

In 1993, Concord spun off the Jazz Alliance label for the purpose of releasing albums of *Marian McPartland's Piano Jazz*. The material on many of the CDs listed here as out of print is now available for streaming at www.npr.org/programs/piano-jazz:

Dave Brubeck (1993). Jazz Alliance TJA-12001. (o.p.) Reissued (2003) as Jazz Alliance TJA-12043.

Teddy Wilson (1993). Jazz Alliance TJA-12002. (o.p.) Reissued (2005) as Jazz Alliance TJA-12052.

Rosemary Clooney (1993). Jazz Alliance TJA-12003 (o.p.) Reissued (2003) as Jazz Alliance TJA-12041.

Bill Evans (1993). Jazz Alliance TJA-12004 (o.p.) Reissued (2002) as Jazz Alliance TJA-12038

Dizzy Gillespie (1993). Jazz Alliance TJA-12005. Reissued (2003) as Jazz Alliance TJA-12042.

Eubie Blake (1993). Jazz Alliance TJA-12006. (o.p.)

Dick Wellstood (1994). Jazz Alliance TJA-12007. (o.p.)

Barbara Carroll (1994). Jazz Alliance TJA-12008. (o.p.)

Clark Terry (1994). Jazz Alliance TJA-12009. (o.p.)

Bobby Short (1994). Jazz Alliance TJA-12010. (o.p.)

Red Richards (1994). Jazz Alliance TJA-12011. (o.p.)

Dick Hyman (1995). Jazz Alliance TJA-12012. (o.p.)

Stanley Cowell (1994). Jazz Alliance TJA-12013. (o.p.)

Mercer Ellington (1994). Jazz Alliance TJA-12014.

Benny Carter (1994). Jazz Alliance TJA-12015. (o.p.)

Milt Hinton (1995). Jazz Alliance TJA-12016 (o.p.)

Jess Stacy (1995). Jazz Alliance TJA-12017 (o.p.)

Jack DeJohnette (1995). Jazz Alliance TJA-12018. (o.p.)

Mary Lou Williams (1995). Jazz Alliance TJA-12019. (o.p.) Reissued (2004) as Jazz
    Alliance TJA-12045-2.

Alice Coltrane (1995). Jazz Alliance TJA-12020. (o.p.)

Kenny Burrell (1995). Jazz Alliance TJA-12021. (o.p.)

Amina Claudine Myers (1995). Jazz Alliance TJA-12022. (o.p.)

Dave McKenna (1995). Jazz Alliance TJA-12023. (o.p.)

Henry Mancini (1995). Jazz Alliance TJA-12024. (o.p.)

Roy Eldridge (1995). Jazz Alliance TJA-12025. (o.p.)

Lee Konitz (1995). Jazz Alliance TJA-12026. (o.p.)

Joe Williams (1996). Jazz Alliance TJA-12027. (o.p.)

Oscar Peterson (1996). Jazz Alliance TJA-12028. (o.p.) Reissued (2002) as Jazz
    Alliance TJA-12033-2.

Lionel Hampton (1996). Jazz Alliance TJA-12029. (o.p.) Reissued (2004) as Jazz
    Alliance TJA-12046-2.

Jay McShann (1996). Jazz Alliance TJA-12030. (o.p.)

Les McCann (1996). Jazz Alliance TJA-12031. (o.p.)

Charles Brown (1996). Jazz Alliance TJA-12032.s (o.p.)

Carmen McRae (2002). Jazz Alliance TJA-12039-2.

Chick Corea (2002). Jazz Alliance TJA-12040-2.

John Medeski (2006). Jazz Alliance TJA-12047-2.

Steely Dan (2005). Jazz Alliance TJA-12048-2.

Elvis Costello (2005). Jazz Alliance TJA-12049-2.

Bruce Hornsby (2005). Jazz Alliance TJA-12051-2.

Shirley Horn (2006). Jazz Alliance TJA-12053-2.

Brad Mehldau (2007). Jazz Alliance TJA-30154-2.

Jimmy McPartland

The Wolverine Orchestra (1924). "When My Sugar Walks Down the Street,"
    "Prince of Wails." Gennett 5620. (o.p.)

McKenzie and Condon (1927). "Liza," "Nobody's Sweetheart." Okeh 40971. (o.p.)
    Reissued (1995) on *Windy City Jazz* Topaz TPZ 1026.

———. "Sugar," "China Boy." (o.p.) Okeh 41011. Reissued (1995) on *Windy City
    Jazz* Topaz TPZ 1026.

The Original Wolverines (1927). "Royal Garden Blues," "A Good Man Is Hard to
    Find." Brunswick BR 4000. (o.p.)

Eddie Condon and His Footwarmers (1928). "Makin' Friends." Okeh 41142. (o.p.)
 Reissued (1995) on *Windy City Jazz* Topaz TPZ 1026.
Benny Goodman's Boys (1928). "Jungle Blues." Brunswick BR 4013. (o.p.)
The Ben Pollack Orchestra (1928). "Futuristic Rhythm." RCA (F) 741101. (o.p.)
 (available as download).
Irving Mills (1928). "Since You Went Away." Brunswick BR 4112. (o.p.)
The Chicago Jazz Album (1939). Decca DL 8029. (o.p.)
Dizzy Gillespie and the Cool Jazz Stars. *Hot Vs. Cool* (1953). MGM E194. (o.p.)
Shades of Bix (1953). Brunswick BL 58049. (o.p.) Original 10-inch EP reissued (1956)
 as 12-inch LP *Jimmy McPartland and His Dixieland Band,* with "In a Mist"
 performed by Marian McPartland. Brunswick BL 54018. (o.p.)
George Wein's Dixie Victors Featuring Ruby Braff (1956). Music from the TV show *The*
 Magic Horn. Jimmy McPartland on "Dippermouth Blues." RCA Victor LPM
 1332. (o.p.)
The Music Man Goes Dixieland (1958). Epic Records LN3463.
More Informal Sessions (1996). MIS-1.
Bud Freeman, Jimmy McPartland, Ted Easton's Jazz Band. *Jazz Meeting in Holland*
 (1975). Circle CCD-10.

Index

MM stands for Marian McPartland (née Margaret Turner). JM stands for Jimmy McPartland.

Aachen, Germany, 63
Abbey Road studios, 34–35
Adair, Tom, 321
Adams, Major, 57, 60
Adamson, Harold, 32
Adderley, Nat, 222
Adrienne (singer), 110
African Americans
    in Chicago, 77
    music of, 30, 150, 265, 412
African Jazz Ensemble, 266
Afro-Cuban jazz, 318–19
After Dark: The Marian McPartland Trio with Strings (album), 161
"Afterglow" (song), 239, 252
After Hours (album), 167
Agnes Scott College, 348
A.G.S.M. degree, 34
Akiyoshi, Toshiko, 138, 219–20, 226, 284, 285
Albam, Manny, 350
Albertson, Chris, 226
Albright, Thomas, 275
The Alcoa Hour (TV show), 168
Alcoholics Anonymous (AA), 108, 114, 121, 159, 231, 246, 335
Alexander, Elmer "Mousie," 113, 116, 139, 140, 145, 146, 151, 280
Alexander, Monty, 304
Alice (maid), 7–8
Alice Tully Hall, New York, 331
Alive! (group), 287
Allen, Beverly, 62
Allen, Fred, 174
Allen, Geri, 352, 385
Allen, Henry "Red," 109, 142, 188
Allen, Steve, 5, 156, 157, 161, 162, 199, 318, 325–26
all-female groups, 283–86
All Girls Band (Benson), 39
All in Good Time (book by MM), 341, 348
Allyson, Karrin, 398, 399
Alter, Lou, 40
Alumni Jazz Band, 217
Ambiance (album), 238, 290
"Ambiance" (song), 252, 384

Ambrose, Bert, 23, 36
America/Americans
    British affection for, 69
    overcoming MM's innate reserve, 170
    soldiers in Britain, 48–49
American Popular Song (book by Wilder), 252, 260, 295
American Popular Song with Alec Wilder and Friends (radio show), 295
American Women in Jazz (book by Placksin), 339–40
Anderson, Ernestine, 304
the Apartment, New York, 227–28, 234, 238
Aquarium club, New York, 98
Argo label, 193
Argyl, Chicago, 109
Arlen, Harold, 187, 249, 252, 260, 280, 356
Armitage, Chris (MM's nephew), 45, 245, 313
Armitage, Mark (MM's nephew), 245, 376, 387
Armitage, Sheila (MM's niece), 24, 112, 245, 377, 417
Armitage, Tony (Joyce's husband), 72, 107
Armstrong, Lil, 308
Armstrong, Louis, 41, 56, 79–80, 82, 83, 85, 87–88, 93, 98, 107, 110, 116, 187, 231, 257, 266, 331, 412
Arne, Thomas, 18
Arriale, Lynne, 349
The Artistry of Marian McPartland (transcriptions by Oddo and Sickler), 350
Artman, Julius, 140
ASCAP, 325, 381, 388
Ashcraft, Edwin M. "Squirrel" III, 90–91, 95, 97, 107–8, 228, 235, 375
Askey, Arthur, 34
"Aspen" (song), 239
Associated Booking Corp, 110, 137
Astaire, Fred, 28, 53–54
Astoria, Queens, N.Y., 87
Atlanta, Georgia, 348
Atlantic Records, 135
At the Top (TV series), 283
Atwell, Father Henry, 253, 315
Atwell, Winifred, 41, 382
Audubon Society, 254

Auld, Georgie, 194
Ausanka, Joellyn, 287–88, 300, 338, 372, 397
Austin, Illinois, 77, 181
Austin, Patti, 325
Austin Blue Friars, 78
Austin High Gang, 82, 84, 94, 102
Austin High School, 77, 95
Avakian, George, 91
Avonclyffe School, 14, 18

Bacall, Lauren, 278
Bach, Jean, 375
Bach, Johann Sebastian, 28, 223
Bacharach, Burt, 240
Bailey, Buster, 125
Bailey, Dave, 197, 199
Bailey, Pearl, 365
Baker, Chet, 158, 256, 304
Baker, Dorothy, 93
Baker, Josephine, 116
Baldwin Piano Company, 296, 378
Ball, Ronnie, 194
Balleras, Jon, 329
Ballew, Smith, 89
Balliett, Whitney, 132, 261, 269, 276, 292, 328, 341
Bampton, Claude, 117
Band Box, Chicago, 109
Band Waggon (show), 34, 409
Band Wagon (variety act), 1, 49, 53
Bankhead, Tallulah, 127, 140
Baquet, Maurice, 54
Barbican Centre, London, 326
Barelli, Aimé, 119
Barnes, George, 92, 270
Barnet, Charlie, 102
Baron, Joey, 330, 331
Barton, Willene, 309
Barty-King, Hugh, 27
Basie, Count, 110, 179, 187, 188
    style of, 152, 330
Basin Street, New York, 149, 160
Bates College, 289, 333
Bateson, Mary Catherine, 371
Battle of the Bulge, 59
Baum, Jamie, 386
the Beatles, 43, 212, 213, 224, 240, 292
Beauvoir, Simone de, 280
bebop, 67, 110, 123
Bechet, Sidney, 22, 23, 41, 117
Beebe, Jim, 358
Bee Hive, Chicago, 110
Beethoven, Ludwig van, 28
Beiderbecke, Leon "Bix," 40, 54, 75, 79, 80, 81, 82, 84, 86, 87, 89, 93, 116, 119, 168, 201, 270, 279, 325, 363, 413
    style of, 158
Bel Canto Foundation, 221
Belleson, Louie, 365
Bellmore, Long Island, N.Y., 262, 310
Bemelmans, Ludwig, 275

Bemelmans Bar, Carlyle Hotel, New York, 275–76, 287
Beneš, Edvard, 65
Benjamin, Dr. William, 207, 210, 230, 231, 242, 247, 261
Bennett, Larry, 135, 137, 138
Bennett, Tony, 34, 228, 235, 250, 251–52, 256, 269, 290–92, 295, 325, 334, 392, 398–99
Benny Goodman Trio, 22
Benson, Ivy, 39
Benson, Warren, 251
Benton, Robert, 187
benzedrine, 111–12
Bergman, Ingmar, 309
Berigan, Bunny, 121
Berklee School of Music, Boston, 217
Berlin, Irving, 252
Bernstein, Leonard, 199, 364
Berry, Chuck, 187
Bertoncini, Gene, 276
Betjeman, John, 5
Beverly Hills, California, 248
Big Dorothy. See Williams, Dorothy
Billboard, 160, 161, 178
Birdland, New York, 113, 132, 142, 145, 149, 154, 349, 385, 398
Black, Scott, 111
Blackhawk, San Francisco, 198
Blackhawk Tavern, Chicago, 84, 85
Blackman, Cindy, 388
Blair, Janet, 131
Blake, Eubie, 269, 302, 331
Blakey, Art, 188, 304
Bley, Carla, 286, 309, 382
Bley, Paul, 156, 383
    style of, 239
Blind Orchestra, 117
Blitz, World War II, London, 69
Blitzkrieg, World War II, 44–45
Blood, Sweat and Tears, 293
Bloom, Jane Ira, 386
Blue Note, Chicago, 109, 113, 146
Blue Note, New York, 167, 172
blues, 177
Blues Alley, Washington, D.C., 249, 250, 258
Blumenthal, Bob, 396
Boccherini, 36
Borders Books & Music, 381
bossa nova, 199
Bossa Nova + Soul (album), 199–200
Boston, 125, 130, 141, 147, 171, 395–96
The Boston Globe, 176
Boston Globe Jazz Festival, 310
Boston Symphony, 132
Bouchard, Fred, 313
Bourgeois, Charlie, 130, 176, 220, 269, 299, 300, 334
Bourne, Michael, 370
Bow Bells (stage show), 18
Bowie, David, 11

Bown, Patti, 229
Boykins, Ronnie, 296
Brackeen, Joanne, 296, 308, 309, 328, 334, 348, 371, 386
Braddy, Pauline, 307–8, 388
Bradley, Curley, 118
Bradley, Omar, 49, 97
Brady, James, 377
Braff, Ruby, 168, 361
Braithwaite, E. R., 348
Brando, Marlon, 123
Brass Rail, Chicago, 94, 104, 106, 108, 109
Braugham, Charlie, 361, 370, 400
Braybeck, Irv, 127
Brice, Fanny, 89
Bridge, Frank, 22
Bridgeford, Buzzy, 152
Britain/British
    audience for jazz, 23
    bathroom humor of, 47
    class system, 8
    preparation for war, 42
    reserve of, 170
    sexuality of, 46–47
    war brides, 69
    See also England
British Broadcasting Corporation (BBC), 23, 29, 34, 39, 41, 117, 143, 159, 169, 324
British Expeditionary Force, 43
"British invasion," 212
Britto, Bill, 166–67, 168, 171, 193, 347
Britto, Carol, 166, 347
Broadbent, Alan, 384
Broadway, New York, 75
Bromley, England, 11, 29
Bromley Music Festival, 21
Bron, Eleanor, 208, 244, 377
Brookmeyer, Bob, 316
Brown, Arthur, 41
Brown, Cleo, 41, 318, 321, 332, 371
Brown, Clifford, 163
Brown, Pamela, 18
Brown, Patti, 322
Brown, Ray, 126, 129, 222, 304, 306, 365
Brubeck, Chris, 320
Brubeck, Dave, 95–96, 128, 141–42, 147, 149, 158, 160, 162, 170, 171, 176, 179, 194, 199, 212, 219, 318, 320, 325, 331, 376, 381–82, 385, 387
Brunies, George, 94
Bruno Walter Auditorium, Lincoln Center, New York, 260
Brunswick records, 84
Bryant, Clora, 283
Bryant, Ray, 199, 380
Buckley, William F., 315, 350
Buckloff, Michael, 47
Buena Vista Lounge, Disney World, Florida, 310
Buenos Aires, Argentina, 271
Bunch, John, 204–5, 242, 361, 380
Burke, Vinnie, 151, 152, 424

Burkhardt, Jay, 110
Burns, Ken, 398
Burr, Jon, 240
Burrell, Kenny, 380
Burton, Gary, 240
Bushkin, Joe, 125, 127, 128, 129, 138, 178
Byard, Jaki, 322
Byas, Don, 117
Byrd, Charlie, 291

Caen, France, 49
Caesar, Irving, 167
Café Bohemia, New York, 149
Café Carlyle, New York, 261
Café Society, New York, 113, 149, 256
Cagney, Jimmy, 1, 48
Cahn, Sammy, 179
Cain, Jackie, 110, 315–16, 325, 380, 398
Callahan, John, 274
Calloway, Cab, 249
Campbell, Elspeth, 19
Campbell, Glen, 237
Cannes, France, 66
Capitol Lounge, Chicago, 103
Capitol Records, 160–61, 168, 178, 179
Capone, Al, 79
Carless, Dorothy, 36
Carlton, Ben, 103, 110, 111, 113, 114, 116, 118, 125
Carlton, Eileen, 103, 118
Carlyle Hotel, New York, 261, 275–76, 286, 287, 305, 308, 313
Carmichael, Hoagy, 125, 237
Carnegie Hall, New York, 114, 126, 309
Carnevale, Ralph and Mary, 49
Carrington, Terri Lyne, 287, 388
Carroll, Barbara, 128, 129, 132–33, 135, 136, 141, 147, 157, 194, 276, 281, 296, 380, 398
Carroll Levis Discoveries (film), 47
Carroll Levis Discoveries (radio show), 43
Carson, Johnny, 204
Carson, Rachel, 196, 254, 352–53
Carter, Benny, 271, 304, 364–65
Carter, Betty, 284, 331
Carter, Bob, 127, 144–45, 151, 420
Carter, Regina, 398
Carter, Ron, 236
Cary, Dick, 168, 185
Catlett, Sid, 145
Cavalli, Max, 227, 248, 257, 273, 274, 369
cello, 160–61
Celtic Bar, Sherman Hotel, Chicago, 90
Central Plaza, New York, 122, 124, 149, 158
Cerruti, Jorge, 346–47, 377, 389
Cerulli, Dom, 180
Chairman's Pianoforte Prize, 34
Chairman's School Composition Prize, 28
Challen piano company, 32, 34
Chamberlain, Neville, 42
Champion, Marge and Gower, 156
Chapí, Ruperto, 36

Charlap, Bill, 389, 398, 400
Charles, Ray, 199, 200, 256, 291, 356–57
Charlie's Tavern, New York, 162, 426
Chiaroscuro label, 259
Chicago, 42, 54, 58, 77–94, 99, 101–21, 146, 147,
    160–61, 172, 181, 289, 387
  gangsters in, 83, 115
  jazz scene, 76, 84–85, 91, 109–11
Chicagoans (Condon's), 91
Chicago Daily Tribune, 125
The Chicago Jazz Album, 91, 415
Chicago Jazz Archive (CJA), 357–58
Chicago Jazz Festival, 310, 370, 387
Chicago Rhythm Kings, 91
Chicago Symphony, 101, 387
Child's Paramount, New York, 142, 149
Choice, Harriet, 310
Chopin, Frédéric, 7, 28, 33, 201, 377
Christian, Jodie, 387
Christmas, 16, 113, 206, 315
Churchill, Winston, 45
Church of England, 11
CIA, 235
Cinderella Ballroom, New York, 81
Cirin, Alex, 327–28
Clare, Alan, 355
Clark, Dave, 212
Clark, Dick, 91
Clark, Tom, 378
Clarke, Kenny, 136, 157
Clarke, Roma, 39
classical jazz, 127–28, 160, 331
the Claviers, 34–37
Clayton, Buck, 227, 280
Clayton, Geoffrey, 31
Clayton, John, 364
Cleveland, Ohio, 82, 147, 231
Clicquot Club Eskimos, 90
Cline, Patsy, 390
Clinton, Bill, 386
Clooney, Rosemary, 156, 304, 356
Clouds of Joy (band), 104
Club DeLisa, Chicago, 109
Club Forrest, New Orleans, 89
Cobb, Ray, 23, 29
CODA, 239, 307
Cohen, Anat, 386
Cohn, Al (reporter), 215
Cold Spring Harbor High School, Long Island,
    N.Y., 218, 240
cold war, 150
Cole, Nat, 129, 178
Coleman, Bill, 119
Coleman, Cy, 157, 318, 321
Coleman, Ornette, 149, 203, 229, 342
Coleridge-Taylor, Samuel, 27
Colette, 166, 244
College Inn, Sherman Hotel, Chicago, 109
Collier, Zena, 68, 253, 255, 309, 361
Collins, Al "Jazzbo," 129

Collins, Judy, 325, 392
Cologne, Germany, 63
Colonial Tavern, Toronto, 121, 126
Coltrane, John, 149, 218, 222, 224, 225, 229, 278,
    325, 341, 378
  style of, 363
Coltrane, Ravi, 398
Columbia, South Carolina, 294
Columbia Records, 35, 256, 290–91
Columbus, Ohio, 120, 125, 147
Comer, Carol, 284, 348
Commodore Record Shop, 124
Como, Perry, 90
the Composer, New York, 149, 180, 427
Concord, California, 303
Concord Jazz Festival, 306, 363
Concord Records, 283, 303, 351, 357, 363, 380,
    383, 384, 385, 399, 400
Condon, Eddie, 72, 79, 83, 84, 86, 91, 92–93, 94,
    95, 97–99, 113, 117, 159, 185, 226, 247, 258,
    280, 326
Condon, Phyllis, 247
Congress Hotel, Chicago, 91
Conniff, Ray, 236
Conover, Willis, 187, 280
Cons, Carl, 91
Conservative Club, Bromley, 29
Conwell, Mary Kay, 260, 393
Cook, Marion, 23
the Cookery, New York, 256, 272, 293
Cooper, Margaret, 22
Copeland, Ray, 239
Corea, Chick, 296, 301, 317, 325
  style of, 305, 328
Corsello, Joe, 254, 260
Coslow, Sam, 236, 250
Costello, Elvis, 390, 391–92, 400
Cousteau Society, 353, 362
cover art, 236, 239
Coward, Noel, 28, 39, 263
Cox, Jim, 370
Crispell, Marilyn, 383
Crosby, Bing, 22, 53, 54, 84, 96, 121, 258
Crosby, Bob, 30, 121
Crow, Bill, 140, 151, 152–53, 156, 160–61, 165,
    166, 180, 187, 197, 378, 380, 385, 398
Crowther, Bosley, 158
Crystal, Jack, 124
Cuenca, Sylvia, 386
Culhane, Tom, 108
Cusatis, Joe, 193

Da Costa, Raie, 41
Dahl, Linda, 309, 340
Daily News (New York), 311
Dale, Zonie, 48, 181
Daley, Mayor, 361
Dalton, Sasha, 331
Daly, Claire, 386
Dameron, Tadd, 304

Damita, Lili, 88
Danitz, Marilyn, 247
Dankworth, Alec, 377
Dankworth, Cleo, 369
Dankworth, John, 143, 326–27, 348, 369, 382
Dardanelle (Marcia Marie Hadley), 132
Dave Clark Five, 212
Davern, Kenny, 270
Davey Jones Locker Room, Minneapolis, 216
David Lipscomb University, 368
Davis, Dorothy (later Nash), 62
Davis, Glenn, 333, 376, 383, 386, 398, 399
Davis, Jean, 340
Davis, Miles, 117, 119, 130, 141, 149, 201, 237, 277, 326
   style of, 238
Davis, Stuart, 93
Davison, Wild Bill, 270
Dawson, Alan, 240
D-Day invasion, World War II, 1, 49
Dean, James, 123
Dearie, Blossom, 235, 262
Debussy, Claude, 28, 168, 201
Deems Taylor Broadcast Award, 381
DeForest, Charles, 228
Delaunay, Charles, 67
A Delicate Balance (radio program), 226
"A Delicate Balance" (song), 252
Delius, Frederick, 28, 33, 37, 229, 320
Delmonte, David, 1, 47–48
DeMichael, Don, 218, 229
Dempsey, Jack, 89, 90, 96
Dennenberg, Marty, 110
Dennis, Matt, 321
De Rosa, Clem, 216–17, 239, 240, 247
Des Moines, Iowa, 82
Desmond, Margaret, 253
Desmond, Paul, 142, 171, 172–73, 176, 203, 209, 218–19, 249, 281, 320, 341
Detour, Chicago, 109
Detroit, 147, 167
Dickenson, Vic, 125, 188, 280
Dietrich, Marlene, 53, 60
Diller, Phyllis, 325
Dimitriou, John, 301
Dinkler Motor Inn, Syracuse, N.Y., 310
Di Pasqua, Mike, 305
disco, 265
Dixieland Jazz Jubilee, 337
Dixieland revival, 94
Dixon, Lucille, 309
Dizzy's Club Coca-Cola, New York, 400
Djangirov, Eldar, 352, 388
Dobrin, Peter, 388
Dodds, Warren "Baby," 78, 102
Dodds Brothers, 85
Dodgion, Dottie, 208–9, 215, 262, 283, 284, 285, 340
Dodgion, Jerry, 208, 225, 284, 330
Doerschuk, Robert, 323, 370–71

Dome Arena, Henrietta, New York, 289
Domínguez, Alberto, 271
Donegall, Lord and Lady, 143
Donegan, Dorothy, 299, 301, 309
Dorham, Kenny, 222
Dorne, Raquelle, 39
Dorritie, Frank, 303, 357
Dorsey, Jimmy, 75, 86, 88
Dorsey, Tommy, 75, 86, 114, 121, 171
Dot label, 236
Douglas, Dave, 398
Douglass, Bill, 349, 383–84, 390, 396, 400
Down Beat, 72, 91, 93, 103, 114, 116, 118, 119–20, 131, 132, 133, 141, 147, 159, 161, 176, 179, 180, 185, 186, 196, 198, 205, 210, 215, 217, 218, 222, 225, 229, 237, 246, 248, 256, 273, 329, 338, 370
   Blindfold Test, 134, 378
Down Beat club, New York, 135
Down Beat Jazz Festival, 224
Down Beat Room, Chicago, 109
Downtown Room, Buffalo, 290
Dreamland Café, Chicago, 82
drugs, 111
Dryden, Ken, 397
Duke, Doris, 186
Dukes of Dixieland, 194
Duke University, 268
Dulles, John Foster, 185
Dunkirk rescue, 43
Dunne, Irene, 39
Dylan, Bob, 34
Dyson, Albert Harry (Harry) (MM's great-uncle), 3–4, 7
Dyson, Arthur Edward (MM's great-uncle), 3
Dyson, Charles Frederick (Frederick) (MM's great-uncle), 3–4
Dyson, Sir Cyril (MM's cousin), 3, 155
Dyson, George Henry (MM's great-uncle), 3
Dyson, Margarette Clara (MM's great-aunt), 3
Dyson, Sarah Annie (Annie) (MM's grandmother), 3, 11–12
Dyson, Thomas (MM's great-grandfather), 3
Dyson, Thomas George (MM's great-uncle), 3
Dyson and Sons, 3
Dyson family, 3–4

Eastbourne, England, 37, 71, 118, 169, 348
Eastbourne Rhythm Club, 118
Eastman School of Music, 253–54, 349–50, 359
Eastwood, Clint, 400
Eddie Condon's, New York
   closing of, 326
   MM's first venue in New York, 149
Eddy, Bill, 47
Eden, Ellie, 139, 154
Edison, Harry "Sweets," 365, 380
Edwards, Phil, 363
85 Candles—Live in New York (album), 399
Eigsti, Taylor, 352, 390

Eisenhower, Dwight D., 54, 67
Eisenhower, Julie, 267
Eldridge, Roy, 59, 109, 128–29, 134, 188, 197, 223, 227, 280, 321, 348
electric pianos, MM's use of, on the road, 196
Elie, Rudolph, 132
Elizabeth II, Queen, 400
Ellington, Duke, 22, 40, 41, 103, 116, 138, 140–41, 157, 168, 176, 179, 185, 187, 201, 222, 229, 237, 249, 258, 265, 266–67, 282, 302–3, 331, 364, 395, 396, 399
    style of, 350, 363
Ellington, Mercer, 267
Ellington, Ruth, 141, 249
Ellis, Beatrice "Evie," 141
Ellis, Don, 245
Ellis, Herb, 303
El Matador, San Francisco, 275
Elmes, Barry, 397
Elmhurst, Illinois, 360
Elwood, Phil, 303, 328, 329, 339, 349
Embassy Four, 90, 93
the Embers, New York, 127, 128, 134, 135, 137, 149, 175
EMI Music, 160
Empire Room, Palmer Hotel, Chicago, 90
England, 159–60, 169, 180–81, 194, 211, 348, 355, 389
    MM not popular in, 159–60
    See also Britain/British
Enstice, Wayne, 377–78
Entertainments National Service Association (ENSA), 2, 44
Ephland, John, 370
Epic Records, 184–85
Equal Rights Amendment, 280
Ertegun, Ahmet, 276, 356
Esquire (magazine), 187, 189, 340
Esquire label, 117
Establishment, The, New York (revue), 208
Eton College Musical Society, 3
Eubanks, Robin, 397
Eugene, Ore., 349
Eupen, Belgium, 56–57, 60, 63
European circuit, 270, 365
Evans, Bill, 201–2, 209, 218, 222, 226–27, 229, 237, 239, 272, 290, 296, 300–301, 303, 341, 430
    style of, 202, 239, 305, 328, 349, 383, 396
Evans, Chick, 110, 111, 113
Ewell, Don, 258

Faddis, Jon, 398
Fairchild, Sherman, 125, 144, 183, 228, 235, 238, 258–59
Falaise Gap, World War II, 97
Farlow, Tal, 304
Farmer, Art, 197
Farnon, Robert, 252
Fauré, Gabriel, 384

Feather, Leonard, 119, 131–32, 133–34, 141, 142, 167, 186, 275, 280, 284, 285, 303, 308, 318, 327, 328, 330, 378
Federal label, 127
The Feminine Mystique (book by Friedan), 195
feminism, 133, 280–87
Fender Rhodes (instrument), 200
Ferguson, Maynard, 226, 228, 248
Ferrer, José, 156
Fettig, Mary, 284, 287, 304, 306, 358, 370
Fields, Dorothy, 87
Fields, Gracie, 39, 44
Fields, Kansas, 358
Fields, Lew, 87
Fifty-second Street jazz clubs, New York, 67
Filoli, Woodside, California, 394
A Fine Romance (album), 291
Fitzgerald, Ella, 109, 194, 198–99, 258, 271, 292
Fitzgerald, F. Scott, 90
Five Play, 386
the Five Spot, New York, 149, 186, 203
Flack, Roberta, 325
Flanagan, Thomas, 296, 299, 348, 366, 380, 385
Florentine Grill, Park Central Hotel, New York, 86
Flynn, Errol, 88
Fonda, Henry, 156, 278
Fonteyn, Margot, 15, 235
"For Dizzy" (song), 319, 350
Forest Room, Columbus, Ohio, 120
Foresythe, Reginald, 40, 42
Formby, George, 39
Forrest, Helen, 131
Foster, Frank, 223
400 Restaurant, New York, 98
Fox, Roy, 23
Fox Lake Casino, near Chicago, 79
France, 42, 134
    jazz in, 67, 116–17
Franklin, Mrs. (Frank Turner's landlady and possible lover during the War), 45–46
free jazz, 203, 229, 383
Freelon, Nneena, 398
Freeman, Bud, 22, 55, 58, 77, 80, 82, 84, 85, 86, 93, 94, 113–14, 124, 156, 168, 185, 187, 188, 194, 270, 278, 310, 346, 360
Freeman, Stan, 147
French Lick, Indiana, 197
Friar's Inn, Chicago, 77, 83
Friedan, Betty, 133, 280
Friedman, Don, 222
Friedman, Janice, 376
Friends of Alex Wilder, 316
Frishberg, Dave, 390
Fritzel, Mike, 83
From This Moment On (album), 304, 440

Gabriel Award, 332
Gardner, Hy, 152
Garlow, Kitty, 59
Garment, Len, 255, 265

Garner, Erroll, 147, 161, 176, 199, 378
Garroway, Dave, 111, 113, 137, 151
General Strike (1926), 14
Gensel, Rev. Peter, 347, 359, 361
George V, King, 4
Germany, 37–38, 63
Gerow, Leonard Townsend, 61
Gershwin, George, 30, 141, 144, 252, 356
Getz, Stan, 152, 185, 199, 269, 295, 304, 316, 364
Giannini, Elena, 381
Gibbons, Carroll, 23, 41
Gibbs, George, 159
Gibbs, Lee, 230
Gibbs, Lenore (JM's niece, née McPartland), 92
Gibbs, Terry, 128
Giddins, Gary, 331
Gielgud, John, 39, 209
Gil, Gosia, 373, 381
Gilberto, Astrud, 364
Gilder, Rusty, 260
Gillespie, John Birks "Dizzy," 67–68, 103, 104, 111, 135, 142, 161, 188, 197, 209, 216, 258, 302, 309, 318–19, 326, 328, 350, 366, 392
Gillespie, Lorraine, 138
Gitler, Ira, 222, 380
Giuffre, Jimmy, 156, 157–58, 159, 187
    style of, 152
Glaser, Joe, 110, 113, 115, 120, 137, 197, 227, 369
Glasper, Robert, 400
Gleason, Jackie, 161
Gleason, Ralph J., 195
"Glimpse" (song), 238–39
Goering, Hermann, 73
Goldblatt, Burt, 131, 146
Goldkette, Jean, 81
Goldman, Jack, 138
Golly, Jack, 113
Gomez, Eddie, 200, 202, 208–9, 227, 230, 248, 303, 322, 341
Gonsalves, Paul, 168
Goodman, Benny, 22, 23, 40, 41, 55, 75, 76, 79, 84, 86, 87, 88, 91, 94, 95, 96, 114, 156, 171, 203–4, 209, 218, 219, 226, 249, 280, 341
    difficulty of working with, 203–4
Goodman, Harry, 86
Gopnik, Adam, 391
Gottlieb, Annie, 285
Gould, Morton, 219
Gourdol, Alexandre (Donna's son), 346
Gourdol, Benjamin (Donna's son), 346
Gourdol, Jacques (Donna's husband), 280, 313, 326, 346, 387
Grammy Awards, 225–26, 400
Grande Parade du Jazz, Nice, 270, 326, 327
Grandview Inn, Columbus, Ohio, 126
Granz, Norman, 126, 219, 292
Grappelli, Stéphane, 41, 270
Graves, Denyce, 376
Great American Songbook, 292, 356

The Great Crepitation Contest of 1946 (comedy album), 165
A Great Day in Harlem (documentary film), 375–76, 378
A Great Day in Harlem (photograph), 188–89, 399
Great Migration, 77
Greece, Helene, 386
Green, Benny, 352, 380
Greenberg, Roland, 119
Gregg, Dianne, 284
Grey, Al, 365
Greystone Ballroom, Detroit, 83
Grieg, Edvard, 7, 37, 287, 288, 313, 330, 377
Griffin, Daniel, 136, 289, 314–15, 325, 357, 366, 368–69, 372, 376
Griffin, Johnny, 188
Grimm, Bill, 79
Gross, Ben, 134
Guaraldi, Vince, 199
Guarnieri, Johnny, 128, 147
Guggenheim Foundation, 339
Guide to Swing Music (book by Panassié), 85
Guildhall School of Music and Drama, 1–2, 25, 27–34, 288
Guild Records, 68

Hackett, Bobby, 72, 92, 194, 205, 227
Haggart, Bob, 345
Haid, Al, 79
Haig, Al, 68, 228
Haigh, Ada Bacon, 18, 21, 24, 29
Halcyon Records, 236, 237–38, 258–60, 270, 273, 305, 435
Hale, Binnie, 18
the Half Note, New York, 149
Hall, Adelaide ("Addy"), 40, 42
Hall, Cliff, 48
Hall, Henry, 23
Hall, Herb, 291
Hall, Jim, 222, 398
Hallock, Ted, 115
Hammond, Dorinda, 12
Hammond, John, 119
Hampson, Tom, 268, 296, 315, 388
Hampson, Zena, 315
Hancock, Herbie, 225, 226, 266, 317, 322, 324, 365
    style of, 238, 328
Handy, Antoinette, 340
Hanna, Jake, 172, 198, 227, 303, 304, 307, 341
Hanna, Sir Roland, 390
Hanon method of piano technique, 28
Harding, Hank, 126
Hardy, Joe, 56
Hargrove, Roy, 398
Harlem, New York, 67, 87–88
Harlequin Records, 72
Harmon, Dave, 81
Harmony label, 116
harp, 160–61
Harris, Fred (JM's uncle), 77, 88

Harris, Gene, 385
Harris, Joe, 91
Harrison, Rex, 209
Hart, Billy, 238, 265
Hartman, Johnny, 295
Hartwell, Jimmy, 81
Hartz, Jim, 312
Harvard University, 276
Hasse, Paul "Frisco," 79
Hassett, Bill, 290–91
Hatchett's club, London, 41
Havana, Cuba, 90
Haverford College, 272–73
Hawes, Hampton, 186
Hawkins, Coleman, 31, 128–29, 134, 188
Hawthorne School, Washington, D.C., 266
Hawthorn road house, Cicero, Illinois, 79
Hay, Bill, 295–96
Hayes, Harold, 187
Heath, Ted, 117
Hebb, Bobby, 240
Heffley, Mike, 349
Heidt, Horace, 89
Heilbrun, Carolyn, 282, 360, 411
Heiser, Catherine, 380–81
Heitler, Mike de Pike, 77
Helleur, Stan, 126
Hello, Daddy (musical), 87
Henderson, Bobby, 258
Henderson, Fletcher, 98
Hendrick, Joe, 238, 260
Hentoff, Nat, 129, 130, 135, 157, 161, 188, 328, 375
Hepburn, Katharine, 278, 334–35
Heppell, Kathleen, 34, 36, 37
Herbst Theatre, San Francisco, 370
Herman, Woody, 111, 114, 127, 157
Herve, Belgium, 60
Hess, Myra, 28
"He's the One" (song), 106
Heywood, Eddie, 109, 128
Hickory House, New York, 62, 138, 144, 149, 151, 154–57, 167, 169, 171, 183, 186, 187, 197, 198, 204, 209, 220, 227, 247–48, 299, 341, 355, 380, 383, 385
Higginbotham, J. C., 109
High Fidelity, 273
Hilton Head Arts and Jazz Festival, 279
Hines, Earl "Fatha," 85, 117, 157, 235, 258, 271, 327
Hi-Note, Chicago, 110, 117
Hinton, Milt, 187, 365
Hipp, Jutta, 132, 138
Hiroshima, 66
Hirschfeld, Al, 392
Hitchcock, Alfred, 39
Hitler, Adolf, 42
Hodes, Art, 76
Hodges, Johnny, 330
Holden, Stephen, 328, 331
Holiday, Billie, 92, 110, 114, 115, 187, 293, 342, 392

Holland, Dave, 363
Hollenbeck, John, 397
Hollins, Miss, 20
Hollywood, California, 49
Holm, Celeste, 66–67, 130
Holmes, John Clellon, 196
Holy Trinity Convent, 18, 29
Holzfeind, Frank, 113
Hookham, Felix, 15
Hookham, Nita, 15
Hookham, Peggy (Margot Fonteyn), 15
Horn, Shirley, 176, 320–21, 322
Horne, Lena, 342, 378
Horowitz, Murray, 399
Horowitz, Vladimir, 334
Hot Club, Paris, 67
Hot Club of Chicago, 102, 105
Hot Feet (revue), 87
Hot Record Society label, 91
housewife ideal, 133, 281
Houston, 206
Huebner, Clarence, 65
Hughes, Ken, 22
Hughes, Langston, 78
Hull House, Chicago, 76, 79
Humboldt State College, California, 365
Humes, Helen, 309, 342
Hunt, Betty Lee, 308
Hunter, Frank, 290
Hunter, Lurlean, 194
Hunter College, New York, 388
Huntington Township, Long Island, N.Y., 218, 239
Hutcherson, Bobby, 222
Hutchinson, Leslie "Hutch," 40, 42, 408
Hutchinson, Shari Craighead, 317, 322–23, 347, 354–55, 364
Hyams, Marjorie, 138
Hylton, Jack, 23, 54
Hyman, Dick, 296, 322, 377, 389

Ibarra, Susie, 388
Ibert, Jacques, 28
"I'll Be Around" (song), 161, 228, 250, 296
"Illusion" (song), 252
improvisation, 383
Improv Records, 291
"In a Mist" (song), 40, 82, 115, 116, 168, 270, 325, 347
Independent School (magazine), 314
In My Life (album), 363
Institute of Jazz Studies, 218
International Art of Jazz, 217, 397
International Association for Jazz Education (IAJE), 397, 436
International Jazz Festival, 365
International Jazz Hall of Fame, 378
International Radio Festival of New York Gold Medal Award, 332
International Sweethearts of Rhythm, 307–8, 341, 388

Interplay (album), 236–37
"In the Days of Our Love" (song), 252, 306
In Town Tonight (radio program), 169
Iron Butterfly, 240
Irving Plaza, New York, 390
Irwin, Pee Wee, 247
Israels, Chuck, 293
Ithaca College, Ithaca, N.Y., 333
Ives, Charles, 229
Izzard, Eleanor, 16

Jackson, Chubby, 111, 188, 216
Jackson, Franz, 358
Jackson, Isaiah, 287
Jackson, Mahalia, 187
Jamal, Ahmad, 193, 199
James, Leon, 158
Janofsky-Patterson big band, 308
Japan, 66, 271, 349, 366
Jarrett, Keith, 271, 272, 332, 400
    style of, 383
Jarvis, Edith, 16
jazz
    avant-garde, 224, 378
    British audience for, 23
    changes in, during the 1960s, 223–25
    as fine art, 292–94, 331
    golden age of (1950–53), 123–48
    golden age of (1953–56), 149–70
    golden age of (1956–58), 171–89
    loss of popularity, 213
    new audiences for, 348–49, 378
    renaissance of (1973–78), 265–94
    revivalist, 94–95
    in schools, 177–78, 215–18, 239–41, 265–68
    teaching of technique, 110, 240–41, 265–68
Jazz (PBS documentary), 398
Jazz Alive (radio show), 299
Jazz Alley, Seattle, 301, 349, 358, 390, 394
Jazz Alliance label, 260, 357, 444
Jazz and Classics Festival, Juneau, Alaska, 353
Jazz Anecdotes (book by Crow), 152
Jazz at 76 Warrenton, Boston, 125
Jazz at Lincoln Center, 331
Jazz at the Hickory House (album), 151–52
Jazz at the Philharmonic, 109
Jazz at the Top (videocassette), 279
Jazz Bakery, Los Angeles, 349, 394
Jazz Band Ball (radio program), 169
Jazz Dance (documentary film), 158, 180
Le Jazz Hot (magazine), 67
"jazz-in," 247
Jazz Institute of Chicago, 365
Jazz Journal, 237
Jazz Ltd., Chicago, 109
Jazz Masters Award, 386
Jazz on a Summer Day (documentary film), 187
Jazz Showcase, Chicago, 109, 387, 397
Jazz Silver Medal, 389
Jazz Suite, Beverly Hills, 248

JazzTimes, 313, 332, 355, 378
Jefferson, Carl, 303–4, 306, 357, 363
Jeffries, Herb, 127
Jessel, George, 89
Jimmy and Marian McPartland Fellowship in
    American Music, 387
Jimmy Giuffre 3, 187
Jimmy Ryan's, New York, 138, 149
Jobim, Antonio Carlos, 377
John, Elton, 292
Johnson, Buddy, 240
Johnson, Bunk, 106, 122
Johnson, Robert, 251
Jones, Amanda, 262
Jones, Hank, 188, 271, 400
Jones, Harold, 364, 384
Jones, Jo, 144
Jones, Jonah, 161, 194
Jones, Margaret, 169
Jones, Max, 71, 169, 212
Jones, Norah, 390, 391, 395, 398
Jones, Quincy, 218, 229
Jones, Rusty, 42, 284, 326
Jones, Spike, 113
Jones, Thad, 225
Jordan, Duke, 322
Jordan, Sheila, 400
Josephson, Barney, 256
Juárez, Mexico, 233
Julius (headwaiter at Hickory Club), 154, 155
Just Friends (album), 373, 385
Just Jazz (annual compilation of essays), 194
JVC Festival, 388

Kahn, Otto, 89
Kahn, Roger Wolfe, 89
"Kaleidoscope" (song), 301, 359
Kane, Art, 150, 187
Kansas City, Missouri, 284
Kansas City Women's Jazz Festival, 284–85, 286,
    295–96, 308, 348
Kappes, Jim, 228, 230, 239, 248
Kappes, Mickey, 271
Kassel, Don (JM's son-in-law, m. Dorothy H.
    McPartland), 105, 106, 112, 142, 164–65, 173,
    182, 236, 245, 335
Kassel, Donna (JM's granddaughter, m. Jacques
    Gourdol), 94, 102, 137, 164, 182, 184, 231,
    244, 247, 273–74, 280, 313, 326, 338, 346,
    353–54, 358, 360, 361–62, 365, 387, 395, 397
Kassel, Doug (JM's grandson), 94, 120, 164,
    174, 182, 184, 187, 193, 224, 244, 245, 273,
    275, 280, 312, 337–38, 358, 361–63, 380, 389,
    394, 397
Kazin, Alfred, 333
Keepnews, Peter, 341
Keezer, Geoff, 352
Kellaway, Roger, 322
Kelly, Gene, 141
Kelly, Grace, 352, 400

Kennedy, Bobby, 223
Kennedy, Jacqueline, 156, 275
Kennedy, John F., 275
  assassination of, 205, 223
Kennedy Center, Washington, D.C., 386, 400
Kenny, Nick, 140
Kenton, Stan, 145–46, 161, 223, 235, 284
Kentucky, 197
Kern, Jerome, 126, 273, 356
Kerouac, Jack, 196
Ketelbey, Albert, 31
Khan, Chaka, 378
Kidney, Doris, 20
Kilgallen, Dorothy, 140, 204
King, B. B., 251
King, Jackie, 390, 398
King, Martin Luther Jr., 223
King, Teddi, 260, 276, 436
King Cat Theater, Seattle, 390
King Records, 127
the Kinks, 211
Kirby, John, 109
Kirk, Andy, 104, 136
Kirkwhite, Iris, 36
Kissane, Ruth, 308
Kitt, Eartha, 281
Knauss, Zane, 288
Kniss, Dave, 222
Kofsky, Frank, 199
Komlos, Bill, 193
Konitz, Lee, 158
Kool & the Gang, 265
Kool Jazz Festival, 309, 310, 313, 316, 328
Kopetz-Korf, Ada, 288, 290
Kosko, Polly, 318
Kovacs, Ernie, 185
KQED-TV, 312
Krahmer, Carlo, 117
Kral, Roy, 110, 315–16, 380
Krall, Diana, 355–56, 391, 400
Krupa, Ethel, 98
Krupa, Gene, 84–85, 94, 96, 98, 138, 188, 194
Krupa, Jane, 330
Kruswick, Don, 113
Kuhn, Steve, 157
Kurzweil 250 synthesizer, 352

Labieniec-Despard, Michelle, 388
Labour Party, 14
Lady Chatterley's Lover (book by D. H. Lawrence),
  18
LaFaro, Scott, 201, 228, 237, 303, 322
Laine, Cleo, 326, 348, 369, 378, 382
Laing, R. D., 313
Lambert, Hendricks, & Ross, 194
Lamond, Don, 127, 129–30, 131
Landowska, Wanda, 196
Lang, Eddie, 62, 270
Lange, Art, 384
Lanigan, Diane (JM's niece), 92, 94

Lanigan, Jim (JM's brother-in-law), 77, 78, 83, 84,
  94, 95, 101, 102, 105, 112
Lanigan, Jim (JM's nephew), 105
Lanigan, John (JM's nephew), 102, 105, 112, 244
Lanigan, Richard (JM's nephew), 105
Lanin, Lester, 256
LaPorta, John, 240
Laredo, Ruth, 377
Larkins, Ellis, 271, 296, 299, 322
La Roca, Pete, 202
LaSpina, Steve, 286, 305, 307, 329, 331, 361
Lawrence, Gertrude, 54
Le Club, New Orleans, 293
Le Down Beat, New York, 136
Led Zeppelin, 240
Lee, Dave, 355
Lee, Peggy, 98, 123, 252, 269
Leigh, Vivien, 39
LeMaire, Jack, 62, 67, 138
Lemon, Brian, 355
L'Engle, Madeleine, 394
Lennon, John, 212–13
Leonhart, Jay, 257
Lepp, Harry "Slip," 116
Les Champs, New York, 227
Levis, Carroll, 43, 47
Levittown, Long Island, N.Y., 182
Lewinsky, Monica, 386
Lewis, John, 271, 274, 280, 295, 296, 366
Lewis, Mel, 225
Lewis, Ramsey, 193, 194, 199
Lewis, Vic, 72, 117
liberal politics, 150
Lienhard, Noreen, 241, 351–52
Life (magazine), 93, 375–76
Lifetime Achievement Awards, 370, 386, 388
Lillie, Beatrice, 45
Limpsfield, England, 15
Lincoln Center, New York, 294
Lincoln Gardens, Chicago, 79
Lincoln Park West, near Chicago, 81
liner notes, 152, 238
Lintz, Paul, 294
Lionel Hampton Jazz Festival, 352
Li Po, 211
Liston, Melba, 309, 388
Little Club, New York, 85, 138
Live at Shanghai Jazz (album), 395–96
Live at the Carlyle (album), 305
Live at Yoshi's Nitespot (album), 383–84
Living Room, Cincinnati, 202
Lloyd, David, 29
Local 802 union, New York, 121, 125, 188
Logan, Arthur, 249
Lombard, Illinois, 102
London, England, 39, 117
London House, Chicago, 167, 192, 193
London Jazz Club, 117
London Symphony, 327
Long Beach, N.Y., 121, 124

Long Island, N.Y., 181
Long Island Jazz Festival, 376
Lorillard, Elaine, 162, 186–87
"Lost One" (song), 252
Louisiana, 206
Lou Terrassi's, New York, 142
Lower Basin Street, New York, 180
Lubinsky, Herman, 130, 152
Luftwaffe, 37
Lutcher, Nellie, 111
Lyttelton, Humphrey, 87, 117

Mabern, Harold, 349
MacDonald, Bernice, 139, 257, 260, 322, 347, 366, 377, 389, 393, 395, 397
MacDowell, Edward, 28
Mackie, Doris ("Mac"), 24–25, 31, 194, 286, 417
Madison, Jimmy, 238
Madonna, 292
The Magic Horn (teleplay), 168
Maher, Barbara, 278
Maher, Jim, 163, 175, 233, 252, 269, 278, 287, 289, 309, 341, 371
Malcolm X, 223
Mance, Junior, 365
Manchester, England, 45
Mancini, Henry, 321, 325
Mangano, Dago Lawrence, 77
Manhattan Transfer, 276
Mann, Herbie, 199, 380
Manne, Shelly, 145
Mansfield, Jayne, 183
Marcille, John A., 328
Mares, Paul, 80
Margaret, Princess, 348
Marian McPartland Day, 376
Marian McPartland/Eastman Jazz Series, 388
Marian McPartland: Live at the Maybeck Recital Hall (album), 359
Marian McPartland Plays the Benny Carter Songbook (album), 364–65
Marian McPartland Plays the Music of Billy Strayhorn (album), 330
Marian McPartland's Hickory House Trio: Reprise (album), 385–86
Marian McPartland's Jazz World (book), 397
Marian McPartland with Strings (album), 178
Marian McPartland with Strings: Silent Pool (album), 384
Mariano, Charlie, 219
Maricle, Sherri, 386
Marienbad, 66
marijuana, 83, 111, 256, 279
Marion, Sid, 48
Markson, Hadassah, 377
Mark Taper Forum, Los Angeles, 274
Maroon Five, 80
Marsala, Joe, 138
Marsalis, Branford, 293–94
Marsalis, Ellis, 386

Marsalis, Wynton, 293–94, 331–32, 377, 386
Marsolais, Joe, 176
Martin, Mary, 312
"Marvin Bonessa" (imaginary drummer), 155
Mary, Queen (consort of George V), 4
Mary Lou Williams Jazz Festival, 325
Mary Lou Williams Women in Jazz Festival, 386
Massey, Gwen, 21, 22
May, Earl, 198
May, Elaine, 197
Maybeck Recital Hall, Berkeley, California, 358–59, 396
Mayerl, Billy, 2, 22, 23, 29, 31–37, 201
Mayerl, Jill, 34, 37
Mazzaroppi, Gary, 376, 386, 395, 398
MCA Records, 127, 137
McBride, Christian, 380
McCann, Les, 223
McCartney, Paul, 224, 273
McClure, Ron, 242, 248, 341
McConnell, Jack "Duff," 116
McCorkle, Susannah, 276, 305, 316, 350
McCoy, W. U., 330
McDonough, John, 385
McFerrin, Bobby, 325
McGhee, Howard, 109
McGlohon, Loonis, 294, 295–96, 315, 329, 359
McHargue, Rosy, 82
McHugh, Jimmy, 32
McKenna, Dave, 194, 272, 273, 296, 300, 347
McKenzie, Red, 84, 86
McKenzie-Condon sessions, 54
McNally, Owen, 260, 329
McPartland, Dorothy Hannah (JM's daughter, m. Don Kassel), 88–89, 92–94, 96, 98–99, 104–5, 112–13, 120, 164–65, 173, 182, 192, 193, 243, 245, 273, 337–38
  (1930) birth, 88
  (1941) stays with Lanigans in Chicago, 94
  (1948) marries Don Kassel, 112
  (1968) suicide, 245, 337–38
  JM as father to, 112, 245, 274
McPartland, Ethel (JM's sister, m. Jim Lanigan), 76, 83, 92, 94, 101, 105
McPartland, Haydon (Richard's son), 113, 310, 346, 361, 387
McPartland, James Clement (JM's father), 75, 77–78
McPartland, James Dugald "Jimmy"
  (1907) birth, 75
  (1921) joins the Austin High jazz band scene, 77
  (1923) plays professionally in Chicago, 79–85
  (1928) in New York, 85–90
  (1930) marries Dorothy Williams, 88
  (1935) return to Chicago, 90–95
  (1942) joins the army in a combat role, 95–97
  (1944) meets MM, 55–58
  (1945) marries MM, 58–65
  (1946) in New York with MM, 140, 142
  (1956–66) in New York, 168, 188, 228

McPartland (*continued*)
(1956) in Boston, 171
(1972) in South Africa, 256, 435
(1974) in Nice, 270
(1975) in New York, 276
(1975) travels, 278
(1975) work with MM, 279
(1977) 70th birthday surprise party, 280
(1980) reunites with MM, 309
(1989) appears on *Piano Jazz,* 347
(1990) lung cancer diagnosis, 357
(1991) remarriage to MM, 359
(1991) death and honors, 360–62
affairs of, 174–75
childlike quality of, 279
death, obituaries, burial, and memorials, 360–62
dementia developing, 347
deterioration of, 335
drinking problem, 80, 92, 105–8, 142, 230–31, 246–47
family background, 54–56, 59, 75–99
final years, 345–73
His Orchestra, 91
horn of, obtained by MM, 394
independent gigs of, not playing with MM, 158
influence on MM's career, 282
lack of ambition, 215
a legendary figure, 54–55, 293
lung cancer diagnosis, 357
meets Marian's parents, 71–72
MM's reminiscences and regrets about, 371–73
MM's writing about, 397–98
musical family background, 76
in Paris, 67
at Paris Jazz Festival, 117
pot-smoking and getting stoned, 279
reaction to MM's affair, 175
relationship with daughter Dorothy, 245, 274
relaxing mood of, 345
revivalist jazz of, 94–95
schooling, 77
tributes to, 387
visits to England, 46
in World War II, 65
McPartland, Josh (Haydon's son), 346, 361
McPartland, Lenore (JM's niece, m. Gibbs), 101
McPartland, Lenore (JM's sister-in-law, m. Richard McPartland), 92
McPartland, Marian (née Margaret Turner)
(1918) birth, 3
(1930s) musical recitals in school, 18
(1935) at Guildhall School of Music and Drama, 27–34
(1938) at Mayerl's school of jazz, 32
(1938) drops out of Guildhall, tours with Mayerl, 32–37
(1938) pickup musical jobs in London, 39–43
(1940–45) in World War II, 1–2, 44–45
(1940) signs up with ENSA, 44
(1942) first affair and sex relations, 47–48

(1943) signs up with USO, 48
(1944) in European campaign, 51–66
(1944) meets Jimmy, 55–58
(1945) marries Jimmy, 58–65
(1946) lands in America, 73
(1946) playing clubs in New York, 97
(1946) in Chicago, 101–21
(1946) first gigs in Chicago, 102
(1946) first studio recording, 72
(1949) visits London, plays gigs, 115
(1950) return to New York, 121–25
(1952) opens at Hickory House, 139–40
(1952) visits London, plays gigs, 143
(1957) house in Long Island, 181
(1958) in *Great Day in Harlem* photograph, 188
(1967) divorces Jimmy, 233–34
(1968) starts own label, 235–39
(1978) starts *Piano Jazz,* 295
(1980) reunites with JM, 309–12
(1988) visit to England, 348
(1991) remarriage to JM, 359
(1992) visits England, 366
(1997) visits England, 377
(1998) 80th birthday celebration, 379–80
(2003) 85th birthday celebration, 396–97
(2008) latest tour, 400
(2009) retires from hosting *Piano Jazz* but remains as artistic director, 400
(2010) OBE to, 396
advocate for musicians, 177
affair with Joe Morello, 162–66, 171–74, 210–11
agents and managers, 227, 257, 366–70
age of, kept uncertain, 314, 379
ambition of, 69–70, 176
assertiveness of, learned in America, 180
as author, 307, 338–41, 371, 397–98
autobiography plan, 261–62, 278, 370–71
business knack of, 235, 249
cats in life of, 215, 312
celebrity status of, 334–35, 378
childlessness of, 137–38, 314
"the divorce was a failure," 263
drinking recreationally, 120
engaging the audience during sets, 277
English upbringing, 2–25
environmental concern, 12–14, 196, 353
family background, 3–5
favorite recipes of (e.g., spotted dick), 283
female glamour look of, 281, 306–7, 314, 380–81
generosity of, 325, 351
health problems and accidents, 336–37, 347–48, 355, 366, 367, 377, 381
home and gardening routine, 311
honors and awards to, 332–33, 370, 379, 386, 400
house in Port Washington purchased, 336–37
illnesses, 15
as jazz educator, 177–78, 216–18, 239–41, 265–68
love of pop music and jazz, 23, 29, 40–42
marital problems with Jimmy, 106–9, 215, 230–33
musical ability, 7, 288

musical training, 16–17, 21–22, 24–25, 27–34, 288

music the main interest of, 196–97, 333–34

nurturing role, 109

occasional cruel, arrogant, and demanding behavior of, 314–15, 317, 367–70

parsimony of, 248–49

philanthropy, 387–88

piano style, 153, 157, 160–61, 201–2, 230, 275, 350, 364, 384

psychotherapy sesssions of, 206–8, 210, 230–34

racial and class prejudice lacking in, 42

raunchy language of, 47, 209, 282

reading books, 394

recognition as a top jazz pianist, 135–37, 147, 324, 328, 342–43

recordings, 125, 130

refusal to retire, 399–400

regret for felt mistreatment of Jimmy, 371–73

as reviewer of recordings, 222–25, 432

reviews of work, 157, 237, 330–31, 365

reviews of work, unfavorable, 327–28

schooling of, 12, 14, 18–21

sexuality of, 18, 29, 37, 46–48, 242, 274, 286

shrinks from intimacy, 353–54

song-centered musical approach, 23–24

songs composed by, 167, 252–53

stage names, 1, 34, 114, 126

stubborn, determined character of, 18

sunbathing love, 17, 182

symphonic career of, 287–90, 313, 330–31, 377

teenage friendships, 22

trio personnel, 144–45, 152, 166

women-in-jazz book project, 338–40

writings about music, 118–19, 176, 179, 194, 218–23, 307–8

McPartland, Richard (JM's brother), 76, 78, 81, 84, 90, 95, 102, 113

McPartland, Ruth (JM's sister), 76

McPartland family, 113, 359

McPartlandize, 254

McRae, Carmen, 199, 308–9, 321

Mead, Margaret, 133, 176

Meadows, Jayne, 156

Meet the Composer, 325

Mehegan, John, 154, 179, 349, 427

Mehldau, Brad, 383

Melody Maker (magazine), 31, 61, 71, 95, 143, 180, 194, 212

Mencken, H. L., 78

Mendelssohn, Felix, 21

Menninger, Karl, 206, 267, 282

Menninger Clinic, 206

Mercer, Johnny, 160, 252

Mercer, Mabel, 280, 295, 316

Mermaid Room, New York, 157

Merrick, Long Island, N.Y., 181–82, 335

Merrill, Alan, 163

Merrill, Helen, 163, 165, 173, 176, 179, 200, 219, 233, 263, 382, 392

Metronome, 116, 159, 161

the Metropole, New York, 149, 156, 157, 425

Metropolitan Music School, New York, 154

Metropolitan Theater, Brooklyn, N.Y., 86

Meyer, Sheldon, 307, 340

Meyer, Sig, 82

Mezzrow, Milton "Mezz," 76, 77, 82, 83

Michael's Pub, New York, 272, 305

The Middle Road (album), 167

MIDI, 352

Milano, Lynn, 283, 284, 285–86

Miley, Bubber, 87

Millennium Evenings (TV show), 386

Miller, Allison, 388

Miller, Bill, 178

Miller, Charlie, 62

Miller, Fran, 315–16

Miller, Glenn, 56, 65, 75, 84, 86, 89

Miller, Max, 92, 110

Miller, Mitch, 255, 269, 316

Milliman, Linc, 236, 237, 239, 248, 249

Mingus, Charles, 149

Minneapolis, 216

Minns, Will, 158

Miss Hammond's School for Young Children, 12

Mitchell, Dwike, 222

Mitchell, George, 83

Modern Jazz Quartet, 176, 187

Monk, Thelonious, 136, 149, 186, 187, 188, 200, 278, 319, 331, 347, 351, 384
    style of, 370, 390

Monterey Jazz Festival, 274, 275, 277, 400

Montgomery, General Bernard, 49

Monticello Room, Rochester, New York, 250, 283

Montreal Jazz Festival, 327

Moody, James, 378

Mooney, Hal, 179

Moore, Dudley, 341

Moore, Garry, 140

Moore, Michael, 238–39, 250, 260, 276

Moore, Vic, 81

Moran, Jason, 398

Moran, Pat, 194, 197

Morello, Ellie, 170, 171, 173, 192

Morello, Joe, 136, 140, 144–45, 151, 152, 154, 160–61, 162, 163–64, 168, 171, 173, 176, 191, 193, 202, 207, 210, 219, 231, 243, 252, 341, 352, 355, 378, 380, 385, 394, 395, 398, 399, 448
    (1952) meets MM, plays in trio, 144–47
    affair with MM, 162–66, 171–74, 210–11
    end of the affair, 192

Morgan, Orlando, 28, 30, 33

Morgen, Joe, 138, 139, 140, 141

Morgenstern, Dan, 136, 218, 225, 237, 297, 378, 389

Morris, Audrey, 103, 104

Morris, Ken, 240

Morris, Scotty, 390

Mossman, Ted, 104

motherhood ideal, 133

Motian, Paul, 201
  style of, 239
Mound City Blue Blowers, 84
Moyle, Willie, 177
Mulligan, Gerry, 166, 187, 188, 209, 276, 316, 321
Multi-Tone (keyboard), 32, 35
Munn, Duigald (JM's grandfather), 75–76
Munn, Jeannie (JM's mother), 75–76
Murphy, George, 289
Musical Express, 116, 117
The Music Man Goes Dixieland (album), 184–85
Myddleton, George, 34, 35, 36
*My Old Flame: Marian McPartland Performs the
  Classic Hits of Sam Coslow* (album), 236

Nardy, Joe, 62, 72
Narita, Cobi, 286
Nash, Lewis, 380
National Academy of Recording Arts and
  Sciences, 226
National Association of Jazz Educators, 217, 265,
  332, 436
National Cathedral, Washington, D.C., 386
National Endowment for the Arts (NEA), 265,
  318, 355, 377, 386
National Endowment for the Humanities (NEH),
  307, 338
National Jazz Ensemble, 293
National Organization for Women, 280
National Public Radio (NPR), 299, 377, 392, 399,
  440
National Stage Band Camps, 240, 351
Nava, Eliseo Cueva ("Cheo"), 243–44
Negri, Ruth, 161
Nelson, Nels, 316, 318
Nelson, Willie, 390–91
Nemirovsky, Irene, 393
the Nest, Soho, London, 31
Nest club, Chicago, 82, 83
New Jersey Jazz Society, 359
Newman, Edwin, 253
New Musical Express, 143
New Orleans, 77, 85, 93, 440
New Orleans Rhythm Kings, 77–78, 83
Newport Jazz Festival, 162, 186, 187, 224, 260,
  269–70, 283, 286
Newsday, 215, 241
New Sound Chicagoans, 119
Newsweek (magazine), 185, 194
New York, 73, 75, 85, 97, 117, 121, 149, 181
  heroic period of the 1950s, 123
  jazz community, 84, 149, 399
The New Yorker (magazine), 194, 261, 304
New York Jazz Repertory Orchestra, 293
New York Public Library, 322, 325, 347–48
The New York Times, 140, 260, 265, 308
Nicholas, Glover, and Wray, 312
Nichols, Mike, 197
Nichols, Red, 84
Nicholson, Agatha Cicely Grantham, 12

Nick's, New York, 92–93
1960s, 223–24
Ninety-second Street Y, New York, 377, 389
Nixon, Pat, 249
Nixon, Richard M., 249–50, 255, 267
Non-Aggression Pact, German-Soviet, 42
Noone, Jimmy, 82, 83, 85
Nora (friend of Doris Mackie), 24
Norman, "Happy," 61
Normandy invasion, 1, 49, 52, 96–97
North, Dave, 77, 78
North Sea Jazz Festival, 326
Northwestern University, 79
Norvo, Red, 121, 194, 227
Novachord (instrument), 34, 41
Now's the Time (album), 283
Nuremberg trials, 73
"Nurse Turner," 7–8
Nuthouse Band, 117

Oak Ridge Boys, 325
O'Brian, Jack, 228, 234, 308
O'Brien, Floyd, 113
O'Brien, Father Peter, 136, 257, 276, 309, 386
O'Connell, Frank, 105, 233
O'Connor, Father Norman, 169, 171–72, 215, 225
O'Connor, Sandra Day, 376
O'Day, Anita, 91–92, 110–11, 117, 187, 235
Oddo, John, 350
Off-Beat, Chicago, 91
the Office, Freeport, 216
Ogden, Herb, 247
O'Hara, John, 93
Ohio State University, 217
Okeh studios, 84
Olivelli's (theatrical hangout, London), 46
Oliver, Joe "King," 78, 79, 82, 85, 102
Oliver, Sy, 382
Olivia's Patio Lounge, Washington, D.C., 176
Olivier, Laurence, 39
Onassis, Jackie, 156, 275
O'Neal, Hank, 235–36, 246–47, 258–59, 359, 360
"100 Golden Fingers," 349, 366
Order of the British Empire (OBE), 400
Original Dixieland Jazz Band, 23
Ormsby-Gore, Sir David, 156
Ory, Kid, 82
Osborne, Mary, 114, 115, 138, 139, 283, 284, 309,
  340
Oshrain, Dr. Carl, 174, 253, 256, 347, 353
Ouellette, Dan, 399
Ouzer, Lou, 253, 254, 315–16
Oxford University Press, 288, 307, 338, 340–41

PACE program, 239
Pacifica stations, 226
Packard, Mary, 235
Pagani's Restaurant, London, 34
Page, Marian (another pianist and singer with the
  same name as MM's stage name), 127

Page, Marian (early stage name of MM), 1, 34, 407
Page, Oran "Hot Lips," 117, 119
Page, Roger, 227
Paley, Bill, 83
Palm Beach, Florida, 210
Palmer, Bea, 86
Palmer Hotel, Chicago, 361
Panassié, Hugues, 85
Panther Room, Sherman Hotel, Chicago, 92
Parenti, Tony, 98, 152
Parham, Truck, 358
Paris, France, 53, 65, 67, 97, 116–17
Paris, Jackie, 155
Paris Jazz Festival, 116–17, 118
Parker, Charlie "Bird," 67–68, 117, 130, 157, 306,
    321, 328, 331
Parks, Aaron, 352
Parnell's, Seattle, 324
Parsons, Pam, 366–70, 376, 381, 445
Pass, Joe, 303
Pathé newsreel, 35
Patton, George S., 63
Paudras, Francis, 143
Payne, Arthur (MM's uncle), 4, 8
Payne, Jack (bandleader), 23
Payne, Janet (MM's mother, m. Frank Turner), 3,
    7–9, 14–18, 24, 37, 45–46, 61, 71, 117, 126,
    192, 194, 211–12, 366
    (1964) death of, 211
    described, 4
    health problems, 38
    musical ability, 7
Payne, John (MM's grandfather), 4
Payton, Nicholas, 386
Peabody Award, 321, 332, 442
Pearl, Jack, 48
Peck, Dave, 240
Pecka, Colonel, 59, 61
Pekar, Harvey, 222
Pershing Hotel, Chicago, 91, 109
Personal Choice (album), 329
Peters, Bernadette, 325
Peterson, Oscar, 126, 129, 147, 156, 179, 222, 272,
    290, 301, 318, 323–24, 333, 397
Petkere, Bernice, 284
Petrone, Rick, 255
Petrucciani, Michel, 341–42
Pettiford, Oscar, 136, 156, 168, 188, 329
Peyroux, Madeleine, 390
Phillips, Nick, 302, 303, 384, 396
Phillips, Russ, 358
Phipps, Dick, 295, 296, 301, 317–18, 322, 363
Piano Jazz, Volume I (book of transcriptions), 350
Piano Jazz (radio program), 42, 220, 241, 295–316,
    317–26, 327, 332, 340, 341–43, 347, 348–49, 351,
    355–57, 364, 381–83, 386, 390–93, 396, 400
    awards to, 321–22, 355, 442
    CDs taken from, 357
    hiatus in production of (1981), 317
    starting of, 226, 295–96

25th anniversary gala concert, 400
    unique features of, 296–303
Piano Playhouse (concert), 271
Piano Playhouse (radio show), 125
piano teachers, MM's aversion to, 24, 218
piano trios, 124, 129, 421
Pickens, Willie, 387, 396–97
Pickwick label, 201
Piket, Frederick, 351
Piket, Roberta, 351
Pilsen, Bohemia, 65–66
Pimsleur, Susan, 313, 366
Pittman, Susan, 19
Pitts, Trudy, 386
Pizza on the Park, London, 377
Pizzarelli, Bucky, 156
Placksin, Sally, 339–40
Plantation club, Chicago, 82
Playboy (magazine), 260
Playboy Club, Los Angeles, 273, 280
Playboy Jazz Festival, 194
Plunkett's speakeasy, New York, 88–89
Pod's and Jerry's, Harlem, New York, 88
Poland, 42
Pollack, Ben, 84, 85, 86, 88
Pollack, Julian Waterfall, 352
Pollard, Terry, 194
Pollock, Bill, 275
Pomeroy, Herb, 240
Popkin, John, 85, 138, 139–40, 154–55, 187
popular music
    British audience for, 23
    mass production of, 292
    neoclassical, jazz-infuenced, 292
Porter, Cole, 127, 252, 300, 383
Portnoy, Donald, 400
Portrait of Marian McPartland (album), 306, 328–29
A Portrait of Rachel Carson (musical piece), 353,
    400
Portraits (album), 392
Port Washington, Long Island, N.Y., 336–37, 345,
    351, 373
Potter, Chris, 363, 398
Powell, Bud, 111, 135, 136, 141, 143–44, 147, 157,
    223, 324, 383, 392, 423
    style of, 146, 396
Powell, Celia, 382–83
Powell, Mel, 41
Pozo, Chano, 319
Pratt, Nancy Brown, 308
Presley, Elvis, 170, 177, 251, 292
"Press On and Persevere" (house song), 21
Prestige label, 125, 420
Prohibition, 75, 76, 83, 90
Public Broadcasting System (PBS), 279, 283, 377,
    386
Purcell, Henry, 27

Quarrymen (later the Beatles), 43
Queen Elizabeth (ship), 107, 112

Queen Elizabeth II (ship), 376
Queen's Tavern, Durban, South Africa, 256

Race, Steve, 116, 117, 195
Rachmaninoff, Sergei, 28, 104
Radio Rhythm Club show, 41, 72
Rag Doll, Chicago, 107
ragtime, 30
Ramsey, Doug, 307
Randall's Island Jazz Festival, 187
Randolph Street, Chicago, 109
Ranier, Lou, 113
Ravel, Maurice, 82–83, 85, 168, 413
Ravinia Festival, 387
Ravinia hall, near Chicago, 366
Ray, Carline, 340
Ray Knapp School, 113
RCA-Victor, 438
Reagan, Ronald, 353
Reckless, Dolly, 49, 53, 54, 56
Record Mirror, 169
Red Barn, London, 313
Redd, Vi, 283
Redman, Don, 321
Reed, Eric, 388
Reed, Leonard, 341
Reed, Rex, 328–29
Regal, Columbus, Ohio, 126
Reich, Howard, 361, 375
Reid, Rufus, 395
Reinhardt, Django, 41, 54, 67, 103, 117, 161, 270,
    328, 416
Rendezvous, Philadelphia, 121
Reser, Harry, 90
Rex, Charlie, 104
Rexroth, Kenneth, 78
Reynolds, Fred, 147
Rhiannon (singer), 287
rhythm and blues, 123
Rhythm Club, Chicago, 90
Rice, Don, 1, 49
Rich, Buddy, 125, 138, 154, 194
Richardson, Ralph, 39
Rick's Café Americain, Chicago, 284
Riley, Ben, 250
Roach, Max, 155, 199
Roaring Twenties, 75, 88
Robbins, Adelaide, 132
Robbins, Jack, 167
Roberts, Judy, 284, 325, 387
Robertson, W. Graham, 21
Robinson, Bill "Bojangles," 82
Robinson, Edward G., 48
Robinson, Janice, 265, 284
Rochester, New York, 177, 250, 253, 279, 290,
    359, 388, 435
Rochester Philharmonic, 287, 289
Rockefeller, John D., 235
rock music, 239, 251
    MM's condescension toward, 224

rock 'n' roll, 123, 178
Rodgers, Richard, 144, 151
Rodgers and Hammerstein Archives of Recorded
    Sound at Lincoln Center, 322
Rodin, Gil, 86–87
Rogers, Billie, 115
Rogers, Shorty, 141
Rogers, Sylvia, 380
the Rolling Stones, 212, 292
Rollins, Sonny, 149
Ronald, Sir Landon, 25, 27, 30
Ronan, Eddie, 103–4
Ronell, Ann, 151, 284
Roosevelt, Eleanor, 69, 112
Rose, Billy, 89
Rose Bowl, Chicago, 103
Rosnes, Renee, 380, 385, 390, 400
Ross, Diana, 293
Rothstein, Arnold, 87
'Round Midnight (film), 324
Roundtable, New York, 197
Rowe, Ellen, 349–51, 360
Rowles, Jimmy, 30, 272, 273, 304
Royal Academy of Music, 27
Royal Air Force, 43
Royal Box, Americana Hotel, New York, 262
Royal College of Music, 27
Royal Roost, New York, 149
Ruark, Robert, 132
Rubin, Lance, 290
Rubinstein, Arthur, 287
Ruff, Willie, 222
Rushen, Patrice, 287
Rushing, Jimmy, 187, 188, 226
Russell, Connie, 131
Russell, Pee Wee, 72, 82, 86, 93, 94, 157, 158,
    185, 202
Russo, Bill, 110

Sachs, Lloyd, 321
Safranski, Eddie, 129–30, 131, 134
St. Agnes boarding school, 104–5
St. Charles Hotel, near Chicago, 102
Saint-Lô, 49, 97
St. Louis, intercollegiate jazz festival, 240
St. Peter's Church, New York, 347, 361
St. Vith, Belgium, 54–56, 59
Salinger, Pierre, 197, 209, 228
Salmins, Ralph, 377
Salvador, Sal, 144, 145, 155
Sam Beers My Cellar, Chicago, 84
Sarka, Patti, 246, 353
Sartre, Jean-Paul, 116
Saturday Review, 237
Saunders, Red, 109
Sauter-Finegan Orchestra, 145
Saving America's Treasures, 392
Savoy Havana Band, 23
Savoy Hotel, London, 41
Savoy Orpheans, 23

Savoy Records, 130–31, 141, 151–52, 160
Scarlatti, Domenico, 162
Schneider, Ellie, 162
Schneider, Howard, 241
Schneider, Maria, 282, 287
Schoenberg, Loren, 398
Schonberg, Harold C., 132
School on Modern Syncopation, 31–32
schools, jazz education in, 177–78, 215–18, 239–41, 265–68
Schreiber, John, 272–73, 279, 380, 398
Schreiber High School, Port Washington, 351, 360
Schuller, Gunther, 316
Schwartz, Diana, 47, 286, 296, 310, 311, 317, 325, 333–34, 336, 345, 352–53, 354, 355, 358, 366
Schwartz, Jack, 310, 352
Schwartz, Jerry, 72
Scotland, 96
Scott, Hazel, 41, 42, 104, 138, 318
Scott, Ronnie, 159, 326
Scott, Tony, 155
Scranton Sirens, 86
Scullers, Boston, 396
Sedric, Gene, 125
Sefcik, Joe, 144
Segal, Joe, 109, 349, 387
Seidel, Wayne, 364
Senior Citizens Symphony Orchestra, 289
SESAC, 429
Shad, Bob, 199
Shaffer, Paul, 392
Shakespeare, William, 18, 20–21
Shalit, Gene, 283
"Shall we play that one together?" (MM's slogan), 296–97, 401
Shank, Bud, 236, 304
Shaughnessy, Ed, 187
Shavers, Charlie, 347
Shaw, Artie, 156
Shaw, George Bernard, 39
Shaw, Martin, 21
Shearing, George, 31, 41, 111, 115, 117, 121, 126, 128, 143, 147, 176, 178, 180, 200, 235, 280, 287, 289, 301, 305, 312, 313, 318, 319–20, 325–26, 328, 329, 331, 347, 365, 366, 385
  style of, 131, 146, 147, 327, 328
Shearing, Trixie, 143
Shepheard's, Drake Hotel, New York, 233
Shepp, Archie, 222, 224, 229
Sheridan, Phil, 357
Sherman, Bob, 272
Sherman, Daryl, 300
Sherman, Joe, 109
Sherock, Shorty, 375
Shirley, Don, 194
Shore, Dinah, 53–54, 62
Shore, Julie, 53, 56
Shore, Willie, 53, 54–55, 60, 70, 97
Short, Bobby, 261, 275, 295, 296, 299, 305

Showboat Sari-S (showboat), Chicago, 234
Shreveport, Louisiana, 206
Sibley Music Library, Rochester, 359
Sickler, Don, 350
Siegel, Janis, 331
Siegel, Joel E., 315
Sierra Club, 254
Silent Pool (album), 13, 384
"Silent Pool" (Song), 13, 291, 384
Silent Pool (in Surrey, England), 13
Silhouette, Chicago, 115
Silver, Horace, 179
  style of, 168
Simeon, Omer, 121
Simmons, Norman, 380
Simon, Carly, 272
Simon, George T., 161
Simpkins, Andy, 248, 384
Sinatra, Frank, 123, 194, 251, 258, 334
The Single Petal of a Rose (album), 20, 396
Singleton, Zutty, 82
Sister Joseph, 19
Slack, Freddie, 109
Sloane, Carol, 222, 276
Slough, England, 3, 5, 404
Smith, Bessie, 116, 331
Smith, Beverly, 69
Smith, Chris, 56
Smith, Johnny, 145
Smith, Liz, 335
Smith, Paul, 147
Smith, Willie "the Lion," 88, 158, 249–50, 258
Smithsonian Institution, 322
Smithsonian Jazz Oral History Program, 70, 196
Sneed, Ann, 217
"Solace" (song), 252
Solal, Martial, 138
Solo Concert at Haverford (album), 273
"So Many Things" (song), 193
Sondheim, Stephen, 273, 398
Sons O' Guns (show), 88–89
Souter, David, 377
South America, 270–71
South Carolina Educational Television (SCETV), 295, 318, 386, 392
Southern, Jeri, 111
Southern Syncopated Orchestra, 23
South Side, Chicago, 77, 85
Soviet Union, 42
Spaatz, Carl Andrew "Tooey," 54
Spanier, Muggsy, 22, 82, 91, 186
Sperazza, Sal, 253, 315
Spivak, Charlie, 98
the Stables, near London, 348
Stacy, Jess, 41, 82, 94, 103, 272, 318
Stafford, Jo, 253
Stage Door, Milwaukee, 113
Stegner, Bentley, 93, 414
Stein, Victor, 272
Steinbeck, John, 93

Steinem, Gloria, 281
Stereo Review, 237, 329
Stern, Bert, 187
Stern, Isaac, 325
Stevens, Dale, 202, 203, 327
Stewart, Buddy, 98
Stewart, Rex, 188
Stigers Curtis, 398
Stitt, Sonny, 194
Stone, Desmond, 252, 253
Stone, Evelyn McGee, 307
Stone, George Lawrence, 144
Stone, Lew, 23
Storyville, Boston, 130, 141, 171–72, 198
"Stranger in a Dream" (song), 167
Stratford House School for Girls, 2, 19–24
Stratham Ice Rink, 31
Strayhorn, Billy, 161, 186, 275, 329–30, 364, 390
strings, with MM's music, 160–61, 384
Strollers Theatre club, New York, 208
Strudwick, Barbara, 21
Stuyvesant Casino, New York, 122, 124
Styne, Jule, 179
Such Good Companions (TV show), 268
Sudhalter, Richard, 85, 87, 95, 276, 293, 347, 360,
    361, 370–71, 376, 384
Sugar and Spice show, 47
Sullivan, Joe, 30, 84, 124, 277, 325
Sullivan, Maxine, 150, 188
Sunday Mirror, 130
Sung, Helen, 352
Supreme Court, performing before justices of,
    376–77
Supreme Headquarters Allied Expeditionary
    Force (SHAEF), 54
Swallow, Steve, 202, 209, 382
Swan Club, Port Washington, N.Y., 348
Swedish All-Stars, 117
Sweet and Low (revue), 89
Sweet Honey in the Rock, 325
Swingle Singers, 228
Sylvia (wife of Cyril Byson), 155

Taboo, Chicago, 103
Taboo, Palm Beach, 197
Talbert, Tom, 127
Tancil, Eddie, 79
Tanglewood festival, 366, 390, 400
Tate, Buddy, 262
Tate, Frank, 227, 276
Tate, Grady, 236, 380
Tatum, Art, 30, 56, 92, 127, 129, 147, 157, 175–76,
    272
Tavern on the Green, New York, 355
Taylor, Billy, 129, 135, 138, 147, 177, 179, 194, 197,
    217, 247, 265, 296, 299, 319, 323, 365, 380, 398
Taylor, Billy Sr., 242
Taylor, Cecil, 229–30, 317, 322, 331, 341–43, 377,
    383
Teachout, Terry, 305, 308

Teagarden, Addie, 197
Teagarden, Jack, 86, 87, 88, 95, 107, 197
Ted Kurland Associates, 369–70
Terkel, Studs, 115, 116, 201, 302, 361
Terminus Hotel, Eastbourne, England, 118
Terrasson, Jacky, 351, 380
Terry, Clark, 280, 309, 361, 366, 398
Terry-Thomas (comedian), 43
Teschemacher, Frank, 77, 78, 82, 84, 89
Thames River, England, 2
Theatrical Lounge, Cleveland, 175
"There'll Be Other Times" (song), 168–69, 329, 384
Thiele, Bob, 158
Thielemans, Toots, 117
Thigpen, Ed, 222
Thomas, Clarence, 377
Thompson, Don, 397
Thompson, Eric, 358
Thornhill, Claude, 153
Thornton, Big Mama, 177
Three Deuces, Chicago, 84, 92
"Three Piano Crossover" (concert program), 377
"Threnody" (song), 384, 392
Tilton, Roger, 158
Time (label), 199
Time (magazine), 94, 140, 146–47
"Time and Time Again" (song), 252
Tippy the cat, 216, 310, 312
Tivoli Gardens, Copenhagen, 326
Tizol, Juan, 377
Tjader, Cal, 222
Today show, 283
Tokar, Norman, 57
Tonight Show, 168
Tony Bennett, the McPartlands and Friends Make
    Magnificent Music (album), 291
Top of the Plaza, Rochester, 279
Top o' the Pole, New York, 195
Torff, Brian, 257, 284, 304, 305, 308
Tormé, Mel, 199
Toronto, 121, 125, 171, 397
Tough, Dave, 58, 78, 82, 83, 94, 111, 114–15, 117,
    144
Towner Art Gallery, Eastbourne, England, 348
Town Hall, New York, 378–79
Townsend, Irving, 135, 158, 277, 285, 295
Tracy, Stan, 355
Traeger, Charlie, 146
Traill, Sinclair, 194
Triangle Jazz Band, 90
Trinity Church, New York, 400
Tristano, Lennie, 110, 111, 121, 124, 130, 161,
    203
Trost, Merrilee, 304, 366–67, 394
Troy, N.Y., 328
Trumbauer, Frankie, 82
Trustees Lifetime Achievement Award, 400
Tubb, Carrie, 28
Tucker, Ben, 198–99, 273
Tucker, Bobby, 114

Turner, Frank (MM's father), 3, 4–7, 10–11,
12–13, 14–15, 24–25, 28, 29, 32–33, 37–38, 43,
45, 61, 71–72, 117
(1958) death of, 191
described, 4
national defense work, 10–11, 38
possible affair with Mrs. Franklin, 45–46
singing by, 10
Turner, Gertrude (MM's aunt, m. Harry Turner),
38
Turner, Harry (MM's uncle), 17, 37
Turner, Henry J. (MM's grandfather), 4
Turner, Mrs. Henry J. (MM's grandmother), 5
Turner, Joyce (MM's sister), 4, 7, 9, 14, 15–16,
19, 22, 24, 29, 37, 42, 45, 46, 64, 72, 107–8,
112, 142, 173, 192, 211, 244–45, 348, 366, 389
(1922) birth, 9
(2000) death, 389
marriage and affair of, 244–45
Turner, Mabel (MM's aunt), 13, 46
Turner, Margaret Marian. See McPartland,
Marian
Turner, Ted, (MM's uncle), 16
Turner, Ted, Jr., 211–12
Turner, Will (MM's uncle), 13, 46
Twilight World (album), 400
"Twilight World" (song), 237, 252, 399
Tyner, McCoy, 327

Ulanov, Barry, 132, 147
Umbria Jazz, 270
Union College, Schenectady, N.Y., 333
Unison label, 115–16, 125
United Service Organizations (USO), 1, 2, 44,
48, 53, 58, 61, 308
United States Navy Band, 266
Universal Jazz Coalition, 286
University of Chicago, 79, 80, 357, 365, 387
University of Michigan, 351
University of South Carolina Symphony
Orchestra, 400
Unterbrink, Mary, 332
U.S. Department of Health, Education and
Welfare, 265

Vaché, Warren, 270
Vallée, Rudy, 31
"Valse Gracieuse" (early composition by MM),
28
Van Gelder, Rudy, 152
Variety, 130, 131
Varney, Bob, 125
Vaughan, Sarah, 109, 110, 115, 201, 322
Ventura, Charlie, 110, 127
Venuti, Joe, 270, 279
Verizon Wireless, 388
VerPlanck, Marlene, 286, 305, 316, 359
Vietnam War, 224, 255
Village Vanguard, New York, 201
Virden, Jenel, 70

Voce, Steve, 318, 324
Voynow, Dick, 81, 84

Wainwright Memorial Scholarship, 28
Walker, Betty, 114
Walker, Norman, 27
Waller, Fats, 30, 31, 40, 41, 56, 92, 179
style of, 72
Wallington, George, 180, 322
Wall Street Journal, 399
Walter, Cy, 125
Wang, Dick, 95, 103, 357–58, 361, 365, 387
Wanted (Live) (album), 291
Ware, Wilbur, 157
Warner, Harry Waldo, 28
Washington, D.C., 97, 176, 265, 386
Washington, Dinah, 331
Waters, Ethel, 84
Waters, Muddy, 251
Watkins, Ralph, 128
Watrous, Peter, 375
Watt, Doug, 162
Watt, James, 353
Wayne, Max, 125, 139, 141, 144, 146
WBAI, 226, 253
WBGO, 318
Webb, George, 41
Webb, Jimmy, 237
Weber, Jon, 400
Webster, Ben, 156, 158
Weems, Ted, 90
Wein, George, 70, 130, 141, 142, 162, 165, 173,
197, 219, 270–71, 283, 293, 310, 313, 380, 398
Welch, Elizabeth, 40
Welk, Lawrence, 179
Werner, Kenny, 316
Wesley, Charles, 8
West, Hollie, 332
West Babylon High School, Long Island, N.Y.,
357
Weston, Randy, 392
Wettling, George, 91, 124, 157, 185, 420
"What Is This Thing Called Love?" (song), 239
White, Andrew, 265
White, Paul, 444–45
White City (amusement park), near Chicago, 82
Whitehead, Edward, 156
White House, Washington, D.C., 197, 249, 255
Whiteman, Paul, 23, 84, 86, 128, 270, 293, 406
style of, 116
Whiting, Margaret, 295
Whittaker, Popsie, 135
Wiggins, Eddie, 103
Wilder, Alec, 40, 161, 226, 228–29, 250–56, 260,
261, 263, 268, 269, 276, 280, 287, 288, 291,
292, 294, 295, 305, 315–16, 341, 350, 352, 359,
364, 434
background of, 250–51
death of and memorial, 315–16
songs written for MM, 251–52

Wilkinson, Eva Georgiana, 19–20, 21
Williams, Dorothy (JM's first wife, "Big Dorothy"), 86, 88, 89, 90, 93–94, 96, 98, 120, 182–83, 394
  (1930) marries JM, and birth of Dorothy H. McPartland, 88
  disintegration of, 93–94
Williams, Fred, 265
Williams, Hank, 250
Williams, Hannah (Dorothy Williams's sister), 86, 89, 90, 182
Williams, James, 196, 297, 380, 398
Williams, Mary Lou, 41, 42, 104, 124, 129, 132, 135, 136–37, 138, 143, 150, 176, 188, 195, 218, 221–22, 256, 272, 276, 281, 283, 284, 285, 290, 296–97, 299, 304, 309, 328, 331, 340, 341, 342, 363–64, 371, 386, 388, 395, 398
  death of, 309
Williams, Ned, 118
Williamson, Freddie, 110
Willingdon, England, 37, 45, 118
"Willow Creek" (song), 252, 290
Willow Creek and Other Ballads (album), 329, 350
Willson, Meredith, 185
Wilmer, Valerie, 245
Wilson, Earl, 130
Wilson, John S., 146, 147, 257, 273, 328
Wilson, Nancy, 153
Wilson, Phil, 216, 240, 254
Wilson, Teddy, 22, 30, 70, 103, 208, 227, 235, 258, 271, 272, 296, 299–300, 318
  style of, 131
Winchell, Walter, 140
Windsor, Duke and Duchess of, 197
Windsor, England, 3–4, 112
Winnipeg, Manitoba, 348
Winter, Paul, 197
Wiswell, Andy, 178
"With You in Mind" (song), 178–79
WJR, 125
WLTR, 299
WMAQ, 111
WNEW, 129
WNEX, 130
Wolf Trap, Virginia, 325
Wolverines, 54, 80, 81–82
women in jazz, 131–37, 150, 176–77, 194–95, 280–87, 338–40, 348–52

books about, 338–40
  MM's advocacy of, 308–9, 349–52
  MM's mentoring of, 305–6, 351–52
  MM's opinion on, 388
  in war service, 43
Women in Jazz (TV show), 308–9
Women in the Arts Festival, 348
women's lib, 280
Wonder, Stevie, 224, 240
Woods, Phil, 144, 398
Woolwich, England, 5–11
Woolwich Royal Arsenal, 3, 5–6, 38, 44
WOR, 147
World of Jazz (book), 281–82
World of Jazz (radio program), 143, 169
World War II, 1–2, 37–38, 42–49, 95
  anticipation of, 5, 37–38
  beginning of, 42
  end of, 66
  and war brides, 69–70, 417
Worshipful Company of Musicians, 28, 389
Wright, Eugene, 209
Wright, Norton, 133, 155
Wright, Ray, 253–54
Wright, Rayburn, 349
Wurlitzer electric piano, 199
WVET, 177
WXXI, 279

Xavier University, 327

Yaffe, David, 388
Yale Oral History of American Music, 324, 332, 336
Yardbirds, 212
Yarrow, Julian, 307
Yoshi's, Oakland, California, 349, 394
Young, Lester, 111, 143, 187, 188
  style of, 153
"You've Come a Long Way, Baby" (autobiographical essay), 281–82, 340, 398

Zawinul, Joe, 225
Zebra Lounge, Green Bay, Wisconsin, 118
Zeitlin, Denny, 222
Zelnick, Mel, 139, 140, 141
Zorina, Vera, 39
Zurke, Bob, 30, 70, 126
Zwerin, Michael, 222